Understanding Crime

Essentials of Criminological Theory

THIRD EDITION

L. THOMAS WINFREE
New Mexico State University, Las Cruces

HOWARD ABADINSKY
St. John's University

WADSWORTH
CENGAGE Learning™

Australia • Brazil • Japan • Korea • Mexico • Singapore • Spain • United Kingdom • United States

WADSWORTH
CENGAGE Learning™

Understanding Crime: Essentials of Criminological Theory, **Third Edition**
L. Thomas Winfree, Howard Abadinsky

Publisher/Executive Editor: Linda Schreiber

Acquisitions Editor: Carolyn Henderson Meier

Assistant Editor: Megan Banks

Editorial Assistant: John Chell

Media Editor: Andy Yap

Marketing Manager: Michelle Williams

Marketing Assistant: Jillian Myers

Marketing Communications Manager: Talia Wise

Content Project Management: Pre-Press PMG

Creative Director: Rob Hugel

Art Director: Maria Epes

Production Technology Analyst: Lori Johnson

Print Buyer: Rebecca Cross

Rights Acquisitions Account Manager, Text: Mardell Glinski-Schultz

Rights Acquisitions Account Manager, Image: John Hill

Production Service: Pre-Press PMG

Copy Editor: Pre-Press PMG

Cover Designer: Tim Heraldo, Riezebos Holzbaur Design Group

Cover Image: John Fox/Stockbyte/ Getty Images

Compositor: Pre-Press PMG

For product information and technology assistance contact us at
Cengage Learning Customer & Sales Support, 1-800-354-9706.
For permission to use material from this text or product,
submit all requests online at **www.cengage.com/permissions**
Further permissions questions can be e-mailed to
permissionrequest@cengage.com

Library of Congress Control Number: 2009928869

Student Edition:

ISBN-13: 978-0-495-60083-1

ISBN-10: 0-495-60083-0

Wadsworth, Cengage Learning
10 Davis Drive
Belmont, CA 94002-3098
USA

Cengage Learning is a leading provider of customized learning solutions with office locations around the globe, including Singapore, the United Kingdom, Australia, Mexico, Brazil, and Japan. Locate your local office at **www.cengage.com/global**

Cengage Learning products are represented in Canada by Nelson Education, Ltd.

To learn more about Wadsworth Cengage Learning, visit **www.cengage.com/wadsworth**

Purchase any of our products at your local college store or at our preferred online store **www.ichapters.com**

Printed in the United States of America
1 2 3 4 5 6 7 13 12 11 10 09

Tom Winfree dedicates this book to his wife, Eileen Jeffery Winfree, whose courage, perseverance, and persistence in the face of life's sometimes-unexpected challenges serve as a beacon of hope for us all.

Contents

8   Labeling and Shaming Theories   223

Preface

Theory is a daunting subject in any academic discipline. Crime theories are no less challenging, but they should at least be interesting. This book represents our attempt to compress what are often complex and bewildering crime theories into a consumable format—the essentials of criminological theory. The frustrations and satisfactions associated with teaching this subject led us to prepare this book. We hope that you receive some positive benefits from our experiences as you learn about crime theories.

ORGANIZATION

We approached these theories, and the theorists behind them, in the following fashion: In the first chapter we provide the tools needed to develop a greater appreciation for crime theories. For example, we describe the structure of theory, including the building blocks of theories—their basic assumptions and assertions. Other topics include the goals and challenges for theories; the relationships between human nature, government, and public policy; the nature of crime and laws; and the origins of crime theories. The first chapter also outlines the organization of this text. A careful review of this chapter will enhance your understanding of crime theories.

The next 10 chapters provide a review of the essentials of criminological theory. We organized the text into 22 clusters of theories or perspectives, what we call theory modules, each containing: (1) an overview of its development, assumptions, and causal arguments; (2) an assessment of tests of these arguments; and (3) a discussion of the implications for public policy and criminal justice practices. Each learning module begins with a series of questions and observations to get you thinking about the relevance of the theories to everyday life. The reader may find it useful to reflect on these bulleted items before and after you read the associated module. You may also find it instructive to compare questions between modules within a chapter to understand the points of divergence and convergence for each cluster's assertions and assumptions.

The final chapter explores the future of crime theories. We approach this task by seeking answers to a series of questions. The questions (and the answers we provide) are intended to be a starting point for your own examination of the future of crime theorizing.

Below is a summary of each chapter and its specific modules:

- Chapter 1 (Theory and the Study of Crime) addresses four important topics: the origins and functions of laws, the key elements in studying crime, the structure of theories, and the central elements in understanding any crime theory. This chapter provides readers with the requisite tools to explore the broad landscape that is criminological theory.

- Chapter 2 (Deterrence and Opportunity Theories) includes three modules. The first looks at deterrence theory, from its origins in classical criminology to contemporary versions, including an introduction to the concept of "free will." The next two add opportunity to the mix. One, rationale choice theory, looks at how criminals structure their choices to commit or not to commit crime; the second, routine activities, emphasizes the everyday aspects of some forms of crime.

- Chapter 3 (Biological and Biochemical Theories) includes a module on the origins of biological explanations, including some theories that, through the lens of time, appear rather nonsensical to the modern mind. Two other modules address, first, the potential genetic basis of crime and, second, the links between biochemistry and crime, providing more contemporary versions of what has been a popular perspective in criminological studies for several hundred years. Standing in sharp contrast to the content of Chapter 2, these theories describe crime-causing conditions within an individual's human physiology or related to the ingestion of a foreign substance that are essentially immutable or resistant to change.

- Chapter 4 (The Psychology of Crime I) provides the reader with two modules, as well as a general introduction to the idea that the origins of criminality may lie within some aspect of the human mind. The first module looks at the psychoanalytic approach, suggesting that the psychological development of criminals is arrested by some force in their immediate environment, which if addressed could result in changes in behavior. The second module centers on the significance of deviant personalities for the study of crime, including historical and contemporary versions of a key term, psychopathy.

- Chapter 5 (The Psychology of Crime II) also contains two separate modules. The first looks at the history and use of IQ (and IQ testing) by criminologists over the past 100 or more years, as well as issues related to the use of such psychometric tests. The second module provides insights into a specialized psychological perspective called behaviorism, and how criminal justice professionals employ the same psychological techniques of conditioning used in the learning of criminal behavior to unlearn it.

- Chapter 6 (Social Organizational Theories) provides three separate but related modules. Each module examines how various sociological features of communities and cultures serve to create crime. The first chapter module explores social ecology and its main theoretical contribution of social disorganization, ideas that were largely discounted by mid-century, only to enjoy a resurgence in the present one. The second module looks at how a macro-level (or societal-wide) sociological idea, anomie, rose to prominence in criminology, only to be eclipsed by other theories and then, like social disorganization, be reborn in a new form at the end of the twentieth century. The third module focuses specifically on how subcultures create or foster rule breaking and criminal conduct by their members or how that behavior comes to be seen as problematic.

- Chapter 7 (Social Process Theories) provides insights into two sociological perspectives on crime and delinquency that have, almost since their origins, been viewed as competing theories. The first module, learning theories, examines how social beings must be taught to be criminals, as crime and delinquency are not part of the normal state of human beings. The second module takes a different perspective: social beings are by nature prone to rule-breaking behavior and it is only through individual and collective control mechanisms that they abide by society's rules.

- Chapter 8 (Labeling and Shaming Theories) also provides the reader with two separate but related modules, each looking at a slightly different use of power by individuals or other societal entities. In the labeling module, we describe how formal agents of social control essentially stigmatize adult criminals and delinquents, and the impact of that stigmatization process on their subsequent lives. The second module looks at one of the oldest forms of social control: shaming. In this module, the emphasis is on shaming practices that are intended to facilitate the reentry of rule breakers back into the community, as opposed to further marginalizing them.

- Chapter 9 (Conflict Theories) provides a look at three types of conflict theory in a single module. Each of the individual conflict theories includes power and laws as critical dimensions. In culture conflict theory, the emphasis is on how contacts between different cultures create situations that sometimes become defined as crime and at other times generate even wider conflicts, such as wars, where genocide and related crimes are likely consequences. Group conflict theory suggests that laws often serve to criminalize the behavior of some groups, particularly those outside the circles of power in a community, or to otherwise threaten the interests of the powerful groups that control both the laws and the law enforcers. The final conflict theory provides even more specific details about how laws can be used to criminalize the behavior of those who resist their regulatory intent.

- Chapter 10 (Marxist and Critical Theories) is the third chapter to look at how power is used to control people generally, but criminals in particular. Marxists base their notions of power and control on responses to capitalism, an economic system in which wealth and the means of producing more wealth are controlled by very powerful individuals identified as capitalists. The legal system and its associated agents of control (e.g., the police and prisons) serve the interests of capitalists alone. The second chapter module delves into late twentieth century and early twenty-first century manifestations of similar critical theories, including left realism and peacemaking criminology, along with their efforts to explain the presence of crimes and criminals.

- Chapter 11 (Gender, Race, and Crime Theories) represents a unique look at two variables that, by themselves, appear to predict low criminality (among women) and high criminality (among ethnic and racial minority groups). However, as this chapter makes clear, the role played by each in theorizing about crime and criminals is complex and merits this special attention (see "New for the third edition" below).

- Chapter 12 (The Future of Crime Theory) presents three questions about the future of criminological theorizing, research, and policy. As we make clear, there are no right or wrong answers, just questions. The challenge lies in the preparation and presentation of your answers to these questions, wherever they take you and criminological theory.

The study of crime theories is all about connectivity, since no contemporary theorist is totally oblivious to the contributions of other theorists. Indeed, we organized this textbook so that the theory modules may be presented in a sequence different from ours. To do so is not a problem; rather, it is a matter of organization and emphasis, and the flexibility built into the self-contained modules allows instructors the freedom to present the material as they see fit.

Theory is important to all academic disciplines, and it can be interesting. Open your mind and cast out preconceptions about theory. If you can accomplish this feat, you will find that understanding crime and criminals is a far more agreeable endeavor.

ADDED FEATURES

Several important features are repeated periodically in this text, including the following:

- *"Comments and Criticisms" Boxes.* Many theories contained in this book have generated deep and abiding controversies about their value to the study of crime or the assumptions they make about human beings, our systems of laws and their administration, and society at large. In these boxes we highlight specific concerns that critics have expressed about the theories.

- *"In Their Own Words" Boxes.* In many instances, no one expresses an idea or responds to a criticism better than the originator of the idea. In these boxes we include the specific remarks of theorists. These are more than random observations on the issues being discussed or simple citations. They will motivate readers to think about terms, concepts, ideas, and theories in different ways; to question the development of a given theory; and to understand the context in which it was developed. In fact, at times we raise the issue with the specific intent to "put a stick in the hornet's nest." These remarks often tell a great deal about the evolution of the specific theory and the controversies in the study of crime and criminals.

■ *Figures.* At times a picture really is worth a thousand words, especially when dealing with theory. We have tried to represent numerous theories in graphic form faithfully. Such images are necessarily simplistic and may not reflect the complexities of some theories. Our intent is to provide a graphic representation of a theory's main ideas and causal premises. These images are meant to be pedagogical, or teaching, devices.

■ *Theory Summary Tables.* At the conclusion of each chapter, we provide tabular summaries for each theory, along with brief statements about the major figures, central assumptions, causal arguments, strengths, and weaknesses of each. These summaries are no substitute for reading the entire chapter, but they should serve to remind readers of the critical differences between the theories explored in each chapter.

■ *Key Terms.* In the body of each chapter, we boldface a number of terms and provide definitions for each. At the end of each chapter, after the summaries, we provide a list of these terms. Mastering the chapter's content includes having a working understanding of these terms and their application to crime theories.

■ *Critical Review Questions.* Following the summary of each chapter is a series of study questions. These are not requests to regurgitate information covered in the chapter. Instead, they encourage you to think critically and analytically about what you have read. The questions both challenge students and represent enjoyable learning exercises. If you apply yourself to these questions, you will master the content of each chapter.

NEW FOR THE THIRD EDITION

Change is inevitable. This is perhaps especially true for textbooks—even ones about theory. While continuing to link crime theories to criminal justice policies and practices, we edited and reorganized every chapter, updating research findings and expanding (or in rare instances contracting) the policy and practical implications of each theory. In the process, we increased *Understanding Crime* from 10 to 12 chapters. This edition also has several new features, including the following:

■ New Boxed Inserts: *Comparative Criminology:* Since the second edition of this book appeared, we have become increasingly convinced that students of crime need to gain a greater appreciation of the globalized status of criminology. Hence, we have included 17 examples of relevant cross-cultural and comparative crime theory research; each chapter now has at least one such example and several have two or more. Some of these examples are single-nation studies outside the U.S., while others include studies of two to more than 100 nations around the globe. If criminological theorizing is to have an impact on public policy and criminal justice practices in the U.S., it must also demonstrate an ability to transcend legal and cultural systems, a goal we address here.

- Reorganized and Expanded Chapter 1: Theory and the Study of Crime: This chapter now includes a new section, "Studying Crime," which provides information related to the definition, classification, and measurement of crime. We added this section in response to requests from instructors who want to include information about the nature and extent of crime in the United States as a way to demonstrate the breadth and depth of the crime problem. A 20-year picture of the Uniform Crime Report and a 30-plus-year view of the National Crime Victimization Survey enables students to separate the myth from the reality of crime in America.

- New Chapter 8: Labeling and Shaming Theory: When we included shaming theory in the second edition, we placed it in the chapter about deterrence. However, critical readers of the text suggested that it should be given a higher profile. As a consequence, we have expanded our discussion of re-integrative shaming and restorative justice, combining this with the labeling theory module. While shaming certainly has elements of deterrence, we felt that pairing it with labeling theory was a better fit. Of course, as in the past, we await your judgment and comments.

- New Chapter 9: Conflict Theories: In the first edition of this book, we included conflict in a chapter on power and crime; in the second edition, we placed it in a chapter with labeling theory. However, instructors and critical reviewers of the textbook have told us that conflict theory, especially in the twenty-first century and in a global context, merits its own chapter, which we provide in this edition. In the second edition, we removed Austin Turk's discussion of norm resistance theory; we have replaced it in this edition, owing to a boom in theoretical and policy-related research, and use it as a theoretical base. Moreover, given the variety of international and intranational conflicts around the globe in the twenty-first century, past adopters suggested expanding this topic, which we have done.

- New Chapter 11: Gender, Race, and Crime: This chapter represents the most ambitious change in the text. Feminist criminology received short shrift in the first edition and shared a chapter with Marxist theory in the second edition. In both previous editions, race was viewed as a variable in the analyses and received little other attention. Adopters of previous editions picked up on these shortcomings and suggested ways to overcome them; the principal one was to expand the book by adding a new chapter, which we have done. In Chapter 11, we address the sometimes thorny definitional issues associated with questions of gender and race (or ethnicity). We also provide a detailed gender- and race-specific crime analysis, emphasizing the intersection of both race and sex in the specific crime of homicide. The majority of the chapter, however, examines both gender- and race-inclusive theorizing about crime, including attempts by mainstream criminology to provide such insights and efforts by critical criminology to show the essential nature of both variables in the study of crime and justice. In the latter category, we include recent theorizing by critical race theorists who seek to bridge the gap between race and gender. As always, we provide assessments of gender- and race-inclusive theorizing, and any implications that such efforts have for policy and criminal justice practices.

ACKNOWLEDGMENTS

As with every book ever written, people other than the author, or in this case the authors, played some role—major or minor—in its preparation. We would like to thank the folks at Wadsworth, but especially our executive editor Carolyn Henderson-Meier. We would also like to acknowledge the great production staff, including Mary Thomas Stone, Cindy Bond, and Mark Mayell.

We must thank countless "generations" of students who, over the past 30-plus years, have put up with our efforts to make sense of crime theories in the classroom and, as a group, pushed us not only to provide the key components of the various theories but also to clarify their practical and policy implications. Tom Winfree would also like to thank Dean Pam Jansma, College of Arts and Sciences, New Mexico State University, for helping to create the kind of intellectual environment in which diverse ideas and scholarship can flourish, and for supporting Tom during his sabbatical leave. Several of Tom's current and past colleagues also commented on different chapters appearing in this edition, including J. Keith Akins, Robert Durán, David Keys, and Christine S. Sellers.

Two other individuals also contributed to this work. Margery Cassidy read and commented on every chapter in the first edition. Her death in 1998 deprived us of our most helpful critic, and we have tried to honor her spirit in subsequent editions. Eileen Winfree checked all citations in this work, and she found mistakes made in previous editions. Thank you, Eileen.

We owe a considerable debt to the collective input of all of these reviewers, commentators, and colleagues; this edition is better for their critical reading of our collaborative work. Any mistakes, however, remain those of the authors.

Tom Winfree
Las Cruces, New Mexico

Howard Abadinsky
Jamaica, New York

About the Authors

Howard Abadinsky is professor of criminal justice at St. John's University, Jamaica, NY. He was an inspector for the Cook County (IL) Sheriff's Office for eight years and a New York State parole officer and senior parole officer for 15 years. He holds a B.A. from Queens College of the City University of New York, an M.S.W. from Fordham University, and a Ph.D. in sociology from New York University. He is the author of several books, including *Drug Abuse*, Sixth Edition, *Probation and Parole*, Tenth Edition, *Organized Crime*, Ninth Edition, and *Law and Justice*, Sixth Edition. Dr. Abadinsky has been teaching crime theory courses for more than two decades.

L. Thomas Winfree, Jr. is professor of criminal justice at New Mexico State University. In 1968, he received a bachelor's degree (sociology) from the University of Richmond. He then joined the U.S. Army, serving in Berlin, Germany. Returning to Richmond, Winfree received a master's degree (sociology) from Virginia Commonwealth University in 1974. He then journeyed to Missoula, Montana, where he earned a doctorate (sociology) from the University of Montana in 1976. Winfree has participated in many theory-testing and theory-extending activities for the best part of two decades, including ones based on social learning, social control, and self-control theories. He has been a principal investigator or research associate for several theory-driven evaluations in the field of criminal justice, including a quasi-experimental assessment of a court-based DWI drug court in Las Cruces, New Mexico, and the National Evaluation of Gang Resistance Education and Training. Most importantly, he has taught a class on crime theories, by several different names, scores of times since 1975.

1

Theory and the Study of Crime

CHAPTER OVERVIEW

LEARNING OBJECTIVES

In this chapter, you will learn the following:

- The legal and social elements that define what a crime is and who is a criminal.

- How theorizing as a process compares to other forms of human inquiry.

- Why theories must be held to higher standards than other forms of conjecture about human behavior.

- The various parts of theories—how they fit together and how they yield insights into crime and criminals.

- The linkages between theorizing about and researching crime, and the role of ethics and government in these important processes.

■ The roles played by different philosophical perspectives in shaping both crime theories and crime control policies.

INTRODUCTION

As you watch the evening news or one of the many "real crime" shows on television, or read a newspaper or one of the thousands of "true crime" books, do you find yourself amazed at what criminals are thinking when they do what you see as stupid things? If you do, then you belong to a club where people seek answers to the age-old question: Why do they do it? You are now a devotee of **criminology,** the scientific study of crime and criminals, and the societal response to both (Sutherland 1973). For example, even the casual observer of crime and justice in contemporary society wonders about:

■ The 19 Islamist terrorists who hijack three airplanes, turning them into weapons of mass destruction and taking not only their own lives, but also the lives 2,998 innocent people. Years later, after thorough investigative work, a biographer describes them as "unexceptional men" and notes the fact "that young men of good backgrounds would leave homes and families without fanfare or discouragement was evidence of the broad support within Saudi Arabia for jihad." All knew they were going to die; all welcomed their martyrdom.[1]

■ An attractive and personable man stalks and kills at least 30 women. When tried for capital murder (and eventually executed), he earns the begrudging respect of the trial judge, who, after sentencing him to death, says to him: "Take care of yourself, young man. I say that to you sincerely… It is an utter tragedy for this court to see such a total waste of humanity as I've experienced in this courtroom. You're a bright young man. You'd have made a good lawyer, and I would have loved to have you practice in front of me, but you went another way, partner."[2]

■ An aging sports celebrity is found not guilty of two high-profile murders in the mid-1990s but is ordered to pay a crushing judgment to the victims' families after later losing a civil "wrongful-death" suit. He eventually finds himself in criminal court once more. This time, a jury convicts him of kidnapping and firearms charges—exactly 13 years to the day after his exoneration on the criminal murder charges.[3]

■ A prostitute turns her rage and hatred of the men who have used her for years into a calling, killing seven men. Over a period of two years, she appears in four trials. The jury convicts her in the first trial; she confesses in the three later trials to killing at least six men (the body of one alleged victim is never recovered). She receives six separate death sentences. After an unsuccessful appeal to the U.S. Supreme Court, this female serial killer spends more than a decade on death row before her death by lethal injection. Before she dies, she says, in essence, that 12 years on death row was long enough and it is time to die.[4]

■ "Mother drowns kids," screams the headline in South Carolina, Texas, New Jersey, and California. In some cases, the defendants claim mental disease or defect; in others, they state that they were protecting their children from a far worse fate—often an abusive partner. Perhaps the children were just an inconvenience. In their subsequent trials, juries convict nearly every one of these women of murder or manslaughter, sentencing them to long prison terms, but not before asking, How could they do it?[5]

Serious scholars of crime sometimes call these events "celebrated cases," crimes that, according to Samuel Walker (2006), consume inordinate attention from the media, the public, and the criminal justice system. Celebrated cases often shape the public's view of crime and justice in the United States, even though they are relatively rare events. We suspect that many of you are aware of other, far less notorious criminal events, ones that perhaps touched you or your community, and you still ask the same question: Why did he/she/they do it? Just because the crime is not a serial killing, a mass murder, a familial homicide, or some other high-profile crime does not make the offense or the offender more understandable. In fact, what might be described as "garden-variety" crimes—a youthful neighbor who shoplifts music from a local retailer, a college student who robs a pizza deliverer but takes only the pizzas, or a neighbor who by "adopting" hundreds of stray animals violates local ordinances restricting the number of live animals on one's property—may trouble us just as much. You may not know a serial killer or an Islamist terrorist, but you may know the perpetrators of these kinds of crimes. Such crimes (and the criminals who commit them) may not receive the same level of attention as the celebrated cases, but they may be no less baffling to those of us trying to understand the offenders' motivations and thought processes.

This book is about crime theories—also called criminological theories—and their infusion into criminal justice policies and practices. Crime theories represent systematic answers to such questions as:

- Why does the definition of crime vary by time and place?

- Why do people commit crimes?

- Why is there crime?

In essence, theories of crime and criminals provide general ideas about what lies behind both phenomena. Specifically, a theory represents systematic speculations or insights into the fundamental causes of an event or class of events. We will necessarily modify this definition; hence, you should only view it as a starting point. Indeed, before we can explore why people commit crimes, it might be useful to look at the origins of laws and their ties to human nature, governments and public policy, as part of the question, Why is there crime? The quick answer is simple: Because members of a society at some point decided to outlaw certain kinds of conduct. The full answer is more complex.

HUMAN NATURE, GOVERNMENT, AND PUBLIC POLICY

Nearly every theory of crime addresses two elemental questions. First, what is the role of human nature ascribed by the theory? That is, we can categorize crime theories by how their supporters conceive of the nature of human behavior. Nearly all theories make assumptions about human nature; these untestable assumptions are, as previously mentioned, essential grounding for crime theory. For example, prominent in any discussion of human behavior is the **nature-versus-nurture controversy.** Both sides in the controversy address the same question: What is the dominant force shaping human behavior? Supporters of the **nature** position argue that most behavior, including crime, is due primarily to genetic, biological causes, or explained by other properties inherent in individuals. In short, human behavior is inheritable. Conversely, proponents of the **nurture** position look to the social environment for the causal factors; that is, human behavior is largely the product of social interaction. Moreover, as we shall see later in this book, some theorists view the **nature-versus-nurture controversy** as irrelevant—many of them see crime as better understood by power relationships in a society.

If a person's nature determines that he or she will be a criminal, then, short of genetic engineering, the policies directed at criminals are limited. For example, if criminals are unchangeable, if nature caused their behavior, all a society can hope to do is warehouse them until, because of age, infirmity or death, they are no longer a threat to community safety and security. However, if the problem lies largely within society's mechanisms of socialization—the family, schools, and other social institutions, then a different set of policy responses would be appropriate. Of course, it might be that nature and nurture are both important, but in different ways and at different junctures in people's lives. For example, nature may limit a person's ability to learn within the traditional educational system; however, that same system may play a large role in ostracizing and penalizing underperformers, further limiting their life choices and chances.

Second, what is the basis of human society? Crime theorists generally view society as based on consensus, pluralism, or conflict (Michalowski 1977). Supporters of the **consensus** view maintain that people do not dispute definitions of right and wrong and law is an expression of this collective agreement, a codification of social norms. Such agreement is necessary for a society to survive—law is functional. According to the consensus view, law serves people equally, and persons who violate the law represent a unique subgroup. Conservatives think of criminals as deserving punishment; liberals see a need to bring them back into conformity. Although consensus advocates argue for universal conduct norms, as we shall see, most of their crime theories have focused on the crimes of young working- or lower-class males.

According to the **pluralist** view, race, ethnicity, gender, geography, economics, and religion constitute the points around which a society's diverse groups cluster. These groups often do not agree on what is right and wrong. Moreover, they may expound different—sometimes competing—interests, values, and goals. Law is the method by which a society manages conflict without threatening its own existence. Moreover, laws and the legal system provide a value-free framework for divergent interests to coexist within a democratic framework. Crime definitions reflect a coalition of interests.

The **conflict** view also emphasizes society's diversity. According to this perspective, diverse groups are often at odds with one another—farmers, industrialists, and union members; atheists and fundamentalists; liberals and conservatives—all competing for power and position within society. One important prize awaits the winners: they get to define crime. Thus, the definition of crime reflects power relationships in society and serves the interests of those in control. In capitalist societies, the owners of the means of production—the wealthy—also maintain the power to define laws and their enforcement.

Origins of Law

Legal scholars believe that *law* derives from the Old Norse *log* or *lag,* the former meaning "to lay down or determine" and the latter meaning "to bind people together" (Aubert 1983). Although it is central to the functioning of society, law defies authoritative definition. Even lawyers and judges have no generally agreed-upon definition of law: "For them it is simply what they practice and what courts do" (Loh 1984:23).

Order is essential for the continued existence of any society (Hoebel 1974:12), and law then becomes simply a body of rules intended to create and maintain social order. Nevertheless, social scientists disagree over the point at which a society is under the rule of law: How is law to be distinguished from social rules and customs, the norms of a society? **Norms** indicate societal expectations of what is right or "normal," of what ought to be (i.e., **prescriptive norms**); norms may also indicate what is wrong or "abnormal," what ought not to be (i.e., **proscriptive norms**).

The American sociologist William Graham Sumner (1840–1910) saw social control as either informal or formal. For Sumner (1906), informal social control promotes conformity not through some rational basis but by nearly automatic adherence, owing to childhood socialization. Violators often must answer to more normative peers, who enact appropriate sanctions or punishments. Yet, not all norms enjoy the same level of endorsement within the community. **Folkways** define socially approved or disapproved behavior, but they do not reflect a sense of moral obligation. Perhaps the following phrase best captures their meaning: Thou *should* or *should not* do something. The penalties that accompany their violation are relatively mild and include ridicule and ostracism. **Mores** (singular, **mos**) are also informal norms, but adherence is obligatory: Thou *must* or *must not* do something. Communities meet a mos violation with a far stronger sense of moral indignation; moreover, the penalties that accompany the violation of mores are far more severe, including, in extreme cases, the death penalty. Neither type of social norm is formalized in the law, nor is there, in most cases, a specialized community institution for enacting penalties. Rather, imposing punishment is the duty of all members of the community.

Formalization of folkways and mores generates law. Sumner saw the process of moving from informal to formal social control as taking thousands of years and involving the development of some form of centralized government. Laws have at least two forms. **Customary laws** are perhaps the oldest form; they represent the codification of traditional practices and include definitions of the condemned act or omission, the procedures for determining guilt or innocence, and the punishments for those found guilty. As described by Sumner, customary laws bear a striking resemblance to common law as practiced by the English and others. When systematically represented in a culture, customary laws never break with tradition, but rather reflect the social intent and moral force of their foundational mores and folkways.

Enacted laws are similar to customary laws, but official representatives of the community deliberately record them; and as such, they are explicit and carry the moral force of the entire community. Sumner saw enacted law as far more advanced; not only did it no longer rely upon customary law for guidance, but it often contradicted the latter. Indeed, he viewed the intent of enacted law punishments as deterring crime rather than merely serving as retaliation or revenge.

Sumner emphasized that law and custom are not the same. The act of creating formal laws "endows certain selected individuals with the privilege–right of applying the sanction of physical coercion" (Hoebel 1974:276). Former Supreme Court Associate Justice Benjamin Cardozo pointed to the necessity of regular enforcement by courts of law. Law, he said, "is a principle or rule of conduct so established as to justify a prediction with reasonable certainty that it will be enforced by the courts if its authority is challenged" (1924:52). The presence of formal mechanisms for enforcement suggests that, for these norms—now called laws, there may be those who do not, or will not, follow them in all instances. At the same time, as the sociologist Max Weber (1967[1925]) pointed out, custom may be far more determinative of conduct than the existence of legal enforcement machinery.

Contemporary law includes formalized and codified rules stipulated by courts of law and coercively enforced by control agents. Some laws restrict behavior; others compel it; still others (e.g., contract law) facilitate voluntary actions by providing guidelines. Laws create benefits, such as Social Security, and empower bureaucratic entities, such as transportation departments responsible for building and maintaining roads. In short, it is difficult to conceive of any aspects of contemporary life that laws do not influence.

Government, Policy, and Practice

Among other things, theory refers to explanations, whereas policy is a planned course of action designed to deal with a problem. For the crime problem, policy creation and implementation is typically government's responsibility. Theory has the potential to support policy; however, conflicting theories can confound policy alternatives. Research that supports or weakens a theory will obviously influence policy. Because we can never prove crime theory in the criminal law sense (i.e., proof beyond reasonable doubt), policy guided by research-grounded theory—what some call **evidence-based practices (EBP)** (see, e.g., Sherman et al. 2002)—will always be tentative. Theory-driven policy must pass a myriad of political tests that are part of a democratic system. What are the alternatives? Policy by public opinion? Policy by "gut feelings"? Policy by the most powerful, for the most powerful? We suggest that each of these forces have, at various times, driven the nation's crime-control policies and practices, and the results have not always been useful, fair, or even made sense (Mays and Ruddell 2007; Walker 2006).

Reformers may seek out theories that focus on that which (given the political will) is subject to change. Yet, important correlates of crime are beyond the ability of policy to affect. Consider the influence of age on crime: "Criminal behavior depends as much or more on age than any other demographic characteristic—sex, social status, race, family configuration" (Wilson and Herrnstein 1985:126). The crime-prone ages are roughly 15–25, and it is unusual to find criminals whose illegal behavior began after the age of 25.

Additional obstacles stand in the way of those who would translate theory into practice. Theories often support alternative policies, which means that drawing policy conclusions from theory-guided research can be problematic. Facts do not speak for themselves; they suffer from definitional issues and subjective influences that determine not only what facts we seek, but also how we measure them. For whom do the researchers work? The government? Corporations? Foundations? Is an ideology involved in the research effort? In practice, the government—local, state, and federal—sponsors most research into criminal behavior. Moreover, the prevailing policies of the administration in control of the executive branch, the legislative branch, or both, may determine who does it, what they look at, and for what purposes.

We can identify four basic positions on the relationship between theory and policy:

1. If crime is the result of individual dynamics that can be changed or modified, then policy may endorse deterring, punishing, or treating the offender.

2. If crime is the result of individual dynamics that are beyond society's ability to change, then policy may endorse incapacitating through incarceration or permanently removing the offender through execution.

3. If criminal behavior is the result of modifiable environmental conditions, then policy may be geared to changing that environment, thereby eliminating or altering the forces creating crime.

4. If criminal behavior is the result of environmental conditions that are resistant to change, then policy may follow a path similar to that endorsed in position #2, expanded to include sterilization and abortion.

Given some of these alternatives and their implications for criminal justice practices, it is not difficult to understand why some criminologists shun the policy aspects of theorizing. To ignore policy, however, is to ignore an element of theory as important as the shared definitions used by criminologists to measure and study crime, our next topic.

STUDYING CRIME

If we agree to study something, the first task we set for ourselves is to define exactly what the thing is. That is, what will we include and why? Moreover, what will we exclude and why? In order to study something as complex as crime, we need to proceed through a series of definitional layers. First, we define crime, a simple-sounding task, but one that hinges on rather arcane and debatable terms. What, we ask, is a crime? Once we have defined our subject matter, we need to find some way to make order out of chaos. Our second task, then, is to classify crime. At that point, the public's need—along with those of the law makers and policy implementers—to know the nature and extent of the "crime problem" leads to an emphasis on measuring that which we have just defined: How much crime is there? We start with the definition of crime.

Defining Crime

Crime has no generally accepted definition. For many people, crime is any *behavior* that is harmful to individuals or groups. This normative definition leaves open the question of what constitutes harm. To be useful, such a definition must also address behavior that only harms the "perpetrator"—using heroin, for example.

In legal terms, crime is any act that violates existing criminal statutes; it is a wrongful act or omission subject to official punishment. This definition raises additional questions:

- Who determines the criminal law?
- What constitutes "a wrong"?
- Can governments commit crimes?

Governments *have* committed many atrocious acts, including the concentration camps of Nazi Germany, the Gulags of Stalin's Soviet Union, and the murderous predations of the Pol Pot regime in Cambodia. Before 1989, border guards were under orders to shoot anyone who violated the law by attempting to flee from East Germany into the West. After the collapse of the Berlin Wall and German reunification, former East Germany border guards who had followed their government's orders were tried as criminals.

Determining what is or is not a crime—and who is or is not a criminal—depends on time and place. From 1920 to 1933, possession and sale of alcoholic beverages were crimes in the United States. Most contemporary Islamic nations ban all alcoholic beverages. Before 1914, trafficking in heroin and cocaine was legal in the United States. The First Amendment protects our ability to express opinions and write books; in other countries, such exercises are illegal or fraught with danger. In the early 1990s, for example, an Egyptian court convicted a writer of heresy and sentenced him to eight years in prison. Around the same time, the Iranian government tried Salman Rushdie, author of *The Satanic Verses,* in absentia and sentenced him to death under Islamic law for apostasy, acts that threaten God's word. In twenty-first century Germany, a person commits a crime if he or she writes anything that denies the Holocaust, the systematic attempt by the Nazis to exterminate all the Jews in Europe. Holocaust denial, however misguided and inaccurate, would be "protected speech" in the United States.

Determining who the criminal is may also rest in the hands of those with the power to do the defining. Were the civil rights protesters in the American South during the 1950s and 1960s criminals because they deliberately violated statutes that supported segregation? Were the antiwar protesters of the Vietnam era criminals? Was the well-known traitor to the English crown, George Washington, a terrorist? Is Osama Bin Laden a garden-variety criminal, a terrorist, a freedom fighter, or a religious warrior?

Ultimately, a crime is whatever the political machinery in a given geopolitical area—a local, state, or national government—says it is. Thus, certain actions constitute a crime if so defined by the criminal statutes, Moreover, it may also be that failing to act when required to do so by law is also legally unacceptable; for example, failing to pay one's taxes. Thus, a **crime** is any act in violation of an existing law, or failure to act when required by an existing law, which, upon conviction in a lawfully constituted court, results in a specific sanction, administered in the name of the entire community.

Classifying Crime

Laws provide a formal mechanism for the creation and maintenance of social order in complex societies. They define crime, whether a crime has been committed, whether a given person is guilty of the act, and the convicted offender's punishment. Criminologists resort to typologies as a means of classifying crime, several of which we have already employed.[6] The level of "evilness" is the basis of one such typology. *Mala in se,* Latin for "evil in itself," refers to crimes that are intrinsically evil, such as murder. Although societies may differ on the details of acts that constitute murder, all prohibit the behavior. This term contrasts with *mala prohibita,* Latin for "wrong because it is prohibited," which refers to activities that have been outlawed not because they are obviously or inherently evil, but because they violate certain societal standards. Insider trading, for example, is a violation of accepted business practices and is not intrinsically evil; rather, some people, through knowledge that is not generally available to everyone, gain an unfair advantage in a business transaction. When does an unfair business advantage become a crime? In 1909, the Supreme Court provided one answer to that question in the first case of insider trading, *Strong v. Repide.* A corporate executive who knew that his company's stock was about to soar in value bought company stock from an outsider without revealing what he knew. The court viewed the executive's actions as constituting fraud.[7]

Law distinguishes noncriminal—or civil—offenses (also called torts) from criminal ones, and criminal law distinguishes misdemeanors from felonies based upon the legalistic idea that the more serious offender should receive the more serious punishment. We can distinguish crimes from one another in terms of the length of punishment and place of confinement. Legally, **misdemeanors** are crimes other than felonies. Courts can punish those convicted of violating misdemeanors by sentencing them to no more than one year of incarceration in a city or county jail or federal correctional center or a fine up to a certain level. **Felonies** are punishable by death or more than one year in a state or federal

---

COMMENTS AND CRITICISMS: Social Harm

Some theorists classify behavior as criminal based on the amount of social harm the behavior causes. Marshall Clinard and associates note that the criminal law reflects differences in power. Burglary prosecutions, for example, routinely invoke more significant penalties than those for white-collar crime. Just one case of corporate law violation may involve millions or even billions of dollars in losses. The injuries caused by defective products, including pharmaceuticals, can involve thousands of persons in a single case. Consider, for example, the following cases:

- From May 1983 through June 1992, the U.S. Department of Justice initiated 102 prosecutions for price fixing involving 100 corporations: 96 pled guilty or were found guilty after trial.
- In 1993, it was revealed that in at least 20 states, executives of the nation's largest dairy companies had conspired, some for decades, to rig bids on milk products sold to schools and military bases. Dozens of executives pled guilty.
- In 1996, Archer Daniel Midlands (ADM), one of the world's leading grain processors with about $13 billion in annual sales, pled guilty to price fixing and paid $100 million, the largest fine ever in a federal antitrust case.

- In 2008, several airlines, including Air France, British Airways, KLM Royal Dutch Airlines, and SAS, pled guilty in the U.S. District Court for the District of Columbia to fixing prices on air cargo. Airline executives had conversations and held meetings for the purpose of monitoring and enforcing adherence to the agreed-upon cargo rates.
- In 2008, three leading electronics manufacturers pled guilty and agreed to pay a fine of $585 million for conspiring to fix the price of Thin-Film Transistor-Liquid Display panels used in computer monitors, televisions, notebooks, and other electronic devices—a $70 billion-a-year market.

The loss from a larceny-theft or a burglary is far less than that of corporate crime, but the persons who are found guilty of committing the former offenses may receive sentences of 10 years or more. The sole punishment for crimes committed by large corporations often consists of warnings, consent orders, or comparatively small fines paid by the corporation. As the title of a book by Jeffrey Reiman aptly points out, *The Rich Get Richer and the Poor Get Prison.*

SOURCES: Clinard et al. (1979); Henriques and Baquet (1993); Millman (1996); Reiman (2007); Ross (1961); Smith (1961a, b); U.S. Department of Justice (2008a, b).

---

prison or correctional institution, and as such represent far more serious crimes than misdemeanors. Other miscreant acts, deemed very minor, call for the creation of **ordinances,** the violation of which are resolved most often by a fine. Such acts include some traffic offenses and violations of local regulatory rules, such as parking regulations, smoking restrictions, and noise abatement rules. Moreover, as the box on social harm makes clear, not all criminologists agree even on the definition of harm.

Measuring Crime

Once we define and classify crime, we still have one important question left: How much crime is there? Today, there are two main sources of crime data on the national level. First, the Federal Bureau of Investigation (FBI) annually publishes *Crime in the United States*, also known as the *Uniform Crime Report* (UCR).[8] The second main source of information about crime and its victims on a national level comes from the National Crime Victimization Survey (NCVS). We begin with a brief review of the UCR.

Uniform Crime Report   The **Uniform Crime Report (UCR)** is the responsibility of the Federal Bureau of Investigation (FBI), which receives data about crime from law enforcement agencies throughout the country. The report provides information on two types of crimes, Part I Offenses and Part II Offenses. Part I Offenses are crimes (1) that victims are most likely to report, (2) that occur most frequently, and (3) that are serious because of their frequency of occurrence. The UCR ranks them in order of seriousness: four personal and four property crimes. Part I Offenses are "crimes known to the police" in eight categories (see UCR1–8 in Table 1.1). In contrast, crimes in the Part II Offense category do not meet the test of frequency of occurrence or seriousness and are summaries of arrest statistics; moreover, they include so-called "victimless" crimes (*mala prohibita* offenses). Thus, Part II Offenses are a measure, not of crime, but of police activity (see UCR9–29 in Table 1.1).

According to the FBI, in the 20 years between 1988 and 2007, the actual volume of violent and property crime declined in the nation, while the population increased by nearly 60 million inhabitants. Moreover, as we learn in Table 1.2, crime rates for most Part I crimes peaked in the early 1990s and then dropped precipitously through the end of the decade and into the early 2000s. For example, murder dropped from its peak of 9.0 (1991) to 5.5 (2000), where it has remained for over eight years.

This official picture of crime is clearly at odds with the popular media's portrayal of high crime and especially high levels of violent crime. There are many technical reasons to question statistics that are essentially the work product of a governmental entity. First, these crime data rely on someone witnessing and reporting the crime. Except in two categories—homicide and auto theft—underreporting of crime occurs for many reasons, including the shame of victims, their involvement in the crime, the fact that the loss or injury was so small as not to be worth reporting, and the use of "private justice" to rectify the matter (Abadinsky and Winfree 1992:58). Generally, homicide data accurately reflect homicide rates since a dead body requires a death certificate signed by a medical doctor listing the cause of death. When the cause of death is not natural or suspicious, the medical examiner will determine if it is a homicide. While the authorities sometimes never find a homicide victim (e.g., Jimmy Hoffa), such occurrences are extremely rare. Almost all owners insure their automobiles against theft, and an insurance company will not entertain a claim unless the insured reports the theft to the police. Auto theft does suffer from overreporting as the result of insurance fraud.

The official picture of crime described in the UCR does not include the "dark figure" of crime, crimes that go unreported and therefore unnoticed by the police. The crime victimization survey is a response to concern about crime data that is missing in the UCR.

National Crime Victimization Survey   The practice of crime surveys is nearly 300 years old (Biderman et al. 1967). Federally funded national crime surveys began in 1972, and initially included both a central city survey of 26 metropolitan areas and a national crime survey, the latter providing details of crime

T A B L E 1.1   **Uniform Crime Reports: Crime Categories (UCR1–29)**

UCR category	Crime description
Part I Offenses	
UCR1	Criminal Homicide: Murder and nonnegligent manslaughter
UCR1a	Murder and nonnegligent manslaughter
UCR1b	Manslaughter by negligence
UCR2	Forcible rape
UCR2a	Rape by force
UCR2b	Attempt to commit forcible rape
UCR3	Robbery
UCR3a	Using a firearm
UCR3b	Using a knife or cutting instrument
UCR3c	Using any other weapon
UCR3d	Strong-arm robbery (mugging)
UCR4	Aggravated assault
UCR4a	Using a firearm
UCR4b	Using a knife or cutting instrument
UCR4c	Using any other dangerous weapon
UCR4d	Using hands, fists, feet, etc. to cause aggravated injury
UCR5	Burglary
UCR5a	Forcible entry
UCR5b	Unlawful entry (no force)
UCR5c	Attempted forcible entry
UCR6	Larceny theft
UCR6a	Pocket picking
UCR6b	Purse snatching
UCR6c	Shoplifting
UCR6d	Thefts from motor vehicles
UCR6e	Theft of motor vehicle parts and accessories
UCR6f	Theft of bicycles
UCR6g	Theft from building
UCR6h	Theft from coin-operated devices or machines
UCR6i	All other larcenies
UCR7	Motor vehicle theft
UCR7a	Automobiles
UCR7b	Trucks and buses
UCR7c	Other vehicles

(Continued)

T A B L E 1.1 (Continued)

UCR category	Crime description
UCR8	Arson
UCR8a–g	Arson-structural (seven different kinds of structures)
UCR8h–i	Arson-mobile (vehicle or other mobile property)
UCR8j	Other
Part II Offenses	
UCR9	Simple assault
UCR10	Forgery and counterfeiting
UCR11	Fraud
UCR12	Embezzlement
UCR13	Stolen property: buying, receiving, possessing
UCR14	Vandalism
UCR15	Weapon: carrying, possessing, etc.
UCR16	Prostitution and commercialized vice
UCR17	Sex offenses (except UCR2 and URC16)
UCR18	Drug abuse violations
UCR19	Gambling
UCR20	Offenses against the family and children
UCR21	Driving under the influence
UCR22	Liquor law (offense)
UCR23	Drunkenness
UCR24	Disorderly conduct
UCR25	Vagrancy
UCR26	All other offenses (except traffic law violations)
UCR27	Suspicion
UCR28	Curfew and loitering law (juveniles)
UCR29	Runaways (juveniles)

victimizations for both homes and businesses. A redesign in 1975 dropped the 26-city survey and the businesses. In 1992, a second redesign resulted in the current **National Crime Victimization Survey (NCVS).**

Each year, trained researchers obtain victimization data from a nationally representative sample of 76,000 households, obtaining information from nearly 135,000 persons. Surveyors ask respondents about the frequency, characteristics, and consequences of criminal victimizations at their address. The Bureau of

T A B L E   1.2   Crime in the United States by Volume and Rate per 100,000 Inhabitants, 1988–2007

Year	Violent crime	Violent crime rate	Murder and nonnegligent manslaughter rate	Forcible rape rate	Robbery rate	Aggravated assault rate	Property crime	Property crime rate	Burglary rate	Larceny theft rate	Motor vehicle theft rate
1988[1]	1,566,221	640.6	8.5	37.8	222.1	372.2	12,356,865	5,054.0	1,316.2	3,151.7	586.1
1989	1,646,037	666.9	8.7	38.3	234.3	422.9	12,605,412	5,107.1	1,283.6	3,189.6	634.0
1990	1,820,127	729.6	9.4	41.1	256.3	441.9	12,655,486	5,073.1	1,232.2	3,185.1	655.8
1991	1,911,767	758.2	9.8	42.3	272.7	427.6	12,961,116	5,140.2	1,252.1	3,229.1	659.0
1992	1,932,274	757.7	9.3	42.8	263.7	391.0	12,505,917	4,903.7	1,168.4	3,103.6	631.6
1993	1,926,017	747.1	9.5	41.1	256.0	361.4	12,218,777	4,740.0	1,099.7	3,033.9	606.3
1994	1,857,670	713.6	9.0	39.3	237.8	324.0	12,131,873	4,660.2	1,042.1	3,026.9	591.3
1995	1,798,792	684.5	8.2	37.1	220.9	309.5	12,063,935	4,590.5	987.0	3,043.2	560.3
1996	1,688,540	636.6	7.4	36.3	201.9	288.6	11,805,323	4,451.0	945.0	2,980.3	525.7
1997	1,636,096	611.0	6.8	35.9	186.2	287.5	11,558,475	4,316.3	918.8	2,891.8	505.7
1998	1,533,887	567.6	6.3	34.5	165.5	385.6	10,951,827	4,052.5	863.2	2,729.5	459.9
1999	1,426,044	523.0	5.7	32.8	150.1	433.4	10,208,334	3,743.6	770.4	2,550.7	422.5
2000	1,425,486	506.5	5.5	32.0	145.0	440.5	10,182,584	3,618.3	728.8	2,477.3	412.2
2001[2]	1,439,480	504.5	5.6	31.8	148.5	418.3	10,437,189	3,658.1	741.8	2,485.7	430.5
2002	1,423,677	494.4	5.6	33.1	146.1	382.1	10,455,277	3,630.6	747.0	2,450.7	432.9
2003	1,383,676	475.8	5.7	32.3	142.5	334.3	10,442,862	3,591.2	741.0	2,416.5	433.7
2004	1,360,088	463.2	5.5	32.4	136.7	318.6	10,319,386	3,514.1	730.3	2,362.3	421.5
2005	1,390,745	469.0	5.6	31.8	140.8	295.4	10,174,754	3,431.5	726.9	2,287.8	416.8
2006[3]	1,418,043	473.6	5.7	31.0	149.4	290.8	9,983,568	3,334.5	729.4	2,206.8	398.4
2007	1,408,337	466.9	5.6	30.0	147.6	283.8	9,843,481	3,263.5	722.5	2,177.8	363.3

1. Population figures are U.S. Census Bureau provisional estimates as of July 1 for each year except 1990 and 2000, which are decennial census counts.
2. The murder and nonnegligent manslaughters that occurred as a result of the events of September 11, 2001, are not included in this table.
3. The 2006 figures have been adjusted since publication of *Crime in the United States, 2006.*

NOTE: Although arson data are included in the trend and clearance tables, sufficient data are not available to estimate totals for this offense. Therefore, no arson data are published in this table.

Source: Federal Bureau of Investigation (2008b).

Justice Statistics (BJS) takes this information and estimates the likelihood of victimization by rape, sexual assault, robbery, assault, theft, household burglary, and motor vehicle theft for the nation as a whole. The BJS also prepares periodic population-specific (e.g., elderly and youth) and crime-specific (e.g., rape, theft) studies from the national data.

Table 1.3 contains a trend analysis for violent and property crime. This table suggests three generalizations. First, from the first surveys through the 1995 redesign, violent crime was relatively stable, peaking several times at about 50 victimizations per 1,000 persons age 12 and older. Second, beginning in 1995, violent crime victimizations began to decline until 2000, stabilizing there for several years. Third, the general trend for property crime has been downward, dropping from a peak of about 570 per 1,000 in 1975 to a relatively stable rate of fewer than 200 since 2000. In short, the NCVS does not describe a nation consumed by increasing levels of either property or personal crime.

Counting crime is not a simple task, even when we share relatively similar definitions, legislative processes, court structures, and a general criminal law system (i.e., common law). There are also good reasons to question both the UCR and the NCVS as reliable and valid sources of information about crime—especially the latter. Indeed, this concern about the reliability and validity of crime data is not restricted to the United States, as the box on comparative criminology makes clear.

If our data on crime is generally an accurate reflection of trends in criminal behavior, how can we explain why crime rates go up or down? The theories discussed in this book will help provide an answer.

THE STRUCTURE OF THEORIES

A **theory** is an attempt to make sense of a real-world occurrence, an explanation in the form of a highly organized statement based on systematic observations about the phenomenon or class of phenomena under study. Theory enables prediction of when the phenomenon or phenomena under study will occur, or retrospectively, why it occurred in the past. A theory can explain the relationship between two or more variables—poverty and crime, for example, a neurotransmitter deficiency and criminal behavior, or IQ and crime—all of which we explore later in this book.

Theories are often abstract and complex. By abstract, we mean that they consist of statements generally unassociated with any material objects, specific circumstances, facts, or observations. Abstractness is both a curse and a blessing. On the one hand, abstractness tends to confuse the uninitiated, especially newcomers to criminology. Detractors describe theories as lacking concreteness, which is often the case. In fact, statements that purport to tell us about crime generally may not *directly* assist those who are responsible for reducing crime. Indeed, theorists sometimes fail to concern themselves with the practical applications of their abstract statements about crimes and criminals.

TABLE   1.3   National Crime Victimization Survey: Violent Crime and Property Crime Trends from 1973–2005

Violent Crime Rates
Adjusted victimization rate
per 1,000 persons age 12 and over

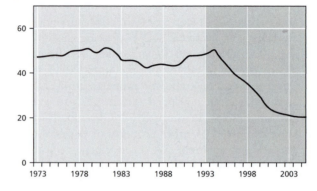

Property Crime Rates
Adjusted victimization rate
per 1,000 households

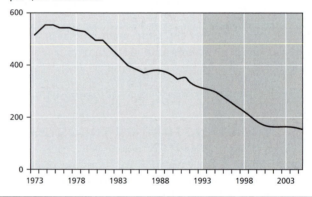

NOTE: Violent crimes include rape, robbery, aggravated and simple assault, and homicide. Property crimes include bur-glary, theft, and motor vehicle theft. The National Crime Victimization Survey redesign was implemented in 1993: the area with the lighter shading is before the redesign and the darker area is after the redesign. The data before 1993 are adjusted to make them comparable with data collected since the redesign. Estimates for 1993 and beyond are based on collection year while earlier estimates are based on data year.

SOURCES: BJS (2009a); BJS (2009b).

REFERENCES:
Bureau of Justice Statistics (2009a). "Trends in violent crime victimizations, 1973-2005." Retrieved at http://www.ojp. usdoj.gov/bjs/glance/viort.htm on April 6, 2009.
Bureau of Justice Statistics (2009b). "Trends in property crime victimizations, 1973-2005." Retrieved at http://www.ojp. usdoj.gov/bjs/glance/house2.htm on April 6, 2009.

On the other hand, criminologists tend to see theoretical abstractness as more of a blessing than a curse because the assertions in theories must go beyond the immediate time and place. A theory about some phenomenon in Indiana should also apply in Maine, and it should apply in both places today, last year, in the last

---

COMPARATIVE CRIMINOLOGY—WORLD VIEWS ON CRIME AND JUSTICE:
Defining, Measuring, and Comparing Crime

Philip L. Reichel tells us that we cannot easily compare crime data between nations, citing four main reasons:

- *Statistics are political statements:* Variability in crime rates might reflect poorly (or well) on the current political regime; hence, officials often check them quite thoroughly before publication. Some nations even give crime data to the United Nations Office on Drugs and Crime that is unavailable to their own citizens.

- *Problems in defining, reporting, and recording:* Some nations have crimes that do not exist in the U.S. legal system (e.g., apostasy or crimes against a deity) or these other nations may define the same crimes in slightly different ways, making comparisons difficult (e.g., blood alcohol levels for drunk-driving charges may vary between nations). In addition, citizens in some countries simply do not report all crimes to the police, often for the same reasons we see cited in the U.S. (e.g., a belief that the police will do nothing or a fear that the offender or even the police may retaliate against the victims). Few nations possess the existing infrastructure for crime defining, reporting, and recording that exists in the U.S.

- *Comparison problems:* The way in which police are organized varies across the globe, including the number of police per capita population. What a nation's crime statisticians count as a crime also varies. In some jurisdictions, they only count crimes forwarded for prosecution and not crimes known to the police.

- *Varying social structures affect crime rates:* Simply the absence of an effective public communications system (e.g., telephones) can influence crime reporting. Nations that have higher levels of insured citizens also report higher crime levels. Finally, the better a nation's medical infrastructure, the lower the homicide rate. Simply put, in some nations people die of injuries sustained in a criminal event that they would not die of had the assault occurred in another nation.

In spite of these problems, some comparisons are possible, and we provide many such cross-cultural examples at appropriate junctures in this text.

Source: Reichel (2008).

---

century, and in the next one. The extent to which a theory is tied to a particular set of events or people may help us understand what is happening here and now, but this same concreteness limits the theory's ability to provide the same types of insights for other places, times, and peoples. This comparison—concreteness versus abstractness—helps explain why most information obtained from the media or other individualistic, unsystematic observations yields few insights applicable beyond a specific set of circumstances.

Assumptions and Assertions: The Building Blocks of Theories

The complexity of theories lies in their assumptions and assertions. As we observed earlier in this chapter, it is important to know what a given theory assumes about human beings and, by extension, human behavior. There are other assumptions at work beyond the ones associated with the nature-or-nurture issue. For example, some theories are rooted in the assumption that people have the ability to choose alternative life paths freely, as they possess **free will.** Alternatively, other theories assume that forces beyond people's control largely shape individual and social behavior. Scientists describe this position as **determinism,** with the specific

---

COMMENTS AND CRITICISMS: What Is the Role of the Economy in Crime?

The economics–crime link provides a quandary for criminologists. What does it show? We know that when confronted with starvation, most of us would engage in law-violating behavior to survive. Short of such extreme situations, what is the economic order's impact on crime? In Chapter 10, the Marxists make much of surplus labor and exploitation of workers. We know there is a correlation between living in poverty and being convicted of crime—the overwhelming majority of persons convicted of crime are poor—but is poverty a *cause* of criminal behavior? Poverty is, after all, subjective and comparative, based on one's economic situation compared to others with whom he or she identifies. Thus, improvement in society's overall economic condition may have no real impact on crime that is economically driven, making a lie of the old saw: "A high tide raises all boats." Alternatively, something undesired could happen: In Western societies, increases in crime rates historically follow reductions in absolute poverty (Roshier 1989).

If not poverty, could the problem be about unemployment? We know that many offenders had jobs at the time of their arrest, albeit low-paying and dead-end ones. Some crimes, such as embezzlement and employee theft, require that the offender have a job. However, under- or unemployment and criminal behavior may have the same underlying cause, making the connection between unemployment and crime a spurious relationship. That is, employment and crime could both be dependent variables; a possible cause could be conflict. For example, those on the losing end of culture or group conflict may find it difficult to find employment, or to find employment that pays a wage sufficient to lift them out of poverty.

Perhaps the distance between the wealthiest and the poorest person in a society better explains the economic–crime connection. In the United States, 15 percent of American families hold 85 percent of the nation's wealth. Nations with greater social welfare benefits and, therefore, considerably higher taxes, such as the United Kingdom, Germany, Netherlands, Denmark, Finland, Norway, and Sweden, report less crime. Figure 1.1 represents this idea.

Research intended to show that economic conditions and crime directly relate to one another has met with mixed results. As Vold and Bernard observed: "[I]n the end it seems best to conclude that there is no direct causal relationship between crime and poverty since crime rates do not consistently increase and decrease as the number of poor people increases and decreases" (p. 141).

SOURCES: Allan and Steffensmeier (1989); O'Brien (1983); Currie (1985); Messner and Rosenfeld (1994); Vold and Bernard (1986); Zuckerman (2006).

Theoretical space between a society's richest and poorest person correlates with crime:

The greater the distance, the greater the rate of crime

FIGURE 1.1 Economic Inequality

---

underlying force signifying the form of determinism. For example, if a theorist proposes biological forces, such as brain functioning or mental illness, as the culprit, then the theory is rooted in biological determinism. It is important to note that a theory's assumptions constitute the theory's core belief system. Assumptions are taken as given and are either accepted or rejected, but they are not generally subject to testing or to modification.

Once the assumptions are stated, understood, and accepted, the next task is to consider the assertions. Theoretical assertions, or the relationships they imply, must be testable. If scientists cannot evaluate the assertions in the "real world" in which we live, then we are talking not about a theory but rather about something akin to an **ideology,** a set of strongly held beliefs that are not subject to testing or, in some cases, critical review of any sort. Some ideas on crime form a **theology,** an even stronger set of beliefs that originate with a god or other spiritual entity. Religious beliefs may offer interesting insights into the cause of crime, but these are usually faith-based and beyond any claim of scientific validity—they are not subject to testing.

Theorists often formalize their assertions as **propositions,** which are generalized statements about relationships, usually between two or more things.[9] In the formal language of logic, we refer to highly verified propositions, ones that receive consistent and strong support when tested, as **laws.** We refer to other propositions, ones for which the body of research is less compelling, as **hypotheses.** For example, we may view economic forces such as poverty or unemployment as leading to crime within the specific segments of society that evidence these characteristics. The economic force is the cause, and crime is the effect; without the former (poverty or unemployment), the latter (crime among the underclass) would not exist. Such a general relational statement about two facts is a hypothesis; this specific one represents an economic theory of crime, and is one we consider in the next box.

Strategies for the Scientific Enterprise

Any explanation of crime that aspires to the level of theory requires an application of the scientific enterprise, whose principles include a series of processes and products. Figure 1.2 summarizes the scientific enterprise in terms of four processes and four associated products (Wallace 1971).[10] First, theory is either the starting point for **deductive research** (i.e., theory-testing studies) or the ending point for **inductive research** (i.e., theory-building studies). Deductive researchers base their work on past theorizing that leads to research questions or testable hypotheses. Inductive researchers allow the data to "speak for themselves," providing findings that may emerge as theory.

Whether criminologists follow induction or deduction, a **research design** guides them toward answers to questions such as: Why are we doing the research? Who or what will we study in our search for answers? What do we want to know about the objects of study? Over what period will we conduct the study? Researchers often adopt a single mode of observation: They collect **qualitative data** (i.e., nonnumerical examinations and interpretations of observations intended to reveal the object of study's essence or basic nature) or **quantitative data** (i.e., numerical examinations and manipulations of observations intended to express the object of study in terms of accurate numerical equivalents). Less frequently, researchers seek both kinds of information. They then follow literally dozens of steps beginning with the decision to test a particular theory or generate information on a particular topic. A detailed elaboration of the process is beyond the scope of this book. However, because many of these

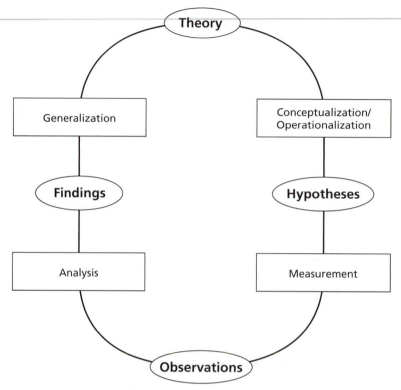

FIGURE 1.2 The Scientific Enterprise
SOURCE: Modified from Wallace (1971).

steps may constitute reasons to question a given study, we will refer to the relevant ones at the appropriate junctures.

Theory Testing: Deductive Reasoning and the Scientific Enterprise   Assume that the task is theory testing. This deductive approach begins with specific statements of causation and proceeds down the right side of Figure 1.2. The first stop—what we refer to as a product—is a hypothesis. To get to this point, criminologists generally follow several processes. Through **conceptualization,** they provide reasonably general and logical definitions for each important term contained in the theory. After defining the **concepts** and specifying their interrelationships, the criminologists-as-conceptualists specify the ways in which they can measure the concepts and actually test the linkages. They sometimes call this stage in the process **operationalization.** Through operationalization, criminologists provide the specific steps that allow for the measurement of the theory's key terms.

The operationalization process transforms concepts—a theory's abstract building blocks—into **variables,** things that can be counted, observed, or otherwise measured.[11] In the social sciences, data collection efforts are limited to what can be measured by smell, sight, taste, touch, or hearing. Intuition cannot provide empirical data, the basis for testing theories. Hence, operationalization refers to the steps by which the researchers ground the concepts in the world of sense impressions; that is, they describe them in terms that make concepts measurable. For example, crime is not, by itself, measurable using the moral, secular, or legalistic definitions previously provided. If, however, we ask *how often* a specific act—say, stealing an object worth more than $25 but less than $500—was committed between January 1, 2008, and December 31, 2008, in Dayton, Ohio, then we have provided an operational definition of crime. This highly restrictive definition does not cover all crimes or legal jurisdictions, but it does qualify as one possible operational definition of the concept of crime.

Hypotheses are another product of operationalization. The theory may provide explicit linkages between concepts called propositions, or it may suggest to the researcher what will happen in comparing two or more variables. Recall the alleged linkages between poverty and crime. In any event, once the concepts are operationally defined and the variables identified, we have one or more hypotheses. Hypotheses, then, are statements that assert specific relationships between certain observable facts.

By this stage in the research enterprise, the process of operationalization has yielded one or more variables for each concept. For example, a crime is a law violation, and a robbery is a type of serious crime; however, both are relatively abstract concepts. In contrast, the exact number of armed robberies reported to police in East Rutherford, New Jersey, in a specific 12-month period is a concrete variable. Bearing in mind the previous statements about poverty and crime, consider the following scenarios:

- Assume that for one 12-month period, the economy of East Rutherford was booming, followed by 12 months of economic bust. The theory predicts that crime, including perhaps armed robbery as an economically based offense, will increase over the second 12 months. In this example, the hypothesis is clear: The sum total of armed robberies in East Rutherford will be higher in the 12 months of economic decline than in the 12 months of economic prosperity.

- Assume that on January 1, New Jersey instituted "enhanced" sentencing for armed robbers: Persons convicted of armed robbery will receive a mandatory 20-year prison sentence. Moreover, the East Rutherford Police Department, which has been plagued in the previous 12 months by a series of unsolved armed robberies, has instituted an Armed Robbery Task Force. Consequently, the severity and certainty of punishments for armed robberies has increased dramatically. The hypothesis for this set of variables is the opposite of the previous one: The sum total of armed robberies in East Rutherford will be lower in the second 12-month period of enhanced deterrent effects than in the prior 12 months.

The theory-testing process continues up the left side of Figure 1.2. We explore these processes and products in detail in the section on theory building, but a brief overview is useful here. Researchers typically subject the resulting variables and hypotheses to measurement. They test the hypotheses, either accepting or rejecting them. Should the analysis stage support rejecting the hypotheses, then, by extension, they must reconsider the propositions and concepts as well. In essence, rejecting the research hypotheses calls into question all or part of the theory, or the operationalization of the variables, or both.

Even if we accept a theory-derived hypothesis, or cannot reject it, we do not consider the theory as proven. Rather, we view the research as contributing to the body of knowledge about the theory in question. This apparent equivocating—"weasel-wording"—is a necessary part of theory-driven research, whether the subject matter is crime or physics. Proof is an elusive goal in the world of theory. Eventually, given sufficient corroborating evidence, the theory's propositions may achieve the stature of a law. As you might suspect, this level of proof for criminological theories does not exist. Does this mean that research efforts are in vain? We think not and suggest that you reserve judgment.

Theory Building: Inductive Reasoning and the Scientific Enterprise   Inductive reasoning starts at the bottom left-hand side of Figure 1.2. The goal is to create generalizable findings that may yield systemic and organized assertions from **empirical observations.** Researchers who use this method also make assumptions about human behavior and the best ways to develop theories. In this case, the researchers do not so much test a theory as build it from the ground up, starting with the data.

Inductive researchers use qualitative and quantitative information. Unlike deductive researchers, who look to pre-existing theory for guidance, these researchers let the observations, no matter how we collect them, paint a picture of the phenomenon under study. **Analysis** is the process by which researchers look for patterns and ways of organizing their observations or data in systematic ways. The products of analysis are the **findings,** which, through a second process called generalization, may yield statements that extend the findings beyond the particular set of circumstances. Theory is the final product of inductive reasoning.

The generalization process is the obverse of operationalization and conceptualization. Here, the researchers essentially take the information gleaned about a specific case and make broad statements about similar objects (i.e., the general class of similar events or phenomena); they synthesize the observations derived from the data collection and make a general statement called an empirical generalization. An **empirical generalization** is, in essence, an individual proposition about or statement of the relationship between facts revealed by the data; moreover, this statement has the potential to go beyond the present case and so has causal implications for all similar phenomena.

Again, it is crucial to reiterate that Figure 1.2 is only a graphic representation of the ties between theory and research. The right half is representative of activities best described as theory testing; the left side represents theory-building activities. Dividing the figure in half, top to bottom, yields a different perspective on the scientific enterprise. The processes and products in the top half are far more abstract and removed from the world of sense impressions than those in the bottom half: The top half involves theorizing, and the bottom half represents research and analysis.

The Goals of Theory

According to our definition, there are at least four separate and equally important goals for crime theories. First, theory *as description* means that the statements embodied in the theory mesh with what we know about crime and criminals. The descriptions must have high levels of accuracy, reliability, and validity. The descriptive questions are framed in a "What is it?" format.

Theory *as explanation* answers a different ("Why is it?") set of questions: Explanation suggests a deeper penetration into the problem of crime, especially compared to simple description. They account for the very being of the things under study, providing the reason or reasons that such phenomena as crimes exist. Any theory—criminological or otherwise—that fails to explain contributes little to the theoretical enterprise. For example, why is it that our prison population, going back more than 200 years, is always overrepresented by persons from an underclass?

Theory *as prediction* shifts the emphasis a bit, in that prediction—the act of foretelling or making known beforehand—emphasizes time. In this context, prediction involves identifying when something will occur by specifying the conditions conducive to its occurrence. As such, prediction involves the "When is it?" question. Social, behavioral, and physical scientists often express prediction in probabilistic terms, stating the likelihood that, given a set of conditions, some event—in this case crime—will occur. It may have a 10 percent or a 90 percent probability of occurring; however, even physical scientists rarely deal in zero probability or 100 percent probability. Thus, greater levels of unemployment or a significant increase in the crime-prone population (e.g., males between 15 and 25) predicts greater levels of criminality.

Achieving the final goal, *theory as control,* is sometimes problematic for criminologists, because they may view themselves not as providers of solutions to problems, but rather as value-free observers of the social world. Consequently, they place a premium on **pure science,** or the creation of knowledge for its own sake, as contrasted with **applied science,** which attempts to address a specific societal need. The nuclear scientists who provided the theoretical basis for atomic, and eventually nuclear weapons, faced this dilemma several generations ago: They failed to establish policies for their use, leaving that decision to the politicians.

Social, behavioral, and physical scientists who study crime, whether they are sociologists, psychologists, physiologists, or biochemists, are becoming increasingly involved not only in the first three goals (i.e., describing, explaining, and predicting crime and criminals), but also in the use of the resulting knowledge to control behavior. The position of those who support theory-guided policy is simple: If those who know the most about the theory do not get involved, then persons who know less about its constituent parts and its strengths and weaknesses will define the policy and practice agenda.

Challenges for Theory Testing and Theory Building

We have summarized some of the logical and practical challenges awaiting anyone who engages in theorizing about physical, behavioral, or social phenomena. Many others are beyond the scope of this text. We turn next to a review of some of the most important remaining challenges. These concerns—correlation versus causation, tautological traps, and the role played by values in both theorizing and researching—often cause the public, policy makers, and even criminologists to stumble in their search for answers.

Correlation versus Causation   When exploring theory, and especially when testing hypotheses, we must avoid confusing causation with correlation. A **correlation** ties two variable measures of events together. To say that two phenomena are correlated means that a change in one precedes a change in the other. Perhaps the presence or absence of alleged cause A is sufficient to alter effect B. In this case, we can express the notion of a correlation as follows: In the presence (or absence) of A, B changes in certain ways. For example, we may observe a close correlation between poverty and birthrates, but low income does not *cause* pregnancy. Similarly, there is a strong correlation between poverty and crime, but it does not *explain* crime. That is, most known criminals—with emphasis on the term *known*—are from an economically deprived background, but they represent only a small fraction of the poor, and criminals come from all economic backgrounds. Another variable, perhaps a biological or sociological one, may explain poverty and crime.

Causation, an equally complex concept, refers to anything that produces an effect. In the language of science, for scientists to view one event as another's *cause*, the first event—the cause—must satisfy three criteria. First, the putative (alleged) cause must precede the effect in time, a requirement referred to as time-order sequencing. The amount of time (e.g., seconds, weeks, months, years, or millennia) is largely irrelevant—except to the person seeking the cause. For example, the child who touches the surface of a hot stove will recoil immediately as the nerve endings send a message to the child's brain. Conversely, the consequences of building homes on landfill poisoned by contaminated waste may not be evident for decades until medical researchers observe increased rates of birth defects or cancer. Being abused as a child may "cause" criminal behavior by the victim when "the victim" becomes an adult.

According to the second criterion, once they establish that the cause indeed precedes the effect in time, researchers must demonstrate the presence of a correlation. If the researchers can count the correlated variables, they may express the resulting relationship in statistical terms and described as strong, weak, or somewhere in between.[12]

The third criterion is the absence of a spurious link between the alleged cause and effect. **Spuriousness** is a quality accorded certain types of relationships. It refers to an observed relationship between two measures (or variables) that is due to the influence of a third measure (or variable). We can make this statement because when we control for the third variable's influence, the relationship disappears. The third variable is "a rival causal factor" (F. Hagan 1989:32). Historically, in areas with more storks, there were more children. While we know that storks do not bring (cause) babies, rural areas have a high number of both storks and babies—farming communities generally see children as an economic asset. Thus, the correlation between storks and babies is spurious

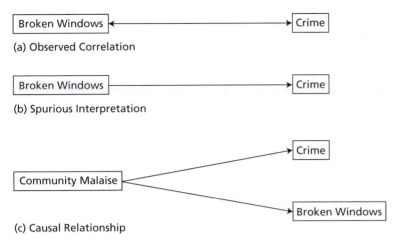

FIGURE 1.3 Correlation versus Causation: The Case of Crime and Broken Windows

while the variable "rural" explains both the high rate of storks and the high rate of babies.

We represent the difference between correlation and causation in Figure 1.3. In this case, the observed relationship between crime and broken windows serves as an exemplar. As observed by James Q. Wilson and George Kelling (1982), when a single window is broken in, say, an abandoned apartment building, and no one bothers to fix it, soon a few more, then dozens more, and eventually all the windows in the building will be broken. Just as importantly, crime in the neighborhood surrounding the building will increase at a rate that approximates that of the breaking of the windows in the building. Diagram (a) in Figure 1.3 represents this correlation. Did the broken windows cause the crime, as this correlation seems to imply? That would represent a spurious interpretation (and defy logic). Wilson and Kelling (1982) maintain that both broken windows and increased crime share a common cause: community malaise. The same sense of uneasiness and disconnectedness within the neighborhood that caused community members not to fix the windows led to increased crime.

The Tautological Trap   One final significant cautionary note about assumed causal ordering remains. When expressing or testing a theory, scientists must avoid tautological or circular reasoning. A **tautology** occurs when the variable under study and its cause are indistinguishable from each other. For example, Sigmund Freud's pleasure–pain principle is often given as an example of a tautology: "If one says that a man does what is pleasurable to him and that he does not do what is painful, then *everything* he does is pleasurable by *definition*" (Simon 1969:211; emphasis in original). Years ago, psychologists observed a strong statistical relationship between psychometric tests for psychopathy, a relatively rare mental condition to which we return later in this text, and subsequent criminality. However, imbedded in their measure of psychopathy was the propensity to break the law. Hence, the researchers used past behavior (i.e., prior rule-breaking

conduct) to predict future behavior (i.e., subsequent illegal conduct). In tautological terms, psychopathic behavior is the behavior of psychopaths.

At times, the issue of tautological relationships can be tricky. For example,
differential association theory argues that the strength of one's patterns of
association—prosocial or antisocial—determines behavior, law-abiding or criminal. According to this explanation, criminal association leads to criminality, but
criminal association is also the result of criminality—"birds of a feather flock
together." Does the use of these variables constitute a tautology? Perhaps, but if it
can be shown that criminality did not exist prior to criminal associations, then a
possible interpretation is that, due to increased criminality in a community, youths
have fewer opportunities to associate with non-criminals. Thus, there is a feedback
loop between criminality and criminal associations, a condition that is not, strictly
speaking, a tautology.

Research, Theory, and Values   The scientific method basic to developing theory presumes neutrality in the search for "truth": The scientist is neither
Republican nor Democrat, liberal or conservative. Is a lack of values possible or
even desirable? What will be the influence of values on the types of scientific
questions and evidence pursued? Although theory is the basic building block
for the advancement of human knowledge, the testing of crime theories is
problematic.

In the natural sciences, such as chemistry and biology, scientific neutrality is
easier to attain than in the behavioral sciences. In the natural sciences, researchers
can subject their theories to rigorous laboratory testing and replication (testing the
effects of certain chemicals on genetically engineered—and nearly identical—
laboratory rats, for example). The social or behavioral sciences are concerned with
behavior that is peculiarly human, and testing is limited accordingly. We could
subject rats to extreme levels of physical stress and then study their reaction to
morphine. However, we would not subject humans to similar levels of stress,
expose them to morphine, and then see if they became drug addicts. Social
scientists often must study the etiology of drug addiction indirectly or in a more
ex post facto (after the fact) fashion, looking at the effects of drug addiction or efforts
to treat the disorder in existing addicts.

The "gold standard" of research is the experimental design using random
assignment (Weisburd, Lum, and Petrosino 2001), an approach difficult to apply
in the study of crime (see Chapter 12). Thus, while conventional wisdom (often
neither wise nor sensible) posits a connection between abuse in childhood and
criminality in adulthood, we could not (ethically or legally) randomly select a
group of children to subject to child abuse and compare them to another randomly selected group whom we have protected from abuse to measure differences in adult criminality between the two. We could, and we did, however,
test the effectiveness of police preventive patrol by doubling the size of the police on patrol while withdrawing all police patrol from similar police beats, and
comparing both to beats that were left unchanged (Kelling et al. 1974).

In the search for causal relationships, theories that are too broad or too complex can be difficult to test, and attempts may yield conflicting results. Even

theories that have not been subjected to empirical research or have garnered little support may be promoted by those who decide crime policy. For example, consider the following purported truth statement: Increasing the number of police officers on patrol will reduce crime. Although a popular policy argument ("Let's put 100,000 more police on the nation's streets"), researchers have questioned it for over 30 years (Kelling et al. 1974). The policy of providing more police as a way of reducing crime may defy logic: It is reasonable to believe that a person will not commit a crime when a uniformed officer is present; it is illogical to believe that this will deter further criminal behavior or reduce crime when the officer is someplace else on the beat.

Consider the following illustration of this logical question. A hypothetical male miscreant, set on illegal enrichment (read: robbery), spots a uniformed police officer and as a result does not commit robbery. However, if he simply goes to an area where no police officer is present or delays his crime to another time, crime simply has been displaced or delayed, not deterred or eliminated. Our hypothetical miscreant, now fearful of the police, gives up on crime completely—deterred—and instead registers for college (and becomes a criminal justice major). Does that scenario appear likely?

The perception of reality often determines the outcome. In other words, if policy makers behave as if a particular theory is correct, then, whatever the objective reality, the theory is real in its consequences. However, research that fails to support a particular theory does not necessarily undermine its validity since the theorists may modify their arguments to account for the findings. Too many modifications, however, may result in a theory that is so broad as to reduce if not eliminate its usefulness to practitioners.

Some theories may be too broad to be tested or too limited in their application to explain crime across social classes, cultures, or history. For example, theories that link a lack of legitimate economic opportunity to criminal behavior fail to account for individual differences among those with limited opportunities. James Q. Wilson and Richard Herrnstein (1985), in a review of crime theories, restricted their search to crime that was predatory and to criminals who committed serious crimes at high rates In other words, they chose those crimes most likely committed by individuals at the bottom of the social scale. Any policy evolving out of their theory, therefore, will be class-specific.

The same would apply to research into corporate crime, acts most likely committed by those at the top of the social scale. The choice of crimes—those most likely committed by persons in the lower or upper strata of society, for example — often reflects a bias of either the researchers or those funding the research. Researchers whose funding source is corporate, for example, may avoid delving into corporate crime. Similarly, government funds for research into crime may avoid angering political benefactors (read: political campaign contributors) by similarly avoiding research into corporate criminality.

Limits of Criminological Knowledge   What are the limits to our ability to generate crime theories that are applicable to criminal justice policies and practices? The answer depends upon whom you ask, as we could array their responses on a continuum from "all theories are useful" to "no theories are useful." However, the reality is that many theories emerge with very practical goals in mind. For example, criminologists in Chicago in the early twentieth century viewed that city as having endemic problems that "caused" crime in certain parts of the city, problems that could be changed by vigorous social action. Later generations of criminologists suggested theories to help probation or parole officers by creating conditions of release that minimized exposure to criminogenic social forces.

As Kurt Lewin (1951) once observed, "There is nothing so practical as a good theory." This statement, however, has generally not taken hold in criminology. Can theories contribute to crime control policies and practices? Glen Leavitt (1999) provided a thought-provoking answer: "No, not at this time." Crime theories are, in his estimation, far too discursive—that is, rambling or digressive in nature (see also Gibbs 1972, 1985). Criminological theorizing, he further observed, while increasingly gaining scientific status, often fails to identify clearly the key assumptions, provides ill-defined concepts and murky propositions, and confuses the assumptions and the assertions. In Leavitt's opinion, one we suspect others inside and outside of academic criminology share, crime theories are more art than science. Hence, the ability of criminology to serve as a "handmaiden of the criminal justice machinery" is quite limited (Leavitt 1999:398). As you read the chapters that follow, we recommend that you reflect on Leavitt's concerns. We also suggest that you independently assess the value of the various theories discussed. Consider the following question as well: If contemporary theories are too discursive *and* of little practical use to criminal justice practitioners, is it not possible that the call to be useful and practical might motivate theorists and researchers to make theories more formal and rigorous? Finally, if theory does not drive criminal justice policy, what is its basis? It is hard to conceive of a policy in criminal justice that does not have theory at its core, although its proponents or those employed to carry it out may not understand or even realize what theory underlies their actions.

The Case for Considering Theory

The basic questions seem so simple: Why is there crime? Why do we have criminals? We should not lose sight of the fact that theory, whatever the specific manifestation, provides the best insights into the "why?" and "how?" of the phenomenon under investigation. It is in testing and applying those ideas that we learn about their "goodness of fit" with reality. Consider the following observations about the possible linkages between crime theory, research, policy, and practice:

- Theories that essentially are untestable are of little use in crime studies, especially if we seek to understand crime, predict its occurrence, and ultimately control it.

- All theories have some policy implications although, for political, moral, economic, or social reasons, it may be impossible to implement the policies suggested by a given theory.

- Research that is atheoretical (i.e., has no connection to theory)—or perhaps is even antitheoretical—may yield interesting, short-term insights into the phenomenon under study. However, unless that phenomenon is static and immutable, the long-term utility of such research and any policy decisions based upon it are limited.

- Policies whose theoretical underpinnings are unknown may have limited utility, as they may meet immediate needs if based on current research, but be unable to meet the demands of a changing society.

- Practices that are not subjected to exhaustive research—especially evaluation research—can undermine the authority of their source, whether that is a specific criminal justice agency (e.g., police misuse of firearms or high-speed chases) or society in general (e.g., laws criminalizing the use of a drug that enjoys widespread use in society or laws increasing the sanctions for violent juvenile offenders).

Figure 1.4 schematically represents the central ties between crime theory, research, policy, and practice. All four elements address the problem of crime. Each one depends on the adjacent elements for basic inputs; however, the information flow is in both directions (e.g., theory depends on research, and research upon theory). The model also suggests that theory impacts practice only indirectly through research and policy. This indirect linkage may account for the reluctance of some practitioners to engage in, let alone be persuaded by, theoretical discussions, leading to the popular—and often disdainful—refrain: That's nothing but theory!

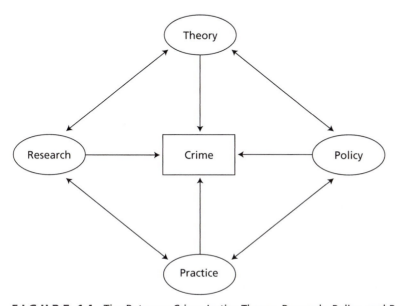

F I G U R E 1.4 Ties Between Crime Justice Theory, Research, Policy, and Practice

In the chapters that follow, we examine theories and their supporting research, as well as any associated policies and practices. By simultaneously considering all four basic elements, we enhance our understanding of crime theory. Before we can evaluate the various crime theories, however, we must briefly and critically examine the underpinnings of most contemporary views on the nature of laws and crimes.

UNDERSTANDING CRIME

This section provides the tools to examine a wide range of crime theories with a critical eye. That is, we predicate our understanding of crime theories in this text on knowledge of the elements of theories, the ability to assess them, and an awareness of their linkages to criminal justice policies and procedures.

Elements of Theories

Theories have many parts. In the first section of this chapter, we explored the role of assumptions and assertions in the structure of theory, as well as the challenges that confront all those proffering a crime theory. In subsequent chapters, we explore each theory's (1) underlying assumptions, whatever their source; (2) causal arguments, including, where appropriate, propositions and hypotheses; (3) implicit concepts and variables; (4) empirical support for the causal arguments, including quantitative and qualitative forms; and (5) fulfilled, unfulfilled, or ignored goals. We suggest that you may wish to refer back to this chapter later in the text when you encounter these ideas as the wellspring for twentieth and even twenty-first century theories of crime and criminals.

Equally important to the theoretical enterprise is the contextualization of theory. That is, we must consider each theory in terms of its historical context, and the forms and types of supporting evidence provided. It is also important to consider the role of the government as an advocate, opponent, or neutral party in response to the theory and its implications for social policy. At times, this activity becomes a history lesson, as we consider theories that emerged over the last three centuries. Unless we clearly understand the social, historical, and political context out of which a theory emerged, it is not possible to appreciate fully that theory's relevance to the study of crime.

The discussion of each theoretical orientation begins with a series of questions related to the theory. We suggest that you review and seriously consider every one of them. They are not rhetorical questions, asked simply as a means of amplifying an obvious point. Embedded within these questions are sample assumptions, propositions (and hypotheses), or concepts (and variables) that provide the gist of each theory. We purposely grounded the questions (and a few statements) in non-theoretical, real-world terms as a means of providing a connection between theory and reality. Spending a few minutes considering these questions will make it easier to understand the elements of the various theories.

Assessing Theories

Criminologists and others often talk about "good theories," as opposed to "bad theories." One meaning of this distinction is that a "good theory" (1) is readily understood and makes sense (i.e., has logical merit); (2) stands up well under empirical scrutiny, whether it is qualitatively or quantitatively; and (3) generally achieves some (or all) of the goals of theory (i.e., describes, predicts, explains, or controls the phenomena under study). A "bad theory" fails to exhibit one or more of these qualities. Some theories that make sense, are logically consistent, and have powerful implications for criminal justice practice have not fared well when subjected to empirical verification. Does this mean that they are "bad" or weak theories? Hardly. What it may mean is that adequate tests have yet to be constructed or that the operationalization of key concepts is incomplete. As a case in point, consider the fate of social disorganization theory, a macro-sociological explanation (see Chapter 6). Shortly after they applied it to urban blight and crime in the 1920s and 1930s, criminologists abandoned the theory as suffering from an intrinsic and fatal error: They could not separate the cause from the effect. In the late 1980s, however, this same theory—complete with a few refinements, better data, and sophisticated analyses—enjoyed an explanatory renaissance.

In each subsequent chapter, we provide two sections on theory assessment. First, after reviewing the assumptions and assertions of each theory, we give an overall assessment of the evidence, highlighting with bulleted items the points most in dispute. The intent is to summarize the key critical themes, the strengths and shortcomings, and the general tenor of the evolving body of theory-specific research. Second, at the end of each chapter, we provide a table summarizing the following information about every theory in the chapter: its name or names, its major proponents (and critics), its central assumptions, its causal arguments (and key terms), and its strengths and weaknesses.

We view the process of assessment in terms of judging, measuring, or evaluating the worth of something. Here we provide (1) the theory's truth claims—what the theory's proponents say it intends to describe, explain, predict, or control—and (2) the body of evidence supporting those claims. Thus, assessing theories in the present context is more of an ongoing, up-to-date appraisal than a final judgment. This goal is in keeping with the spirit of the theoretical enterprise.

The discussion of each theory concludes with a section on criminal justice policies and procedures. Certain theories are ripe with implications for the criminal justice system. In some cases, lawmakers have formulated laws in response to crime theories; in others, legislative responses mimic the theories, but have no direct connection. Crime theories also help us understand law enforcement, judicial, and correctional agencies. Indeed, we can understand sometimes the law-violating and law-abiding actions of individuals within these entities in terms of crime theory. Some theories have few direct implications for criminal justice policies or procedures; but even then, they allow for a better general understanding of why the system responds as it does to certain threats to the social order.

SUMMARY

You now know the basic definitions and philosophical orientations we employ in subsequent chapters, along with the organizational structure and rationale for reviewing a wide array of theories—all intended to generate a better understanding of crime. In addition, this chapter contains three important lessons. First, we must not lose sight of the fact that crime theories are developed, tested, and rejected or accepted in a sociopolitical context. We can enhance our understanding of a specific crime theory by knowledge of its implicit, and sometimes explicit, social and political implications. Second, we must clearly understand the link between crime theory and crime research, an understanding that is essential either to test or to build theories. Studying theories without reviewing the related research (or data), with all due respect to Arthur Conan Doyle's character Sherlock Holmes, is akin to making bricks without clay.[13] Third, if we are to gain a full sense of the links between crime theory and research, we must also clearly delineate the ties of each to crime policy and "crime fighting" practices.

The theories presented in this text are valuable for their contributions to our understanding of human social behavior, including crime and delinquency. However, in the minds of some criminologists and criminal justice practitioners, crime theories should also contribute to the control of crime. Our goal, then, is to provide a comprehensive view into both the theory and practice of crime, one that will yield a better understanding of how society views—and responds to— crime and criminals in the new century.

KEY TERMS

analysis

applied science

causation

concepts

conceptualization

conflict

consensus

correlation

crime

criminology

customary laws

deductive research

determinism

empirical generalization

empirical observation

enacted laws

evidence-based practices (EBP)

felonies

findings

folkways

free will

hypotheses

ideology

inductive research

laws

mala in se

mala prohibita

misdemeanors

mos/mores

National Crime Victimization Survey (NCVS)

nature

nature-versus-nurture controversy

norms

nurture

operationalizations

pure science

proposition	qualitative data	theory
ordinance	quantitative data	typology
pluralist	research design	Uniform Crime Report (UCR)
prescriptive norms	spuriousness	
propositions	tautology	variables
proscriptive norms	theology	

CRITICAL REVIEW QUESTIONS

1. What are the elements that constitute law?
2. How can we distinguish laws that compel conduct from laws that facilitate voluntary actions?
3. Why is it so difficult to define crime?
4. What are the elements of a theory?
5. How can we distinguish correlation from causation?
6. What is a tautology and why is it important to theories of crime?
7. Why is theory testing in the natural sciences easier than in the social sciences?
8. How do the consensus, pluralist, and conflict views of society differ?
9. Why might it be comforting to believe in theories that explain crime according to qualities inherent in the individual criminal actor?
10. Go to the Internet and research "Three Strikes" legislation and its impact in your state. How does that impact compare to the national picture provided in the text?

NOTES

1. These "criminals" or terrorists, if you will, are of course the 9/11 hijackers, whose short lives and horrible acts McDermott (2005) describes so well.

2. Ted Bundy's story as a serial killer with a propensity for sadism and necrophilia continues to attract the attention of laypeople and criminologists (see also Rule 2000; Keppel 2005). Physically attractive and intellectually gifted, his outward persona did not fit the stereotype of the twisted killer portrayed in popular media.

3. Orenthal James Simpson's double-homicide trial in 1995 shaped how a generation saw the American criminal justice system. Scholars, journalists, and others wrote thousands of pages about the failures of Los Angeles police and prosecutors to bring Simpson to justice (Hunt 1999). The criminal trial verdict highlighted the racial divide on justice issues in America, revealed in a national survey prior to the

trial: most African Americans believed Simpson was not guilty, while most white American held the opposing view. Perhaps Simpson's 2008 fall into the abyss was due in no small measure to his own internalized belief that he was above the law, if not beyond its reach.

4. While Aileen Wuornos was the subject of two television documentaries and a feature-length film (*Monster*), Reynolds (2004) tells her story in riveting detail. However, Wuornos was certainly not the first female serial killer or even the worst. In the 2008 movie "Changeling," director Clint Eastwood tells the poignant story of a mother's search for her kidnapped son. Missing from the movie is Sarah Louise ("Louisa") Northcutt. The grandmother of chief perpetrator Gordon Northcutt, Louisa actively participated in most if not all of the homicides at the Wineville Chicken Ranch, but perhaps for cinematic and dramatic reasons, she is missing from the movie. Spared the death penalty, authorities in California paroled her fewer than 12 years into her life sentence.

5. There are too many cases in American true crime history of mothers drowning their children to catalog here. Two "infamous" cases illustrate this form of criminal act. South Carolina's Susan Smith, who in 1994 drowned her two sons in a lake, received life in prison. Texas's Andrea Yates, who drowned her five children in a bathtub, also received life in prison, although the state of Texas sought the death penalty. Popular culture has found the "drowning-mother" syndrome too powerful to resist, as it was the basis for episodes of the television show *Law & Order* and musical groups of various genre have performed songs about these murdering mothers.

6. A **typology** is a systematic method of classifying information according to clearly specified rules; it allows for the collapsing of information into more manageable and logical clusters or groups.

7. The 1909 Supreme Court decision did not settle the matter of what is insider trading. Over the course of the next 70-plus years, it and other appellate courts heard dozens of cases. However, it was the "merger mania" of the 1980s that propelled insider trading into the lexicon of average Americans. As Newkirk and Robertson (1998) observe, the significance of this legal concept has grown tremendously on both the domestic and international stages since the end of the 1980s, especially in the face of globalized business and economic interests.

8. In 1988, the FBI director acknowledged that the nation needed better data to fight crime in the upcoming millennium. The result was the National Incident-Based Reporting System (NIBRS), which consisted of 46 specific crimes, including all Part I Offenses and most important Part II Offenses, along with 11 other "lesser crimes." NIBRS data included details about each criminal event, all parties to the crime and victims. After two decades of work, the NIBRS effort has stalled, as only 26 states are NIBRS-compliant, that is, their data collection and reporting systems comply with FBI standards. As the FBI acknowledges on its website: "Although participation grows steadily, data are still not pervasive enough to make broad generalizations about crime in the United States" (FBI 2008a).

9. For some philosophers of science and theoreticians, the distinction between a proposition and a hypothesis is as important as how the term *fruit* is different from *apple:* The former is more abstract and generalizable than the latter. For our purposes, we will distinguish between them only insofar as a given theorist may provide general propositions for the theory in question or for testable hypotheses.

10. We base the following discussion largely on the works of Wallace (1971) and the use of his "Wheel of Science" by others (Babbie 2007; Hagan 2005).

11. Not all variables are created equal. Some variables, like gender, are *nominal* in nature and reflect only observable characteristics. Statisticians rank *ordinal* variables; such measures reflect more or less of the item under study. For example, we may rank crimes from very serious crimes, such as the UCR's Index Crimes, to less serious ones, such as non-Index Crimes. With *interval* variables, the differences between values are equal. For example, the Army classifies a private first class (PFC) as an E-3 while a three-stripe sergeant is an E-5; the sergeant is two ranks, or intervals, above the PFC. Finally, *ratio* variables have all of the previous qualities and one more: There is an absolute absence of the variable under study, or a real zero value. Money is a ratio-level variable. You may have 10 dollars; your friend, who won the lottery, may have a million dollars; and your sister may have no money.

12. Statisticians employ a variety of measures of association, often related to the type of information under analysis. For example, we might want to know how often members of certain racial groups are arrested; however, the strength of this relationship would be difficult to estimate because group memberships are nominal data and arrest rates are ratio data. These statistical requirements and limitations aside, researchers prefer statistics that range from zero (no association) to 1 (maximum association) with the sign (plus or negative) indicating the direction of the relationship, where appropriate. They summarize these associations using terms like "very strong," "moderately strong," "moderate," "weak" and "very weak," among others.

13. Faced with a perplexing conundrum about which he had insufficient information to reach a conclusion, Holmes turned in exasperation to his colleague Dr. Watson and said: "Data! data! data!... I can't make bricks without clay."

2

Deterrence and Opportunity Theories

CHAPTER OVERVIEW

Deterrence Theory

Classical and Neoclassical Theory

Defining Deterrence

Assessing Deterrence

Deterrence, Public Policy, and Criminal Justice Practices

Rational Choice Theory

Fundamentals of Choice and Choice Structuring

Assessing Rational Choice Theory

Choices, Public Policy, and Criminal Justice Practices

Routine Activities/Opportunity Theory

Routine Activities Theory

Assessing Routine Activities/ Opportunity Theory

Routine Activities, Opportunity, Public Policy, and Criminal Justice Practices

LEARNING OBJECTIVES

In this chapter, you will learn the following:

- The origins of ideas about deterring criminals.

- The ties between classic deterrence theory and modern versions.

- That for some people, crime is but one of many choices and, given a particular set of circumstances, a reasoned and reasonable choice.

- The routine nature of some offending, and the role of opportunity plays in defining its routineness.

INTRODUCTION

Most organized religions describe the fate of those who fail to follow the rules laid down by a supreme being. Ancient laws not only are prescriptive and proscriptive, telling people what they must and must not do, but also describe the sanctions that befall those who stray from the righteous path. Historical and archeological evidence of such rules—and often-graphic accounts of accompanying corporal and capital punishments—suggests a longstanding belief in their power to promote compliance.

The eighteenth-century Italian social critic Cesare Beccaria provided one of the first treatises on the ties between formal sanctions—those flowing from governments and enforced by their social control agents—and compliant behavior. Criminological interest in the deterrent affects of formal sanctions diminished 100 years ago as positivists searched for the causes of crime in other venues. Rediscovered in the 1960s, deterrence has become a mainstay of criminological research, especially that funded by state and federal governments.

Over the final two decades of the twentieth century, criminologists described two deterrence-related processes. Rational choice suggests that some people have already decided what laws they will break, given a certain set of circumstances and rationalizations. As with deterrence, society must make the choice of crime as unpleasant as possible. The second theory, routine activities, views crime as a response to life's opportunities. The supply of criminals and victims is constant. More importantly, we are bombarded with clues about where and when crime is likely to occur—clues available to potential criminals and victims and to social control agents. The central policy response is to reduce or eliminate the opportunity to offend.

The theories in this chapter explore the choices people make. All assume some level of volition or the exercise of *free will*, and all have deep roots in Western history and culture. These theories explore the mechanisms that shape and influence individual choices either to engage in normative behavior or to violate rules, norms, and laws. We begin with deterrence theory, an idea that has proved to have great longevity.

DETERRENCE THEORY

- Have you ever wondered why people commit illegal acts even when they know the specific punishment for the act, perhaps from prior experience or from knowledge of what happened to friends who committed the same crime?

- What about people who know someone who commits a crime and gets away with it? What does this situation have to do with deterrence? Is it a reflection of the failure of deterrence, the failure of the criminal justice system, or something else?

The search for answers to these questions begins in the eighteenth century and the quest to understand the criminal mind begins in the age of reason.

Classical and Neoclassical Theory

Classical theory is an outgrowth of the eighteenth century European Enlightenment (sometimes referred to as the "Age of Reason"), when adherents rejected spiritual and religious explanations of crime. During this epoch, philosophers such as Charles-Louis de Secondat, Baron de La Brede et de Montesquieu (1689–1755), and François-Marie Arouet Voltaire (1694–1778) spoke out against the French penal code and punishments that were both inhumane and inequitable. Jean-Jacques Rousseau (1712–1778) and Cesare Bonesana, marchese di Beccaria, usually referred to as Cesare Beccaria (1738–1794), argued for a radical new concept of justice. Social critics such as these demanded *justice* based on equality and *punishment* that was humane and proportionate to the offense. This doctrine of equality helped foment the American Revolution with the declaration that "all men are created equal," and the French Revolution, during which the National Assembly enacted a "Declaration of the Rights of Man and Citizen" (1789). We find the roots of this philosophy in the concepts of *natural law* and the *social contract*.

Natural Law   Universal elements of natural law exist in the Ten Commandments revealed to Moses on Mount Sinai. The term **natural law** refers to a legal theory that holds the following to be morally irrefutable: some rules and principles derive from more than the experiences of men and women, but rather nature itself creates them and humankind discovers them. Given this perspective, the search for absolute justice is possible (Levy 1988:3). At its core, natural law posits the belief that humans have an inborn notion of right and wrong; therefore, law's very essence does not rest upon the arbitrary will of a ruler or upon the decree of the masses (Rommen 1998). Natural law, while not requiring belief in a deity, refers to a higher law, primordial or natural—in other words, rules for living that are binding on all societies.

Thomas Aquinas (1225–1274) united natural law doctrines, derived from Aristotle and other ancient philosophers, into a Christian framework. In his *Summa Theologica*, Aquinas asserts that if **positive law** (i.e., law derived out of the political process) violates natural law, it is not law but a corruption of law. According to Church doctrine, natural law is rooted in human nature; divine law is written on the human heart (Fuchs 1965), the principles of which are known or at least knowable by anyone (J. Boyle 1992).

During the Middle Ages (from the fall of the Roman Empire to the Renaissance), the natural law concept served the interests of the Roman Catholic Church in its dealings with secular powers. In the hands of the Papacy, it was an impediment to the growth of nation-states (Aubert 1983). According to Church doctrine, the source of all natural law is divine and, thus, "the Church in her own Code emphatically refuses to recognize any legislation that contradicts the natural law" (Fuchs 1965:8). An emerging middle class used the concept of natural law to counter the feudal nobles' power and later the monarch's divine right, thus preserving individual freedoms from the power of the state (MacDonald 1961:4). Natural law necessarily places limits on political power. Natural law transcends all formal human constructs, and any law contrary to the natural law derives from the coercive force of the state, not the voluntary compliance of the governed. According to the *Commentaries* of William Blackstone (1723–1780), any human law contrary to natural law has no validity, a statement similar to that made by Aquinas 500 years earlier.

Social Contract   Classical European Enlightenment expresses natural law in the **social contract:** a mythical state of affairs wherein each person agrees to a pact, the basic stipulation of which is that all men are created equal. "The social contract establishes among the citizens an equality of such character that each binds himself on the same terms as all the others, and is thus entitled to enjoy the same rights as all the others" (Rousseau [1762] 1954:45).

The natural law concepts of John Locke (1632–1704), which states that all men are by nature free, equal, and independent, and that no one can be subjected to the political power of another without his own consent, should sound familiar to most citizens of the U.S. We find them in the Declaration of Independence: "all men are created equal" and "governments are instituted among men, deriving their just powers from the consent of the governed." The idea that man is free by nature and endowed with natural rights is the philosophical basis for the first ten amendments to the Constitution (the Bill of Rights).

Classical Theory   The **Classical School,** standing in opposition to the manner in which laws were being enforced at the time, argued that laws should recognize neither rank nor station—all men are created equal. Beccaria formalized this premise in *An Essay on Crimes and Punishments* (1963 [1764]: English edition, 1867), when he wrote that laws should be drawn precisely and matched to punishments applied equally to all classes of men. The law, he argued, should stipulate a particular penalty for each specific crime, and judges should mete out identical sentences for each occurrence of the same offense.

According to the classical position advanced by Beccaria and Jeremy Bentham (1748–1832), a society can justify the punishment of any offender only if that person is rational and endowed with free will. Moreover, they concluded that every person has the ability to choose between right and wrong, between being law-abiding and criminal conduct. Law-violating behavior is, therefore, a rational choice made by a reasoning person with free will.

Classical theory argues that human beings tend toward **hedonism**—that is, they seek pleasure and avoid pain. The fear of punishment restrains the populace from unlawful albeit pleasurable acts. Crime is "caused" by the inability of laws— and the punishments they endorse—to deter would-be criminals from committing their crimes. Accordingly, the purpose of law is not simply retribution, but also deterrence.

Beccaria's classical theory requires three essential elements for lawful punishments to deter future criminality: certainty, celerity, and severity. **Certainty** refers to the probability that offending persons will receive a sanction for their miscreant deed. If deterrence is to work as intended, the certainty of capture, trial, and, ultimately, punishment must be high. Beccaria's **severity** was a complex idea. The pain of any sanction must outweigh the pleasure received from engaging in the associated illegal act. This idea proved a difficult balancing act even for Beccaria, as, for example, he opposed the death penalty as a case of the state declaring war on the individual. While classical theory emphasizes the certainty of punishment over its severity, the reality of criminal justice is the reverse: Severity is more easily achieved than is certainty.

The fusion of two requirements—certainty *and* celerity—rounds out the classical position. **Celerity,** or promptness, refers to the elapsed time between the act and the sanction. In order for sanctions to deter, the elapsed time must be short, as the offender must associate the sanction with the crime, and if too much time has elapsed, this logical connection is less likely to occur. This forms the basis of behaviorism, a psychological theory that we review in Chapter 5. As we shall see in Chapter 2, the gap in time between committing a serious (felony) crime and punishment, if it occurs at all, is often quite wide.

In sum, Cesare Beccaria saw the choices between good and evil as simple and straightforward. Several assumptions about humankind led him to this conclusion.[1] First, he saw all *men* as possessing free will; that is, they could choose to act or not to act of their own volition.[2] Second, he believed that humans are capable of rational thought. They possess the ability to weigh alternative courses of action and, depending on which one was most advantageous, select it from among the available choices. Third, he viewed humans as virtual slaves to their own base desires—humanity is hedonistic by nature, seeking pleasure and avoiding pain. The concept of hedonism leads to his fourth and most critical assumption. In Beccaria's view, a system of just punishments, based on the principles of certainty, celerity, and severity, was needed to control people's conduct, cloaking humanity's hedonistic proclivities under a shroud of deterrence, counteracting the prevailing system of justice (see In Their Own Words: Beccaria on the Inequality of Justice in Eighteenth-Century Europe).

Neoclassicalism According to classicalists, society can justify punishing lawbreakers because those who violate the social contract are rational, endowed with free will, and responsible for their actions. The focus is on the legal system, not the nature of criminal motivation. Under most justice systems, an explanation is not a justification unless it reaches the level of a (legal) compulsion, at which point the law does not blame the perpetrator, as they do not possess a guilty mind, meaning *mens rea* is absent.

Classicalism had one annoying shortcoming: Implementing a criminal code based on it proved elusive. This problem became apparent when the drafters of the 1791 French Code attempted to implement Beccaria's reforms. Equality and proportionality proved more difficult in practice than in theory, and the French added to the discretionary powers of judges, resulting in a type of neoclassicalism (Roshier 1989). The resulting **neoclassicalism** maintains classical theory's emphasis on free will, while paving the way for the entry of mitigation or aggravation into law based on past criminal record, insanity, retardation, and age. The neoclassicalists believed that a society ruled by law can justify punishment only if crime is reasoned behavior. Their revisions created a need for nonlegal experts, such as psychiatrists, psychologists, and social workers (Taylor, Walton, and

---

IN THEIR OWN WORDS: Beccaria on the Inequality of Justice in Eighteenth-Century Europe

Classicalism led to a revolution in criminal justice. The injustices of late eighteenth-century European laws and penal practices motivated Beccaria to write his *magnum opus, On Crimes and Punishments.* Laws at the time were different for people based on their station in life, and the existing laws often exempted members of the nobility from any criminal responsibility. However, it was the behavior of judges that most enraged Beccaria, and it was for them that he reserved his harshest criticism. Judges of his day frequently gave very different punishments for identical offenses, practicing an extreme form of individualized justice. Moreover, most punishments accorded offenders at the time were harsh by any standards and at times barbaric.

The 26-year-old Beccaria made a series of recommendations for the administration of justice throughout Europe. He believed that legislatures should define the crimes and associated punishments, and that government must inform the public about the crimes and associated punishments, thereby

eliminating secret accusations and torture. Punishments should equal the threat of the crime to society—no more, no less—as **proportionality** was essential for deterrence to work. Beccaria saw punishments that exceeded proportionality as tyrannical and evil, and as undermining the purposes of deterrence.[3] Governed by just laws, the judge's role would be to determine of guilt or innocence. Given a finding of guilt, the judge would simply consult the law and pronounce the sentence. Finally, he proposed that imprisonment replace capital punishment and that living conditions in jails and prisons be more humane. Beccaria (p. 99) summarized these ideas as follows: "In order for punishment not to be, in every instance, an act of violence of one or of many against a private citizen, it must be essentially public, prompt, necessary, the least possible given the circumstances, proportionate to the crimes, dictated by laws. "

SOURCES: Beccaria (1963[1764]: English edition, 1867); Martin et al. (1990).

Young 1973:8). Such experts determine the presence of mitigation, while maintaining a fundamental belief in free will, creating a bit of wiggle room for neoclassicalists.

Classical and neoclassical philosophies underwrite the U.S. criminal justice system. Contemporary crime theories also reflect many of the ideas originally laid down by Beccaria and Bentham more than 200 years ago, including modern deterrence and opportunity theories. The idea that people are responsible for their own actions—and that society, through its social control mechanisms, can make clear that lesson—has proved to be quite resilient.

Criminologists' interest in deterrence theory waned in the last quarter of the nineteenth century. The works of Charles Darwin, Herbert Spencer, and Cesare Lombroso, whose contributions we explore in the next chapter, led to a revolution in explanations of human behavior. Criminologists shifted from the study of laws and punishments to the study of criminals, both in society and in its prisons, a locus largely maintained until the 1960s. For 100 years criminologists took one path, and policy makers followed an entirely different one.

The 1960s brought changes to American society, ranging from desegregation to near political anarchy. In those tumultuous times, two social scientists shifted criminologists' attention back to deterrence theory. In 1968, Jack Gibbs published "Crime, punishment, and deterrence," in which he tested the **perceptual deterrence hypothesis.** Also in 1968, economist—and eventual Nobel Prize winner (1992)—Gary S. Becker published "Crime and punishment: An economic approach," an article that generated great interest in a perspective called

cost–benefit analysis. With the publication of these two works, deterrence theory was once more on the agenda of criminologists. One irony in this rediscovery of deterrence is that positivistic criminologists began applying the scientific method in an attempt to reveal punishments' deterrent effects.

Defining Deterrence

Beccaria's ideas about deterrence were simple and straightforward. Beginning in the 1960s, a series of works reviewing past deterrence research and suggesting new avenues of exploration provided new insights into the mechanisms of deterrence (Gibbs 1975; Zimring and Hawkins 1973). For example, **general deterrence** reflects the idea that persons watching, hearing about, or otherwise becoming aware of a sanctioning process will view the outcomes as too costly and not engage in the punished conduct. The saying "There but for the grace of God go I" reflects this idea. In years past, when punishments were carried out in public and most offenses resulted in either corporal punishment or the death penalty (or both), being present was thought to have an ameliorative impact on potential offenders, including those who had committed previous offenses but had not been caught and those contemplating them. In fact, public executions usually included the convicted person's recitation of the sins that had led them to the gallows. A minister, preacher, or priest often facilitated the confession.

The target of **specific** (or **individual**) **deterrence,** the second major form, is chiefly persons who have been caught, convicted, and punished. The intent of imprisonment or, prior to the mid-twentieth century, corporal punishment, was to encourage offenders to change their life paths to noncriminal ones. Otherwise, they would suffer increasingly harsh sanctioning at the hands of the court for their misdeeds.

Social scientists added two other concepts to the mix: absolute and restrictive deterrence. According to **absolute deterrence,** once individuals come to see either the error of their ways or the potential losses they face, they will refrain from all crime. Just as importantly, those who have never been caught in a criminal act, as well as those who have been caught and punished, may exhibit the effects of absolute deterrence. For example, suppose a young man spends 10 years, from age 18 to 28, in federal prison for dealing crack. At the time of his mandatory release, thanks to the federal prison industries program, he knows how to build furniture. He subsequently secures a good-paying job and leaves behind his life as a drug dealer. Meanwhile, a 16-year-old friend back in the neighborhood, who was also contemplating a career as a drug dealer, hears about the 10-year sentence and decides to return to high school, where he gets his degree, and then goes on to college. The same day his old friend is released from federal prison, the wannabe drug dealer assumes a position as a criminal justice professor at the local community college. In both cases absolute deterrence is at work.

The second concept is **restrictive deterrence,** whereby offenders may refrain from the act that previously landed them in trouble or that threatens trouble, but modify their criminal conduct rather than abandon it. For example, suppose our hypothetical 18-year-old drug dealer decides, upon release from prison, to stop selling crack because the police are targeting that particular drug and embarks on a new career in marijuana sales. He has not entirely given up criminal ways, but he has modified them to reduce his risks to more manageable levels.

Mark Stafford and Mark Warr (1993) offered another modification to the deterrence model, as depicted in Figure 2.1. Stafford and Warr catalogued the flaws in previous conceptualizations, which failed to take into account people who "got away" with crime. That is, each time someone escapes notice or punishment, what is the implication in terms of that law's ability to deter? Warr and Stafford suggested several possible answers. First, people who commit crimes and escape apprehension (or conviction), thereby having personal experience with attempts to deter them, may view this as license to commit more crimes. Second, individuals who know of others who escaped paying for their crimes may be disposed to engage in crime as they see no downside to criminal activity. Third, individuals with personal or vicarious experience with a sanctioning process that was effective should be deterred. For example, a juvenile might be deterred from further offending as an adult by a stay in juvenile hall, or learning about a neighborhood friend who was sent to "juvie" might serve as a deterrent to other juveniles.

Deterrence conceptualizing in the 1960s and 1970s benefited from the collective work of Jack Gibbs, Richard Hawkins, Franklin Zimring, and Stafford and Warr, among others (cf. Geerken and Gove 1975; Meier and Johnson 1977; Nagin 1978; Silberman 1976; Tittle and Rowe 1974). They demonstrated that, if there was a deterrent effect to sanctioning, it was not the simple process envisioned by Beccaria. The power of simple messages from formal sanctioning authorities is largely a myth. Raymond Paternoster and Ronet Bachman (2001:16) observed the following about the complex processes at work whenever sanctions

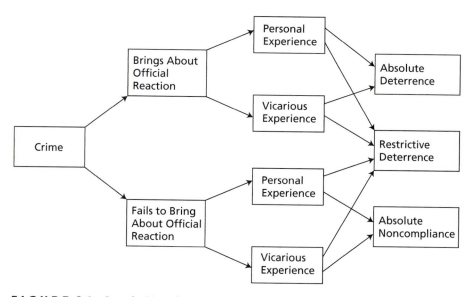

FIGURE 2.1 Complexities of Perceptual Deterrence

are threatened or applied: "It is not difficult to see that the deterrence message may get mixed because often our personal and vicarious experiences are at odds." Present-day deterrence conceptualizing little resembles Beccaria's ideas. Whether the world has become more complex or they were simply optimistic about the power of a fair and just state to deter crime is beyond testing. Contemporary researchers have added to the debate, one that is far from resolved.

Assessing Deterrence

Beginning in the 1960s, deterrence studies focused on punishments' certainty and severity effects (Blumstein, Cohen, and Nagin 1978; Gibbs 1975; Tittle 1969). Researchers have evaluated the links between what people think about the certainty and severity of punishments and their subsequent self-reported criminal behavior and deviance (Paternoster 1987; Waldo and Chiricos 1972). In his review of perceptual deterrence studies, Paternoster (1987) found that the theory did not fit the data, largely because of poor research designs. The operationalizations of punishments' certainty or severity effects were inadequate.

Nearly 20 years later, Paternoster, working with colleagues (Wright, Caspi, Moffitt, and Paternoster 2004), found better data. Employing the longitudinal Dunedin (New Zealand) Study, the researchers explored the links between criminal propensity, perceived risks and costs of punishments, and subsequent criminal behavior. Given the longitudinal nature of the Dunedin Study, they used deterrence-related perceptions at 18 and 21 and self-reported criminality at 26 years of age for the same individuals. They reported that deterrent-effect perceptions worked best for those with the highest crime propensity (Wright et al. 2004:205). Indeed, among those with low propensity to crime, perceptions of risk and costs were unimportant. If one is not sufficiently prone to crime, then the justice system's presence, and its accompanying sanctioning processes, may be irrelevant, as other inhibitions and informal social controls are more important.

Prisoner studies provide insights into the experiential component of deterrence (i.e., specific deterrence). For example, Julie Horney and Ineke Marshall (1992), in a study of the experiential interpretation of sanctions by a sample of prison inmates, addressed the meaning of punishments for persons with a high propensity for crime. High involvement in crime should lead to perceptions of low certainty of punishment only in situations in which the offenders go unpunished for their criminal acts. The researchers found that, consistent with deterrence theory, active offenders, or those who reported any involvement in a given crime, formulated their perceptions of punishment probabilities based on their past experiences with legal sanctions.

The certainty of a sanction must not be in doubt for deterrence to work. However, when does certainty take hold? Deterrence generally assumes that all people look at time in the same way. That is, we all calculate events in the future in the same way: we worry about all future events equally, good or bad. Those persons not deterred, but arrested and punished, just made bad decisions. **Time discounting,** an idea from economics, has implications for how deterrence operates (Read and Read 2004). What if an offender sees a current event (think crime) as highly valued (think hedonism) and some future negative event (think prison or worse) as a long way off and not worth the bother? The future is deliberately devalued (Nagin and Pogarsky 2004). The near event (pleasure from the crime) is more important than the far-off (and possibly avoidable) event (punishment). Consider another example: A person offers you $20 in a week or $5 today; you take the $5, reflecting your time-discounting rate. It is possible that experience influences time discounting. Hence, if your friend takes the $20 in a week, and you take the $5 and see the error of your ways, next time you may defer to the future choice (Klochko 2006; 2008; see also Horney and Marshall 1992). In this way, time discounting is important to choices, but rarely acknowledged; rather, we often see it linked to another theory, Chapter 7's self-control theory (Nagin and Pogarsky 2004).

In sum, early research on the ability of sanctions to deter offending was generally inconclusive. Employing new conceptualizations of deterrence arguments or longitudinal data, more recent studies have met with more success. Critics of deterrence research, nonetheless, stress several thematic questions, including:

- *Is it a theory or a hypothesis?* Deterrence is often called a hypothesis, meaning that it is a testable idea but lacks fully developed theoretical arguments—mainly propositions—about its putative operation and effects (Tittle and Rowe 1974). As Matthew Silberman (1976:442) noted, classical deterrence employs strongly stated arguments steeped in untested assumptions about human nature and philosophical treatises on the use of punishments to secure normative conduct. This is hardly the level of conceptual thinking that leads to empirical verification.

- *Whether theory or hypothesis, can deterrence stand on its own, or must it be tied to other theories?* Modern tests of deterrence include variables never envisioned by Beccaria or Bentham, including opportunity structures discussed later in this chapter. Deterrence theory is often integrated with other ideas about human beings, such as Chapter 3's genetic arguments, Chapter 4's notions of psychopathic personality disorders, and Chapter 5's IQ–crime links. That is, owing to various biological or psychological anomalies, certain people are undeterred by penal sanctions. Larry Sherman and associates (1992), attempting to explain the variable deterrent effects of arresting spousal abusers, joined deterrence and labeling theory (see Chapter 8) to control theory (see Chapter 7). Theory integrations such as these reinforce the observation that deterrence is a hypothesis with limited utility to explain behavioral choices on its own merits.

- *Is the theory's conceptual base too narrow?* Classic deterrence theory addressed compliance flowing from formal sanctions. This narrow view of human behavior, generally ignoring as it does the role of informal social control mechanisms and social disincentives to illicit conduct, is perhaps the theory's biggest weakness (Roshier 1989).

- *Does deterrence work to control only minor forms of conduct but not crimes that are more serious?* The general absence of studies supporting the utility of severe sanctions, including the death penalty, to deter homicides suggests that even when it works, the deterrent effect of criminal sanctions has limits (e.g., Bailey 1998; Glaser and Ziegler 1974; Kleck, Sever, Li, and Gertz 2005; Pratt et al. 2006; Sorensen et al. 1999). As Paternoster (1988) suggests, "perceptions of certain punishments may have a deterrent effect on some forms of common, nonserious delinquency."

Deterrence research continues in spite of lackluster support (Nagin 1998). For example, the certainty of punishment may exhibit a correlation with the frequency of criminal behavior, but that correlation is low (D'Alessio and Stolzenberg 1998). The severity of punishment has even less support. Several meta-analyses—a statistical technique that allows researchers to pool the estimates of a number of studies in order to find the trend in the research findings for a given topic—report little support for punishment's deterrent effects (Pratt and Cullen 2005; Pratt et al. 2006). Several researchers suggest that, although the death penalty may serve as a deterrent for some types of homicide, executions may actually cause the homicide rate to rise. They report increased stranger homicides following executions, suggesting that the exercise of capital punishment may incite murders (cf. Bailey 1998; Cochran, Chamlin, and Seth 1994). This **deterrence/brutalization thesis** is interesting, given Beccaria's opposition to the death penalty.

Despite questions about whether deterrence works for both formal *and* informal sanctions, the absence of complete tests of the theory, and its utility for both major *and* minor crimes, deterrence remains one of the most appealing crime theories. It makes sense to laypersons and practitioners alike. After all, the threat of criminal sanctions deters them. Its impact on those likely to or engaging in crime remains less clear.

Deterrence, Public Policy, and Criminal Justice Practices

The deterrence model has dominated U. S. criminal justice policies for most of the nation's history. From the time of the nation's founding to World War II, deterrence defined criminal justice policies and practices. From 1945 to 1975, however, various jurisdictions experimented with rehabilitation and treatment models, which differed considerably from the deterrence approach. According to these philosophies and practices, humans are malleable and redeemable. Psychology and social psychology provide the theoretical and practical rationale for most treatment modalities, ideas explored in later chapters. By the mid-1970s, faith in rehabilitation was shaken (cf. Cullen and Gilbert 1982; Farabee 2002; Lipton, Martinson, and Wilks 1975; Martinson 1974, 1979), and, as importantly, new, far more punitive philosophical positions on offenders emerged, including just deserts and retributive justice (Fogel 1975; van den Haag 1975; von Hirsch 1976).[4] Law violators deserved harsh punishments, irrespective of whether those punishments deterred them or others. Society demanded and deserved the sanctioning of those who posed threats to the safety and security of its citizens.

Deterrence coexisted with rehabilitation and continued to provide a legitimate rationale for punishment in the 1980s and 1990s and into the new century. Merged with an old idea, *lex talionis,* or "just desserts," deterrence resumed its age-old position at the pinnacle of penal philosophies: Deter criminals, and if you cannot deter them, then give them the punishment they deserve. The idea that fear of punishment and respect for the law deter most people is popular with the public, politicians, and other policy makers. Deterrence provides the primary justification for the nation's "get tough" crime policy, initiated in the mid-1970s and continuing to the present (Hagan 1995).

Law Enforcement Practices Municipal police departments allocate most of their resources to patrol, whose primary purpose is to deter crime. The presence of highly visible police cars or uniformed patrol officers may deter a would-be miscreant from committing a crime at that time and place. However, does it deter the crime—so it *never* occurs—or does it simply displace it to another time or place? If the latter is true, then the practice does not really deter crime. A 1970s study of police patrol patterns conducted in Kansas City, Missouri, failed to show that highly visible proactive patrols deterred crime (Kelling, Pate et al. 1974). Nevertheless, many other police practices have deterrence theory ties (Gay, Schell, and Schack 1977). Consider, for example, the placement of police cars, sometimes with lights flashing, in high-visibility locations on highways as a way of slowing traffic. The intent is not to catch speeders, but to remind them about the certainty of apprehension. The same goal is what's behind informing local radio and television stations about DUI checkpoints or random stops on local streets and highways. The public policy of funding more police and placing them on the streets (e.g., "100,000 more police") should both increase the actual certainty of arrest and raise perceptions of certainty.

From cruising by local parks, recreational centers, and school grounds to stopping and questioning "suspicious persons," the intent of nearly all police patrol practices is as a deterrent. Other police investigative and intervention practices, including arresting the aggressor in misdemeanor domestic violence cases, have roots in deterrence theory (Sherman and Berk 1984a, b). In summary, many police activities—and many police officers—are invested in the assumptions and operating principles of deterrence theory.

Judicial Practices Since the 1970s, mandatory sentencing laws decreased judges' sentencing discretion. **Mandatory sentencing** defines punishments for certain crimes (usually violent and drug offenses), meaning convicted offenders may not be placed on probation and must serve a specific sentence prior to release on parole, if parole is an option. In 1993, Washington became the first state to adopt formally a policy whereby a person convicted of a third felony charge would face life in prison without parole (see the following box for an analysis of the law's impact). Within a decade, 24 states and the federal government adopted "three-strikes" sentencing laws, and every other jurisdiction in the United States considered related legislation, earning the strategy the label of "politicized crime control policy" (Benekos and Merlo 1995). The net result is that courts in the United States at the start of the twenty-first century closely resemble Beccaria's eighteenth-century vision of the ideal court. That is, judges' sentences are more often based solely on penal statutes and less often on judges' discretion and interpretation of the best interests of the offender and the community.

COMMENTS AND CRITICISMS: The Impact of Three-Strikes Laws

What has been the impact of three-strikes legislation on crime and criminals? This question addresses two important concerns related to "three-strikes" laws that arose when states began implementing them. First, critics expressed concern that imprisoning persons for life would result in an increase of geriatric prisoners and prisoners overall, something that the nation's crowded prison system could ill afford. Second, supporters argued that by practicing selective incapacitation and general deterrence, the crime "bottom-line" would go down.

In 2004, the Justice Policy Institute, a nongovernmental organization (NGO), issued a policy brief on three strikes. After examining 21 of 23 states using three-strikes sentencing practices, it concluded the following about their impact:

- Only California has extensively employed three-strikes legislation, incarcerating four times as many people under its provisions as all other three-strikes states combined. Its incarceration rate (119.3 per 100,000 residents) is 18 times greater than the average for all other three-strikes states (6.7 per 100,000 residents).

- Except for California, Florida, and Georgia, none of the other 18 three-strikes states for which data were available had more than 400 three-strikes prison inmates.

- Every state that enacted three-strikes laws already had a "career-offender" statute on the books; hence, this legislation was, in the words of Austin and associates, "much ado about nothing." The practice is unlikely to produce prisons full of geriatric inmates.

The second issue was the law's impact on crime. Crime did not go down in states that had three-strikes laws compared to states without such laws. Specific observations include:

- In California, where it could reasonably be expected to have the greatest impact, serious crime rates did not decline below what would reasonably be expected, given national trends.

- National crime rate comparisons between three-strikes and non–three strikes states failed to demonstrate a significant decline in crimes by violent repeat offenders.

- Three strikes–less New York outperformed heavy–three strikes California, as the former experienced greater declines in index crime and violent crime than did the latter.

Three-strikes laws, representing a popular law-and-order response to unique high-profile crimes, do not appear to have had the positive crime-reducing effects hoped for by proponents, and may not have further crowded prisons as feared by opponents. What they may have done, however, was unintended and certainly undesired. Researchers studied 188 large cities from 1980 to 1999, comparing homicide rates in those with access to three-strikes laws to those without such laws. That is, cities in states with three-strikes laws experienced both short- and long-term increases in their homicide rates compared to cities in states with no such sentences. The reasoning: If you are facing life in prison without the hope of parole, why leave any witnesses?

SOURCES: Auerhahn (2001, 2002); Austin et al. (1998); Kovandizic, Sloan, and Vieraitis (2002); Greenwood and Hawkins (2002); Macallair and Males (1999); Marvell and Moody (2001); Schiraldi, Colburn, and Locke (2004); Stolzenberg and D'Alessio (1997).

Correctional Practices   We could argue that the entire correctional system serves a specific deterrent function, if not a general deterrent one. Beyond those in prison and those bound for prison, there exists the concept of shock and its ability to deter. A shock corrections program gives an at-risk person or actual perpetrator a "taste" of prison life, and then, after a very short or somewhat longer period, returns them to free society (Waldron and Angelino 1977). This theory was the basis of such programs as shock probation/parole, where judges sentenced offenders to prison, and then after a brief stay conditionally released them back into the population. The underlying idea was that, after experiencing prison life, they would not want to return.

Two other well-known correctional practices owe their existence to deterrence theory. The first have been called **"scared straight" programs,** the practice of exposing young, and presumably impressionable, adolescents to the "horrors" of crime, usually by putting them in a room with prison inmates. One of the first systematic programs of this nature operated at New Jersey's Rahway State Prison and was the subject of a 1978 documentary film, *Scared Straight,* and a series of evaluations. The film gave the impression that the program was highly successful. However, evaluators of New Jersey's Juvenile Awareness Program found two things: (1) Most participants were low-risk, middle-class children, and (2) those youths who participated in the program later committed four times the number of offenses as members of a control group who had no exposure to prison inmates (Finckenauer 1982). Programs in other states similar to that at Rahway State Prison also failed to show a deterrent effect (Jensen and Rojek 1998).

Boot camp or **shock incarceration** is a second popular program heavily indebted to deterrence theory and shock probation/parole for its theoretical underpinnings. Boot camp is a sentence accorded first-time felony offenders, who go to a special prison where they are subjected to three to six months of military-style basic training. In some jurisdictions, educational, vocational, and treatment programs supplement basic training. Following successful participation in the program, "graduates" return to the community under some form of enhanced supervision. The actual mechanisms vary across the nation; some jurisdictions use probation (i.e., conditional release from the sentencing court, which is part of the judicial branch), and others prefer parole (i.e., conditional release from the correctional system, which is part of the executive branch). In practice, the conditional release often translates into intensive supervision, with several contacts per month between the probationer/parolee and the supervising agent.

Do boot camps deter youthful offenders? The evidence suggests that they do not (cf. MacKenzie 1993; MacKenzie, Gover, Armstrong, and Mitchell 2001; Peters, Thomas, and Zamberlan 1997). Youthful participants may exhibit some prosocial attitudes and orientations because of participating, but it does not appear that boot camps achieve their primary goal: deterring future offending (Bottcher and Ezell 2005).

RATIONAL CHOICE THEORY

- Juan cannot find a job. His wife is pregnant and has special dietary needs. They have tried to get help from local and state social service agencies, but as newcomers to the city, they have experienced difficulty obtaining the needed documentation. Juan's command of English is poor, and he cannot read or write in any language, so he often simply leaves the social services office in embarrassment. Upon entering a grocery store, he puts what his family needs in a basket and runs out the door with it. What might Juan have been thinking before he committed this crime?

■   It is the winter holiday season. The bleak economy has yet to bottom out but Jim has: he was laid off from his job of 18 years last week. His family faces the prospect of skipping Christmas entirely. To avoid this embarrassing and disheartening situation, Jim is cruising the parking lot of a shopping center close to his home. He is looking for a car filled with packages, where the shopper neglected to lock the car. Jim does not want to break into a car, as that would be stealing. If he just takes what he finds unattended and un-guarded, it is not as big a deal. What mental processes helped Jim negotiate his moral dilemma and facilitate his decision to become a criminal?

Economists, who view crime as they do any decision that has associated costs and benefits, provide another perspective. If someone analyzes the costs and ben-efits associated with purchasing any household item, goes the logic, then he or she will perform similar cost–benefit analyses prior to committing crime (Becker 1968; Sullivan 1973). For example, Isaac Ehrlich (1975) applied cost–benefit analysis to the death penalty. His conclusion: Executing one person saves seven to eight other lives (Ehrlich 1975); however, flaws in Ehrlich's data largely dis-credit this finding (Forst 1983; Klein, Forst, and Filatov 1978). Critics point to the Ehrlich study as an example of manipulating data to prove a specific point (Klein et al. 1978).

Gary Becker provided the groundwork for a new crime theory by suggest-ing that decisions to commit crimes involve the same decision-making processes as in buying a car, for example. Even absent all needed information about possi-ble outcomes (e.g., the roadworthiness of the car or its repair history), people make decisions based on an **expected utility principle.** They glean informa-tion about cars (or crimes), store it in their memory, and use it to analyze a given decision (e.g., buy the car or commit an illegal act). The rationality they employ may be imperfect, but it is framed by the information they possess, recall, and act upon in a given situation at a given time. They may make imperfect decisions (e.g., buy a bad car or get caught committing a crime), but it is the best decision at the time. In other words, the cost–benefit analysis made by stupid people will result in stupid decisions. In computer lingo, garbage in, garbage out.

Criminology saw a resurgence in deterrence ideas in the late 1970s, thanks to Becker's (1968:170) simple and elegant suggestion that criminologists consider "the economist's usual analysis of choice" and Ehrlich's cost–benefit analysis. These new-generation deterrence theories, called the **Neuve Classical School** (Paternoster and Bachman 2001:19), were manifested in two primary forms: ratio-nal choice theory and routine activities theory.

Fundamentals of Choice and Choice Structuring

In *The Reasoning Criminal*, Derek Cornish and Ronald Clarke (1986:1) observed (1) that offenders seek to benefit themselves by their criminal behavior; (2) that this involves the making of decisions and choices, however rudimentary these pro-cesses might be; and (3) that these processes exhibit a measure of *rationality,* albeit constrained by limits of times and ability and the availability of relevant informa-tion. Cornish and Clark merged the economists' idea of cost–benefit and the classical/deterrence theorists' idea of free will, forming rational choice theory. This theory is a restatement of Becker's expected utility principle, framed in terms of a crime decision-process. There are also psychological forces at work in these rational choices. Indeed, Cornish and Clarke included such background factors as intelligence, temperament, and cognitive style in their explanatory schema.

Given Cornish and Clarke's emphasis on criminal acts as possible sources of rewards or punishments, you might think that this is only a property theory; however, nothing could be further from the theory's intent. Proponents claim that violent crimes with no apparent motivation are explained by this theory. Even crime that appears purely impulsive has rational elements. For example, graffiti artists enjoy not only the act of creating their art, but also the dangers associated with it (e.g., the possibility of contact with law enforcement, rival gang members and other graffiti artists, or just working over a highway overpass) and the notoriety that follows a successful act. Nonutilitarian violence appears to be rewarding to those who engage in such acts, perhaps due to the domination of the victims and the acts' senseless (and unpredictable) nature. In addition, the risks involved in criminal behavior can be exciting—in the jargon of behavioral psychologists, "reinforcing"—a topic to which we return in Chapter 5.

The theory *is* crime-specific, meaning that different crimes provide different offenders with varying means of meeting their needs. Extending this idea to its logical conclusion, offenders actually choose specific crimes based on their personal characteristics, needs, and skills (e.g., previous experience and learning, background, and needs) and offense characteristics (e.g., proximity to a victim and likelihood and severity of punishment).

Choice Structuring   **Choice structuring** occurs when individuals assess their own skills and needs in light of a specific crime's characteristics. Cornish and Clark asserted that each crime has a unique choice-structuring process associated with it. Even the crime of burglary is not a single generic crime, they claimed, as "it may be necessary to divide burglary simply into its residential and commercial forms" (Cornish and Clarke 1986:2). It may also be necessary to distinguish between burglary committed in middle-class suburbs, in public housing, and in wealthy residential enclaves. Having followed a choice-structuring process for one type of burglary does not lead automatically and inevitably to the choice to commit another type. Empirical studies suggest that the kinds of individuals committing different forms of residential burglary, as well as their motivations and their methods, differ considerably. Figure 2.2 contains a graphic representation of this model of the choice-structuring process.

Involvement Decisions   The **involvement decision** is a multistage evaluation process that ends with the decision to get involved in crime. In this step, a person's demographic, social, familial, and psychological backgrounds constitute the interpretive context for crime involvement decisions. These background factors, along with various experiences (e.g., direct or vicarious criminal behavior, contact with police, and conscience and moral attitudes), provide the means to evaluate legitimate and illegitimate solutions for achieving generalized needs felt by everyone (e.g., money, sex, friendship, status, and excitement).

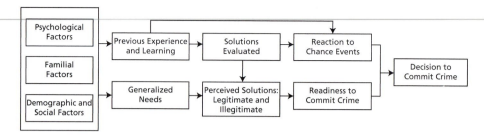

FIGURE 2.2 Cornish and Clarke's Rational Choice Theory

The evaluation of solutions includes an appreciation for (1) the amount of work involved (i.e., too much or just the right amount), (2) the amount and immediacy of the reward (i.e., too little reward too far in the future versus the right amount immediately), (3) the likelihood and severity of punishment (an element easily recognized from classical deterrence theory), and (4) moral costs (i.e., values tied to one's upbringing, especially family factors). Once the individual evaluates a particular illegitimate solution as acceptable, a readiness to commit the crime is said to exist. Crimes occur when individuals with such readiness or a preexisting involvement decision react illegitimately to chance events, such as an easy opportunity, a need for cash, persuasive friends, drunkenness, or quarrelsome demeanor, among others.

Event Decisions   Immediately before the commission of a crime but after the involvement decision, the criminal makes an **event decision,** based on information about the possible criminal act. This step occurs quickly and without much thought on the offender's part. This decision becomes a rational response to chance events, a decision that is based on preexisting inclinations and a readiness to engage in illegitimate acts.

Opportunity is an important event element. Without the opportunity to engage in a crime, the involvement decision is, in sports parlance, all windup and no pitch. Cornish and Clarke did not see crime, even economic crime, as well planned and carefully executed. The rationality associated with crime goes into the decision to get involved in crime. Certain factors—including previous punishments—constrain choices, moving the individual away from a decision to get involved in crime. After the initial decision has been made to commit a particular crime, however, the person moves quickly to its commission, given the right set of circumstances.

Assessing Rational Choice Theory

Rational choice theory is itself the source of definitional problems. These problems cluster in terms of the questions they elicit for those studying rational choice theory:

■ *Can rational choice theory overcome the definitional shortcomings of deterrence theory?* Grasmick and Bursik (1990:439–42) suggested that individuals take into account three kinds of potential costs in the rational choice process: (1) state-imposed physical and material deprivation (i.e., fines and incarceration), (2) self-imposed shame, and (3) social embarrassment. Their variant of rational choice theory extends the deterrence model to include both legal and nonlegal costs associated with crime; the latter are not dependent upon imposition of the former. In a study of tax cheating, drunk driving, and petty theft, Grasmick and Bursik found support for the idea that shame has "a strong deterrent effect" while embarrassment does not. However, their measures of rational choice were overly simplistic, lacking Cornish and Clarke's multistage process.

- *Is the theory too narrow, being merely an application of a utilitarian theory of economics?* To critics, rational choice theory traces its roots more closely to economic theory (i.e., expected utility) than to behaviorism (see Chapter 5). The economist's utilitarian view of choice is the basis of a test by Irving Piliavin and associates of both deterrence *and* rational choice models. They summarized the model using variables such as the actor's expected utility from a contemplated activity, the likelihood of punishment, the anticipated return (material or psychological), and the anticipated penalty if punished. Thus, a person engages in a criminal act when the expected utility of that act is greater than for any alternatives (Piliavin, Gartner, Thornton, and Matsueda 1986:102).[5]

- *Does the addition of new sociological and psychological elements expand the theory's utility?* A third approach links rational choice and deterrence to both sociological and psychological variables (cf. Bachman, Paternoster, and Ward 1992; Paternoster 1989a, b). Paternoster (1989a) tested a deterrence/rational choice model of delinquent offending, which he described as incorporating deterrence into "a more general rational choice model of offending" (Paternoster 1989a:305). To accomplish this task, Paternoster employed variables new to rational choice, such as attachment to family members and peer involvement in delinquency, that some critics felt were more closely linked to social learning and social bonding (see Chapter 7) than to either deterrence or rational choice theories (Akers and Sellers 2009:30).

- *What is meant by the word "rational"?* About the only thing the rational choice supporters and detractors agreed upon was that *rational* did not mean "careful thinking and sensible decisions by someone's standard" (Felson 1993:1497). Rather, rational choice proponents argued that offenders may think, but not necessarily with great care, preferring to engage in "illegal decision analysis" (Felson 1993:1497). Offenders often engage in behavior that can only be described as "unrealistic," as in the case of repeat property offenders who demonstrated little planning or, for that matter, understanding of the penalties for their crimes (Tunnell 1990, 1992). The issue may be a too-narrow definition of rationality, using only its instrumental meaning (i.e., what is the benefit gained from the act?), rather than its noninstrumental forms (i.e., what does engaging in the crime mean to the person doing it?) (Boudon 2003).

- *What would constitute an adequate test of rational choice theory?* Akers (1990:663) further noted that even Cornish and Clarke "assert a very minimal assumption of rationality, which does not seem to differ very much from the level of rationality assumed in most criminological theories." In short, there is very little agreement in the literature as to what constitutes an adequate test of rational choice theory. Simply including a number of reward and sanction models does not necessarily capture the full intent of either the rational decision-making process or the economists' idea that actors behave in ways that maximize their own expected utility (Akers 1990, 1994; Heineke 1988).

Recasting deterrence theory in econometric terms has silenced some critics, while others are less impressed, seeing new logical flaws in terms such as rational, restrictively narrow definitions related to its economic origins, or the conceptual commingling of rational choice with other theories. Moreover, finding empirical support for rational choice has proven difficult, a view reinforced by a meta-analysis of research on rational choice theory (Pratt and Cullen 2005).

Choices, Public Policy, and Criminal Justice Practices

Rational choice theory adds to the basic deterrence theme. First, knowledge of the possible legal and social costs is essential, just as Beccaria maintained more than 200 years ago. This translates into greater emphasis on legal education in primary and secondary schools. Second, the theory spells out the processes by which offenders makes choices to get involved in crime and to engage in specific crimes. In these ways, rational choice theory expands our understanding of how deterrence works or does not work for some individuals.

Terrorism is another topic that has caused criminologists to reexamine their theories in an effort to provide policy makers and antiterrorist practitioners with guidance for effective practices. The rational choice has provided researchers with a view into the occurrence of airplane hijackings (Dugan, LaFree, and Piquero 2005). Combining original data with information obtained from the Federal Aviation Administration and the RAND Corporation, a nonprofit research firm, Dugan and associates explored 1,101 attempted aerial hijackings from 1931 to 2003. They looked at the ability of major counterhijacking strategies, including the certainty of apprehension (e.g., metal detectors and law enforcement around passenger check-in points) and the severity of punishments to impact, in the former case, new hijacking attempts and, in the latter case, diversions to Cuba. While police interventions may reduce non-terrorist hijackings, they did not have the same impact on terrorist hijacking. The researchers suggest that rational choice theory may not be capable of piercing the motivational choice structuring of persons motivated by "martyrdom and eternal bliss" (Dugan et al. 2005:1059). Indeed, later in this book, we look at two other theories (Chapter 6's anomie theory and Chapter 7's social learning theory) to provide alternative understandings of this phenomenon.

As Travis Pratt (2008) observes, rational choice theory has come a long way from simplified predictions about the presence of formal criminal sanctions and criminal behavior, especially those predictions made by Beccaria. Over the past few decades, criminologists have described the conditions under which sanctions work best, often based on calculations of what influences offenders' choice decisions. The problem, notes Pratt, is that policy makers have gotten the wrong message. Criminologists consistently demonstrate that writing harsher laws does not yield positive crime control outcomes; policy makers like the language of rational choice theory without considering its subtleties. Criminologists, including those supporting rational choice theory, argues Pratt (2008:46), need to "get the word out" about what works and why, but, he also warns, in order to achieve this goal they must learn to "talk like a real person again," something that has proven difficult for some theorists.

ROUTINE ACTIVITIES/OPPORTUNITY THEORY

- Willy Sutton, a famous bank robber, was once asked why he robbed banks. Willy's reply: "That's where the money is!" What does this statement suggest to you about criminals?

- Are there places in your city you know to avoid? Are they "dangerous places," which is part of their attraction? If you answered yes to the second question, you should enjoy the next chapter. You are probably a risk taker or thrill seeker, and theories about impulsivity may interest you more.

Routine Activities Theory

In the late 1970s, criminologists began to pull together several disparate theoretical ideas and empirical findings under an umbrella called opportunity theory or routine activities theory. Armed with the findings of victimization surveys and motivated by a general interest in better understanding the fate of crime victims, Lawrence Cohen and Marcus Felson (1979) first proposed routine activities theory. They expressed the belief that both criminal motivation and the supply of potential offenders are constants: There is a never-ending supply of individuals who are ready, willing, and able to engage in **predatory crime,** that is, violent crimes against persons and crimes of theft in which the victim is present. The statistical summaries of criminal victimizations, however, showed that crime was not evenly distributed throughout society.

Cohen and Felson assumed that predatory crime depends on the *coincidence* of (1) a **motivated offender** (e.g., someone who feels the need for cash, items with immediate liquidity, or other items of value such as clothing or cars), (2) a **suitable target** (e.g., a well-heeled pedestrian in the wrong part of town, a rental car in search of the interstate, or a house with valuable goods), and (3) the absence of a **capable guardian** (e.g., no homeowner present, no police, or a lone traveler). Cohen and associates (1981) later stipulated that target suitability has four dimensions: (1) **exposure,** or the visibility and physical accessibility of the target; (2) **guardianship,** or the ability (and presence) of persons or objects to prevent crime from occurring; (3) **attractiveness,** or the material or symbolic value of persons or property; and (4) **proximity,** or the physical distance between potential targets and populations of potential offenders. Figure 2.3 graphically depicts routine activities theory.

Cohen and Felson's theory offers an explanation for why crime rates increased between 1960 and the early 1980s, and what the future is likely to hold. For instance, they observed that in the post–World War II era, increasing numbers of women entered the workforce, taking their children to day care and leaving their homes unguarded. Furthermore, the number of people living in single-household dwellings located in impersonal suburban neighborhoods increased. Traditional neighborhoods declined, and there was a further erosion of guardianship. Basic demographics also influenced the number of motivated offenders. During the period from 1960 to 1980, the "baby boomer generation," the large group of post–World War II babies, experienced a "coming of criminal age" (Felson and Cohen 1980:396–99). There was, as a result, a surplus of motivated offenders. Finally, the increased opportunity to commit predatory crimes substantially reduced the ability of the criminal justice system, the community, and the family to respond effectively to the increased threat. That is, the certainty, celerity, and value of the rewards of crime are vastly greater than the certainty, celerity, and severity of any punishments (Cohen and Felson 1979:606).

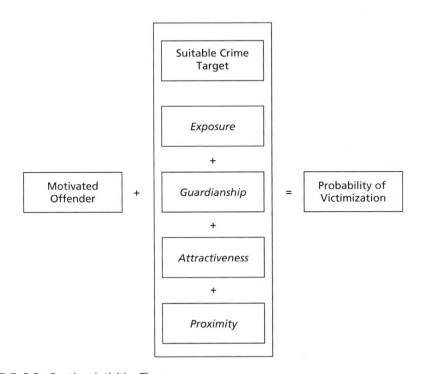

F I G U R E 2.3   Routine Activities Theory

COMPARATIVE CRIMINOLOGY—WORLD VIEWS ON CRIME AND JUSTICE:
Routine Activities and Victimization in China

In 2004, researchers anonymously polled 2,500 randomly selected residents of a Chinese city. The researchers included lifestyle measures often associated with increased victimization, including increased visibility and accessibility as a crime target (e.g., activities conducted away from home, such as eating out or traveling out of town) and greater target attractiveness (e.g., carrying valuable property); moreover, they assessed personal guardianship (e.g., self-assessed physical strength and self-defense capabilities). They measured victimization risk by exposure to four types of crime (i.e., personal theft, robbery, assault, and swindles or confidence games).

The Chinese subjects underreported some activities associated with victimization experiences in the West, including dining out and traveling. When explored for their theoretical import, these elements of routine activities *perform* as they do in the West: Eating out and traveling increase the risk of certain crimes, including personal theft; traveling for both work and pleasure increases the risk of being swindled.

The researchers noted that China is going through a modernization phase, and with modernization comes changes to both routine activities and increased opportunity for crime. They concluded that "these changes are likely to play an even more important role in the future, insofar as consumer lifestyles penetrate society more deeply" (p. 514).

SOURCE: Messner, Lu, Zhang, and Liu (2007).

Traditional law-and-order policies to reduce predatory crime, then, may be doomed. Those features of modern life that improve the quality of life—such as better transportation, more electronic durable goods, and greater opportunities for recreational activities outside the home—may increase the opportunity for predatory crime, result in lower guardianship, and increase the pool of suitable targets. Cohen and Felson (1979) also disdained the idea that crime is related to the breakdown in the social structure of large cities: "Rather than assuming predatory crime is simply an indicator of social breakdown, one might take it as a byproduct of freedom and prosperity as they manifest themselves in the routine activities of everyday life" (p. 606).

Assessing Routine Activities/Opportunity Theory

Routine activities theory has proved to be a most popular theory for testing. One trend is to apply qualitative research designs. For example, Leslie Kennedy and Stephen W. Baron (1993) used the case study approach and unstructured field interviews to study delinquent street groups. They reported that the routine activities model alone is insufficient to explain escalating street crimes committed by these youths. Rather, the authors suggested that routine activities theory should be integrated with rational choice and subcultural theories (see Chapter 6). "Behavior is sometimes guided by choice, sometimes influenced by cultural norms and processes, and at other times by routine activities" (Kennedy and Baron 1993:108–9). Escalation of violence is related not only to motivated offenders, suitable victims, and low guardianship but also to subcultural definitions of what is acceptable and tolerable within these interactions (Kennedy and Baron 1993:108). The entry of youths into a criminal subculture "influenced their routine activities, exposing them to situations where the chances of victimizations are increased, but their decision to engage in violence appeared to be made on the basis of rational choice: Respond or be beaten" (Kennedy and Baron 1993:109).

Another trend is to use the theory to explain previously observed phenomena. For example, Dennis Roncek and Pamela Maier (1991) extended routine activities theory to examine so-called **hot spots.** Bars, taverns, and cocktail lounges known to "attract" unseemly and troublesome customers are hot spot prototypes; many fights, brawls, and even murders occur there as well (Roncek 1981; Roncek and Bell 1981; Roncek and Pravatiner 1989; see also Sherman, Gartin, and Bueger 1989). Analyzing residential blocks, Roncek and Maier found links between crime and the presence of taverns and lounges. After eliminating the potentially confounding effects of being located in high-crime environments, they reported that all crime types were significantly higher on residential blocks with taverns or lounges than on others. They reaffirmed the importance of dangerous places in understanding crime rates.

A third use of the theory is to look at macro-level trends and crime-related issues (Jackson 1984; Stack 1995). Taking this approach, Steven Messner and Judith Blau (1987) examined the variability in leisure-time activities and crime rates in the nation's largest Metropolitan Statistical Areas. They predicted that household-bound leisure activities would be negatively related to crime rates because people would primarily stay at home and out of harm's way. They also predicted that the aggregate volume of nonhousehold leisure activities would positively relate to crime rates, given the increased opportunity for victimizations provided by engaging in leisure activities outside the home. Their findings strongly supported these hypotheses.

As a general observation, then, routine activities theory has proved itself a rich conceptual base from which to view crime and crime-fighting efforts. Several central issues related to the testing of routine activities theory reappear in the literature:

- *Is this a crime theory or a victimization theory?* This is not a trivial point. As first stated, the theory explored why crimes occur, where they are likely to occur, and who is likely to engage in them. Some **victimologists**—researchers who study crime victims—have linked routine activities concepts to activity-specific risks of property and personal crime victimizations (Miethe, Stafford, and Long 1987; Miethe and Meier 1990; Wilcox, Madensen, and Tillyer 2007), gender-specific risks for victimization (Mustaine 1997), college student lifestyles (Mustaine and Tewksbury 1998), community disorganization (Moriarty and Williams 1996), and gang membership, gun carrying, and violent victimizations (Spano, Freilich, and Bolland 2008). Researchers suggest that principles of routine activities (e.g., nature and extent of engaging in the life-course patterns found among the sample as a whole) may provide key insights into subsequent victimization experiences: those whose life-course patterns differed from their peers reported more victimization experiences than those reporting more homogeneous patterns, irrespective of prior victimizations (Wittebrood and Nieuwbeerta 2000). Although nothing about the theory restricts tests to the explanation of criminal motivation and behavior, its use as a victimology theory is an important shift in emphasis.

- *Are the indicators of opportunity measuring what we want them to measure?* Terance Miethe and associates (1987) observed that the indicators of criminal opportunity theory are the same ones used in other theories of crime. For example, a household activity ratio that involves the number of female labor force participants with a husband present and those with an absent husband, divided by the total number of households, reflects social disorganization theory (see Chapter 6) and opportunity theory. This ratio exhibits a linkage to burglary, but given the prior status of disorganization theory, it is unclear what opportunity theory adds to our understanding of burglary.

- *Where are the offender motivation studies?* Wayne Osgood and associates (1996) reported that participation in routine activities—including the presence of peers, absence of authority figures, and lack of time-delimited structure in their lives—accounted for much of their youth sample's involvement in deviant behavior. Few other tests of routine activities hypotheses include measures of offender motivations (Bryant and Miller 1997).

- *Where are tests that include all the central elements of routine activities?* Tests rarely include more than one of the theory's central elements. Richard Bennett (1991), for example, explored target suitability, proximity to a pool of motivated offenders, and guardianship, using a sample of 52 nations over a 25-year period. He found that the routine activities model is crime-specific and does a better job of explaining property crime than personal crime. Bennett's work demonstrates the importance of considering as many elements of routine activities as possible (see also Anderson and Bennett 1996).

- *How does the "hot spot" interact with its residents to create a place where crime becomes routine?* Wilcox and associates (2007) added neighborhood-level measures of guardianship to individual-level ones, focusing on physical (target hardening), person (home occupancy), social (informal control), and natural (surveillance through environmental design). Using census tract and individual resident data from Seattle, Washington, they found that burglaries decreased as individual-level target hardening, placement management, and natural surveillance increased; however, these relationships only held true when the neighborhood-level indicators of target hardening, informal social control. and natural surveillance also increased. In spite of these successes, a piecemeal approach to the testing of routine activities may lead to a false sense that the theory has been tested when, in fact, only limited hypotheses drawn from it have been subjected to empirical verification.

- *What is the role of formal guardians?* The general absence of suitable guardians creates problems, but the absence of the police could signal broader community-level problems. In later works, Felson (2002) tended to devalue formal guardians, preferring to emphasize the informal guardianship that occurs when people interact as a part of everyday life. Sociologists have long accentuated informal social control, even if Felson initially failed to acknowledge it (Akers 2000:32).

Routine activities/opportunity theory has proven to be resilient when tested. Certain elements remain underdeveloped, including the role of informal social control in both creating and eliminating "hot spots," and the absence of complete tests of the theory. Nonetheless, the theory is rich in its implications for both policies and practices, especially within local communities and for policing agencies.

Routine Activities, Opportunity, Public Policy, and Criminal Justice Practices

According to Felson (2002), routine activities theory provides broad-ranging policy implications for structuring communities and lives. He described his contribution to criminological theory as "a very versatile theory of crime" (2001:43). Some level of victimization is inevitable, as the supply of victims and perpetrators is a constant. Where and when those crimes take place, however, is within the control of citizens at large, especially through collective guardianship and control of exposure.

Routine activities theory serves as the conceptual undergirding for afterschool programs intended to prevent delinquency and victimization (Gottfredson, Cross, and Soulé 2007). As Osgood and Anderson (2004) argue, unsupervised teens engaged in socializing activities have both the opportunity and motivation for delinquent behavior; the amount of time teenagers spend in unsupervised activities predicts delinquency involvement (see also Haynie and Osgood 2005). Gottfredson and associates (2007) studied the impact of 35 after-school programs on self-reported substance use, delinquency, and victimization experiences, controlling for the participants' individual characteristics (e.g., race, gender, and time participating in the program). Program size (i.e., smaller) and structure (i.e., more structured programming) predicted program success—less drug use, victimizations, and delinquency. Also, unstructured socializing exhibited strong ties to victimization, but it was only partially related to delinquency. Providing alternative "routine activities" with fewer opportunities for misbehavior can reduce delinquency.

Law Enforcement Practices   The targeting of hot spots by an influx of specialized police units—what police call **hot-spot patrols** (Sherman and Weisburd 1995)—is one practice that has evolved from fusing routine activities and rational choice. Flooding an area identified as being a statistical outlier in crime rates with higher-than-normal levels of police patrols and specialized anti-crime units, goes the logic of this practice, not only results in more arrests, but also forces choice decision by offenders. Staying put and engaging in more crime will have the likely effect of an arrest and possibly a criminal sanction. The result, claim the proponents, is lower crime (Sherman et al. 1997; Weisburd and Eck 2004). Moreover, there is the possibility that increasing enforcement in one area will drive down the crime rates of nearby areas as well, what has come to be called the **diffusion of crime-control benefits hypothesis** (Clarke and Weisburd 1994; see also Braga et al. 1999; Sherman and Rogan 1995; Weisburd and Green 1995).

The **spatial displacement hypothesis** suggests that hot-spot practices may reduce one area's crime rates, but only because the criminals move to nearby areas, where crime-control efforts are less aggressive (Reppetto 1976). Empirical studies of possible crime displacement tend not support this hypothesis (Barr and Pease 1990; Eck 1993; Hesseling 1994). Focused anticrime efforts rarely yield total crime displacement, and even where it does occur, it seems to be relatively minor and not wholesale (Clarke 1992; Gabor 1990).

In an effort to resolve the issue, researchers simultaneously examined both displacement and diffusion hypotheses (Weisburd et al. 2006). They closely monitored two areas in Jersey City, New Jersey, with substantial street-level crime and disorder, and watched for displacement into two neighboring locales designated as "catchment areas." The catchment areas did not receive the enhanced police activities provided to the target areas. The researchers subsequently collected systematic observational data, supplemented with interviews and ethnographic field observations, for the both target and catchment areas. While the limited focus of the study restricts its generalizability, the researchers reported that "for crime markets involving drugs and prostitution, crime does not simply move around the corner. Indeed, [their] findings support the position that the most likely outcome of such focused crime control efforts is a diffusion of crime control benefits to nearby areas" (Weisburd et al. 2006:584). In other words, the displacement that occurs does not undermine the use of enhanced police services in specific high-crime areas.

SUMMARY

Life is a series of choices, or so claim the theorists in this chapter. This emphasis on choosing between alternatives—one right and one wrong—has proved to be a powerful and enduring idea, based on equally powerful assumptions about human behavior, as suggested in Table 2.1.

Even in the absence of definitive proof, deterrence theory remains a powerful icon in crime theory. The new incarnations of deterrence, extensions into rationality and opportunity, have extended the theory's life into the twenty-first century. Even without these new conceptualizations and attendant research findings, the political appeal of deterrence arguments likely accounts for most of its popularity with policy makers and the public.

T A B L E 2.1   Deterrence Theories of Crime

Theory	Major Figures	Central Assumptions	Causal Arguments (Key Terms)	Strengths	Weaknesses
Formal deterrence	Beccaria, Bentham, Gibbs, Tittle, Becker	Humans are rational beings, endowed with free will and capable of making informed choices between good and evil; humans are also hedonistic beings, seeking out pleasure over pain.	Hedonistic tendencies threaten the social order unless crime penalties are certain, swift, and appropriately severe—elements modified by some theorists.	Intuitively correct, as most people abide by the law; widely supported by the public, who fear punishments; criminal justice system reflects its philosophical premises.	Hypotheses generated by the theory proved hard to test, largely due to operationalization difficulties.
Rational choice	Cornish, Clarke	Crime is, for many some, a reasonable alternative to other less palatable and possibly more costly outcomes.	Offenders' *choice structuring* lays the foundation for the kind of crime (*involvement decision*) they are willing to commit, followed by the *event decision* at the time of the crime.	Provides a logical decision-making context to deterrence ideas; explains how some crime occurs so quickly when the opportunity presents itself to potential offenders.	May be little more than deterrence theory cast in econometric terms (costs versus benefits), ones that sound suspiciously like the words of Bentham.
Routine activities/ opportunity	Felson, Cohen	Criminal motivations and supply of potential offenders are constants; supply of potential victims varies and determines crime level in a given community or geographic area.	Predatory crime depends on timely convergence of: (1) a motivated offender, (2) a suitable target (high exposure, low guardianship, high attractiveness, and close physical proximity), and (3) absence of a capable guardian.	Explains increased crime rates from 1960s to 1980s; the theoretical base for "hot spots" hypothesis; includes concept of opportunity, which implies prevention strategies; allows for integration with other theories, including rational choice.	Primarily addresses only predatory crime, leaving out a great deal of the breadth and depth of crime.

KEY TERMS

absolute deterrence

attractiveness

boot camp

capable guardian

celerity

certainty

choice structuring

cost–benefit analysis

Classical School

determinate sentencing

deterrence/ brutalization thesis

diffusion of crime control benefits hypothesis

event decision

expected utility principle

exposure

general deterrence

guardianship

hedonism

hot spots

hot-spot patrols

individual deterrence

involvement decision

mandatory sentencing

motivated offender

natural law

neoclassicalism

Neuve Classical School

perceptual deterrence hypothesis

positive law

predatory crime

proportionality

proximity

restrictive deterrence

"scared straight" programs

severity

shock incarceration

social contract

spatial displacement hypothesis

specific (individual) deterrence

suitable target

time discounting

victimologists

CRITICAL REVIEW QUESTIONS

1. Which of Beccaria's ideas might explain problems with mandatory sentencing?

2. Why do you think the classicalists profoundly influenced U.S. penal philosophy?

3. What kind of research would convince you that the death penalty either deters crime or creates a brutalization effect?

4. What do you see as the greatest flaw in deterrence research?

5. Do you believe people are calculating machines, constantly doing cost–benefit analysis?

6. "Choice structuring is like when a student considers what classes to take (e.g., X amount of work for Y credit and Z knowledge equals too much work for too little gain)." How accurate is this statement?

7. If you broke the law, whom would you be more concerned about finding out—your family or the police?

8. How might rational choice theory expand our understanding of the relationship between routine activities and predatory crime?

9. Which deterrence-related criminal justice practices strike you as most likely to be successful? Support your answers with insights gleaned from this chapter.

10. Which ones are likely, in your opinion, to fail? Support your answers with insights gleaned from this chapter.

NOTES

1. The following derives from Martin, Mutchnick, and Austin (1990) and Monachesi (1955).

2. The use of gender-specific pronouns in discussions of classical theory is consistent with the philosophy, in that the theorists did not view females as having the same rationality as men. French neoclassical law largely exempted females from the legal expectations accorded males.

3. Beccaria opposed the death penalty since he saw it as a case of the state essentially declaring war on the individual, an unfair struggle given the state's resources.

4. Fogel, von Hirsch, and others supporting the use of sanctions for their own sake—as just desserts—are sometimes called neoclassicalists (Einstadter and Henry 1995:46).

5. Piliavin and his associates found support for the opportunity and reward elements of the rational choice model, but failed to find support for risk, which included personal and formal risks. Indeed, the deterrence elements were the weakest, with choice proving to be stronger. In spite of positive findings about rational choice theory, they worried that it oversimplifies the cognitive process behind criminality: "Persons' evaluations or imputed meanings of sanctions are important in determining their behavior. These evaluations or meanings may be *conditioned* by elements within the immediate situation confronting the individual" (Piliavin et al. 1986:115; emphasis added).

3

Biological and Biochemical Theories

CHAPTER OVERVIEW

Origins of Biological Explanations

Evil Spirits and Crime

Nature and Crime

Criminal Anthropology

Criminals and Body Types

Assessing Primitive Biological Theories

Primitive Biological Explanations, Public Policy, and Criminal Justice Practices

Genetics and Crime

Genetic Factor Studies

Karyotype Studies: The XYY Chromosome Abnormality

The Future of "Crime Genetics"

Assessing Genetic Explanations

Genetics, Public Policy, and Criminal Justice Practices

Biochemistry and Crime

Substance Abuse

Neurotransmitters and Criminal Behavior

Other Biochemical and Neurological Explanations

Assessing Biochemical Explanations

Biochemistry, Public Policy, and Criminal Justice Practices

LEARNING OBJECTIVES

In this chapter, you will learn the following:

- The role of positivistic determinism in shaping contemporary criminology.

- The appropriate historical and social context for biological theories of crimes and criminals, past and present.

- The nature and extent of genetic theories of crime, particularly how these theories answer criticisms leveled against earlier biological crime markers.

- Whether scientific advances can confirm the role of biology in crime.

- The extent to which chemicals shape human actions.

INTRODUCTION

The moment we entertain the possibility that criminal behavior is *caused* rather than *chosen,* we move away from free will, a central concept in all theories that evolved from classicalism, and toward **determinism,** the idea that all human behavior results from antecedent conditions and events. Determinism is either "hard" (complete) or "soft" (partial) (Matza 1964); that is, forces beyond human control cause either all or some human social behavior. In the nineteenth century, determinism merged with positivism to form **scientific determinism.** According to **positivism,** the scientific approach, which has proven so successful in the study and control of the physical world, has equal validity and promise in the study of humanity and society. Following the precepts of scientific determinism, science can separate out the various deterministic forces—be they biological, economic, psychological, or social in origin—that cause antisocial behavior.

Scientific determinists place great stock in the notion that only our five senses can provide knowledge of natural phenomena in the physical world. They rely on the scientific method to reveal natural laws governing these physical and social phenomena (Michalowski 1977:28). As positivists, they search for underlying causes that are applicable universally. With respect to crime, this process should allow for the prediction of criminal behavior and suggest ways of preventing or controlling it.

Throughout the twentieth century, American society turned to science and technology to solve a wide range of social problems, including crime. Two sciences have long interested positivistic criminologists. Biology and chemistry provide systematic knowledge of nature and the physical world. *Biology* addresses, among other things, the physiology, origins, and development of animal and plant life; *chemistry* deals with the composition and properties of substances, and with the reactions that create substances or convert them into others. Criminologists have also shown an interest in *biochemistry,* the branch of chemistry that deals with plants and animals, and their life processes, especially their susceptibility to natural and artificial chemical compounds. Chemicals, such as alcohol, heroin, and cocaine, have well-documented ties to criminal conduct. We also know that humans must manufacture certain chemicals to maintain normal physical, psychological, and social states—that is, **homeostasis.** Too much or too little of these chemicals is bad. The physical environment also can contain many toxic substances, chemicals linked by scientific research to crime and other forms of antisocial behavior.

Before biologists and chemists began studying crime, other deterministic explanations dominated punishment philosophies and practices. Some were the forerunners of primitive scientific theories about crime. Their central themes, including assumptions about human behavior and the causal forces at work, have existed for millennia. Sociologists dominated late twentieth-century criminology and tended to dismiss biological explanations for criminal behavior. Nicole Rafter (2008:199) argues that biological theories are gaining ground and "threatening not to eclipse sociological theories but to break their monopoly."

ORIGINS OF BIOLOGICAL EXPLANATIONS

- Have you ever crossed the street to avoid a dangerous-looking person because the person's physical appearance intimidated you?

- After reading a newspaper article or watching a television report on a particularly heinous crime, have you thought that the perpetrator was not human?

Thousands of years in the past, before there were laws as we know them, community elders, religious leaders, and others with special insights into human nature blamed something within those who misbehaved for their conduct. They believed that evil spirits, demons, and devils caused a wide range of unacceptable and otherwise troublesome behavior. Such theories were deterministic, individualistic, and prescientific.

Evil Spirits and Crime

Humans have long blamed evil forces for troubling events. Graeme Newman (1978:130) summarized the issue: "Myth is part of culture, and as such has shaped human response to crime for thousands of years." Early humans believed that supernatural powers caused life's harsh conditions and the natural disasters that added to its unpredictability, a belief that evolved into spiritualistic explanations: Where gods reign, demons also exist.

Attempts to rid a community of demons and other evil spirits often overlooked the welfare of the "victim." Punishments based on spiritualistic explanations are especially instructive. **Apotropaic punishments,** or actions intended to ward off evil spirits, were common. Practitioners believed that **corporal punishment,** where they subjected the evildoer's body—the demon's host—to excruciating pain, drove out the demon. Similarly, the demon, as much as its host, was the target of capital punishment. People living in the Middle Ages believed that hanging protected the community from the condemned person's demonic powers (Newman 1978:37). On the way to the gallows, the condemned could not have direct contact with the earth. The executioner often left the body to rot on the rope, allowing it to return naturally and harmlessly to the earth.

Throughout history, societies executed unknown numbers of people accused of demonic possession.[1] Punishment often followed canonical (religious) or secular (civil) trials. Many scholars believe that such demonological explanations reached fever pitch in medieval times. According to the criminologist George Vold (1979:5), European theocracies of the Middle Ages fused demonism with the political and social organization of feudalism. One element, the Inquisition, was a type of state-sponsored witch-hunting.

Unlike earlier involuntary demonic possession, Renaissance-era witchcraft involved the exercise of free will. Witches, having made a pact with the devil, freely gave up the faith (Currie 1968). Apotropaic punishments continued with the emergence of Protestantism in the sixteenth-century's Reformation (Sharpe 1997). Perhaps the most famous episodes in the American colonies occurred at Salem in New England (Erickson 1966).[2]

Nature and Crime

For thousands of years, **naturalistic explanations** coexisted with those based on spiritualistic origins. The ancient Phoenicians, Greeks, and Romans developed naturalistic explanations, which, unlike those developed by spiritualists, sought causal arguments in the physical and material world. Greek physician Hippocrates (c. 460–370 B.C.E.) based his conclusions about healing on objective observations and deductions. Greek philosopher Democritus (c. 460–370 B.C.E.) held that all living things were made of tiny indivisible particles, called atoms, and that their constant motion explained the creation of the universe. He accomplished this feat without an electron microscope or orbiting satellite telescope. Like Hippocrates, Democritus had keen powers of observation and deduction.

Naturalists sought to understand the "nature of things." Later generations adapted this philosophy, refined it, and made it science. Even in times dominated by demonology, naturalistic explanations gained popularity. With naturalistic explanations, however, it was easy to deduce that a person's exterior, which naturalists could observe, corresponded to an unobservable inner self.

Physiognomy: Crime and the Human Face   Practitioners of **physiognomy** made judgments about individuals' mental qualities, character, and personality based on external physical characteristics, especially facial features. An early adherent, J. Baptista della Porte (1535–1615), like many positivists of the day, developed his ideas from examining criminals' cadavers. He concluded that specific characteristics, including small ears and bushy eyebrows, indicated certain criminal types. Being a determinist, della Porte held out little hope for changing offenders. Criminals were victims of their physical features, and no amount of moral persuasion could alter that fact.

In 1775, the Swiss theologian Johan Caspar Lavater (1741–1801) published a four-volume work titled *Physiognomic Fragments,* in which he classified people according to certain physical qualities called **fragments.** For example, shifty-eyed, beardless men with weak chins were untrustworthy. Interestingly, Lavater's main contribution to criminology was to point to another science of the day as having more promise than physiognomy, that science being phrenology (Vold 1979:53).

Phrenology: Curing Criminal Tendencies   The followers of **phrenology** looked at the skull's shape and protuberances, with the latter supposedly suggesting either latent or manifest criminality. According to phrenologists, persons with these characteristics were now, may once have been, or were likely to become criminals. Franz Joseph Gall (1758–1828), an Austrian anatomist, described his study of the human skull as **cranioscopy.** Gall visited prisons and insane asylums, physically examining inmates' skulls for bumps, lumps, and other abnormalities. He then codified and systematized his observations, publishing a series of works on the brain's physiology and function. His greatest contribution may have been his student John Gasper Spurzheim (1776–1832), who emphasized the skull's shape and any facial imperfections. In refining his master's work, Spurzheim became phrenology's greatest proponent.

Unlike della Porte's immutable conditions, phrenologists held that a regime of moral exercise and "right living" could divert those diagnosed through phrenological screening from the path to criminality. In the late nineteenth century, American phrenologists were still conducting phrenological readings and constructing treatment plans for the "afflicted," much like medical doctors (Schafer 1969; Vold 1979).

Today, criminologists reject physiognomy and phrenology as unscientific. In the opinions of some scientists, however, physiognomists and phrenologists were looking in the right place: the human brain. Rather than "brain organs," today's scientists explore the neurochemistry of the central nervous system (Morse 1997; see also Chapter 4).

Criminal Anthropology

Charles Darwin's (1809–1882) *The Descent of Man* (1871) included the idea that **natural selection** shaped humanity. Nature specifically eliminated a species' weaker members or, given an uncorrectable flaw, an entire species—the fittest survive to reproduce. The English philosopher Herbert Spencer (1820–1903) advanced Darwin's thesis by placing natural selection in a social context. Spencer (1961) believed that artificially perpetuating society's weakest members through public welfare or private charity did them—and society—a disservice. (See In Their Own Words: Spencer on Survival of the Fittest.) Darwin and Spencer wrote about human evolution and its effect on society, but not specifically about crime. It remained for Cesare Lombroso to use evolution in his new science of criminal anthropology.

Criminal Man: Lombroso's Atavistic Human   Cesare Lombroso (1835–1909), a Venetian physician, studied thousands of convicts, using **anthropometry,** a branch of anthropology based on taking body measurements to determine individual differences. In 1876, pulling together his diverse findings on diseases of the nervous system, the brains of criminals, and their anthropometrical measurements, Lombroso published *L'uomo delinquente* (*Criminal Man*) (1876[2006]). Lombroso concluded that crime derived from arrested evolution; he called this state **atavism,** from the Latin word for "ancestor."

IN THEIR OWN WORDS: Spencer on Survival of the Fittest

Spencer used Darwin's thesis in a social context, expressed as **Social Darwinism,** and condemned the emerging practice of **social engineering.** Spencer believed, among other things, that the suffering of the poor was the inevitable price for the struggle of existence and the advancement of the stronger stock—a struggle destined to end in the survival of the fittest and the elimination of the unfit. Consider the following ideas, also expressed by Spencer, as you examine the development of criminal anthropology:

- *On the relationship between sociology and biology:* "There can be no rational apprehension for

the truths of Sociology until there has been reached a rational apprehension of the truths of Biology" (p. 334).

- *On the dangers of engaging in programs for the poor:* "If the unworthy are helped to increase, by shielding them from that mortality which their unworthiness would naturally entail, the effect is to produce, generation after generation, a greater unworthiness" (p. 344).

SOURCES: Andreski (1971); Spencer (1961).

According to Lombroso, atavistic man had peculiar physical characteristics, which he called **stigmata.** He included the following among dozens of stigmata: facial asymmetry; an enormous jaw; prominent cheekbones; large ears; fleshy, swollen, and protruding lips; abnormal dentition; a receding or excessively long chin, or a short and flat one, as in apes; excessive arm length; and more than the normal complement of fingers, toes, or nipples. He also included a series of predatory habits, including a craving for evil for its own sake and a desire not only to kill but also to mutilate victims. Lombroso stressed that these were not the *causes* of crime, but simply the signs of atavism.

Facing mounting criticism, Lombroso modified his position to include environmental factors in later editions of *L'uomo delinquente.* He concluded that, given access to money and the ability to steal, even the wealthy are tempted to commit crimes; moreover, they avoid discovery or prosecution by exercising influence. Although no longer ascribing all criminality to atavism, Cesare Lombroso argued that atavists pose the most serious threat to society. Gina Lombroso-Ferrero, his daughter, included many of these modifications in her English-language version, *Criminal Man* (1979[1911]). As the following box on COMPARATIVE CRIMINOLOGY makes clear, his contributions were worldwide.

The English Convict: Goring's Refutation of the "Born Criminal"   The shortcomings of Lombroso's "research" became obvious even in his own time. Charles Goring (1870–1919) examined 3,000 convicted offenders and a comparison group of unconvicted Englishmen in a 12-year effort; he presented his findings in *The English Convict: A Statistical Study* (1972[1913]). Goring was looking for statistical correlations between the objective measures of physical and mental anomalies and known criminals. Not only was he unable to distinguish offenders from nonoffenders using these anomalies, he also failed to find significant differences between types of offenders, as predicted by Lombroso (e.g., comparing burglars to forgers or murderers).

COMPARATIVE CRIMINOLOGY—WORLD VIEWS ON CRIME AND JUSTICE: The World View of Lombroso: Past and Present

By the time of his death, much of the criminological world had discounted Lombroso's contributions to the study of crime and criminals. Indeed, his concept of the "born criminal" was widely denounced by French criminologists at the 1889 International Congress of Criminal Anthropology. As recent historical analyses suggest, this enmity was not surprising, given contemporary European politics. National pride and not necessarily critical science may have precipitated this French response, a rebuke echoed for similar reasons in Germany. It appears, through the lens of history, that Lombroso's criminal anthropology may even have had an influence on British criminology of the early twentieth century, long thought to have ignored all European criminology.

Nicole Hahn Rafter suggests that criminologists outside of Europe also liked Lombroso's ideas. As we have seen, American criminal anthropology, and perhaps American criminology itself, owes Lombroso a large and generally unrecognized debt. Latin American criminologists also benefited from his work at the turn of the twentieth century, after its translation into Spanish and the Italian positivist Enrico Ferri's Latin American lecture tours.

Lombroso has been dead for nearly a century. Nonetheless, criminologists, historians, and others interested in the crime continue to debate the contributions and costs associated with his criminal anthropology.

SOURCES: Lombroso (2006); Rafter (1997).

Goring's criminals were shorter in stature and lower in body weight than were people in his comparison group, differences he attributed to hereditary inferiority, the "real" source of criminality. As for the "born criminal," Goring (1972[1913]:173; emphasis in original) observed, "Our results nowhere confirm the evidence [of the born criminal], nor justify the allegations of criminal anthropologists... Our inevitable conclusion must be that *there is no such thing as a physical criminal type.*"

The American Criminal: Hooton's Rejoinder   In response to Goring's critique, Harvard physical anthropologist Earnest Albert Hooton (1887–1954) published *The American Criminal: An Anthropological Study* in 1939. For years, he and colleagues at other universities collected body measurements from 17,000 individuals, including roughly 14,000 prison inmates. His control group was a cross-section of college students, police officers, and firefighters. Hooton performed many meticulous comparisons between the inmates and the control group. He concluded that there were significant differences between criminal and civilians on more than half of the anthropometric measurements. The physical inferiority of the criminals, compared to the control group, was important for its link to mental and moral inferiority.

Hooton also analyzed body types as they related to crime type. He concluded that tall, thin men were more likely to be murderers and robbers, and that tall, heavy men were more likely to be killers and to commit fraud and forgery, as well. What Hooton failed to note was that over half his prison subjects were repeat offenders, and many had previously committed different offenses (Vold 1979:63). Hooton (1939:309) nonetheless concluded that criminal were an organically inferior class of human beings.

Hooton compared apples to pears, both fruits, but obviously different. He failed to appreciate that police officers and firefighters, especially during the Depression when such positions were prized, would be physically superior (e.g., had to meet weight and height requirements) to prison inmates, who were often from economically deprived circumstances. College students, especially those at Harvard, represented an advantaged population with good nutrition and opportunities for physical recreation.

American Criminal Anthropology   Between 1893 and 1909, a group of U.S. anthropologists took Lombroso's work and "Americanized" it (Rafter, 1992). Their central assumption was clearly Lombrosian in nature, but tempered by the Victorian-Edwardian times in which they lived: "The body must mirror moral capacity" (Rafter 1992:535). They integrated Lombroso's ideas of atavism with **generation theory,** arguing that socially problematic groups inherited their tendency toward various forms of devolution, a type of backward evolution. Moreover, poverty, mental illness, and crime were symptoms of the underlying organic malaise found in these degenerate groups.

The origins of American criminology in criminal anthropology yielded three long-term problems. First, criminal anthropologists kept the boundaries of their discipline extremely fluid, where specialists moved easily from one area to another, regardless of their expertise (Rafter 1992). While these cross-disciplinary forays may have strengthened criminology, some scientists see the lack of a disciplinary boundary as a weakness. Second, criminology lacks a central, generally agreed-upon method of study. This fact derives from the criminal anthropologists' inability to define the nature and practice of their science, a fact not lost on critics. Lastly, criminal anthropology's ties to eugenics troubles many people. **Eugenics** is the practice of ridding the human species of unfit biological stock, largely through sterilization, life sentences in prison, or death. Figure 3.1 summarizes Lombrosian-style explanations of crime.

Criminals and Body Types

During the 1930s and 1940s, the physician William Sheldon (1898–1977) studied criminal man by **embryonics.** An embryo, he noted, is like a tube with three layers of tissue, each becoming a different bodily function or part. The endoderm yields the digestive tract; the mesoderm gives bone and muscle; and the ectoderm provides the nervous system. One element can dominate, yielding a specific body type, or **somatotype,** and an accompanying temperament.

Sheldon measured the body types of 200 boys housed in a small residential rehabilitation home and 200 male college students. Based on comparisons between these known juvenile delinquents and noncriminal students, Sheldon (1949) found a correlation between body type and criminality. In his study, the delinquents were **mesomorphs** (i.e., having muscular bodies and aggressive tendencies) and far less often **ectomorphs** (i.e., having fragile, skinny bodies, small faces, and introversive tendencies) than the noncriminal comparison group. However, some students were mesomorphs, and some delinquents were ectomorphs.

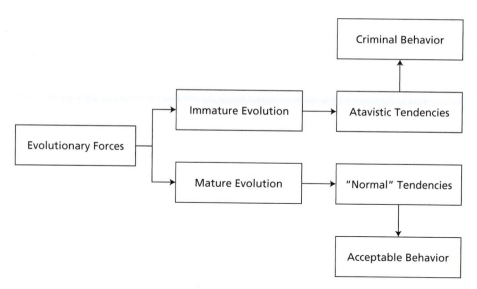

FIGURE 3.1 Lombrosian Explanations of Crime

Eleanor Glueck (1898–1972) and Sheldon Glueck (1896–1980), two Harvard-based criminologists, supported the connection between mesomorphy and delinquency. Assessing the body types of 500 delinquents and 500 "proven nondelinquents," they identified more than half of the delinquents as mesomorphs, as compared to less than a third of the nondelinquents (Glueck and Glueck 1956:9). They found that mesomorphs had personality traits that made them likely to engage in aggressive acts without remorse or self-doubt (Glueck and Glueck 1956:226). They also reported that several sociocultural factors, all related to the home, had ties to mesomorphic delinquency.

The Gluecks were not true biological determinists, but rather viewed biological features as creating a situation in which other social forces could act upon the individual (Laub and Sampson 1991:1423). That is, body types cannot motivate criminal behavior, but they may be a factor in determining the direction of any set of behaviors, including crimes. **Endomorphs,** whose bodies tended to be soft and round, were rarities within the population of known delinquents. Sheldon (1949), for his part, associated each body type with a tendency toward a specific temperament. For example, endomorphs tended to seek comfort and love luxury; mesomorphs were dynamic and assertive and tended to behave aggressively. Ectomorphs tended to be introverts, and were sensitive to noise and other distractions. Temperament and body type combined to form a person's propensity for delinquency. Figure 3.2 summarizes theories of body type and crime-proneness.

Assessing Primitive Biological Theories

The major weakness of primitive biological explanations is also, paradoxically, an enduring strength: There is virtually no way to test them. True believers accept as

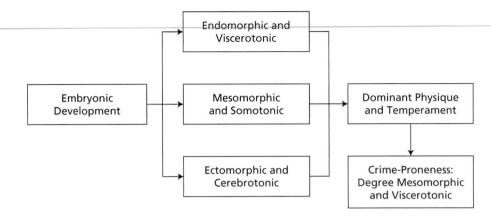

F I G U R E 3.2   Body Types and Crime-Proneness

an article of faith the alleged causal factors. Even the pseudoscientific phrenologists admitted that their entire discussion of the "physiological organs of the mind" was hypothetical. They could construct no meaningful tests (Vold and Bernard 1986), meaning these theories had more in common with theology than biology.

In the late nineteenth and early twentieth centuries, criminal anthropologists applied the best science of their day, but this does not mean their critics were silent on what constituted good science. Goring failed in his attempt to find a link between Lombroso's stigmata and crime. Lombroso maintained that some stigmata defied measurement and that only "trained observers" could detect them (Vold and Bernard 1986). Goring may have been too eager to disprove Lombroso (Driver 1972:440). Although Goring demeaned Lombroso's data, the samples used in *The English Convict* would hardly satisfy contemporary survey research standards. In addition, Hooton used a method similar to Goring's procedure. Consequently, the generalizability of both Goring's and Hooton's research is suspect. For his part, Hooton saw the differences between his sample of white male prisoners and his far smaller and no more representative control group as signs of criminal degeneracy, an inherited trait. This process is a classic illustration of circular reasoning: criminals are inferior, thus inferiority must cause criminality (Vold and Bernard 1986:57; see also Gould 1981).

Body typing, too, was not without its critics. Edwin Sutherland (1951) reanalyzed Sheldon's calculations, classifying each youth in the case histories according to offense seriousness and consistency of delinquency involvement. He argued that Sheldon's methods for doing these tasks were questionable, that the selective manner by which Sheldon included cases for examination called into question the entire study. Sutherland concluded that Sheldon had failed to show any real differences between the physical appearances of offenders and nonoffenders.

Sutherland was also critical of the Gluecks' research. However, his criticisms may have had ideological roots, given that he viewed their work as representing a dangerous trend in criminological research. Sutherland had no interest in the biology of crime and demeaned the work of those who suggested even the possibility of biological factors, a characterization that circumscribed the Gluecks' work (Laub and Sampson 1991:1422).

The use of subjective body measurements to identify crime potentialities seems odd because the human body is subject to many external forces. Moreover, Sheldon's study focused exclusively on boys, a shortcoming corrected by the Gluecks. Nonetheless, the mutability of the human form and its susceptibility to environmental forces make body typing a dubious proposition at best. One recent study, however, found mesomorphs overrepresented in the Arkansas prison system—62 to 72 percent of about 5,000 inmates fell into that category as measured by body mass index (Nagourney 2008). Was this a study of body typing or bodybuilding?

Primitive Biological Explanations, Public Policy, and Criminal Justice Practices

Darwin, in *The Descent of Man*, emphasized a hierarchy among human societies, an idea that lent support to the rampant racism of the nineteenth century. Various strains of social Darwinism relegated all efforts for physical, mental, or social improvement as predestined to fail. By logical extension, this led to the conclusion that the destruction of the physically, mentally, and socially weak would serve to improve the human species. Indeed, natural selection justified both slavery and imperialism (Degler 1991).

Judicial and Political Practices   State sterilization laws ensured control over reproduction of inferior stock, with Indiana enacting the first such law in 1907. By 1915, 13 states had such laws; by 1930, 30 states permitted sterilization of certain criminal offenders and so-called mental defectives in public institutions (Degler 1991). The Supreme Court upheld these laws in *Buck v. Bell*, a 1927 decision. Carrie Buck was the daughter of a "mental defective" and the mother of a daughter adjudged feebleminded. Referring to this situation, Justice Oliver Wendell Holmes famously wrote for the majority: "Three generations of imbeciles is enough." In 1932, Vivian Buck, Carrie's "imbecile child," died of an intestinal disorder, but not before she had completed the second grade, and her teachers had judged her to be "very bright" (Locurto 1991).

The view that criminals derive from poor biological stock supports eugenics. Being a runaway slave in the pre–Civil War United States meant being a criminal, in much the same way that a Jew in Nazi Germany held criminal status. Defining behavior as criminal, then, is a legal act, not a scientific one. Consequently, eugenics is more social prejudice than objective science (Gould 1981). In the United States, before sterilization laws fell into disuse in the mid-1960s, more than 65,000 reputedly mentally ill and developmentally disabled people underwent the procedure in 33 states. Hitler modeled Germany's sterilization policies on California's 1909 sterilization law (Bruinius 2006).

Law Enforcement Practices   Whether we can discern a biological basis of crime, current informal police practices may reflect such arguments. Police often use body typing and criminal anthropology in their work, if informally. For example, the arresting officers described Rodney King at his 1993 civil rights trial as "a monster" largely due to his physique and alleged drug use. He was, in the terminology of the street, "buffed-out." Police may learn from experience to look for physical characteristics that mark a person as a threat. These markers could include well-developed physiques (mesomorphic somatotype); "shifty" eyes (a physiognomic fragment); and twisted, upturned, or flattened noses (atavistic anomalies). Just as with the primitive biological researchers, the employment of these markers by police is very much a hit-and-miss proposition. Informal discussions with police, however, reveal that physical markers continue to set off alarms. Singling out persons for vehicle stops by police officers because they fit a physical profile not only may violate suspects' civil rights, but also places the officers at legal risk (Del Carmen and Walker 2006).

GENETICS AND CRIME

- Do you question if crime is due to *either* nature *or* nurture, or perhaps both?
- Is genetic theorizing a modern-day search for the "criminal man," similar to the ones conducted by Lombroso and Hooton?
- What kind of evidence would convince you that crime has genetic origins?
- Do you think that a crime gene exists?

Genetics is the study of heredity. The science emerged in 1900 when researchers rediscovered Gregor Mendel's (1822–1884) work on inherited characteristics or traits. Mendel viewed every trait as potentially transmittable within a species. He believed that both parents, as hereditary units, contributed some of their respective traits to their offspring through reproductive cells called gametes. In the field of genetics, two key technical terms are *chromosomes* and *genes*.

Chromosomes are high-density genetic storage devices, the carriers of human hereditary characteristics that reside in all of the body's cell nuclei. Males have an X and a Y chromosome in each cell; females have two X chromosomes. An ordinary body cell contains 23 pairs of chromosomes each with thousands of genes. **Genes** are chromosome segments—humans have about 70,000 genes—by which living organisms transmit inheritable characteristics to the next generation. Genes consist of **deoxyribonucleic acid (DNA)** and array themselves along the length of each human chromosome.

One way to visualize gene segments is to think of a spiral staircase with two intertwining rails, described by geneticists as the double helix (Watson 1990). One rail contains subunits called **nucleotides,** and the opposing rail has a mirror image of subunits, arrayed in chemically bonded groups that form traits or **alleles.** The human organism has more than 3 billion nucleotides. Scientists believe that about 300,000 of these DNA bases form human genes. Hence, every human cell, except red blood cells, contains an exact copy of an individual's DNA. We refer to the sum of these DNA genes as the **human genome**—instructions, written at the molecular level, for constructing an entire human being.

The science of genetics is at the core of two types of criminological studies. The first type looks at inheritable genetic factors. These studies, which began before the 1953 discovery of DNA, may seem primitive by today's standards. The second type of study looks at the arrangement of sex chromosomes inherited from one's mother and father, the so-called X and Y **sex chromosomes.** Collectively, they form the genetics of criminology.

Genetic Factor Studies

Genetic factor crime studies take one of two main forms. The first is the **twin study.** Twins exist in two genetic versions: (1) identical or **monozygotic twins,** which evolve from a single fertilized ovum or egg and share the same genetic material, and which resemble each other; and (2) fraternal or **dizygotic twins,** which evolve from two separate eggs, fertilized by different spermatocytes, and which have less genetic material in common. Twin studies assume that, if the criminal activities of identical twins are more similar than those found in fraternal twins, then hereditary factors are the cause. It also possible, however, that identical twins do not share identical genetic profiles—close but not identical—that is, they do not have identical DNA (O'Connor 2008).

The **adoption study** is the second main form. Researchers compare the crime and delinquency rates of these children with those of both their biological *and* their adoptive parents. When the adopted children's behavior more closely resembles that of their biological parents, supporters point to this as evidence of a genetic predisposition.[3] Twin studies rarely take into account the interaction of genetics and the home environment. Studying the criminality of adopted children separated from their biological parents at an early age can overcome this weakness.

Twin Studies Concordance,   the key measurement in twin studies, is the degree to which twins share some behavior or condition. We do know that there are many more behavioral similarities among reunited identical twins than among reunited fraternal twins (Rowe 2002). What about criminal behavior? The ideal research design would be to separate identical twins at birth and have them randomly assigned to adoptive parents, something forbidden by researcher ethics (Rowe 2002). We must settle for twins separated by circumstances. Germany's Johannes Lange published the first such criminological twin study in his 1929 book *Crime as Destiny.* Of monozygotic twins, 75 percent were concordant pairs on subsequent criminality, but only 12 percent of the dizygotic twins were also concordant.

Patricia Brennan and her associates (1995:69) reported on eight twin studies, three from Germany, and one each from Holland, the United States, Finland, England, and Japan. These eight studies, published between 1929 and 1979, examined 138 pairs of monozygotic twins and 145 dizygotic twins, and included many mentioned by Bartol (1999). Brennan and her associates identified crime concordance levels for monozygotic twins ranging from 50 to 100 percent, with most between 60 and 70 percent. Crime concordance levels for fraternal twins were much lower, ranging from zero to 60 percent, with most between 10 and 15 percent. Indeed, the overall average was 52 percent for monozygotic twins and 21 percent for dizygotic twins (see Raine 1993:79).

The twin studies have several important shortcomings. For one thing, those reporting very high concordance for identical twins involved as few as two to four sets of twins. There are relatively few separated identical twins available for study. The three studies with the largest numbers of identical twin pairs, between 28 and 37 sets, exhibited concordance levels between 61 and 68 percent. The highest level of concordance (54 percent) for dizygotic twins was in the same study that reported only an average concordance level among the monozygotic twins (66 percent). Few medical researchers would accept so few cases as definitive. Moreover, the chief outcome variables—crime, delinquency, or some other indicator of misconduct—rely on the timely intercession of the criminal justice system or a judgment by a researcher. These facts make the conclusions of the twin studies highly suspect.

When a major Norwegian study failed to show a significant difference between the criminality of identical and fraternal twins, Karl Christiansen, who studied Danish twins, was troubled. Christiansen (1977:82) suggested that perhaps "some special conditions exist in Norway that would dampen the expression of genetic factors." Given the high level of cultural and racial homogeneity found in most Scandinavian countries, this is a remarkable statement. The same qualification is true for nearly all such genetic studies because the largest and most sophisticated ones have taken place in Scandinavian countries. These findings beg an important question: What are the researchers measuring? Is it, perhaps, the impact of nationality or geographic boundaries on genetics?

Adoption Studies   The adoption studies yielded the same general findings: Adopted children whose natural parents have criminal records are much more likely to be convicted of a crime than when the natural parents have no criminal records (Hollin 1989). Barry Hutchings and Sarnoff Mednick (1977) compared adopted children who had a criminal biological father and a noncriminal adoptive father with those who had a noncriminal biological father and a criminal adoptive father. The former were twice as likely as the latter to become criminals themselves.

Mednick and his associates (1984, 1987) found support for the genetic transmission of crime traits. However, the type of crime committed by biological parents was unrelated to their child's specific crime. If the police had arrested either biological parent, the child of that union, no matter the gender, was much more likely to have a criminal record. Most offspring in all categories had no criminal conviction record; moreover, using arrest records introduces the confounding factors of police activity and criminal ability.

Proponents of a gene–crime link believed that adoption studies would control for environmental effects, particularly those that made the findings of twin studies suspect. The evidence is consistent with the heritable-factors thesis. However, researchers cannot rule out the interactive effects of the biological parents' social status and such factors as prenatal alcoholism (Duyme 1990; Van

Dusen, Mednick, Gabrielli, and Hutchings 1983). That is, child-rearing patterns in different social classes and communities compound the problems rather than eliminate them. According to Lee Ellis and Anthony Walsh (2000), adoption studies provide evidence of the interaction between genetic and environmental factors, the result being, in some cases, criminal behavior.

Karyotype Studies: The XYY Chromosome Abnormality

Karyotype studies address the number and type of chromosomes in individuals. In 1965, P. A. Jacobs and associates (1965) resurrected Lombroso in *Nature,* a British scientific journal, when they pointed to a genetic abnormality as a possible key to some criminal behavior. The researchers based this claim on the fact that sex chromosomes determine gender: An XX pairing is a female, and an XY is a male. Using karyotyping, they observed that a chromosomal abnormality occurs when the fertilized ovum receives an extra Y chromosome. Jacobs and associates speculated that the extra Y chromosome created an XYY pattern, which is extremely rare (Hoffman 1977). The **XYY male** is usually over six feet tall, exhibits low mental functioning, suffers from acute acne, and is often clumsy (Clark, Tefler, et al. 1970; Hoffman 1977; Horgan 1993; Hunter 1977).

Criminologists focused on XYY males for two main reasons. First, the XYY pattern occurred 5 to 10 times more often among prison inmates than predicted by chance alone (Jacobs et al. 1965; see also Ellis and Walsh 2000). Researchers subsequently found high proportions among mental hospital patients (Price, Strong, Whatmore, and McClemont 1966). However, it is possible that the observed overrepresentation of XYY males in certain environments is due to certain aspects of the XYY males' physical appearance and intellect. It is easy to envision two criminals engaging in an armed robbery; the first is of average height without any outstanding physical characteristics and a normal IQ; the other is an XYY male. Which one are the police more likely to catch? In other words, XYY predicts "getting caught," not criminality.

The XYY karyotype may also be class-biased, given that this anomaly appears most often among those in lower-class living conditions (Kessler and Moos 1970). Social class, and not genetic makeup, may account for their higher-than-expected showing: Most inmates are members of the lower class. Finally, marginal mental functioning may be yet another cause of this alleged overrepresentation (Hunter 1966).

XYY males are allegedly more aggressive than XY males (Jacobs et al. 1965). By the late 1970s, however, the scientific consensus was that the hyper-violent XYY male was a myth. Indeed, such individuals, when compared to genetically normal males, tend to exhibit higher levels of passivity (Sarbin and Miller 1970).

The Future of "Crime Genetics"

James Watson and Francis Crick discovered DNA in 1953. Mapping the human genome was an elusive goal until the invention of automatic genetic sequencers in the 1990s. More than 1,000 scientists at 16 laboratories in six countries completed the **Human Genome Mapping Project (HGMP)** at a cost of $250 million. It took four years to map the first billion markers, four months to move to 2 billion, and 12 weeks to finish the task, mapping all 3.2 billion chemical nucleotide base pairs in 2003 (Human Genome Project 2008). The function of more than 50 percent of the pairs is at present unknown.

Scientists have mapped dozens of diseases and genetic defects with a hereditary basis. Some birth defects associated with dietary problems or poisoning, like fetal alcohol syndrome, may have no location on the human genome. However, genetic markers may show who is most at risk for developing problems due to environmental factors. Few markers exist for social behavior, except some forms of mental retardation. The discovery of other behavioral markers, particularly inheritable predispositions for depression and related neurological conditions, awaits further scientific advances (McInerney 1999).

What does the HGMP mean for criminology? Pondering the crime gene's existence, Ellis and Walsh (2000:436) responded: "No. In this sense, there is still no proof that criminal/antisocial behavior is genetically influenced. However, scientists have not yet located any specific genes for height, either. Yet, there is no reason to doubt that height is genetically influenced." Ellis and Walsh point out that height may come from several genes and not one "height gene," and that the same could be true of crime.

Assessing Genetic Explanations

Figure 3.3 summarizes the genetic explanations of crime. As with any crime theory, the true test of these explanations lies in the demonstrated links between what theorists believe and what researchers discover. Genetics–crime link assessments generally take two forms. First, as happened with XYY theory, critics may challenge the theory's basic premise. For instance, does the addition of an extra Y chromosome really suggest a supermale? Skeptics argue that the extra Y chromosome does not predict criminality, but at best predicts the likelihood of apprehension. Since only 3 percent of the prison population has the XYY pattern

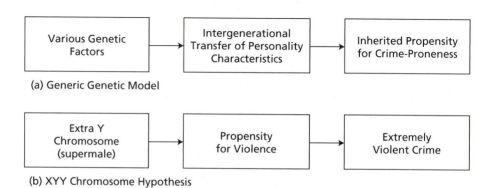

(a) Generic Genetic Model

(b) XYY Chromosome Hypothesis

F I G U R E 3.3 Genetic Explanations of Crime

(Jacobs et al. 1965), the theory, even if correct, explains very little criminality. Moreover, the research on XYY individuals suggests that they are usually passive and *underrepresented* in the noninstitutionalized criminal population (Sarbin and Miller 1970). Perhaps labeling theory (Chapter 8), and not biology, better explains XYY as a correlate of prison placement.

Second, genetic researchers' methods receive special attention. According to David Rowe (1990), genetics cannot explain criminal behavior in a single person, but it can provide reasons why some *groups* are more prone to commit crime. Rowe and D. Wayne Osgood (1984) found significant links between genetic factors and the self-reported criminality of twin pairs. Rowe (1990) concluded that neither family nor other environmental factors serve as suitable causal factors in explaining adult crime or delinquency. Genetics may predispose children toward antisocial behavior, as heredity accounts for one-third to two-thirds of the explanation (Rowe 1983, 1990; Rowe and Gulley 1992). Diana Fishbein (1990:45) observed that the methods used by sociobiologists, especially in twin studies, failed to provide consistent patterns of genetic influences.

The general criticisms of crime gene research, then, fit into these clusters:

- *Sampling issues.* The samples in twin and adoption studies are, as a rule, small. When researchers employ larger samples, the differences are less significant. Mednick and associates (1984, 1987) overcame this deficiency in a study of 14,427 Danish adoptees (but see "measurement problems" below); however, few researchers achieve this sample size, especially with twin studies.

- *Alternate explanation issues.* Studies of the potential links between genetics and crime rarely employ sophisticated statistical controls or use sufficiently matched control groups. Environmental variables, from social class and family to contaminated living conditions, are strong candidates to explain the findings attributed to genetics. Moreover, the role of the police in determining who will have a criminal record confounds the problem.

- *Measurement problems.* Michael Gottfredson and Travis Hirschi (1990:60), after calculating the correlation in Mednick's adoption study, concluded that "the magnitude of the 'genetic effect' as determined by adoption studies is near zero."

- *Overstated cases.* **Biocriminologists**, as criminologists who seek to understand crime using biological explanations, cite statistically significant differences as proof that heredity determines behavior. However, the fact that two groups exhibit statistical differences on a given characteristic is not proof of causation. Research on Danish identical and fraternal twins that considered social factors estimated the effects of heredity as very modest and, in one case, nearly zero (Carey 1992).

- *Misstated science.* Perhaps the most stinging rebukes of biocriminology's genetic claims come from the scientific community. Garland E. Allen (2001), a biologist and historian, notes that he has never seen a behavioral genetics theory linking corporate embezzlement with genetics. Rather, biocriminologists focus on the crimes of the poor. Geneticist Ayesha E. Gill (1978) argues that those who use genetics to explain the low IQ recorded for certain races engage pseudoscience and have little true understanding of genetics. (We return to the question of the IQ–crime link in Chapter 5 and the race–IQ–crime link in Chapter 11.)

The greatest genetic variability exists at the individual level, not the racial level (Cavalli-Sforza 2000). In contrast to the tiny number of genes that determine a person's skin color, perhaps tens of thousands of genes shape traits such as intelligence (Angier 2000). These facts hardly bolster the credibility of crime gene arguments. As Glenn Walters (1992) observed nearly two decades ago in his meta-analysis of the gene-crime connection, and which appears to hold true today: Earlier, poorly designed studies revealed far more support for the connection than better-designed and more recent studies. However, it is also likely that American criminology has a decidedly anti-biological bias, as suggested in the following Comments and Criticisms.

Genetics, Public Policy, and Criminal Justice Practices

Public policies derived from modern genetics are as controversial as earlier variants. The ethical and philosophical arguments against "biomedical" crime factors are widely recognized (Brennan, Mednick, and Volavka 1995:65–66). First, as noted previously, biological explanations have ties to nineteenth-century social Darwinism and to twentieth-century Nazi ideology and practice, such as Josef Mengele's horrific experiments on twins at Auschwitz.[4] The racist legacy of genetics lingers. Second, some critics decry the genetics–behavior link because it eliminates free will and criminal responsibility—in legal parlance, *mens rea*. Third, the nature-versus-nurture controversy "created an 'either/or' context of research on crime causation" (Brennan, Mednick, and Volavka 1995:66). A **nature-plus-nurture model** allows for the effects of free will.

COMMENTS AND CRITICISMS: Is There an Anti-Genetic Bias in Contemporary Criminology?

Early in the twenty-first century, Wright and associates began testing the genetics–crime link with large, longitudinal datasets, particularly the National Longitudinal Study of Adolescent Health (Add Health). The Add Health study included a sample of twins. The researchers explored the extent to which being a twin accounted for variations in delinquent peer formation and delinquency. Wright and associates reported that both genetic influences and nonshared environmental influences can account for the variability in the outcomes they examined. While they found many similarities in the monozygotic and dizygotic twins included in the Add Health sample, there were also significant differences. Generally, their research supported a convergence of biogenetic and social/

physical environmental factors on the study of crime and delinquency.

This group, along with several additional associates, also criticized contemporary graduate education in criminal justice and criminology, suggesting that the true legacy of Lombroso is the near avoidance of any biocriminological arguments in the career training of the next generation of criminology. They call this phenomenon the "miseducation of criminologists," accusing sociological criminologists of misstating the theorizing of biocriminologists and ignoring the findings of biocriminologists—all in an attempt to enforce disciplinary boundaries. Who said the politics of criminology was boring?

SOURCES: Wright, Beaver, DeLisi, and Vaughn (2008); Wright, Beaver, DeLisi, Vaughn, Boisvert, and Vaske (2008).

Patricia Brennan and her associates (1995) identified several policy implications with regard to genetics and crime. They pointed out that we can predict antisocial behavior from the interaction of perinatal factors (i.e., those occurring during a child's delivery) and unstable family environments. Providing prenatal health care to mothers and early hospitalization should help to reduce perinatal problems. According to Brennan and associates (1995), such programs could halt or severely restrict the potentially adverse social conditions that children with perinatal complications might otherwise encounter.

Even in the event that geneticists could identify a crime gene, what should society do about it? Currently, the DNA analyses of millions of convicted and even accused criminals reside in the nation's DNA database, called the Combined DNA Index System or CODIS (National Institute of Justice 2008; Peterson and Hickman 2005; Steadman 2001). At some point in the not too distant future, a new generation of "social engineers," much like the well-meaning social activists of late nineteenth- and early twentieth-century America, could scour these databanks, looking for people with a particular marker, and therefore deserving of special treatment by the criminal justice system. This special treatment could include extended and length periods of protective incarceration—already justified for sex offenders who are continuing threats to the community—or gene therapy to reverse their alleged propensity to repeat the offense.

From a criminal justice perspective, such practices should be limited to convicted offenders. However, it is that possible that for various well-intended purposes, including the identification of biological parentage or as a means to identify abducted children, DNA typing will become a far more common, perhaps automatic, procedure at birth. Without sounding too conspiratorial or, for that matter, paranoid, some governmental agency could scan this database looking for potential criminals, based on the presence of "the crime gene." What would be their next course of action? One possible choice could be between mandatory and elective gene therapy. Another alternative could be early selective incapacitation for those with the gene.

Bioethicists and others concerned about civil rights question the search for disease genes, let alone behavioral ones (Gold 1999; Knoppers and Chadwick 2005; Weiner 2001). Geneticists tell us that a genetic predisposition does not mean that a specific outcome is inevitable. Genes are not destiny (Steen 2001; Owens 2006). Perhaps by the time scientists give us more genetic markers for behaviors, society will come up with answers as to how we use that information. However, geneticists already looking for underlying human phenotypes related to known diseases suggest that this task, while more likely now that the human genome project is complete, is far from easy (Botstein and Risch 2003; van Ommen, Bakker, and den Dunnen 1999). Looking for a crime gene may be accorded less priority than certain cancers or other life-threatening diseases, and prove even more difficult to find.

A meta-analysis of studies conducted around the world concluded that violent criminal behavior never emerges from a single cause (Strueber, Lueck, and Roth 2007: 22). Rather, it results from a complex web of interrelated of risk factors, "among them an individual's inherited tendencies, brain anatomy, and childhood experiences." Genetic *and* environmental factors interact and aggravate one another; however, the studies also concluded that positive environmental influences may offset those that promote violence.

In Chapter 2, we examined the economist's view of the decision to engage in criminal behavior as based on a rational process—a calculus of risk to reward. If, in the criminal's subjective thinking, the reward significantly outweighs the risk, then crime is a likely outcome. Recent studies have found that the immature brains of adolescents may be responsible for much of the risky behavior that young people engage in. Adolescents tend to weigh benefits more heavily than risks: "So, after carefully considering the risks and benefits of a situation, the teenage brain all too often comes down on the side of the benefits—and chooses the risky action" (Reyna and Farley 2007: 60). We consider the idea that most adolescent delinquents mature out of crime as adults with drift theory (Chapter 6) and labeling theory (Chapter 8).

Judicial Practices   Genetics-related affirmative defenses meet with judicial skepticism, as Richard Speck's case highlights. The State of Illinois tried and convicted Speck in 1967 for the murder of eight Chicago nurses. His lawyer claimed that Speck was an XYY male. Speck and others who have attempted to blame their criminal deeds on their chromosomal structure have been unsuccessful. The plea "I am a victim of my genes" has fallen on deaf judicial ears.

BIOCHEMISTRY AND CRIME

- How do you respond to the claim that alcoholism and other forms of drug abuse are diseases meriting treatment, not punishment?

- Even if you are willing to view these forms of behavior as addictions and medical problems, can you understand why some people resist this idea?

- Alcohol and controlled substances are only a few of the many chemicals in the environment. Do you think that exposure to other chemicals also has the potential to alter human behavior?

Human life depends on a wide array of chemicals—their actions, interactions, and reactions. For example, the *autonomic nervous system (ANS)* governs digestion, respiration, and heartbeat, and **neurochemicals** enable these processes to work. The *central nervous system (CNS)* consists of the brain and spinal column. Other neural stimuli are necessary to operate the smooth muscle groups, which require cooperation between the ANS and the CNS. A delicate balance of neurochemicals maintains the information flow between the ANS and the CNS, keeping humans alive and functioning.

Human brains are susceptible to biochemical imbalances, particularly as related to antisocial behavior. The brain, weighing three pounds and containing 10 billion neurons, performs two functions: (1) It integrates and processes information, and (2) it serves as a storage and retrieval system for information. The ANS and CNS, but especially the brain, are similar to a computer system. Change the current, alter the direction of that current, or somehow misdirect the incoming messages, and unpleasant consequences will result.

Substance Abuse

Understanding substance abuse—and perhaps even controlling it—is important because substance-involved criminals account for the majority of those arrested (U.S. Department of Justice 1994, 1999). Moreover, when they enter the criminal justice system, these individuals pose unique jail and prison management problems (Mays and Winfree 2009). Alcohol use and criminality are positively correlated both nationally and cross-culturally for property crime, violent offenses, and delinquency; the same is true for self-reported offenses (Ellis and Walsh 2000).

Any understanding of substance abuse begins with an examination of the central nervous system's operation and the significance of neurotransmitters. CNS cells, or neurons, come in many sizes and shapes, and form chains of specialized and excitable cells. The body's 100 billion neurons differ from other body cells in that they can send signals or impulses in the form of electrical energy.

Neurotransmitters carry CNS information; they inhibit or enhance the release of ions, electrical charges, and communication between neurons when these electrical impulses activate a sufficient number of synapses—microscopic gaps between neurons—causing the release of neurotransmitters. They are fast-acting neurochemicals. For example, if you touch something that is very hot with your finger, neurotransmitters allow your brain to define and react to the incident. They accomplish this feat by passing an electrochemical signal or message between millions of nerve cells that finally arrives at your brain. A key part of your brain then interprets this signal as an unpleasant event that causes the brain to send out instructions to improve the situation, such as "move your finger." These messages travel at light speed.

The CNS contains roughly 100 neurotransmitters. Some, such as dopamine, epinephrine, and norepinephrine, excite or speed up the "firing" of ions between neurons; others, such as endorphins, slow down this "firing." The body uses these chemicals to trigger anger or to regulate the operation of different organs. Each neurotransmitter has a receptor site—proteins located on the surfaces of neurons—designed to receive it, and the ensuing reaction may stimulate or inhibit a specific bodily function.

Dopamine (DA), one of many neurotransmitters found in the CNS, has received special attention from psychopharmacologists because of its apparent dual roles in the regulation of (1) mood and affect, and (2) motivation and reward processes. Researchers have found that the reinforcing effects of psychoactive drugs in humans are associated with increases in brain DA (Volkow et al. 1999). Although the brain contains several DA systems, the mesolimbic DA system appears to be the most important for motivational processes. Some addictive drugs produce their potent effects on behavior by enhancing mesolimbic DA activity. Scientists speculate that some forms of clinical depression may result from unusually low DA levels, which legal or illegal chemicals can offset.

Repeated use of psychomotor stimulants (e.g., cocaine) and depressants (e.g., heroin) can deplete the mesolimbic DA system, causing normal rewards to lose motivational significance. As a result, the mesolimbic DA system becomes even more sensitive to pharmacological substances (Addiction Research Unit/SUNY at Buffalo 1998). Abstinence from cocaine and morphine in the wake of repeated administration may decrease DA levels in the brain system. Lower levels of brain-bound DA, in turn, may amplify the intense cravings associated with withdrawal in drug-dependent humans. Relapse into drug-taking behavior following abstinence correlates with the subjective experience of craving and is an important factor in drug addiction.

Stimulants may compensate for a deficiency in the dopamine, serotonin, and norepinephrine—neurotransmitters that determine a person's mood. Cocaine or amphetamine users, according to this theory, attempt to stave off the apathy and depression caused by a chemical deficiency (Khantzian 1985), drug use being homoeostatic. Chronic cocaine users, in self-administering doses throughout the day, counteract DA deficiency (Gold, Washton, and Dackis 1985:133). In extroverted persons with high levels of DA, even small doses of cocaine are intensely rewarding, exposing them to higher risk of dependence (Goleman 1990).

During the 1970s, scientists discovered morphine-like neurotransmitters within the brain, along with CNS-specific receptor sites programmed to receive them. These **endorphins** (short for "endogenous morphine") relieve pain when they reach receptor sites in the spinal cord and brain. Although these sites receive naturally occurring neurotransmitters, or endorphins, they are receptive to external ones, such as heroin, as well.

Endorphins also enable people to deal with psychological stress by curbing autonomic overreactions and promoting a sense of calm. They slow respiration, reduce blood pressure, and lower the level of motor activity, which sometimes leads to feelings of inadequacy and sadness (Levinthal 1988:149). Persons at risk for opiate addiction may suffer from endorphin deficiency. Their predisposition to heroin addiction could be a biological response to a genetically acquired deficiency, or it could represent a temporary or permanent impairment of the body's ability to produce endorphins. This finding helps account for the puzzling individual variability in the addictive power of opiates.

If an endorphin deficiency exists, however, the question remains about what precipitating circumstances might lead to such a deficiency. Among the possible causal forces are the environment, genetics, or both (Levinthal 1988).

The National Institute on Drug Abuse (1998) sponsored research revealing that an individual's genetic makeup is a major factor in drug abuse vulnerability. The researchers found that, although family and social environmental factors determine whether an individual will begin using drugs, progression from use to dependence is largely due to genetic factors, particularly for males. In addition, the genetic influence for heroin addiction surpasses that of any other drug (Zickler 1999). Thus, even though drug abuse is the result of a complex interplay of environmental, social, psychological, and biochemical factors, genetics plays an important role in individual vulnerability to drug use—the more severe the abuse, the greater the role of genetic factors (Comings 1995). While genes do not directly cause a person to become a drug user, some researchers suggest that genes produce a predisposition to respond in a specific way to a given drug, including becoming an alcoholic or drug addict (Pickens and Svikis 1988:2).

Neurotransmitters and Criminal Behavior

Two other neurochemicals have ties to criminal behavior. We can easily see how a lack of impulse control—impulsivity—could result in antisocial behavior, and the condition has been associated with low levels with such important neurotransmitters, such as serotonin. **Serotonin** is a stimulating neurotransmitter sometimes connected to violence. Persons with low serotonin levels compared to those with levels that are more normal are inclined toward aggression and violence. We do not know how serotonin influences behavior—whether it has a direct impact or lessens impulse control. In any event, because of this link, serotonin levels are a rough predictor of criminality. Although the correlation between serotonin and crime is clear, it is unclear whether the environment influences serotonin levels. It is also possible that serotonin levels (and other biological factors) have social roots, such as extreme poverty and accompanying malnutrition.

Monoamine oxidase (MAO) is a neurologically active enzyme tied to criminality since the 1970s (Ellis 1991). The enzyme, found throughout the human body, apparently helps regulate key neurotransmitters. MAO, in two forms, works on serotonin, norepinephrine, and dopamine, which in turn influence behavior. No one knows what the exact nature of MAO activity in the brain is or how it influences human behavior (Roth, Breakefield, and Castiglione 1976). Biologists have only studied what they call "peripheral MAO," or MAO outside the nervous system.

Although it may be important to criminologists and have a genetic link, scientists do not agree on how genetics influence MAO levels or if this is even important to criminality (Ellis 1991:230–31). An MAO deficiency is associated with borderline retardation; furthermore, low-MAO persons exhibit a tendency toward aggressive outbursts, often in response to anger, fear, or frustration. Finally, several studies report relationships between MAO deficiency and abnormally aggressive behavior in males (Brunner et al. 1994). Studies looking at the impact of MAO levels on crime have, to date, suffered from an important methodological shortcoming: They have only examined peripheral MAO, which limits the generalizability of their findings (Ellis 1991). Nonetheless, some researchers link MAO levels to crime and race, a topic explored in Chapter 11.

Other Biochemical and Neurological Explanations

The potential list of biochemical and neurological influences on criminality is extensive (Ellis and Walsh 2000; Walsh and Ellis 2007). Among the various explanations, three yield interesting insights into biology-based criminality. The

first involves chemical substances other than psychoactive drugs. Their ingestion may be environmental or it may result from purposive acts, such as eating
or drinking. The chemical either is nontoxic in low doses but toxic in higher
doses or is toxic at any level. The underlying premise is that toxicity may
negatively influence behavior. A second biochemical hypothesis involves abnormal hormonal levels. When something interferes with the production,
movement, or absorption of hormones, physiological and behavioral alterations
often result. The third involves defects in brain functioning. That is, a childhood trauma, such as witnessing or being a victim of violence, can affect brain
development and later criminal behavior. As Rafter (2008:206) notes, "events
completely external to the child can become internalized in his or her brain
and personality."

Foods, Toxins, and Crime   Criminals and delinquents often exhibit vitamin deficiencies, poor eating habits, and low blood-sugar levels, all conditions—particularly
low blood sugar or hypoglycemia—related to hyperactivity and aggression
(Hippchen 1978, 1982; see also Shah and Roth 1974). The exact causal links to
crime are unclear. One case exemplifies the confusion about these ties. In 1982,
former San Francisco supervisor Dan White, the assassin of Mayor George
Moscone and Supervisor Harvey Milk, blamed the murders on his consumption
of too many Hostess Twinkies. White did not deny that he committed the crimes,
but argued that something intervened to eliminate the necessary *mens rea* component of criminal responsibility. The media-dubbed **Twinkies defense** resulted in a
finding of guilty on lesser charges. In the wake of this trial, the idea of a chemically
based defense gained popularity. Other courts, however, have shown less inclination
to accept this as a legitimate mitigating factor or an affirmative defense. In any
event, the questionable methodology of most hypoglycemia studies casts doubt on
the central argument that low blood sugar, caused in part by an excess sugar intake,
causes violence (Kanarek 1994).

Heavy metals, including lead, mercury, and cadmium, are environmental toxins.
Biochemists have long recognized the toxicity of these metals even in small doses,
and they are pandemic in our environment, largely in lead-based paints and industrial waste. Speculations about their possible ties to antisocial behavior are of recent
origin. For example, a postmortem laboratory analysis of an alleged mass murderer's
hair revealed significantly elevated lead and cadmium levels. After eliminating other
possible medical explanations, the researcher concluded that heavy-metal poisoning
might have affected the accused's inhibitory mechanisms (Hall 1989).

The **neurotoxicity hypothesis (NH)** holds that "chemical imbalances in
heavy metals and other toxins may contribute significantly to antisocial behavior
by disrupting the normal functioning of a person's brain chemistry" (Crawford
2000:6; see also Denno 1993; Masters 1997). NH proponents view lead, manganese, and cadmium as likely candidates. Pulling together several biological hypotheses, they suggest that genetic makeup and psychoactive chemicals, especially
alcohol, along with heavy metal poisoning, can interact to cause antisocial behavior. Researchers even link lead to homicide and other violent crimes (Reyes
2007; Stretesky and Lynch 2001).

This hypothesis may contain a class and race bias. Members of the lower class are at greatest risk from the primary environmental sources of lead: lead-based paints and lead plumbing. Scientists believe that manganese lowers the levels of serotonin, dopamine, and norepinephrine, (Masters, 1997; Masters, Hone, and Doshi 1997). Individuals with diets low in calcium and other essential vitamins are especially vulnerable to manganese uptake and neurotransmitter depletion. Such dietary deficiencies are common in African American and Hispanic American infants (Masters, Hone, and Doshi 1998:158).

Hormonal Influences and Crime   Another biochemical explanation of criminality focuses on abnormal hormone levels. **Hormones** are also chemical messengers secreted by the endocrine system, a series of ductless glands in the body that include the pituitary and thyroid glands, pancreas, kidneys, ovaries, and testes. They move through the bloodstream or pass slowly through cell walls to various parts of the body, where they regulate cell metabolism—speeding up, maintaining, or slowing cell activity. Hormones are secondary chemical messengers and are generally slow-acting.

In 1850, scientists observed the physiological and psychological effects of the **endocrine system**'s hormones (Vold and Bernard 1986:98). Scientists also noted the importance of hormonal balance—and imbalance—for human behavior early in the twentieth century. Louis Berman (1938) later suggested that institutionalized offenders in New York State had glandular problems at a rate two to three times greater than that of a control group. However, a series of studies conducted in New Jersey on incarcerated and "normal" juveniles found no such differences (Moltich 1937).

The **PMS defense** is an extension of the hormonal imbalance theme. Premenstrual syndrome is a little-understood medical condition that afflicts some women around the onset of their menses, perhaps leading to irrational, bizarre, or aggressive behavior. Katherine Dalton (1964) viewed natural chemicals in women suffering from PMS as the cause of their aberrant, law-violating behavior. The menstrual cycle creates large fluctuations in female biochemistry (Fishbein 1992). In the early stages of menstruation, women experience a depletion of female hormones (ovulation marks the highest level), and reduced levels of estrogen are associated with aggressiveness. Doctors give many women who suffer from the symptoms of PMS progesterone and estrogen therapy.

Without more research, it is impossible to state that PMS, alone or in concert with environmental factors, actually "causes" criminal behavior. Researchers could inform the separate legal issue of whether society should excuse persons so afflicted from criminal responsibility for their acts (Horney 1978). However, conducting ethically responsible research on the influence of hormones on criminal behavior remains a considerable barrier. For a definitive study, researchers would have to assign subjects—women—to either a control or experimental group, and how to achieve this without endangering the health and welfare of both groups remains an elusive practical and ethical goal.

Research scientists have also linked testosterone, an essentially male hormone, to inappropriate conduct in teenagers and adults, ranging from excessive aggressiveness to violent behavior (Dabbs, Frady, Carr, and Beach 1986; Olweus, Maattson, Schalling, and Low 1980; Udry 1990). For example, a study of prison inmates revealed strong correlations between testosterone levels and violent criminal behavior (Dabbs, Carr, Fray, and Riad 1995). This testosterone–crime linkage is especially appealing because a high testosterone level signifies a "super-male." However, the testosterone–deviance link remains more of a statistical association than a single variable statement of cause and effect; the role of testosterone in producing antisocial behavior is not clear (Booth and Osgood 1993:95). Rather than ruling out social explanations, Alan Booth and D. Wayne Osgood (1993) suggested that a combination of biological and social explanations is helpful. This mixing of social experience and hormonal effects has also been proposed by researchers studying the testosterone levels in male and female youths engaged in violent urban subcultures (Banks and Dabbs 1996). This argument envisions a balanced-influence model in which testosterone contributes indirectly to crime. Specifically, the hormone affects temperament, interpersonal relationships, and even performance of important social roles, which relate to criminal and other antisocial behavior.

Neurological Crime Theories Neurophysiology looks at both the central nervous system (CNS) and the autonomic nervous system (ANS) in seeking explanations of criminality. Biocriminologists, using neurophysiology, trace criminality to events in early childhood. Injuries to the brain—what doctors call *brain insults*—can lead to defective brain functioning. Intrusive agents such as gunshots and knives, brain and spinal-column injuries, and even fevers brought on by infectious diseases qualify as brain insult. Brain lesions and tumors, whether malignant or nonmalignant, are also candidates in the search for neurological origins of crime. People with these types of injuries or disorders—especially to the cerebral cortex—exhibit, among other things, psychotic episodes, depression, homicidal urges, massive personality alterations, and even hallucinations (Walsh and Ellis 2007; Yeudall 1977).

CNS disorders, such as **learning disabilities, attention deficit disorder (ADD)**, and **hyperactivity**, although not inherently criminogenic, are statistically linked to antisocial behavior. For example, some researchers maintain that learning-disabled children violate the law at the same rate as the non–learning disabled (Murray 1976). Others, however, report that the learning disabled exhibit high official delinquency and crime rates (Buikhuisen 1987; Holzman 1979). Each set of researchers studied the same condition but reached different conclusions.

Behaviors related to brain dysfunctions include aggressiveness, dyslexia, and other rapid onset disorders that threaten an individual's well-being or lifestyle. ADD and childhood brain dysfunctions amplify the problem. ADD-related behaviors include lack of attention to details and tasks, outbursts of impulsivity and instances of "acting without thinking," and hyperactivity (e.g., the classic fidgety child who shows excessive motor activity even during sleep). This disorder manifests itself in poor school performance, stubbornness, and an unwillingness to obey authority figures. About 3 percent of the nation's children suffer from

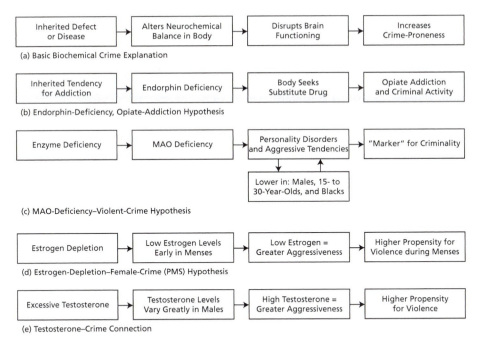

F I G U R E 3.4 Biochemical Explanations of Crime

ADD, mostly boys. Both ADD and brain dysfunctions may relate to growing up in dysfunctional families although the causal ordering is elusive (Moffitt and Silva 1988). Early diagnosis and treatment may lower the risk for antisocial and criminal behavior. Figure 3.4 summarizes biochemical explanations of crime.

Assessing Biochemical Explanations

The idea that chemical imbalances cause behavioral changes in humans is very intuitive. We know that severe brain damage will affect behavior (Mednick, Brennan, and Kandel 1988). There are documented cases of otherwise normal persons receiving brain injuries, followed quickly by changes in aggressiveness, demeanor, personal attitudes, mental functioning, and conduct. However, in amount of crime committed annually (see Chapter 1), brain trauma can account for only a small portion. Even the observation that a specific mass murderer suffered from a brain trauma may be of little help except to understand that single case. Conversely, a predisposition to alcoholism or other forms of addiction may show strong ties to criminality, but we must carefully review any conclusions. Crime is a *correlate* of addiction, and there may be a *biological predisposition* to addiction. However, a predisposition to addiction does not *cause* crime—or even addiction—as many addicts commit no crimes and many criminals are not addicts.

In fact, for most drug-abusing criminals, criminality preceded addiction (Abadinsky 2008). Alcohol may also be a crime's immediate precursor, the proximate cause. That is, alcohol lowers individuals' inhibitions and hinders their judgment, which facilitates the commission of a crime and, often, the subsequent arrest. What is the causal link? Did alcohol provide "liquid courage" for an act that was already being planned? We know that alcohol consumption can lead to the loss of inhibitions, but what distinguishes the "life of the party" from a felonious assaulter? Alcohol can also impair the processing of information, thereby causing a misinterpretation of events or the behavior of others, resulting, for example, in assault or aggressive sexual behavior (e.g., date rape). Although we may not want to make too much of the intoxication levels of arrestees, they do not diminish the importance of biochemical susceptibility to alcoholism or other drug addiction. Susceptibility by itself does not tell us why someone who drinks to excess then commits crime, while others do not. Nevertheless, it does suggest treatment modalities to eliminate the proximate cause of both the crime and the arrest.

The neurotoxicity hypothesis may eventually explain some criminality. For example, in comparing U.S. counties with no reported release of lead or manganese to countries with toxic releases, one researcher found that the former had violent crime rates below the national average, while the latter's rates were four times greater than the national average (Masters 1997:32). While interesting, the researcher drew individual-level inferences from group-level data: most persons exposed to high toxin levels committed no crimes.

Major criticisms of the biochemistry of crime follow now familiar patterns:

- *Methodological issues.* Much biochemistry–crime research suffers from methodological shortcomings. Only carefully controlled clinical studies can help to eliminate this concern, and then only if successfully replicated. Of course, designing a controlled experiment that manipulates and analyzes the level of heavy metals in humans may pose insurmountable ethical and practical challenges, ones shared with other biochemistry studies, such as research into the effects of PMS (Crawford 2000). The samples used in these studies are often unrepresentative, and generalizing to the population at large is nearly impossible. Biocriminologists also employ contestable criminality indicators, especially official crime records, or vague surrogate measures such as "antisocial behavior."

- *Causal ordering problems.* Researchers may also confuse cause with effect—for example, the alleged PMS–female crime link, whereby irregular menstruation brings on both the psychological and physical stressors associated with aggression (Dalton 1961, 1964). Perhaps the psychological and physical stresses associated with aggression bring on irregular menstruation (Horney 1978).

- *Overstated cases.* Hormone–crime studies yield inconsistent and unremarkable results. At best, testosterone–crime ties are negligible; they also have nonchemical explanations (Rowe and Osgood 1984). One study did find higher testosterone levels for violent offenders—including rapists and armed robbers—than for nonviolent offenders or nonoffenders; however, testosterone levels for *all* subjects were within normal ranges (Rubin 1987). Drugs do lower testosterone levels and offending for some sex offenders, but they do not affect their nonsexual violence (Rubin 1987). Generally, criminologists reject the endocrine system secretion thesis as lacking theoretical foundations and, when applied to crime, unsupported by the evidence (Hurwitz and Christiansen 1983; Wolfgang and Ferracuti 1967).

Biochemistry, like genetics, is the domain of physical scientists. Problems emerge when criminologists tie biochemistry to crime, which is, after all, human social behavior.

Biochemistry, Public Policy, and Criminal Justice Practices

If humans are, at their most fundamental level, chemistry experiments, holding persons accountable for their behavior—or *mens rea*—is illogical (although incapacitation would be logical.) Critics of this deterministic position reject the notion that humans are not responsible for their actions, that they do not have free will. The centrist position is that behavior is the result of nature-plus-nurture, but the role of volition remains ambiguous. Society and the legal system have walked a fine line between these positions, generally favoring free will over "the devil (or genes or chemistry or diet) made me do it." Although the medical community recognizes alcoholism as an addictive state, society does not legally excuse individuals who commit crimes while intoxicated. However, it may mitigate their punishment, resulting in a shorter prison or jail term, probation, or other creative sanctions.

Public policy on biochemically induced crimes generally boils down to a single issue: If actions beyond the control of the alleged perpetrator induced the physical state, then the act lacks the element of criminal responsibility. For example, accidental exposure to chemicals may poison the accused and induce paranoia or other aberrant thought processes, leading the judge or jury to find the defendant not guilty. Similarly, someone could have forced the accused to take a drug or administered it without his or her knowledge and consent, in which case the same outcome is likely: The accused is not guilty. In this way, the legal community recognizes that some physical states are nonvolitional. However, most chemical-inducement arguments are reasons for the mitigation of punishment, not its nullification. The neurotoxicity hypothesis may challenge ideas, especially on questions of criminal responsibility (Crawford 2000).

There is also the self-medication issue—some neurological theories describe the drug abuser as a person whose body is malfunctioning with respect to the production of crucial neurotransmitters, making drug use a form of self-medication (Abadinsky 2008). If the drug is alcohol or a legally prescribed substance, the public and the criminal justice system do not see the victim of this physical disability as a criminal. However, if the substance is illegal, the results often are quite different. Policy considerations that address his anomaly are at the heart of the controversial legalization/decriminalization debate. The use (actually possession) of certain psychoactive chemicals, such as heroin or cocaine, is a crime only if society defines it as such. Until 1914, heroin and cocaine were legal in the United States; alcohol was illegal from 1920 to 1933.

Judicial Practices   The implications for judicial decision making are unclear. Trial courts may hold drug addicts or abusers accountable for their acts. However, convicted offenders may receive more lenient sentences than may sober offenders. Drunk drivers are one exception to this observation. Given citizen groups such as MADD (Mothers Against Drunk Driving) and "get tough" state laws, the trial courts are less forgiving and the mandatory penalties far stiffer (Walker 1994:108–16). Yet even here, the trend may be toward forms of treatment, as DWI-drug courts and programs intended to offer first-time drunk drivers a combined second chance and treatment gain in popularity (Breckenridge, Winfree, et al. 2000; Taxman and Piquero 1998).

Any biological explanations of crime will meet with limited acceptance in court, especially those intended to exculpate the offender. Society bases the law, as we have learned, largely on the concept of free will. Legislatures more closely relate the law's philosophical base to classicism than to empiricism or science: "As long as the law rejects science and remains committed to concepts of punishment, revenge and the mind rather than concepts of prevention, treatment, and brain defects, the crime problem will remain exactly where it is today" (Jeffery, Myers, and Wollan 1991:6). The widespread use of biogenic defenses or even mitigating circumstances is unlikely. Instead, a piecemeal and occasional use of certain affirmative defenses is the more likely course.

Correctional Practices   The strong association between crime drugs has been the focus of much research since the 1980s. For example, in 1987, the National Institute of Justice established the Drug Use Forecasting program to measure drug use among arrested persons, which for more than a decade found that yearly about one-half of all arrestees in DUF-reporting cities were under the influence of one or more drugs at the time of arrest (U.S. Department of Justice 1999). Other studies have revealed links between drugs, crime, and criminals (Brounstein, Hatry, Altschuler, and Blair 1990; Brownstein and Goldstein 1990; Fagan 1989; Fagan and Chin 1991), especially violent crimes committed by users of crack (McBride and Swartz 1990).

In spite of the evidence, drug treatment programs for high-risk persons, especially inside prisons, currently receive low priority (Abadinsky 2008; Inciardi 2007; Mays and Winfree 2009). The U.S. Bureau of Prisons operates more than 100 facilities and incarcerates nearly 200,000 inmates; it provides three types of institution-based, voluntary drug treatment programs. In a given year, thee programs reach less than 15 percent of the federal inmates (Mays and Winfree 2009:171). Nearly all state prison facilities operate some form of counseling program, with (about 90 percent) most addressing drug and alcohol issues (Mays and Winfree 2009:178). While perhaps up to 85 percent of state prison inmates need drug treatment, only slightly more than 10 percent receive it in a given year (Office of National Drug Control Policy 2001). The current system of institutionally based drug treatment is clearly not getting to the target population, in spite of research to suggest that it works (Bhati, Roman, and Chalfin 2008).

SUMMARY

Contemporary biocriminology clearly is not the same biological theorizing of 100 or even 50 years ago. Serious methodological and logical problems remain, and biocriminologists face daunting tasks. Bioethicists tell us that many issues must be resolved, in terms of both the types of allowable research and the ways in which policy makers and practitioners use the resulting knowledge. The lessons of nineteenth-century social Darwinism and twentieth-century fascism are too important to ignore. According to Rafter (2004; see also Rafter 1997), we cannot afford to ignore the contributions of the biological tradition, whether they are from Lombroso, Hooton, Sheldon, the Gluecks, or more recent contributors. Whether science has or will invalidate their ideas is irrelevant from this perspective. Their work constitutes an important piece of the puzzle that is criminology.

In spite of important scientific advances, the influence of genetics and biochemistry on human social behavior, but particularly crime, remains largely speculative, a fact reinforced by the summary of this chapter's biologically based explanations contained in Table 3.1.

TABLE 3.1   Primitive Biological, Genetic, and Biochemical Explanations of Crime

Theory	Major Figures	Central Assumptions	Causal Arguments (*Key Terms*)	Strengths	Weaknesses
Physiognomy	della Porte, Lavater	Human behavioral characteristics have external physical manifestations, especially related to facial features.	Facial features (*facial fragments*) reveal a person's inner criminal tendencies.	Better than spiritualist theories; eliminates society's responsibility.	Untestable; criminalized people due how they looked.
Phrenology	Gall, Spurzheim, Caldwell	*See Physiognomy.*	Bumps and dips in skull reveal amoral and criminogenic tendencies.	Mental or moral exercise reverses natural tendencies.	*See Physiognomy.*
Social Darwinism	Spencer	Biology determines behavior; state should not interfere with nature.	Only the fittest should survive; all others, including those who only drain society's resources, should perish (*natural selection*).	Tends to reinforce existing prejudices and racial/ethnic stereotypes.	*See Strengths.*
Criminal anthropology	Lombroso, Hooton	Biology determines men's and women's ultimate destinies.	Criminals are born, a throwback to more primitive life forms (*atavism, born criminal*).	Provides simplistic answers: those with unusual physical features are evil.	Measures are subjective and prone to mismeasurement; test samples highly suspect.

(Continued)

T A B L E   3.1   **(Continued)**

Theory	Major Figures	Central Assumptions	Causal Arguments (*Key Terms*)	Strengths	Weaknesses
Criminal body types	Sheldon, the Gluecks	The adult body derives from embryonic tissues developed during gestation.	Criminals more mesomorphic than the general population.	Explains why criminals are physically tougher than victims.	*See Criminal anthropology*; uses highly subjective body-type placement.
Genetic explanations	Brennan, Rowe, Hutchings, Mednick, Hunter, Lee, Walsh	Criminal tendencies may be passed from one generation to the next through genetic mechanisms, including but not limited to DNA.	Some people, given genetic predispositions, are more likely to succumb to crime than those without such genes.	Adoption studies reveal that some criminal tendencies are inheritable.	Employs suspect research methods; too few XYY men to explain much crime; may be based on a poor understanding of genetics; twin studies generally inconclusive.
Biochemical explanations	Levinthal, Ellis, Hippchen, Berman, Dalton	Humans are cauldrons of biological chemicals, many of which are susceptible to external influences and internal disturbances or imbalances.	Disturbances or imbalances in electrochemistry and biochemistry (e.g., hormones and neurotransmitters) may cause socially unacceptable behavior or even criminal conduct.	Provides logical explanations; the scientific community seems to support many of these arguments; provides answers to irrational criminal conduct.	Has the same problems as noted for genetic research; alternative explanations abound; even if there is a biochemical basis, is society willing to view them as non-volitional medical conditions?

Biogeneticists may rewrite the book on biology–crime links in the next decade or less. New research in biocriminology may alter criminological thinking about nature versus nurture. The trend is toward a view of biologically induced human susceptibility to criminality. The current consensus favors this nature-plus-nurture perspective, one in which biology determines individual susceptibility to other crime-causing forces (Fishbein 1990; Plomin 1989; but see also Wright and Beaver 2005; Wright et al. 2008).

KEY TERMS

adoption study

alleles

apotropaic punishments

anthropometry

atavism

attention deficit disorder (ADD)

biocriminologists

chromosomes

corporal punishment

cranioscopy

deoxyribonucleic acid (DNA)

determinism

dizygotic twins

dopamine (DA)

ectomorphs

embryonics

endocrine system

endomorphs

endorphins

eugenics

fragments

generation theory

homeostasis

hormones

human genome

Human Genome Mapping Project (HGMP)

hyperactivity

karyotype studies

learning disabilities

mesomorphs

monoamine oxidase (MAO)

monozygotic twins

natural selection

naturalistic explanations

nature-plus-nurture model

neurochemicals

Neurological Crime Theories Neurophysiology

neurotoxicity hypothesis (NH)

neurotransmitters

nucleotides

phrenology

physiognomy

PMS defense

positivism

scientific determinism

serotonin

sex chromosomes

Social Darwinism

social engineering

somatotype

stigmata

Twin Studies Concordance

Twinkies defense

XYY male

CRITICAL REVIEW QUESTIONS

1. What are the modern versions of physiognomy and phrenology?

2. What do you make of Lombroso's shift to environmental influences? What would he have made of Hooton's attempts to find the "criminal man"?

3. How would you respond to someone who suggests that body typing is simply a more modern version of phrenology?

4. Summarize the strengths and weaknesses of genetic–crime linkages. Which one is most damaging to the arguments? Which one is most supportive?

5. Can you see a way to make twin or adoption studies more definitive in the search for a genetic basis of crime? Can we do it ethically?

6. Are you optimistic or pessimistic about the future of genetic theories of crime? Explain your answer.

7. Describe the basic ideas behind the biochemistry–crime linkage. What are their practical implications for criminal justice?

8. Which do you think plays a larger role in helping us understand criminal behavior—neurotransmitters or hormones? Explain your answer.

9. How does the neurotoxicity hypothesis change the search for solutions to the crime problem? Explain your answer.

10. Which of this chapter's policy implications do you think poses the greatest threat to democratic ideals? Which one holds the greatest promise for reducing crime?

NOTES

1. The precise number of persons executed for witchcraft is unknown. In some parts of Europe, exact figures were kept because the supposed witch's possessions reverted to the Crown, went to the accuser, or were shared by both parties (Currie 1968). Credible estimates put the number at about 90,000 (Sharpe 1997).

2. Erickson (1966) argued that the Salem witch trials were less about the devil than about politics. According to Hoffer (1997), they were motivated by true believers who feared the devil's power.

3. A confounding factor is that adoption agencies, particularly with a surplus of potential adoptive parents, engage in a matching process to find homes similar to the biological homes.

4. The German twin studies inspired Mengele, the so-called "Angel of Death."

4

The Psychology of Crime I

CHAPTER OVERVIEW

Psychoanalytic Theory

Psychosexual Development and Crime

Psychoanalysis and the Treatment of Psychic Disorders

Assessing Psychoanalytic Theories

Psychoanalysis, Public Policy, and Criminal Justice Practices

Deviant Personalities and Psychopathologies

Personality and Crime

Assessing Personality Theory and the Psychopathy Hypothesis

Personality, Public Policy, and Criminal Justice Practices

LEARNING OBJECTIVES

In this chapter, you will learn the following:

- The distinctions between psychology and psychiatry, and the importance of those distinctions for criminology and criminal justice.

- The psychoanalytic origins of human internal conflicts.

- The unique role played by psychometric testing, both for diagnosing and classifying offenders and for selecting and promoting criminal justice personnel.

- The strengths and weaknesses of *psychopathy,* a term rich in visual imagery but poor in definitional preciseness.

INTRODUCTION

In Greek and Roman mythology, Psyche, a beautiful wood nymph elevated to the status of an immortal, was the living personification of the soul. (The Greek word **psyche** means "soul.") Two distinct forms of scientific inquiry and practice have addressed questions of the human mind, that which ancient Greeks and Romans saw as the human soul. **Psychology** examines individual human and animal behavior; it is concerned chiefly with the mind and mental processes—such as feelings, desires, and motivations. Psychology is both an area of scientific study and an academic behavioral science, although some clinical psychologists engage in the treatment of mental disorders. Clinical psychologists generally have a doctoral degree, although states do license them with lower levels of education. **Psychiatry**—literally "healing the soul"—is the branch of medicine primarily concerned with the study and treatment of mental disorders, including **psychoses,** or very serious personality disorders, and **neuroses,** or milder personality disorders. Psychiatrists possess the medical doctor (M.D.) degree. In summary, psychology explores both normal and abnormal behavior, whereas psychiatry, as a branch of medicine, employs the disease model and deals principally with abnormal behavior.

Few **psychogenic theories,** or behavioral explanations of the mind's functioning, have evolved as explanations of crime. Crime is a *legal* term, not a *medical* one. Accordingly, psychologists and psychiatrists seek explanations of individual human behavior, not criminal behavior by itself. Like biogenic explanations, psychogenic theories focus on individual differences. Psychogenic theories are also deterministic: the causal factors associated with criminality are beyond individuals' control.

Two themes dominated psychological thinking about crime through the first half of the twentieth century. The philosophical and explanatory roots of the first lie deep in *psychoanalysis,* a psychogenic theory that often provokes strong mental images. According to this theory, some criminals suffer from arrested or interrupted psychological development, particularly their emotional and *psychosexual development.* **Psychoanalytic theories,** as psychological theories grounded in psychoanalysis, suspend the notion of free will; crime becomes far more deterministic and far less volitional than in other theories examined in this text. The reason is simple: The motivation to commit the crime is unknown to the offender, and resides in the *unconscious.*

Deviant personality theories, the second major psychological explanation reviewed in this chapter, became a significant analytical tool during the second half of the twentieth century. **Personality** "is a dynamic organization, inside the person, of psychophysical systems that create a person's characteristic patterns of behaviour, thoughts, and feelings" (Carver and Scheier 2000:5). In other words, personality is the sum total of an individual's habitual patterns and behavior, expressed in that person's physical and mental activities. This concept is central to *deviant personality theory,* with its associated inventories, and to the *psychopathy hypothesis.*

Conventional psychiatry largely ignores crime and criminals, except for the twin issues of *insanity* and *sanity.* Those adjudged to be sane are responsible for their actions (in legal parlance, they have *mens rea*); however, as a matter of principle, the law cannot hold the insane accountable for crime. Of course, they can be held against their will for psychiatric observation. Hearkening back to English common law, the medical profession established the definitions of sanity and legal competence. Trial lawyers often use medical terms to define the legal notion of insanity, including the landmark *McNaghten* case of 1843 (Simon 1967), whose modern equivalent is the Durham Rule (*Durham v. United States,* 1954). This rule includes the phrase "the accused is not criminally responsible if his unlawful act was the product of mental disease or mental defect." This merger of law and medicine in the courtroom troubles practitioners of both disciplines. Psychogenic theory moved into the realm of criminality in the early twentieth century, just as psychoanalytic theory was gaining prominence.

PSYCHOANALYTIC THEORY

- What do you think when you hear the term *psychoanalysis?*
- Have you ever heard the quip, "Oops, your Freudian slip is showing," directed at someone who says something very revealing about his or her personality? The implication is that the person unconsciously meant to be revealing, so the revelation, however accidental it may appear, was intentional.

Psychoanalysis, the common element in these questions, is a treatment method based on the work of Sigmund Freud (1856–1939). Over the years, both theory and method have undergone changes, although Freud's basic exposition of unconscious phenomena in human behavior remains unchanged. He viewed the unconscious as "essentially dynamic and capable of profoundly affecting conscious ideational or emotional life without the individual's being aware of this influence" (Healy, Bronner, and Bowers 1930:24). People are not aware of the origins of their misbehavior. In stark contrast to classicalists, psychoanalysts believe that reason does not rule human behavior (Cloninger 1993).

Freud postulated unconscious processes, which, while not directly observable, he inferred from actual case studies. He divided unconscious mental phenomena into three groups:

1. The **conscious**—those phenomena about which we are currently aware

2. The **preconscious**—thoughts and memories, just below the surface, that we can easily call into conscious awareness

3. The **unconscious**—repressed memories and attendant emotions that we can pull into the conscious level only with much effort

According to Freud, the unconscious serves as a repository for painful memories and the highly charged emotions associated with them. We accumulate these repressed memories and emotions as we pass through life on our way to adulthood or **psychosexual maturity.** The stages of psychosexual development are repressed and, therefore, unconscious. Yet, they serve as a guiding force of conscious behavior. Moreover, they are a source of anxiety and guilt, the basis for psychoneurosis and psychosis.

Psychosexual Development and Crime

Some people, then, are victims of breakdowns in the "normal" stages of psycho-sexual development. Most psychoanalysts identify five stages of **psychosexual development:**

- The **oral stage** (birth to 18 months). The mouth, lips, and tongue are the predominant organs of pleasure for the infant. In the normal infant, the source of pleasure becomes associated with the touch and warmth of the parent who gratifies oral needs. Infants enter the world as asocial beings, not greatly dissimilar to criminals: unsocialized and without self-control.

- The **anal stage** (age 1–3 years). The anus becomes the primary source of sexual interest and gratification. Children of this age closely connect pleasure to the retention and expulsion of feces, to the bodily process involved and the feces themselves. During this stage, the partially socialized child acts out destructive urges, breaking toys or even harming living organisms, such as insects or small animals. Disruptions at this stage may be the sources of psychological problems in the adult, including violent behavior and sociopathological personality disorders, topics covered in this chapter.

- The **genital stage** (age 3–5 years). The genitals are the main sexual interest, continuing to function as such in "normal" adults. During this stage, the child experiences **Oedipus** (in boys) and **Electra** (in girls) **wishes,** or fantasies about the opposite-sex parent. Normal psychosexual maturity involves relinquishing paternal or maternal attachment and overcoming the subsequent sadness.

- The **latent stage** (age 5 to adolescence). The child experiences a lessening of interest in sexual organs. Nonsexual, expanded relationships with same-sex and same-age playmates become paramount.

- The **adolescence/adulthood stage** (age 13 to death). Genital interest and awareness reawakens. Late adolescents and young adults repress incestuous wishes, now replaced by mature sexuality or erotic interest in adults who are not close relatives.

These stages overlap, as the transition from one to another is gradual, and the spans of time are approximate. As people develop, they leave each stage behind, but it is never completely abandoned. Some amount of **cathexis,** or psychic energy, remains linked to earlier objects of psychosexual attachment. When the cathexis is strong, psychiatrists call it a **fixation.** For example, rather than transferring affection to another adult of the opposite sex in the adolescent–adult stage, the child may stay fixated on the opposite-sex parent. Psychoanalysts refer to the state when a person reverts to a previous mode of gratification as **regression.** We can see this type of behavior in young children who revert to thumb sucking or have elimination "accidents" when a sibling is born.

Psychic Development   While a child is passing through the first three stages, his or her mind concomitantly undergoes the development of three psychic phenomena:

1. **Id.** The id consists of impulses or instincts that have parallels in classical theory. The id impulses define humans as hedonistic. This mass of powerful drives seeks immediate discharge or gratification, devoid of restraints.

2. **Ego.** The ego is the great mediator. Infants modify their id drives through contact with the world around them and through parental training. Psychoanalysts call this stage **ego development.** Infants can obtain maximum gratification with a minimum of difficulty from the restrictions in their environment. For example, the ego controls an id drive (desire) to harm sibling rivals by providing an awareness of the consequences of such action—the punishment that may result. Without the ego to act as a restraining influence, the id would destroy the person through its blind striving to gratify instincts with complete disregard for others. A person may remain at the ego level of development if he or she experiences disturbance in psychosexual development. Feelings of rage and aggression associated with the anal stage lurk in the background, awaiting an opportunity to erupt.

3. **Superego.** During normal development, the child integrates outer (social) discipline and self-imposes it. As personal control gains the upper hand over instinctual impulses, the child experiences the beginnings of a superego (Smart 1970). Psychoanalysts view the superego as a conscience-type mechanism, a counterforce to the id, creating a sense of morality for the ego.

Psychoanalytic theory links the superego to the incestuous feelings of the genital stage. Control becomes an internal matter, no longer exclusively dependent upon external forces (e.g., parents). A healthy superego is the result of identification with a parent or parents during the genital stage. Conversely, an unhealthy superego can support criminality when the child internalizes the actions of antisocial parents (Smart 1970). The superego may fail to develop sufficiently because of abuse or neglect.

Psychic Drives   Id drives impel a person (via the ego) to activity, leading to a cessation of the tension or excitement caused by the drives. The person seeks discharge, or gratification. For example, the hunger drive will cause activity through which the person hopes to gratify his or her appetite. Psychoanalysts divide these drives into two categories, but elements of each appear with the activation of basic drives. The **primary process** tends toward immediate and direct gratification of the id impulses. The **secondary process** shifts the focus from the original object or method of discharge when something—including the superego—blocks a drive. A shift may also occur when gratification is simply inaccessible by legitimate, acceptable means.

In the Freudian scheme, the mind has several defense mechanisms initiated by the secondary process that allow it to adapt to the environment. Included among these mechanisms are these:

■   **Denial.** This state exists when an individual refuses to acknowledge a painful reality, resulting in a distortion of reality.

- **Displacement.** In this case, an individual expresses unacceptable id impulses through an acceptable outlet. For example, the individual may unconsciously transfer, or displace, a desire to play with feces to playing with mud or clay.

- **Repression.** This ego activity prevents unwanted id impulses, memories, desires, or wish-fulfilling fantasies from entering the conscious-thought level. Psychoanalysts believe that the repression of highly charged material, such as incestuous fantasies, requires much psychic energy; and the result is often a permanent conflict between the id and the ego. The delicate balance between the charged material and the opposing expenditure of energy, called **equilibrium,** generally causes great stress. When the means of repression are inadequate to deal with charged material, psychoneurotic or psychotic symptoms develop.

- **Reaction formation.** This mechanism allows an individual to replace socially unacceptable behavior with behavior that is socially acceptable. As distinct from displacement, reaction formation involves behavior that is the opposite of that expressed by the original desire or drive. For example, a child who wants to kill a sibling will become very loving and devoted. In adulthood, a sadistic impulse can result in a person becoming involved in the care and treatment of highly dependent persons or animals.

- **Projection.** This mechanism allows an individual to attribute her or his own wishes or impulses to others. For example, John may say to Mary, "Fred wants to ask you out on a date," when, in fact, it is John who wants to ask her out. Paranoia is an extreme and dangerous form of projection.

- **Sublimation.** An individual who cannot experience a continuous drive in its primary form employs this mechanism. A sadist might overcome the urge to cut people, for example, by substituting acceptable alternatives, such as becoming a surgeon or a butcher.[1]

According to psychoanalysts, the unconscious maintains a delicate balance as people experience the sociocultural and biological aspects of life. However, this balance is easily upset—there is a thin line between normal and neurotic, and between neurotic and psychotic. When repressed impulses begin to overwhelm the psyche and threaten to enter the conscious, external defense mechanisms come into play as neuroses and, in extreme cases, psychoses. These responses take the form of **phobias,** or unreasonable fears, involving heights, insects, closed spaces, and the like. Employing reaction formation, for example, a person may channel the destructive urges of the anal stage into prosocial activities, such as becoming a vegetarian. Failing in this, the person may succumb to the threat posed by the repressed wishes and desires, and resort to extreme antisocial behavior, such as that of serial killers. The same unconscious drive may explain the behavior of the serial killer and the surgeon; choice of expression is the difference.

Crime and the Superego   According to August Aichhorn (1973[1935]:221), the superego takes its form and content from identifications that result from the

---

COMMENTS AND CRITICISMS: "Freudian Slips"

He entered Commerce Bank in Manhattan in 2008, passed a note to the teller—"No alarms. No heroes"— and ran off with $2,500. As he ran, the thief tossed his do-rag hat, glasses, and hooded sweatshirt. When the police searched the sweatshirt, they found two forms of photo ID as well as his Social Security card and a pay stub ("Robber not ready for crime time," 2008).

In 2007, the victim of a residential burglary returned to his Connecticut home to find a piece of paper titled "Conditions of Probation," which listed the suspect's name, and a second piece of paper with the name of the suspect's probation officer on it.

SOURCES: "Robber not ready for crime time" (2008); Bruen (2007).

---

child's effort to emulate the parent. It reflects not only the parent's love of the child but also the child's fear of the parent's demands. However, Freud (1933:92) stated that "the superego does not attain full strength and development if overcoming of the Oedipus [in males] complex has not been completely successful."

The superego keeps most people from acting on primitive id impulses. Only the ego restrains persons with poorly developed superegos; however, the ego alone cannot exercise adequate control over id impulses. Such a person suffers almost no guilt from engaging in socially harmful behavior. Similarly, the person whose superego is destructive cannot distinguish between *thinking* bad and *doing* bad.

Unresolved conflicts between earlier development and id impulses that people have normally repressed or dealt with through reaction formation or sublimation create a severe sense of (unconscious) guilt. They experience this guilt (again at the unconscious level) as a compulsive need for punishment. To alleviate this guilt, the criminal commits acts for which punishment is virtually certain. Delinquents of this type are victims of their own morality (Aichhorn 1973[1935]). For example, employees of the criminal justice system often see cases in which the offenders apparently desired capture, so poorly planned and executed were the crimes.

In summary, psychoanalysts relate criminal behavior to the functioning of the superego, which is the result of the offenders' abnormal relationships with their parents (or parental figures) during early childhood. Parental deprivation— through absence, lack of affection, or inconsistent discipline—hinders the proper development of the superego. Deprivation during childhood thus weakens parental influence; in adulthood, the individual is unable to adequately control aggressive, hostile, or antisocial urges. Rigid or punitive parental practices can lead to the creation of a superego that is likewise rigid and punitive, leading the person to seek punishment as a means of alleviating unconscious guilt.

Psychoanalysis and the Treatment of Psychic Disorders

Psychoanalysts treat psychic disorders using **psychoanalysis.** According to Freud, psychoanalysis "aims at inducing the patient to give up the repressions that belong to his early life and replace them with reactions of a sort that would correspond better to a psychically mature condition." To accomplish this, the psychoanalyst attempts to get the patient to "recollect certain experiences and the emotions called up by them which he has at the moment forgotten" (Reiff 1963:274). The psychoanalyst ties present symptoms to repressed elements of early life—the primary stages of psychosexual development. The symptoms will disappear when the patient discloses the repressed material under psychoanalytic treatment.

Free Association   To expose repressed material, psychoanalysts use several techniques, including free association, dream interpretation, and transference. With **free association,** the patient verbally expresses ideas as they come to mind. The psychoanalyst then works with the patient to understand why he or she uttered the words or phrases—that is, to learn their true meaning.

Dream Interpretation   Dream interpretation encourages patients to recall and analyze dreams. Freud believed that dreams hold the key to an individual's makeup. He also saw a difference between the experienced content of the dream and its actual meaning: The former is what the patient was doing or having done to him or her, and the latter is the actual meaning of the dream, which the unconscious mind conceals. It is up to the therapist to help the patient understand the repressed meaning.

Transference   With **transference,** the patient develops a negative or positive emotional attitude toward the psychoanalyst. This attitude is a reflection or imitation of emotional attitudes that the patient experienced in relationships during his or her psychosexual development. Thus, the patient may unconsciously come to view the therapist as a parental figure. By using transference, the therapist recreates the emotions tied to early psychic development, unlocking repressed material and freeing the patient from his or her burden. As Freud noted, transference "is particularly calculated to favor the production of these (early) emotional conditions" (Reiff 1963:274).

Freud created the psychoanalytic perspective. For a generation, his theories were paramount. However, as we see in the following box, he was not the only proponent, and many others were more influential in shaping how criminologists saw the links between the unconscious mind and crime than was Freud. An open question remains unanswered: What is the evidence supporting the contentions of psychoanalysts about the ties between unconscious states and crime? It is toward that question that we next turn.

Assessing Psychoanalytic Theories

During the 1930s and 1940s, penologists and juvenile justice experts considered classic psychoanalytic theory—with its roots imbedded in the work of Freud, Jung, Horney, and Rank—to be one of the best hopes for understanding the criminal mind (Schaefer 1969:214-6; Vold 1979:133–38). August Aichhorn (1878–1949), a psychoanalytic psychologist, described delinquents as "wayward youth," children who needed convincing that society cared about them (1973 [1935]). Kurt R. Eissler (1908–1999), a follower of Freud who often expressed

---

COMMENTS AND CRITICISMS: Freudian, Adlerian, or Jungian: Does Form Matter?

Does the psychoanalyst's orientation make a difference? The short answer to this question is, yes, orientation is important. For example, Freudian criminologists view sex as playing a major role in shaping criminals' responses to their environments, just as does the need for apprehension and punishment. Followers of Alfred Adler (1870–1937), an associate of Freud, reject sex, placing the emphasis on feelings of inferiority. In *The Individual Psychology of Alfred Adler,* Adler wrote that this sense of inferiority derives from restrictions on the individual's self-assertion. Adler's work influenced a generation of gang theorists in the 1950s, including Albert K. Cohen, James F. Short, Richard A. Cloward, Lloyd E. Ohlin, and Walter B. Miller, who all depicted the status-seeking delinquents in Adlerian terms.

Carl Gustav Jung (1875–1961) also rejected Freud's emphasis on sex. Jung believed that the unconscious, which holds the key to individuals' adjustment to life, consists of the repressed or forgotten parts of their lives. However, he added an element missing from Freud's perspective: the collective unconscious acts and mental patterns shared by all members of the human species. Whereas for Freud and Adler dreams represented a personal reality, Jung believed that inborn mental structures—what he called archetypes—shape dreams, and that these archetypes originate in the collective unconscious of the human species. As Jung observed in *Psychological Types,* the harmony achieved between the conscious and unconscious is the key to

understanding behavior. Interestingly, Jung also wrote a book that reflects back on the moral roots of psychology: *Modern Man in Search of a Soul.*

Other disciples and colleagues of Freud formed their own variants on strict psychoanalysis. Karen Horney (1885–1952) placed far greater emphasis on cultural and interpersonal experiences. She believed that feelings of helplessness naturally arise in a hostile world and lead to anxiety. Culture creates the hostility, and some members of society simply deal with it better than do others. Otto Rank (1884–1939), a member of Freud's inner circle, argued that the trauma of the birth event, and not a hostile world, gives insight into the crises and conflicts that people experience. Rank assigned the will a central role in conflict resolution: When the will fails, guilt surfaces.

As a rule, then, each variant of psychoanalytic theory has its own view of the origins of the crime problem. Freudians blame psychosexual development, Adlerians address feelings of inferiority, and Jungians look at shared innate structures. The followers of Horney, Rank, and other psychoanalysts, in turn, emphasize different forces. The solution, however, is generally the same: psychoanalysis that will reveal the deep-seated, unconscious cause of the unwanted behavior.

SOURCES: Adler (1927; 1963); Jung (1921; 1961[1933]); Schaefer (1969); Vold (1979).

---

sociologically oriented ideas, believed that aggression was an abnormal reaction to society's value system.[2]

Franz Alexander (1891–1964) and William Healy (1869–1963) provided an account of seven criminals in *Roots of Crime* (1935). The ages, crimes, and psychological histories of the offenders differed. However, the cause of the criminality was identical in each case: Crime was a necessary substitute for something tied to a repressed and unconscious conflict, deeply felt by each offender. Healy later teamed up with Augusta F. Bronner in *New Lights on Delinquency and Its Treatment* (1936), a massive empirical study that matched 105 sets of same-sex siblings, one delinquent and the other nondelinquent.[3] Healy and Bronner psychoanalytically assessed each pair. Their principal finding was that 9 out of 10 delinquent youths expressed significant emotional disturbances, compared to roughly 1 out of 10 nondelinquents.

The Healy and Bronner study was not without critics. Edwin Sutherland and Donald Cressey (1974:164) based their challenge of Healy and Bronner's findings on three points. First, the researchers had a predisposition to find emotional

---

IN THEIR OWN WORDS: Lindner on Psychoanalysis and Crime

Robert M. Lindner's *Rebel without a Cause* is perhaps the best-known psychoanalytic work on crime and deviance that employs a strict Freudian methodology. Lindner claimed to have caused a nearly miraculous cure of Harold, a virtually blind prison inmate. He explained that Harold's criminal career was the result of feelings of anxiety, fear, and guilt stemming from having witnessed, at the age of 8 months, his parents having sex. When the inmate realized this fact, claimed Lindner, his eyesight improved, along with his hope for rehabilitation.

■ *On crime causation:* "Modern analytic theory predicates criminality and all other activities of an aggressive or debasing order upon the prepotency of the *Death Instinct,* which is believed to exert an

influence sufficient to catapult an individual toward self-destruction" (pp. 8–9).

■ *On traditional rehabilitative practices:* "We have glimpsed the utter futility, the sheer waste, of confining individuals in barred and turreted zoos for humans without attempting to recover [their] secrets. Harold's case makes a mockery of current penological pretense. It points the finger of ridicule at the sterile corridors of modern prisons ... in brief, the whole hollow structure of rehabilitation that is based upon expediency, untested hypotheses, [and] unwarranted conclusions from a pseudoscientific empiricism" (p. 228).

SOURCE: Lindner (1944).

---

disturbances, and they knew the identities of group members. Second, even if emotional disturbances were present, Healy and Bronner could not state categorically that they were the *cause* of the delinquency. Finally, the researchers did not investigate the alleged emotional disturbance beyond noting its presence.

Edwin Sutherland and Donald Cressey were also critical of Healy and Bronner's evidence, the case study. Linder's prototypical case study, which gave the world of literature and popular culture a great phrase, stands as a classic example of the psychoanalytic case study (see In Their Own Words). Forty years later, Flora Schreiber's (1983) detailed look at the criminal career of shoemaker Joseph Kallinger provides a contemporary look at the tendency toward overstatement and hyperbole common to case studies. Kallinger, along with his son, engaged in a string of robberies, burglaries, and murders. Schreiber concluded that the elder Kallinger was "driven to kill" by the psychological and physical abuse heaped on him by his adopted parents. At the age of four, following a surgical procedure to repair a hernia, Kallinger's parents told him the goal of the surgery was to rid his penis of the devil. It was Schreiber's conclusion that these and subsequent statements by Kallinger's parents effectively performed a psychological castration on the boy, a psychosis from which he never recovered: "Joseph Kallinger would never have become a killer without this psychosis" (Schreiber 1983:17).[4]

Criminologists challenge psychoanalytic-based arguments about crime and criminality on many grounds. General criticisms of psychoanalytic theories follow a familiar pattern.

■ *Operational definitions are unclear.* According to Susan Cloninger (1993), psychoanalytical theories have not clearly specified the operational definitions of their theoretical ideas, making conclusions based on observations scientifically questionable (see also Pallone and Hennessy 1992). Scientific testing may not be possible because psychoanalytic theory purports to explain *all* observations, so *no* observation is inconsistent with the theory. For example, consider the so-called students' dilemma: Those who arrive early to class are anxious; those who arrive late are hostile; those who arrive on time are compulsive.

- *Diagnosis is subjective.* Diagnosis, a weakness related to operational definitions, is also extremely subjective, because descriptions of a subject's mental state may reveal more about the training of the psychologist than the condition of the patient. The psychologist's training and orientation determine where he or she looks for the causes of misbehavior. How, then, does a third person—not the psychoanalyst or the patient—address the reliability and validity of the diagnosis? This high level of subjectivity leads to unstable and untrustworthy patient classifications (diagnoses) as psychically disturbed.

- *Small (and perhaps unrepresentative) samples are problematic.* Few psychoanalytic studies involve more than a dozen or so subjects. How generalizable, critics ask, are the findings from such studies? If we examine 2 people or even 20, can we generalize to the U.S. population at large? Besides misinterpretation and overgeneralization, there is also the question of misrepresentation. Subjects are patients and enjoy confidentiality, so verifying that the psychotherapist has given an accurate and faithful account is virtually impossible. Ultimately, we are unable to determine with any degree of reliability the extent to which these case studies reflect problems with psychic development in the general population (Pallone and Hennessy 1992).

- *Psychoanalytical theories are examples of the tautological trap.* Perhaps the greatest shortcoming of psychoanalytic theories is its inherent *tautological trap*. What psychoanalysts define as antisocial instincts, repressed urges, or unresolved complexes may be alternative labels for the behaviors they seek to explain. This tautology makes the theory essentially untestable (Pallone and Hennessy 1992; Shoham and Seis 1993).

For these reasons, and given the lack of confirmatory evidence, psychoanalytic theories have fallen out of favor with criminologists (Andrews and Bonta 1998; see also Akers and Sellers 2009:74). Nevertheless, they provide important insights into a host of human maladies, and their explanation for such problematic behavior as substance abuse has strong intuitive appeal (Abadinsky 2008). They are also the basis for therapeutic efforts in many treatment disciplines. Figure 4.1 summarizes the classic psychoanalytic perspective.

Psychoanalysis, Public Policy, and Criminal Justice Practices

Absent compelling supporting evidence, beyond anecdotal revelations about serial killers and other horrific offenders and a few studies employing questionable samples with little generalizability, classic psychoanalytic theories are generally ignored by most contemporary policy makers and many practitioners in the field

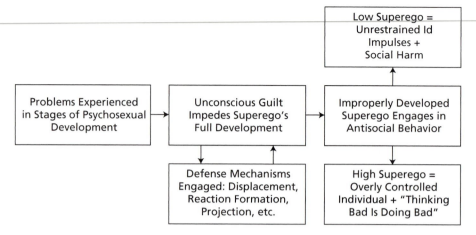

FIGURE 4.1 Psychoanalytic Perspective on Crime

of criminal justice. However, some in the mental health field find the arguments persuasive and logical:

> Psychoanalytic theory is concerned with the early developmental years of a child. Dysfunctional adults, including those whose neurotic behavior is criminal, are the sum of their early childhood experiences. An environment that fails to nurture, or perhaps that is characterized by neglect and abuse, will yield an adult whose behavior is likely to conflict with social norms.

Considerable doubt remains about the strength of the ties between childhood neglect and abuse, such as that mentioned by Schreiber as instrumental in Kallinger's case; moreover, it is also unclear whether childhood neglect invariably leads to criminality as an adult (cf., Kelley, Thornberry, and Smith 1997; Widom 1989; Zingraff, Leiter, Myers, and Johnsen 1993). Nonetheless, there are clinicians who emphasize such linkages.

Court Practices   Recovered memory is an area of considerable controversy that could provide insights into the psychoanalytic elements of crime. The significance of this concept for criminology is this: If criminals are, as psychoanalysts suggest, the victims of repressed memories, is the same true of victims? Clinical psychologists describe this as memories long forgotten or suppressed but subsequently recalled; they often link it to very traumatic events, such as rape, incest, and other sex-related or violent crimes, particularly childhood abuse. The debate over recovered memory centers on two questions (Coughlin 1995): First, is it possible to suffer a horrible trauma, repress that memory, and subsequently recall it? Second, is that memory reliable?

At the heart of this controversy is Freud's concept of repression. *Repression,* like many Freudian ideas, elicits high levels of skepticism from many contemporary psychologists and psychiatrists. For his part, Freud largely discounted the stories his female patients told him about sexual abuse by their fathers, viewing the "memories" as repressed sexual fantasies. However, contemporary memory experts question the extent to which courts of law should consider recollections tied to traumatic events as reliable (Coughlin 1995; Monaghan 1992). Consequently, they question whether recovered memories are even recollections of true events, the fruit of seeds planted by well-meaning psychotherapists, or simply scrambled messages in the brain. No less an authority on memory than Elizabeth Loftus, writing with Katherine Ketcham (1994), called repressed memory a myth. The debate has led some skeptics—and "victims"—to form the False Memory Syndrome Foundation, an advocacy group for accused parents (Coughlin 1995: A9). As the debate continues, criminal courts continue to hear the testimony of victims who have suddenly and often spontaneously recovered supposedly long-forgotten memories. Is it possible that the same is true of offenders? Do therapists and others implant "memories" of repressed or interrupted psychic development in offenders, using the same processes as found in victims suffering from false memory syndrome?

The psychoanalytically disturbed offender, whose "criminal insanity" is rooted in maladapted psychosexual development, remains a popular image in fiction and in some case studies of criminal offenders, from Lindner's "rebel without a cause" to Schreiber's murderous shoemaker. In the final analysis, however, the significance of the psychoanalytic window into crime and criminality may not be in its ability to explain crime and treat offenders, although proponents might argue that we simply do not yet know how these mechanisms operate. Rather, this was one of the first psychogenic theories applied to criminology, and it merits our attention for this reason.

DEVIANT PERSONALITIES AND PSYCHOPATHOLOGIES

- Have you ever taken a personality inventory such as the Minnesota Multiphasic Personality Inventory? If you are bound for a career in criminal justice, the odds are good that you will encounter such a test.

- The term *psycho* has a negative connotation, often serving as a warning to stay away from a particular person. Can you think of any books or movies with a psychopath as the main villain? Whether you prefer fiction or nonfiction, you have probably encountered examples of the remorseless killer.

- Are you a person who craves excitement, lives on the edge, and challenges yourself physically? If so, we have a theory for you.

The study of individuals who are psychologically deranged but appear to be normal has a long and convoluted history (Arrigo and Shipley 2001a). This notion took shape and form in a little over 100 years. At the start of the nineteenth century, French physician Phillipe Pinel (1745–1826) observed that some of his patients committed impulsive acts, engaged in episodic violence, and harmed themselves (Davies and Feldman 1981; Millon, Simonsen, Birket-Smith, and Davis 1998). He called this specific mental disorder *manie san délire* ("insanity without delirium") (Millon et al 1998).

Thirty years later a British physician, J.C. Prichard (1786–1848) used the expression **moral insanity** to describe people who had "a morbid perversion of the natural feelings, affections, inclinations, temper, habits, moral dispositions, and natural impulses, without any remarkable disorder or defect of the intellect or knowing and reasoning faculties, and particularly without any insane illusions or hallucinations" (1837/1973:16).

At the turn of the twentieth century, German psychiatrist J. L. A. Koch (1841–1908) was the first to describe this condition using the term psychopathic; he viewed people who had emotional and moral aberrations derived from congenital factors as suffering from **psychopathic inferiority.** Koch's goal in using this term was to rid the condition of the moral condemnation associated with Pritchard's moral insanity.

Finally, German psychiatrist Emile Kraepelin (1856–1926) expanded Koch's basic diagnosis so that it could contain categories for especially vicious and wicked offenders; moreover, his categories of **psychopathic personalities** closely resemble those currently in use. Kraepelin also reinstituted a moral component, calling psychopaths "the enemies of society" (quoted in Millon et al. 1998:10).

Most psychologists tie the modern era of psychopathic theorizing to the 1941 publication of *The Mask of Sanity* by American psychiatrist Hervey M. Cleckley (Arrigo and Shipley 2001:334). Like his predecessors, Cleckley (1903–1984) used a list of the **psychopath**'s "essential characteristics," among which were such descriptors as grandiose, callous, superficial, and manipulative. Psychopaths lacked empathy, guilt, or remorse. They were as likely to be successful in the world of business as to turn to crime, since other characteristics such as glibness and emotional detachment could come in handy in either vocation (Arrigo and Shipley 2001:335). Behind the mask of sanity was the psychopath.

Cleckley's timing was propitious. Following World War II, questions about personality traits became increasingly important in the work world and elsewhere. Owing to emerging management science in the postwar era, managers increasingly turned to psychometric screening devices. The idea was to identify only those candidates who had the right personality traits for the job (Houston 1995:17–18; Swanson, Territo, and Taylor 1998:101–6). American correctional philosophy and practices were also undergoing a revolution of sorts, with scientific management practices also extending to correctional facilities (no longer called prisons). Interestingly, employees were not the only subjects of screening: Correctional case-managers also screened the "clients" of that system for entry into rehabilitative programs and general institutional management (Clear, Cole, and Reisig 2009; Mays and Winfree 2009).

Personality theory, including Cleckley's diagnostic category of the psychopathic personality, also suited the criminal justice system's needs. Policy makers and practitioners observed empirical ties between personality theory and crime after applying it to employee screening. Most importantly, personality theorists generated psychometric diagnostic instruments that gave uniform, reliable, and quick—and some would argue overly simplistic—answers about personality traits.

Personality and Crime

A central assumption of **personality theory** is that the ways in which people express their habitual patterns and behavioral qualities hold the key to understanding their behavior. These habitual patterns and qualities are physical or mental, behavioral or attitudinal.

Psychopathy, Sociopathy, and Crime   In 1952, the American Psychiatric Association officially abandoned the term psychopathy, substituting for it the term **sociopathic personality disturbance,** shortened to **sociopathy;** however, both terms essentially refer to the mental condition psychologists currently classify as **psychopathic personality disorder (PPD).** The occasion was the publication of the first DSM, or *Diagnostic and Statistical Manual of Mental Disorders.* The DSM criteria for sociopathy varied little from Cleckley's personality inventory for psychopathy. The terms psychopathy, sociopathy, psychopathic personality disorder, and antisocial personality disorder are frequently used to describe the same constellation of traits, although, as Anthony Walsh and Heui-Hsia Wu (2008) argue, while they overlap, they are different: by definition, unlike **sociopaths,** psychopaths are criminals.

Psychiatrist Samuel Guze (1923–2000) offered a concrete definition of *sociopathy.* Sociopathy exists "if at least two of the following five manifestations were present in addition to a history of police trouble (other than traffic offenses): a history of excessive fighting … school delinquency … poor job record … a period of wanderlust, or being a runaway. … For women, a history of prostitution could be substituted for one of the five manifestations" (Guze, 1976:35–36). Clinical definitions—the means by which the disorders are diagnosed—center on behavior (Vold and Bernard 1986:122). Even when objective tests are used, however, the definitions are arbitrary, and personality researchers have little agreement as to their use (Meier 1989). The "absence of easily readable signs has led to debate among mental-health practitioners about what qualifies as psychopathy and how to diagnose it" (Seabrook 2008:64).

In general, usage **psychopathy** and *sociopathy* denote unpredictability, untrustworthiness, and instability.[4] When combined with *criminal,* each term takes on a new meaning: The psychopathic criminal is totally without conscience, capable of unspeakable acts, but shows no external signs of psychoses or neuroses. Paul Tappan (1960:137) described psychopathy as "a condition of psychological abnormality in which there is neither the overt appearance of psychosis nor neurosis, but there is a chronic abnormality of response to the environment." This rather vague definition and description aside, psychologists call the resulting body of work either the **psychopathy hypothesis** or **sociopathy hypothesis.**

Definitions of *sociopath* and *psychopath* are so broad that psychologists can apply them to any criminal (Cleckley 1976:137). Indeed, members of Congress, covert operatives in the Central Intelligence Agency, soldiers in elite Special Forces units, and university administrators all may share these characteristics. It would be difficult to find a prison inmate lacking all five of Guze's manifestations. If all inmates are sociopaths, it could be costly for taxpayers, given Guze's recommendation that society should lock up all sociopaths until they reach middle age (Guze 1976:137).

Arousal Theory   Lee Ellis's **Arousal theory** represents a major expansion of the ties between psychopathy and crime. A key difference between arousal theory and garden-variety psychopathy theory is that the former provides a biopsychological explanation for antisocial and asocial conduct, whereas the latter is primarily a diagnosis and treatment in search of a cause. Ellis's arousal theory looks to the stimulation levels sought by individuals. Some persons need more stimulation than do others, owing to problems with their **reticular activating system (RAS),** the part of the brain responsible for attentiveness to the surrounding world. Psychopaths may need excessively high levels of stimulation, the kind provided only by behavior that generates pathological levels of excitement and thrills. As Ellis (1991:37) observed about his theory:

> According to arousal theory, persons who are most apt to be reinforced for engaging in criminal behavior (and less likely to learn alternative behavior patterns) have reticular [the brain's information intake system] functioning patterns that quickly habituate to incoming stimuli. Persons with this genetic makeup are very susceptible to reinforcement when they engage in antisocial behavior, and less likely to learn alternative behavior patterns. Subjectively, such persons regard many ordinary environments as "boring" and "unpleasant," and thus should be motivated to seek novel and/or intense sensory stimulation to a degree most people would choose to avoid.

High-arousal persons, Ellis (1990) claimed, (1) exhibit impulsive and hyperactive behavior, (2) are prone to take risks and seek excitement at virtually any cost, (3) are inclined to use psychoactive drugs to modify their mental state when other means of doing so are not viable, (4) prefer chaotic and varied social and sexual experiences, and (5) consider academic tasks boring. In short, high-arousal persons show few qualities or personality characteristics that hold out much hope for prosocial behavior.

Interestingly, underaroused psychopaths, whose RAS barely keeps them awake, may be relatively immune to efforts intended to alter their undesired behavior. Psychologists believe that only increased stimulation leads to corrective learning. Researchers report that punishment administered in low-arousal contexts, including prisons and classrooms, have little aversive influence; consequently, the psychopath seems unable to benefit from both learning and punishing activities conducted in such environments (Bartol 1991; see also Chesno and Kilmann 1975). Figure 4.2 summarizes the main theoretical approaches to deviant personalities, psychopathologies, and crime.

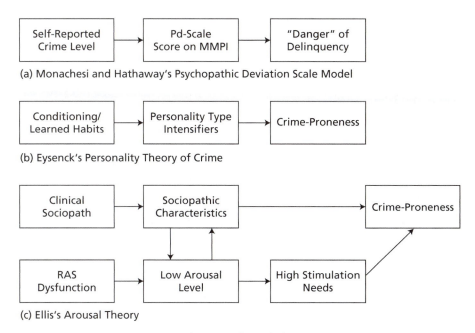

(a) Monachesi and Hathaway's Psychopathic Deviation Scale Model

(b) Eysenck's Personality Theory of Crime

(c) Ellis's Arousal Theory

F I G U R E 4.2   Deviant Personalities, Psychopathologies, and Crime.

Assessing Personality Theory and the Psychopathy Hypothesis

Sociologically trained criminologists generally view the definitional imprecision of psychopathy and sociopathy as rendering the terms virtually meaningless for criminology and, by extension, criminal justice. Sutherland and Cressey (1974:169) saw psychopathy as a kind of "trash-can" category for people whom psychiatrists could not otherwise diagnose.

Research findings on psychopathy are mixed. Early studies of psychopathic characteristics, even among prison inmates, failed to provide a useful basis for distinguishing the least psychopathic from the most psychopathic (Cason 1943, 1946). One prison-based study, which used a nonprison comparison group, found that psychopathy was concentrated among males age 20–29. This finding suggests that what researchers described as an unalterable condition decreases after the age of 30 (Cason and Pescor 1946). In the late 1990s, clinical comparative studies of brain activity revealed differences in the brains of persons diagnosed as psychopaths (Raine and Mednick 1997; Raine et al. 2000). For whatever reason, their brains seemed to work differently from nonpsychopaths and other psychologically disordered persons.

A longitudinal study of over 500 patients in a children's clinic found that, compared to "normal school children," those in the clinic led far more disordered lives as adults; 1 in 5 of the clinic's patients was diagnosed as sociopathic, compared to 1 in 50 for the control group (Robins 1966). The researchers could not determine unequivocally whether a personality disorder "caused" the subsequent criminality or whether the intervention of the juvenile courts and guidance clinic were instrumental in classifying the children as psychopaths (Gibbons 1977:175). William McCord and José Sanchez (1983), who followed a juvenile institution's former residents for 25 years, found little evidence to support the notion that those defined as psychopathic were more crime-prone than were other delinquents.

Psychologists continue to see value in psychopathy as a diagnosable psychological condition. In a recent meta-analysis, researchers reviewed the findings of 59 different studies conducted from 1963 to 2000 and reported that several dimensions of psychopathy bear a moderate resemblance to **antisocial behavior disorder (ASBD).** Psychologists Joshua Miller and Donald Lyman defined ASBD broadly to include self, parent, and teacher ratings. However, like many psychopathology researchers before them, they also included "personality scales" from personality inventories. Lastly, they included studies employing the **antisocial personality disorder (APD)** diagnoses or criteria. They acknowledge the existence of high intercorrelation between the various measures of ASBD. Miller and Lyman (2001:780) offered the following description of the personality traits of persons with ASBD characteristics: "Individuals who commit crimes tend to be hostile, self-centered, spiteful, jealous, and indifferent to others.... They tend to lack ambition, motivation, and perseverance, have difficulty controlling their impulses, and hold nontraditional and unconventional values and beliefs."

Proponents of psychopathy's application to criminal justice point to the Hare's **PCL-R (Psychopathy Checklist-Revised),** a 20-item rating scale based on semistructured interviews, case-history information, and specific diagnostic criteria related to each item. Hare's (1998:99) own claim is definitive and unequivocal: "Psychopathy is the single most important clinical construct in the criminal justice system." The problem, maintains Hare (1996a, 1996b, 1998), is with the use and measurement of antisocial personality disorder (ASPD) in the DSM-III and DSM-IV. With its 1980 publication of the DSM-III, the American Psychiatric Association (APA) abandoned the term psychopathy, preferring the more value-neutral ASPD diagnosis. Because of dissatisfaction with the conceptualization and criteria for ASPD, the APA reevaluated both before publication of the DSM-IV. The result was a description that, in Hare's (1996b) opinion, leads to a diagnostic nightmare. He argues for the use of the **psychopathic personality disorder** and his PCL-R (or a juvenile version, the PCL-JV), when the issue is to determine the threat to community; the two-stage ASPD diagnosis is better suited for diagnosing a persons' suitability for treatment of antisocial personality disorder (Hare 1996a, 1996b).

Ellis's arousal theory, also called sensation-seeking theory, tells us that we can expect people who seek sensation for its own sake to engage in higher levels of criminality. Biological research supports the idea that risk taking and impulsivity have a biological basis and a further connection to crime and illicit drug use (King, Curtis, and Knoblich 1996; Knoblich and King 1992; Magnusson, Klinteberg, and Stattin 1992). As importantly, convicted offenders describe an elevated neurophysical state—being high—during the course of committing crimes (Gove and Wilmoth 1990; Wood, Gove, and Cochran 1994), which may help to explain the connection between doing drugs and doing crime (Fishbein 1990; Fishbein and Pease 1988). Some people just seem to exhibit more need for sensation seeking than do others (David, Schnur, and Birk (2004). As was the case for psychopathy, however, arousal theory does not allow us to distinguish between the street criminal who makes a big score, the white-collar criminal who steals hundreds of millions from unsuspecting investors, and the long-shot presidential candidate who wins the election. All may seek to maximize sensations through risk taking, but why do some choose crime and some do not? Sensation seeking and risk taking are also central concepts in other crime theories, but especially self-control theory (Chapter 7).

The fault, however, may not lie with the theories, as the following key criticisms suggest:

- *There is little consensus about which definition of psychopathy to use.* A key problem with psychopathy is the lack of consensus in the psychological community as to its definition and prognosis. As Walters (2004:143) observes: "There is no definitive proof that psychopathy can be diagnosed, studied, and applied similar to the medical diseases that serve as its standard of comparison."

- *Concepts drawn from the theory have low prospective prediction power.* Less than 3 percent of nearly 1,000 deinstitutionalized mental patients adjudged to be "criminally dangerous" returned to mental hospitals with a new diagnosis of criminally insane (Steadman 1972), although studies using the Hare PCL-R claim higher prediction power (Hare 1996b; Hare et al. 2000).

- *The measurement techniques seem prone to circularity.* In addition to an inability to predict "future dangerousness," circularity is a key concern in the diagnosis of psychopathy. That is, the clinical method or test used to diagnose the condition (i.e., the PCL-R or PCL-JV) has in it the very symptom defined as problematic, including such things as pathological lying, promiscuous sexual behavior, and commission of deviant or delinquent behavior (Hare 2003; Walters 2004). As a result, a given diagnostic test result is often highly correlated with known, self-reported, or even future criminality or delinquency in that individual. What may be at work is one of the most profound truisms in all the behavioral and social sciences: Past behavior is the best predictor of future behavior.

- *Personality theories, like most psychogenic explanations, are prone to tautologies.* Given the observation that psychopathy diagnostic instruments include the same behavior as predictive and outcome measures, this criticism comes as no surprise (Walters 2004). The symptoms of the personality disorder are evidence of its existence, and vice versa. That a psychopath is someone who acts psychopathic is hardly a helpful observation.

- *The inclusion of neural elements adds unknown variables.* Many psychogenic theories, including Ellis's arousal theory, include biological elements based on little-understood neural and neurocognitive processes (Blair and Frith 2000). Abandoning a pure nature or pure nurture position is not a problem; the

COMPARATIVE CRIMINOLOGY—WORLD VIEWS ON CRIME AND JUSTICE:
European Use of Psychopathy Diagnoses

The popularity of psychopathy continues to grow, in spite of its predicted demise in the 1970s. Much of the work has focused on prison inmates and much of that has used Hare's PCL-R. Hare and associates claim considerable cross-cultural generalizability for the PCL-R's ability to predict recidivism, violence, and treatment outcomes. While many of these claims rest on North American samples, supporting research has also come from the United Kingdom, Spain, and Portugal. For example, a study of male batterers with and without the diagnosis of psychopathy confined in a Spanish prison tended to confirm the construct's cross-cultural generalizability. The use of psychopathy diagnostic instruments is not without its concerns in the European context, especially given its reliance on morality, the central question being, Whose morality do we use?

Still, the psychopathy concept in general, and the Hare PCL-R in particular, seem to enjoy a strong following in Europe. Felicity de Zulueta sees problems with current attempts to integrate psychopathy diagnostic labels into British prevention and intervention practices: the former talks about increasing self-esteem, neighborhoods, bad peers, and school failure; the latter focuses on psychotropic medications, genetic influences, and psychometric measures. In de Zulueta's words, this artificial and politically induced division creates an illusion of unrelated causation.

SOURCES: Cooke, Hart, and Michie (2004); Echeburua and Montalvo (2007); Hare, Clark, Grann, and Thornton (2000); Harris et al. (2001); Moore and Hogue (2000); Vermeiren, Jones, Ruchkin, Deboutte, and Schwab-Stone (2004); Vermeiren, Deboutte, Ruchkin, and Schwab-Stone (2002); Vien and Beech (2006); de Zulueta (1993; 2001).

inclusion of factors from highly limited studies of the human brain may be a poor substitute, as that work remains speculative (Blair and Frith 2000; Martens 2000).

Through its various incarnations, psychopathy has demonstrated an amazing resilience to critics and, as the following Comparative Criminology box suggests, perhaps due in no small way to the breadth and depth of support around the world.

Personality, Public Policy, and Criminal Justice Practices

For decades, personality inventories—such as the **Minnesota Multiphasic Personality Inventory (MMPI)** and the **California Personality Inventory (CPI)**—and more general psychological tests—such as the **Rorschach Inkblot Test** and the **Thematic Appreciation Test (TAT)**—have plumbed the depths of the human personality. The goal has been to identify "crime personality" markers or characteristics. Those who interpret the tests and inventories point out that certain response patterns suggest specific personality disorders.

Assessment for crime-proneness using the Rorschach and TAT is rare (Siegel 1992). These tests require clinicians trained in the subjective interpretation of test results. More common is the use of checklist personality inventories, based on DSM-IV definitions of various psychiatric diagnoses of mental conditions. Key among these inventories is the MMPI, first used to study crime by R. Starke Hathaway and Elio Monachesi (1953). Their work supported the use of the **psychopathic deviation (Pd) scale** as a delinquency correlate. However, some researchers question the MMPI's ability to predict criminality or delinquency. For example, in a review of 94 MMPI-based personality studies published between 1950 and 1965, Gordon Waldo and Simon Dinitz (1967) found that more than 8 in 10 studies reported significant differences between delinquent and nondelinquent youths. Nonetheless, the researchers reported that the evidence about the MMPI's predictive usefulness was inconclusive. A major reason for this conclusion may be that the Pd scale includes self-reported acts of delinquency. In other words, the use of the MMPI to predict delinquency status is a tautology. The MMPI may be inappropriate because any significant differences between the psychology of criminals and noncriminals "are based on tautological arguments" (Tennenbaum 1977:228). That is, criminals are those persons reporting to have engaged in criminal behavior.

The MMPI–delinquency link assumes official delinquency as the outcome, or dependent, variable. The following scenario suggests itself: The MMPI's Pd scale may tap into those personality characteristics among delinquents—aggressiveness, irresponsibility, lack of maturity—associated with the chances of getting caught and punished by the criminal justice system (Tennenbaum 1977). The scale creates a problem with circular reasoning. Hindelang (1972:81) reported that youths who commit delinquent activities are "impulsive, shrewd, uninhibited, aggressive and pleasure-seeking." When we add a tendency to disregard social mores, the result is an interesting but relatively useless description of delinquents. The purpose of criminological theory is to find out why youths and adults engage in crime. The CPI and MMPI seem to do little more than *describe* characteristics associated with the commission of crime and delinquency.

The creators of the CPI based it less on such negativistic ideas as the "psychopathic deviate," and relied instead on the extent of individual socialization, expression of self-control, and acceptance of responsibility for personal actions. Although not created with this purpose in mind, practitioners also use the CPI to distinguish between offenders and nonoffenders (Gough 1965; Megargee 1972, 1977).

The personality-based psychogenic theories offer scant hope for changing behavior. Their focus is more on what we can do *to* offenders than what we can do *for* them or the general population to prevent crime. For example, consider the implications of psychopathy/sociopathy and arousal theories. Beyond identification and separation from the general population, what can we do for individuals who have basic personality flaws that will not respond to any known treatment? Perhaps psychotropic drugs will ameliorate this condition, as they have for other behavioral maladies with organic causes.

As with IQ testing (see Chapter 5), the attractiveness in psychometric personality testing may be the appearance of impartiality. These tests are also quick, uniform, and reliable even if their validity remains in question (i.e., we are not sure exactly what is being measured). Nevertheless, when it comes to employment and promotion decisions, they are a policy maker's dream. Commonly and widely used, and generally accepted by the scientific community, such tests are difficult to attack in the courts.

For the clients of the criminal justice system—from the accused to the ex-con—such tests have become a way of life. Again, policy makers rely heavily upon psychometric tests, which provide neat, clean, and impartial means of making all sorts of decisions about system clients. Testing removes the specter of discrimination or arbitrary judgment. Prison and jail administrators use these tests to inform decisions about everything from inmate classification to treatment program access to release on probation and parole.

The criminal justice system bases many policies and practices on these theories. The fact that there is little associated empirical support or generalizable data does not seem to faze policy makers or implementers.

Law Enforcement Practices   Police work has strong ties to psychological explanations. First, police departments frequently use personality inventories to screen job applicants and determine the suitability of candidates for promotion. In fact, the 1967 Presidential Commission on Law Enforcement recommended the MMPI as an appropriate device, and the 1973 report of the National Advisory Commission on Criminal Justice Standards and Goals reinforced this opinion. The initial purpose of such psychometric tests was to screen in candidates with highly desired qualities and screen out candidates who possessed characteristics deemed less desirable; however, the former goal often lost out to the latter (Benner 1986).

Geoffrey Alpert (1993:103) observed this about the MMPI's ability to screen police candidates: "The selection and promotion of police candidates must move beyond political patronage and approach a scientific method. A balance must be reached among screening in, selecting out, and avoiding discriminatory practices. It is to be hoped that the psychological test will be used simply to screen out [unsuitable] candidates." A late-1980s study revealed that half of all major law enforcement agencies use psychological testing; furthermore, of the 72 larger metropolitan law enforcement agencies surveyed, nearly half used the MMPI (Strawbridge and Strawbridge 1990).

If such tests enjoy widespread use, what about deceptions—attempts by candidates to "beat the test"? Researchers report such efforts, especially attempts at "faking good" among prison inmates (Gendreau, Irvine, and Knight 1973), general offenders (Wasyliw, Grossman, Haywood, and Cavanaugh 1988), and police recruits (Grossman, Haywood, Orlov, Wasyliw, and Cavanaugh 1990). Recent studies suggest that checking for internal consistency makes "faking good" more difficult. Such attempts are especially difficult when the test interpreter differentiates "healthy defensiveness from the intentional effort to ignore or minimize difficulties" (Borum and Stock 1993:159). Skilled administrators and test interpreters are important. They not only screen in (or out) certain kinds of candidates but also ascertain the veracity of applicants' answers.

The **police personality** concept describes undesired police characteristics— the chief one, according to Arthur Niederhoffer (1969), being authoritarianism. Psychologists popularized the term at the end of World War II to help understand how the Germans cooperated with Hitler and his goals. **Authoritarianism** refers to a personality type characterized by undemocratic tendencies, cynicism, and a readiness to condemn others solely based on race or ethnicity (Adorno, Frenkel-Brunswick, et al. 1985). Personality researchers report that police officers are more authoritarian than are members of the public. However, it is not clear whether high authoritarians are drawn to police work or whether policing creates high authoritarianism (Lipset 1969; Van Maanen 1973).

Some social psychologists view the police personality using a more general personality syndrome called **dogmatism.** Milton Rokeach (1956:3) described this condition as "(a) a relatively closed cognitive organization of beliefs and disbeliefs about reality, (b) organized around a central set of beliefs about absolute authority, which in turn, (c) provide a framework for patterns of intolerance and qualified tolerance toward others." It is unclear whether all aspects of authoritarianism, cynicism, or dogmatism are out of place in the police work world (Anson, Mann, and Sherman 1986).

Law enforcement agencies, including violent-crime task forces and special investigative units, often use personality theory to develop **criminal profiles,** often using descriptors associated with psychopathy (Egger 1990; Hare 1996b; Holmes 1990; Ressler, Burgess, and Douglas 1988). The application of these psychogenic theories may be perfectly acceptable and appropriate because the goal of profiling is to bring together all relevant information on a single subject and identify a pattern of human behavior. A major criticism of personality theory and the psychopathy hypothesis is that they are overly concerned with using past behavior to predict future behavior, something police investigators need to do, especially in the pursuit of serial offenders (e.g., rapists, burglars, and murders). Police investigators are less concerned with learning why a crime was committed than with developing a list of possible suspects or potential victims.

Correctional Practices   Correctional psychology is a major area of study and practice. Personality inventories, such as the MMPI, are regular features of the intake process for newly arrived prison inmates (Hawkins and Alpert 1989; Mays and Winfree 2009). Such tests allow for the separation of certain inmates from the general population in order to treat their ailments and protect them. Given the limited psychotherapeutic resources of most prisons, this task may be an exercise in futility. However, it may be possible to place such inmates in a protective custody unit, away from predators.

One function of psychometric-based testing at intake and classification is to measure an inmate's ability to adjust to prison life and determine a suitable security level. The Megargee Inmate Typology (Megargee and Carbonell 1985), based on the MMPI, classifies inmates into 1 of 10 prisoner types and predicts the likelihood that the inmates will violate prison rules or otherwise act aggressively during incarceration. Researchers question this instrument's ability to achieve its stated goals (see also Farrington and Tarling 1985; Gottfredson and Gottfredson 1988; Louscher, Hossford, and Moss 1983). Nonetheless, they remain staples of prison classification systems.

Moreover, a comparative test of the Megargee Offender Classification System using a sample of Belgian federal male prisoners suggests that several of the specific types of offenders identified by the system enjoy reasonable reliability and generality; however, some of the inmate types failed to perform as they did with the U.S. samples (Rossi and Sloore 2008). In order to demonstrate the

TABLE 4.1   Theories of Psychological Abnormalities and Crime

Theory	Major Figures	Central Assumptions	Causal Arguments (Key Terms)	Strengths	Weaknesses
Psychoanalytic	Freud, Healy, Aichhorn	The unconscious self can shape the conscious self in profound ways.	In developmental stages (*oral, anal, genital, latent, adolescent, adult*), imperfect passage may create problems, especially if weak *superego* gives in to hedonistic and antisocial id (see *displacement, repression, reaction formation,* and *sublimation*).	Suggests that, by unlocking the unconscious, psychoanalysis may change antisocial criminals; this approach has much commonsense appeal, especially when we view the offender as crazy: "No normal person would commit a crime like that."	Based on questionable definitions (e.g., repression); studies include few people; theories are largely tautological; therapy is expensive.
Deviant personality	Monachesi, Hathaway, Megargee	The key to normal and abnormal behavior lies in the way we express our valued habitual patterns and qualities in life; psychological tests can reveal these personality markers, including those associated with crime.	Exactly how personality causes crime is missing.	Provides a way to determine the risk for criminal behavior (e.g., MMPI's psychopathic deviation scale score); MMPI and similar tests have widespread uses in criminal justice, for both system clients and personnel.	May be tautological: Self-reported delinquency yields a score on the MMPI that indicates danger of delinquency.
Psychopathy (sociopathy) hypothesis	Cleckley, Guze, Hare	Some people are totally without conscience, capable of acting without concern for others and without any external manifestation of mental illness.	Owing to a lack of conscience, *psychopaths* (*sociopaths*) can commit a wide range of unacceptable acts, from lying with impunity to mutilation murders.	Provides a rationale for social sanitation: We can do little for psychopaths except to institutionalize them; enjoys popular appeal; "The person who did this must have been psycho!"	Has imprecise definitions; research findings are mixed; practitioners use the term as a classification of the last resort, reinforcing the idea that this is another tautology.
Arousal	Ellis	See *psychopathy*. (The theory is an extension of psychopathy.)	See *psychopathy*. Criminals have brains that quickly habituate to incoming stimuli; they are under aroused psychopaths; arousal theory adds a biopsychological explanation to the psychopathy hypothesis.	Explains why some criminals adjust well to prison or jail (low stimuli) but cannot adjust to the free world (high stimuli); also explains why they are relatively immune to rehabilitation (i.e., they are barely awake in low-stimuli environments).	Is an interesting idea that has yet to receive a great deal of empirical support; prisons and jails are boring environments.

wisdom exhibited by U.S. prisons with their wholesale adoption of this system, we need more cross-national and intranational studies, especially ones that allow comparisons between samples.

SUMMARY

This chapter focused on explanations that look primarily within the individual for answers. Biogenic and psychogenic theories of crime share a common history: They emerged from the naturalistic (positivistic) explanation of crime that replaced earlier spiritualism. However, even the most modern psychological theory has not entirely escaped the idea that residing within the individual is some characteristic, identifiable by modern scientific methods, which could cause the undesired behavior. For these reasons, crime theory taxonomists classify psychogenic theories as individualistic and deterministic, as is clearly evident in Table 4.1.

The theories reviewed in this chapter alert us to several important linkages to theories examined later in this book, and they serve as cautionary reminders of the limitations of theories. Psychogenic explanations increasingly have included an "appreciation" for environmental influences. Contemporary tests of these and related theories have yet to show the predictive efficacy of the combined models. Many criminologists view this development with mixed feelings.

Finally, Clemens Bartollas and Simon Dinitz (1989) provide an insightful analysis of both biological and psychological positivism. They suggest that as the medical profession grew in stature, practitioners medicalized certain forms of deviance. By "medicalization," Clemens and Bartollas mean that certain forms of deviant and criminal behavior were no longer viewed as moral problems but rather as medical ones. Consequently, medicine could aid in controlling these "illnesses." Badness became an illness. Eventually, the medical model fell out of favor with criminologists, but the search for biological and psychological explanations continues.

KEY TERMS

adolescence/adulthood stage

anal stage

antisocial behavior disorder (ASBD)

antisocial personality disorder (APD)

arousal theory

authoritarianism

California Personality Inventory (CPI)

cathexis

conscious

criminal profiles

denial

deviant personality theories

displacement

dogmatism

dream interpretation

ego

ego development

Electra wishes

equilibrium

fixation

free association

genital stage

id

latent stage

Minnesota Multiphasic Personality Inventory (MMPI)

moral insanity

neuroses

Oedipus wishes

oral stage

personality

personality theory

phobias

police personality

preconscious

primary process

projection

psyche

psychiatry

psychoanalysis

psychoanalytic theories

psychogenic theories

psychology

psychopath

psychopathic deviation (Pd) scale

psychopathic inferiority

psychopathic personality disorder (PPD)

psychopathic personalities

psychopathy

Psychopathy Checklist–Revised (PCL-R)

psychopathy hypothesis

psychoses

psychosexual development

psychosexual maturity

reaction formation

regression

repression

reticular activating system (RAS)

Rorschach Inkblot Test

secondary process

sociopathic personality disturbance

sociopaths

sociopathy

sociopathy hypotheses

sublimation

superego

Thematic Aptitude Test (TAT)

transference

unconscious

CRITICAL REVIEW QUESTIONS

1. What is the difference between psychology and psychiatry? Why is this distinction important to criminology? Why is it important to criminal justice?

2. What is the importance of unconscious phenomena to human behavior? How does the preconscious differ from the unconscious?

3. What role does psychosexual development play in creating a criminal?

4. What is a key criticism of the psychoanalytic approach to crime causation?

5. What is the most important criticism of the psychopathy hypothesis?

6. Which psychological theory contains social policy implications that not only would be difficult to implement, but also might raise serious constitutional issues?

7. Should the criminal justice system increase or decrease its reliance on psychometric testing in selecting personnel for the criminal justice? Why do you feel this way?

8. From its nineteenth-century beginnings to the present day, the diagnosis of the condition we know as psychopathy has undergone many name changes. Can you suggest more than one reason why this is the case?

9. Which theory examined in this chapter is the most logical one to you? Explain your selection and your criteria.

10. What is the single most important idea that you learned from this review of psychoanalysis, personality, and psychopathy? Explain your answer.

NOTES

1. Not all surgeons or butchers are sadists engaging in sublimation, but we suspect that you already knew that.

2. Stephen Schaefer (1969:211) observed that, had he lived longer, Freud might have become "one of the greatest sociologists." Schaefer saw in Freud's later writings a declaration for the role of societal factors in human behavior, including aggression. Perhaps this shift had an impact on followers like Eissler.

3. An interesting metaphor emerges from criminological studies that use psychoanalysis: bringing light to darkness. Both Eissler's and Healy and Bronner's books included the word *light* in the title. This metaphor is interesting, given the emphasis psychoanalysts place on the darker recesses of the unconscious.

4. Flora Schreiber, an English professor at the John Jay School of Criminal Justice in New York, also wrote *Sybil* (1973), a story about a woman with 17 distinct personalities, and the basis for the made for television movie "Sybil." After the publication of *The Shoemaker* in 1983, the family of one of Kallinger's victims sued Schreiber. She lost the case at trial, and the judge ordered Schreiber to pay the family not only the 12.5 percent of profits promised to Kallinger, but also her share of the earnings and those of the publisher, Simon & Schuster. An appellate panel reversed the ruling's final two conditions, but turned Kallinger's profits over to the victim's family, under New Jersey's so-called "Son-of-Sam Law," a legislative act intended to stop criminals benefiting in any way from their criminal acts.

5

The Psychology of Crime II

CHAPTER OVERVIEW

Introduction

Intelligence and Crime

  Feeblemindedness and Early IQ Tests

  Contemporary Explorations of the IQ–Crime Connection

  Assessing IQ and Crime Links

  Intelligence, Public Policy, and Criminal Justice Practices

Behaviorism and Learning Theory

  Operant Conditioning

  Behaviorism and Crime

  Assessing Behaviorism

  Behaviorism, Public Policy, and Criminal Justice Practices

LEARNING OBJECTIVES

In this chapter, you will learn the following:

- The history and use of IQ testing.
- The complex biological, psychological, and sociological interconnections that determine measured intelligence.
- The various specifications of the IQ–crime link.
- The development of behaviorism and psychological learning theory.
- The application of both behaviorism and learning theory to the explanation of crime and delinquency.

INTRODUCTION

This chapter is about two sets of psychological factors that have worked their way into the criminological literature. The first concerns measures of human intelligence and what it portends for their behavior. When Cesare Lombroso was writing about born criminals, psychologists and others interested in the crime phenomenon in the United States began investigating an inherited mental condition—feeblemindedness—characterized by low mental functioning. Early advocates of treating the feebleminded differently from others in society rarely looked for any explanatory factors. What they acted upon was an often-reported correlation: the lower the mental functioning, the higher the criminal activity.

By the end of the first quarter of the twentieth century, just even as intelligence testing was finding broader practical applications in U.S. society, psychologists had largely abandoned the concept of feeblemindedness. The persistent IQ–crime correlation continued to intrigue criminologists and eventually formed the basis of several different explanations of criminality examined in this chapter.[1]

The second psychological factor derives from learning theory. In addition, at the turn of the twentieth century, psychologists began to observe and theorize about how living organisms—including humans—learned, placing great emphasis on the objective, measurable investigation of individual actions and reactions. Eventually called behaviorists, these psychologists study the unique learning mechanisms associated with various stimuli, those forces in the environment that influence human behavior. Behaviorists did not set out to explain crime, but their theories—and the behavior-modifying practices they suggest—have found their way into the criminological literature and criminal justice practice.

We begin our look at "normal" psychological processes with the evolution of intelligence testing and its eventual application to the study of crime.

INTELLIGENCE AND CRIME

- By the time most people enter college, they have taken at least one standardized intelligence test. Have you? Did you find out the results? If you did, were they beneficial?

- Should jail and prison administrators deny inmates access to certain kinds of programs or treatments based on their IQ scores?

- Do you believe that IQ tests provide a reasonably accurate measure of a person's native intelligence? If so, how widely should they be used?

These questions center on an idea that gained popularity during the first decade of the twentieth century: Low intelligence, an inherited condition, is a correlate of crime. For the idea to take hold, an "objective" measure of intelligence was needed. In 1905, the French psychologist Alfred Binet (1857–1911), working in collaboration with Théodore Simon (1872–1961), provided this measure as a series of tasks of increasing complexity, from those intended for children through those for adults. Three years later, Simon assigned a mental age to groups of tasks.

In 1912, a colleague suggested that he divide mental age by chronological age and multiply the results by 100, and the intelligence quotient, or **IQ** score,[2] was born. Smarter people had IQ scores above 100, while duller ones were below that figure.

Herbert H. Goddard (1866–1957), using a modified Binet-Simon test, studied IQ score distributions in American society. He concluded that as few as 28 percent and as many as 89 percent of the nation's prison inmates had IQ scores of 75 or less (Goddard 1914). The perceived link between weak morals and weak minds gained in popularity during the early decades of the twentieth century (Degler 1991).

By the start of World War II, intelligence testing had found a strong foothold in American society, and its popularity has carried over into the twenty-first century. The contemporary search for the links between IQ and crime, however, has its roots in the far older studies of feeblemindedness, a term popularized in the nineteenth century.

Feeblemindedness and Early IQ Tests

Nineteenth-century students of **feeblemindedness** defined it as a condition of mental deficiency and often used value-laden terms such as *imbecile, moron,* and *idiot* to describe those so afflicted. Proponents of **mental degeneracy,** the late nineteenth-century idea that some people simply fell below the expected level of mental and moral competency, supported their assertions with family histories. In this form of research, "the crime and deviance of the members were explained by hereditary mental degeneration, based on a methodologically dubious collection of data" (Schafer 1969:205). For example, Richard L. Dugdale's study of the Juke family stressed the high incidence of both crime and feeblemindedness. Originally published in 1877 in *The Jukes,* Dugdale's claims were highly speculative and imaginative, based on faulty definitions of both crime and feeblemindedness (Vold 1979).

Goddard was the leading proponent of the use of feeblemindedness as legal and social categories, as well as an ironic figure in the IQ–crime debate. Goddard provided two types of support for his thesis. First, in 1912 he published *The Kallikak Family: A Study in the Heredity of Feeble-Mindedness.* In the Dugdale tradition, he detailed the crimes and other aberrations of 976 descendants of Martin Kallikak and two women. During the Revolutionary War, Kallikak had an affair with a "feebleminded" girl who bore him an illegitimate son, a pairing that yielded 480 descendants. After the war, he married a Quaker girl from a "good family," a union that led to 496 descendants. In the former family, Goddard found 143 feebleminded descendants and dozens of criminal or immoral persons; in the latter, he found only one mental defective and no criminals. As was the fate of Dugdale's *The Jukes,* later investigations revealed that Goddard's revelations were at best composites of other social histories and at worst works of fiction.

Two years after *The Kallikak Family,* Goddard published *Feeble-mindedness: Its Causes and Consequences,* in which he reported on intelligence tests given to the inmates at the New Jersey Home for the Care and Education of Feeble-Minded Children (see Comments and Criticisms). No inmate had a mental age greater than 13. Goddard (1914) deduced that the upper limit for feeblemindedness was a mental age of 12 or an IQ of 75. In *Feeble-mindedness,*

> **COMMENTS AND CRITICISMS: From the School for Feeble-Minded Children to Community Corrections Center: The Story of Vineland Training School**
>
> The New Jersey Home for the Care and Education of Feeble-Minded Children in Vineland, New Jersey, opened in 1888. The facility, with a capacity of 55 boys and girls, was the first of its kind in the United States. Originally housing children in dormitories, the training school changed in 1891 to the "cottage system," an organizational plan whereby children lived in small cottages intended to mimic a family home.
>
> In 1906, Goddard left his position as a university professor of psychology and moved to Vineland, where he became director of the school's newly formed Psychological Research Center. It was here that Goddard supervised the translation of the Stanford-Binet IQ test into English and began testing it on the school's residents. Later, he used public school students from the surrounding community of Vineland to validate and norm the instrument. Goddard continued his work on refining IQ testing at Vineland for 12 years, taking time out to publish *The Kallikak Family* and to supervise the IQ testing of immigrants at Ellis Island. In 1917, Goddard and Vineland hosted a meeting of the American Psychological Association, which convened to devise the IQ-testing procedure that the U.S. Army eventually used on all recruits during World War I.
>
> After Goddard's departure in 1918, the Vineland Training School remained at the center of psychology's involvement in crime and delinquency studies. The center's next director, Australian psychologist Stanley D. Porteus (1883–1972), conducted many tests of heredity, race, intelligence, and delinquency.[4] During the 1920s, the center was known around the world for its studies of feeblemindedness, epilepsy, biochemistry, neuropathology, metabolism, blood chemistry, idiocy, speech pathology, birth injury, and criminology; agricultural research also took place at the school.
>
> After nearly closing down in the early 1980s, Elwyn Institutes, a not-for-profit human services organization, intervened. It restored the school's dilapidated buildings and reopened it as the Training School at Vineland. By the mid-1990s, as national criticism of institutional-based correctional programming grew, the school began to shift operations to community-based group homes, a transition that ended in 1996. Today, the school operates 43 group homes in New Jersey.
>
> The Training School at Vineland played a prominent role in the early development of both IQ testing as a practice and the establishment of a link between low IQ—initially defined as the condition of feeblemindedness—and both adult crime and juvenile delinquency, among other problematic forms of behavior. That the school survived the trend toward the deinstitutionalization of juveniles to be reorganized as the organizational structure for community-based group homes is ironic, given the connection between IQ testing and the penal harm movement discussed below.
>
> SOURCE: The Training School at Vineland (2009).

Goddard also reported on many studies linking feeblemindedness and crime. These prison-based studies typically found high levels of feeblemindedness, and Goddard believed that they firmly established the IQ–crime connection, a conclusion confirmed by others (Davenport 1915). His research convinced him that *positive eugenics*, in this case meaning the sterilization of the feebleminded, was a policy that the nation should adopt, and, as we saw in Chapter 2's discussion of eugenic practices in the United States, many legal jurisdictions did adopt it.[3]

Goddard, when writing about a study of wartime draftees, observed that a high proportion of the men had IQ scores of 75 or lower, a finding that called into question his operational definition of feeblemindedness. Goddard could not accept that nearly a third of the draftees—and perhaps all Americans—were feebleminded. He reckoned that the feebleminded accounted for only 1 percent of the U.S. population (Goddard 1921:173). Faced with these results, he concluded that mental defectives had IQ scores far below 70, a finding that also cast doubt on his IQ–crime link.

IN THEIR OWN WORDS: Goddard on Feeblemindedness

Henry H. Goddard was in a unique position to assess the utility of feeblemindedness for two reasons. First, he used data drawn from both qualitative and quantitative sources to support feeblemindedness as a precursor for crime and deviance. Second, he lived long enough to see his own benchmark for feeblemindedness crumble under the weight of evidence provided by his own IQ tests. His insights on the role of feeblemindedness in causing crime and delinquency are instructive, nonetheless.

■ *On the role of the environment in criminal responsibility:* "Environment will not, of itself, enable all people to escape criminality. The problem goes much deeper than the environment. It is the question of responsibility. Those who are born without sufficient intelligence to know either right from wrong, or those, who if they know it,

have not sufficient willpower and judgment to make themselves do the right and flee the wrong, will ever be a fertile source of criminality" (p. 7).

■ *On the merger of environment and temperament:* "Whether the feebleminded person actually becomes a criminal depends upon two factors, his temperament and his environment. If he is of a quiet, phlegmatic temperament with thoroughly weakened impulses he may never be impelled to do anything seriously wrong. . . . On the other hand, if he is a nervous, excitable, impulsive person he is almost sure to turn in the direction of criminality. . . . But whatever his temperament, in a bad environment he may still become a criminal" (p. 514).

SOURCE: Goddard (1914).

Few criminologists or psychologists today take seriously the idea of feeblemindedness, except for its historical ties to IQ testing. Moreover, its links to *positive eugenics* further lessened its appeal among many in the academic community. Whatever its failings, the concept was the progenitor of contemporary IQ–crime arguments.

Contemporary Explorations of the IQ–Crime Connection

Between the 1920s and the 1960s, criminologists acknowledged the tie between IQ and crime, but speculated little about what it meant. This was when sociology dominated criminological studies, and most challenges to sociological theories came from criminal anthropology and related biological arguments (Wright and Miller 1998; see Chapter 2). Sociologically trained criminologists focused on macro-level forces, such as poverty, cultural conflict, and disruptive neighborhood-level social forces, as the precursors for crime and delinquency. For decades, they relegated the IQ–crime correlation to the status of an interesting but invalid and spurious connection (Bartol 1999:39).

IQ as a Crime Correlate: Travis Hirschi and Michael Hindelang   Travis Hirschi and Michael Hindelang (1977) pointed to the sociologically trained criminologists that decried criminal anthropology early in the twentieth century as helping to bias criminologists against IQ-testing. They pointed out that an early and vocal opponent of the IQ–crime link, Edwin Sutherland (1931), argued that imprecision in the idea of a normal mental age meant that the concept was of little use in crime studies. To learn more about criminality, claimed the criminological mainstream, criminologists should study social forces and not individual factors.

Hirschi and Hindelang reviewed the available studies on the IQ–crime connection and concluded that (1) a low IQ is at least as important as low social class or race in predicting official delinquency, but more important in predicting self-reported offending; (2) within social classes and racial groups, persons with a low IQ are more likely to be delinquent than individuals with a higher IQ; and (3) the relationship between IQ and crime is mediated by negative school experiences. Overall, Hirschi and Hindelang's work supported the view that IQ is important, but only as mediated by what happens to a child in school, irrespective of race or social class.

The Bell Curve: Richard Herrnstein and Charles Murray   In *The Bell Curve,* psychologist Richard Herrnstein and social scientist Charles Murray argued for a clear and consistent link between low intelligence and criminality. Since the 1940s, IQ tests have consistently placed the offender population at between 91 and 93, and the general population at about 100. Herrnstein and Murray (1994:235) saw this as an incontrovertible fact:

> Among the most firmly established facts about criminal offenders is that their distribution of IQ scores differs from that of the population at large. . . . The relationship of IQ to criminality is especially pronounced in the small fraction of the population, primarily young men, who constitute the chronic criminals that account for a disproportionate amount of crime.

Herrnstein and Murray (1994:235) acknowledged the possibility that a high IQ could provide "some protection against lapsing into criminality for people who otherwise are at risk." In reanalyzing the National Labor Youth Survey, a longitudinal study of young males, Herrnstein and Murray (1994:235) found that offenders caught committing crimes differed little in terms of their measured IQ from those getting away with crimes.

Herrnstein and Wilson found intelligence to be correlated with socioeconomic status (SES): the lower the SES, the lower the IQ. However, the lower the SES, the more likely the identification as a criminal, a fact that skews the IQ–crime connection. What are we measuring, IQ or SES? Herrnstein and Murray believe that, independent of SES, IQ predicts criminality.

Assessing IQ and Crime Links

What do IQ tests measure? Do environmental and cultural factors influence IQ scores? If, as we suspect, the corporate offender's IQ differs from that of the street criminal, what are the implications? IQ tests predict success in school, but they may be reliable predictors because such measures also predict middle-class status. Middle- and upper-class children tend to score higher on IQ tests than lower-class youths. We might expect that those who are less successful in school (i.e., children with a lower IQ) would be more likely candidates for criminal behavior. In addition, education positively correlates with economic opportunity. Intelligence quotients, argued Charles Locurto (1991), are also very malleable, easily influenced by many social, physical, and environmental forces.

COMPARATIVE CRIMINOLOGY—WORLD VIEWS ON CRIME AND JUSTICE: Can We Use Standardized IQ Tests in Other Cultures?

For decades, researchers have warned about possible problems with using social and psychological constructions—along with the techniques used to measure them—in cross-national research. There is a potential that the studied groups do not share an understanding of the subject matter. Translation problems, even when multiple forward and backward translations occur, could further cloud the issue. Finally, in the case of psychometric testing, test norms, that is, the "average" figure against which the researcher compares the observed or reported ones, may prove problematic.

IQ testing is no exception to these concerns. For example, persons from two cultures with contrasting views of what constitutes problem-solving ability and innate intelligence might perform quite differently on a standardized IQ test. Comparative studies that link suicide-related behavior—for example, suicide ideation, suicide plans, and even attempted suicide—to IQ suggest that such differences cloud the linkages, even when the samples come from nations that share similar cultural origins, such as Western Europe.[5]

We observed the presence of similar concerns about the cross-national transferability of psychometric testing in Chapter 4, particularly when we discussed psychopathy and derivatives of it, such as the MMPI Pd-scale and the Megargee Offender Classification System. In later chapters, we return to the measurement of IQ as a correlate of other conditions related to crime and criminality—such as race or ethnicity (Chapter 11) or various individual factors in life-course criminology (Chapter 12). We suggest that the concerns addressed here remain relevant for those discussions as well.

SOURCE: Flynn (1986); Voracek (2004; 2007).

He suggested the need for a serious reevaluation of IQ centered on a single question: How do we know that IQ is a measure of intelligence?

As Curt Bartol (1991:132; emphasis is the original) observed, "IQ scores and the concept of intelligence should *not* be confused. The term *IQ* merely refers to a standardized score on a test. Intelligence, on the other hand, is a broad, all-encompassing ability that defies any straightforward or simple definition." Herrnstein and Murray (1994) believed that a place exists for everyone in society, but that some individuals may be destined, due to their low IQs, to occupy lower positions than is the case for those with higher IQs. Not surprisingly, academics and the media have attacked this position (Fraser 1995; see also Allman 1994; Cose 1994; Hancock 1994; Mercer 1994; Morganthau 1994).

Unlike skeptics of IQ (Gartner, Greer, and Reissman 1974; Locurto 1991), Herrnstein and Murray cited questionable studies of IQ and heredity. More recently Bernie Devlin and associates (1997), in a meta-analysis of IQ studies, observed that perhaps less than 50 percent of IQ is the result of genetics, with the rest determined by the environment, a chief contender being prenatal care. Devlin and associates saw these figures as challenging key contentions of *The Bell Curve*.

Some critics of *The Bell Curve* see the book as fraught with logical and empirical shortcomings (Fraser 1995). Herrnstein and Murray place great faith in the representative accuracy of self-reports of crime—a faith not shared across the discipline of criminology. "Smart" criminals do not boast or otherwise reveal their criminal behavior, particularly to strangers. An alternative conclusion is that the criminal justice system ensnares the least capable criminals: stupid criminals commit stupid crimes and get caught. Once identified as the "usual suspects," these criminals become more vulnerable to arrest and serve to populate and repopulate our prisons.

Most prison inmate samples, such as those discussed by Herrnstein and Murray, have high numbers of members with low intelligence. Society has detected, apprehended, and convicted these law-breakers; they are *failed* criminals. We could speculate that those who avoid detection, arrest, prosecution, or conviction are smarter. Alternatively, they may have chosen crimes with a lower probability of detection or successful prosecution. The ability to postpone gratification, a middle-class value, may also be at work: Successful criminals may plan their activities, and the payoff comes later. Less intelligent criminals may go for the quick money—for immediate gratification—with all its attendant risks. Corporate criminals, in particular, pose problems for the purported IQ–crime link. It would be reasonable to assume that in order to pull off a $50 billion Ponzi scheme, the perpetrator would need a relatively high IQ. To be in a position to engage in multimillion- and even multibillion-dollar fraud, the would-be criminal must possess at least average intelligence and possibly professional degrees, qualifications that do not fit the criminal type presented in *The Bell Curve*.

Three positions dominate the debate on the IQ–crime connection—yes, no, and maybe:

- *The IQ–crime link exists.* Many studies support the claim that IQ is a significant delinquency predictor. For example, studies in Denmark and Sweden found strong relationships between IQ and delinquency, even significantly predicting officially recorded crime up to the age of 30 (Moffitt, Gabrielli, Mednick, and Schulsinger 1981; Stattin and Klackenberg-Larsson 1993). Deborah Denno (1985) reported that chronically violent youthful offenders scored lower on verbal and general IQ tests than one-time offenders.

- *The IQ–crime link does not exist.* Some studies report no causal link. For example, Scott Menard and Barbara Morse (1984), using a longitudinal research design, concluded that IQ does not cause delinquent behavior. Rather, IQ is one of humankind's individual characteristics that social institutions—schools, colleges, and universities, and even the workplace— may or may not reward with tangible measures of success. Menard and Morse's research is not without its critics (Harry and Minor 1985). Nonetheless, they (1985) maintain that the IQ–crime correlation is a statistical artifact that owes its existence to the fact that IQ is something tangible to which social institutions can respond.

- *IQ influences criminality, but only due to the action of other, intermediate factors.* While students' IQ test scores predict school achievement, researchers can find no direct link between mental ability and delinquency (Denno 1985). It is possible that delinquents do poorly in school *and* on IQ tests. If IQ has an indirect impact on delinquency, it is probably through school performance, a conclusion that supports the Hirschi–Hindelang hypothesis about the mediating effects of education (Farrington 2005; McGloin, Pratt, and Maahs 2004).

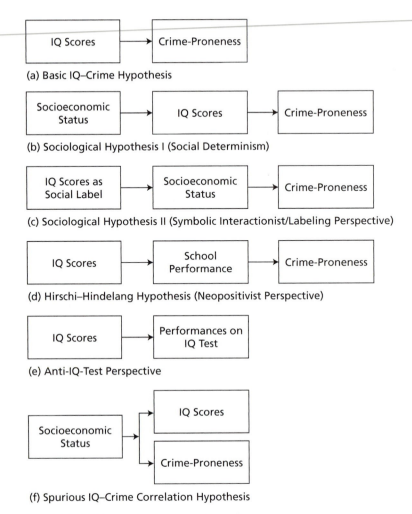

(a) Basic IQ–Crime Hypothesis

(b) Sociological Hypothesis I (Social Determinism)

(c) Sociological Hypothesis II (Symbolic Interactionist/Labeling Perspective)

(d) Hirschi–Hindelang Hypothesis (Neopositivist Perspective)

(e) Anti-IQ-Test Perspective

(f) Spurious IQ–Crime Correlation Hypothesis

FIGURE 5.1   Various IQ–Crime Hypotheses

Despite widespread corporate crime, the use of IQ scores to predict criminality is limited to crimes most likely committed by persons with limited intelligence. So pervasive is the problem, that in 2002 President George W. Bush created the Corporate Fraud Task Force "in response to a number of high-profile acts of fraud and dishonesty that occurred in corporate executive suites and boardrooms across the country" (Corporate Fraud Task Force 2008:iii). We could confidently predict that corporate crime, organized crime, or even political and computer crime require superior intelligence. We could also conclude that IQ and crime may share a common cause, but while high or low intelligence may influence the choice of crime and the probability of being caught, intelligence is not the *cause* of crime. Figure 5.1 summarizes the various IQ–crime hypotheses.

Intelligence, Public Policy, and Criminal Justice Practices

Intelligence testing may be one of the most powerful legally sanctioned instruments of discrimination created in the twentieth century. In a society that seems to live and die by quantitative information, IQ tests fit right into the cultural mainstream. They provide a simple and seemingly objective means to make what is often a difficult decision.

Overreliance on IQ testing may create a situation in which everybody loses and nobody wins. Those whom IQ tests exclude or misclassify may have career doors closed to them or be denied access to training that would change their lives for the better. Indeed, some prison inmates find themselves ineligible for job training or other career-related opportunities while incarcerated because they are not intellectually up to the task—at least as determined by IQ and other psychometric tests. Employers may lose potentially valuable employees, and educational programs may lose unique students.

For more than 100 years, the causal links between intelligence and offending have been tenuous at best. Even with the best, most current IQ–crime studies, the conclusions seem to point in all directions at once. A statistical correlation may exist between a person's IQ score and likelihood of offending, but the reasons are unclear. We have posited several interpretations of this correlation. Given the various potential answers, building public policy on an idea that points in so many different directions is imprudent, a form of social Darwinism that supports deliberate neglects of those in society with the greatest need for assistance, and by extension, a form of passive eugenics.

Several Scandinavian countries established eugenics programs in the 1930s. Between 1935 and 1976, the Swedish government authorized the sterilization of no fewer than 60,000 Swedish women deemed as mental defectives to halt the propagation of their weak genes (Gallagher 1998). About 11,000 Danish women met a similar fate, along with 1000 Norwegians (Broberg and Roll-Hansen 1996). In the United States, public health officials estimate that perhaps 60,000 women underwent forced sterilization during the 1930s (Reilly 1991; Sofair and Kaldjian 2000). The Nazis also practiced several types of eugenics, ranging from involuntary euthanasia for German citizens to genocide for members of undesired races (Sofair and Kaldjian 2000).

What is needed next, the authors of *The Bell Curve* claimed, are simpler rules and a far simpler criminal justice system, with less "ambiguously administered punishments that give short shrift to personal excuses or social circumstances" (Cullen, Gendreau, Jarjoura, and Wright 1997:401). Francis Cullen and his associates saw such logic as adding to the problems already created by the **penal harm movement** (see also Chapter 9). That is, a raft of punitive policies and practices, adopted on the state and federal level since the 1970s, has resulted in the rapid expansion of institutional-based criminal sanctions as a way of protecting society against the predations of criminals arguably committed to a life of crime. The financial costs of this expansionist policy on prison construction are colliding with a severe economic downturn. Moreover, an IQ-based public policy "seeks to lock up stupid people" (Cullen et al. 1997:403), hardly the basis of a good crime control policy, let alone one rooted in solid criminological theory or sound research.

Law Enforcement Practices   For more than 85 years, intelligence testing has been an integral part of police officer selection. Stanford University psychologists used IQ evaluations of police applicants in 1916 for the San Jose (California) Police Department. Because the average applicant had an IQ of 84, they recommended setting the minimum standard at 80 (Wrightsman, Nietzel, and Fortune 1994:116). Officers have challenged the tests as culturally biased and discriminatory, which are not new arguments in this ongoing controversy. What is interesting is that "many departments ... cling to tradition and use some form of multiple-choice IQ test for initial screening purposes" (Roberg and Kuykendall 1993:284).

Judicial Practices   Persons with low intelligence are legally not insane; however, they may not recognize that what they did was wrong, appreciate the quality of the illegal act, or understand why they are punished. Trial courts have convicted individuals with low IQs—below 75—of homicide, sentenced them to die, and ultimately executed them. Consider the case of Morris Odell Mason, a retarded African American male with an IQ of 66, who was executed in 1985 for multiple rapes and murders. If a defendant is profoundly retarded, should he be subjected to the full force of the law? Can we conclude that he does not have *mens rea*? If he is incapable of distinguishing right from wrong, should the courts sanction him at all? Don't we excuse the very young, those under 10 years of age, from any criminal or even juvenile justice processing? What if the person is the mental equivalent of a 10-year-old or even a 5-year-old?

Trial and appellate courts, including the U.S. Supreme Court, historically have been unimpressed with these questions. Writing for the majority in *Penry v. Lynaugh* (1989), Associate Justice Sandra Day O'Connor noted, "There is insufficient evidence of a national consensus against executing mentally retarded people convicted of capital offenses for us to conclude that it is categorically prohibited by the Eighth Amendment." In *Penry,* Texas convicted the accused of capital murder. At the time of his trial, Penry had the mental age of a 6½-year-old; socially, he was 9 or 10. The Supreme Court did find that the trial judge should have instructed the jury that mental retardation could be a mitigating circumstance, and issued a new sentencing order for Penry. As a footnote to this case, the Texas Supreme Court overturned Penry's third death sentence in 2005, the second one having been overturned by the Supreme Court in 2002 owing to the *Atkins* case.

In 2002, the Supreme Court reversed itself, claiming that the nation had achieved the missing consensus. The case involved a 1996 abduction, armed robbery, and capital murder for which Daryl Renard Atkins was convicted and sentenced to death. At trial, a forensic psychologist concluded that Atkins was "mildly retarded," and according to school and court records and a standard intelligence test, he had an IQ of 59. In a 7–2 decision, the Court, led by Justice

John Paul Stevens, held that "such punishment is excessive and that the Constitution 'places a substantive restriction on the State's power to take the life' of a mentally retarded offender" (*Atkins v. Virginia* 2002:17). One reason cited by the Court in reversing itself—and the trial court's decision in *Atkins*—was the fact that by 2002, 21 states and the federal government had enacted laws prohibiting the execution of those with mental retardation, a clear majority, in the opinion of the justices. The methods by which various states will implement *Atkins* are unknown. Indeed, in 2007, Texas executed James Lee Clark, deemed mentally retarded, resulting in an international outcry against Texas's policies and practices in light of *Atkins*. The judge in the case determined that while Clark may have suffered developmental problems, his level of retardation was not sufficient to compel an *Atkins* ruling.

Court officers often use IQ tests, along with personality inventories such as the MMPI and the TAT (see Chapter 4), to assess suitability for probation—that is, in measuring **dangerousness.** Given the attitude of the nation's highest court, the most that low-IQ defendants can hope for is that at sentencing, judges may view their affliction as a mitigating circumstance. Judges may choose to ignore it; in fact, given the average IQ of prison inmates, that seems to occur with regularity. Researchers have estimated that between 2 and 10 percent of the nation's prison population are mentally retarded or developmentally disabled (Davis 2000). Given these estimates, on any given day, state and federal prisons in the United States hold between 24,000 and 120,000 mentally retarded inmates (Beck and Karberg 2001:1).[6] Jails may have even higher percentages than prisons because they have become a holding area for the nation's mentally impaired citizens (Mays and Winfree 2009).

Correctional Practices   As in law enforcement, candidates for entry-level correctional system positions, including correctional officers and other staff in prisons and jails, may have to take IQ tests. Test results also help staff manage inmates. Prison and jail classification schemes, which may include IQ tests, establish new security levels for inmates. These tests also may be used to judge suitability for facility-based treatment or rehabilitation programs, including education, job training, and drug or alcohol treatment. As Clemens Bartollas and John Conrad (1992:525) noted:

> The IQ tests are not reliable instruments to administer to men and women who have just arrived in prison, many of them depressed, many of them unskilled at reading, and many quite unmotivated to do their best on the batteries of tests that are impersonally administered to the newly arrived "fish." Still, the results give a rough—very rough—idea of the intellectual capabilities of the new prisoners.

Low-functioning individuals may find that in prison or jail they are again at the mercy of IQ test results, unable to "pass muster" for the few available programs (Bartollas and Conrad 1992; Mays and Winfree 2009). However, Cullen and associates (1997) identified two areas in which one's IQ score may have a positive impact. The first involves the **responsivity principle,** under which "services designed to reduce offender recidivism will be enhanced if the style and modes of service are matched to the learning styles and abilities of the offender" (Cullen et al. 1997:403; see also Andrews and Bonta 1994; McGloin and Pratt 2003). In this context, IQ is but one of a series of personality factors, including anxiety, depression, and mental disorder, which may play important roles in the delivery of treatment. Recall Bartollas and Conrad's observation about IQ tests given in prisons and jails: They are notoriously inaccurate. Nonetheless, the results may be important predictors of the receptivity of a given offender to correctional treatment (Cullen et al. 1997:404).

In addition, Cullen and associates (1997) suggested expanding IQ to include practical intelligence (see also Gould 1981, 1995). For example, we may possess verbal intelligence, linguistic intelligence, mathematical intelligence, and emotional intelligence. **Practical intelligence** is "a person's ability to learn and profit from experience, to monitor effectively one's own and others' feelings and needs, and to solve everyday problems" (Cullen et al. 1997:404; see also Gardner 1983; Sternberg 1985). Practical intelligence may be more amenable to change than conventional IQ. Cullen and associates (1997:405) viewed the inclusion of practical intelligence measures in correctional treatment as a positive way to influence an offender's future by taking into account his or her individual differences, which included intellectual competencies.

BEHAVIORISM AND LEARNING THEORY

- As a small child, you sipped a cup containing a beverage that was so hot that it scalded your lips. You learned to check similar cups, blowing into them before tasting the contents. What elements of this process have criminological implications?

- You watch a news report about a major forest fire. Inmates from a local prison volunteered to fight the fire even though this exposed them to considerable danger. After discounting their community spirit as an attempt to escape (who can escape into a forest fire?), you ask yourself another question: Why can't prison inmates learn to be contributing members of society in other ways?

These questions relate to **behaviorism,** a branch of psychology. John B. Watson (1878–1958) first used the term nearly 100 years ago, in 1913, when he penned an article titled "Psychology as the behaviorist sees it."[7] Watson later wrote, "Learning in animals is probably the most important topic in the whole study of behavior" (1914:45). Watson (1930:2) contrasted the subject of "old" psychology—consciousness—with his variant in the final edition his classic text on the topic, *Behaviorism*: "Behaviorism, on the contrary, holds that the subject matter of human psychology is the behavior of the human being." It was learning, and not instincts, that earned the most praise from Watson. Understanding the means of habit formation was the key, Watson (1914) believed, to controlling human activity.

The Russian psychologist Ivan Petrovich Pavlov (1849–1936) influenced Watson. Pavlov experimented with dogs; the most famous dog was the one he taught to associate food with bell chimes, so that the dog salivated at the sound of the bell alone. For Watson, behavior was merely a physiological response to a given stimulus. The theories discussed in Chapter 4 notwithstanding, Watson saw no place in this process for the conscious or the unconscious, and he spent much of his career debunking what he saw as the psychoanalytic myth, translating psychoanalytic ideas into Pavlovian conditioning (Rilling 2000). It remained for others, but especially the American behavioral psychologist B. F. Skinner, to explain the complex nature of these learning mechanisms, and for still others, including Julian Rotter, Albert Bandura and Hans Eysenck, to tie this perspective to crime.[8]

Operant Conditioning

Behaviorists typically dismiss psychoanalytic theory as unscientific; that is, psychoanalytic theory lacks the rigorous testing associated with learning theory. Indeed, measurement of objective behavior is intrinsic to **learning theory,** which proceeds on the basis that all forms of behavior are conditioned: the result of learned responses to certain stimuli. B. F. Skinner (1904–1990), America's foremost behaviorist, argued that psychoanalytically oriented therapists "rely too much on inferences they make about what is supposedly going on inside their patients, and too little on direct observation of what they do" (Goleman, 1987:18). If a person's aggressive behavior has been rewarded, at least part of the time, no further explanation in terms of internal needs is necessary; he or she has simply learned to behave aggressively (Nietzel et al. 2003).

Behaviorists stress—and have been able to prove—that they can modify animal behavior through the proper application of operant conditioning: positive and negative reinforcement. Behavior is "strengthened by its consequences, and for that reason the consequences themselves are called 'reinforcers'" (Skinner 1974:40). Behaviorists also see all behavior as resulting from learned responses to distinct stimuli. As noted by Skinner, when some aspect of behavior (animal or human) is followed by a certain type of consequence—a reward—it is more likely to recur. The reward is a **positive reinforcer.** However, a reward becomes a positive reinforcer, and punishment becomes a **negative reinforcer,** only when it actually influences behavior in a specified manner. These concepts form the basis for operant conditioning, whereby reinforcement incrementally shapes behavior patterns. The following box provides examples of classical and operant conditioning.

Disturbed behavior results from learning inappropriate responses, which may be due to either learning them directly from others (e.g., peers) or the failure to discriminate between competing lawful and unlawful norms owing to inappropriate reinforcement. When conforming behavior is not adequately reinforced, or is perhaps negatively reinforced, competing, albeit antisocial, sources of positive reinforcement, can more easily influence an actor.

Under controlled conditions, such as when one is conducting an experiment or training animals, the reinforcement, if it is to be effective, needs to occur as

COMMENTS AND CRITICISMS: Classical and Operant Conditioning

Behavioral psychology recognizes two basic types of processes associated with learning:

Classical conditioning involves pairing two stimuli, one that elicits a reflex and one that is neutral (e.g., food and the sounding of a bell). With repeated pairing of the two stimuli, the previously neutral stimulus (bell) becomes a conditioned stimulus and elicits the response (e.g., salivating) in absence of the original eliciting stimulus (food).

Operant conditioning involves the repeated presentation or removal of a stimulus following a behavior to increase the probability of the behavior (i.e., **reinforcement**). A reinforcer is a stimulus that increases the probability of a behavior. If the probability of a behavior goes up following the presentation of some stimulus, then positive reinforcement has occurred. If the probability of a behavior goes up after the *removal* of a stimulus, then negative reinforcement has occurred.

SOURCE: Tilson (1993:2).

close to the event as possible. Our criminal justice system's effectiveness as a conditioning agent, therefore, may be limited due to the question of timeliness: How long does it take to discover the undesired or desired behavior and either extinguish it or reinforce it?

According to Skinner (1974:63), "Punishment is easily confused with negative reinforcement. The same stimuli are used, and negative reinforcement might be defined as the punishment of not behaving, but punishment is designed to remove behavior from a repertoire, whereas negative reinforcement generates behavior." For example, in the event that an offender is fined or put in prison, what is actually occurring is not the presentation of a negative stimulus, but rather the removal of a positive one, a situation that has thus far positively reinforced the aberrant behavior (Skinner 1974:63). Skinner believed that those who were punished still possessed a tendency to behave as before but now they would attempt to void punishment by acting in a different manner to escape detection. In other words, punishment is effective in controlling behavior only in the short term unless the subject can be continually monitored and punished. Effective behavioral changes require reinforcing alternative behavior. Figure 5.2 summarizes the basic behaviorist models.

Behaviorism and Crime

Antisocial behavior is merely the result of learning directly from others (e.g., peers) or the failure to learn how to discriminate between competing norms, both lawful and unlawful, because of inappropriate reinforcement. When conforming behavior is not adequately reinforced, an actor can more easily be influenced by competing, albeit antisocial, sources of positive reinforcement (e.g., money and excitement from criminal behavior). To be effective for learning, however, reinforcement must follow rather closely the behavior that is to be influenced. "Generally, operant conditioning is most likely to occur when reinforcers and punishers follow immediately after an operant" (Baldwin and Baldwin, 1998:89). Offenders have problematic reinforcement contingencies and often

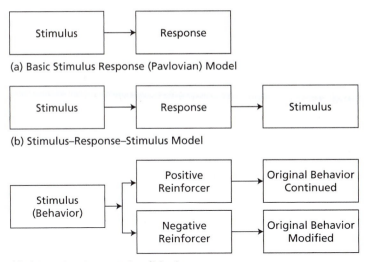

(a) Basic Stimulus Response (Pavlovian) Model

(b) Stimulus–Response–Stimulus Model

(c) Skinnerian Operant Conditioning

F I G U R E 5.2 Behaviorist Models

engage in behavior that provides an immediate payoff but has negative long-term consequences: If criminal behavior is usually rewarding, significant but intermittent punishment is unlikely to suppress it.

Hans Eysenck saw the *conscience* as controlling antisocial behavior. This is not the mechanism that Freud ascribed to the superego, but instead is the result of conditioning, a process that often sounds like an admixture of classical deterrence, atavistic determinism, and modern behaviorism. As Eysenck put it:

> The young child, as he grows up, is required to learn a number of actions which are not, in themselves, pleasant or pleasurable and which in fact go counter to his desires and wishes. . . . In every society there is a long list of prohibitions of acts which are declared to be bad, naughty and immoral, and which, although they are attractive to him and are self-rewarding, he must nevertheless desist from carrying out. . . . In childhood it is possible to administer such punishment at the right moment of time; the child who does something wrong is immediately slapped, told off, sent upstairs, or whatever punishment it may be. . . . [A]fter a number of repetitions of this kind, the act itself would produce the conditioned response. . . . The child acquires, as it were, an "inner policeman" to help in controlling his atavistic impulses and to supplement the ordinary police force which is likely to be much less efficient and much less omnipresent (quoted in Taylor, Walton, and Young 1973:48–49).

Most conventional crime involves substantial risk and relatively modest external rewards. Therefore, reinforcement for such activity may involve internal rewards through the release of potentially pleasant neurotransmitters such as endorphins and dopamine (Gove and Wilmoth 1990). Eysenck (1973) noted the need for timeliness in order for reinforcement to be effective: Immediate rewards could offset delayed punishments.

Behaviorism has several implications for criminology. We begin with Eysenck's criminal personality theory.

Criminal Personality Theory   Hans Eysenck created **criminal personality theory,** a mix of behaviorism, biology, and personality theories, to explain the links between aberrant personality conditions and crime. A critic of sociological crime theories (Eysenck and Gudjonsson 1989), Eysenck saw crime as an interaction between environmental conditions and inherited nervous system features. Like many other psychobiologists, Eysenck (1973:171; see also Eysenck 1977) believed that focusing on the nature-versus-nurture controversy was no way to resolve the crime-causation debate. In another divergence, Eysenck asked, "Why doesn't everyone commit crime?" To this point, psychologists have concerned themselves with a different question: What made this person commit crime?

Eysenck suggested that, although criminality is not an inherited trait, certain inherited characteristics make crime more likely. He used the nervous system to explain different personality types. Eysenck divided the controlling of behavior into two kinds: (1) that which is the result of the quality of conditioning and (2) that which is inherited. Part of what we inherit is our nervous system. As we learned in Chapter 3, the *autonomic nervous system (ANS)* regulates involuntary bodily functions (e.g., heart, lungs, and digestion), including ones that have opposing effects. For example, sympathetic functions act or, more correctly, react to mobilize the organism for action, as in the classic "fight or flee" scenario; parasympathetic functions deal with the digestive system and act to conserve bodily resources. The central nervous system (CNS) is the brain and spinal chord; it contains the majority of our nervous system and controls behavior.

The ANS and CNS, then, help delineate between personality types. Eysenck believed that personality depends on four "higher-order factors," including **ability,** or intelligence (a quality he called **g**), and three temperaments: **extraversion, neuroticism,** and **psychoticism.** Although g is important in understanding crime, Eysenck claimed that the three temperaments are far more critical. Two of these, extraversion and neuroticism, are related; the third, psychoticism, is unique. For Eysenck, extraversion reflected basic central nervous system (CNS) functioning. Neuroticism depended on nerve pathways outside the CNS; in particular, the ANS. Psychoticism had no specified neural links.

According to Eysenck, two personality types exhibit the greatest proneness to crime. The first includes **neurotic extraverts,** or persons who—because of their biology—require high stimulation levels from their environments. Moreover, their sympathetic nervous systems are quick to respond without much counterbalancing from the parasympathetic system. The second type, the **psychotic extraverts,** are persons who—due to reasons of unknown physiological origin—are cruel, hostile, insensitive to others, and unemotional, but not necessarily "out of touch with reality." By themselves, however, these personality types do not explain *why* crime occurs.

Eysenck merged his genetically determined personality types with instrumental learning, or behaviorism, to provide a complete answer to his key question, *Why doesn't everybody commit illegal acts?* Instrumental learning occurs in the individual's environment; some action must be engaged in that elicits either a reward or a punishment. About this process Curt Bartol (1991:51) observed:

> Most people . . . do not participate in criminal activity . . . because after a series of trials they have made strong connections between [criminal activity] and aversive consequences. On the other hand, those persons who have not made adequate connections, either because of poor conditionability (e.g., extraverts) or because the opportunity to do so was not presented (socialization), are more likely to display deviant or criminal behavior. According to Eysenck, these people do not anticipate aversive events strongly enough to be deterred; the association has not been sufficiently developed.

Criminal behavior, in Eysenck's model, is thus the product of environmental factors (conditioning/learning habits) and biology (personality type intensifiers).

Cognitive Learning Theory   Human behavior is more complex than the relatively simple responses of lower species, as symbols and beliefs often mediate it. The readiness to fight or die for a "cause" or a strongly held belief system, such as those associated with religious symbols, embodies some of the most abstract complexities of human behavior. This recognition has led to **cognitive behavior theory,** based on the idea that "human behavior is mediated by unobservables that intervene between a stimulus and a response to that stimulus" (Gold 1980:8). Many mediating constructs are important to a full understanding of emotion and behavior, including beliefs, strategies, attributions, and expectancies. The way a person evaluates a given situation, in light of these mediating constructs, determines the affective and behavioral response (Gold 1980). For example, based on past learning, a twisted cross (swastika) may have different meaning to a Jew (for whom it is a symbol of the Holocaust) than to a member of the Navajo Nation (for whom it is a cosmic religious symbol). As Susan Cloninger (1993:369) observed, to "describe people's overt behavior without paying attention to what people are thinking cannot provide an adequate model of personality. Behaviorism that does not involve extended consideration of cognitive variables risks neglecting much that is human."

Julian Rotter (1954) proposed that a cognition or expectation leads to a certain outcome or consequence. People weigh the possible consequences of their actions in terms of recollections about what has happened previously in similar circumstances. The possible rewards—how much value they attach to the outcome—may determine whether people engage in certain behaviors. These "generalized expectancies" are relatively stable in similar situations (Mischel 1976).

Rotter's **expectancy theory** describes how people make decisions, and not just crime. As for applying the theory to crime, Curt Bartol (1999:120) wrote:

> We would say that when people engage in unlawful conduct, they expect to gain something in the form of power, security, material goods,

or living conditions. The violent person, for example, may elect to
behave that way in the belief that something will be gained. The serial
murderer might believe that God has sent him on a mission to eliminate
all "loose" women; the woman who poisons an abusive husband looks
for an improvement in her life situation.... Usually when people act
violently, they do so because that approach has been used successfully in
the past (at least they believe it has been successful).

Humans use their cognitive powers to look simultaneously into the past and the
future, make decisions about likely outcomes, and act upon them. What happens if
they lack the experience to draw conclusions about the future? Bandura provides
one answer.

Psychological Modeling Theory   Albert Bandura is best known for his Bobo
doll experiments. In this experiment, children first watched while an adult model
attacked a plastic clown doll called Bobo, kicking it and committing other aggressive acts against it using toys in the room. Next, the children were placed in a
room with attractive toys that they were not allowed to touch until they grew
visibly agitated and frustrated. They were then moved to another room containing a Bobo doll and the same toys used by the adult model to attack Bobo.
Bandura found that nearly 9 in 10 children imitated the attack on Bobo, and
about 4 in 10 reproduced the behavior when placed in a similar physical situation
eight months later (Bandura and Huston 1961; Bandura, Ross, and Ross 1963).

Bandura's learning theory blends reinforcement theory with cognitive psychology.[9] "By representing foreseeable outcomes symbolically people convert
future consequences into motivations of behaviour" (Bandura 1974:859). He
called the process by which this happens **observational learning** or **modeling,**
a process that need not involve direct reinforcement. Instead, humans are capable
of learning vicariously (Bandura 1977, 1989). For example, a handful of magazines catering to both the hardcore outlaw subculture and "wannabe" outlaws
promote the lifestyles and traditions of outlaw bikers. Biker magazines "make it
possible for a man to construct a biker identity and develop a sense of loyalty to
that image without having met another biker" (Wolf 1991:37).

Bandura's research and theorizing largely involved aggression. The person
most likely to learn to be aggressive is the individual who observes much aggressive behavior, is reinforced for acting aggressively, and is the object of aggression.
Bandura identified the primary models as family members, members of one's
subculture, and symbolic models provided by the mass media. Behavioral diagnosis and treatment, especially for aggression in children, were best undertaken
during childhood (Bandura 1977). Treatment involved modeling socially acceptable behavior.

Behaviorism as an explanation for crime is uncritical of the social order,
the legal system, and its enforcement apparatus, and adopts a consensual view
of society. Much of what is done in the name of behaviorism is dependent on
one's definition of the situation. As a technique for altering behavior, it is amoral

or politically neutral and easily lends itself to misuse. In *The Gulag Archipelago,* Alexander Solzhenitsyn (1974) described the prison hospitals maintained in the former Soviet Union and their reliance on modified Pavlovian behaviorist principles as a means of eliminating dissent. Behavior modification has met with varying degrees of success in helping to maintain prison discipline and order in the United States as well (see the following discussion).

Applying Learning Theory: Behavior Modification   The behaviorist stresses client analysis to discover the variables that are reinforcing and then attempts to discover the situational demands and emotions that are related to the patient's behavior. The analysis deals with the day-to-day functioning of the subject in order to discern the cause (independent variables) of the maladaptive behavior (dependent variables). The therapist attempts to elicit specific descriptions of actual events that constitute a problem—functional analysis—so that he or she can evaluate which components of the situation are amenable to change by behavioral techniques (Nietzel et al. 2003). The specific description, whenever possible, is based on direct observation or interviews with the client and/or significant others (e.g., parents or spouse), and a review of any relevant records. Maladaptive behavior is analyzed in terms of intensity and frequency and is often presented in the form of graphs.

The therapist teaches the client to conduct his or her own functional analysis for subsequent self-produced modification of the environmental contingencies that are reinforcing the maladaptive behavior. The functional analysis can be combined with self-monitoring techniques. A highly motivated client maintains a daily log of the specific problem—for example, lack of temper control—and records the number of times that he or she exhibits the specific manifestations of a lack of temper control. Although therapists can combine this technique with other forms of therapy, alone it seems to have the power to modify behavior owing to the fact that it makes clients aware of their problem. This increased level of self-motivation actually encourages clients to reward or punish themselves, depending on how close they are to their personal goals. The intent, then, is that such activities provide clients with the opportunity to suppress the undesired responses and any associated behaviors. The logs—as a form of personal journal—have proven important as aids in helping the clients achieve their goals (Bootzin 1975).

Cognitive behavioral therapy (CBT), a dominant therapeutic practice in psychology, reduces recidivism (Lipsey, Chapman, Landenberger 2001; Pearson et al. 2002; Wilson, Bouffard, and MacKenzie 2005). CBT maintains that an understanding of behavior is to be found within a person's thoughts, memory, language, and beliefs, placing the emphasis on inner rather than environmental determinants of behavior (Hollin, 1990). Albert Bandura (1974) argues that to ignore the influence of covert reinforcement in the regulation of behavior is to deny a uniquely human capacity. According to the cognitive view, a human being is an active participant in his or her operant conditioning processes—the individual determines what is and what is not reinforcing. For example, to become a drug abuser, one must *learn* that ingesting certain chemicals is desirable

(Abadinsky 2008). In other words, human behavior is complex and reinforcement often abstract. Humans have a unique capacity to use abstractions, or symbols, that can serve as important reinforcers, such as the medals and trophies dear to any amateur athlete. People can learn behavior vicariously through observation without *obvious* reinforcement (Nietzel et al, 2003).

The use of CBT with criminal offenders focuses on coping and problem-solving skills. The offender is suffering from faulty thinking patterns and lacks a level of social competence that is necessary to cope adequately with a variety of situational demands. "Their behavior may be guided by dysfunctional assumptions about how one should behave, for example, 'you have to punish people for messing with you or they won't respect you,' 'you have to rebel against authority or they will break you'" (Lipsey, Chapman, Landenberger 2001:145). Cognitive behavior therapy seeks to correct dysfunctional and criminogenic thinking patterns.

People can monitor and change their cognitive activity (i.e., "think crime") and resulting behavior (i.e., "do crime"). The therapeutic process begins with an assessment of positive and negative aspects of their behavior. The assessment focuses on the behavior's social, physical, and emotional environments. After the assessment, the role of the therapist is to enable the person to deal with cues that trigger problem behavior in a manner that avoids resorting to illegal activity, with the patient's own report of the negative aspects (e.g., arrest, incarceration) serving as a motivator for adopting more positive coping strategies (Donovan, 1988). Negative reinforcement in the form of avoidance strategies prevents the occurrence of influences that trigger criminal behavior.

Assessing Behaviorism

Most behaviorist contributions to crime and justice issues have been largely indirect, through other theories such as social learning (see Chapter 7) and rational choice (see Chapter 2). The exception is the work of Bandura (1973), whose theory of aggression includes the influence of symbolic models, particularly the mass media (i.e., television and movies). Research on Bandura's learning model has linked exposure to TV violence with increased aggression in children and adults, although this relationship is clearer for short-term effects and among those who were already aggressive (Freedman 1984, 1986; Freidrich-Cofer and Huston 1986; Pearl, Bouthilet, and Lazar 1982).

Researchers also fail to support Eysenck's personality theory. Research design flaws make any findings about personality theory research highly suspect (Passingham 1972; see also Farrington, Biron, and LeBlanc 1982). In particular, adequate control groups are generally missing. Even the experimental groups employed—in some cases prison inmates—may be incapable of accounting for confounding factors, such as the type of crime committed. Indeed, penologists find few "pure type" offenders prison; few offenders are guilty of only one type of criminal activity. In at least one study, criminals scored lower than did members of the control group on a personality scale derived from Eysenck's work (Bartol and Holanchock 1979).

Besides noting somewhat inconclusive results between experiments about learned aggression and later acts of misbehavior, critics of behaviorism have noted the following problems:

- *Failure to consider the role of biology.* Although Bandura and Eysenck acknowledged that genetic endowment could influence the rate at which learning takes place, biological theorists complain that behaviorists largely ignore the individual's biological state. What, they asked, are the individual differences in learning given variations in genetics, brain functioning, and learning (Jeffery 1985)? Not everyone, observed critics, is equally prepared to learn. Moreover, two people witnessing the same violent event (e.g., a hanging or a murder) might respond in very different ways.

- *Questions of manipulation and ethics in research.* The Bobo doll experiments have been criticized as manipulative (i.e., the children were teased and became frustrated because they could not touch the toys); moreover, the research may have been unethical in that it trained children to be aggressive (Worthman and Loftus 1992:45).

- *The catharsis effect.* Bandura and other cognitive behaviorists expressed concern about television violence because of the opportunity to model aggressive behavior. But many researchers have reached the opposite conclusion, suggesting that the act of viewing violence may lower aggression (Feshbach and Singer 1971). According to the **catharsis effect,** viewing violence allows some people to release aggressive thoughts and feelings by relating to those engaged in violence (Gerbner and Gross 1976, 1980).

- *The inclusion of neural elements adds unknown variables.* This criticism, also mentioned in Chapter 4 as a problem with Ellis's arousal theory, is equally true of Eysenck's criminal personality theory: To include highly speculative biological elements based on little-understood neural and neurocognitive processes in highly problematic (Blair and Frith 2000; Martens 2000).

In sum, learning is a logical process to link to human behavior, even human social behavior, and perhaps especially to criminal behavior. The processes by which we learn to interact with others in the community should work for criminals as well as those who act within society's norms, rule, and laws. However, showing exactly how conditioning occurs in the context of crime and delinquency has proven difficult.

Behaviorism, Public Policy, and Criminal Justice Practices

The role of operant conditioning principles—negative reinforcers and positive punishers—in criminal justice policy is far from clear. Equally unclear is whether, issues of due process aside, the criminal justice system is capable of responding quickly and consistently enough to accomplish the desired modifications in the behavior of those who are caught, convicted, and punished. Similar problems confounded deterrence theory's system of rewards and punishments (see Chapter 2). Behaviorism adds operant conditioning language to the punishment process. The complex psychosocial nature of reinforcers and punishers suggests why sanctions alone may not deter offenders. Good behavior helps people avoid a visit to the local jail or revocation of parole or probation. Such negative reinforcers are intended to promote continued good behavior. Similarly, punishments entail the loss of something valued (e.g., the prospect of a particular job, perhaps in the field of criminal justice, which requires the absence of a felony conviction record) should the undesirable behavior continue or reach a certain level. In short, behaviorism exerts considerable influence on criminal sanctions. The problem is that small, immediate rewards tend to be repeated even though they are followed by large, painful but delayed punishments.

Behaviorism holds much promise as a mechanism for changing problematic behavior. Schools use **token economies,** a form of **behavior modification,** to teach students the rewards of good behavior. However, most behaviorists place less faith in the capacity of punishers to extinguish behavior than in the capacity of rewards to encourage it. This lesson is often lost on policy makers, who tend to emphasize positive punishers and neglect the other elements of operant conditioning, cognitive learning, or behaviorism generally. Just as importantly, most of these theories emphasize early intervention, especially Bandura's. Modifying adult behavior through behaviorist principles may be a difficult task.

Correctional Practices   The constructs of behaviorists play a major role in programs of inmate change and institutional control. Juvenile justice specialists have long used CBT (Bartol 1991:366). **Reality therapy (RT)** is a form of self-control therapy posited by the correctional psychiatrist William Glasser (1975), who stated that offenders must take responsibility for their own behavior. From this perspective, crime is viewed as irrational, rather than the result of a mental disease or disorder. Many mental problems, Glasser argued, are symptomatic illnesses that have no presently known medical cause. They act as companions for the lonely people who *choose* them from a lifetime of experiences residing in the unconscious. The RT practitioner proposes first substituting the term *irresponsible* for mental health labels (e.g., *neurotic, personality disorder,* or *psychotic*). A "healthy" person is called *responsible,* and the task of the therapist is to help an irresponsible person to become responsible. Glasser (1980:48) saw RT as "based upon the theory that all of us are born with at least two built-in psychological needs: (1) the need to belong and be loved, and (2) the need for gaining self-worth and recognition."

RT is widely accepted and applied in corrections. The therapy flows easily from the need to hold the offender accountable for his or her behavior. Some critics maintain that RT's emphasis on values coincides with the traditionally paternalistic and perhaps authoritarian attitudes of correctional workers (Bersani 1989).

Although Glasser did not deal with theory, and RT is practice-oriented, its theoretical underpinnings are quite close to those of behavior modification. Instead of manipulating the environment or using tangible reinforcers, the therapist develops a close relationship with the client and uses praise or concern as the positive and negative reinforcers. For this method to be carried out effectively, the practitioner needs to be a genuinely warm and sympathetic person, able to relate to offenders who may have committed very unpleasant acts and whose personalities may leave a great deal to be desired.

Behavior modification is also important to prison administrators. For example, the punishments most often used in prison are (1) loss of privileges (e.g., commissary privileges, use of recreational facilities, and visitations by family and friends), (2) loss of good time (i.e., time off one's sentence due to good behavior in prison), and (3) confinement in punitive segregation (i.e., solitary confinement) (Clear and Cole 1986:362). Two of these punishments are not, strictly speaking, positive punishments, but rather negative punishments that are withdrawn only if bad behavior replaces good behavior. Punitive segregation is clearly a positive punishment.

Some prison programs directly integrate behavior modification principles in unique ways. In a procedure that sounds like it might have been dreamed up by *A Clockwork Orange*'s Anthony Burgess, some inmates have been "deconditioned" from inappropriate behavior by involuntary injections of a vomit-inducing drug. This specific treatment—unless (1) it is voluntary, (2) a physician administers the drug, and (3) a staff member witnesses the rule-violating behavior—has been ruled cruel and unusual punishment (Wexler 1975).

Constitutional questions are not germane to token economies, programs in which inmates earn privileges and even experience certain living-arrangement inducements (Wexler 1975). For example, during the 1970s, inmates in one multitiered building at Louisiana's Angola State Prison started prison life on a tier with only the most basic human needs (i.e., shelter, clothing, food, and security). Inmates displaying good behavior "graduated" to surroundings that were far more comfortable.

Community-based programs play an important role in the corrections process (Mays and Winfree 2009), and psychogenic theories are no less important in these settings. Treatment specialists use behavior modification to treat criminals in semisecure residential treatment settings located between the prison environment and the "free" world, as well as those who remain at large, outside the nation's prisons and jails. For example, probation—the conditional release from a judicial authority (court system)—and parole—the conditional release from an executive authority (prison system)—both employ key elements of operant conditioning to control participants (Abadinsky 2009; Mays and Winfree 2009). Such conditions include the following:

- Those offenders who follow the written conditions of their release remain in the community, but violating the rules can mean immediate confinement (negative reinforcer, positive punisher).

- At the beginning of supervised release, clients may have to report in person on a weekly basis. With good behavior, reporting periods become less frequent and may be accomplished by letter or phone (positive reinforcer).

- If the person being supervised is a drug-involved offender, probation/parole supervisors may use routine and random drug testing. Positive outcomes could result in weekends in jail, loss of certain privileges, or confinement for the duration of the original sentence (negative reinforcers, positive punishers).

- The release conditions generally include restrictions on (1) movement, such as leaving the supervision area to take a vacation, visit a friend or relative, or move to a new residence; (2) specific activities that require licensing, such as driving a car, getting married, or going hunting or fishing; (3) rights of assembly, such as getting together with friends who are also convicted felons; and (4) various other behaviors, including but not limited to owning or possessing a firearm and voting. The inclusion of any given conditions constitutes a positive punisher, and their exclusion—or later restoration for good behavior—serves as a positive reinforcer.

Intermediate sanctions may also modify behavior. Offenders under home detention/house arrest stay in their homes except when they are working or shopping for necessities (Ball, Huff, and Lilly 1988). Often, these programs are combined with electronic monitoring systems, allowing "community control officers" to oversee offenders with increasingly sophisticated technology. In the absence of electronic monitoring, officers might make unannounced visits to the detainee's home (Flynn 1986). The underlying idea is that the prospect of losing one's freedom and the threat of incarceration control and modify law-violating behavior. Despite the lack of definitive studies about program success, correctional experts remain optimistic that home confinement and electronic monitoring programs serve the interests of society (McShane and Krause 1993:115–148).

SUMMARY

Psychological factors play important roles in creating and maintaining criminal tendencies and in changing criminals as well. This statement may seem self-evident, although demonstrating which factors work to bring about prosocial change—and exactly how they work—has proven difficult. In the previous chapter, abnormal personality development, along with the role of the unconscious, provided answers to key questions about who was likely to offend and why. The theories in this chapter shifted the focus to forces that all of us face: questions of intellect, how to measure it and what it means, and the psychological process of learning, with the specific subject—whether it's mathematics or criminal violence—being irrelevant.

Criminologists continue to include IQ test results—with their putative although poorly understood ties to criminality—in their studies of crime and delinquency well into the twenty-first century (Farrington 2005). The IQ test has found favor and disfavor among correctional practitioners as a means of determining an offender's suitability for certain treatment or ruling it out entirely. Behaviorism, too, has assumed high visibility within the criminal justice system, especially in terms of correctional practices. The cognitive and behavioral modeling theorists suggest specific ways in which humans make decisions, as well as factors that may influence or disrupt the decision-making processes (Timmerman and Emmelkamp 2005). However, it is unclear whether some people are more susceptible to the cues and processes than others, and if they are, why this is the case. Nonetheless, the proponents of other theoretical perspectives on crime rarely match the behaviorists' contributions to specific correctional practices.

T A B L E 5.1   Psychological Learning and Developmental Theories

Theory	Major Figures	Central Assumptions	Causal Arguments (*Key Terms*)	Strengths	Weaknesses
Feeblemindedness thesis	Dugdale, Goddard	Mental functioning is inherited and weak minds run in certain families.	Low-functioning individuals (i.e., the feebleminded) seek out crime to compensate for an inability to gain money through honest labor.	Explains why whole families seem to turn to crime as vocation.	May have fabricated studies; is an overly simplistic representation of the role of intelligence in daily life.
IQ–crime hypotheses	Jensen, Herrnstein, Hirschi, Hindelang, and Wilson	IQ tests measure innate intelligence, which is human destiny's major delimiter.	Criminals have lower IQ scores than non-criminals; three crime links exist: (1) IQ predicts criminality; (2) the IQ–crime link is an artifact of other forces such as SES; and (3) IQ affects performance at school, which is related to delinquency and, later, crime.	Reports some version of IQ–crime links; gives policy makers something to respond to (i.e., IQ score is an overt indicator of innate criminogenic tendencies; enables society to then classify and categorize people by IQ scores).	The validity of IQ tests remains highly questionable; the wide range of tests makes meaningful comparisons difficult; there are few studies of serious offenders who have no formal criminal justice system contacts; largely ignores social factors as causes of criminality.
Behaviorism and learning theories	Pavlov, Watson, Skinner, Rotter, Bandura, Eysenck	All forms of behavior are learned in response to certain stimuli; in order to change behavior, change stimuli; Eysenck's theory views crime-proneness as the product of conditioning/learned habits multiplied by personality type intensifiers (e.g., *neurotic extraverts* and *psychotic extraverts*).	Children learn, by rewards and punishments, to repeat some behaviors and avoid others (*conditioned response*); an inner "policeman" controls atavistic leanings.	Appeals to those who hold that punishments and rewards should shape behavior (see also the discussion of deterrence theory in Chapters 1 and 2); Eysenck's theory was specifically created as a psychological crime theory.	Receives little empirical support outside of animal experiments; human behavior—especially crime—is complex and hard to fit in classic behaviorist models; tests of Eysenck's theory failed to include adequate control groups.

KEY TERMS

ability (g)

behavior modification

behaviorism

catharsis effect

classical conditioning

cognitive behavior theory

cognitive behavioral therapy (CBT)

criminal personality theory

dangerousness

expectancy theory

extraversion

feeblemindedness

IQ

learning theory

modeling

mental degeneracy

negative reinforcer

neurotic extraverts

neuroticism

observational learning

operant conditioning

penal harm movement

positive reinforcer

practical intelligence

psychometric intelligence (PI)

psychotics

psychotic extraverts

psychoticism

reality therapy (RT)

reinforcement

responsivity principle

token economies

CRITICAL REVIEW QUESTIONS

1. How might low intelligence, including feeblemindedness, influence criminal behavior? Why is this linkage a poor theoretical explanation?

2. Discuss the ties between early IQ testing and the bio-anthropological theories of the late nineteenth and early twentieth centuries?

3. Why is any sample of prison inmates likely to be skewed in favor of the less intelligent? Can you think of a way to create a definitive link between intelligence and crime?

4. Do you believe that we should treat law violators with very low IQs differently from those who fully appreciate the nature of their illegal acts? Why or why not?

5. How does behaviorism explain criminal behavior? What criticisms most damage behaviorism's ties to crime and delinquency? How do they do the most damage?

6. What specific part or element of behaviorism is its strongest contribution to crime theory? What is its weakest part or element?

7. Which of the policies reviewed in this chapter do you think poses the greatest threat to democratic ideals?

8. Which of the policies reviewed in this chapter do you think holds the greatest promise for reducing crime?

9. You have been asked by your employer, the Division of Youth Services (or the equivalent agency in your state that develops statewide policy

for children, youths, and families), to prepare a proposal to fund early-intervention programs for at-risk families and their children. What do you include as theoretical and empirical support?

10. Over the past 100 years, many academics and other scholars have lent their time, talents, and reputations to testing theories that are of questionable scientific value. How would you respond to someone who said that this was a perversion of the goals of science? (NOTE: Keep your answer to this question and reexamine it after reading Chapter 11.)

NOTES

1. We could easily have included intelligence in Chapter 3, as some claim that it is a biologically determined human factor (see, e.g., Akers and Sellers 2009:55–7). However, as currently measured, intelligence (i.e., IQ) is a psychological construction, and as it is used today, it has both psychological and sociological implications. Hence, we feel that it better fits in this chapter.

2. Psychometrics, or mental measurements, is an important and useful tool for mental health professionals and psychologists, who prefer the term **psychometric intelligence (PI)** or even the term g, the term for intellectual ability discussed in Chapter 4, to IQ. In the interests of clarity and continuity with the literature, we employ the latter term.

3. Support of eugenics and similar practices by scientific researchers, academicians, and scholars did not end in the 1920s, 1930s, or even the 1940s. Questionable scholarship, including the work of Herrnstein and Wilson, reviewed in this chapter and in Chapter 11, continues to find its way into criminological debates on biological and psychological origins of criminality. One resource in this debate is the Institute for the Study of Academic Racism at Ferris State University, which maintains a website on the topic at http://www.ferris.edu/HTMLS/staff/webpages/site.cfm?LinkID=249&eventID=34

4. Porteus is something of a controversial figure in psychology, much in the same way as is Goddard. Porteus studied cognition and intelligence in aboriginal populations, especially in Hawaii. Many of his conclusions, reached over a career that spanned decades after he left Vineland, supported apartheid and segregation. For more information on Porteus, consult the website of Ferris State University's Institute for the Study of Academic Racism.

5. We recognize that not all nations consider suicide to be a crime. However, suicide is, in the Western European context of suicidology, much like homicide: The definitions of both are relatively similar legally and socially.

6. Mental health treatment and the use of psychotropic drugs are only proxy measures for mental retardation and other psychological disabilities among inmates; however, in 2000, 1 in 8 state prisoners received mental health therapy or counseling, and nearly 1 in 10 received antidepressants, stimulants, sedatives, tranquilizers, or other antipsychotic drugs (Beck and Maruschak 2001:1).

7. We based much of the following discussion on Rilling (2000).

8.   Not all psychologists see behaviorism, especially Watson's version, in a positive light. John Mills (1998) suggested that it is an ideology of science without much vision (see also Mos 1999; Smith 2001). He saw evidence of this shift in the resistance of 1960s neobehaviorism to speculation about the perspective's pragmatism and concern with prediction. For more on these ideas as applied to theory and crime, see either Chapter 1 or Chapter 10.

9.   Bandura's contribution is also called social learning theory; however, we reserve the use of this term for Akers' social learning theory.

6

Social Organizational Theories

CHAPTER OVERVIEW

CRIME AND SOCIAL ECOLOGY

Social Disorganization Theory and Crime

The Legacy of Social Disorganization Theory

Assessing Ecological Theories

Ecology, Public Policy, and Criminal Justice Practices

CRIME AND SOCIAL STRUCTURE

Structural Functionalism, Anomie, and Crime

Anomie Theory Rediscovered

Assessing Strain Theory

Social Structure, Public Policy, and Criminal Justice Practices

CRIME AND SUBCULTURES

Delinquent Subculture Theories

Subcultural Delinquency Theories

Assessing Subcultural Theories

Subcultures, Public Policy, and Criminal Justice Practices

LEARNING OBJECTIVES

In this chapter, you will learn the following:

- The social-ecological roots of social disorganization, an outlook on criminality with practical implications.

- That society's formal structure—its roles and statuses—provides unique insights into all behavior, including crime and deviance.

- The two distinct ways used by criminologists to understand the crime and delinquency of groups called subcultures.

- That in the twentieth century, macro-sociological theories shaped local and national policies, and these ideas still intrigue criminologists and policy makers.

INTRODUCTION

One way to look at crime is to step back and see the "big picture." Crime becomes part of the big-picture, a **macro-sociological** orientation in which society and social processes hold the key to understanding criminality. That is, if we wish to understand crime, we must know society's role in shaping its members, only some of whom are criminals. Society is not "blamed" for crime—crime emerges from the social cauldron.

This chapter addresses three sociological theories. *Social ecology* uses the ecological model as a social prism through which to view a city's crime patterns. In this context, sociologists study all of the interrelated social and physical elements of the immediate community in which crime is an endemic problem. Crime is thus a social phenomenon that exists apart from the people who presently reside in the community and continues long after they are gone and replaced. *Structural functionalism* stresses that every element in society is either part of the solution or part of the problem. When social conditions change dramatically, crime and other forms of social disorder can be the result. Emergent groups within society are at the core of the third orientation, in which two views dominate. First, *delinquent subculture* theorists suggest that the misbehavior exhibited by a subordinate group comes from friction between that group's values and those of the dominant culture. Second, *subcultural delinquency* theorists do not limit their scope to subordinates, but rather look at how both subordinates and superordinates take the dominant culture's values and push them to the extreme, creating group-specific values that are both exciting and threatening, and often illegal.

We begin our exploration of sociological explanations with the ecological approach of the Chicago School, which helped found American criminology.

CRIME AND SOCIAL ECOLOGY

- Are there identifiable ethnic or racial neighborhoods in your community? Are they low- or high-crime areas? Do you believe there is a relationship between the qualities of these neighborhoods and crime? What are these qualities?

- Have you noticed homes and businesses in your community with barred windows or other security devices? Do you encounter buildings that have guarded entrances, speed bumps, curvy streets, or small green areas instead of large open parks? Each of these anticrime techniques has its roots in an ecological perspective on crime.

- Have the police in your community adopted a high profile in certain neighborhoods? Although this approach to policing comes from several sources, one in particular exhibits strong ties to the material in this chapter.

Early in the twentieth century, Robert Park proposed a parallel between human societies and the plant and animal kingdoms, one that reflects principles of ecology. **Ecology** is the branch of biology that studies the relationships between organisms and their environment. To understand plant or animal life, one must master plant or animal ecology. Similarly, to achieve insights into human life, one must focus on human ecology.

Using the multicultural and racially diverse city of Chicago as a social laboratory, Park and his colleagues at the University of Chicago saw "natural areas" where vastly different types of people lived. Robert Burgess, Park's colleague, divided the city into five **concentric zones,** differentiating each zone according to land use, population types, and other physical, economic, and social characteristics. Burgess referred to the central business district as Zone 1. Surrounding the industrial and business base was Zone II, the zone in transition. Burgess described it as an **interstitial zone,** a slum area with high levels of social deterioration; for most urban immigrants Zone II was their first home. Moving outward, the next area was Zone III, home to the city's working class, where living costs were higher and housing was better. Two characteristics distinguished Zone IV residents from those in Zone III: even higher incomes and smaller families. Arrival in Zone V, also called the commuter's zone, signified economic prosperity and stability.

Eventually the inner-city community ceased to function as an effective social control agent, while the interstitial zone exhibited few characteristics of a neighborhood and had little social cohesion. These inner-city zones had high concentrations of social ills (e.g., crime, poverty, illiteracy, mental illness, and alcoholism). They also had the highest levels of what Park and Burgess called **social disorganization,** which is "any disturbance, disruption, conflict, or lack of consensus within a social group or given society which affects established social habits of behavior, social institutions, or social controls so as to make relatively harmonious functioning impossible without some significant intermediate adjustments" (Elliott 1967:280–81).

Social Disorganization Theory and Crime

Clifford Shaw and Henry McKay used social ecology to study the geographic distribution of crime and delinquency in Chicago. They equated social disorganization with weak community controls, which led to geographic areas with high levels of law-violating behavior. They did not view people as inherently bad; rather, the problem was the area. Once a high crime rate became established, no matter who lived in these areas, the rate remained high. It was as if a crime pathogen had infected the very soil of the community, as one generation of residents passed along a tradition of deviance to successive generations. What they found were not high-delinquency *groups,* but rather high-delinquency *areas.*

To prove their claim, Shaw and McKay collected massive amounts of quantitative data on delinquency. They studied court actions, arrest statistics, and commitment rates, which they overlaid on city maps. **The Chicago School** (as this group was known) complemented these quantitative studies, including *Juvenile Delinquency and Urban Areas* (1942), with first-person accounts of criminal careers, such as *The Jackroller* (1930) and *Brothers in Crime* (1938). This approach, especially the first-person accounts, became a significant part of the Chicago

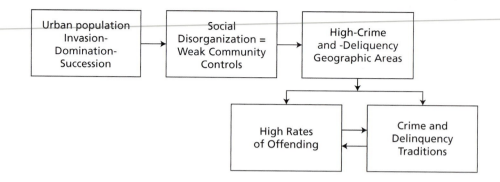

F I G U R E 6.1 Shaw and McKay's Social Disorganization Theory

tradition. Autobiographies, or life histories, allowed the juveniles to tell their "own story" as a part of a total case history. The veracity of the life histories was never at issue. As Shaw (1930:3) observed, "Rationalizations, fabrications, prejudices, exaggerations are quite as valuable as objective descriptions, provided, of course, that these reactions be properly identified."

The Chicagoans painted a picture of chronic social disorganization. Whether looking at arrests, commitments, or court processing, they noted that, as the distance from the Chicago Loop—the **zone of transition**—increased, the rates decreased (Shaw and McKay 1942). Shaw reported that the community of the "brothers in crime" was neither unique nor unusual. He described it as just another part of the physical deterioration that characterized the entire area, including the high level of truancy, delinquency, and crime. Figure 6.1 summarizes social disorganization theory.

The Legacy of Social Disorganization Theory

The University of Chicago's social ecologists had several long-lasting effects. First, their efforts generated richly descriptive ideas for later generations of criminologists. Second, an entire approach to crime reduction, called environmental criminology, owes a major intellectual debt to social ecology. Finally, during the 1980s, criminologists rediscovered social disorganization theory and placed it in a more contemporary community context.

From One Generation to the Next: The Cultural Transmission Thesis   Three findings reported by Shaw and McKay set the stage for later **cultural transmission theories.** First, Shaw and McKay (1972:174) described socially disorganized neighborhoods as brimming with attitudes and values conducive to delinquency and crime, particularly organized crime, which provided pathways to adult crime:

> The presence of a large number of adult criminals in certain areas
> means that children there are in contact with crime as a career and
> with the criminal way of life, symbolized by organized crime. . . . The

heavy concentration of delinquency in certain areas means that boys living in these areas are in contact not only with individuals who engage in proscribed activity but also with groups which sanction such behavior and exert pressure upon their members to conform to group standards.

Second, they observed that one generation passed on their attitudes, values, and crime techniques to the next. Trapped in their neighborhoods, children saw not only the delinquency present in similarly aged youths but also the actions of older offenders. As Shaw and McKay (1972:174) stated, "This contact means that the traditions of delinquency can be and are transmitted down through successive generations of boys, in much the same way that language and other social forms are transmitted." Shaw and McKay suggested that conflict was inevitable in this mix of cultures that characterized the city of Chicago. The values of the larger, more conventional society may have held little meaning for the youthful residents of these inner-city areas.

Third, Shaw and McKay (1972:172) viewed the community as a source of many conflicting messages: Children should obey laws, even if their parents and other adults do not; crime does not pay, but sometimes it does; people should obey the law, unless it runs counter to what their local neighborhood expects of them. How could society expect youths living in these environs to be anything but confused? This was the position of the Chicagoans and later generations of cultural transmission theorists.

Environmental Criminology   Beginning in the 1960s, environmentalists connected crime to land use. Jane Jacobs (1961) theorized about the connection between the use of residential and commercial land. In analyzing the quality of interactions along residential streets, she noted that interaction increased surveillance, which, in turn, increased safety and reduced crime. The diversity of land use, especially the establishment of commercial use close to residential use, was the key to safety and low crime levels. When property owners used their land strictly for commercial purposes, they essentially abandoned their property for long periods, creating opportunities for crime.

Throughout the 1960s, researchers conducted a series of architectural design studies in public housing projects. They looked for a relationship between residential social interaction and levels of self-policing, but their findings were inconclusive (Leudtke and Lystad 1970; Rainwater 1966; Wood 1961). However, these early studies lacked a conceptual base upon which to build an ecological theory of crime and space.

Oscar Newman (1972) provided key concepts in *Defensible Space,* including the four elements of **defensible space.** First, **territoriality** means that one's home is sacred. Second, **natural surveillance** links the physical part of an area to the residents' ability to view the area. Third, **image** refers to the capacity of the physical design to impart a sense of security for residents and potential "invaders." Finally, **milieu** addresses other features that might influence security, such as the proximity of a park or shopping mall (Newman 1972:50; see also

Davidson 1981; Greenberg and Rohe 1984). The physical design of an area enhances or inhibits the inhabitants' feelings of control and sense of responsibility.

C. Ray Jeffery, in *Crime Prevention through Environment Design* (1971), expressed the idea that a three-part strategy could prevent crime. First, he believed that physical design could make an area more defensible. Second, he emphasized the importance of higher levels of citizen involvement in preventing crime. Finally, he advocated for a more effective criminal justice system. Jeffery saw heightened police effectiveness in detecting and arresting criminals as essential, and suggested that more efficient court and correctional systems would buttress the work of the police and complete the punishment cycle. Figure 6.2 summarizes Newman's and Jeffery's models.

Redefined Social Disorganization Theory   During the 1980s, social disorganization proponents redefined its conceptual base. For example, Robert Sampson and W. Byron Groves (1989) developed a community-level version. Besides economic status, ethnic heterogeneity, residential mobility, family disruption, and urbanization, they tied community social disorganization to the strength of social network systems in those communities. These systems include *informal controls* (e.g., friendship ties), *formal controls* (e.g., participation in religious or civic groups), and the *collective supervision* related to troublesome local concerns (e.g., youth groups). In sum, neighborhoods that "have their act together" have less crime. Figure 6.3 contains a schematic representation of this theory.

Sampson and Groves (1989) tested their ideas using crime surveys from the United Kingdom. They found that communities in Great Britain with few friendship networks, unsupervised teenage groups, and low organizational participation

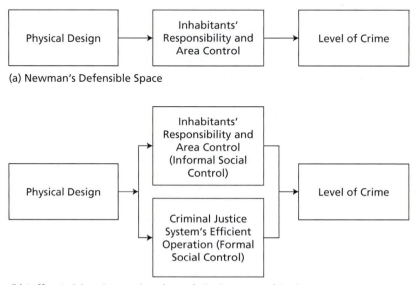

(a) Newman's Defensible Space

(b) Jeffery's Crime Prevention through Environmental Design

F I G U R E 6.2 Environmental Criminology

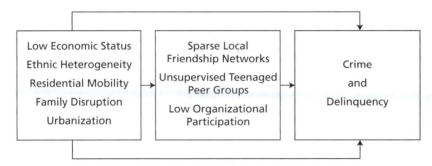

FIGURE 6.3 Causal Model of an Extended Version of Shaw and McKay's Theory of Community Systemic Structure and Rates of Crime and Delinquency

had disproportionately high crime and delinquency rates. Sampson and Groves (1989:799) demonstrated the social disorganization's "vitality and renewed relevance" as a macro-level crime theory.

Assessing Ecological Theories

Three measurement problems plagued early statements of social disorganization theory. First, later generations of criminologists dismissed the theory as a *tautology,* since Shaw and McKay's model had few independent measures of social disorganization. If an area was crime-ridden, this alone was evidence of a lack of social controls and social disorganization; socially disorganized areas were crime-ridden. Robert Bursik (1988) wondered, given its natural tautological tendency, how we could measure social disorganization. Social scientists now use a different definition: *Social disorganization* is "the capacity of a neighborhood to regulate itself through formal and informal processes of social control" (Bursik 1988:527; Sampson and Groves 1989).

Second, critics noted the presence of the **ecological fallacy,** which involves making inappropriate *individual*-level inferences from *group*-level data. For example, suppose we find that for 200 communities the extent of participation in civic organizations relates to the level of reported crime. We may commit the ecological fallacy if we state that a given community has a greater likelihood of high crime because rates of participation in civic organizations are low or that increasing participation rates can reduce crime. What is true for the group may not be true for the individual.

Third, obtaining, compiling, and analyzing the macro-level information needed to test social disorganization theory is a difficult undertaking. The findings from smaller-scale studies, often including only a few neighborhoods, support Shaw and McKay's predictions (Bursik 1988:532). However, questions remain about the validity and reliability of available crime statistics. Even in the 1930s criminologists questioned official statistics (Robison 1936). Criminologists have long argued that reliance on official data is a bad practice because the police and courts may have community-specific biases. We do not know the extent to

COMMENTS AND CRITICISMS: Does It Matter Who Provides the Guardianship?

In the Italian section of New York's Greenwich Village, for example, "street corner boys" enforced the social order, making the streets safe. The formidable reputation of the neighborhood's late 20th century organized crime figures backed their self-appointed role. In one Brooklyn neighborhood, a stronghold of the Lucchese crime family, informal social control, devoid of the restraints of due process, provided a form of justice that was swift and final: On a dark night, the young man following her did not realize that he was being watched. Several large men foiled his attempt at a knifepoint robbery by quickly carrying him up the stairs. An observer recalls: "I could make out the small roof wall on the front of the building—it was made of brick—and then I saw the guy launched right over it into the air. He hung there for just a second, flailing arms like a broken helicopter, and then he came down hard and splattered all over the street" (Pileggi, p. 40). As ex-FBI agent Joe Pistone notes: "Neighborhoods that are dominated by wiseguys are considered to be under the protection of these wiseguys. There are far fewer robberies, rapes, or muggings in wiseguy neighborhoods than even the safest precincts of the city" (p. 76). Moreover, that would extend to some Chicago suburbs, where selling drugs resulted in mutilated corpses. Despite their effectiveness, no one has seriously suggested we turn over neighborhood crime control to the organized crime families or the Hell's Angels, but in Japan, a *quid quo pro* policy leaves effective control over street crime in entertainment areas to organized crime, the ferocious *yakuza*.

SOURCES: Abadinsky (2010); Pileggi (1990); Pistone (2004); Tricarico (1984).

which neighborhood crime and delinquency rates are artifacts of local decision making. For example, one consequence of placing more police in a neighborhood may be more arrests and, therefore, a higher reported crime rate.

Exploring Defensible Space   Measurement of defensible space created a methodological problem for researchers. Early studies, which did not include residents' attitudes and behavior, concluded that crime varied with environmental design. How they measured design—as a general location, a street, or even the neighborhood level—was irrelevant (Bevis and Nuttler 1977; Greenberg, Rohe, and Williams 1982). A later study found that "physical, social, and attitudinal (territorial) variables as *relevant to crime and fear at the level of the street block*" (Taylor, Gottfredson, and Brower 1984; emphasis added). Contrary to what Newman believed, then, we cannot rely upon physical factors alone to preserve the local order and promote feelings of security. Territoriality tends to provide more insights into crime and fear than does defensible space features (Taylor, Gottfredson, and Brower 1984; see also Taylor and Gottfredson 1986).

Gerald Suttles (1968) used territoriality to study "defended neighborhoods" as recognized ecological niches in which inhabitants form cohesive groups and seal themselves off through the efforts of delinquent gangs, restrictive covenants, and a forbidding reputation. A reputation for territoriality, and not necessarily the neighborhood's physical qualities, provided effective crime control, a point amplified by the following box.

Macro–Level Studies of Social Disorganization Principles   Social disorganization has figured prominently in several innovative studies. For example, Darrell Steffensmeier and Dana Haynie (2000) looked at gender differences in crime rates by applying a structural disadvantage model that included gender-specific poverty measures, income inequality, female-headed households, percentage black, and joblessness as social structural elements of status and class. They examined intercity variations in the 1990 rates for 178 cities.[1] The patterns they found were essentially the same for men and women: the greater the disadvantages, the higher the rates of offending.[2] Conventional wisdom, admittedly often wrong, would expect that those with less have a greater incentive for remunerative criminal behavior.

Paul Bellair (1997) explored serious crime rates in 60 urban neighborhoods, examining the level and type of social interaction found in each neighborhood. He reports that neighbors' getting together once a year or more had the strongest positive impact on burglary, motor vehicle theft, and robbery rates. This finding suggests that residents' general willingness to provide supervision and guardianship in the neighborhood is important: know your neighbors.

Wayne Welsh and his associates (1999, 2000) investigated disorder in Philadelphia's middle schools. Their study included community-related predictors such as poverty, residential stability, and community crime. The researchers looked for both within-group and between-group differences in violence and its precursors. Welsh and associates (1999:106) conclude that "the thesis 'bad' kids or 'bad' neighborhoods directly import violence into any school is unsupported by our results." They also report that "the effects of community variables on school disorder were strongly mediated by school stability, illustrating that analyses of institutional processes have much to add to the explanation of school disorder" (Welsh, Stokes, and Green 2000:243).

Ruth Peterson and associates (2000) explored whether local institutions influence crime rates in disadvantaged neighborhoods in Columbus, Ohio. The researchers included such stabilizing factors as libraries, recreational facilities, and retail businesses, and a single destabilizing one—bars; they looked for each in every census tract. They found that only recreational facilities had a stabilizing influence on violent crime rates. They also reported that the impact of economic deprivation and residential instability on violent crime did not depend on the institutional structures. Local institutions may be ameliorative, but they proved ineffective in countering the macro-structural factors that generated economic deprivation and subsequent crime.

Finally, after reexamining Sampson and Groves' data, Bonita Veysey and Steven Messner (1999) failed to find the same level of support for social disorganization theory, particularly the observation that social disorganization is a single construct. Much of what Sampson and Groves reported came from a single piece of information: community perception of unsupervised teens. Veysey and Messner (1999:171) concluded that the supporters of social disorganization theory overstated their claims. They nonetheless concurred with Sampson and Groves' final observations about the "vitality and renewed relevance" of social disorganization theory for criminology, particularly its focus on processes that influence macro-level variations in crime. Clearly, the final word on social disorganization theory's utility has not yet been written.

Ecology, Public Policy, and Criminal Justice Practices

If community disorganization causes crime and delinquency, perhaps communities should strengthen local social control mechanisms. In the 1930s, Shaw initiated the Chicago Area Project (CAP) to encourage grassroots organizing against crime. Local community leaders provided recreational opportunities. CAP workers improved the area's physical appearance by removing trash and cleaning property, and they mediated among the courts, schools, and communities to reduce conflict and incarceration. They also promoted conventional behavior, particularly among young people.

As urban architects plan new areas of expanding cities, they may wish to apply defensible-space concepts. For example, increased mobility in and around modern cities has long been associated with increased crime (Walker 1983:13–14). Restricting vehicular traffic by limiting access to residential areas or controlling traffic flow in commercial areas could reduce the incidence of some forms of crime (Poyner 1983). Gated communities, in which guards allow only residents, guests, and service and delivery vehicles to enter, are also becoming increasingly common.

Creating defensible space is possible for existing neighborhoods as well. In the early 1990s, planners in Dayton, Ohio, invited Newman to create defensible space for Five Oaks, a neighborhood in decline. Newman designed a series of gated mini-neighborhoods, reasoning that smaller neighborhoods enhanced the sense of community and made anonymous crimes harder to commit. These changes decreased community traffic by 67 percent, and total crime declined by 26 percent, with violent crimes cut in half (Cose 1994:57).

Patricia and Paul Brantingham imported Crime Prevention through Environmental Design (CPTED) to Canada, where plans for new housing projects, businesses, and even schools in British Columbia conform to the principles of CPTED (Brantingham and Brantingham 1991, 1993). They recommended locating malls and schools far from each other to prevent school children from congregating during lunch hours and after school, high-prevalence times for vandalism and drug use. The popularity of the CPTED model has resulted in its application to a wide range of environmental settings, including event facilities, retail businesses, and playgrounds (Crowe 2000).

Law Enforcement Practices   Observations about **community malaise** and **disorder** have reshaped the police role in the community. In challenging the police to regain control of the nation's cities, neighborhood by neighborhood, James Q. Wilson and George Kelling (1982) made two key observations. Community disorder—including public drunkenness, vagrancy, suspicious persons, and youth gangs—creates a climate of fear. Crime and disorder also "are usually inextricably linked, in a kind of developmental sequence" (Wilson and Kelling 1982:30). The key is to understand the significance of the broken window. According to this metaphor first described in Chapter 1, if one window in a building is left broken, then soon all the windows will be broken; if a neighborhood is left unattended, then disorder will grow, and with it crime.[3] In other words, if the "quality of life crimes" are not aggressively policed, the net result will be higher rates of more serious crime.

The specific programs, sometimes called "Broken Windows Policing," that flowed from this idea, exhibited close kinship to ecological theories. For example, **community policing** is an approach to police work designed to bring officers and the community they serve into closer contact. Such programs have at least five goals: (1) Decrease fear of crime, (2) increase citizen satisfaction with the police, (3) develop programs that address the problems of a community's residents, (4) reduce social disorder at the neighborhood level by using the police as informal social control agents, and (5) reduce crime by addressing the first four goals (Riechers and Roberg 1990).

Community policing necessarily involves improvements in neighborhood ecology. The police help broker services that improve the appearance of, and thus the pride residents have in, a community. This includes better trash collection, removal of abandoned vehicles, and the boarding up and destruction of abandoned structures. An emphasis on policing street disorder—in the form of aggressive panhandlers and streetwalkers, and disorderly or intimidating youths—encourages residents to spend more time on the streets, thus raising natural surveillance levels. If residents believe the streets to be safer, they will become safer as more people interact with their neighbors.

Does it work? Community policing programs include foot patrols, "storefront" police stations, and problem-oriented policing of a single community-level problem such as drugs or prostitution (Bowers and Hirsch 1987; Eck and Spelman 1987; Hayeslip 1989; Moore and Trojanowicz 1988; Spelman and Eck 1987). These programs meet with generally positive results—an enhanced public perception of police, in particular.

Houston's community policing program is an interesting case in point. This early 1980s program included community police substations, a victim re-contact program, a community newsletter, a citizen contact patrol, and a community response team (Brown and Wycoff 1986; Skogan and Wycoff 1986). It had the most positive impact on those who already had favorable images of the police (i.e., whites, homeowners, and older people). One reason cited for the failure of the Houston experiment to lower crime was that the city had an "almost nonexistent neighborhood life" (Skogan 1990).

Correctional Practices   The environmental lesson that we can design crime in or out is applicable to prisons and jails as well. Two primary facility designs keep inmates (and staff) safe and secure (Mays and Winfree 2009:157–59). **Linear-design** facilities arrange individual cells or dormitories along hallways. However, these facilities, owing to their sterile and impersonal environment, are a major source of both physical and psychological stress (Mueller 1983). The environment they create bears a striking resemblance to the criminogenic areas described by environmental criminologists.[4] **Podular-design** facilities feature more open, self-contained environments, in which inmates reside in "pods" or small, self-contained housing units. In addition, a constant staff presence provides direct supervision of all inmates in each pod. Podular facilities, particularly those with direct supervision, report lower victimization rates and lower rates of vandalism to the facility (National Institute of Corrections 1983; Nelson 1988; Sigurdson 1985, 1987; Zupan 1991). Inmates and staff respond positively to the far less rigid and alienated environment of the podular design with direction supervision (Zupan and Menke 1988; Zupan and Stohr-Gillmore 1987). We can view prisons as micro-ecological systems in which the environmental criminologists' social forces are at work.

CRIME AND SOCIAL STRUCTURE

- Did you ever wonder why, during your grade school days, you pledged allegiance to the flag? Why does every nation believe it necessary to have a flag and a national anthem?

- What society-wide condition may confront both the victors and the vanquished after a war? Could these conditions apply equally to a suddenly prosperous society or one in an economic downturn?

- Are you pursuing the "American Dream"? What is that dream? Is it all about material things or consumer goods?

Beginning in the late nineteenth century, sociologists searched for answers to these questions. They explored the structure and functions of different parts of society. According to *structural functionalists,* society consists of various institutions, and groups that, owing to their constant contact with one another, shift, move, and alter their mutual influence. The result is a unified social system. Any given practice or tradition persists over time because it is functional—that is, it provides something beneficial to society; anything that threatens to destroy society is dysfunctional.

Structural Functionalism, Anomie, and Crime

Emile Durkheim (1858–1917) considered structural elements as central to any analysis of society and its ills. As a society moves from mechanical solidarity to organic solidarity, Durkheim (1961[1925]) claimed, unstable relationships evolve. **Mechanical solidarity** is a primitive stage of societal development in societies characterized by traditional family- or tribal-based social relationships, which also exhibit a strong **collective conscience,** or consensual ways in which the group views the social and physical world. **Organic solidarity** is common in more advanced industrial societies, which are characterized by a high degree of differentiation and specialization. An inverse relationship exists between the collective conscience and individualism: As one increases, the other declines. Societies with high levels of organic solidarity experience greater difficulties in socializing members, in promoting a feeling of "us." Therefore, social cohesiveness requires an external mechanism, the state with its active promotion of devotion to country—in place of family or tribe—through symbols such as flags, oaths, and anthems.

The Anomie Tradition and Deviant Behavior   Can a valued behavior such as ambition be the cause of crime? For Durkheim, the answer is yes: **unrestrained ambition**—individualism at its worst—causes deviance.[5] He saw the process by which ambition is set free in structural functionalist terms.[6] The collective conscience assists in governing a community's members. However, societal disturbances or transitions, even ones that seem beneficial, could upset the balance and alter or even diminish the collective conscience's ability to control social behavior (Durkheim 1951[1897]:252). The problem centers on disturbances in the collective order or **social equilibrium** that set people adrift; patterns are upset and people no longer have the comfort of knowing their place in society. When this happens, society cannot immediately improvise an acceptable new balance. It takes time for the collective conscience to reclassify people and things, to create a new social equilibrium. In the interim, unbridled individualism, absent social restraints on behavior, becomes the norm, as old values and norms become irrelevant.

Such disturbances are problematic, whether they are negative (e.g., an economic depression or failure in war) or positive (e.g., economic prosperity or success in war). Durkheim called the resulting societal condition **anomie,** meaning a relative absence or confusion of norms and rules. Given society-wide stresses, nothing in humankind's experience sets limits on the quantity of comforts craved. Excited appetites are freed of social constraints and threaten social stability.

For Durkheim, anomie explained deviance in times of war and rapid industrialization and urbanization. The breakdown in social controls throws many people's lives out of whack. The society devolves to a condition of "normlessness," or anomie, a feeling of being adrift without customary social guideposts or constraints on behavior. Readjustments eventually restore social controls and moderation; however, until that time, a lag occurs, during which society can expect high levels of deviance, including crime.

Strain Theory: The Americanization of Anomie   Robert K. Merton, who "Americanized" anomie in 1938, during the Great Depression, believed that "good" can cause "evil." In this case, unrestrained ambition was a prime cause of crime in the United States. Merton (1910–2003) argued that U.S. society considers economic success as a near absolute value; moreover, the resulting pressure to achieve success may eliminate effective social constraints on the means employed to this end. The "end-justifies-the-means" doctrine becomes a guiding tenet for action when cultural structure unduly exalts the end, and social organization unduly limits possible avenues to approved means.

Merton, who saw "American culture" as generally uniform throughout all classes, posited that a differential social structure is the source of the lower class's high crime rates. Social structure determines access to **legitimate opportunities** (i.e., acceptable means to achieve economic success): they are most available in the higher social classes and absent in the lower social classes. According to Merton's **ends–means schema,** anomie results when people confront the contradiction between culturally defined goals and societally restricted means. Normlessness arises out of the disjuncture or *strain* between goals and means—hence the name **strain theory.**

How do individuals respond to this **anomic trap**? Most simply "grin and bear it"—that is, they make the best of the situation and suffer in silence. These **conformists** accept both the goals (ends) and the means, and they strive to achieve success within the rules even if this necessarily limits their goals. Others become **ritualists,** rigidly adhering to and accepting their station in life. Three adaptations to anomie, however, have implications for criminology:

- **rebels** reject the goals and attempt to overthrow the existing social order and its cultural values, joining a revolutionary group or a countercultural commune, for example.

- **retreatists** abandon all attempts to reach conventional social goals in favor of a deviant adaptation (e.g., dropping out or abusing drugs).

- **innovators** use illegitimate, and sometimes illegal, means to gain societally defined success goals, because their experiences limit access to legitimate means.

For innovators, crime becomes a utilitarian adaptation to the anomic trap. Rebels, especially those who seek change by force, are also a threat to formal social control mechanisms. Retreatists can create difficulty for control agencies, ranging from police to social services. Dropping out of society may place them at odds with various codes and laws. For example, the homeless often do not send their children to school.

Differential Opportunity Theory   Richard A. Cloward (1926–2001) and Lloyd E. Ohlin (1918–2008) integrated Merton's strain theory with the Chicago School's ideas about the cultural transmission of criminality and Albert Cohen's work on negativistic subcultures.[7] Merton viewed lower-class youths as striving for monetary rewards, whereas Cohen saw them as conflicting with middle-class values. Cloward and Ohlin maintained that both money and status are important but that they operate independently of each other. Cloward and Ohlin (1960: 106–7) saw the dilemma of many lower-class people: they are unable to find alternative avenues to success goals: "Delinquent subcultures, we believe, represent specialized modes of adaptation to this problem of adjustment." Criminal and conflict subcultures provide illegal avenues to success, the former through illicit income, the latter through violence. Meanwhile, the retreatist "anticipates defeat and now seeks to escape from the burden of the future" (Cloward and Ohlin 1960:107). Crime is not an individual endeavor, but part of a collective adaptation.

Cloward and Ohlin (1960:145) pointed out that the societal distribution of illegitimate *and* legitimate means of success is not equal. Failing with legitimate opportunity structures, despondent youths cannot simply turn to a wellspring of **illegitimate opportunities.** For the average lower-class adolescent, a career in professional or organized crime can be as difficult to attain as a legitimate lucrative career.

Cloward and Ohlin understood that both system injustice and system blaming occur when youths perceive little opportunity for success, when they perceive a discrepancy between formal ideology—expectation of economic success—and unfair practices that deny them the ability to achieve this goal. The former may promise equality of access, while the latter reflects the realities of prejudice and discrimination. Some youths regard this blockage as an injustice. For differential opportunity proponents (Cloward and Ohlin 1960; see also Simons and Gray 1989), lower-status persons, *especially lower-class minorities,* are more likely to respond negatively to blocked opportunities, viewing them as part of a continuing pattern of exclusion.

Finally, Cloward and Ohlin described the **double failure,** the person who is unsuccessful in both legitimate and illegitimate pursuits—those individuals who populate and repopulate our prisons. They suggested that such people are "more vulnerable than others" to retreatism, including joining hedonistic, drug-using subcultures. Retreatism may also manifest itself in other ways. Failed criminals may unconsciously retreat to prisons because of their inability to succeed using either means. Periodically they emerge, fail, and then return to prison. Cloward and Ohlin (1960:184) recognized that some double failures adopt conventional lower-class lifestyles, becoming conformists. Figure 6.4 summarizes traditional anomie-based theories of crime.

Anomie Theory Rediscovered

In the late 1980s and early 1990s, the view that anomie theory was passé came under reconsideration. Recent restatements have taken several approaches.

General Strain Theory and Delinquency   In **general strain theory,** Robert Agnew (1985, 1992) redefined the goals of American youths to include short-term aspirations such as popularity with the opposite (or same) sex, good school grades, and athletic achievements; this helped to explain conditions of middle-class strain, as these goals may not be class-linked. For adults, the failure to achieve expected goals causes strain that, in some persons, leads to anger, resentment, and rage—emotional states that can lead to criminal behavior (Agnew 1992). Agnew suggested that social injustice or inequity might be at the root of strain; a sense of being treated unfairly—others are the source of adversity—and not simply an inability to reach goals, creates strain.

The difference between traditional strain theory and general strain theory is crucial to understanding Agnew's insight into the process. Traditional strain theory is like a person running *toward* something—in most cases, societally defined success goals, such as money, fame, cars, and jewelry. General strain theory, in contrast, suggests that some people are running *away from* something, such as undesired parental punishments or negative relationships at school. Thus, adolescents are *"pressured into delinquency by the negative affective states—most notably anger and related emotions—that often result from negative relationships"* (Agnew 1992:49; emphasis in original). The fact that Agnew has provided a social psychological explanation of the emotional condition most likely to precipitate delinquency resulting from general strains moves anomie theory further from both Durkheim's macro-level and Merton's mid-level explanations. Children clearly saw and felt general strains within their physical and social environment.

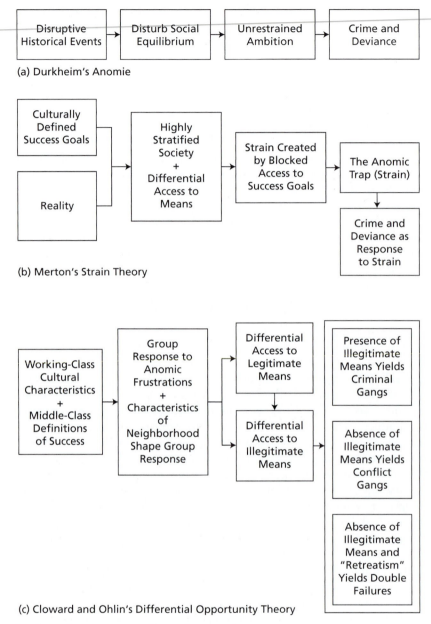

(a) Durkheim's Anomie

(b) Merton's Strain Theory

(c) Cloward and Ohlin's Differential Opportunity Theory

F I G U R E 6.4   Anomie-Based Theories of Crime

Agnew identified three major types of strain:

1. *Strain as the failure to achieve positively valued goals.* This form of failure includes a) strain as the disjunction between aspirations and expectations or actual achievements (rewards); b) strain as the disjunction between expectations and actual achievements; and c) strain as the disjunction between just or fair out–comes and actual outcomes.

2. *Strain as the removal of a positively valued stimuli from the individual.* This state occurs with the actual or anticipated loss of something valued (e.g., the loss of a close friend, death of a relative, or suspension from school, if school is valued.)

3. *Strain as the presentation of negative stimuli.* Delinquency may ensue when a youth attempts to avoid or escape negative stimuli, terminates or alleviates the source of the negative stimuli, or seeks revenge against the source.

In all cases, actual and anticipated strains may create a *predisposition* for delinquency or function as a *situational event* that instigates a particular delinquent act. These strains are, in Agnew's opinion, so strong that they mediate or condition the effects of other forces in a youth's life, such as societal labels and delinquent peers.

As youths attempt to avoid the problems created by the strain, four factors predispose them to delinquency (Agnew 1992:61). First, their normative coping strategies are at their absolute limit. Second, chronic strain lowers the threshold for tolerance of adversity, meaning that the youths are unable to deal with increasing levels of discomfort. Third, repeated or chronic strain may lead to a hostile attitude. Finally chronic strain increases the likelihood that the youths will be high in negative effect/arousal at any given time—that is, prone to fits of anger that focus the blame for bad outcomes on others. Figure 6.5 summarizes general strain theory.

Institutional Anomie Theory   The connections between anomie and crime are central to Steven Messner and Richard Rosenfeld's (1994) restatement of anomie theory. They described the "social reorganization" of American society as the **American Dream** in what we now call **institutional anomie theory.** This process would lead to a "mature society," one that maximizes the talents and capabilities of its citizens "on the basis of mutual support and collective obligations" (Messner and Rosenfeld 1994:111).

Like other social structural theories, institutional anomie theory contends that a community works best when all of the various institutions contribute equally to the welfare of its citizens. If one dominates, and Messner and Rosenfeld stated that

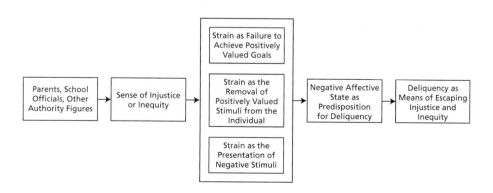

F I G U R E 6.5   Agnew's General Strain Theory

the economic sphere dominates American society, then the results are generally bad for some citizens. Crime devolves from this situation owing to four value orientations. First, the American dream's economic sphere emphasizes achievement, whereby citizens are valued in terms of what they have done and what material goods they have accumulated. Second, American society emphasizes that we must do it (i.e., achieve material success) on our own, rather than cooperate with others. Third, in spite of an emphasis on individualism, American society endorses universal normative expectations—we are all striving (albeit independently) toward the same goals. Lastly, American society has made money the "metric of success," creating a form of monetary fetishism (Messner and Rosenfeld 2001:63–64). The dominance of the economic institution has created a situation which, when combined with crime-endorsing cultural values, makes crime a natural product of a social system that is out of balance.

Messner and Rosenfeld proposed a two-step program for crime reduction through social reorganization. First, society must reform its social institutions. Crime reduction would be a logical consequence, claimed Messner and Rosenfeld (1994:103), of "policies and social changes that vitalize families, schools, and the political system, thereby enhancing the 'drawing power' of the distinctive goals associated with these institutions and strengthening their capacity to exercise social control." Second, they called for a redefinition of the American Dream to reduce the cultural pressures toward criminality and society's overemphasis on materialism. Concurrently, society must develop a greater sense of altruism so that other practices—parenting, teaching, and learning—become more highly valued and desired.

Messner and Rosenfeld urged that we must view the social role of parenting as an end unto itself. Pundits are quick to note that we require no license to have children and that children do not come with instructions. Perhaps, Messner and Rosenfeld suggested, public and private entities could fill this void, encouraging, placing greater value on, and rewarding quality parenting. Whose standards should apply? That is, who decides what skills and techniques are good or bad, positive or negative, constructive or destructive? In short, the enhancement of general parental management sounds intuitively appealing, but its accomplishment may be very difficult.

These revisions of anomie theory force us to go beyond the traditional views espoused by Durkheim, Merton, and Cloward and Ohlin. Agnew's proposal represents a partial recasting of strain theory in social psychological terms (i.e., reinforcements and punishments, aversive and rewarding conditions); consequently, a new theory emerges. Messner and Rosenfeld's suggest a restructuring of society's basic values and the adoption of a new belief orientation, resulting in a restatement of the classic American Dream.

Assessing Strain Theory

Durkheim's theory is rarely tested. Comparative criminologists have examined crime in developing nations, which experience social and normative changes, but they are more speculative than definitive, focusing on official data pertaining to crime, industrial development, and urbanization. Louise Shelley (1981) reviewed many comparative studies of the crime-and-modernization hypothesis. She found that the patterns of crime first observed in western European countries were occurring in the emerging nations of Asia, Latin America, and Africa, due in large measure to recent economic development.

Reconstituted anomie theory has given criminologists new insights into crime. Mitchell Chamlin and John Cochran (1995) explored Messner and Rosenfeld's idea that structural and cultural pressures to secure monetary rewards—amid weak controls from noneconomic social institutions—promote high levels of property crime. They studied the 1980 property crime (i.e., robberies, burglaries, larcenies, and auto thefts) rates for all states. They merged this information with state-level measures of noneconomic social institutions, such as divorce rates, voting behavior, and religious membership, and then measured economic deprivation as the percentage of families below the poverty level. Chamlin and Cochran found tentative support for institutional anomie theory, since the relationship between economic and other social institutions determined the level of anomie, and subsequently the level of property crime.

Two final studies addressed the quest for monetary status. Robert Agnew and associates (1996) focused on dissatisfaction or frustration with achieved monetary success. Using a sample of adults living in a single city, they explored several strain determinants, including the importance of monetary success, social class position, expectations for future monetary success, and comparisons with the success of others. The level of monetary dissatisfaction should have predicted incoming-generating crime, and this is precisely what they found. As the researchers observed, their study suggested a new direction for anomie studies: the individual's level of anger/frustration or dissatisfaction.

Steven Cernkovich and associates (2000:135) surveyed a group of 12- to 19-year-old youths living in Ohio in 1982 and resurveyed them again in 1992. Part of the 1982 sample resided in juvenile correctional facilities. The researchers explored both success goal orientation, as a measure of the American Dream, and economic satisfaction. Although blacks appeared to "buy into" the American Dream, their self-reported offending rates were not related to either materialism or career importance. Overall, the strain measures revealed far more about white than black offending. Cernkovich and associates (2000) provided a series of possible explanations: the lack of candor by blacks, the high levels of frustration felt by whites at failure, the lower expectations of blacks, and a more well-developed repertoire of survival strategies for blacks. The relative power of strain theory to explain norm-violating behavior among whites but not blacks led the researchers to argue for more research into this disparity.

The evidence tends to provide conditional support for the idea of strain, but most of it points to the revised rather than traditional versions of the concept (Lanier and Henry 1998:222). As a rule, most critics of strain theory focus on the following shortcomings:[8]

- *Deviance is a relative concept.* Merton's emphasis on the importance of economic success is misplaced. Coming to Merton's defense, Messner and

Rosenfeld (1994:60) contended that critics offered only a caricature of his work. However, they overlooked Merton's own statement that it would be "fanciful to assert that accumulated wealth alone stands as a symbol of success" (Merton 1968:190). Discounting the importance of economic success in relation to individual behavior in modern America would also be wrong. Alternatively, as a street philosopher might assert: "Money is important only when you don't have enough."

- *Class-biased.* Anomie assumes that crime is disproportionately more common in the lower socioeconomic classes, where gaps between goals and means are greatest. Ruth Kornhauser (1978) reported that, although anomic theory predicts that delinquents will have higher aspirations than expectations, they often possess low expectations *and* low aspirations. Her assessment: Delinquents do not want or expect much, and so they do not experience the anomic trap. Still, Ron Simons and Phyllis Gray (1989:99) reported a relationship between *anticipated* occupational success and delinquency, but "only for lower-class youth, and particularly lower-class minority youth, as these are the individuals whose life expectations are apt to lead to system blaming."

- *Not a general theory of misbehavior.* Anomie may not explain crime by elites, including white-collar and corporate crime, or nonutilitarian crime, such as vandalism and violent offenses. Recent thinking about anomie, however, suggests that it exists even in corporate boardrooms (Passas 1990). What is price-fixing or other forms of corporate crime if not "organizational innovation"? Perhaps we need to ask, How much wealth is enough?

- *Too simplistic an answer to a complex problem.* The supposed linkage between retreatism and misconduct may represent an oversimplification of a complex process. For example, retreatism confuses cause and effect about drug use and abuse. Do drug users retreat *to* drugs, or do they retreat *because* of drugs? Elliott Currie (1993) noted an interconnection between drug abuse and anomie's breeding conditions, conditions exacerbated by the growing gap between the nation's wealthiest citizens and its poorest. Of course, anomie does not explain why people select one adaptation over another.

- *Untested.* Due to measurement problems, Merton's anomie theory remains untested. It is unclear whether individuals experience anomie or whether it is a social condition.

- *Few tests of adult samples.* Most anomie researchers study juveniles. Yet, strain is more about adults than for children, especially Merton's anomie (Agnew 1995).

- *Possibly racist, sexist, or both.* A key problem with traditional strain theory has been its focus on minority-male delinquency. Recent forms of anomie theory, including the general strain and institutional strain versions, move beyond class and race. However, its gender bias remains an issue. Are females immune to strain? We return to both issues in Chapter 11.

- *The failure of general strain theory to serve as a mediating force.* Several researchers report that general strain measures do not mediate the impact of other social forces on the level of crime and delinquency (Neff and Waite 2007; Paternoster and Mazerolle 1994). Akers and Sellers (2009:202) see this as general strain theory's greatest failing.

Social Structure, Public Policy, and Criminal Justice Practices

Theories of social structure have been among the richest sources of public policy initiatives in the history of criminology (Akers and Seller 2009; Lanier and Henry 1998). The idea of extending opportunities to the disadvantaged fits with the liberal view of good government. For example, the work of Cloward and Ohlin (1960) led to significant public policy initiatives. Attorney General Robert Kennedy, after reading *Delinquency and Opportunity,* asked Ohlin to develop a program that addressed the nation's juvenile delinquency problem. The Juvenile Delinquency Prevention and Control Act of 1961 was a direct attempt to extend legitimate opportunities for success to lower-class youths. After the death of President John F. Kennedy, President Lyndon B. Johnson extended the act to all lower-class citizens through his **War on Poverty.**

A key goal of this initiative was to empower local antipoverty groups to open up opportunities using rent strikes, demonstrations, voter registration, and political mobilization. However, Cloward and Ohlin's work may have inadvertently created an "us versus them" mentality on both sides. Federally funded community legal services sued local and state governments, and rent strikes and demonstrations sponsored by federally funded antipoverty groups generated considerable publicity. The nation's business and political sectors opposed these programs. Finally, although Washington funded no evaluations, President Richard Nixon declared the programs a failure and dismantled them.

These programs exhibited three fatal flaws. The first culprit, claimed Daniel Patrick Moynihan (1969), was a philosophical shift away from providing access to political and social empowerment. Program leaders assumed increasingly activist positions on behalf of the poor and disenfranchised. These changes brought them into conflict with local and federal politicians, a conflict they were destined to lose. As Lamar Empey (1982) observed, "Influential members of Congress made it clear that the mandate of the President's Commission was to reduce delinquency, not to reform society or try out sociological theories on American youth." Second, the goals of the opportunity-based programs created obvious problems. If such programs increase the education and job skills of participants, only an expanding economy allows them to secure a level of economic success sufficient to negate the anomic trap. Failure to secure such employment, after investing considerable time and effort, may escalate the anomic condition. Finally, Stephen Rose (1972) believed that the War on Poverty failed because the established and entrenched poverty-serving bureaucracies transformed it to serve their own interests.

Law Enforcement Practices   Beyond macro-level national polices, the concept of strain also provides insights into police corruption. Society's desire for law and order contrasts with its antipathy toward governmental authority. This often places police officers in an anomic trap, caught between competing goals: the arrest, indictment, and conviction of offenders on the one hand, and the rule of law on the other. Consequently, some perjure themselves, engage in entrapment, falsify evidence and incriminating statements, and even plant evidence at crime scenes. Sometimes they administer "street justice," a form of extra-legal force—for example, executing street-level drug vendors. David Carter (1990) contrasted this form of behavior with corrupt practices self-serving (and illegal) acts, such as accepting bribes, drugs, and protection money from these same offenders. Officers also may suppress evidence or information that might lead to an arrest. In either case, we can understand police deviance as resulting from strains created by an ambiguous social system that pressures the police to respond efficiently to crime but restrains their ability to do so with a host of due process protections.

CRIME AND SUBCULTURES

- Did you know people in school who seemed to lack the same values as most of the other students and who were always rebelling, going against the rules?

- Do members of the lower social classes have different values from those in the middle class? If so, what are their theoretical and policy implications?

- The media often portray certain persons or groups that are inclined to use violence to resolve disputes. Do these images have a basis in fact?

Culture refers to a society's beliefs and moral values. Not everyone in a modern pluralistic society supports them all, especially members of some **subcultures,** a term that refers to both a set of normative expectations and a group. "Subcultures are patterns of values, norms, and behavior which have become traditional among certain groups" (Short 1968:11). As a group, James Short noted (1968:11), subcultures "may be of many types, including occupational and ethnic groups, social classes, occupants of 'closed institutions' [e.g., prisons, mental hospitals] and various age grades. [They are] important frames of reference through which individuals and groups see the world and interpret it."

The term *subculture* has enjoyed widespread popularity in relation to studies of work and occupations, adolescence, social class, political organizations, and any number of other academic applications. In criminology, the term has different roots and applications.

Delinquent Subculture Theories

Delinquent subculture theories share the wholesale rejection of the dominant culture's values. Yet, even within this theoretical perspective, criminologists often disagree about the origins of the conflicts or the manner of their resolution.

Reaction Formation Thesis   Albert Cohen (1955:13) saw the lower-class delinquent subculture as "a way of life that has somehow become traditional among certain groups in American society. These groups are the boys' gangs that flourish most conspicuously in the 'delinquent neighborhoods' of our larger American cities." Gangs, from this perspective, are primarily male lower-class phenomena, in which status is dependent upon repudiation of the mainstream culture's conventional norms. No physical attributes distinguish a gang boy from a Boy Scout. The difference is in the culture each endorses.

Cohen suggested that the delinquent subculture takes the larger culture's norms, ones he described as middle-class values, and turns them upside down in a process psychoanalysts call **reaction formation.** The anal stage's destructive urges remain unresolved, and conflict with internalized middle-class norms is the result. The subcultural delinquent's conduct is correct "by the standards of his subculture, precisely because it is wrong by the norms of the larger culture" (Cohen 1955:28). Delinquent activities are nonutilitarian, malicious, and negativistic, and delinquents have little regard for profit or personal gain (Cohen 1955:26). Rather, the goal is status. According to Cohen, delinquents see the broader society's rules as not something merely to evade. They must *flout* them, with elements of active spite, malice, contempt, ridicule, challenge, and defiance.

The lower-class delinquent is at a distinct disadvantage as he progresses into adulthood. Certain cultural characteristics are necessary to achieve success in our society, and the upbringing of a middle-class child is more likely to develop these characteristics, such as ability to postpone gratification, skills for achievement, industry and thrift, control of physical aggression, and cultivation of manners and politeness.

Lower–Class Culture Thesis Walter Miller (1958) argued that street-corner adolescents in lower-class communities *do not flout* conventional middle-class norms. Instead, they conform to behavior defined as acceptable by *their* community. The delinquent subculture, according to Miller, did not rise in conflict with the larger, middle-class culture, nor does it to deliberately violate middle-class norms. Rather, lower-class culture is simply *different,* the focal characteristics being (1) **trouble,** or law-violating behavior; (2) **toughness,** or physical prowess and daring; (3) **smartness,** or the ability to "con" and act shrewdly; (4) **excitement,** or a tendency to seek thrills, risk, and danger; (5) **fate,** the idea of being lucky or unlucky; and (6) **autonomy,** or the desire to be independent from external control.

Collectively, these characteristics dictate behavioral norms. Trouble for men often involves fights, police encounters, or sexual promiscuity; trouble for women frequently means sexual activities with disadvantageous consequences, including rape and unwanted pregnancies. For both genders, the excessive consumption of alcohol plays a facilitative or enabling role. Miller contended that members of the lower class rarely seek to avoid troublesome behavior based on a sense of commitment to social order norms or laws. Instead, they try to avoid the possible negative consequences. Although trouble-producing behavior is a source of status, trouble avoidance is necessary to forestall legal complications. Individuals may, in an attempt to resolve this conflict legitimately, become part of highly disciplined organizations, such as the military or law enforcement.

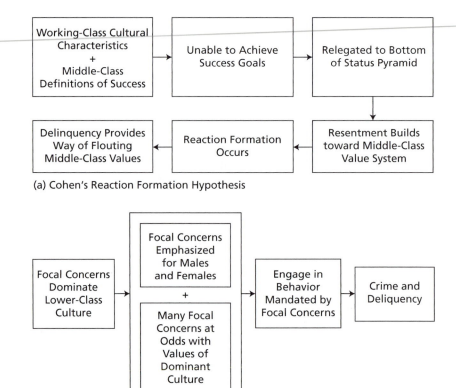

(a) Cohen's Reaction Formation Hypothesis

(b) Miller's Lower-Class Focal-Concerns Thesis

F I G U R E 6.6 Delinquent Subculture Theories

Miller pointed out that lower-class attachments to peers and commitments to their norms prevent lower-class youths from moving into middle-class (i.e., conventional) society. The larger society stifles their upward mobility unless they can break free, and it supports this stratification. Because the lower class does the dirty work of an industrial society, members are encouraged to indulge their whims in liquor, sex, and violence. Crime and delinquency are the costs of a smooth-running industrial machine. Figure 6.6 summarizes these theories of delinquent subculture.

Subcultural Delinquency Theories

Delinquent subculture theories limit their descriptions and explanations to the misbehavior of subordinate members of society. **Subcultural delinquency theories** provide insights into misbehavior by the social structure's subordinates and superordinates. According to this argument, white-collar criminals were super-ordinates who took business norms and twisted them to suit their needs. It re-mained for David Matza, Gresham Sykes, and John Hagan to ground these ideas in youthful transgressions.

Subterranean Values and Delinquency   Sykes and Matza (1957) shed light on the process whereby criminals of all sorts are able to maintain support for prevailing cultural values and at the same violate the law. As they stated, "Values or norms appear as qualified guides for action, limited in their applicability in terms of time, place, persons, and social circumstances" (Sykes and Matza 1957:666).

Sykes and Matza (1957) studied the mechanisms that permit delinquents to accept society's norms and, simultaneously, to violate them. Delinquents, they observed, used various **techniques of neutralization** to deny in moral terms that a crime or rule violation had taken place. According to Sykes and Matza, delinquents are not necessarily committed to their misdeeds, nor do they necessarily see themselves as outside the law. Rather, they justify their misdeeds in a way that, although not valid for the larger society, is valid for them. Specific justifications include the following:

- *The denial of responsibility*. The offender may point to the absence of intent, suggesting that it was an accident or that the injured party "got in the way." At other times, forces outside the youth's control are to blame, including uncaring or abusive parents, a failed educational system, and an indifferent community.

- *The denial of injury*. The perpetrator carefully suggests that, in fact, no one was hurt. This technique plays well for victimless crimes, such as drug abuse or underage consumption of alcohol and cigarettes. In the case of pranks or vandalism, the youth may point out that no real harm occurred: no harm, no foul.

- *The denial of a victim*. If no injury occurs, it follows that there can be no victim. Alternatively, even if an injury occurred, the perpetrator may claim that it was a righteous act of retaliation, that the victim—although this term is avoided—"had it coming." Individuals earn this status by race, gender, sexual orientation, and even economic status. For the latter, the youth defines an act of thievery as redistribution of the wealth. The key is to transform the victim into someone deserving of injury.

- *The condemnation of the condemners*. The delinquent shifts the blame to the person doing the complaining, no matter who it is. This offender views the condemner as just as bad and, what is worse, hypocritical. If the condemner is a police officer, all police are brutal and corrupt; if a schoolteacher condemns the youth, all schoolteachers are lazy and incompetent. The intent is to shift attention from the delinquent's behavior.

- *The appeal to higher loyalties*. Friends, siblings, and youth gangs often provide the content of the final technique. Faced with obeying either society's rules or those of a peer-based entity, the perpetrator often comes down on the latter's side. Such people do not reject society's norms; rather, other norms take precedence.

Matza and Sykes (1961) expanded on subcultural delinquency theory by including **subterranean values** and their role in leisure-time activities. They noted that certain values set delinquents apart: "Juvenile delinquency appears to be permeated by a cluster of values that can be characterized as the search for kicks, the disdain for work and a desire for the big score, and the acceptance of aggressive toughness as proof of masculinity" (Matza and Sykes 1961:715). They argued that these values, often thought to be uniquely juvenile, have parallels in the dominant culture, particularly in leisure-time activities. For example, the search for "kicks" is a subterranean value that parallels middle-class thrill seeking. One set of values represents living on the edge; the other is far more centrist in the middle-class value system.

Delinquency and Drift   Do juvenile delinquents move on to become adult criminals or do they mature into law-abiding citizens? Matza (1964) viewed delinquents as moving between criminal and conventional actions but behaving most of the time in a noncriminal mode, a process he called **drift.** Such youths often feel ambivalent about their episodic criminal conduct. Matza believed that juveniles experience less alienation than adults and are not yet committed to an oppositional culture. He was also highly critical of most delinquent subculture theories, which paint a picture of nonstop delinquent behavior, especially for gang youths. Most of the time, delinquents engage in law-abiding activities. How do these theories account for the fact that most delinquents seem to grow up and out of delinquency?

Although Matza did not entirely reject the idea of delinquent subcultures, he did not see it as a binding force on its members: "Loyalty is a basic issue in the subculture of delinquency partially because its adherents are so regularly disloyal. They regularly abandon their company at the age of remission for more conventional pursuits" (1964:157–58). Many if not most delinquents abandon their misbehaving peers in favor of adult prosocial or conventional behavior. As he observed earlier with Sykes, the youths' subterranean values reflect the core values of society. As edge values, they are distortions of those values, but part of them nonetheless. The move to more traditional and less threatening centrist values is not a long or a difficult journey.

Assessing Subcultural Theories

The *subculture of delinquency* theorists' focus is on subgroups within society that are relatively powerless and economically disadvantaged. Whether it is a rejection of middle-class values or adherence to unique cultural expectations and norms, this perspective seizes on the idea that those in positions of power criminalize the threatening actions of certain groups, but especially lower-class youth gangs. (We return to the topic of power and conflict in Chapter 9.) The *subcultural delinquency* theorists see the essential issue as the social threats resulting from the subterranean values of certain groups.

Critics question whether the assumptions of subcultural theory about social class are correct. Does a lower-class culture exist? Lower- and middle-class families apparently socialize their children in similar ways (Leacock 1971; Piven and

---

IN THEIR OWN WORDS: Subculturalists on Structure, Culture, and Delinquency

Sociologists express many opinions about cultural support for juvenile misconduct. The following excerpts from the two groups of "subculturalists" highlight these differences.

- *Shaw and McKay on the conflict of values:* "Conflicts of values necessarily arise when boys are brought in contact with so many forms of conduct not reconcilable with conventional morality as expressed in church and school. A boy may be found guilty of delinquency in the court, which represents the values of the larger society, for an act which has at least tacit approval in the community where he lives" (p. 166).

- *Miller on "focal concerns" and ties to the immediate culture:* "Focal concerns of male adolescent corner groups are those of the general cultural milieu in which it functions. As would be expected, the relative weight and importance of these concerns pattern somewhat differently for adolescents than for adults" (p. 15).

- *Matza and Sykes on the idea of an oppositional subculture:* "Rather than standing in opposition to conventional ideas of good conduct, the delinquent is likely to adhere to the dominant norms in belief but render them ineffective in practice by holding various attitudes and perceptions which serve to neutralize the norms as checks on behavior" (p. 712).

- *Hagan and associates on subterranean values:* "A recurring theme in American social theory is that core values in American society contain an undercurrent that can cause subcultural delinquent and criminal behavior. . . . The core of this theoretical tradition is the idea that subterranean versions of market oriented values stimulate subcultural crime and delinquency" (p. 334).

SOURCES: Hagan et al. (1998); Matza and Sykes (1961); Miller (1958); Shaw and McKay (1942).

Cloward 1971). "Subcultural theories may be a better reflection of middle-class stereotypes about the poor than an empirically accurate depiction of a 'lower-class lifestyle'" (Curran and Renzetti 1994:158). After all, members of the lower class typically condemn rather than condone violence, perhaps more than those in society's upper strata (Erlanger 1974; Curran and Renzetti 1989).

John Hagan (1997) viewed the techniques of neutralization and subterranean values as providing a shield—albeit only a temporary one—from the anomic condition reviewed earlier in this chapter. He disputed the causal order espoused by most strain theorists, linking the defiant stance of the subcultural delinquent to an engulfing sense of despair provoked by educational and employment problems. As Hagan (1997) noted, the subculture of delinquency may serve to insulate members from socioeconomic stresses, delaying their impact until adulthood. It is only at this point, observed Hagan (1997:133), that they feel the full impact of subcultural involvement: "The same subculture that in adolescence is a source of confidence, or defiance, leads to a loss of confidence, or despair, in adulthood."

Hagan (1991) contended that youths might drift in and out of different kinds of subcultures, some of which (e.g., party subculture), have net positive effects on youths. Other subcultures (e.g., delinquent subcultures), he admitted, have far more damaging effects. In Hagan's view, a party subculture socializes nonworking-class males to participate in social networks that are essential for success later in life. Intervention and prevention strategies that fail to recognize those differences may lack important socializing features from a youth's environment.

Besides these specific observations, we frequently see the following general criticisms of the subcultural perspective:

- *Not clear that lower-class delinquent groups constitute countercultures.* Cohen and Short (1958) suggested that the progeny of the "parent male subculture" includes several criminal variants. Empey (1967) questioned these characterizations, saying that there is more empirical support for the idea of an amorphous "parent" subculture than there is for the idea of highly focused delinquent subcultures. Neither gang members nor other delinquents work to create and maintain a unique, antisocial culture (Akers and Sellers 2009).

- *Too much "blame" attributed to poverty and minority status.* As a rule, subcultural theorists tend to "blame" the poor and minorities for their troubles and ignore two key points: (1) structural factors contribute to both poverty and crime; and (2) the various social classes are heterogeneous in their beliefs, values, and norms (Curran and Renzetti 1994:158). Tittle (1983) warns that those who insist that poverty causes crime may also view poverty as immoral and inferior, a biased view at best.

- *Are these gang theories or delinquency theories?* Criminologists use both types of subculturalist theories to explain youth gangs in urban centers (Akers and Sellers 2009). This characterization is especially true of Cohen, Matza, Cloward and Ohlin, and to some extent Miller's work. While gang delinquency is by definition the work of youth gangs, young people engage in delinquency that has nothing to do with gangs. In other words, these theories fall short of an explanation for delinquency, and do not explain much at all about adult criminality.

Possible class and race/ethnicity biases temper the lasting contributions of subcultural delinquency theories. Recent examinations of subcultural influences tend to broaden the groups captured by such theories, although tests remain rare. For an exception to this generalization, see the following Comparative Criminology box. Conflicts, particularly over culture, race, and ethnicity, may provide a deeper understanding of exactly what the subculturalists observed, a theme to which we return in later chapters.

COMPARATIVE CRIMINOLOGY—WORLD VIEWS ON CRIME AND JUSTICE:
Subterranean Values in Germany

Hagan and associates explored the cross-cultural utility of subterranean values. Employing school-based surveys conducted in the former East Germany and West Germany, they tested the subterranean influence of self-interest and anomic amorality. They found evidence that the former creates the latter. Moreover, anomic amorality leads to inequality acceptance and a repudiation of societal out-groups. In parts of Germany, this has led to attacks on "marginalized groups," such as Turkish residents. Group delinquency is a likely final stage. The researchers concluded that "none of these forces alone is overwhelming, but they combine to form a subterranean causal web that is linked to the core values of market society, and the strands of this causal web can lead to subcultural delinquency" (p. 335).

SOURCE: Hagan, Hefler, Classen, Boehnke, and Merkeas (1998).

Subcultures, Public Policy, and Criminal Justice Practices

While subcultural theories may provide some insight into the concentration of crime among the nation's poor, what are those who fight crime to do with this information? Conduct norms and values are at the core of all subcultures, and policy options for eliminating this problem appear limited.

Law Enforcement Practices   Culture and social structure are important to the police. Many researchers have noted the existence of an insulated and isolated police subculture. For example, the violence of the police work world can spill over into officers' encounters with citizens. Just as represented in the subculture-of-violence thesis, small insults become large ones, and a lack of respectful tone takes on greater symbolic meaning for police officers. They may not only accept and respect the use of force by brother and sister officers, but also may require such acts for full membership in the police subculture (Dorschner 1989; Hunt 1985).

Researchers have also described a **police subculture,** a subset of the police community that promotes a sexist and macho role perception (Martin 1980). Moreover, managing the stress of police work takes subcultural forms. Outsiders can easily interpret the ridiculing of suspects and the use of racial or sexual joking as callous or worse (Moyer 1986; Pogrebin and Poole 1988). The police subculture does little to deflect this criticism. One response to these multifaceted problems is to increase police cultural awareness by means of multicultural education. Academy programs and in-service training address this problem by educating police about the multiple meanings attached to various acts within lower-class and minority communities (Roberg and Kuykendall 1993).

Training addresses only part of the issue. The nation's police forces are overwhelmingly Caucasian (Sullivan 1989; Walker 1992). Minority recruitment may help sensitize officers to a wider range of subcultures, but this practice over-looks the issue of occupational socialization. Police work has evidenced an ability to shape those who wear the shield (Bennett and Greenstein 1975; Rokeach, Miller, and Snyder 1977; Van Maanen 1973). Researchers also have shown that minority officers working with minority populations to be rougher and more assertive than are white officers (Alex 1976; Kephart 1957; Sullivan 1989). This pattern, however, may be changing (Berg, True, and Gertz 1984). In short, sub-cultural norms and values are powerful instruments, including those found in the police subculture (Felkenes 1991).

Correctional Practices   Like anomic persons in the free society, inmates must deal with unique strains. John Irwin (1980) described four lifestyle adaptations that prisoners commonly use. First, **doing time** means that the inmates view prison as a temporary break in their criminal careers. Second, **gleaning** involves taking advantage of every opportunity to improve one's resources. Third, **jailing** resembles colonization, whereby inmates who have little commitment to conventional life adjust well to institutional life and live more comfortably than most inmates. Finally, **disorganized criminals** are inmates who, because of low intel-ligence, or physical or mental disabilities, develop no real adjustment pattern in prison and often are the prey of other inmates.

Contemporary prisons resemble inner cities. They contain many subcultures, ranging from the ethnic gangs (e.g., Crips, Bloods, Mexican Mafia, Latin Kings, and Black Guerrilla Family), to white supremacist groups (e.g., Aryan Brotherhood), to motorcycle gangs (e.g., Hell's Angel's, Gypsy Jokers), to religious groups (e.g., Black Muslims). This extreme heterogeneity not only makes inmate survival difficult (Austin and Irwin 2001; Irwin 1980), it also creates problems for correctional staff. Inmates often control the day-to-day functioning of the institution. The members of prison staff who fail to recognize the variability in inmate responses to incarceration are in for a hard time. They may bend to the pressures, or inmates may coopt them (Hawkins and Alpert 1989). Prison guards are clearly "the other prisoners" (Hawkins 1976).

The significance of cultural-based theories extends beyond prison walls. For example, probation or parole agreements, or participation in other community-based programs, may require participants to refrain from contacts with known criminals. Often a location, such as their "home turf," is off-limits. This requirement is hard to enforce when community programs meet with local resistance. The call often becomes "not in my backyard." In other words, local residents may meet attempts to disperse correctional clients into low-crime areas—a goal consistent with subcultural theories—with resistance.

SUMMARY

Several themes emerged from this review of macro-level theories, as summarized in Table 6.1. First, each theory has well-deserved criticisms. For example, the early social ecologists provided poor independent measures of social disorganization, social controls, and crime. In addition to proposing a theory that seemed to be a tautology, the Chicagoans may have committed the ecological fallacy. Subculturalists engaged in a long-running debate about whether they should study delinquent subcultures or subcultural delinquency. The differences are more complex than simply the proper ordering of words: delinquent subculture theories imply that only subordinates are delinquent; subcultural delinquency extends concerns about misbehavior to both superordinates and subordinates.

Second, all three theoretical traditions experienced rediscovery, transformation, and revitalization in the 1990s, the most important elements of which were definitional in nature. The anomie tradition received an infusion of new ideas, especially with respect to the American Dream and monetary acquisitiveness.

Third, we found many connections between the theories reviewed in this chapter. The Chicago School and anomie theory heavily influenced delinquency subcultural theorists, and subcultural delinquency theorists used elements of the anomie theory and the American Dream. The strong interplay between theories, especially in the 1950s and 1960s, predates the current interest in integrated theories, a theme we explore in Chapter 12. Even disagreements between theorists resulted in contributions to the criminological enterprise, as theorists tried to clarify their respective positions.

TABLE 6.1   Social Organizational Theories to Crime

Theory	Major Figures	Central Assumptions	Causal Arguments (Key Terms)	Strengths	Weaknesses
Social disorganization theory (SDT)	Shaw, McKay	*SDT:* Relationships between humans and their environs yield best understanding of human social life; cities are ecological spheres; people are not crime-prone but areas of the city are.	*SDT:* Sees the cause of crime as poor sense of community and weak social controls; crime is greatest around *interstitial zones.*	*SDT:* Fits with what the Chicagoans observed in their living laboratory; causal arguments are logical; supported by research during the 1930s and 1940s.	*SDT:* Has two main flaws: (1) lacking independent social disorganization measures, the theory may be a tautology; (2) early researchers may have committed the ecological fallacy.
Revised social disorganization theory (RSDT)	Bursik, Groves, Sampson	*RSDT:* Includes the idea that crime and a broader community-level frame of reference can explain other social ills.	*RSDT:* Focuses on a community's capacity to regulate itself.	*RSDT:* Revitalized urban studies of crime; enjoys high theoretical relevance and reasonable empirical support form urban studies of crime and delinquency.	*RSDT:* Must resist temptation to make the same mistakes as early proponents of SDT.
Environmental criminology (EC)	Brantinghams, Jacobs, Jeffery, Newman	*EC:* Designing out crime's ecological factors may be possible.	*EC:* Physical and social environs create opportunities conducive to crime and delinquency.	*EC:* Includes plans to reduce crime by promoting a watchful public and an involved criminal justice system.	*EC:* Needs further studies to support basic ideas about impact of urban planning on crime control.
Anomie theory (AT)	Durkheim	*AT:* Society viewed in terms of its structural parts and functions; society exists in a state of equilibrium that it prefers to others; society must address imbalances.	*AT:* Disruptive historical and social events yield disturbances in the *social equilibrium,* leading to unrestrained behavior and deviance.	*AT:* As the precursor to social deviance, AT seemed to fit with historical, anecdotal, and cross-cultural evidence.	*AT:* Is difficult to define or measure society-wide anomie; the idea remains intuitively interesting, but empirically hard to prove.
Strain theory (ST)	Merton, Cloward, Ohlin		*ST:* Contradictions between *goals and means* can create the *anomic trap;* ways of responding to it may be deviant or criminal.	*ST:* Made sense during the Great Depression, and even in the 1950s with the "beat generation."	*ST* and *GST:* Are somewhat easier to measure than anomie; neither theory has yielded definitive results, although results with GDT are promising.
Institutional strain theory (IST)	Messner, Rosenfeld	*IST:* A mature society maintains balance between all societal institutions, including economic, family, educational, and political institutions.	*IST:* Institutional interplay is critical; *dominance* by one institution weakens the control function of others; strains combine with cultural values endorsing criminal motives and crime results.	*GST:* Provides a micro-level application of strain; accounts for actions of children whose avoidance actions attempt to reduce sources of strain in their lives; research results are promising.	*IST:* Attaining the ultimate goal suggested by IST, a mature society with balance between its institutions, may prove illusive; empirical validity of the theory is weak and uncertain.
General strain theory (GST)	Agnew	*GST:* People experience multiple strain forms at the micro-level.			

T A B L E   6.1   **(Continued)**

Theory	Major Figures	Central Assumptions	Causal Arguments (Key Terms)	Strengths	Weaknesses
			GST: General strains cause people to run from something that is undesired; actual or anticipated strains create predisposition for delinquency or function as a *situation* event that instigates a delinquent act.		
Subcultural delinquency theory (SDT)	Sutherland	*SDT:* Subcultures, consisting of subordinates or superordinates, engage in norm-violating behavior that reflects general social norms taken to the extreme.	*SDT:* Groups marginalize certain social norms by taking specific elements of their content to the edge of normalcy and beyond; at times, these *subterranean values* promote deviance and neutralize offenders.	*SDT:* Removes the class and race biases common in structural theories; explains how those who violate some laws also obey others; shows a logical tie to other structural theories, especially anomie.	*SDT:* Remains an interesting if poorly refined theory, although Hagan's recent reformations address this issue.
Subterranean values	Matza, Sykes, Hagan				
Drift	Matza, Hagan				
Delinquent subculture theory (DST)	Sellin	*DST:* Subgroups engage in norm-violating behavior that threatens the dominant group and its values.		*DST:* Offer graphic images of youthful misconduct, whether it is delinquent gang-specific or class-specific behavior.	
Reaction formation (RF)	Cohen	*RF:* Children engage in group behavior for status; cannot measure up to a middle-class measuring rod.	*RF:* Delinquents turn middle-class values on their head; delinquency is okay because it is wrong; status is the goal.	*RF:* Provides integration of strain's intuitive appeal with Chicagoan's descriptive energy.	*RF:* Is possible that delinquent gangs may merely discourage conventional values, not flout them; juveniles lack a singular loyalty to delinquent subcultures, appearing instead to drift between conventional and unconventional.
Lower-class culture hypothesis (LCH)	Miller	*LCH:* The lower class has unique norms and rules different from those of the dominant class.	*LCH:* Class-based dictates (e.g., *being tough*) may put members on a collision course with the legal system.	*LCH:* Applies the eye of an anthropologist to crime problems.	*LCH:* A lower-class culture may not exist; ultimately, crime may be common to all levels of society and not the unique domain of one.
Differential opportunity structures (DOS)	Cloward, Ohlin	*DOS:* Variable opportunities exist for both legitimate and illegitimate means; uses ideas of Merton, Cohen, and Chicagoans.	*DOS:* Gangs are responses to problems of adjustment created by limited access to legitimate and illegitimate means to achieve success goals.	*DOS:* Has appealing logic; by increasing legitimate opportunities, society can reduce crime.	*DOS:* Gangs based on retreatism, populated by double failures, may not exist, calling into question DOS's basic premise.

The future for macro-level criminological theories remains an open question. First proposed at the end of the nineteenth century, they remain vital at the start of the twenty-first century. This observation is even more remarkable given that, at various times, criminologists declared each one a theoretical or empirical dead end.

KEY TERMS

American Dream

anomic trap

anomie

autonomy

Chicago School

collective conscience

community malaise

community policing

concentric zones

conformists

cultural transmission theories

culture

defensible space

delinquent subculture theories

disorder

disorganized criminals

doing time

double failure

drift

ecological fallacy

ecology

ends–means schema

excitement

fate

general strain theory

gleaning

illegitimate opportunities

image

innovators

institutional anomie theory

interstitial zone

jailing

legitimate opportunities

macro-sociological

mechanical solidarity

milieu

natural surveillance

organic solidarity

podular design

police subculture

reaction formation

rebels

retreatists

ritualists

smartness

social disorganization

social equilibrium

strain theory

subcultural delinquency theories

subcultures

subterranean values

techniques of neutralization

territoriality

toughness

trouble

unrestrained ambition

War on Poverty

zone of transition

CRITICAL REVIEW QUESTIONS

1. What is the basic assumption embodied in the ecological approach to the study of crime? What are the major criticisms of this approach?

2. What did the Chicagoans see as the links between a city's physical and social development and its incidence of crime and other social ills?

3. How would you characterize ecological theories in general? Which ones seem to provide the greatest insights into contemporary urban crime problems?

4. How might some neighborhoods that sociologists characterize as disorganized actually be quite well organized?

5. How does Durkheim's theory of anomie explain criminal behavior? How did Merton's "anomic trap" differ from these earlier ideas about anomie?

6. Which do you think is the most important new variant of anomie theory: general strain or institutional anomie? Explain your choice.

7. Explain how the following, individually or collaboratively, link culture, crime, and delinquency: Cloward, Matza, Miller, Ohlin, Reiss, and Short.

8. For each of the following groups of theories, identify its most important policy implication: social ecology theory, social structural theory, and subcultural theory. Why is it more important than are the others?

9. Who do you think "got it right"—the subculture of delinquency theorists or the subcultural delinquency theorists? Explain your answer.

10. For each of the following groups of theories, identify the most important practical application: social ecology theory, social structural theory, and subcultural theory.

NOTES

1. The researchers were able to break down, or disaggregate, the arrest statistics for men and women; they then used gender as a variable.

2. They did note two differences, however. First, the model worked slightly better for males. Second, it explained female homicide and robbery rates very well, and female aggravated assault, burglary, and larceny rates moderately well.

3. Skogan (1990) observed two main types of urban disorder: (1) disorderly human behaviors included public drinking, corner gangs, street harassment, and commercial sex; and (2) physical decay referred to vandalism, dilapidation, and abandonment of dwellings and other buildings, and rubbish-filled streets and alleys. This description reverberates with the imagery of social disorganization.

4. Environmental criminology is also closely allied with routine activities/opportunity theory, a topic explored in Chapter 2.

5. Durkheim sought to demonstrate the power of sociology in explaining suicide.

6. Francis Cullen (1988) suggested that Cloward and Ohlin's theory owes more to the Chicago School than to Merton.

7. This lack of a community spirit is at the core of another theory about crime, *shaming*, which we explore in Chapter 10.

8. The following assessment comes from Bernard (1984); Cernkovich and Giordano (1979); Clinard (1964); Clinard and Meier (1985); Cohen (1965); Kornhauser (1978); and Simons, Miller, and Aigner (1980).

7

Social Process Theories

CHAPTER OVERVIEW

Learning Theories

Differential Association Theory

Social Learning Theory

Assessing Learning Theories

Learning Theories, Public Policy, and Criminal Justice Practices

Control Theories

Early Control Theories

Social Bond Theory

Self-Control Theory

Assessing Control Theories

Control, Public Policy, and Criminal Justice Practices

LEARNING OBJECTIVES

In this chapter, you will learn the following:

- How social processes create or work against crime problems in society.

- How offenders learn crime propensities, including the various mechanisms involved in the learning process.

- How society's control mechanisms, ranging from individual to group controls, collectively and individually stand as a bulwark against crime propensities.

- Various expansions on the social control theme, including the effects of effective (and ineffective) parenting and too little self-control.

INTRODUCTION

A **social process** is any identifiable, repetitive pattern of interaction between humans in a group or social context. The theories in this chapter emphasize individual responses to social interactions. In several cases, the social process theorists are at odds with one another, as they look at the same problem and see different forces at work. Some contend that social forces produce crime by endorsing or failing to stop the learning mechanism behind criminality; others see breakdowns in the control mechanisms associated with social institutions as the chief culprits.

The theories in this chapter start with the premise that to understand crime we must understand the social processes by which people become criminals. What, they ask, are the social forces behind these processes? We begin with learning theories of crime.

LEARNING THEORIES

- There are no born criminals. Rather, as children, criminals must be taught evil ways, lessons that are best learned in close contact with those who endorse law breaking. Can a theory tell us where, when, and in what context this learning is likely to take place? What exactly do those who commit crimes learn?

- Although we are all exposed to ideas, information, and definitions that support law violations, why do only some of us commit crimes?

If there are no "born criminals," what explains the presence of criminals amongst us? Perhaps all social behavior, including crime, flows from a learning process. According to the claims of this paradigm, while most of us are learning to read, write, and do arithmetic, others are learning the ABC's of delinquency. How is crime learned? Edwin Sutherland addressed this question early in the twentieth century.

Differential Association Theory

Edwin L. Sutherland (1883–1950) proposed **differential association theory** to explain the transmission of criminality. According to Sutherland, criminal behavior is learned. His was an unyielding belief in the need for close personal contacts between "teachers" and "students" for learning to occur. While these two terms were not part of Sutherland's vocabulary, he believed that the same mechanisms that support any learning are at work in criminal learning. He did not think it possible to learn criminal behavior through the mass media (e.g., motion pictures, newspapers, or, more recently, television and videos). Such mechanisms, he claimed, cannot provide the required social context for learning.

Criminal behavior ensues when the motives, drives, and rationalizations direct the individual to view the law unfavorably. Sutherland's (1947:7; emphasis added) Chicago roots—and the influence of culture conflict theory's Thorsten Sellin—were showing when he stated:

> In some societies an individual is surrounded by persons who invariably define the legal codes as rules to be observed, while in others he is surrounded by persons whose definitions are favorable to the violation of legal codes. In our American society, these definitions are usually mixed and consequently we have *culture conflict* in relation to the legal codes.

The conflict, said Sutherland, was between definitions we learn from those close to us that are at odds with the legal codes. The principle of differential association explains how one set of definitions comes to dominate our thinking.

The Principle of Differential Association At the heart of Sutherland's theory is the **principal of differential association,** in which he claims that an excess of definitions favorable to law violations compared with unfavorable ones determines a person's criminality People turn to crime "because of contacts with criminal patterns and also because of isolation from anticriminal patterns" (Sutherland 1947:8). He also believed that the "lessons" must include normative or socially evaluative content—questions and answers addressing issues of right and wrong that had to be learned—or else the learning was neutral and had little effect.

Sutherland observed that differential associations vary in terms of frequency, duration, priority, and intensity. The first two, **frequency** and **duration,** are "modalities of associations." How often one has these contacts and how long the contacts last are self-explanatory. What Sutherland meant by priority, and especially by intensity, however, has proved to be more problematic for those interested in testing the theory. That is, Sutherland believed that early childhood socialization was critical; we learn many of the most important definitions of "right" and "wrong" then and hold them throughout our lives. The associations someone has first in life—those with the highest **priority**—may be the most important ones. Sutherland (1947:7) further stated that **intensity** "is not precisely defined but it has to do with such things as the prestige of the source of a criminal or anticriminal pattern and with emotional reactions related to the associations."

In sum, differential association theory views criminal behavior as resulting from the strength (i.e., frequency, duration, priority, and intensity) of an individual's criminal associations and is a cumulative learning process. A scale that starts out balanced provides a metaphor for differential associations. Criminal and noncriminal associations accumulate over time. At some theoretical point, criminal activity will ensue when the scales reach a tipping point, and the definitions favoring law violations pushes the scale downward to crime. Figure 7.1 summarizes Sutherland's differential association theory.

Variations on a Theme: From Differential Identifications to Differential Reinforcements After Sutherland's death in 1950, sociologists and criminologists critiqued several of his basic assumptions, suggesting that others were at work. For example, Daniel Glaser (1956) questioned the necessity of intimate personal contacts in learning and further suggested that merely identifying with criminal roles may be sufficient. As a modern case in point, during the 1990s, members of the Serbian militia who had never met Nazi Adolf Hitler nonetheless emulated his philosophy and methods, especially with respect to the "ethnic cleansing" of Muslim-Bosnians. Glaser (1965:335) used the phrase **differential identification** to describe the role-taking process, whereby people took on the characteristics of others with whom they had no physical contact.

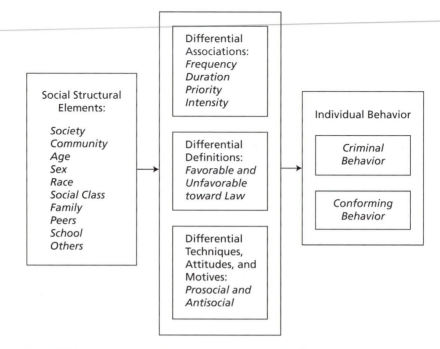

FIGURE 7.1   Sutherland's Differential Association Theory with a Little Help from Akers (1994)

Glaser refined differential identification and renamed it **differential anticipation theory.** Expectations, wrote Glaser (1978), determine behavior and derive from several sources:

- Procriminal and anticriminal "social bonds," or punishments and rewards for law-violating behavior that conforms to the expectations of others.

- Differential learning, by which one is exposed to the attitudes, orientations, and behavior associated with the gratifications of criminal and noncriminal activities.

- The perceived opportunities for success or failure in criminal pursuits.

Glaser (1978:237) wrote that "a person will try to commit a crime wherever and whenever the expectations of gratification from it—as a result of social bonds, differential learning, and perceptions of opportunity—exceed the unfavorable anticipations from these sources." Glaser's **differential expectations** replaced differential associations.

C. Ray Jeffery's **differential reinforcement theory** ties psychological learning processes (i.e., behaviorism and operant conditioning) to differential association theory. He believed that "criminal behavior is operant behavior; that is, it is maintained by the changes it produces on the environment" (Jeffery 1965:295). Social *and* physical environmental changes are important; the latter include material gains.

According to Jeffery (1965:296), the environment in which the act occurs is critical. If, in the past, the actor has had his actions reinforced and the aversive consequences do not control or prevent it, a crime is likely to ensue. For example, an armed robbery may produce not only the reward of money, but also the aversive consequences of physical injury, arrest, conviction, or imprisonment. The robber will stop only after associating the act with aversive consequences; moreover, punishment only works if applied in a consistent manner, soon after the act occurs, which the contemporary criminal justice system typically fails to achieve (Jeffery 1965).

Social Learning Theory

Sutherland's emphasis on crime as *learned* behavior led Robert Burgess and Ronald L. Akers (1966) to offer **differential association/differential reinforcement theory.** Burgess and Akers (1966:140) restated the principle of differential association in operant conditioning terms: "Criminal behavior is a function of norms which are discriminative for criminal behavior, the learning of which takes place when such behavior is more highly reinforced than noncriminal behavior." They also added nonsocial factors to Sutherland's social factors. Burgess and Akers believed that the metaphorical scale's balance is not simply dependent on the definitions for or against following the law, but rather the level of reinforcement accorded one set of definitions over the other.

Social Learning's Content and Context   In 1973, Akers renamed and expanded certain elements of the theory: **Social learning theory** addresses the how, the what, and the where of learning. As for *how,* the answer lies in **instrumental conditioning,** a process identified as "Skinnerian, operant conditioning, reinforcement, or simply behavior theory" (Akers 1973:45). Human behavior takes two forms: (1) **operant behavior,** which is voluntary and mediated by the brain (i.e., food-seeking); and (2) **respondent behavior,** which is automatic and reflexive (i.e., blinking). Operant behavior depends largely on instrumental conditioning, acquired (or conditioned) by the "effects, outcomes, or consequences it has on the person's environment" (Akers 1985:45). Instrumental conditioning has two associated processes:

1. **Punishments,** including punishments received (e.g., when a law violator receives a prison sentence) and rewards lost (e.g., when a law violator has property confiscated), decrease illicit behavior.

2. **Reinforcements,** including rewards received or punishments avoided, increase behavior (e.g., when a law violator scores "the big one" or avoids a conviction, criminal activity is likely to continue). Social reinforcements are often symbolic and abstract, such as gaining ideological, religious, or political goals; nonsocial reinforcements may be physiological, unconditioned, and intrinsically rewarding, such as the feelings and emotions associated with sexual intercourse or the use of controlled substances. Akers believed that

social reinforcements are more plentiful in one's environment and so play a larger role in learning than do the nonsocial.

Social learning occurs in two ways. The first is by **imitation** or **modeling:** Observing what happens to others, people can be vicariously reinforced and may imitate the rewarded actions. They may also develop new behavior without other forces at work simply by modeling what others do. The **principle of differential reinforcement** represents a second method: Given two or more forms of behavior, the one retained and repeated is the one most highly rewarded.

Akers' theory addresses the content—the *what*—of learning. The importance of techniques is elementary. Unless one knows how to commit a crime, motivation and intent are meaningless. **Motivating definitions** form the basis of what Akers called **discriminative stimuli,** two forms of which define the reinforcement process. First, some definitions place the crime in a positive light, defining it as acceptable and permissible. Second, some stimuli, resembling Sykes and Matza's (1957) *techniques of neutralization* (see Chapter 6), serve to "*counter or neutralize definitions of the behavior as undesirable*" (Akers 1985:50; emphasis in original) and may originate through negative reinforcement, providing a means to escape the social disapproval of others and oneself.

Akers believes that learning takes place—the *where*—primarily among **differential associations.** This emphasis is behavioral (i.e., associating directly and indirectly with people who engage in various types of legal and illegal behavior) and attitudinal (i.e., coming to know the normative beliefs and orientations of these people). One's associations provide sources of reinforcements and punishments. Those that occur most often and in the greatest number—and that enjoy the greatest probability of reinforcement—tend to be the ones that guide behavior. Akers believed that this element represented not peer pressure, but rather peer influence (Akers and Sellers 2009).

Social Learning Processes   Social learning theory outlines a process that describes how people move from nonoffender status to offender status and back again (Akers 1998; see also Winfree, Sellers, and Clason 1993). The reinforcements and punishments assume roles that are more prominent once an initial act is committed, and imitation becomes less important. People's personal definitions solidify after repeated exposure to reinforcements and punishments. The commission of a specific act in a given situation depends largely on the individual's learning history, along with the reinforcing or punishing actions of the associated discriminative stimuli.

Feedback is also important, such as when one's own actions influence personal definitions. The first, tentative criminal acts are free of feedback. Afterwards, both responses to the behavior and emerging personal definitions become cues for future behavior. People initially have both deviant and nondeviant peers. After instrumental conditioning, the balance may shift to one group over the other (Akers and Sellers 2009).

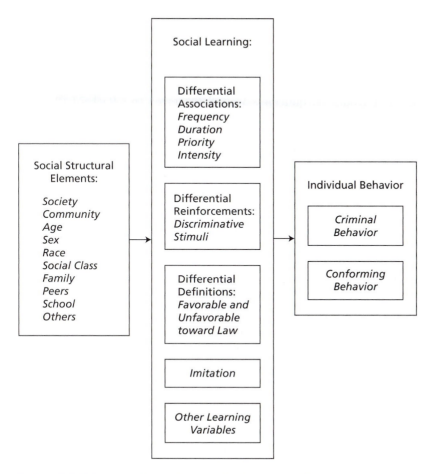

FIGURE 7.2 Akers' Social Structure/Social Learning Theory

Finally, Akers (1998) acknowledged the role of social structure. Society, community, and even individual characteristics—race, gender, religion, and class—create the individual's learning context. Akers (1998:322) assumed that "social learning is the primary process linking social structure to individual behavior." Figure 7.2 summarizes Akers' theory.

Assessing Learning Theories

Differential association and social learning both have received much attention from criminological supporters and detractors.

Differential Association Theory   Shortly after Sutherland's death, criminologists began dissecting the propositions of differential association, examining the theory's conceptual and operational limitations.[1] Sheldon Glueck (1956) doubted if researchers could ever measure the ratio between definitions that are favorable and unfavorable to law-violating behavior; if they can never test the theory's main element, the theory was of little value. Even Sutherland (1947:7), who was interested in quantifying the theory as a "mathematical ratio," admitted that this formulation would be difficult.[2] Melvin De Fleur and Richard Quinney (1966:20) claimed that the theory, far from being untestable, was capable of generating "more hypotheses than could be adequately tested in several lifetimes." What the critics and supporters often overlooked was the fact that "theories—being sets of interrelated propositions explaining a given phenomenon—are rarely tested as a whole. What are tested are specific hypotheses, propositions or empirical implications of a theory" (Matsueda 1988:285).

Within a decade of Sutherland's death, empirical studies tested the "differential association hypothesis" or "differential association theory." The dependent variable for these early studies was always delinquency. As a rule, this body of work supported the principle of differential association, as researchers reported that juveniles with delinquent peers also tended to commit—or at least report—more delinquent acts than those who had no such contacts.[3] Later cross-sectional studies also supported Sutherland's basic tenets (Griffin and Griffin 1978; Jensen 1972; Tittle, Burke, and Jackson 1986), as did longitudinal studies of drug use (Sellers and Winfree 1990) and experimental evaluations of correctional treatment programs intended to help offenders learn ways of conforming to lawful standards (Andrews 1980; Empey and Erickson 1972).[4]

In spite of a large body of work, testing, and even supporting parts of differential association theory, major criticisms of Sutherland's argument include the following:

- *Lacks sufficient operationalization for testing.* Sutherland's stated propositions are not testable, mainly because he failed to operationalize important concepts (e.g., "definitions" and "an excess of definitions").

- *Not a generally applicable theory of crime.* Differential association theory does not explain all crimes (e.g., what about crimes of passion and most violent crimes?). As such, it has severe limitations for a theory that purports to provide insights into all crime.

- *Humans respond exclusively to social stimuli.* Sutherland, suggest some critics, based the theory on an oversocialized view of human beings; it does not account for individual motives.

- *May be inherently tautological.* Criminal-norm learning is central, but the theory views behavior as evidence of those norms; independent evidence of learning is often missing in tests of the theory.

Beginning in the late 1980s, studies of only Sutherland's learning theory became increasingly rare, as researchers interested in the criminal learning process began turning their attention more to social learning theory.[5]

Social Learning Theory   There are at least four approaches to testing social learning, each predicated on a criticism or concern with some aspect of the theory.[6] For example, many early tests focused on drug use, causing critics to question the theory's scope and generalizability of the theory (Alarid, Burton, and Cullen 2000; Warr 2002). About half of 133 published articles using elements of the theory that were published between 1974 (after Akers' reformulation of differential association/differential reinforcement theory as social learning theory) and 2003 focused on self-reported drug use, while about one-quarter looked at serous delinquency (Pratt, Cullen et al. 2008).

In response to claims that the theory's reach seemed limited to drug use (e.g., recall the emphasis on nonsocial reinforcement, such as those associated with the intense high of using certain drugs), the first approach extended the theory's explanatory reach into behaviors not previously considered. As a case in point, William Skinner and Anne Fream (1997) employed social learning to study computer crime among college students. They reported that measures of differential association, differential reinforcements, and punishments, as well as definitions and sources of imitation, performed well in predicting self-reported computer crime (e.g., engaging in software piracy, guessing passwords, inserting viruses, modifying computer files without permission, and accessing accounts or files without permission). Other researchers report similar results for studies of cheating and crime among college students (Payne and Salotti 2007), youth gang membership (Winfree, Vigil-Backstrom, and Mays 1994), and rape and sexual aggression (Sellers, Cochran, and Winfree 2002).[7] In the wake of 9/11, some suggest that it may be applied broadly to politically inspired acts of violence and terrorism (Akers and Silverman 2004; Castle and Hensley 2002; Winfree and Akins 2008).

A second approach is for researchers to examine key subelements of the theory, particularly the claims that differential reinforcements are both social and nonsocial (Akers 1985). In his first full test of social learning theory, Akers and associates found that differential reinforcements, including social and nonsocial elements, contributed to the overall explanatory power of the theory, although they were less important than, for example, differential associations and definitions. Subsequent studies by others (Winfree and Griffiths 1983; Winfree et al. 1993) found that differential reinforcements performed with less consistency, although, like Akers, these studies involved only illicit or illegal drug use and not other forms of delinquency.

Recent tests of the differential reinforcement hypothesis looked at serious crimes. Three studies are particularly instructive. First, Wood and associates (1997) addressed nonsocial reinforcement of habitual criminal conduct, studying the self-reported violent and nonviolent crimes of nearly 300 convicted habitual offenders. The neurophysiological high offenders associated with the act suggests that physiological sensations are instrumental in continuing criminal conduct. Second, following the nonsocial reinforcements theme, David May (2003) studied the ability of nonsocial reinforcements to predict violence in a statewide cross-sectional sample of adolescents. He measured these reinforcements by

COMPARATIVE CRIMINOLOGY—WORLD VIEWS ON CRIME AND JUSTICE: Social Learning Theory and French, Indian, and Chinese Youths

Researchers have subjected social learning theory to tests in Western and Eastern cultures. Concerning the former, Clayton Hartjen and S. Priyadarsini administered items derived from the culturally grounded version of the U.S. National Youth Survey to a sample of middle and high school students in rural central France. They used questions that reflected the arguments of both social learning theory and a theory examined later in this chapter, social bonding theory. They found that while the elements of social bonding failed to create a reliable scale for the French youths, social learning provided reliable and quite interesting insights into self-reported delinquency among both the boys and girls. The authors suggest that the performance of social learning theory in their study supports "social learning/differential association theory as (or as part of) a universal explanation of youth crime and delinquency and possibly criminality as such" (p. 402).

Hartjen and Sesha Kethineni applied elements of strain, bonding, and social learning theory to a representative sample of high school students in Madras, India, which included upper-, middle-, and working-class children. Self-reported delinquency was again the dependent variable, as measured by a version of the U.S. National Youth Survey which colleagues helped ground in the experiences of contemporary Indian youth. Hartjen and Kethineni compared the responses of these Indian adolescents with a sample of U.S. children who completed a previous National Youth Survey. Only variables drawn from social learning theory performed consistently across nations and gender.

Finally, Shu-Neu Wang and Gary F. Jensen provided an elaborate test of social learning theory in a large representative sample of junior high school students in Taipei, Taiwan. As with the two previous studies, the researchers solicited self-report information on juvenile misconduct. Their findings were remarkably similar to those reported in the similar cross-sectional studies of American youth. Particularly salient for this chapter is their observation that the basic elements of learning identified by Akers and others performed as expected within this sample of Taiwanese children.

SOURCES: Hartjen and Priyadarsini (2003); Hartjen and Kethineni (1999); Wang and Jensen (2003).

asking about the intrinsic value associated with forms of misconduct (e.g., "Sometimes I enjoy going against the rules and doing things that I am not supposed to"). The dependent variable was self-reported involvement in violent behavior, which nonsocial reinforcements predicted best, outperforming either differential associations or social control variables. Finally, Cesar Rebellon (2006) examined the longitudinal effects of social reinforcements by using the logic of operant conditioning. Rebellon looked at two waves of the National Youth Survey, a representative survey of the nation's youth conducted periodically during the 1980s. As measures of social reinforcements, he included the significance of and time spent in socializing activities with friends. Rebellon's analysis did not support the direct-reinforcement hypothesis. Rather, if social reinforcing is occurring, it is vicarious, meaning that individuals are likely to adjust their behavior based on what they see as the social consequences of misbehaving for peer-perpetrators.

A third approach examines the cross-cultural applicability of social learning theory. In a series of studies, Winfree and associates demonstrated the theory's ability to predict delinquency and drug use when the groups studied include minority-group members. That is, social learning variables performed well in predicting drug use among junior high and high school students, irrespective of race or ethnicity (Sellers, Winfree, and Griffiths 1993; Winfree and Bernat 1998;

Winfree and Griffiths 1983; Winfree, Griffiths, and Sellers 1989). Tests involving youth gang involvement and serious delinquency by high school students in cities with large Hispanic American populations yielded similar results. Gang involvement and self-reported delinquency are also best understood in social learning terms, regardless of the respondents' race or ethnicity (Sellers et al. 1993; Winfree, Bernat, and Esbensen 2001; Winfree et al. 1989; Winfree et al. 1994). Learning variables performed best when the self-reported behavior was "group-context offending" (e.g., group fighting or drive-by shootings). As the above international box suggests, social learning theory crosses not only cultural barriers within the U.S., but also provides similar insights into the misbehavior of youth in other nations as well.

Longitudinal studies of social learning theory constitute a fourth research track. Given the processual nature of social learning, longitudinal tests are essential. Marvin Krohn and associates (1985) found that social learning variables predicted changes in the cigarette smoking exhibited by junior high and high school boys at two different times. Winfree and associates also found support for social learning principles as predictors of adolescent drug use in successive cohorts of children (Winfree and Griffiths 1983) and panels of the same youths through time (Sellers and Winfree 1990; Winfree 1985).[8]

The conclusions of a social learning theory meta-analysis provide backing for Akers' main contentions: Support was high for differential associations and differential definitions; however, support was lower for differential reinforcements and modeling (Pratt et al. 2008). Critics of this application of operant conditioning to Sutherland's crime-learning process, nonetheless, point out several general shortcomings:

- *Does not specify workings of punishments and reinforcements.* Early versions of social learning theory misled sociologists and criminologists about the principles of operant conditioning (Adams 1973). Other critics observed that social learning theory fails to state what is rewarded and not rewarded, as well as what is considered rewarding and not rewarding (Chambliss 1988). Akers (1985:43) concurred: "The theory is ... incapable of accounting for why anyone or anything is socially defined as undesirable.... The theory does not say how or why the culture, structure, and social patterning of society sets up and implements certain sets and schedules of reactions to given behavior and characteristics."

- *May be inherently tautological.* Social learning, like differential association, may be tautological. Some learning attributes crime to deviant norms and proceeds to take the forbidden behavior as evidence of those norms (Goode 1984:30).

- *Rarely applied to serious law-violating behavior.* Most tests involve relatively minor forms of social deviance (e.g., youthful cigarette smoking); largely missing are tests that involve serious delinquency or crime (Curran and Renzetti 1994:196). A corollary of this criticism is that social learning, like differential association theory, cannot help society deal with serious crime, as few tests involve behaviors beyond minor forms of youthful rule breaking.

Social learning theory challenged social bonding theory through the final three decades of the twentieth century as the most tested criminological theories (Akers and Sellers 2009). Perhaps as important (for our purposes) we can find implications drawn from social learning theory throughout contemporary criminal justice policies and practices, even if, as we discuss next, those implications trouble some policy makers and practitioners.

Learning Theories, Public Policy, and Criminal Justice Practices

The differential association/social learning tradition troubles some policy makers. On a commonsense level, the "crime-as-learned-behavior" argument seems clear, but some policy makers miss key parts of the theory. Perhaps the best example involves the concept of "bad companions." This oversimplification of the social learning model is promoted in families, public schools, businesses, and other social institutions, including the military. Often this concept operates in the following manner: When we are young, our parents encourage us to avoid bad companions. Early in school we learn to avoid contact with children identified by teachers and other friends as troublemakers, especially classmates often suspended or expelled from the school. Later, as we start our careers, we continue to encounter warnings against bad companions, especially "slackers" and others with poor work habits. We get promoted; they get fired.

This conceptualization overlooks the fact that social learning involves more than steering clear of bad companions. Controlling the sources of definitions favorable to law-violating behavior is a far more difficult task than avoiding bad companions, although some zealots may attempt this task by censoring music, books, and movies. Sutherland, Akers, and other proponents of social learning might argue that such efforts will meet with limited success because social groups, and not the mass media, are a necessary ingredient.

Other elements of social learning find their way into the lexicon of our social and public institutions, including families and schools. For example, parents, schoolteachers, social workers, correctional officers, and corporate leaders use operant conditioning, with its reinforcement and punishment processes. Few of these individuals know the formal terms for the processes or their related elements, but they appreciate the method and understand the expected results. If this discussion sounds a little like deterrence theory, the similarities are intended. Indeed, Akers (1990) believed that all of the causal elements embodied in deterrence theory and rational choice theory are contained in social learning theory. In any event, social learning principles of criminal conduct, given their ties to general learning principles, are an integral part of the nation's sociolegal fabric.

Akers and Christine Sellers (2009:110–18) maintain that social learning's influences are evident in a wide range of early delinquency prevention and intervention programs. For instance, at Highfields, an alternative residential treatment program for delinquent boys in the 1950s, counselors attempted to create prosocial peer groups using a technique called Guided Group Interaction (GGI). The intent of these sessions was to create prosocial definitions, attitudes, and behavior (Weeks 1958). The boys in the program fared better than did those in a control group. A similar program operated at nonresidential facility called Essexfield. In this setting, experimental subjects fared no better than controls; however, the boys at Essexfield were better at staying out of trouble than boys sent straight to the state's reform school.

Other classic experiments intended to change the lives of delinquent boys evolved from operant conditioning generally and social learning theory specifically. LaMar T. Empey (1972) used a mix of differential association principles and GGI at the Provo and Silverlake experiments. The Oregon Social Learning Center (OSLC) operates one of the longest-running and most ambitious crime prevention programs based on learning principles. Using a "coercive family model," Gerald Patterson and colleagues at the OSLC both research social learning and deliver services based on social learning (Patterson 1975; Patterson, Debaryshe, and Ramsey 1989; Snyder and Patterson 1995; Reid, Patterson, and Snyder 2002). The program's uses cognitive and behavioral programming to enhance a range of parenting skills and general behavioral responses to intrafamilial and extrasocietal stress points. For example, some of the "courses" built problem-solving skills for children or equipped parents with specific skill sets to deal with family problems in fair and consistent ways.

In terms of delinquency prevention, particularly gang and violence reduction efforts, few programs match the longevity and scope of Gang Resistance Education and Training (G.R.E.A.T.). Created in the early 1990s, the first iteration of G.R.E.A.T. put specially trained police officers into middle school classrooms to administer a cognitive-based program consisting of nine lessons. While not addressing specific learning constructs, the lessons clearly reflect their intent (Winfree, Esbensen, and Osgood 1996; but see also Akers and Sellers 2009:119). The goal, much like the previously mentioned GGI and learning model programming, was to equip the participating children with an arsenal of attitudes, behavioral cues, and conflict-resolution skills, among others, that would arm them against both community gangs and violence. A multiyear, multisite assessment of G.R.E.A.T., however, failed to show that the program achieved its stated goal of inoculating children from the influences of gangs (Esbensen, Osgood et al. 2001).[9]

Law Enforcement Practices In addition to *what* they do, *who* the police are and *how* they perceive their world seems to have links to the processes implicit in differential association and social learning theories. Whether police work attracts certain types of people or the job shapes the people is at the center of a longstanding debate. If police work attracts certain types of people, then society must rely on psychological screening devices to keep out the undesirable one, assuming the psychological devices are accurate. If who police officers are is related to police work, then we need to study professional socialization. For example, as we learned in Chapter 4, police researchers often describe officers as cynical, although there is disagreement among researchers as to the implications of police cynicism (Anson, Mann, and Sherman 1986; Niederhoffer 1969; Regoli 1976). A cynical cop is one who views the public and other institutions, including the Supreme Court, with a measure of distrust and perhaps even hostility. But is this necessarily bad? Samuel Walker (1992:333) suggested that cynicism might be a positive attribute protecting officers from certain aspects of their work that are unpleasant or difficult to deal with, including the victims of crime. Does this sound familiar? If not, we suggest that you review the techniques of neutralization.

Process theories help us understand police corruption, or the misuse of authority by police officers for personal gain or the benefit of others. This behavior is most likely to occur in heterogeneous societies with high levels of conflict and dissensus (Walker 1992:268). Police corruption is often linked to pressures emanating from deviant peers and the need for group solidarity. Officers who refuse to "play along" may be ostracized or worse (Stoddard 1968; Walker 1992; Westley 1970). Thus, police deviance may be understood in terms of social learning theory: Rewarded behavior is repeated behavior.

Judicial Practices   Researchers suggest that differential association/social learning principles are at work throughout the judicial system. Attorneys must learn to work with the courtroom work group—all the key players in the judicial system—or suffer potentially negative consequences (Clynch and Neubauer 1981; Eisenstein and Jacobs 1977). Jurors, as novices to the process, must quickly learn both the practice and the philosophy of their fact-finding roles (Balch, Griffiths et al. 1976). Finally, probation/parole officers must learn what judges expect in their presentence investigations (Abadinsky 2009; McShane and Krause 1993; Rosencrance 1987).

Some legal scholars have suggested that lawyers are subject to the same social learning forces as criminals; only the direction traveled is different (except in the case of unethical conduct and corruption) (Pollock 2003; Wrightsman, Nietzel, and Fortune 1994). Central to this position is legal education. Thanks largely to the efforts of the American Bar Association, legal education in this country is extremely homogeneous. This uniformity is not necessarily a bad thing; it ensures that attorneys share a common understanding of the law and its application to meet the needs of a rational legal system. Lawyers can predict what a court will do; judges treat cases according to shared guidelines so as to earn the respect of the legal community. The courts' operations are made far more predictable by the homogeneous nature of legal education.

In law school, would-be attorneys learn what is acceptable and unacceptable from law professors, their most immediate role models. One survey of law students found that "the ability to think like a lawyer" was the skill on which they rated themselves highest (Gee and Jackson 1977). They were able to think unemotionally in the sense that they could put aside or repress the human element in complex issues (Willging and Dunn 1982).

Consider the links between learning theory and the role of prosecuting attorneys. Research on legal interns in prosecutors' offices suggests that as they immerse themselves in "real-life" legal situations, would-be prosecutors quickly learn that, after making a decision to prosecute, there can be no turning back (Winfree, Kielich, and Clark 1984). Some legal scholars define this as "conviction psychology" (Felkenes 1975). Legal interns and new prosecutors alike must learn definitions that place prosecutorial work in a positive light; they are protected from the possible negative implications of prosecutorial work by other definitions, all of which function as discriminative stimuli (Hubka 1975; Winfree and Kielich 1979; Winfree et al. 1984). Few careers reflect a greater appreciation for the concept of differential associations than the law: Lawyers work together, socialize together, and often live in the same neighborhoods.

The significance of learning theory extends into the judge's chambers; researchers have identified five stages of judicial professional socialization, most of which involve elements of learning theory (Alpert 1981). The first stage, *general professional socialization*, begins in law school. Elevation to the bench begins *initiation*, the first of four on-bench stages, wherein the judge-initiate learns about being a judge. Next, the judge enters the *resolution* stage, as he or she moves from being an advocate to being an arbiter. In the fourth stage, the judge enters the establishment phase, when he or she settles into being a judge. The final stage, *commitment*, is a time when the judge really begins to enjoy the act of judging, a phase demarked by comradeship with other participants (Alpert 1981). What the judge has learned along the way is more than merely how to be a judge. The less tangible expressive content of judgeship—the unique values, ideologies, decorum, and coping strategies—must also be learned. Law school faculty does not teach the expressive aspects of being a judge; a new judge must learn them on the job (Holten and Lamar 1991).

Correctional Practices   Learning theories provide insights into the lives of correctional clients. Every probation and parole agency requires offenders under supervision to avoid associating with people with a criminal record. Many of the conditions of release to which a parolee or probationer must agree reflect some aspect of differential association/learning theory's concern for peer influences (Abadinsky 2009).

Prisons and jails provide many examples of social learning at work. For instance, "prisonization" is the process of embracing, to a greater or lesser extent, the prison's culture (Clemmer 1940; Thomas 1970). Prison researchers contend that negativistic prison and jail inmate societies (1) derive from attitudes and orientations that inmates bring with them into the institution, (2) emerge within the group as a result of the deprivations of institutional life, or (3) are a result of the actions of both forces (Akers, Hayner, and Grunninger 1974; Thomas 1970). It seems highly likely that the ability of prison society to shape inmate responses to incarceration is a reflection of the principles of differential reinforcement and differential association: rewarded behavior is repeated behavior, especially given omnipresent and omnipotent inmate peer groups.

Therapeutic drug communities, located inside and outside correctional facilities, provide drug-using criminals with support, understanding, and affection from people with similar life experiences. They find a *community* with which they can identify and people toward whom they can express their best human emotions rather than their worst (Yablonsky 1989). Such programs rely heavily on social learning principles. Treatment does not eliminate the negative behavior patterns and attitudinal orientations. Instead, it offers appropriate alternative approaches to resocializing individuals, teaching them behaviors and orientations that will promote prosocial adjustment, and offering a new lifestyle. This process includes reinforcements to continue acceptable behavior and punishments to extinguish the unacceptable. Program participants have lower-than-typical recidivism (Lipton 1994; see also Andrews and Bonta, 1998; Andrews, Zinger et al. 1990).

CONTROL THEORIES

Most criminologists acknowledge the roles played by informal control mechanisms, such as family members and neighbors, and formal control mechanisms, such as schools, police, and the courts: the weaker the former, the greater the reliance on the latter (Black, 1976). The strength of the criminal justice system is rarely sufficient to do more than react to crime, let alone prevent it. Social control theorists assume that, if left to their own devices, all people would violate norms. For them the key question is: Why don't more people commit crimes? This question has several answers.

Early Control Theories

In the 1950s and early 1960s, four criminologists examined the social control factors associated with delinquency. In looking to the individual offender for answers, they laid the groundwork for social control theories.

Personal Control   Albert Reiss (1951) observed that youthful probation revocations are more likely when juveniles receive poor psychiatric evaluations. He attributed both poor psychiatric conditions and probation revocations to failures in **personal control.** Low-control youths meet their personal needs in a manner that conflicts with community rules. However, Reiss himself found little empirical support for this contention.

A Stake in Conformity   Perhaps the problem is a weak **stake in conformity.** Jackson Toby (1957) believed that, although every youth is tempted to break the law, some—particularly those doing well in school—risk a great deal by giving in to temptation. Being caught means possible punishment and threatens the future career being contemplated. Poor school performers risk only punishment: Their futures are less bright, so their stake in conformity is lower. Toby speculated that there is more delinquency in urban areas than in suburban areas because low-stake urban youths are exposed to similarly disposed peers; in contrast, suburban low-stake youths, with fewer similarly disposed peers, are "merely unhappy" and not necessarily delinquent.

The Family and Social Control   Reiss and Toby barely acknowledged the family as a source of control. In contrast, F. Ivan Nye (1958) saw ties between family, social controls, and youthful misbehavior. According to Nye, social control has four manifestations: (1) direct controls, such as family-level punishments and restrictions; (2) indirect controls, such as affectional identification with one's parents and noncriminals generally; (3) internal controls derived from one's conscience; and (4) the availability of the means necessary to gratify personal needs. Nye found impressive support for his theory: Misbehavior was greatest among those youths with poor family relationships and weak social controls. However, as critics, principally Toby (1959), have pointed out, Nye failed to study serious delinquency. Moreover, actively delinquent youths may have been more willing than others to report poor family relationships, thus creating a bias that resulted in high support for Nye's theory.

Containment Theory   Walter Reckless (1961) took the search for social controls to a new level with **containment theory.** He saw forces pulling people away from conventional society or pushing them toward misbehavior, including these:

- **Social pressures,** such as poor living conditions, minority-group status, poor lifestyle opportunities, and family conflicts.

- **Social pulls** that keep the individual away from acceptable behavior, such as criminal and delinquent subcultures or bad companions.

- **Biological** or **psychological pushes,** such as inner tensions, hostility, and aggressiveness.

- **Rebellion against authority** that originates within the individual and leads to unacceptable norms of living.

Given these forces, only outer and inner containment stands between any individual and a life of crime. Reckless saw these restraining forces as sufficient to control most behavior. **Outer containment** comes from the family and other support groups; it involves, among other things, a consistent moral front, reasonable norms and expectations, effective supervision and discipline, and group cohesiveness. **Inner containment,** a psychological concept, operates to balance ego strength, the superego, a sense of responsibility, and goal orientation, providing an internal locus of control over an individual's behavior.

Social Bond Theory

Social bonding theory emerged in the turbulent 1960s, and it would become one of the longest-lived and most researched control theories in criminology (Akers and Sellers 2009). Travis Hirschi, the theory's progenitor, wrote: "The bond of affection for conventional persons is a major deterrent to crime" (1972:83). In essence, the **social bond** is the sum total of the forces in a person's social and physical environment that connects him or her to society and its moral constraints. For example, a lack of attachment to others frees an individual from moral constraints, a concept that has direct ties to Durkheim's anomie but which is now expressed in individual terms rather than at the societal level. Absent such bonds, people are free to deviate, to act without "moral" restraint. According to

Hirschi's variant of social control theory, weak bonds do not predict deviance, but simply make it possible or probable.

Hirschi believed that humankind's natural propensity was to engage in hedonistic pursuits. Understanding the social bond's key elements, then, was crucial to understanding how it worked (or failed to work) in moving individuals away from their natural propensities toward legal conformity.

The Social Bond's Key Elements   Hirschi saw the social bond as curbing a natural human propensity for misbehavior. Youths who are bonded to social institutions, including family and school, are less inclined to engage in delinquency. Hirschi's bond has four elements, all of which are tied to conventional norms, rules, activities, and significant others:

- **Attachment** is affection for and sensitivity to social group members. Without attachment, there is no internalization of norms and values. The child who exhibits no affective, or emotional, bonds to others and who is not particularly sensitive to his or her own feelings, may feel, in Hirschi's (1969:18) words, "free to deviate." Researchers measure attachment by the level of parental supervision or discipline, the quality of child–parent communications, or attitudes toward school and school authority.

- **Commitment** refers to investment in conventional norms and rules; this concept recasts Toby's stake in conformity. Attachment and commitment reflect personal attitudes or orientations. Researchers measure commitment by two methods. First, children's engagement in adult activities, including smoking, drinking, and sex, indicates a lack of commitment. Second, educational or occupational aspirations and expectations—two strain concepts—also find their way into social control tests as measures of commitment to conventionality.

- **Involvement** is behavioral and measures the level of conventional activity, a modern version of the age-old dictum "idle hands are the devil's workshop," which includes an opportunity element (Curran and Renzetti 1994:200).

- **Belief** contrasts with Sykes and Matza's neutralization techniques. For Sykes and Matza, conventional moral beliefs are paramount, and to engage in misbehavior, youths must neutralize their moral force. According to Hirschi, belief in the correctness of norms is variable; he questioned whether everyone feels bound to adhere to the dominant moral beliefs. He hypothesized that delinquency is more likely when a youth attaches less significance to conventional moral beliefs.

Delbert Elliott and associates (1985) conclude that the strength of delinquent peer bonding derives from the actor's ties to conventional groups. We would expect delinquent behavior when familial bonds are overcome by bonds to the peer group. The strength of the bond can be observed: If any of the social bond elements are weak, even if other strong ones are present, there is a heightened probability of misconduct. Figure 7.3 summarizes the social bond and its ties to conformity and misbehavior.

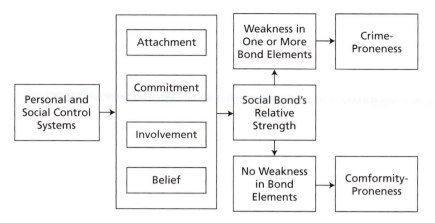

F I G U R E 7.3   Social Control Theory: Hirschi's Social Bond

Self-Control Theory

In the late twentieth century, Hirschi and Michael Gottfredson took on the criminal justice and criminological establishment by questioning the value of the career criminal concept. In so doing, they challenged many contemporary crime control policies and intervention strategies, including the policy of selective incapacitation and "three-strikes" legislation (see Chapter 2). They also challenged much of the life course and developmental criminology that flowed directly from the career criminal research (see Chapter 12), ideas that have been linked to the frequency of offending.[10] In place of traditional social organizational or social process theories, Gottfredson and Hirschi (1990) proposed a "general theory of crime," one that they claimed comported well with the observed stability of crime propensity and versatility, now called both **self-control theory** and **event–propensity theory** (Gottfredson and Hirschi 1989; 1990).

Hearkening back to classical rational theories, Gottfredson and Hirschi explain that self-interest motivates human behavior and further reflects a universal desire to secure pleasure and avoid pain. Sounding like conventional control theorists, they described criminality's origins in child rearing. These early beginnings, claim Gottfredson and Hirschi (1989:61), "suggest that criminality is more or less naturally present, that it requires socialization for its control." They saw crime and analogous acts (e.g., drinking, smoking, drug use, illicit sex, and even serious accidents) collectively and individually offering short-term pleasures (e.g., money, altered states of consciousness, thrills, and excitement) for little effort. Unrestrained individuals, or those with little commitment to conventionality and equally low concern for the long-term consequences of their behavior, are thus attracted to crime. They exhibit called low self-control, a precursor for crime and delinquency (Hay and Forrest 2006).

Defining Self-Control   Self-control's causal elements are straightforward: Parental management and child-rearing practices are central because they are

---

IN THEIR OWN WORDS: Process Theories of Crime and Delinquency

Social process theorists had unique ways of viewing the attainment of criminal status. An important difference was that one group—the learning theorists—observed that humans must be exposed to intense and personal socialization forces before becoming criminal. Conversely, the control theorists placed great stock in the role played by social institutions in maintaining control over otherwise hedonistic and mischievous humans. The following quotes by key control theorists help to clarify these differences.

- *Sutherland on crime and opportunity:* "The tendencies and inhibitions at the moment of the criminal behavior are, to be sure, largely a product of the earlier history of the person, but the expression of these tendencies and inhibitions is a reaction to the immediate situation as defined by that person. The situation operates in many ways, of which perhaps the least important is the provision of an opportunity for a criminal act" (p. 327).

- *Burgess and Akers on criminal behavior:* "We know from the Law of Differential Reinforcement that that operant which produces the most reinforcement will become dominant if it results in reinforcement. Thus, if lawful behavior did not result in reinforcement, the strength of the behavior would be weakened, and a state of deprivation would result, which would, in turn, increase the probability that other behaviors would be emitted which are reinforced, and such behavior would be strengthened" (p. 143).

- *Hirschi on control theory:* "Control theories assume that delinquent acts result when an individual's bond to society is weak or broken. Since these theories embrace two highly complex concepts, the *bond* of the individual to *society,* it is not surprising that they have at one time or another formed the basis of explanations of most forms of aberrant or unusual behavior" (p. 16; emphasis in original).

- *Hirschi and Gottfredson on the role of parents:* "First, the parents may not care for the child….; second, the parents, even if they care, may not have the time or energy to monitor the child's behavior; third, the parents, even if they care and monitor, may not see anything wrong with the child's behavior; finally, even if everything else is in place, the parents may not have the inclination or the means to punish the child" (p. 98).

SOURCES: Burgess and Akers (1966); Gottfredson and Hirschi (1990); Hirschi (1969); Sutherland (1947).

---

instrumental in establishing self-control as early as age 10 or 11. Adequate parental management includes (1) the monitoring and recognition of deviant behavior in a child, (2) appropriate punishment in response to inappropriate behavior ("let the punishment fit the crime"), and (3) emotional investment in the child (Gottfredson and Hirschi 1990). They conclude that inadequate parental management results in low self-control, which influences an individual's choices when faced with an opportunity for immediate gain through little investment. In the end, low-self-control persons exhibit a wide variety of inappropriate behaviors, including crime, because such activities hold the promise of immediate pleasure for minimal effort.

Low-self-control individuals—the unrestrained—share six common characteristics:

1. *A need for immediate gratification.* They seek short-term, immediate rewards (pleasures); the concept of deferred gratification, or postponing of pleasures and rewards to a more appropriate time or even renounced entirely, is foreign to them.

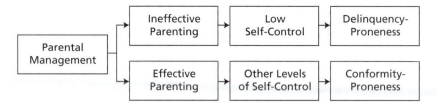

FIGURE 7.4   Gottfredson and Hirschi's Self-Control Theory

2. *Simplicity*. They avoid complicated tasks and decisions, preferring to seek easy answers and easy work.

3. *Physicality*. They prefer to keep physically active.

4. *A need for risk taking*. They are supreme risk takers. They tend to be impetuous and impulsive; they enjoy taking their lives in their own hands, and they seek excitement and danger over sameness and safeness.

5. *Self-centeredness*. They tend to emphasize personal needs, wants, and desires while ignoring those of even significant others, such as relatives and friends.

6. *Anger*. They have a low frustration tolerance and exhibit a tendency to resort to aggressive coping strategies when faced with frustrating situations or events.

In summary, ineffective parenting determines whether children will seek out crime and analogous behavior largely before they enter their teenage years. By the time they are 10 or 11 years of age, the bedrock of low self-control, as summarized in the six characteristics, is well established and largely immutable, claim Gottfredson and Hirschi. Figure 7.4 summarizes Gottfredson and Hirschi's self-control theory.

Assessing Control Theories

The two primary forms of control theory at the start of the twenty-first century were social bonding and self-control theory, although some criminologists view the latter as an extension of the former (Akers and Sellers 2009). Nonetheless, we provide separate assessments of each tradition.

Social Bond Theory   Since 1969, Hirschi's social bond has dominated tests of social control, while few studies have explored more than one control theory. For example, in a study of adolescent drug use, Anastasios Marcos and Stephen Bahr (1988) combined belief in conventional values and attachment to parents, religion, and school with Reckless's inner containment. The inclusion of inner containment resulted in a significant improvement in predictive ability, but results remained modest. Other criminologists, recognizing the natural links between control and strain theory, and their mutual impact on school performance, have incorporated both elements in their tests (Cernkovich and Giordano 1992; Elliott and Huizinga 1984; Elliott, Huizinga, and Ageton 1985; Rodriguez and Weisburd 1991).[11] We return to theory integration in Chapter 12.

Early social control studies placed great emphasis on parental attachment and yielded considerable empirical support.[12] Nonetheless, social bond theory excludes two critical aspects of parental control. First, Hirschi dismissed direct parental controls, ranging from parental specification of rules and constraints to physical punishments, as inconsequential. The important question for him was "whether the parent is psychologically present when the temptation to commit a crime occurs" (Hirschi 1969:88). Others have suggested that direct parental control plays a role in reducing proneness to delinquency, either in concert with strong parental bonding (Patterson 1982) or independently (Rankin and Wells 1990; Williams, Clinton et al. 1992).

Second, social bonding theory ignores parental influences as models of youthful misconduct (Foshee and Bauman 1992). In Hirschi's (1969:73) words, "We honor those we admire not by imitation but by adherence to conventional standards." At least in the case of adolescent cigarette smoking, children honor those they admire by imitation: Strongly attached children of nonsmokers view nonsmoking as conventional and imitate their parents; strongly attached children of smokers view smoking as conventional and imitate their parents (Foshee and Bauman 1992; Jensen and Brownfield 1983).

Attachment to peers does not necessarily guarantee conventional behavior unless the peers themselves are conventional. Attachment to deviant peers, however, may weaken the social bond to conventional society: Youths attached to delinquent friends are themselves more likely to be delinquent (Conger 1976; Elliott et al. 1985). The inclusion of attachment to delinquent peers in any test of social bond theory increases the model's overall predictive power; however, this inclusion makes the test virtually indistinguishable from one of differential association theory.

Since the 1969 publication of Hirschi's *Causes of Delinquency*, researchers and theorists have expressed several general concerns about the social bond:

- *Conventional versus unconventional involvement.* Involvement has proved problematic since Hirschi's first test. Involvement in conventional activities, he reported, was directly related to delinquency: the greater the involvement in dating, reading, working, watching television, and playing games, the higher the reported frequency of delinquency. Perhaps the theory "overestimated the significance of involvement in conventional activities" (Hirschi, 1969:230–31). However, comparing youths involved in conventional activities (e.g., supervised social events and noncompetitive sports) with those involved in nonconventional and unsupervised peer-oriented activities revealed that the former group is less delinquent than the latter (Agnew and Peterson 1989).

- *Natural aggression assumption.* That humans possess innately aggressive or violent tendencies is a much debated assumption in the social and behavioral sciences (Vold and Bernard 1986:247).

- *Trivial versus real delinquency.* Tests of social control theory tend to employ "relatively trivial offenses committed by essentially nondelinquent youths" (Vold and Bernard 1986:245), a fact attested to by Hirschi (1969:41):

COMPARATIVE CRIMINOLOGY—WORLD VIEWS ON CRIME AND JUSTICE: Social Bonding and Turkish Youth

Studies of crime and justice are rare in Islamic nations, even secular Islamic ones such as Turkey. Theory-driven studies are even less common. Özden Özbay and Yusuf Özcan obtained a representative sample of high school students in Ankara using a self-administered questionnaire.[13] For the dependent variable, the researchers included a range of items, largely drawn from the now ubiquitous National Youth Survey (see also Elliott and Ageton 1980). For predictors, they used attachment to parents and teachers, conventionality of peers, family supervision, school commitment, normative beliefs, and school involvement, the latter measured by hours spent on homework. The final sample represented a cross-section of high school age boys and girls living in Ankara.

The researchers explored the ability of the social bond variables to predict total delinquency, assaultive crimes, school-based delinquency, and public disturbances. Their aim was to determine whether a theory created in the West would work in a nation that blends secularism and Islam. Contrary to their

concerns, the theory indeed provided good insights into the four forms of misconduct, confirming what others have found using Western samples. In particular, attachment to teachers, family supervision, school commitment, and belief in conventional values were consistent performers in their analyses. Conversely, the variables of attachment to family, conventionality of peers, and school involvement did not yield consistent relationships with the measures of misconduct.

Finally, it is important to note that in Özbay and Özcan's analyses, the control variables (i.e., measures of differential association) mediated the effects of all the significant social bonding measures on the dependent variables, except public disturbances. Interestingly, the researchers suggest additional tests in rural Turkey (see the test of social learning theory in rural France above), given the higher levels of familial control likely in such environs.

SOURCES: Özbay and Özcan (2006).

"Delinquents are so obviously underrepresented among those completing the questionnaires that the results need not be taken seriously." In tests with *both* minor delinquency (e.g., alcohol and marijuana use) and serious delinquency (e.g., property and violent offenses), social control theory better explained the former than the latter (Krohn and Massey 1980; Rosenbaum 1987; Rosenbaum and Lasley 1990).

- *Social control versus differential association.* Early studies comparing the relative merits of differential association and social control tended to support the latter over the former. Matsueda's (1982) reanalysis of Hirschi's data, along with reconceptualizations of key differential association elements, yielded the opposite results. Gerben Bruinsma (1992), using a sample of Dutch youths, reported findings very similar to those of Matsueda. Yet, Costello and Vowell's (1999) reanalysis cast doubt on the work of Bruinsma and Matsueda. This issue—whether a theory that attempts to explain how humans who are basically *tabla rasa* (i.e., blank slates) at birth become criminal or how society controls humans who are basically hedonistic—is likely to continue unabated.

Criticisms aside, social bonding is one of the most influential crime theories of the twentieth century. The characterization of the empirical findings ranges from "moderate" to "good" (Akers and Sellers 2009). Moreover, the theory is rich in its implications for criminal justice policies and practices. As the following box suggests, this theory also has implications for crime and delinquency in other cultures.

Self-Control Theory   Tests of self-control also fit into several distinct categories. First are those that address the theory's ability to yield insights into a variety of analogous behaviors. For example, Dana Lynskey and associates (2000) found an inverse relationship between self-control, as measured by an index of impulsivity, risk-seeking behavior and physicality, and self-reported youth gang involvement among a sample of eighth-grade students. The strongest single predictor of self-control was the level of parental monitoring: the greater the monitoring, the higher the self-control. Christine Sellers (1999) studied intimate violence within a sample of college students; she reported significant ties between courtship aggression and low self-control, opportunity, and perception of immediate gratification. Other topics addressed in self-control tests include cheating by college students (Cochran, Wood et al. 1998; Gibbs and Giever 1995), youthful drug use (Winfree and Bernat 1998; Wood, Cochran, Pfefferbaum, and Arneklev 1995), drunk driving (Keane, Maxim, and Teevan 1993), and accidents (Tremblay, Boulerie et al. 1995). In general, tests of analogous behavior and self-control provide at least modest support for self-control theory (Pratt and Cullen 2000).

A second type of test has provided indirect, inferential insights into self-control. Gottfredson and Hirschi predicted that low-self-control people will have higher rates of delinquency, regardless of any other characteristic. Terence P. Thornberry and his associates (1993), in a study of the role of youth gangs in facilitating delinquency, reported that gang members do not appear to be recruited based on their high propensity for delinquency. Gottfredson and Hirschi's theory recognizes that gang membership might provide the opportunity for any underlying delinquency propensity to be manifested more often and so accounts for the higher delinquency rates of active gang members. However, they have difficulty coming to grips with the fact that these gang members are *not* more delinquent than are nongang members before or after they are active in the gang (Thornberry, Krohn et al. 1993). Similarly, David Evans and his associates (1997) reported higher misbehavior by low-self-control individuals, irrespective of other community or individual characteristics. The quality of their lives and their life outcomes were also negatively impacted, including reduced church involvement, lower educational and occupational attainment, and diminished interpersonal communications with friends and relatives.

International and comparative tests represent a third form. Teresa LaGrange and Robert Silverman (1999) supported self-control in a Canadian study of self-reported delinquency; they also reported variations by gender, a finding replicated in the United States (Longshore, Turner, and Stein 1996; Lynskey et al. 2000). That is, females may have lesser inclination and fewer opportunities, findings consistent with the theory. (We return in Chapter 11 to gender-based differences in theoretical explanations.)

A subcategory of international studies involves more than one theory. For example, Bradley Wright and associates (1999) explored the effects of social bonds and self-control on a sample of Dunedin, New Zealand, residents, following them from birth to age 21. Low self-control in childhood predicted disrupted social bonds and delinquency in adolescence; however, social bonds apparently

COMPARATIVE CRIMINOLOGY—WORLD VIEWS ON CRIME AND JUSTICE: Self-Control Theory and Hungarian, Dutch, Swiss, Japanese, and American Youths

The general trend throughout the boxes dedicated to comparative criminology has been to highlight research in one other nation at a time. Researchers rarely possess the information to do true comparative studies, which would be to compare and contrast identical theoretical and behavioral measures across two or more nations. In an exception to this generalization, Alexander Vazsonyi and Lara Belliston examined levels of self-control and deviance for middle and late adolescents in Hungary, the Netherlands, Switzerland, Japan, and the United States. The samples consisted of children living in medium-sized cities; the youths in the European samples included both university-bound students and those participating in vocational/technical training, while the U.S. sample included high school, community college, and university students. The subjects constituted more of an available sample rather than a representative sample (i.e., sample members picked for their availability); however, its size (over 8,400 subjects) and cross-national nature make it unique. They used the Normative Deviance Scale, created by a group of international researchers, which provided seven different independent variables (i.e., vandalism, alcohol use, drug use, school misconduct, general deviance, theft, and assault), as well as an overall measure of normative misconduct.[14]

Their findings were consistent with the theory, supporting the culture-free nature of self-control concepts. The self-control variables, especially when considered with family processes (e.g., closeness, support, and monitoring) provided greater insights into the self-reported misconduct of the sampled youths than similar U.S.-based studies report, even though the measures of the independent variable (i.e., the six elements of self-control) were identical. However, the self-control measure revealed more about minor offending than serious delinquency. This study strongly suggests that current operationalizations of self-control theory, like social learning theory, transcend national boundaries.[15]

SOURCES: Reichel (2008); Vazsonyi, Pickering, et al. (2001).

mitigated (i.e., caused a temporary reduction in) these effects on adult criminality. Charles Tittle and associates provide two interesting international tests of self-control; one in Russia (Tittle and Botchkovar 2005), and the other in Ukraine (Antonaccio and Tittle 2008). In the first, the researchers examined whether motivations, such as target attractiveness, or controls, such as deterrence or self-control factors, were more important. Tittle and Botchkovar reported that the explanatory power of self-control was about what others observed it to be in Western samples; however, the attractiveness of the target far overshadowed either sanction fear or self-control levels in predicting criminal behavior. As the authors (2005:307) conclude: "The results suggest that in the production of criminal behavior, motivation may be more important than controls inhibiting criminal impulses." Working with Olena Antonaccio, Tittle (2008) adds morality to the mix, which they define as a cognitive conceptualization where they asked respondents to judge if certain acts seemed "right" or "wrong" to them.[16] Much like the study in Russia, the researchers reported that while self-control performed in concert with expectations (confirming again its cross-cultural relevance), its influences were weaker than morality. Morality's influences were strong and independent. As the saying goes: Always a bridesmaid, never a bride.

Overall, international research suggests that self-control translates reasonably well into non–American cultures, and performs much as it does in U.S.-based studies. The above box contains a unique five-country study of self-control.

Opponents and supporters generally focus on one or more of the following issues:

- *Generalness of self-control.* As articulated by Gottfredson and Hirschi, self-control theory is a general theory that explains all criminal behavior. But critics have pointed out that much crime does not fit the theory. Gottfredson and Hirschi, claim some critics, carefully tailored their crime facts to fit their theory. For example, Ken Polk (1991) observed that there is no "typical" homicide, and whatever exists is far from the two forms described by Gottfredson and Hirschi (i.e., homicides as the result of a heated argument and pursuant to a burglary). Similarly criticisms abound of Gottfredson and Hirschi's claim that white-collar crime is uncommon and that its participants conform to the same age and race distributions of other criminals. White-collar and corporate crimes simply do not work well within a self-control model (Ermann and Lundman 1992; Polk 1991; Reed and Yeager 1996; Steffensmeier 1989; see also Hirschi and Gottfredson 1989). Organizational offending must take into account factors not acknowledged by Gottfredson and Hirschi, including the actions of political, economic, and bureaucratic systems (Reed and Yeager 1996:377).

- *Self-control versus criminal personality.* Larry Siegel (1992:237) noted that "saying someone 'lacks self-control' implies that they suffer from a personality defect that makes them impulsive and rash." How does this characterization differ from the "criminal personality," a generalized description that is of little use to psychological clinicians or criminal justice practitioners?

- *May be inherently tautological.* Akers (1994:122–23) saw self-control theory as a tautology. He observed that Gottfredson and Hirschi used terms like "low self-control" and "high self-control" when they referred to the "differential propensity to commit or refrain from crime." According to Akers, reduced to its basic causal elements, the theory posits that low self-control is caused by low self-control. The lack of separate definitions for low self-control, crime propensity, and crime measures makes the theory untestable.

- *Multidimensionality versus unidimensionality of self-control.* Almost since its inception, criminologists have debated answers to an important measurement question: Is self-control a single dimension, as suggested by Gottfredson and Hirschi, or are the various characteristics of low self-control equally important? Early evidence supported the unidimensionality position (Arneklev, Grasmick, and Bursik 1999; Grasmick, Tittle et al. 1993); however, Peter Wood and his associates (1993) suggested that disaggregating self-control elements provides more insights into self-reported criminal conduct. This debate is far from resolved; indeed, we see the split between those who treat self-control as a unitary factor and as a multidimensional one in the studies we have just reviewed.

- *Ignores biopsychological origins.* Biocriminologists question the claim that parental management and not biological and genetic influences determine self-control; self-control appears to be part of a constellation of "executive functions" performed by the brain's prefrontal cortex (Beaver, Wright, and DeLisi 2007). Research using twins suggests that genetic and nonshared environmental factors strongly influenced self-control levels (Wright, Beaver et al. 2008).

- *Weaknesses in current operationalizations.* Hirschi (2004) suggests that most measures to date fail to capture what Gottfredson and he intended. Self-control reflects the immediate situation, as it is the "set of inhibitions one carries with one wherever one happens to go" (Hirschi 2004:543). Measures of low self-control conforming to his prescription have removed the attitudinal element and shown considerable utility, in particular, future research must consider self-control in a situational manner (Piquero and Bouffard 2007).[17]

- *Immutability of self-control measures.* The claim that self-control levels, established early in one's youth, do not change—the immutability-of-self-control hypothesis—is one of the theory's more controversial elements. Preliminary analyses of self-control measures over time support the stability position, although the time frames employed are relatively short (Arneklev, Cochran, and Gainey 1998; Arneklev, Grasmick, and Bursik 1999); however, research that extends the time period of several years finds less support for the immutability of self-control (Winfree, Taylor et al. 2006).

During the 1990s, dozens of studies explored the utility of self-control theory. Travis Pratt and Frances Cullen (2000) conducted a meta-analysis of 21 empirical studies of self-control theory, all published between 1993 and 1999. They reported that low self-control was an important predictor of crime and analogous behavior, irrespective of the sample employed. However, the constructs fare poorly in longitudinal research, and, when self-control theory is compared with social learning theory, the latter receives more empirical support than the former.

Control, Public Policy, and Criminal Justice Practices

According to Hirschi's social control theory, delinquent acts result when an individual's bond to society is weakened or broken. Attachment for conventional persons is, from this perspective, a major deterrent to crime, whereas lack of attachment frees others from moral constraints. In areas of poverty in urban America, increasing numbers of children live with neither a mother nor a father, creating what Jane Gross (1992) called America's "new orphans." Parents are institutionalized—in prisons, jails, or residential drug programs—or living marginal existences under the influence of heroin or other drugs. When they are present in the home, parents may be unwilling or ill-equipped to care for their offspring. These children are farmed out to relatives, friends, foster care, or institutions, and experience little stability and few, if any, lasting emotional ties.

Adding parental management, opportunity, and rational choice to the social control debate creates a new set of policy implications, but ones mirrored in the concerns of social bonding theory. The rational choice component of self-control theory portends many of the same policy implications found in rational

COMMENTS AND CRITICISMS: Did They Both Get It Wrong? The Effects of Mediator Variables

The exact nature of parental and peer influences have long eluded criminologists, even those studying learning, bonding, and self-control theories. The fundamental question, as framed by James D. Unnever, Francis Cullen, and Robert Agnew is simple: Why is "bad" parenting criminogenic? Answers to this question abound in the theories contained in this chapter, and find support in the comparative exemplars. Yet there are empirical problems: Bonding theory, for example, predicts that school attachment will mitigate the influences of prior physical abuse, but a study of Australian youths did not support this contention. Moreover, self-control theory predicts that self-control should come in between and influence the effects of parental efficacy on delinquency, but researchers employing a nationally representative sample of U.S. children failed to support this contention. Research on social learning theory consistently finds support for social learning/differential association's links between "bad" parenting practices (e.g., modeling bad behavior) and delinquency, even if the empirical support for modeling of behavior is generally lacking and almost nonexistent for studies of serious crime and delinquency.

In order to substantiate a theory's claim to be a general theory of crime, researchers must discredit the causal links of rival theories (i.e., show them to be spurious). Unnever and associates, using a sample of middle-school children living in Virginia, look at two rival perspectives on the influence of parenting—self-control and social learning theory—and ask a simple (appearing) question: Do they mediate the effects of "bad parenting"? They also used a modified version of the self-report instrument developed by Delbert Elliott and colleagues for the National Youth Survey. To measure parenting, the researchers explored intrafamilial conflict, parental monitoring,

parental involvement with their children, and level of coercive parental practices. The aggregate version of Grasmick and associates' six-item scale provided a single indicator of self-control; the extent to which the youths endorsed aggressive attitudes suggested that they had learned the definition of such attitudes through the process of social learning. The researchers then explored the extent to which either or both social learning and aggressive attitudes intervened between "bad" parenting and self-reported delinquency.

Unnever and associates found that, indeed, both ineffective parenting and aggressive attitudes were related significantly to violent and nonviolent delinquency, supporting the view that both theories have general effects on misconduct. However, their findings suggest that low self-control is not simply a case of parents failing to instill high self-control; rather, parents may model low self-control, principally by coercive, angry punishments and erratic and impulsive interactions with their children. Importantly, much of the influence of ineffective parenting on misconduct was direct and not mediated through either self-control or aggressive attitudes. Unnever and associates note too what they call a most ironic finding: "bad" (i.e., ineffective) parenting produced low self-control and aggressive attitudes in many subjects. In other words, the findings are more consistent with the view that internal controls and aggressive attitudes are complementary rather than competitive forces, questioning their status as theoretical rivals.[18] Moreover, since neither theory can discredit the claims of the other, Unnever and associates question whether either one is truly a general theory of crime and delinquency.

SOURCES: Elliott et al. (1985); Jensen (1972); Perrone, Sullivan, et al. (2004); Unnever, Cullen, and Agnew (2006).

choice theory (see Chapter 2). That is, rational choice supporters see merit in educating the public as to the consequences of certain acts and, when that fails, providing for the swift and certain imposition of those punishments on transgressors—easier said than achieved. State legislatures enacted policies that reduce the economic supports associated with large dependent families, and federal welfare reform limits the length of time recipients can receive funds under the Aid to Dependent Families program. Parents are being encouraged to take responsibility for their acts and their creations. As Gottfredson and Hirschi have pointed out, the processes of education and reinforcement begin with a solid foundation of parental management.[19]

In sum, the theory suggests that policy makers need to focus on strengthening social bonds to conventional groups, institutions, and activities. Indeed, this strong ideological appeal may help explain the longevity of social bond theory more than the empirical evidence marshaled in its support (Greenberg 1999).

Law Enforcement Practices   Control-based explanations define prosocial elements of police work. For example, the Police Athletic League (PAL) allows youths to interact with off-duty officers, so that the police and youths have positive contacts with one another. PAL emphasizes positive, supportive interactions rather than negative, confrontational ones. This perspective is rooted in social bonding. Other programs involving uniformed police officers, including Drug Abuse Resistance Education (DARE), provide similar attachments to police and promote participation in conventional activities and development of prosocial beliefs.[20] In the case of DARE, police officer-instructors expose youths to "hard lessons" of drugs from empathetic police officers. One could argue that the intent of such programs is to reinforce ideas associated with rational choice, which is a key component in self-control and other theories.

Judicial Practices   The family is at the center of most control theories, including both bonding and self-control theories. In some it was blamed; in others it was viewed as the key to preventing delinquency. Since their inception in 1899, juvenile courts have played an interesting role in this debate, with the preservation of the family, perhaps at any cost, a nearly universal mandate (Mays and Winfree 2006). Judges remove children from the family only when they believe that it serves the child's best interests (Krisberg and Austin 1993). A better outcome may be a forced separation or perhaps emancipation of the child; however, such actions are generally the choices of last resort. In short, the juvenile courts, by following a policy of family preservation, may be creating the very condition they seek to prevent.

SUMMARY

This chapter reviewed a wide range of social process theorists. (See Table 7.1.) Learning theorists emphasized the mechanisms and processes by which otherwise normative people become delinquent and criminal. How, they asked, are people socialized into law-violating behavior? Control theorists turned the crime causation question around: Why isn't everyone a criminal?

Each perspective's assumptions are central to the orienting questions. For example, answers to the first question review the processes by which we learn definitions favorable and unfavorable to law violations, as well as the role of interpersonal relationships. Sutherland's differential association theory provided a fertile base for other learning theories, including Akers' social learning theory, which integrated differential association propositions and operant conditioning. Although the evidence has tended to support differential association and social

TABLE 7.1   Social Process Theories of Crime

Theory	Major Figures	Central Assumptions	Causal Arguments (Key Terms)	Strengths	Weaknesses
Differential association theory (DAT)	Sutherland	Like all behavior, criminal behavior is learned, and by the same mechanisms.	Misbehavior due to excess of definitions favorable to law violations over those unfavorable to it (*principle of differential association*); *differential associations vary by frequency, duration, priority, and intensity*.	Commonsense answer; provides propositional statements and conceptual base for other criminological theories; suggests ways to change behavior; is not class-bound.	Difficult to test; may not prove useful for explaining certain types of crime (e.g., violent crimes or "irrational" crimes); does not include individual motives; may be tautological.
Social learning theory (SLT)	Akers	Criminal behavior learned through a process of operant conditioning; some behavior is reinforced and other behavior is extinguished.	Probability that a person will commit crime increased by normative statements, definitions, and verbalizations that become *discriminative stimuli* through the process of *differential reinforcements*.	Adds operant conditioning to DAT; may be applied to situations intended to alter undesirable behavior; tests of theory support causal process.	Critics, depending on their orientation, see SLT as bad sociology and too psychological or bad psychology and too sociological; cannot explain how one behavior is rewarded and another punished; may be tautology; there are few serious crime tests.
General social control	Reiss, Toby, Nye	Left alone, people engage in hedonistic, self-serving, and often criminal conduct; culture provides glue that holds society together.	*Reiss:* Personal control troubles yield psychiatric issues; low-control persons may meet personal needs by rule-breaking acts. *Toby:* Some youths have a lower *stake in conformity* as their futures are not bright; they risk only punishment. *Nye:* Family's role in *direct controls* (e.g., family-level punishments) and *indirect controls* (e.g., family affection) are part of conscience.	Logical answers to the crime problem for those persons who assume that people are prone to evil; appeals to those who believe dysfunctional families are at the center of the crime problem; stake in conformity makes sense to those who have never seriously challenged rules because they have too much to lose; increase social controls and support for families and crime will decline.	All have little or questionable empirical support.

Containment	Reckless	See general social control.	Biological and social forces push and pull youth toward crime; only *outer containment* (e.g., the family, other support groups) and *inner containments* (e.g., a sense responsibility, a conscience) stop them.	See *general social control;* is appealing to supporters of psychological factors because the theory includes inner containments.	See general social control.
Social bonding	Hirschi	See general social control.	The *social bond* curbs the natural propensity for misbehavior; it consists of *attachment, commitment, involvement,* and *belief;* when any bond element weakens, crime ensues.	See *general social control;* one of the most frequently tested social process theories; one of the few "traditional" criminological theories to explore differences between male and female delinquency rates, as well as differences in observed rates for various ethnic and racial groups.	Ignores parents as models and barely addresses peers; natural aggression may be overstated and oversimplified; tests often use trivial acts; less support when tested against other theories.
Self-control theory (SCT)	Gottfredson, Hirschi	Self-interest motivates all human behavior and reflects the universal desire to secure pleasure and avoid pain; those unrestrained by society's norms create its problems.	The unrestrained, or persons searching for immediate gratification, simplicity in all tasks and decisions, who are anger-prone, are likely to engage in acts, including crimes, that offer short-term pleasures for little effort; the fact that they have little commitment to conventionality or concern for long-term consequences of their acts makes crime all the more attractive; origin of *low self-control* found in poor *parental management* (e.g., inadequate monitoring or poor emotional ties to their children).	Restatement of free will concepts in the language of social psychology; continues the popular "family values" theme by emphasizing parental management.	Doubts about theory's generalness (i.e., its ability to explain all crime); leaves unanswered critical differences between persons with low self-control and those with a criminal personality; inconsistencies between Hirschi's social bond theory and self-control theory; may be a tautology (i.e., the terms *low self-control* and *high self-control* may be labels for differential propensity to commit or refrain from crime); attempts to test theory have been mixed.

learning, criticisms of causal sequencing, conceptual fuzziness, and tautologies plague both theories. Nonetheless, learning theories have contributed much to criminal justice policies and practices.

What this chapter reveals more than anything else is the following: An original idea, brilliant in its simplicity and design but vaguely stated and incompletely operationalized, can give rise to many different views of the same phenomenon. There seems to be little doubt that the lack of social control and social learning are *somehow* responsible for crime. But precisely how they function and whether they work in concert or at odds with one another remain to be seen.

KEY TERMS

attachment

belief

biological pushes

commitment

containment theory

differential anticipation theory

differential association theory

differential associations

differential association/ differential reinforcement theory

differential expectations

differential identification

differential reinforcement theory

discriminative stimuli

duration

event-propensity theory

frequency

imitation

inner containment

instrumental conditioning

intensity

involvement

meta-analysis

modeling

motivating definitions

operant behavior

outer containment

personal control

principle of differential association

principle of differential reinforcement

priority

psychological pushes

punishments

rebellion against authority

reinforcements

respondent behavior

self-control theory

social bond

social learning theory

social pressures

social process

social pulls

stake in conformity

CRITICAL REVIEW QUESTIONS

1. List and discuss the propositions inherent in differential association theory. How is this theory related to the Chicago School's cultural transmission theory?

2. How did Glaser and Jeffery modify differential association theory to produce their respective theories?

3. According to social learning, when is someone most likely to commit a crime?

4. Describe the key processes associated with instrumental conditioning.

5. Compare and contrast tests of differential association and social learning theories.

6. Describe how the various social control theorists might answer this question: Why don't more people commit crimes?

7. How does self-control theory differ from bonding theory?

8. How does social bonding theory differ from social learning theory?

9. How does self-control theory differ from both social bonding and social learning theory?

10. Describe how each theory reviewed in this chapter conforms to the idea of social process theories. In what ways does one or more diverge from this central theme?

NOTES

1. Among these critics were Cressey (1965), De Fleur and Quinney (1966), Glaser (1956), and McKay (1960).

2. Sutherland (1973) became so convinced that differential association theory was doomed never to be tested that in 1944 he wrote an essay entitled, "The swan song of differential association," in which he sounded the theory's death knell.

3. Among the researchers offering early empirical tests of Sutherland's differential association theory were Glaser (1960), Reiss and Rhodes (1964), Short (1957, 1958, 1960), Stanfield (1966), and Voss (1964).

4. Criminologists test competing theories—differential association usually "wins" (Matsueda 1982; Matsueda and Heimer 1987)—or integrate different theories (Elliott, Huizinga, and Ageton 1985; Marcos, Bahr, and Johnson 1986). We return to the "competition" approach later in this chapter and to theory integration in Chapter 12.

5. Sutherland saw differential association theory as a learning theory (Sutherland and Cressey 1960:87; see also Akers and Sellers 2009:87; Akers and Matsueda 1989).

6. Researchers testing social learning theory, including those reviewed below, have used both cross-sectional and longitudinal data. Given the processual nature of social learning theory, it could be argued that only longitudinal data, especially a panel of subjects studied over a relatively lengthy period, could adequately test social learning theory. Except where noted, the studies reviewed are cross-sectional and therefore subject to this criticism.

7. Akers (1998:262) reported that the theory did better in predicting the proclivity to use nonphysical coercion than actual physical force in rape.

8. Although these studies addressed longitudinal elements of social control, they also looked only at the use of illegal psychoactive substances.

9. In light of this longitudinal evaluation, G.R.E.A.T. was redesigned and redeployed as a far different program; an evaluation of it by Finn-Aage Esbensen is underway.

10. This "debate" took the form of a back-and-forth exchange, largely between Al Blumstein and his colleagues and Gottfredson and Hirschi (cf., Blumstein and Cohen 1987; Blumstein, Cohen, and Farrington 1988; Cohen and Vila 1995; Gottfredson and Hirschi 1986; Hirschi and Gottfredson 1986).

11. Other theorists acknowledge "natural links" between different theories. For example, at the end of his career, Merton (1997) wrote that he saw the major part of differential association theory as quite compatible with anomie theory, a fact attested to by Cloward and Ohlin's integrated theory of differential opportunity structures.

12. The researchers claim a 99 percent response rate, a phenomenal rate by Western and U.S. standards. A recent survey of school children in Bosnia-Herzegovina enjoyed a similarly high response rate (Mujanovic, Nash, and Winfree 2008). The reason for such high response rates could be twofold: (1) the naïveté of the subjects (i.e., they are not surveyed about misbehavior as often as students in the West) and (2) the fact that students in eastern European and Islamic cultures rarely refuse to participate in something that seems even remotely official. These observations are highly speculative but deserve further examination.

13. For more on these tests, see Hindelang (1981), Krohn and Massey (1980), Thomas and Hyman (1978), and Wiatrowski, Griswold, and Roberts (1981).

14. In our review of IQ testing in Chapter 5, we asked whether such techniques work in a cross-cultural context. In the opening chapter, we noted that some crimes simply do not translate well in the context of other nations. It is important, therefore, to note that the Normative Deviance Scale provided reliable estimates of youthful misconduct in all four nations (Vazsonyi et al. 2001:119–20).

15. In an earlier study without the Japanese children, Vazsonyi and associates (2001) supported the view that self-control is a multidimensional rather than unidimensional measure (see issues section below).

16. Antonaccio and Tittle (2008:492) phrased the acts in terms of their "moral acceptability" to the subjects.

17. Hoffman (2002) questions the context in which social control, differential association, and social strain theories work. Too often, he suggests, researchers ignore the institutional and social structural elements that may influence the "causal" factors.

18. Unnever and associates (2006) suggest that while Gottfredson and Hirschi, as "preeminent control theorists," would be unwilling to concede anything to social learning/differential association, Akers would in all likelihood view positively the inclusion of self-control into his paradigm.

19. These policies can also be understood in terms of an earlier concept: social Darwinism.

20. Akers and Sellers (2009) also see G.R.E.A.T. as having ties to social bonding theory.

8

Labeling and Shaming Theories

CHAPTER OVERVIEW

LEARNING OBJECTIVES

In this chapter, you will learn the following:

- The processes by which society comes to define certain people as criminals.

- The significance of criminal labels for both those doing the labeling and those being labeled.

- The role of shaming in controlling crime is complex, and it can result in various outcomes, depending on whether the goal is to bring those persons being shamed back into the community or further isolate them.

- How shaming and labeling work for and against society's interests.

223

INTRODUCTION

In this chapter, two theoretical perspectives explore the community's role in "creating" crime and delinquency. The first perspective has several names, including labeling theory and the societal reaction perspective, and is one of the most intuitively comprehensible crime theories. While its roots date to the 1930s, labeling rose to prominence in the 1960s and 1970s, mainly due to the work of American sociologists Howard Becker, Edwin Schur, and Edwin Lemert. The key to understanding law-violating behavior, they claimed, was in the ways social institutions—including the family, schools, and criminal justice system—respond to conduct which is viewed as outside acceptable behavioral parameters. The theory acknowledges the power of such institutions to limit a person's life choices by stigmatizing adults as criminals or minor children as delinquents. When stigmatized individuals realize that they have few paths to follow other than law-violating ones, they may take on the deviant role completely, finishing the labeling process.

Reintegrative shaming, the second perspective, is relatively new, having emerged in the 1980s, mainly through the work of Australian John Braithwaite. Braithwaite's central thesis is that reintegrative shaming functions at both the macro-level and the micro-level; that is, the theory explains why some societies have higher crime than others *and* why some people are more likely than others to engage in crime. In communities that employ shaming that stigmatizes, crime rates are higher and those stigmatized are far more likely to engage in subsequent crime. Conversely, in communities that practice reintegrative shaming, which allows offenders to rejoin the community as fully functioning members, crime is lower than where the shame is stigmatizing; recipients of reintegrative shaming are less likely to return to crime compared to those who are stigmatized.

These two perspectives share a focus on the community's role in creating the very conditions that laws exist to control: crime and delinquency. Both acknowledge that communities have immense power to harm and to heal. How the theories view this power and the processes of creating criminals and delinquents, as well as the resolution of those spoiled identities, take the theories in rather different directions.[1]

LABELING THEORY

- Did you ever wonder how you escaped adolescence without being labeled as a delinquent? (For those of you who received this label, you probably know the answer to the next question.) Is who does the labeling or name calling important?

- Did friends, family members, teachers, or others in positions of authority over you ever call you unpleasant or even cruel names? Did you internalize the names or did you ignore both the labels and the labelers?

While these questions imply informal and formal processes, our focus is on the latter. Before we examine how communities formally designate acts and actors as problematic for good social order, we first look at the significance of symbols for social interaction.

Symbolic Interactionism and Labeling Theory

Symbols are an essential part of any culture—it is how we communicate. Words have no intrinsic meaning, only the meaning that we impute. Thus, persons who understand English share a common meaning for the color red. The letters "r-e-d" symbolize a color for those who understand English, while *rojo* serves the same purpose for those who understand Spanish. Simply put, a **symbol** is something that stands for something else. A symbol usually captures the essential meaning of a cluster of more abstract ideas, ideologies, beliefs, practices, and concerns. Consider the symbolism in the following:

> If someone sets fire to a structure for profit, the act is arson. But if the building is a church, mosque, or synagogue, it is a **hate crime,** a criminal act precipitated by victim's race, gender, sexual orientation, or other protected status. Crimes are bad, but hate crimes are even worse: the former is only about money, but the religion's symbolism is the target in the latter.

To understand these apparent contradictions, we must consider the origins of labeling theory in **symbolic interactionism,** a perspective that explores how individuals render the world meaningful (Mead 1934; see also Matsueda 1992). While the term may appear daunting, it is actually simple and literal: people interact through symbols, including language.

According to symbolic interactionists, human beings gradually internalize the expectations of the groups with which they socialize as social definitions, largely in reaction to rewards and sanctions. For example, we praise children who act politely, and chastise those who do not. "Polite," however, is a socially determined behavior whose elements differ from society to society. Consider the propriety of wearing shoes or a head covering, for example, when entering someone's home or place of worship. Possessed of these now internalized social definitions, people can evaluate their own conduct from the group's perspective, meaning that they now view themselves as a social object (Quadragno and Antonio 1975:33). The focus is not on the behavior of any social actor, but on how others, including the criminal justice system, view that behavior or actor. No behavior is inherently deviant; rather, deviance is a property given to the behavior by others who have direct and indirect contact with those engaged in it (Erickson 1966:6).[2]

Symbols have the power to galvanize social action. W. I. Thomas and Florian Znaniecki (1918) observed that objective reality is less important to our definition of a social situation than is our subjective belief about it. If we believe something to be true and act accordingly, it does not matter if that belief is true. Thus, the *innocent* but convicted will be treated the same as the *guilty* and convicted. Symbolic interactionists are less interested in "truth" than in the societal reaction to beliefs. Consequently, deviance—a term that is broader than but includes crime—is important for its symbolic contribution to our interpretation of our social world.

Societal Reaction: From Tagging to Labeling

Frank Tannenbaum (1938) was among the first to articulate formally the idea that social institutions can cause society to view some people as criminals. His specific focus was the social-psychological implications of the *delinquent* tag. The principal difficulties, he observed, are definitional ones. What a youth views as a lark or an adventure the community may define as a nuisance or evil. Such divergent views can create rifts between the parties involved. If definitional differences persist, a shift occurs within the community, from the deed-as-evil to the person-as-evil, a process Tannenbaum described as the **dramatization of evil.** He also suggested that this redefinition occurs through the intervention of an institution created for the task—the criminal justice system. Exposed by police, courts, and correction to various dramatization rituals, the child receives the delinquent "tag" and now must live in a new and unexplored environment, the world of crime and criminals (Tannenbaum 1938:20).

Successive generations of symbolic interactionists addressed society's power to redefine social situations. Erving Goffman, for example, described how people respond to so-called **spoiled identities**—both the community at large and those whose identities were spoiled—through the process of **stigmatization.** Goffman (1963:43–44) distinguished **prestige symbols,** which convey "a special claim to prestige, honor or desirable class position," from **stigma symbols,** which draw "attention to a debasing identity," negatively altering how society views that person, spoiling his or her identity.

Consider the following examples of both prestige and stigma symbols. Honor societies traditionally award pins or keys to their members as an indication of their special status. Universities and colleges bestow honorary degrees upon persons they wish to designate as having led exemplary professional or personal lives. Conversely, in many states, convicted and released sex offenders have their pictures, offense records, and current addresses posted on public Web sites. These prestige and stigma symbols send strong messages to society: *These people bear watching!*

Important, too, are the processes by which stigma symbols become the defining criteria for a person's identity. Harold Garfinkel (1956:421; emphasis in original) saw **status degradation ceremonies,** including trials and prison intake procedures, as providing ritualistic and public denunciations of individuals viewed as unworthy. The publicness of such ceremonies is an essential element, without which the community might not come to know who was now less human than the rest of us.

Goffman and Garfinkel placed societal reactions in a symbolic interactionist framework. Howard Becker, Edwin Schur, and Edwin Lemert reveal the essence of labeling theory.

Deviance as Social Status

Howard Becker (1963:9) wrote that "deviance is *not* a quality of the act the person commits, but rather a consequence of the application by others of rules and sanctions to an 'offender.' The deviant is one to whom that label has successfully been applied; deviant behavior is behavior people so label." According to Becker, negative societal reactions result in tarnished and even damaged self-images, deviant identities, and a host of negative social expectations. Think about how members of your community typically react to the terms *ex-con, parolee, child molester,* and *serial killer.* We all play many community roles, including teacher or student, child or parent, and worker or boss. What if we traded one of the positive statuses for one of the more negative ones? Which one would define how others view us or, as importantly, how we see ourselves?

This distinction is the master status. According to Becker, the **master status** defines how others view us and how we see ourselves, our defining social position. The criminal label can become a master status, overriding all others (Becker 1963). For example, consider the fallout if the police arrested your favorite professor on child molestation charges. At that point, all of the professor's education, rank, status, and professional standing would cease to have meaning. The professor would be an accused pedophile, a damning master status, likely to elicit high stigmatization no matter whether there is a trial, guilty verdict, or legal sanction.

Not all stigma symbols are of equal social significance and, in spite of powerful status degradation ceremonies, may not have a negative impact on the person labeled. Even a successful status degradation ceremony may not result in a new master status. Consider, by way of illustration, the following hypothetical situation. A faculty member at your college or university decides that the local community is not doing enough to help the homeless. Moreover, the police seem to target the homeless for arrest and removal from the community. Because of strongly held beliefs, your professor decides to join a noisy picket line outside the city council meeting hall, while inside the city council meets to consider new, even tougher "antiloitering" ordinances. The police order the picketers to disperse. They take the protestors, including your professor, into custody; the charge is creating a public disturbance. At trial, your professor enters a plea of no contest, pays a $10 fine, and serves 10 days of community service at the local homeless shelter. Rather than viewing the professor as an outcast and a criminal, colleagues and students praise the individual as a victim of conscience. What are the labels? What are the costs?

Becker (1963) pointed out that many labeled individuals are indeed deviant; they have earned the label of **true deviants.** They have few advocates, other than those who would see that they receive a just and fair review before imposing a sanction. Society labels other individuals as deviants who, in fact, have not committed the specified act; these are the **falsely accused.** In the minds of many critics, the presence of falsely accused persons in prison and jail justifies unrelenting vigilance. Society also sees some persons as innocent of any wrongdoing when in fact they have committed no deviance; these are the **true innocents.** Finally, some members of society are **hidden deviants;** that is, they have committed an evil act, but society perceives them to be nondeviant, so they escape labeling. Perception creates its own reality. Thus, a pedophile who escapes detection escapes stigma, while a person falsely accused of the crime does not.

Labeling as Social Process

The damaged self-image and its meaning for the individual can result in a **self-fulfilling prophesy,** or the idea that what people believe to be real becomes real in its consequences (see Merton 1957:421–24; see also Thomas and Thomas 1928). Edwin Lemert and Edwin Schur provide two versions of how this movement from normal to criminal occurs, ones that are not at odds with each other, but rather provide complementary views of labeling as a social process.

Lemert's Primary and Secondary Deviation   An initial foray into a criminal activity, unless it involves an extremely heinous crime, may be nothing more than what Lemert (1951) called **primary deviation,** a condition in which the actor has little commitment to a deviant career. Some individuals do not stop here, but the decision may not be entirely their own. The accusations may appear on the newspaper's front page, but the exonerations are on the back page. Many ex-convicts find it difficult to secure employment, or at least meaningful and rewarding jobs, increasing the attraction of crime and the likelihood of subsequent labeling. According to Lemert (1951:76), the labeled may reorganize their behavior according to society's reactions and respond to society in terms of that negative label. Lemert called this condition **secondary deviation.**

Moving from primary to secondary deviation generally follows a seven-step process (Lemert 1951:77):

1. Primary deviations bring out penalties, usually of a mild nature, which often

2. stimulate further primary deviations, which

3. elicit stronger penalties and rejections by a wide range of groups and individuals,

4. causing further deviations, possibly including hostilities and resentment toward those doing the penalizing, which

5. creates a crisis in the tolerance quotient, expressed in formal action by the stigmatizing body,

6. meaning harsher reactions to misdeeds, further strengthening the deviant act as a reaction to the stigmatization and penalization, and ultimately

7. yielding psychological acceptance of the deviant status and reorganization of one's social-psychological makeup around that deviant role, or secondary deviation.

If the initial act is especially troubling to the public, a rape or homicide for example, the accused may skip several steps, resulting in a far faster journey to secondary deviation.

Schur's Elements of Labeling Schur (1971) believes that successful labeling requires four elements. First, **stereotyping** is essential in helping people make sense out of that which is new and unfamiliar. A stereotype is a simplistic and unchanging mental image or pattern resulting from the presence of certain cues, visual or auditory. Moreover, stereotypes are biased generalizations about a group or individuals that are often unfavorable or exaggerated. For example, a conservatively dressed, middle-aged couple, passing a car thumping with loud music, might denigrate both the car's occupants and their music as "trash." Schur's (1971:38) concern was with a far more damning form of stereotyping that begins with police observations of or encounters with youths and culminates in the use of prejudicial stereotypes at sentencing.

Second, labeling can continue after the fact, and it may require reinforcing. This is the case when the media describe a person accused of a horrible act as "a former mental patient"—as if to say: "Now we understand why that person did it." Schur (1971:152) uses the term **retrospective interpretation** to describe the process of looking to the past for previously unseen causes of present undesired behavior. The implication is that society should have suspected that the person was different from prior clues, such as a stint in a mental hospital. Even unseen clues, like the presence of a brain tumor, allow society to "understand" the deviance, albeit after the fact. In fact, few such persons actually commit crimes, but society rarely lets facts get in the way of a good retrospective interpretation. Rather, this mechanism allows us to make sense of the otherwise unfathomable, providing a partially exculpatory medical, psychological, or social fact about an offender, and making the crime more easily understood.

Schur's (1971:56) third element consists of **negotiations** between the labeled and the labelers. Superficially, the parties involved are negotiating the formal charge, the plea, and the eventual sentence; in fact, they are negotiating the label. Stereotypes and retrospective interpretation play major roles in the negotiation process. The negotiation process includes how the police defined the youth upon detainment or arrest and what the probation officer can piece together about the youth's life before the offense. Occasionally the youth may promote a negative stereotype by acting belligerent and unresponsive to officials, an indication of role engulfment.

Role engulfment, Schur's fourth element differs from Lemert's secondary deviation. Secondary deviation includes *both* the impact of labeling on the individual's self-concept and "secondary expansion of deviance problems at the situational and societal levels" (Schur 1971:69). Role engulfment, a narrower facet of secondary deviation, relates to society's response to individuals now recognized as deviants, criminals, or delinquents. **Role engulfment** is the social-psychological process by which the individual assumes the master status; it is the sum total of stereotyping, retrospective interpretation, and negotiation. Because legitimate roles are no longer available to the individual, the only alternative is total engulfment in the deviant role, to the exclusion of all others. Schur believes that this step stabilizes one's self-concept. Figure 8.1 depicts labeling as a process.

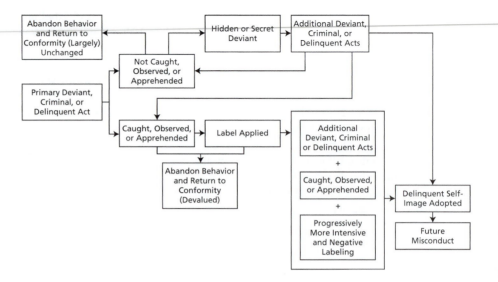

FIGURE 8.1 Labeling as a Process

Labels and Their Consequences

The movement from tentative acts of misconduct into role engulfment and secondary deviation clearly has implications for both the labeled individual and, in the case of criminal justice processing, the system doing the labeling.

Labeling: A Deviance Amplification System? Leslie Wilkins (1965) described **deviance amplification,** a system by which misbehavior is magnified and made worse. Less tolerance leads to more acts being defined as crimes, which leads to more action against criminals, which leads to more alienation of deviant groups, which leads to more crime by deviant groups, which leads to less tolerance of deviants by conformists—and the cycle continues. In short, the individuals' actions, once defined as deviant, limit their options in many areas, including choice of companions. Those whom the system has condemned and excluded can hardly be expected to feel a part of it. The continued criminal acts of the "outliers" (outlaws), and the amplifying effects of self-perception, typically result in even harsher responses by conforming groups.

Jock Young (1971) proposed that, in the case of illegal drugs, police serve as deviance amplifiers. Because the police occupy a socially isolated position in the community, they are susceptible to stereotypes about a variety of social behaviors such as drug use. Given their inherent power, officers negotiate the evidence— the reality of drug-taking behavior—to fit preconceived stereotypes. Given repeated police interaction with members of the drug culture, the latter's misbehavior becomes a transition to a self-fulfillment of the drug-user stereotypes. As Young (1971:28) saw it, due to police actions, these stereotypes go from fantasy to reality.

COMMENTS AND CRITICISMS: Labeling and Radical Nonintervention

Edwin Schur viewed the delinquent label as so detrimental to future conduct that he argued for a policy of **radical nonintervention.** The focus should be on keeping adolescents away from contact with the official (labeling) agencies of social control. Symbolic interactionists are especially concerned with the process by which official control agents—particularly psychiatrists, police, and judges—label behavior. Do the police uniformly enforce the law when they encounter similar behavior, or do the persons or circumstances influence decisions about whether to intervene or arrest? Aaron Cicourel found that many juvenile activities are indeed minor pranks, until observed by juvenile officers, as the youths may fit a specific type of child targeted by that officer. Hence, what is for the child, and perhaps even the community at large, just routine juvenile misbehavior, becomes for the officer serious delinquent acts. Ignoring such minor misbehavior, Schur suggests, poses no serious threat to good social order, and avoids the spiral that can eventually lead to a full-blown delinquent/criminal career.

SOURCES: Cicourel (1976); Schur (1971).

Long-Term Effects of Labeling   For those who cannot avoid the "convict" label, the consequences can be serious and long-lasting, particularly in terms of securing lawful employment. Richard Schwartz and Jerome Skolnick (1962) provide a rare look at the impact of criminal convictions; they studied the effects of a criminal record on the employment opportunities of unskilled workers. The researcher provided four groups of 25 potential employers with one of four employment folders, which were identical in all respects other than the criminal records of the applicants. The documents in one folder stated the applicant had been convicted of and sentenced for assault; in a second folder, he had been tried for assault and acquitted; the third also indicated that he had been tried for assault and acquitted, with a letter from the judge certifying the not guilty finding; and the final folder did not mention any criminal record. In the case of the employers shown the "no record" folder, 36 percent gave positive responses. In the case of employers shown the "acquitted" folder with the judge's letter, 24 percent expressed an interest in the applicant. Among the employers assessing the "acquitted" folder, 12 percent expressed an interest in the applicant. Finally, only 4 percent of the possible employers expressed an interest in the applicant previously convicted of a crime.

Florida allows judges to withhold adjudication of guilt for those who have been found guilty of a felony and are being sentenced to probation. Such persons lose no civil rights and may lawfully assert that they are unconvicted of a felony. Research comparing offenders sentenced under this process with those sentenced to probation without it, and thus labeled felons, found that those escaping the label "felon" had a significantly lower rate of recidivism (Chiricos, Barrick, Bales, and Bontrage 2007:571).

Assessing Labeling Theory

In spite of the fact that many criminologists declared labeling theory "dead" in the 1980s, new conceptualizations account for its resurgence a decade later

(Paternoster and Iovanni 1989). The first, the **status characteristic hypothesis,** proposes that certain personal characteristics, such as race, sex, and social class, determine whom social control agencies label. Researchers using the status characteristics hypothesis studied "label applications" by different agencies within the criminal justice system, including police, prosecutors, and courts in arrests, trials, and postadjudicatory dispositions. Their findings suggest that, given certain contexts and stages in the criminal justice process, a person's race, ethnicity, gender, or social class functions to ease the label's application. For example, a black male accused of harming a white female may stand in greater legal jeopardy than if his victim had been another black male (Baldus, Pulaski, and Woodworth 1983; Smith, Visher, and Davidson 1984; Vito and Keil 1988). In addition, the importance of social class and race increases during the later stages of processing for juvenile suspects (McCarthy and Smith 1986). We return to these topics in Chapter 11's review of race-based theories of crime.

Raymond Paternoster and Lee Ann Iovanni (1989) also propose the **secondary-deviance hypothesis,** which focuses on the criminal label's stigmatizing and segregating *consequences*. This hypothesis infers that as official labeling occurs, individuals may experience changes in personal identity and in accessibility to conventional persons and employment opportunities, yielding greater involvement in crime and delinquency (see the ideas of role engulfment, secondary deviation, and deviance amplification).

Jon Lofland (1969) believes that the probability of assuming a criminal identity and engaging in further criminality increases when the individual has (1) a criminal self-identity, (2) low self-esteem, and (3) emotional ties to *both* normal and deviant others. To explore these contentions, Frances Palarma and associates (1986) studied two groups of youths. One group had no police contacts at the start of the study; the other group had such contacts. By the study's end, not only did the officially labeled youths exhibit more delinquency, but also they had higher levels of psychological impairment compared to those of the youths not previously labeled. This study highlights the problems of disentangling the causal ordering of labeling theory. It is possible that those with police contacts were more delinquent or committed before the study.

Douglas Smith and Paternoster (1990) tested a court-based deviance amplification model for juvenile suspects. They reported that court appearances by higher-risk juveniles, the ones with more extensive youthful misconduct records, linked directly to their recidivism. Apparently, through their interactions with juvenile suspects, officials sometimes *cause* future misbehavior.

Tests of other labeling subelements have qualified some of labeling's claims. For example, mere contacts with the juvenile court may not be as detrimental as claimed. One study found that most of the children whose first referral was a status offense (noncriminal misbehavior such as chronic truancy) did not graduate to more serious delinquency (Sheldon, Horvath, and Tracey 1989:214). Another study found that youngsters adjudicated delinquent in juvenile court on their first referral were less likely to have criminal records as adults than those whose referrals were delayed until further offenses (Brown, Miller, Jenkins, and Rhodes 1991).

Social scientists also have explored the utility of Becker's master status (Miethe and McCorkle 1997; Zatz 1985). The master status of a gang member, in particular, fits Becker's original notion of a status that overwhelms and neutralizes all others. Terance Miethe and Richard McCorkle (1997) compared gang and nongang felony prosecutions. However, the direction of that impact was unexpected: Although other offender and offense characteristics play less crucial roles in the dispositional decisions made about gang members compared to nongang defendants, gang members received the *less* harsh outcomes of the two groups, including a higher dismissal rate and less severe sentencing decisions (Miethe and McCorkle 1997:420). Faced with these anomalies, Miethe and McCorkle considered and rejected two explanations: (1) pressures to clear cases meant that weaker ones were dismissed (i.e., the sentencing outcomes were also less severe), and (2) a benevolent criminal justice system rendered more lenient treatment to youths who were victims of economic inequality (i.e., elected judges, faced with a climate of "gang-banging" youths, would be unlikely to render "soft justice" to gang members). Instead, the researchers speculated that the judiciary viewed the offenses of gang members as wholesale crimes. **Retail crimes** are expensive and include crimes that outrage the public; **wholesale crimes,** in contrast, cost little and involve victims and perpetrators who have low status in the community. The latter characterization reflected the types of offenses resulting in the court appearances of gang members. When gang members prey on one another, it is wholesale crime and so receives different justice than retail crime would (Miethe and McCorkle 1997:423).

Since its "rediscovery," labeling theory has provided considerable insights into how the government's power creates the very class we expect them to control: criminals. These new labeling advocates have broken down the theory into key parts and looked at how those elements function. As we can see in the following criticisms, concerns remain about labeling's place in criminological knowledge and theory.

Skeptics of labeling theory focus on several themes:

- *Theoretical shortcomings*. Critics point to labeling theory's poor or missing conceptual definitions, to its tautological nature by which evidence of labeling is the presence of a label (i.e., crime is behavior so labeled, or the criminal is the person so labeled), and the lack of formal propositions as causal statements from which to derive testable hypotheses (Paternoster and Iovanni 1989; see also Gibbs 1968; Gove 1980; Wellford 1975).

- *Theory-generated research problems*. Theoretical shortcomings lead to substantial empirical problems. For example, Milton Mankoff (1976) was quite explicit about the links between one theoretical shortcoming—the initial rule breaking and the application of the label. The significance of the initial rule breaking, and whatever caused it, disappears after it has occurred. At that point, the theory's focus becomes the societal reaction (Mankoff 1976:247). Perhaps, observed Mankoff (1976:248), rule breakers continue their evil ways because of "positive attachment to rule breaking." Crime may provide monetary rewards, immediate gratification, and excitement (see the discussion of operant conditioning principles in Chapter 5).

- *Poor research results.* Those who have tested "labeling hypotheses" and failed to find support for them often call for the theory's death (Hagan 1974; Wellford 1975). However, others have argued that "for the most part, empirical tests of labeling propositions have been conducted with grossly misrepresented hypotheses that are more caricature than characteristic of the theory" (Paternoster and Iovanni 1989:360). Recent longitudinal studies of labeling effects suggest that calls for its demise as a theory are premature: the fate of convicted felons is consistent with labeling theory (Chiricos et al. 2007).

- *Missing mediating forces.* It is also possible that labeling overlooks the significance of deviant peers in shaping a person's possible life choices. That is, labels do not play a direct influence on deviant behavior; rather, they bring about conditions that often lead to lives of crime and delinquency. Bernberg and associates (2006; see also Bernberg and Krohn 2003) explore this idea in a four-wave panel of nearly 1,000 adolescents living in upstate New York. Being in a street gang and being formally labeled as delinquent was linked to the movement of some youth into serious delinquency. The researchers conclude that while the deviant status may not be permanent, it can still have significant consequences for developing serious patterns of offending throughout the life course, ones that peer networks can mediate during adolescence.

- *Overstatement and misstatement of labeling's importance.* Akers (1968) observed that many youth gang members have well-formed deviant identities but have never been formally labeled. Mankoff (1976) noted that those aspiring to a criminal career may achieve criminal status, rather than have it ascribed to them. For some of the most violent norm violators—terrorists and revolutionaries—an official label may mean that they have received recognition for their deeds. Gang jackets and other gang paraphernalia serve as reminders that for some persons deviant labels are valued. Consider, too, the antithesis of labeling—deterrence theory (Tittle 1975). Some children do "go straight" and never engage in subsequent misconduct after an encounter with the juvenile justice system (see the discussion of correctional uses of behaviorism in Chapter 5). For a graphic statement of this effect, we refer you to the Comments and Criticisms box.

Several key questions remain unanswered. Why has labeling theory research shown so little support for the substance of its assertion that society's reaction to deviance causes further deviance? When is the label sufficiently stigmatizing to ensure a deviant career? Do some persons, including members of delinquent gangs, outlaw motorcycle clubs, and organized crime groups, seek this lifestyle not in spite of the label that goes with it, but *because of it?* Labeling theory fails to answer fully these questions. Nevertheless, as anyone who has worked with ex-offenders knows, the criminal label can have a devastating impact on individuals attempting to "go straight." We do not yet understand all of the mechanisms by which labels take shape and form. Nonetheless, we recognize and understand the pragmatic effects of stigmatization as a criminal.

COMMENTS AND CRITICISMS: Value of a Bad Reputation

Labeling theory must consider the "value of a bad reputation" (Reuter 1987). In the Hobbesian world inhabited by criminals, members of an organization with sufficient martial capacity (read: dangerous and scary) can offer services typically reserved for government, such as contract enforcement and adjudication of disputes. Members of criminal organizations are also in a position to enforce extralegal social norms (Abadinsky 2010). In Chicago, when the police failed to adequately respond to complaints about reckless driving by youngsters in a particular neighborhood, several

residents went to see their neighbor, Joseph ("Joey the Clown") Lombardo. This ranking member of the Windy City's crime family (the "Outfit") resolved the problem with a few carefully chosen words to the young men. One of the authors (Abadinsky) has a law enforcement-source photo of a Harley Davidson motorcycle with the following plaque attached: "This motorcycle belongs to a Hell's Angel—fuck with it and find out."

SOURCE: Abadinsky (2010).

Labeling, Public Policy, and Criminal Justice Practices

Labeling has proven to be one of the richest theoretical perspectives generated by American criminologists. From cops to judges to correctional officers, nearly all system personnel intuitively understand the negative stigmata associated with the criminal (or delinquent) label. Indeed, this is one argument for "sealing" juvenile offenders' records once they turn 18 or 21, depending on state laws and practices.

Proponents of public policy based on labeling theory seek to reduce the stigma that attaches to those labeled a delinquent or criminal. For example, **decriminalization** refers to a reduction in the number of outlawed behaviors (e.g., possession of small amounts of marijuana for personal or medical use). **Diversion** attempts to avoid unnecessarily stigmatizing persons who violate the law by providing alternatives to official criminal justice processing. The police or prosecutor's office can operate diversion programs for both adults and juveniles, referring certain offenders to treatment, counseling, or employment training programs instead of official processing. However, many observers of the criminal justice system criticize diversion for contributing to **net widening.** That is, the police would not have arrested these individuals, nor would the prosecutor's office have charged them in the first place, absent diversion programs. In effect, critics argue, diversion efforts may add to the number of people caught in the "criminal justice net" (Austin and Krisberg 1981:171; see also Blomberg 1980).

Labeling theorists are all too aware of incarceration's negative effects. Given that incarceration may facilitate secondary deviation, many labeling theory supporters rally around **deinstitutionalization,** the removal of inmates from prisons, jails, and juvenile detention centers. Most states no longer incarcerate **status offenders.**[3] Also, the Juvenile Justice and Delinquency Prevention Act of 1974 and subsequent federal legislation mandates the removal of juveniles from jails intended to house adults, although many states have been slow to act (Mays and Winfree 2006).

Labeling theorists also recognize the state's power over the individual. Consequently, it is not surprising that during the 1960s and 1970s, labeling supporters also championed the extension of **due process guarantees.** This effort met with notable successes (e.g., *Kent v. United States* 1966; *In re Gault* 1967; *Breed v. Jones* 1975) and failures (e.g., *In re Winship* 1971; *McKiever v. Pennsylvania* 1971; *Schall v. Martin* 1984). As courts decide whether to try youthful offenders in an adult court, they enjoy many of the rights accorded adults, and adult penalties and institutional placement upon conviction.

Critics argue that juvenile court intervention does not help youngsters because the services are often inadequate, and intervention intensifies existing problems by stigmatizing children. In other words, a juvenile may not be able to discern the subtle differences between the juvenile court and the criminal court—differences that have been seriously eroded as society moved in favor of harsher treatment of juveniles. Thus, the child, as well as the child's parents, friends, and community, may react to juvenile court intervention as if the child were facing charges in criminal court.

Edwin Schur (1973:30) warns that the "labeling" that results can set in motion "a complex process of response and counter-response with an initial act of rule-violation and developing into elaborated delinquent self-conceptions and a full-fledged delinquent career." As noted earlier, however, there is research indicating that the majority of those whose first referral to juvenile court was a status offense did go on to more serious acts of delinquency. "If anything, they became something considerably less than serious delinquents" (Sheldon, Horvath, and Tracy, 1989:214). Brown and associates (1991) also contradict the labeling argument: Youngsters adjudicated in juvenile court on their first referral are less likely to have criminal records as adults than those whose referrals are delayed until further misbehavior occurred.

Is there a way out of the labeling dilemma? Can labeling truly be undone? The philosopher and social psychologist George Herbert Mead (1863–1931) argued that society will not accept back into its fold those labeled as criminals. Nearly 100 years ago, Mead (1918:591) stated that "hostility toward the lawbreaker inevitably brings with it the attitudes of retribution, repression and exclusion. These provide no principles for the eradication of crime, for returning the delinquent to normal social relations." Mead believed that, owing to the psychology of punitive justice, adjudged criminals can never regain society's trust. You may wish to reflect on this idea when you read about restorative justice in the next section of this chapter.

Law Enforcement Practices   Law enforcement officers are central figures in labeling's early stages, especially the movement from primary to secondary deviation.[4] Police patrol officers' discretionary decisions often determine whether a person will enter the criminal justice system. Officers opting for a warning or reprimand instead of formal processing, particularly with both juveniles and adults who engage in minor law-violating behavior, may prevent deviance amplification. Upon what facts do police base these decisions?

Labeling theory may also help to explain police responses to various identifiable groups, particularly ethnic and racial groups, a topic to which we return in Chapter 11. For now, suffice it to say, much police street work has its foundation in stereotyping and the related issue of racial profiling. So much so, in fact, that this process has become an integral part of the police culture, since officers must often make immediate, reactionary-style decisions after processing very few cues—for example, being more likely to stop a young black male driving a luxury vehicle than an older white male driving the same car. Offender types—**symbolic assailants**—elicit different responses from the police than do normal citizens. Thus, the Los Angeles officers' responses to Rodney King are recognizable, if excessive, examples of stereotyping and labeling in action.

Judicial Practices   Throughout the trial process, court actors—ranging from the judge or jury, to the attorneys, to witnesses, to the defendant—exercise significant roles in the labeling process. Adjudication itself serves as "an interpretive process" in which legal authorities, especially attorneys and judges, present and assess evidence as a way of determining the defendant's suitability for sanctioning (Swigert and Farrell 1976:90). Trial courts formalize and popularize criminal stereotypes through the trial process. Appellate courts, including the Supreme Court, may have less power in reversing this process, even when they fail to certify a guilty finding. In some cases, a finding of guilty by a jury or by the defendant's plea and admission, may be reversed by the courts as the result of procedural errors such as a violation of the *Miranda* decision or the *exclusionary rule*. In such cases, the accused is a criminal in fact but, not in law.

In addition to the role of the trial in the definitional process, many labeling theorists view it as a public degradation ceremony (Garfinkel 1956). The trial's purpose is to finish the criminalizing process begun with arrest, arraignment, and indictment. The "discreditable" become "discredited" by symbolic interaction with the court (Goffman 1963). As for formal labeling, the court has the power to change the adjective "accused" to "convicted," effectively altering the individual's master status as well. For example, accused murderers become convicted murderers and accused child molesters become convicted child molesters only through the intercession of the court. Garfinkel's (1956) entire description of the "denunciation" process sounds like a trial. The "denouncer" (i.e., the prosecuting attorney) introduces him- or herself to the primary audience (i.e., the judge or jury members) as a public representative speaking for society. In the final stage—sentencing—the court displays the denounced as outside the legitimate order, an outlaw.

Another judicial practice based on diversion is deferred sentencing, which usually involves a plea of guilty followed by either restitution or some form of community service. Satisfactory completion of the deferred sentence generally results in the dropping of charges. Failure, in contrast, can result in immediate incarceration.

Finally, labeling depends on negotiation, an idea critical to court proceedings. As Schur (1971:56) observed, at the beginning of the process it is not clear which labels attach. Robert Emerson (1969) detailed three statuses for juvenile defendants: (1) "normal" children, whose involvement with the law is ruled "accidental"; (2) "criminal-like" children, who consciously pursue criminal ends and evidence intense distrust of and dislike for society through their actions; and (3) "disturbed" children, whose actions seem senseless and irrational, thus requiring more of a psychological treatment approach than a criminal justice response. Emerson contended that the status awarded a child was not "proved" in the classic sense of the laws of evidence. Rather, the concerned parties, including the court, the public school, the reform school, the social services system, and other community agencies, negotiated it.

Correctional Practices   Labeling theory also provides insights into two related aspects of corrections. First, labeling makes it easier to understand why convicted felons who spend time in an antisocial, violent environment—contemporary prisons—are unlikely to emerge as better persons or productive members of society. About all that we can hope for, it seems, is that they have paid their debt to society. Negativistic social systems dominate prisons that punish rather than reward adherence to prosocial goals (Bartollas and Conrad 1992; Champion 1990). A prison has few equals as a place in which to complete the process of secondary deviation and role engulfment.

Second, **penal harm reduction** advocates focus on the problems facing adults because of criminal convictions. We earlier reviewed research that supports the notion that criminal convictions can affect hiring potential (Schwartz and Skolnick 1962). It was equally clear that avoiding a formal conviction and the attendant conditions associated with that status could increase a defendant's survivability after trial (Chiricos et al. 2007). To reduce the legal harm caused by an adult criminal record, some states have removed various statutory restrictions on gaining licenses necessary for employment. A few have even enacted "fair employment" laws for former offenders. New York, for example, prohibits the denial of employment or a license because of a conviction. There are, however, exceptions to this practice, including a direct relationship between the crime and the specific employment or license such that employment involves an unreasonable risk to persons or property. According to the direct-relationship requirement, the nature of the instant offense must have a direct bearing on his or her fitness or ability to carry out the job's duties or responsibilities (e.g., a drug offender working in a hospital pharmacy or a convicted sex offender working as an elementary school janitor). The statute requires that a public or private employer provide, upon request, a written statement setting forth the reasons for denial of license or employment. The New York State Commission on Human Rights enforces the statute.

Labeling involves the use of power informally by groups and individuals and far more formally by the state. Without the ability to act upon or control the fate of others, one definition of power, labeling would be merely a largely ineffectual naming process, with no consequences attached to it. Given the involvement of the powerful criminal justice system, and its equally significant subordinate system of juvenile justice, the effects of formal labeling are far from inconsequential.

REINTEGRATIVE SHAMING AND
RESTORATIVE JUSTICE

- Have you ever been so embarrassed by something you did that you found it hard to rejoin the group that witnessed the unbecoming act?

- Have you heard about drunk drivers sentenced to place a license plate on the front of their car indicating that they are convicted drunk drivers? Do you think that such public embarrassment will help the drunk drivers mend their ways?

- If someone in your inner circle of friends (BFF) does something wrong (for example, shares a secret about a group member with someone outside the group), what actions would your circle of friends take to exclude this person? What would your friends do if they wanted to reinclude that person in the inner circle?

Anthropologists sometimes describe situations where cultures must respond to two countervailing sets of rituals. Inclusionary rituals help hold together the communities. When someone violates a group norm, the community finds a way to bring the offender back into the fold, as any other course of action would have devastating consequences for both the group and the individual. The offender suffers more than a symbolic punishment, depending upon the significance of the norm violated, but the ultimate goal is the reintegration of the offender. For example, it might be that other valued community members are relatives of the offender, or that the individual performs an essential role in the community's survival. To push that person to the group's fringes or beyond, to exclude him or her entirely, would be counterproductive to the community. Hence, they must find some way to punish the person and keep the group intact.

Other cultures place less emphasis on inclusiveness as a community value and greater emphasis on the role of law and sanctions. Short of killing the transgressor, appropriate punishments may involve the imposition of real or symbolic stigmata that signify the rule-violating nature of the person and the associated act, as in the case of branding offenders, cutting off their noses, or requiring them to wear other symbols associated with their transgressions. In cases where the community wishes to make a permanent example, the offender may suffer banishment, which is usually irreversible. Whether the sanctions are physical stigmata or banishment, their intent is clearly exclusionary, the removal of the offender symbolically or physically from the community.

At their core, these rituals are about shame. Exclusionary rituals use shame to isolate offenders, identifying them as objects of distain and even hatred. Inclusionary rituals use shame to embrace the offender, restoring them to the community, demonstrating an entirely different set of emotions, including warmth, friendship, and love.

Crime, Shaming, and Social Disapproval

Shame is a very old idea. Nearly all the world's religious and cultural traditions refer to shame's behavior-shaping role. **Shame** is an internal emotional response to embarrassing actions, ideas, words, or thoughts that, when made public, threaten to diminish a person's value or standing in the family or community. Darwin viewed shame as a key self-monitoring activity. He saw blushing, an external marker for shame, as resulting when humans perceive the evaluations of themselves by others as either positive or negative. Other early twentieth-century sociologists and psychologists explored the capacity of shame to control behavior. For example, William MacDougall (1908) saw shame's capacity to control human behavior as second to no other emotion. Charles Horton Cooley (1922) viewed pride and shame as central "social self-feelings," with shame closely tied to his concept of social fear. Embodied in **social fear** is the notion that people engage in crimes—and continue to do so—out of concern that their misconduct will be disclosed to others, resulting in great losses in social standing.

Thomas Scheff (1988) noted the classic anthropological distinction between shame cultures and guilt cultures. However, he also believed that "shame is *the* social emotion, arising as it does out of the monitoring of one's own action by viewing one's self from the standpoint of others" (Scheff 1988:398; emphasis in the original).[5] Even though shame is relatively rare in contemporary Western societies, it has the capacity to achieve conformity through informal but pervasive rewards (e.g., deference from others and inner pride) and punishments (e.g., lack of deference and inner shame) that arise out of the interactions between the individual's assessments and those of others. Perceiving that they are doing something right, human beings sense deference and a feeling of pride for conformity to exterior norms; perceiving that they are doing something wrong, they sense disrespect and shame for violating exterior norms.

Reintegrative Shaming

John Braithwaite (1989) provides the theoretical grounding for shame's contemporary role in maintaining social order. He noted that African and Asian cultures continue to use shame as a means of maintaining social control over a host of behaviors. Braithwaite (1989:100) further stated that **shaming** involves "all social processes of expressing disapproval which have the intention or the effect of invoking remorse in the person being shamed and/or condemnation by others who become aware of the shaming." Shaming is stigmatizing (or disintegrative) if it blames offenders and denies them reentry into the group. Shaming processes are reintegrative if they first establish the deed's wrongfulness (as opposed to the person's evilness) and then provide an equally public and ritualistic means to restore the offender to the group. The key to **reintegrative shaming** is the ritualistic reinforcement of the person's status within the group. The last step is **gestural forgiveness,** where members of the harmed community extend ceremonially to the shamed person. For example, after an offender has served his or her sentence, made public amends to the victim or the victim's family and to the community, a representative of the community must physically and publicly embrace the ex-offender, signifying that person's return. This step is missing in **disintegrative shaming,** as are affective contacts between those doing the shaming and the shamed person. Figure 8.2 depicts the consequences these processes.

Integrative or disintegrative shaming are not minor sanctioning processes. Such rituals of both types can involve painful and lengthy processes, virtually indistinguishable from one another. The actual rituals are irrelevant; rather, the goals of the rituals and their operational processes merit close inspection.

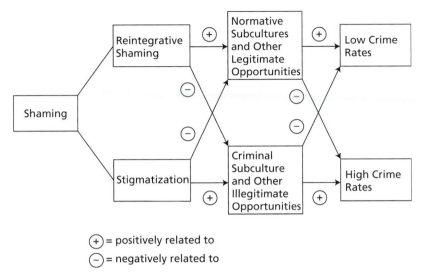

(+) = positively related to
(−) = negatively related to

F I G U R E   8.2   Reintegrative Shaming versus Stigmatization

Communitarianism and Shaming Processes

Braithwaite describes two sets of processes, one operating at the societal (macro) level and the other at the individual (micro) level, as underlying shaming. Braithwaite suggests that contemporary urban communities with high levels of mobility typically exhibit low interdependency among residents. In Braithwaite's (1989:100) terms, these communities lack **communitarianism,** or the interdependencies generally characterized by high levels of mutuality and trust.

High communitarian communities view dependency as a positive social force. Such communities view the characteristics of dependency and dependability as integral to a healthy community (Braithwaite 1989, 2000). Low-communitarian communities widely practice shaming that is stigmatizing or disintegrative. The result is that groups of stigmatized individuals form mutually reinforcing criminal subcultures, groups that provide the learning environments for illegitimate activities.[6] Low levels of communitarianism, and the growth of criminal subcultures, further erode the existing communitarianism, exacerbating the crime problem.

Communities high in communitarianism typically practice reintegrative shaming. For example, the Japanese not only practice *amaeru* (to be succored by others), but also *amayakasu* (to be nurturing to others) (Wagatsuma and Rosett 1986). A contemporary restorative program in China, *bang jiao,* which literally means "help education," starts out with stigmatizing encounters, but tends to end with reintegrative ones (Lu 1998; Wong 1996; see also Braithwaite 1999). Other Asian and traditionalist cultures with similar levels of communitarianism practices parallel rituals of reintegration (Braithwaite 1989; 1999). Public shaming is important for effective social control, and public ceremonies help promote a shared understanding of acts defined as criminal or immoral. However, moralizing and shaming should occur informally within the offender's social network. Heavy reliance on public forums invites disintegrative shaming, since, at this level, the interdependency may be lower, yielding lower communitarianism.

At the individual (micro) level, disintegrative shaming has the most negative impact on individuals who already possess little connectivity to conventionality—young, unmarried, unemployed males with low educational and occupational aspirations. Such individuals lack the interdependencies that negate stigmatizing shame and foster reintegration. Disintegrative shaming further weakens their already attenuated ties to conventionality. Absent effective social controls, they join subcultures that endorse antisocial, criminal values. Thus, in Braithwaite's view, disintegrative shaming, owing to its stigmatizing power, results in continued and perhaps even increased crime. As Braithwaite (1989:1) warned: "Shaming is the most potent weapon of social control unless it shades into stigmatization. Formal criminal punishment is an ineffective weapon of social control partly because it is a degradation ceremony with maximum prospects for stigmatization."

Given reintegrative shaming's collaboration with prosocial elements in the community, criminal subcultures are less attractive to potential members. Moreover, the individual who enjoys multiple interdependencies is most susceptible to reintegrative shaming.

Assessing Reintegrative Shaming Theory

Tests of reintegrative shaming typically take one of two paths. One way is to look at macro-level forces in the community. Mitchell Chamlin and John Cochran (1997) tied social altruism levels to crime rates in a sample of several hundred U.S. cities. **Social altruism** is a community's willingness to "share scarce resources to the aid and comfort of their members, distinct from the beneficence of the state" (1997:204). In a test of the theory's macro-level claims, Chamlin and Cochran hypothesized that crime would vary inversely with altruism levels, a prediction consistent with communitarianism. This linkage was present for both property and personal crimes, leading them to speculate that "communities that effectively teach their members to respect and engage in behaviors that promote the welfare of others enjoy relatively lower rates of crime" (Chamlin and Cochran 1997:221).

Another path is to look at forces within one's own family that may be reintegrative. Carter Hay (2001b), investigating the extent to which the reintegrative shaming practices of parents explained the projected deviance of their children, looked at parental reintegrative practices and shaming. For reintegrative practices, he examined situations where a parent showed a child respect, thought that the child was good, even when they did bad, and eventually forgave the child. Shaming occurred when the parent tried to convince the child that the act was immoral or unfair, made him or her feel guilty or ashamed, or made the child "make up" for the bad deed. Parent–child interdependency was, as the theory predicted, strongly related to parents' use of reintegrative practices and, to a lesser degree, their use of shaming. However, the research generated more questions than answers about the influence of shaming. For example, Hay reported that the data supported the idea that reintegrative sanctioning of children leads to high parent–child interdependency, rather than the reverse relationship as predicted by the theory. In addition, the negative effects of shaming on offending were independent of the reintegration level, a finding also not supportive of reintegrative shaming. Hay proposed that stigmatization may be important but that shaming's moralizing effects may be overstated: an unknown force is the source of harmful stigmatization (Hay 2001b:148).

Perhaps the most comprehensive test of reintegrative principles occurred in Australia. Lawrence Sherman and associates (1998) conducted an experimental study called the Re-Integrative Shaming Experiment (RISE), which followed 1,285 offenders and their victims, the former assigned randomly to either traditional processing or involvement in the RISE. Treatment consisted of face-to-face restorative sessions with the victim, based on the group conferencing model. The offender had to consent before seeking the victim's consent. The researchers reported mixed results. The RISE property experiments yielded increased recidivism (2003), while for other crimes, there were no effects on recidivism, although victims felt better about their participation when contrasted with nonparticipants (Strang 2002; Tyler, Sherman, and Strang 2007).

As a general observation, empirical testing of reintegrative shaming's central themes of gestural forgiveness and communitarian values remains rudimentary. Even when those tests have focused on key provisions, the results have been somewhat limited. Part of the problem may lie with the theory's reliance on existing communitarian values (see Comparative Criminology—World Views on Crime and Justice: Communitarianism and Recidivism in Iceland). Beyond these possible weaknesses, there are other specific concerns about the theory, which we will discuss next.

Concerns about reintegrative shaming fall into several categories:

- *Is this a new theory or a new way of looking at old theories?* Braithwaite argues that disintegrative shaming establishes fertile ground for other social forces to act upon individuals, leading to crime. Hence, it is difficult to describe reintegrative shaming as an entirely new theory, as it has obvious ties to subcultural theories (Chapter 6), control and learning theories (Chapter 7), and labeling theory.

- *Is this solely a theory about predatory crime?* A central reintegrative shaming assumption is that the consensus surrounding a rule-breaking act generates the shame: no consensus, little shame. Thus, the theory's scope is limited to explaining predatory offenses against persons and property (Hay 2001b:135).

- *Where are the tests of the theory's macro-level constructs?* Barriers to tests of reintegrative shaming theory's macro-level constructs are significant (Braithwaite 1989:120–21; Hay 1998:424). Large-scale surveys of shaming across communities, cultures, or societies would be prohibitively expensive. Just as importantly, measures of the levels of reintegrative shaming do not currently

---

COMPARATIVE CRIMINOLOGY—WORLD VIEWS ON CRIME AND JUSTICE: Communitarianism and Recidivism in Iceland

Nations high in communitarianism, suggests Braithwaite, should also exhibit reintegrative shaming and restorative practices, resulting in lower crime rates. Eric Baumer, Richard Wright, Kristrun Kristinsdottir, and Helgi Gunnlaugsson examined a logical corollary of this thesis: high communitarianism should yield higher levels of reintegrative shaming without permanent stigmatization for convicted offenders, leading to lower recidividism levels among sanctioned offenders. They conducted their study in Iceland, an independent country located in the northern Atlantic Ocean, and a prime example of a nation dedicated to both collective duties and individual rights. Whether due to its geographic isolation, harsh climate, or sea-faring traditions, Iceland has a strong tradition of commitment to social interdependency or communitarian social values.

Baumer and associates looked at information collected about all persons sentenced to and released from Icelandic prison between 1994 and 1998. They estimated the recidivism rates of 1,176 offenders. They reported that while other researchers suggest that the presence of a reintegrative-shame culture yields lower crime rates, the same is not true of recidivism rates.

Icelandic rates suggest that shaming cultures do not reintegrate offenders better than others, if recidivism reflects reintegration.

In the final analysis, Baumer and associates suggested that recidivism performs a functional social process. That is, having identifiable and unreintegrated criminals increases social solidarity, since **criminals-as-scapegoats** reinforce the boundaries between acceptable and unacceptable behavior. Baumer and associates reflected, too, on Cohen's observations about exclusionary control, an idea conceptually the same as disintegrative shaming, which he saw as "symbolically much richer; stigma and status degradations are sharper, deviants are clearly seen as different from nondeviants and, above all, there is the promise that they will … not just keep coming back to be reintegrated." They did not interpret their findings as a repudiation of reintegrative shaming; rather, it confirmed the powerfully symbolic nature of shaming that punishes and isolates, even in the presence of high levels of communitarianism.

SOURCE: Baumer, Wright, Kristinsdottir, and Gunnlaugsson (2002).

---

exist.[7] Nonetheless, Braithwaite's theory about the role of shame in producing or reducing crime remains interesting and worthy of further study.

- *Lack of empirical support suggests refinements of theory are in order.* The results of testing reintegrative shaming alone, versus tests of restorative justice programming, suggest that as used in this context, shaming theory may need refining to explain the negative findings, as both types of shaming can lead to criminality (Botchkovar and Tittle 2005).

Other crime theories reflect reintegrative shaming concepts. For example, Sherman (1993) has argued that sanctions based on reintegrative principles promote deterrence, and that stigmatizing sanctions elicit defiance in those who are punished. Still other theories, including conflict theories (see Chapter 9) and developmental/life-course criminology (see Chapter 12) acknowledge macro- and micro-level forces.

Reintegrative Shaming, Public Policy, and
Criminal Justice Practices

Reintegrative shaming provides the theoretical base for **restorative justice (RJ).** The notion that rule violators can be brought back into the community fold,

---

COMMENTS AND CRITICISMS: The Role of Emotion in Reintegrative Shaming

Critics of reintegrative shaming suggest that the theory's emphasis on emotive responses may trigger negative feelings on the part of the offender, and this outcome may constitute a possible inherent weakness. Responding to this concern, Harris and associates used the example of group conferencing, a prototypical application of reintegrative shaming's principles. In the group conference, the offender—and his or her support group—meets with the victim—and his or her support group, along with members of the local community and the formal criminal justice system. They address two elements: (1) the extent to which disapproval is noted by victims, the community, and justice system authorities; and (2) the extent to which such disapproval is accomplished in a reintegrative fashion.

The authors contend that the inability to express remorse is often associated with recidivism; hence, the expression of shame by an offender during the group conference extends beyond remorse to include sorrow and compassion for the victim. The extent to which the facilitators of group conferences are able to insure that emotions and communications between the conference participants engage reparative and positive behaviors—and do not harm the offender's self-esteem and confidence—should overcome the critics' claims that remorse may be more effective than the totality of the reintegrative shaming process.

SOURCE: Harris, Braithwaite, and Walgrave (2003).

---

healing the rifts that their misbehavior caused, has roots in long-standing Western and non-Western cultural traditions (Braithwaite 1999). Ancient Arabs, Greeks, Romans, and Germanic peoples practiced restorative or healing rituals. Buddhists, Hindus, Taoists, and Confucianists all recognize the importance of restoring community harmony and balance after a wrongful or disruptive act. In many nations around the world, contemporary aboriginal peoples employ peacemaking and reintegration models.

From a policy standpoint the world has embraced RJ. We find programs based on its principles in the current criminal justice systems of such politically diverse nations as Austria, Australia, Belgium, Canada, the Czech Republic, Germany, Great Britain, and New Zealand, to name a few. In 1999, the Committee on Ministers for the Council of Europe adopted the language and principles of RJ for penal matters. As early as 1997, the United Nations considered the need for basic principles to guide member states in the adoption of RJ operating principles and programs, and in 2001 the United Nations formally adopted these principles. Whether the model receives even broader acceptance is an open question. Critics express concern that by placing so much emphasis on an emotion, shame, the offender may take on additional guilt or suffer lowered self-esteem and confidence, making successful post-conviction adjustment more difficult to achieve (Harris and Maruna 2006). For an answer to these critics, see Comments and Criticisms: The Role of Emotion in Reintegrative Shaming.

Two recent meta-analyses suggest that RJ practices have met with more than moderate success. Latimer, Dowden, and Muise (2005) examined 22 studies of 35 separate RJ programs. They found that when compared to nonrestorative ones, RJ programs had higher mean effects for victim and offender satisfaction, restitution participation, and recidivism. However, Latimer and associates suggest that psychological treatments show higher mean effects, especially ones that address clinically relevant risk factors, needs, and individual responsiveness to treatment (see also Andrews, Zinger, et al. 1990). They observed that the RJ programs studied, which included conferencing and victim-offender mediation programs, may have a self-selection bias: those who participated may have been more receptive do and endorsing of restorative principles, which helped explain why they volunteered in the first place.[8]

A second meta-analysis by Sherman and Strang (2008) used a British modification of the well-regarded Maryland technique for classifying evaluations based on the extent to which they followed good methodological procedures. Sherman and Strang also report considerable success for RJ programming, and included specific observation about the successes and failures. For example, the results for repeat offending ranged from moderately successful reductions in recidivism to no differences to, in at least one case, increased offending following face-to-face conferencing. They conclude that RJ works best with more serious offending, compared to less serious offending, and shows more consistent results for violent rather than property offending. In their meta-analysis, Sherman and Strang reported that victims had the best effects from face-to-face conferencing, achieving significant short-term reductions in their post traumatic stress symptom. However, improvements in offender satisfaction were less significant. Finally, offering arrested persons RJ programming improves system processing (the number of cases resolved by the court) by two to four times that normally reported.

Restorative processes depend on victims' active participation. They must perform a role more emotionally demanding than that of the complaining witness in a conventional prosecution, which many, perhaps most, victims avoid. When either victim or offender is unwilling to participate, or when the offense is too heinous or the injury too severe, the offender meets with other victims—rather than his or her own victim(s)—often through victim advocate organizations. In some programs, victim–offender discussion occurs through videotaping or written dialogue.

We can find RJ programming at most junctures in the administration of justice in the U.S. and, indeed in the rest of the world, with RJ having achieved the status of a social movement by the early twenty-first century (Bazemore and Shiff 2001; Van Ness and Strong 2006). Below we review several RJ practices based on reintegrative shaming.

Law Enforcement Practices   Braithwaite (1997) observed that the police are crucial gatekeepers in RJ. He stressed that the process must include both the police and offenders; police should be essentialized and not stigmatized. Indeed, the police in several nations participate formally in RJ programs. For example, in the Navajo Nation, members of the tribal police force who view themselves as traditionalists are far more likely than are modernists to make recommendations for peacemaking courts, a form of RJ based on Navajo religious principles (Gould 1999). Police officers in New Zealand play pivotal roles in **family group conferencing,** a program that brings all parties together to begin healing the wounds caused by criminal events. The sentencing of an accused juvenile requires the family group conference's recommendation, in which a youth service officer reads the charges and participates in the decision-making process (Goenner 2000). We find similar programs in Australia, several U.S. states (e.g., Minnesota, Montana, and Vermont), and several Canadian provinces (Bazemore and Umbreit 2001:5). Preliminary results from programs that involve the police directly in RJ goal attainment are promising (McCold and Wachtel 1998; Sherman, Strang, et al. 1998). Officers who are willing to participate in RJ programs may find themselves undervalued within their departments (Winfree 2003b), or decentralization of policing services may serve as an impediment to its widespread adoption in some nations (Winfree 2009).

Judicial Practices   Victim–offender mediation (VOM) programs provide a safe environment in which victims can confront offenders and begin the healing process. Offenders learn about the crime's impact on their victims and take responsibility for their actions. Judges, probation officers, victim advocates, prosecutors, and law enforcement officials make recommendations. Just as critically, they provide an opportunity for both parties to develop a plan that addresses the harm done by the crime that is agreeable to all. More than 300 VOM programs operate in the United States and Canada, and another 700 in Europe (Bazemore and Umbreit 2001:2). Victims report that, although restitution is important, the most significant aspect of VOM programs is that they enable the victims to talk about the impact of the crime, meet the offender, and learn the offender's circumstances (Coates and Gehm 1989; Umbreit 1994).

Circle sentencing—sometimes called **peacemaking circles**—has its roots in the customs of North American aboriginal peoples. This practice is used in several Canadian provinces and in Minnesota (Pranis 1997). Circle sentencing involves five steps: (1) a request by the offender to participate in the process, (2) a healing circle for the victim, (3) a healing circle for the offender, (4) a sentencing circle to establish a consensus on an effective sentencing plan for the offender, and (5) follow-up circles to monitor the offender's progress. Circle participants include the "keeper" of the circle (e.g., a respected community member skilled in peacemaking), the offender and the offender's support group, members of local police and correctional agencies, a judge, the prosecutor and defense attorneys, the victim and the victim's support group, and community leaders. The goals include promoting healing among all parties, empowering all participants, and addressing the underlying causes of the crime.

Correctional Practices   RJ-based corrections programs operate in many U.S. states, including Minnesota, Vermont, Texas, and Oregon (Kurki 1999). To date, no state has incorporated RJ principles into statewide services. Except for a few programs in the United States and in Europe, prison-based restorative programming is quite rare. It is important to note that faith-based groups, such as Prison Fellowship International, have adopted RJ as a guiding principle (Van Ness n.d.; Van Ness and Strong 2006). Faith-based efforts, including those using reintegrative shaming and RJ principles, tend to place greater emphasis on personal change and reform than is the case for other, more secular restorative justice programs (Cullen, Sundt, and Wozniak 2001). One such program is the InnerChange Freedom Initiative (IFI), which teaches restorative principles through confession, repentance, forgiveness, and reconciliation, but does not embrace all of the elements of either reintegrative shaming or a more secular form of RJ; given its Judeo-Christian ethic, it may not be for all inmates (Cullen et al. 2001).

Not all correctional practitioners view RJ programs in the same way, even those who support it in principle. Some see it as a better way to do what they have been doing all along; others see an entirely new paradigm for corrections (M. Smith 2001:2). Some who advocate merging RJ principles into corrections worry about its relegation to minor forms of misbehavior; moreover, they fear its trivialization as a correctional philosophy and practice. Finally, not everyone embraces RJ. Although there can be no denying the progressive ideals of RJ and reintegrative shaming, the risk is very real that they will be corrupted to serve nonprogressive goals and thus do more harm than good (Leverant, Cullen, et al. 1999). Moreover, the extant research fails to support the idea that RJ-based programs will reduce recidivism. Perhaps these concerns and problems reflect Braithwaite's warning that without a normative theory, reintegrative shaming—and programs derived from it—may be corrupted.

SUMMARY

The theories reviewed in this chapter (summarized in Table 8.1) share several features. Power is an obvious one, as labeling theory and reintegrative shaming theory purport to explore the community's ability to define crime and criminals. Although the definitions differ slightly between theories, power's role is undeniable. Second, labeling theory focuses largely on society's responses. After all, crime is behavior so labeled; the criminal is the person so labeled. Reintegrative theory forces us to consider how those sanctioning criminals may use shame constructively. Finally, both theories have broad implications for criminal justice policies and practices.

This chapter's theories provide distinct and unique insights into the use of power by the state. In the case of labeling theory, those who see the application of criminal labels as problematic suggest minimizing their isolating and stigmatizing functions. Proponents of reintegrative shaming argue that the power to shame is not at issue, but rather point to the intent of the shame—to either integrate or isolate the offender—as the crux of the problem. In the 1970s, labeling theory's challenges of the *status quo* yielded a laundry list of programs (e.g., the 4-Ds of diversion, deinstitutionalization, due process, and decriminalization). In the new century, reintegrative shaming has led to the literal worldwide adoption of RJ practices. The ability of both theories to shape criminal justice policies and practices is clearly beyond dispute.

TABLE 8.1   Labeling and Shaming Theories of Crime

Major Figures	Central Assumptions	Causal Arguments (*Key Terms*)	Strengths	Weaknesses
Labeling	Tannenbaum, Goffman, Becker, Lemert, Schur	Social interpretation is highly subjective: What we believe to be true becomes true if we organize our responses or behavior to that interpretation.	Initial acts of deviance, when observed (*primary deviation*), elicit social penalties; any further observed acts "up the ante," increasing the sanctions and devaluing the actor's social worth; at some point the actor assumes the deviant's *master status* (*secondary deviation*).	Popular with practitioners (e.g., social workers, juvenile officers); public intuitively understands the power of labels; many policy implications, including decriminalization, deinstitutionalization, and diversion; new versions have empirical successes.
Reintegrative shaming	Braithwaite	The most effective way to secure rule compliance is to use informal social groups; people care more about what their relatives and friends think of their actions than a judge or jury; power to exclude is bad; power to include is good.	*Reintegrative shaming* leads to legitimate subcultures and other prosocial contacts, and low crime; *disintegrative shaming* leads to illegitimate subcultures, other antisocial contacts, and high crime.	See *deterrence;* reflects the idea that what is feared is not a formal sanction alone, but also the loss of respect and the shame that follow being caught; supports inclusionary social and formal rituals, such as RJ practices.

KEY TERMS

circle sentencing

communitarianism

criminals–as–scapegoats

decriminalization

deinstitutionalization

deviance amplification

disintegrative shaming

diversion

dramatization of evil

due process guarantees

falsely accused

family group conferencing

gestural forgiveness

hate crime

hidden deviants

master status

negotiations

net widening

peacemaking circles

penal harm reduction

prestige symbols

primary deviation

radical nonintervention

reintegrative shaming

republican freedom

restorative justice (RJ)

retail crime

retrospective interpretation

role engulfment

secondary deviation

secondary-deviance hypothesis

self-fulfilling prophesy

shame

shaming

social altruism

social fear

spoiled identities

status characteristic hypothesis

status degradation ceremonies

status offenders

stereotyping

stigmatization

stigma symbols

symbol

symbolic assailant

symbolic interactionism

true deviants

true innocents

victim–offender mediation (VOM)

wholesale crimes

CRITICAL REVIEW QUESTIONS

1. Compare and contrast Tannenbaum's dramatization of evil, Goffman's stigmatization, and Garfinkel's status degradation ceremonies.

2. What is the value of Becker's use of the term *master status* in the study of crime and delinquency? Do you agree with his ideas about perceived and actual behavior? Explain why you feel the way you do.

3. Compare and contrast Wilkins' deviance amplification with Schur's labeling process.

4. What is the greatest shortcoming of labeling theory? Explain your thinking.

5. Labeling theory is important to the courts, police, and corrections. In which specific case do you believe that labeling theory best explains what is happening?

6. Shaming seems like such a natural phenomenon. Why do you think it works to curb behavior, even crime, in some situations but not in others?

7. "Reintegrative shaming is both a normative theory and a causal theory." Explain what this statement means to you. Do you find the duality of reintegrative shaming as troubling as do some criminologists?

8. What are the primary strengths found in RJ that most impressed you? What made them stick out in your mind?

9. What are the primary weaknesses found in RJ that most concerned you? What made them stick out in your mind?

10. Critics of RJ suggest that while its intent is benevolent, it could result in even greater harm than existing practices within the criminal justice system. What do you think concerns these critics? (HINT: Review the net widening of labeling.)

NOTES

1. In an earlier edition, we included reintegrative shaming with deterrence. Thanks to Lode Walgrave, we see labeling and reintegrative shaming as related but countervailing forces.

2. Symbolic interactionism focuses defining certain behaviors as socially unacceptable or morally repugnant. Deviants are the actors whose behavior is outside the parameters of social conduct norms; criminals violate law.

3. A status offender is a juvenile who has committed law violations that would not be offenses at all were it not for the offender's young age.

4. One criticism of official labeling is that it does not account for those criminals who move from primary to secondary deviation without a societal reaction; they are hidden secondary deviants overwhelmed by their deviant roles.

5. Scheff (2001) felt that along with biology and individual psychology, shame and a lack of community were central components of major forms of mental depression. This link is important for Braithwaite's conception of reintegrative shame.

6. Braithwaite (2000:295) saw deterrence as dangerous. He endorsed a normative element called **republican freedom,** a citizenship status associated with dominion, or the complete freedom of choice. In Braithwaite's opinion, reintegrative shaming absent this normative element could be nearly as dangerous as deterrence.

7. Recall that Chamlin and Cochran (1997) looked at altruism, which at best reflects communitarianism and not the presence of reintegrative shaming.

8. As random assignment is not possible when victims and perpetrators work together, the researchers suggest that future evaluations survey all participants prior to participation as to reasons for participation, allowing evaluators to control for motivation as a proxy for self-selection.

9

Conflict Theories

CHAPTER OVERVIEW

LEARNING OBJECTIVES

In this chapter, you will learn the following:

- Conflict is multilayered and contextual: An individual, group, value, idea, or relationship may create conflict.

- When responding to the threat of conflict or actual conflict, the more powerful group may criminalize the "offending" party—the weaker group.

- Social facts—language, religion, culture—that define who we are as a community can and often do serve to create conditions that are divisive and even destructive.

- Laws embody the interests and values of powerful groups in society, sometimes to the detriment of less powerful groups.

- Whether a law receives full enforcement, or whether those convicted of violating it are given a severe penalty may depend on the threat posed by offenders to those making decisions about the level of enforcement and types of sanctions.

INTRODUCTION

This chapter is about the haves and the have-nots, and what transpires because of these disparities. We can express these inequities in terms of **power,** which is, in this context, the ability of a group to carry out its wishes or policies, attain its goals or intentions, and influence the behavior of others, whether those others share the same vision, goals, intentions, or desires. Some groups have power and wish to keep it; other groups have little to no power and no interest in it; still others may covet more power, which often leads to a struggle with either or both of the other two types of groups.

Conflict exists when two or more social, political, or cultural groups—each having common identity, interests, and goals—compete for the same physical space, resources, power base, or social position in a community, nation, or geographic region. Sociologists examine how the groups with power use and abuse it against those without it, the result sometimes being conflict. Criminologists are interested in the connection between conflict and crime, the latter occurring when the group with power invokes the formal legal process to criminalize their weaker opponents. In the wake of such actions, the less powerful group's unique values, beliefs, or behaviors are now illegal, contravening the legal authority (Vold and Bernard 1986; Williams and McShane 2004). The goal of this process is to recast *outsiders* as *outlaws,* and place them and their conduct beyond the law's protection, solidifying and strengthening the in-group's position within the community, nation, or region: us—the "good guys"—versus them—the "bad guys."

While power is central to understanding conflict, so too are *oppression* and *coercion,* the means by which those with power maintain and extend it. **Oppression** refers to the imposition of excessive, severe, or unreasonable burdens on others; **coercion** is a form of hindrance or a compulsive requirement, often but not exclusively imposed by a legal authority. Those who are most powerful in a society control the laws and other key social institutions, including the society's religious, educational, and economic systems; they use both oppression and coercion to achieve their goals.

In this chapter, we present three types of generic **conflict theory,** all emphasizing the use of power to subjugate others, but each differing in terms of its assumptions, scope, rationales, and processes.[1] As a class of theories, conflict theory specifies that different social entities in society seek the same limited goals, and the competition for these goals often criminalizes members of the group with less power. Before looking at these theories, we must examine the origins of conflict theory.

ORIGINS OF CONFLICT THEORY

The conflict perspective is one of the oldest continuously functioning theoretical orientations. History provides many examples of conflicts between cultures that practice a particular religion and those within the same geographic area that do not. Conflicts between nation-states have similar origins: The faithful subjected nonbelievers to coercive or oppressive measures intended to bring them to the new faith or eliminate them as a threat to the established social or economic order. Many of these conflicts occurred in the distant past, while others continue into the twenty-first century. Even those who share the same religion, as least in terms of theological classification, may have conflicts over specific sets of beliefs that only a "true believer" understands: for example, conflicts between Christians—Catholics or Protestants—or between Muslims—Sunni and Shiite. Alternatively, consider the conflicts between Episcopalians who endorse same-sex marriages and those who do not.

Can theory help us understand these theological and ideological battles? Can it suggest ways to reduce the underlying tensions or the crimes committed in the name of one group with power against another group with less or none? Does a way exist to defuse the conflict before it gains momentum? Theories may provide questions, but before detailing them, we must revisit the origins of conflict and consensus.

Crime, Consensus, and Conflict

For much of the early twentieth century, structural-functional and consensus views of law and social control dominated sociology and, consequently, criminology. For instance, nineteenth-century anthropologists A. R. Radcliffe-Brown (1881–1955) and Bronislaw Malinowski (1884–1942) carried on a lengthy debate about the value of **organicism,** or the idea that society was structurally similar to a biological entity (Turner 1978). The interdependent parts of this human social system, or the organs, makes up the totality of society, each part serving its function. The French sociologist Émile Durkheim (1858–1917) refined this idea, as we learned in Chapter 6. He felt that crime and deviance served a purpose in an organic social system—or else they would cease to exist. However, communities seek stability through consensus, striving for equilibrium (*homeostasis*), which balanced the interests of all parties.

Eschewing the functionalist's organic model, Max Weber (1864–1920), a German lawyer and sociologist, studied conflicts between social classes (Coser 1971). Many topics attracted Weber, including sociology of religion, economic sociology, social stratification, social change, complex organizations, and sociology of religion. One outgrowth of his studies was the **ideal type,** a mental construction intended to capture the essence of a class of phenomena used in social analysis, which may not represent any single case found in society, serving rather as a descriptive model.

One area of interest to Weber was **authority relations,** or why people claim or relinquish power and authority, and why they feel that others should obey them. In the **rational-legal authority** type, he created a model that has come to characterize most modern states and their relations with those they represent, govern, and control (Coser 1971:227). The ultimate purpose of law, in such a system, is to insure the fair and equal application of legal principles and procedures to all under its dominion. Nonetheless, Weber saw conflict as inevitable and acceptable, having many sources (e.g., business, religion, government, and law). Under a rational-legal authority, those governed obey rule laws not because they achieve expected or desired effects; rather, they obey them because they are in force, a form of blind obedience (Weber 1947). If we blindly obey old laws, the creation of new laws is a difficult proposition and sets up conditions ripe for conflict. Law, then, is the means by which powerful persons impose their will on all others. Crime becomes a political struggle whereby different groups attempt to promote their interests and, in so doing, preserve or improve their position in society.

German sociologist Georg Simmel (1858–1918) emphasized **group interests**—the needs, goals, status, power, influence, and other concerns related to the collective's continued existence—in his study of the sociology of conflict. Simmel (1955) believed that when individuals recognize that they have interests or needs in common with others, they form groups. The group then seeks, through collective behavior, to further its interests and fulfill its needs. Eventually, they develop group loyalty and form emotional attachments. Those who infringe on the interests and needs of the group become its enemies. From this perspective, group members exhibit loyalty to and identification with the group's interests or needs, with the result often being intergroup conflict. Simmel observed that consensus is an illusion that masks the underlying conflict.

While German and French sociologists laid conflict theory's foundation, it remained for sociologists and criminologists working in America to formulate how such conflict translated into crime and criminality. Those efforts began in the 1930s, with the pioneering work of Swedish-born but American-trained sociologist Thorsten Sellin.

CULTURE CONFLICT THEORY

- Did you or your family immigrate to the United States? Did members of your immediate family have trouble adjusting to American culture, preferring instead to keep to the "old ways"? If you or your family are not recent immigrants but still celebrate a different culture, do these actions pose problems?

- Have you traveled to another country and found yourself confronted by laws that criminalized conduct that is not a crime back home, such as possessing alcoholic beverages?

- Besides race, ethnicity, or nationality issues, do you hold beliefs or engage in cultural practices or rituals that some might question or even condemn? Could someone from another nation see these beliefs or behaviors as crimes?

Societal conduct norms require that in a given situation certain people act in a specific manner (Wirth 1931). Thorsten Sellin (1938) claimed that such **conduct norms** express the group's cultural values. In a homogeneous society, conduct norms express group consensus: There is general agreement about what is right or wrong. In more heterogeneous societies, disagreements may exist about what is right and wrong, as well as what is to be valued and what is to be condemned. **Culture conflict**—the mental and physical clash between groups—is inevitable because "differences in mode of life and the social values evolved by these groups appear to set them apart from other groups in many or most respects" (Sellin 1938:63). Sellin believed that culture conflict had at least two separate and distinct sources, which he identified as *primary culture conflict* and *secondary culture conflict*. As you look at this 70-year-old-plus theory, think about current world and national events. What Sellin wrote about in the 1930s is just as relevant for criminologist in the twenty-first century as it was for his contemporaries.

Primary Culture Conflict

Primary culture conflict exists when one culture brings its legal norms to bear on people socialized in a different culture and has three specific forms.

Cross-Border Primary Culture Conflicts   *Cross-border culture conflicts* can occur when two distinct cultures share a physical border with one another. This condition creates opportunities for those with different conduct norms to clash directly and openly. The extent to which the differences include religion, ideology, language, and political systems only serves to exacerbate the problem. Long-standing enmity toward the *cultural outsider,* a form of a stereotypical representation of those living across the political barrier, makes the likelihood of open conflict even greater, especially if the land on which the border sits is part of the dispute.

Current world events provide examples of cross-border culture conflicts. In the part of eastern Europe that was once Yugoslavia, predominantly Roman Catholic Croats, Eastern Orthodox Serbs, and Bosnian Muslims variously clashed and cooperated with one another throughout the 1990s and into the new century. Predominantly Hindu India and Muslim Pakistan have a long-standing border dispute that periodically erupts into open warfare; acquisition of nuclear weapons by both countries has only worsened tensions on the Indian subcontinent.

We can find an example of this primary culture conflict closer to home. The United States and Mexico share a long border. Conflict along this border, from water and land disputes to smuggling, existed even before the 1848 Treaty of Guadalupe Hidalgo that formalized the boundaries after the Mexican–American War, and has yet to end. Recent efforts by the federal government to build a physical barrier across the region in the name of homeland security and border integrity have done little to reduce the level of conflict.

Colonialism-Derived Primary Culture Conflict   The term **colonialism** refers to a philosophy, process, policy, and practice whereby one nation establishes **hegemony**, a claim of political dominance, over a geographic area, generally followed by the settlement—**colonization**—of its own citizens in that area with the intent of using or even exploiting the region in perpetuity. This practice leads to a second form of primary culture conflict, *colonialism-derived culture conflict,* which is especially oppressive when the colonizing power declares the indigenous culture to be inferior.

The Greeks and Romans famously colonized each other's territory, as well as other parts of the "known world." Greek colonization efforts were relatively benign, but the Romans created a long-standing empire by threat of military action and conquest (Palmer and Colton 1965). The Romans often "encouraged" the people they dominated and absorbed into their empire to follow Roman laws and Roman customs. Indeed, there were two sets of laws in the Roman world: One for citizens of Rome (*jus civile*) and another for dealing with all others under their control (*jus gentium*).[2]

Colonialism reached its zenith in the **Colonial Era,** when it merged with **imperialism**, or the idea that some nations have the natural right to both form and maintain empires at virtually any cost in order to extend their military and trade advantages. Britain, France, Portugal, Spain and the Netherlands variously warred and cooperated with each other from 1500 to 1800, planting their flags and placing their people in faraway places, generally ignoring the rights of the original inhabitants to rule themselves and their lands (Wolny 2005). When indigenous residents resisted colonization, the imperialist power swiftly and decisively defined their actions as criminal and responded with often brutal police and military actions. The European powers maintained these "outposts" into the 1960s, or until they found the political, economic, and social costs of keeping them outweighed their benefits (Englebert 2000, Lange, Mahoney, and vom Hau 2006).[3] In other words, they got their metaphorical "butts" kicked in streets and jungles from Asia to Africa. The indigenous population took control of the legal process, redefining themselves as freedom fighters and their colonial overseers as imperialist-criminals.

The relationship between American Indian tribes and the U.S. government highlights this colonialism-derived primary culture conflict. The government's paternalist and colonialist treatment of the indigenous peoples of what would become the United States resulted in physical genocide (e.g., General Philip Sheridan's infamous quote that "the only good Indian was a dead Indian") and cultural genocide (e.g., the creation of Indian Schools to "assimilate" Indian children into the American mainstream, forbidding indigenous languages or religious practices). Unless they are successful in seizing the power to define crime, those who resist often find themselves branded as criminals by the colonial authority and subject to its coercive power: might makes right.

Immigrant-Status Primary Culture Conflict   The third form of primary culture conflict can occur whenever immigrants leave one culture for another. For example, Sellin described a Sicilian father who avenged his family's honor by killing the "despoiler" of his daughter. Sellin viewed the father's reactions as an

---

COMMENTS AND CRITICISMS: Primary Culture Conflict in the U.S. Today

Two current practices suggest that culture conflict theory is equally relevant in the twenty-first century. First, recent immigrants from certain African nations that circumcise female children (i.e., remove all or part of the clitoris) at an early age, a practice included under the general rubric of **female genital mutilation (FGM)**, run the risk of primary culture conflict. A female child who has not had this operation would, in all likelihood, be unacceptable in marriage. In some parts of the world, this practice is commonplace, with estimates ranging as high as 130 million women undergoing some form of FGM. Many other nations, including the United States, and worldwide groups, such as the World Health Organization and the United

Nations Commission on Human Rights, consider these practices to be mutilation and child abuse. Since 1996, seventeen states and the federal government have adopted legal measures targeting FGM.

Second, among members of the Hmong people from Southeast Asia, traditional shamans are preferred over modern medical practitioners, even when reliance on the former may result in death. Most U.S. legal jurisdictions view failure to secure medical treatment for underage children as a crime, placing many Hmong immigrants to this country at odds with local authorities.

SOURCES: Armstrong (2000); Faderman (1998); Little (2003); Fadiman (1997); Tsai (2001).

---

example of primary culture conflict. The father could not understand why the police viewed him as a criminal while in the eyes of his cultural peers he was exacting expected and demanded retribution (Sellin 1938). As the above box points out, *immigrant-status culture conflicts* did not end with the great U.S. immigration waves of the early twentieth century.

Secondary Culture Conflict

Secondary culture conflict occurs whenever a group emerges within a dominant culture that has significantly different values and conduct norms from the dominant culture. According to Sellin, such developments are normal and natural outgrowths of social differentiation, creating many "social groupings, each with its own definitions of life situations, its own ignorance or misunderstanding of the social values of other groups" (Sellin 1938:105). Sellin did not view the law as a consensus of all views; rather, it was a reflection of the dominant culture's conduct norms. When an emergent group's behavior conflicts with these norms, the dominant culture can declare the behavior a crime.

In Sellin's view, culture conflict is a mental construct, "primarily the clash between antagonistic conduct norms incorporated in personality" (Sellin 1938:66). For this mental condition to exist, the individual must acknowledge the conflict. In both kinds of culture conflict the conflict is external, between cultural codes and norms: the norm-violating individual is entangled between two conflicting sets of conduct norms. Figure 9.1 summarizes Sellin's primary and secondary culture conflict.

GROUP CONFLICT THEORY

- Are you a member of a racial or ethnic minority group? What does the term *minority* mean? Is it all about numbers, or does it involve something else?

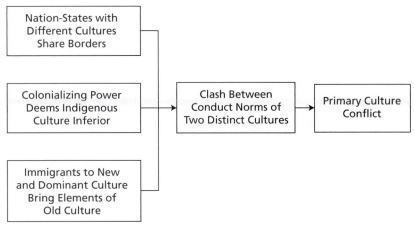

(a) Sellin's Primary Cultural Conflict

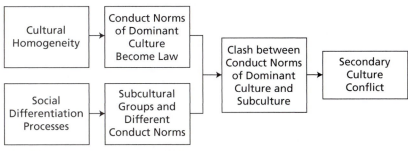

(b) Sellin's Secondary Cultural Conflict

FIGURE 9.1 Sellin's Primary and Secondary Culture Conflict

- Have you ever participated in a political or work action, such as a strike against an employer? Did you uneasily watch nearby police officers, wondering what they were thinking or going to do?

- You have probably seen protesters on television expressing their intense dislike for any number of authority figures, from employers to the U.S. government. Can you recall how and why you reacted to what you saw?

Georg Simmel's work influenced American criminologist George Vold (1896–1967), who focused on group interests and the problems they create. Vold (1958) saw the group itself as a source of conflict, much like a pitched battle between persons seeking the same limited goals. He incorporated a *pluralistic* view in his theory: society consists of many different groups, with some overlapping and compatible interests; however, other interests are distinct and incompatible. Groups conflict when they seek to expand or protect their group's interests, and as they do, in-group loyalties intensify. Vold saw conflict of this sort is healthy, inevitable, and continuous, as groups seek redress for wrongs, improvement in status, and redistribution of power (Vold and Bernard 1986).

Law and Group Conflict

What is the relationship between group conflict and criminality? According to Vold's **group conflict theory,** groups in positions of authority have their values woven into the law to protect that which they hold dear. Because those in position of authority base laws on their values and interests, the likelihood of criminalizing their behavior is low, but increases for those with conflicting values.[4]

Vold saw the legislature, an arena of compromise and accommodations, as a key battleground. For example, while one group wishes to criminalize that which threatens its interests and needs, another may view these efforts as threats to its interests and needs. In the resulting conflict, the group with the most power or votes wins—or there is compromise. In the end, the law intrudes on the losers' interests. Group interests and differences in relative power help us understand why legislatures outlaw certain substances, such as marijuana, while taxing freely available tobacco and alcohol (Abadinsky 2008). However, the poor, lacking the ability to influence lawmakers, often find their behavior— usually *mala prohibita* or victimless crimes—criminalized. Historically, numbers betting—a form of street-level gambling that allows for very small bets with a potentially high (but elusive) return—was common among the poor. Its promise of quick riches for little money clashed with middle-class values of hard work and thrift, and local and state governments criminalized it. Late in the twentieth century, cash-strapped state governments reinvented it as legal lotteries.

Crime as Minority Power-Group Behavior

Vold supported the view that crime is the behavior of **minority power-groups,** groups that lack sufficient influence to promote or defend their interests and needs. Finding themselves disconnected from the law-making process, they are more likely to violate existing laws, which may conflict with their own interests, needs, and purposes ("If it's not my law, why should I do as it says?"). For example, inner-city youth gangs may feel disenfranchised from the power structure represented by the dominant majority. They may engage in behavior that the law prohibits, such as underage drinking and illicit drug sales. At odds with the dominant majority, youth gangs conflict with the police, who represent the majority's interests. As in most conflicts, police actions against gangs help to solidify them and intensify in-group loyalties (Vold and Bernard 1986). It is important to note that Vold was not talking about minority racial or ethnic groups *per se,* but rather about groups that were in relative positions of powerlessness.

In summary, for Vold's form of conflict to operate, the laws must play a central role, as do group loyalty and identification. The law defines certain minority group actions as crime. It is critical to note that Vold believed his theory only explained certain kinds of crime: individual criminal acts that result when two groups with opposing views collide and the members of each act out of loyalty, upholding their group's interests.

IN THEIR OWN WORDS: Conflict Theorists on Inevitability of Conflict

Georg Simmel: "Just as the universal needs of 'love and hate,' that are attractive and repulsive forces, in order to have any form at all, so society, too, in order to attain a determinate shape, needs some quantitative ratio of harmony and disharmony, of association and competition, of favorable and unfavorable tendencies."

Thorsten Sellin: "We have noted that culture conflicts are the natural outgrowth of processes of social differentiation, which produces an infinity of social groupings, each with its own definitions of life situations, its own interpretations of social relationships, its own ignorance or misunderstanding of the social values of other groups."

George Vold: "The result [conflicting group interests] is a more or less continuous struggle to maintain, or to improve, the place of one's own group in the interaction of groups."

SOURCES: Sellin (1938:654); Simmel (1955:15); Vold (1979:228–229).

CRIMINALIZATION THEORY/ NORM RESISTANCE THEORY

A decade after Vold proposed group conflict theory, the U.S. was deeply involved in an unpopular war in Vietnam. Some criminologists during these turbulent times discovered the intuitive appeal of labeling theory; others turned to conflict theory to understand the use of power and coercion to extract lawful conduct. Marxist and critical conflict theories grew more influential in this period (see Chapter 10), and the two latter threads often intertwined (Akers and Sellers 2009; Williams and McShane 2004). For example, Richard Quinney (1970) rejected pluralism in his *social reality theory,* suggesting that the crime–conflict link derives from the competition for power.[5]

Of the post–World War II generic conflict theories, the one most closely tied to criminology is Austin Turk's *theory of criminalization,* what some call the *theory of norm resistance.*

Theory of Criminalization

Turk looked critically at the role of law in creating conflict, calling his work the **theory of criminalization**. He saw merit in German conflict theorist Ralf Dahrendorf's (1959) distinction between those who derive power from social institutions and those who do not. The law, wrote Turk (1976), equals power—*law-as-power* is a weapon in social conflict. While consensus and pluralist perspectives view law as a means of settling or precluding disputes, law also has the ability to generate conflict or make disputes even worse. In Turk's (1976:288) law was "a set of resources whose control and mobilization can in many ways … lead to conflict instead of away from conflicts." Law was a coercive weapon, used against certain groups for the advantage of others.

To Turk (1969), conflict's focus is on those in power (the authorities) and those in weaker or subordinate positions in society. His theory describes the conditions causing the criminalization of certain behaviors, the circumstances that determine who becomes a criminal (i.e., arrested, prosecuted, and punished for their behavior), and the rates at which these events occur. Those with little power are likely to feel the full force of the law, which is especially true when their cultures differ from that of the authorities. This situation creates a struggle over whose norms have precedence over the others.

Cultural and Behavioral Norm Concordance

According to Turk (1969), law consists of both written cultural norms and behavioral social norms. Given these arrangements, social order represents only a temporary resolution of conflicts between various groups, each with its own incompatible desires. Three conditions set the stage for conflict:

- Conflict is most likely to occur when the group in power, the **authorities**, exhibits high agreement between the cultural and social norms or **norm concordance**; that is, agreement between what the group says and does.

- Another group, the **resisters**, is subject to the authorities' cultural norms or law; this group is just as adamant about the sanctity of its own set of unique cultural and social norms.

- Each group, both authorities and resisters, exhibits high concordance about its own set of norms, but not about the same set of norms.

Three characteristics of resisters and authorities determine the likelihood of conflict. First, the higher the *level of concordance* between each group's cultural norms and behavioral norms, the greater the probability of conflict: Do both groups not only "talk the talk, but walk the walk?" If neither group exhibits high concordance, the probability is lowest; if one exhibits high concordance, but not the other, the probability is higher; but if both exhibit high concordance, the probability is highest. The *level of organization* also influences the probability of conflict. When resisters are organized, conflict is more likely to occur. Finally, conflict is dependent on the *level of sophistication* evidence provided by either party. Highly sophisticated resisters or authorities know how to manipulate each other in order to get what they want without resort to overt coercion or strong resistance. When both parties are unsophisticated, conflict is more likely.

The Role of Enforcers and Resisters

Three sets of factors determine whether the conflict results in criminalization. First, the principle way conflict criminalizes is by meaning attached to the resister's act by the authorities' **first-line rule enforcers** (i.e., the police), and the extent to which **higher-level rule enforcers** (i.e., prosecutors and judges) share this meaning. If it is not important to the police, then the probability of enforcement is low; if it is not important to prosecutors and judges, then the penalties sought or pronounced are minimal.

Second, the power of rule enforcers relative to resisters is critical. **High-power resisters**—the wealthy or politicians—are less likely to find their illicit activities criminalized than are the less powerful. For example, in Europe during the late Middle Ages, a land-owning member of the gentry—the ruling class—could beat an unproductive servant to death without concern for a criminal sanction. **Low-power resisters** are far more likely to see their illicit and sometimes even normal, daily behaviors criminalized. For example, indigent street people, setting up shanty-town communities under interstate highway bridges, may find themselves uniquely subjected to long disused vagrancy laws based on a financial-means test.

Turk called the third factor **realism of conflict moves**. Criminalization is most likely when one side or the other does not exhibit realism about the likely outcome. Enforcers are realistic when they do not have to resort to coercive enforcement, relying instead on their positions of authority. Resisters are realistic when they pursue their goals without limiting the enforcers' options. Crime, then, becomes a status conferred upon resisters by enforcers, and becomes a secondary measure of the level of conflict in a community. Figure 9.2 graphically represents Turk's theory of criminalization.

An example from recent world events may help frame this process. In 1989, Chinese college students conflicted with their government over basic human rights. In that year, the Berlin Wall collapsed; communism in Europe was on the brink of destruction. Chinese college students, perhaps emboldened by unfolding world events, stood up to their government in a series well-publicized public demonstrations between early April and early June 1989, including an event called by the world media "the Tiananmen Square massacre." The precipitating event in April was safe enough: A peaceful demonstration upon the death of a prodemocracy and promarket Chinese official, resulting in 100,000 marchers appearing in Tiananmen Square. Communist government officials had long used the Square for its own purposes; hence, they did not view the initial actions as

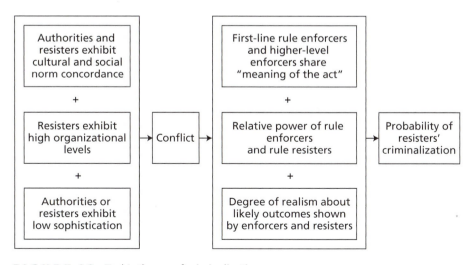

F I G U R E 9.2 Turk's theory of criminalization

threatening. Over the next weeks and months, the demonstrations continued and increased in their criticisms of the government. The student-demonstrators, emboldened by the absence of a governmental response, become even more militant and public in their demands. Power and conflict collided on June 4, 1989, when Chinese Army tanks famously cleared the square of demonstrators. Estimates of the number of dead and injured ranged from 200 to 300 (by the Chinese government) to 2,000 to 3,000 (by the International Red Cross).

The events that unfolded in the spring of 1989 were a textbook example of how Turk's theory criminalizes the behavior of resisters. In this case, the Chinese authorities waited too long to act and badly misjudged the resolve of the students-resisters. By the time the authorities decided to reign in the resisters, they could not rely solely on authority and had to use extreme—and often violent—control measures. The government justified its actions by defining resisters as criminals, casting hundreds, perhaps thousands, into prison, banning the press from the nation, and purging its own party (the authorities) of those who supported the students. Ultimately, the government crushed the student-protest movement in China for decades.

ASSESSING CONFLICT THEORIES

Research involving conflict theories defies categorization. The evidence concerning conflict theories fits into two distinct groups. The first centers on historical analyses and anecdotal evidence of conflict in its various forms. The second consists of survey data gathered from participants in conflict situations. The goal of this second body of work is to determine the extent to which theoretically relevant concepts provide insights into the conflicts reported within the samples studied.

Historical and Anecdotal Evidence of Conflict

Russia under the Czars provides unique insights into culture conflict's power to create criminals and increase crime. Historian Stephen Frank (1999) looks at the interactions between the ruling elites in Russia and the peasant class between 1856 and 1914, a turbulent time in Russian history. He suggests that peasants were far more sophisticated than the elites believed, as the peasants knew exactly how the government viewed them. For all of their attempts to manipulate the elites' images of them, the peasants found themselves under the thumb of Imperial Russia, which employed a colonialist model, such as that described by Sellin in his second form of primary culture conflict. The adoption of this colonialist strategy perpetuated negative stereotypes of rural criminals terrorizing the countryside. The Imperial Russian justice system was not available to the peasants, who were relegated to a secondary system of courts with peasant judges, peace mediators, and extrajudicial functionaries. This practice reinforced the peasants' subservient position relative to other, more modernized groups in Russia, and only served to reinforce elite Russia's poor opinion of the peasants. This policy led to heightened cultural and material conflicts between the peasants and the bureaucrats who enforced the Czar's policies, conflicts that eventually contributed to the end Imperial Russia with the 1917 revolution and a reversal of power: The winners "criminalized" the Czar and his bureaucrats, executing them.

Contemporary history provides additional examples that avoided the bloody reprisals that often accompany revolution:

- In the Republic of South Africa, anti-Apartheid groups engaged in political struggle, rebellion, and revolution for decades. The authorities defined members of these groups as criminals; this included Nelson Mandela, who spent decades in South African prisons. In 1990, as the white-supremacist government announced major land and liberty reform, Mandela walked out of prison a free man. Violent uprisings and reprisals wracked the nation until the peaceful elections of 1994, when 20,000,000 South Africans turned out to vote, and by a large majority, Nelson Mandela became its first democratically elected president. Mandela and Frederik Willem DeKlerk, the last apartheid-era president of South Africa, received the Nobel Peace Prize for their efforts to end apartheid and transfer power peacefully.

- In the former Soviet Union, a crazy quilt of political groups struggle for power, more than 15 years after its collapse. These groups variously condemn and praise those previously in power, from Czar Nicholas to Stalin. Even the transfer of power from Mikhail Gorbachev, the last head of state for the USSR, to Boris Yeltsin, the first popularly elected president of what would soon become Russia, was unsteady, marked by open conflicts, as old-line communists and ultranationalists waited for signs of weakness. The 1993 attempted coup by Communists to retake the Russian government resulted in the arrest of coup leaders; they avoided punishment, although some "committed suicide." In Russia, today's criminals are tomorrow's heroes, and vice versa.

On one level, it makes sense to think about individuals committing illegal acts in the furtherance of a group's goals and intentions. For instance, a member of an embattled labor union, a conscientious objector, or a status-offending juvenile might commit a criminal act to further the group's interests. If both sets of actors are members of minority power-groups and their interests collide, Vold's perspective may provide the best insights into what is happening. On the other hand, such actions might threaten powerful interests. If powerful groups use the law to criminalize the conduct of those doing the threatening, then the social forces described by Turk may be at work.

Survey Evidence of Conflict

Two large-scale surveys provide support for parts of culture conflict theory. The first looks at possible cultural rifts created by gun ownership in the United States. Actually, two positions have long characterized the gun control debate: the right of citizens to own and bear arms (Second Amendment position) and the belief

---

COMPARATIVE CRIMINOLOGY—WORLD VIEWS ON CRIME AND JUSTICE:
Conflict Resolution in East Europe

Since the fall of the Soviet Union, many eastern European nations have adopted Western legal systems. In some, the new ways of conflict resolution ran into long-held cultural traditions that survived communist rule, as was the case in areas populated by ethnic Albanians, parts of Albania, Kosovo, and Macedonia. With the introduction of Western legal systems, crime began to increase in areas with large ethnic Albanian populations. In a survey of the Albanian regions of all three nations, Jana Arsovska and Philippe Verduyn sought to clarify whether this was a case of a Wolfgang's *subculture of violence* (See Chapter 6) or Sellin's *culture conflict*. They reported that violent crime rates seem tied to an endemic subculture of violence; a conflict of conduct norms better explained the recent increases in all crime in the regions where ethnic Albanians resided.

Source: Arsovska and Verduyn (2008).

---

that widespread gun in is itself a danger (gun control position). Gary Kleck tested an alternative thesis: Support for gun control policy is a clash of cultures between those who believe that guns are an integral part of their way of life and those who do not. Employing a national survey, representative of the U.S. as a whole, Kleck reported: "Instead of gun control support being seen as a response to crime, it would seem more useful to see it as a product of membership in culturally conflicting social groupings." (Kleck 1996:401). What were these groupings? Gun control was higher among better-educated, higher-income liberals who did not own guns or hunt. Kleck could not rule out the possibility that support for gun control has ties to the belief that removing them would reduce crime; however, support for the policy was not dependent upon personal experience with crime, directly or indirectly.

Tests of Turk's theory generally focus on the responses of the first-line rule enforcers. Such studies examine police–citizen encounters, including domestic violence calls (Greenleaf and Lanza-Kaduce 1995; Lanza-Kaduce and Greenleaf 1994; 2000) and general police stops of citizen with various outcomes, including warnings, tickets, or arrests (Weidner and Terrill 2005). Overall, the researchers report general support for measures of sophistication and organization levels: social support for the police and social complexity (i.e., organization) are important to our understanding of police-citizen conflict, in much the same way as Turk proposed. Norm concordance and its obverse form, norm resistance, did not perform as uniformly. In one study, a measure of deference norms (Weidner and Terrill 2005), an indirect measure of norm concordance that included race (i.e., African Americans deferring to whites), age (i.e., younger deferring to older), sex (i.e., females deferring to males), and wealth (wealthier-appearing deferring to less wealthy) did not perform as predicted. That is, conflict was not less likely when this aggregate measure of deference reinforced the officer's positional authority as a first-line rule enforcer. A second study did find the officer's race related to norm resistance and increased tensions between the officers and the citizens (Greenleaf and Lanza-Kaduce 1995).

Unresolved Issues in Conflict Theorizing

Several general themes dominate critiques of culture conflict theory:

- *Reliance on questionable methods with limited generalizability.* Some critics see generic conflict proponent's reliance on historical and event analyses, such as that used by Frank, and the anecdotal evidence reviewed above, as weaknesses. The reports by Kleck and by Arsovska and Verduyn somewhat blunt this criticism.

- *A lack of attention to individual motivations.* Although we learn much about the creation of law, the conflict perspective tells us little about *why* people commit crimes. Because the conflict theories provide group-level (macro-level) explanations, they more clearly articulate the motivation of social groups and government officials than those designated as offenders (micro-level).

- *An incorrect and biasing interpretation of culture conflict.* Sellin's theory "blames" immigrants for failing to assimilate properly, hanging on to their vestigial culture as a safety net to calm their fears about the new culture. Following the creation of the European Union and the reduction in border checks between EU nations, the authorities and news media have tended to blame immigrant groups for heightened crime levels. For many social critics, the current interpretation of culture conflict becomes the fruit of state-based biases (Brion and Tulkens 1998), and may in fact lead to racist immigration practices (Tsoukala 2002; Sayad 1999; see also Martinez and Lee 2000).

- *Focus of Vold's theory is too narrow.* Vold contended that group conflict theory only worked to explain "those kinds of situations in which the individual criminal acts flow from the collision of groups whose members are loyally upholding the in-group position" (Vold, Bernard, and Snipes 2001:230). Thus, the theory may provide insights into events such as conflicts between reformists and hard-liners in the old Soviet Union, protesters dissatisfied with their government's position on a global issue, or union workers with grievances against their employers. However, given the volume of crime in the United States (see Chapter 1) and elsewhere, its general utility as a theory of crime may be quite limited.

- *The level of abstraction present in Turk's theory of criminalization precludes testing of its core propositions.* Providing concrete, valid, and valid measures of, for example, concordance or sophistication is a daunting operational task, one that has proven quite elusive (cf., Lanza-Kaduce and Greenleaf 1994; Orcutt 1983).

- *Turk's theory has provided little guidance for policy makers and criminal justice practitioners.* This criticism is somewhat related to the first one: a theory characterized as abstract is hard to translate into policy and practices (Akers and Sellers 2009; Liska and Messner 1999). However, as we demonstrate later in this chapter, this criticism may be shortsighted (see also Greenleaf and Lanza-Kaduce 1995; Weidner and Terrill 2005).

- *Laws do not "cause" behavior.* Without laws, crime would not exist, but the presence of laws does not *create* crimes (Clinard and Meier 1985:91). Certain behaviors have always troubled society, and some more than others. Those that require a formal response because of the nature of the threat to social cohesion or the social order become crimes, but only with the passage of laws.

- *While the theory may explain past events, particularly using historical analysis and anecdotal methods, it may have limited efficacy in predicting future events.* The conditions that explain conflict do not tell us why one set of circumstances produces crime and another does not. In hindsight, conflict theory— whatever form it takes—reveals a great deal about the costs of conflicts and their resolutions; used prospectively, it may be less useful as a predictive tool.

These criticisms and concerns aside, the impact of conflict theory on criminology is undeniable. Specialized conflict theories, which we explore in Chapter 11, have helped unravel questions about the links between race, gender, and crime that threaten the core values of the nation: equality and equity in treatment before the law. Moreover, conflict theory is a popular theoretical underpinning for many unique criminological studies, including those that look at the relationship between economic factors and crime. As the next section makes clear, the generic conflict theories in this chapter by themselves provide important insights into the operation of the nation's system of criminal justice.

CONFLICT THEORIES, PUBLIC POLICY, AND CRIMINAL JUSTICE PRACTICES

Policies such as *colonization* and *imperialism* no longer define the world political stage, although some critics of the international policies and practices of certain world powers might argue with this statement. The vestiges of both policies, however, are real (i.e., the social, political, and economic difficulties faced by some development of former colonies into nation status), as are the continuing culture conflicts. The acts of colonial powers may have served to mute intranational culture conflicts during the colonial period, but afterwards, the original conflict reemerged, often with horrific consequences.

Immigration policies have been the source of considerable divisiveness not only in the United States, but also around the globe, as nations deal with massive migration patterns, sometimes caused by the intranational culture conflicts such as those in Rwanda and Sudan, to mention but two. Currently, in the United States, the nation's policy on immigration has merged with the War on Terror, so that securing the nation's border against terrorists and illegal immigration are viewed as compatible policies. Sometimes, individuals, groups, and even nations turn to formal methods of conflict resolution, such as those described in the following Comments and Criticisms box.

COMMENTS AND CRITICISMS: Methods of Conflict Resolution

In modern, complex societies, group conflicts are endemic. Policies related to generic conflict theories necessarily emphasize power sharing, a difficult idea to sell to those who wield power. An *interested* third party could step in to resolve issues in a coercive fashion. As shown in Africa, the Middle East, and the Balkans, such measures often fail spectacularly or end up creating new conflicts.

From a policy perspective, how is conflict resolved? Steven Vago identified various methods, several of which have implications for criminal justice:

- *Negotiation.* The parties attempt to resolve their differences without the intercession of a third party, normally through a process of compromise. Prison officials often use this method to resolve prison uprisings (although sometimes mediation is employed) and governments use it to end military stalemates (e.g., the Korean conflict and the Vietnam War).

- *Mediation.* An impartial mediator acts as a facilitator and advisor to help the conflicting parties work out an agreement. For instance, neighborhood dispute resolution centers provide a local-level means for mediating everything from personal disputes to minor crimes. Judges, police, and prosecutors refer most participants.[6]

- *Arbitration.* This process also uses an uninvolved and neutral third party; however, unlike in

mediation, the results of arbitration are binding on all parties. For example, if during a police strike officers and management cannot reach a settlement through negotiations or mediation, a court may order binding arbitration. In some jurisdictions, disputing parties may employ retired judges as arbitrators.

- *Adjudication.* This represents a public and formal method of resolving disputes. Whether a judge or jury is present, civil law litigants place their fates in the hands of others. They become relatively passive participants in the proceedings, especially compared with other methods of peaceful conflict resolution. In criminal matters, the state represents the interests of the injured party—in legal parlance, the state is the victim; this interpretation effectively limits the actual victim's role in the proceedings. In addition, adjudication has a "zero sum" outcome: a winner and a loser.

At each juncture in the criminal justice system, opportunities emerge to use one or more of the methods to avoid conflict, minimize its impact, or resolve it. The specific forms may vary from agency to agency, but the basic processes are the same.

Source: Abadinsky (2008); Goldberg, Green, and Sanders (1985); Vago (2009).

Conflict sometimes results in other resolutions, one being crime. For example, conflict theory can yield unique insights into the nation's drug laws and drug control policy. It was Turk's (1969) position that the authorities perceive culturally and racially dissimilar subordinate groups as threatening. Allen Liska and Jiang Yu (1992:55) contend that the size of the dissimilar group was important: smaller dissimilar subordinate groups pose nowhere near the level of threat as a larger one, composing perhaps 20 to 30 percent of the population. The danger is specific: Such groups threaten the social and political order, as established by the power-elites. During the 1980s, when the media portrayed the nation as in the midst of a crack cocaine epidemic, states enacted different sentencing guidelines for persons convicted of possessing crack cocaine versus powder cocaine. The legal battle that ensued over the next 20 years is a classic representation of Turk's theory at work, with a little help from Vold (1958) and Liska and associates (Liska and Chamlin 1984; Liska, Chamlin and Reed 1985).

Crack cocaine and powder cocaine are chemically identical, but crack provides a different delivery system from powder cocaine, and changing cocaine into crack geometrically expands the amount of "product" available for sale at a lower price than powder cocaine. Moreover, the delivery system—one smokes crack, as compared to snorting cocaine powder—is more efficient. However, crack is especially popular among the nation's minority power-groups. Culture conflict: Sentences for crack are far in excess of those for possession of a chemically identical substance. It takes 100 times the weight in powder cocaine to trigger the same penalties as for crack (U.S. Sentencing Commission 1995). Those who made the laws—and their children—were far more likely to use powder cocaine than crack, although in reality the statistical probability of using either drug is low. For example, in the mid-1990s, among crack cocaine defendants, nearly 90 percent were black, but only 7 percent were Hispanic and 5 percent were white; for powder cocaine, 40 percent were black or Hispanic and 18 percent were white (U.S. Sentencing Commission 1995).

The nation's appellate courts long ignored challenges to the sentencing laws as unfair and inequitable (*Edwards v. United States* 1997; The Sentencing Project 2004). After all, the litigants, mostly poor, black and urban, were unsophisticated and disorganized. However, in late 2007, the Supreme Court affirmed (*Kimbrough v. United States*) the right of a judge to give Derrick Kimbrough a shorter sentence than was required by the sentencing guidelines. At the same time, the U.S. Sentencing Commission called for a thorough revamping of the sentencing disparities for crack and cocaine.

Beyond its implications for domestic criminal justice policies and procedures, we can use the theories of Sellin and Turk to gain a better understanding of world events and international criminal justice policies. For example, as suggested by the following Comparative Criminology box, conflict theory can help us understand how alleged intranational law enforcement efforts can serve as a mask for genocide. In this unique piece of scholarship, John Hagan and associates not only use conflict theory to frame the genocide in Darfur, exposing the actions of the Sudanese government, they also manage to castigate several generations of criminologists, from the 1940s to the present, for ignoring war crimes and genocide in their research.[7] Interestingly, this criticism suggests that criminologists have been pawns in dozens of culture, social, and group conflicts, where they could have served as the voice of those less powerful and incapable of representing their group's interests, as is the case for the natives of Darfur during the Sudanese "police action" and the Jews of Europe during the Holocaust.

Law Enforcement Practices

Vold's conflict theory helps us understand both disputes between officers and management and problematic interactions between police and citizens. First, when police officers disagree with management about any number of mutual concerns, ranging from salaries to fringe benefits to shift work, conflicts of group interests are said to exist. On those rare occasions when the officers and management cannot reach an agreement (see negotiations and arbitration above), a strike

COMPARATIVE CRIMINOLOGY—WORLD VIEWS ON CRIME AND JUSTICE:
Genocide and Conflict Theory

According to Article II of the Geneva Genocide Convention, **genocide** consists of the various actions of an aggressor that are intended to bring to the victims—who are identifiable by nationality, ethnicity, race, or religion—conditions of life calculated to bring about the latter's physical destruction in whole or in part. Darfur is a region in western Sudan. The indigenous residents of this area are African tribal groups, while much of the rest of Sudan is of Arab extraction. In February 2003, the Sudanese military, aided by the **Janjaweed**,[8] a militia group composed primarily of Arab Abbala tribesmen from northern Sudan, initiated a concerted military campaign against the primarily black residents of Darfur. The tacit reason for the campaign, said the Sudanese government, was a counterinsurgency against rebel groups in the region. Since 2003, an estimated 200,000 to 500,000 people have died and some two million have been displaced.

John Hagan and associates, employing Turk's "conflict moves," contend that the Arab-dominated Sudanese government "has used systematic killing and rape as instruments of power and control over the tribal African men and women of Darfur" (p. 531). The government has used the counterinsurgency pretext to mask their **genocidal conflict moves,** an idea with direct ties to Turk's theory of criminalization.

In 2004, after both houses of Congress had officially condemned the Sudanese government without legal or scientific evidence of genocide, Secretary of State Colin Powell commissioned the Coalition of International Justice to interview nearly 1,200 randomly sampled households from among the refugees of war-torn Darfur, some still living in Sudan and others in refugee camps in nearby Chad. Hagan and associates restricted their analyses of these data to a sample of 501 refugees for whom questions were asked about the government's rationale for the attacks (e.g., "Was there rebel activity in or near your village"). Their conclusions: The attacks "have been racially motivated, lethally destructive, state supported and militarily unjustified" (p. 552). The Sudanese military and Janjaweed used systematic killings and rapes, the latter having the specific intent of eliminating the "African-ness" of Darfur, as weapons of terror.

The government, by using the counterinsurgency and rebel terminology, clearly operated according to principles that any conflict theorist—but especially Turk—would recognize. The African residents of Darfur, as low-power resisters, were unorganized and unsophisticated; the authorities sent their first-line enforcers, in this case military and paramilitary groups, into Darfur with the specific intent of committing genocide. Both groups exhibited high levels of normative concordance; hence, the genocidal conflict moves of the authorities (i.e., the Sudanese government) were inevitable.

As a follow-up, the world community now recognizes the Sudanese government's actions as genocide. Since Sudan has not ratified the Rome Statute, the International Criminal Court (ICC) could not investigate the "alleged" crimes in Darfur without a request from the United Nations Security Council, an action that occurred in 2005. By 2007, the ICC had issued warrants for members of the Sudanese government. On March 4, 2009, the ICC issued an arrest warrant for the Sudanese president. Yet even these indictments fit within a conflict model: Many Arab nations see them as politically motivated actions by the former colonial powers of Europe. Others ask why the ICC is not investigating the actions of these same powers in Iraq and Afghanistan.

SOURCES: Hagan, Rymond-Richmond, and Parker (2005); International Crisis Group (2009).

may result. Management can criminalize the striking officers' behavior because in most jurisdictions the police cannot legally strike. In the face of a court order, normally an injunction against the illegal strike, officers have two choices: (1) continue the strike and risk arrest, or (2) end the strike. Occasionally the officers have opted to continue the strike and suffer the legal consequences. Several such strikes have turned violent when the police believed that their peaceful efforts to resolve the dispute were failing. As Vold (1958) observed, police may feel disconnected from the lawmaking process and in conflict with the existing laws.

Moreover, this feeling of disconnection from the public can result in violence, as was the case for the police strikes in Cincinnati (1918), Boston (1919), and San Francisco (1975) (Ayers 1977; Bopp, Chignell, and Maddox 1977).

Police face complaints arising from their interactions with the public. There has been criticism from the minority community of the police strategy of "stop and frisk," a conflict between society's desire for safety and "racial profiling." In New York City, in 2008, members of the NYPD frisked over 500,000 persons, more than 80 percent of them young black or Latino men—they arrested only 4 percent of those frisked (Powell 2009). Such disputes, depending on the nature and extent of harm, can involve the same conflict-resolution processes describe by Vago. The idea that officials must quickly resolve conflicts between police and the community, and that those resolutions should reduce the conflict without reducing the power of the police, substantially supports conflict theory.

Greenleaf and Lanza-Kaduce (1995) suggest that norm resistance is more likely to occur when, in a domestic dispute, the police arrest both parties. In an era of mandatory arrest policies, police are far more likely to arrest both and let the courts straighten out the matter (Sherman 1992). Thus, the unintended consequence of the practice of dual arrests is an increase in the level of conflict between offices and citizens.

Ultimately, any attempts to implement policies based on Turk's theory of criminalization would face serious impediments. Both groups, including the police—as first-line rule enforcers—and law resisters—whether criminalized or not, must clearly understand that the process of conflict management has rules that one must play by, like those outlined by Turk. Intractability and inflexibility by either or both parties could "up the ante" in any direct confrontation. Just as important, rule enforcers should gauge clearly and correctly the levels of organization and sophistication present among resisters. For example, when dealing with gangs, local police should consider Turk's admonitions about possible outcomes, especially when faced with a group that is intractable and inflexible upon initial contacts. If the police adopt a similar stance, increased levels of conflict may not be far behind.

Judicial Practices

As described in the general policy section on conflict theory, the role of the judiciary varies. For example, courts play a central role in adjudicating competing or conflicting group interests only when one or more of the parties bring that issue to the attention of the court. An example is abortion, in which both sides have attempted to use the courts in support of their respective positions. In the 1990s, appellate courts in several states upheld laws restricting abortion, and at the same time awarded abortion clinics million-dollar judgments against anti-abortion groups. While the conflict view does not explain all crime, it helps us understand the distinctions between laws that control behavior that most citizens view as problematic and those that do not enjoy such widespread endorsement (Hagan 1994; Vold 1958).

In the case of the theory of criminalization, courts are essential since, as Turk describes (1976), the higher-level rule enforcers' "meaning of the act" is crucial to criminalization. When the defendant stands accused of serious legal misconduct, then it is the court's responsibility to reinforce the gravity of the offense, sometimes by means of a jail or prison sentence. As was argued in the case of the sentencing disparities for crack and powder cocaine, the case was ultimately decided by a mixture of legislative and executive actions. However, it is an interesting footnote to the controversy that a federal judge's unwillingness to use the existing sentencing guidelines, which in effect dictated the meaning of the act for the higher-level rule enforcer, was central to its resolution.

Correctional Practices

Prisons and jails are "total institutions" in that they exercise control over virtually all aspects of inmate life. By their nature, community-based corrections and other alternatives to incarceration are less controlling. Nonetheless, the role of power in corrections is undisputed. This highly charged, closed environment magnifies group interests. That is, correctional officers have interests they wish to preserve, as do inmates, civilian employees, treatment staff, and administrators. From an administrative point of view, one set of interests outweighs all others: the desire to maintain control over the inmates, or custody interests. All others are secondary, a fact that can generate conflict even among different types of staff. For example, treatment staff may feel as if their work is seen as unimportant, exacerbating existing tensions between them and custodial staff (Hawkins and Alpert 1989).

Prison-based gangs do create conflict situations in prisons. Group and culture conflict theories do not explain why people join them, explanations perhaps better left to other theories (e.g., Chapter 5's psychological learning theories, Chapter 6's subcultural theories, or Chapter 7's social learning theories). However, these theories can provide insights into why gangs exist in prison and how they function. The traditional view of prison inmates is that they are members of a subculture that is solidly against both normative society and prison administrators, but especially correctional officers (Sykes and Messinger 1960). We can easily understand this animosity from a group conflict perspective. Correctional officers, as the ones with power, see inmate attempts to thwart their authority and undermine their position in the prison structure as threatening. Inmates are a classic minority power-group, confronting an institutionally more powerful entity, the guards. Moreover, members of prison gangs with close ties to criminal street gangs may be even more threatening than are other inmates. Correctional officers are more likely to criminalize the conduct of the inmate gangs that threaten the orderly operation of the correctional facility.

Culture conflict theory also helps explain prison life and inmate–staff conflicts. The majority of prison inmates are minority-group members (Mays and Winfree 2009). Most of the nation's prisons are located in rural counties, drawing personnel from a rural population that is unlikely to have much in common racially or culturally with the prisoners. It is widely believed, for example, that correctional officers at Attica State Prison, in rural, upstate New York had few insights into minority inmates from downstate New York, a shortcoming that exacerbated the traditional guard–inmate conflict and sparked the 1971 prison riot (New York Special Commission on Attica 1972; Winfree 1995). In other words, culture conflict existed on top of group conflict. This description may not be limited to Attica Prison in 1971. Given the multicultural nature of contemporary prison gangs (e.g., the Mexican Mafia, Black Guerrilla Family, and Aryan Brotherhood), it is possible that group *and* culture conflict combine to exacerbate historical differences between guards and inmates (Mays and Winfree 2009). Reports of recent increases in assaults on staff support this contention (U.S. Bureau of Labor Statistics 2003; Stephan and Karberg 2003).

Finally, prison uprisings—from dining-room food fights to full-blown riots—represent another case where conflict theory, especially Turk's variant, might yield significant insights into both appropriate and inappropriate responses by authorities. Earlier, we described how culture conflict might have lit the fuse on the 1971 Attica Prison riot. Similar culture problems existed at a Bureau of Prisons operated facility in Talladega, Georgia, that housed Cuban detainees and few guards who literally spoke the Cuban language or understood the Cuban culture (Useem, Camp, Camp, and Dugan 1995). While these forces might have been the precipitating forces in these and other prison riots, how the first-line rule enforcers respond—and the outcomes resulting from those responses—might better be understood in terms of Turk's theory of criminalization. If the authorities misjudge the intransigency of the rioters, the levels of their organization and sophistication, and the nature of their leadership, then the conflicts (i.e., riots) may end badly for all parties, as at Attica and Santa Fe (Colvin 1982; Hawkins and Alpert, 1989).

SUMMARY

Generic conflict theory has earned a special place in the pantheon of criminological theories. Few theoretical perspectives have demonstrated such clear applicability to cross-national studies of crime and criminality. Conflict theories also tell us much about individual (micro-level) and societal (macro-level) offending and offenders. They are enjoying a resurgence of interest by criminologists seeking to understand the role of power and conflict in the creation of crime and criminals.

The theories in this chapter extend our understanding of the use, misuse, and abuse of power (see Table 9.1). At times, conflict theory, labeling, and shaming all seem to overlap conceptually. That is, groups identified as problematic for society may be on the receiving end of negative labels that devalue the groups, their members, and their respective values. Shaming mechanisms may come into play, as those threatened by the groups try to marginalize them and push them out of their communities. Authorities may miscalculate the composition, strength, organization, and leadership of the group, responding in ways that simply exacerbate an already delicate social situation. In short, it may be that no single theory can provide all we need to know about such groups, whether they are youth groups, street gangs, international terrorists, or state-sponsored criminals; rather, we need an appreciation of them all to see the total picture.

TABLE 9.1   Conflict Theories of Crime

Major Figures	Central Assumptions	Causal Arguments (*Key Terms*)	Strengths	Weaknesses
Sellin	Conflict is inevitable because power is a scarce and valued resource; conduct norms express the consensus of the group; laws represent dominant culture's norms in a hetero-geneous society.	One of two conditions exists: (1) *primary culture conflict* occurs when the laws of a culture control people socialized into another culture and the two norm sets are incom-patible or (2) *secondary culture conflict* occurs when a subculture emerges within a dominant culture and the subculture's values *and* conduct norms conflict with the dominant subcul-ture's law; conflict between the law and the subculture may be defined as crime.	Provides rich under-standing of the historical roots of crime and con-flicts; it allows insights into the origins of and solutions for conflict between nation states, cultural groups that do not observe national boundaries, and even emergent subcultural groups; it has proven itself a fertile source of ideas for other crime theories based on conflicting values and norms.	Different analyses of events used to sup-port theories often yield different conclu-sions about the value of the theories for explaining crime; may be exploited by authorities to justify poor treatment of immigrants.
Vold	Conflict is inevitable; groups form when individuals recognize they have common interest; groups tend to advance their interests over those of other group; power is not equally distrib-uted in society.	*Crime* is the behavior of *minority power-groups*; the powerless feel disen-franchised from the law and free to violate it.	Good insights into law formation.	Not all laws protect only the interests of select groups; law does not cause beha-vior; gives few insights into indivi-dual motivations.
Turk	Law serves as the primary basis for solidifying power in a society.	The powerful criminalize threatening conduct; agreement between what *authorities* say and do often determines who and what is criminalized; actions of *first-line rule enforcers* determine if *higher-level rule enforcers* get involved; *resisters* are either high power or low power, which can influence whether their behavior is criminalized; *norm resis-tance* is central to theory.	Good insights into how authorities use laws to control unwanted beha-vior and troublesome groups; helps explain why some confrontations become open conflicts and others are resolved more peacefully.	Highly complex theory that resists testing; has limited policy implications.

KEY TERMS

authorities

authority relations

coercion

Colonial Era

colonialism

colonization

conduct norms

culture conflict

female genital mutilation (FGM)

first-line rule enforcers

conflict theory

genocidal conflict moves

genocide

group conflict theory

group interests

hegemony

high-power resisters

higher-level rule enforcers

ideal type

imperialism

Janjaweed

minority power-groups

norm concordance

oppression

ombudsman

organicism

power

primary culture conflict

rational-legal authority

realism of conflict moves

resisters

secondary culture conflict

theory of criminalization

CRITICAL REVIEW QUESTIONS

1. "The origins of conflict theory are at the crossroads of consensus and conflict sociology." Explain what this statement means. (NOTE: For you to answer nothing is not a good response to this question.)

2. Sellin's statements about culture conflict include three sets of conditions. Which one seems to best explain certain types of crime in the United States? Explain your choice.

3. Which single general policy implication associated with either type of generic conflict theory seems to pose the greatest threat to the fair administration of justice? Explain your answer.

4. All three forms of conflict theory are important to the courts, police, and corrections. In which specific instance or practice do you believe that conflict theory best explains what is happening?

5. Culture conflict is often used to explain international conflicts, ones between nation-states and between groups within one nation who have cultural, linguistic, or other ties to people in a second nation. Why is this not an appropriate use of criminological theory? Now take the opposite position and argue it as well.

6. What do you see as the greatest shortcoming of conflict theory?

7. Compare and contrast the assumption made about human behavior found in Sellin's culture conflict theory, Vold's group conflict theory, and Turk's theory of criminalization.

8. Which single policy implication associated with conflict theory seems to pose the greatest threat to the fair administration of justice? Explain.

9. The various forms of conflict theory reviewed in this chapter all have implications for the courts, police, and corrections. In which specific instance or practice do you believe that conflict theory best explains what is happening? Explain your choice.

10. "Conflict theory seems especially useful as a tool to understand international conflict, between or within nations." What is it about all generic conflict theories or one specific generic conflict theory that supports this statement?

NOTES

1. Criminologists use power in several different ways. For example, *Marxists* blame the economic system known as *capitalism* for crime, arguing that those who own the means of production use their considerable power to maintain control over that economic system, often to the detriment of the working class. The forms of conflict in this chapter reference no such ideological statements about the conflict's driving force. Rather than use the awkward conventions of non-Marxist conflict and Marxist conflict, we describe the conflict examined in this chapter as *generic conflict*, and that explored in Chapter 10 as *radical conflict*.

2. It is an interesting footnote of history, that the latter, more flexible law eventually took precedence over the former.

3. That the world is in a "postcolonial" era is open to debate (cf., Ang and Stratton 1996a, 1996b; Chen 1996). At issue is the role of such superpowers as the United States, China, and Russia, and to a lesser extent the old colonial powers of Great Britain and France.

4. Vold excluded impulsive, irrational crimes as beyond conflict theory's scope.

5. A related concept has to do with the **ombudsman**, an official associated with a public agency that receives complaints against that agency and investigates them. For example, an ombudsman in the public prosecutor's office may be asked to investigate a citizen complaint about a particular case that was dropped or to resolve disputes between other officials in the office. Ombudsmen in the employ of law enforcement or correctional systems may investigate complaints and charges made against the actions of police, correctional officers, or other employees.

6. Given Quinney's ties to Marxist theory, we examine this precursor to critical conflict in the next chapter.

7. The politicization of criminology is not new. In the 1930s, social action groups, using social disorganization theory as a guide, ran into trouble with local politicians as radicals (Chapter 6), as was also the case for those using Cloward and Ohlin's differential opportunity theory (Chapter 6) in the 1960s. Efforts to implement policies that were based largely on labeling theory, such as deinstitutionalization and decriminalization (Chapter 8), suffered similar political resistance.

8. The term "Janjaweed" literally mean men with guns on horses or camels; Africans in Sudan use it colloquially to mean "the devil on horseback."

10

Marxist and Critical Theories

CHAPTER OVERVIEW

LEARNING OBJECTIVES

In this chapter, you will learn the following:

- The social, political, economic, and historical context of Marxist theorizing about crime.

- Not all Marxists are strict followers of Karl Marx, as some contemporary Marxist-oriented criminologists have modified his nineteenth-century philosophy to fit today's multilayered society, a social system not predicted by Marx.

- Some Marxist-criminologists wearied of idealizing criminals and began to work toward a more realistic view of crime and criminals.

- The ways that criminologists apply peacemaking as a philosophy and practice to crime and justice issues.

INTRODUCTION

The theories described in this chapter stand at the core of **critical criminology,** a perspective or paradigm that defines crime in terms of power and oppression. While we find both power and oppression in Chapters 8 and 9, critical criminology fuses them, focusing on those who wield the power and the ends to which they use the resulting oppression: the mechanism is economic oppression and the goal is economic domination. Capitalism is the offending economic system, and capitalists are the enemy. Critical criminologists spotlight capitalists as exploiters of those providing the labor that turns the wheels of commerce and industry, usually members of the working class. To maintain their dominant position, capitalists form alliances amongst themselves in an ongoing conspiracy against the interests of the working class. These ideas provided the philosophical underpinnings for international Marxism during most of the twentieth century. They are also at the core of *Marxist criminology.*

Near the end of the twentieth century, several new threads of Marxist-related thinking began to emerge and take hold in criminology. In Great Britain, leftist-criminologists questioned the idealism often associated with Marxist thinking on crime and justice. Many criminals were, at the end of the day, bad people doing bad things. The emergent *left-realist criminology* started working with the state, in this case the British government of the 1980s, to bring about a just and fair system of justice. At roughly the same juncture, another group of critical criminologists began to question why society could not apply larger principles of peacemaking to crime and justice, creating *peacemaking criminology.* As both groups retained close philosophical ties to Marxist principles, we begin with the general contributions of Marx to the study of crime.

MARXISM AND CRIME

- Have you looked at the nation's prisons and jails? Besides tending to share a common race or ethnicity, the inmates also have similar class origins.

- Do you believe that the United States government has ever violated the law? If so, what law? Who determines guilt or innocence? What is an appropriate punishment for a government that commits a crime?

- Have you followed the troubles of the cigarette or handgun industries? Both have struggled with their public image. One Marxist theory should help you better understand this phenomenon.

The common element in all these questions is the German political philosopher Karl Marx (1818–1883) and his sociopolitical philosophy, known as **Marxism.** During the nineteenth century, Marx, working alone and with German philosopher and social scientist Friedrich Engels (1820–1895), described industrialized nations as divided societies in which **capitalists** own the means of production, and workers, or the **proletariat,** provide the labor. For Marx, power derived from ownership of property and control over the means of production. Capitalists use power to subjugate the workers, guaranteeing consolidation of wealth in their hands. Thus, society is characterized by a class struggle between capitalists and the proletariat. In this struggle or what Marxists refer to as a **class war,** capitalists mobilize the resources of government and religion to protect their positions of advantage. As capitalism advances, so does the gap between the capitalists and the workers, with the former gathering wealth at the expense of the latter.

Outside these two classes—owners and workers—is the **lumpenproletariat,** a parasitical group whose predations are based on selfish concerns and the need to survive. Capitalists are most likely to define the threatening behavior of the lumpenproletariat and the working class as "crimes." Over time, Marxists defined the **bourgeoisie,** or middle class, and the **petite bourgeoisie,** or shopkeepers and government officials, between the capitalist and worker classes—two emergent classes whose influence on society the Marxists failed to predict adequately.

A crucial idea to Marxists is **false consciousness.** This condition exists when workers, and even members of the middle class, believe that there is a societal consensus about critical social issues like crime and justice. A key part of false consciousness is the notion that everyone benefits from capitalism and its political underpinnings in the form of democracy. As part of their package of selling points, capitalists may promote positive-sounding doctrines such as freedom of the press—whose primary benefit goes to those who control the press—and freedom of speech—whose primary benefit goes to those who control the mass media. Of what import is freedom of the press and freedom of speech to the unemployed or the worker without medical insurance? Marxists believe that an inevitable revolution will signal the end of capitalism and the beginning of communism. To achieve this end, Marxists must expose the false consciousness and, in so doing, the capitalist system's inequities.

Marxist Views on Criminality

Marx wrote little about crime and criminals, although he did write treatises on capital punishment (1993[1853]) and the dissemination and impact of criminal law (1964[1862]). His collaborator, Friedrich Engels (1958[1845]), wrote that crime was a reflection of the inherent inequities created by capitalism. Those who followed in their philosophical footsteps, however, eventually distilled a great deal about crime from the combined work of Marx and Engels. In fact, traditional Marxists distinguished between three types. First, the crimes of the proletariat are usually directed at capitalists and so are revolutionary. Second, the crimes of the lumpenproletariat are typically directed against the working class and so, to the extent that we can define them as "political," are reactionary. Third, the crimes of the capitalists—the *real* crime—are acts of greed and avarice, and typically involve actions directed against the workers and harmful to the common good (e.g., industrial pollution). Not all Marxists, however, shared the same lockstep views of crime and criminals; as the following box suggests, anarchist-communists had some rather intriguing perspectives on crime, justice, and sanctions.

IN THEIR OWN WORDS: Kropotkin on Anarchy and Crime

Peter Kropotkin (1842–1921) was a member of the Russian royal family and a nineteenth-century revolutionary. He was sometimes called "the Anarchist Prince." **Anarchism** dates from Ancient Greece. Basic to the philosophy and practice is the idea that people are intrinsically good and that social institutions corrupt them, which means the best way to achieve change is to abandon all social conventions. Anarchism is often associated with lawlessness. For example, after the 1901 assassination of President William McKinley (1843–1901) by American-born anarchist Leon Czolgosz (1873–1901), U.S. immigration officials forbade anarchists from entering the country.

In pre-revolutionary Russia, anarchist-communists advocated the abolition of the state, private property, and capitalism; their solution was for everyone to own everything. As anarchists, these unique communists believed in the dissolution of all political power, hierarchy, and domination, even that by communism. They believed that all citizens of such a utopian society would recognize the benefits of communal enterprises and come to the aid of all others in need. After the overthrow of the czar in 1917, the Bolsheviks outlawed anarchists in the Soviet Union, effectively silencing them as a force in European communism.

The following are several seminal quotations about crime and justice from Kropotkin:

- *On criminal sanctions:* "We are continually being told of the benefits conferred by law and the beneficial effects of penalties, but have the speakers ever attempted to strike a balance between the benefits attributed to laws and penalties, and the degrading effects of these penalties upon humanity?" (p. 216).

- *On the ties between prison and future crime:* "Another significant angle is that the offense for which a man returns to prison is always more serious than his first. If, before, it was petty thieving, he returns now for some daring burglary, if he was imprisoned for the first time for some act of violence, often he will return as a murderer" (p. 221).

- *On society's role in creating criminals and glorifying crime:* "Society itself daily creates these people incapable of a life of honest labor, and filled with anti-social desires. She glorifies them when their crimes are crowned with financial success. She sends them to prison when they have not 'succeeded'" (p. 233).

SOURCE: Kropotkin (1970[1927]).

Marxists view crime as capitalism's inevitable by-product. They condemn criminologists who are interested in only minor forces in crime causation, and who fail to see the larger social context of crime—the bigger picture in which capitalism leads to a class system of severely differentiated wealth. The resulting social system is one in which the behavior of the weak has a greater chance of being defined as criminal than do the actions of the powerful. Wealth and power inequities also cause alienation and demoralization. **Alienation,** for Marxists, is a generalized feeling one has of noninvolvement in and estrangement from society, but especially the products of one's own labor (Theodorson and Theodorson 1969:9). **Demoralization** is a product of alienation, whereby there is a weakening of the person's spirit, will, productivity, discipline, and a general loss of feelings for other humans (Bonger 1969[1916]). Members of the alienated and demoralized underclass react in ways defined by capitalists as deviant: Some abuse alcohol and other drugs, while others seek more destructive means to escape capitalism's crushing power. The resulting demoralization generates criminal behavior.

In sum, all conflict theorists share a focus on power and its use to create self-serving laws that reflect the interests of those in control. The powerful organize and control the criminal justice system to serve their interests. One point at which they differ is in their assumptions about humankind. Radical conflict theorists, using a language of their own creation, look at offenders as essentially born **perfectible,** that is, capable of perfection, but as persons moved in different directions by social structural forces; for their part, conflict theorists view humans as amoral, neither good nor bad (Lanier and Henry 1998:238). Radicals also see humans as purpose-driven, capable of shaping their physical and social environments by revolutionary means if necessary, a view not shared by all conflict theorists (see Chapter 9).

By the late twentieth century, two themes dominated Marxist criminology. The first focused on the role of law, law enforcers, and government in subjugating the working class. This perspective was popular during the late 1960s and early 1970s, when the government, along with other social and economic institutions, came under scrutiny and attack. Class war and revolution were espoused by radical antiwar groups such as the Weather Underground in the late 1960s and early 1970s. Radical civil rights spokespersons and groups—from prison inmates Eldridge Cleaver and George Jackson to Black Panthers Bobby Seale and Huey Newton—espoused revolutionary Marxist doctrines. Moreover, events such as the riot at the 1968 Democratic Convention in Chicago, confirmed for them that the police were the "running dogs" of capitalism, oppressing the working class and their supporters at every turn. Oppression, conflict, and state control were common themes in the works of early instrumental Marxists (Krisberg 1975; Quinney 1973; Taylor, Walton, and Young 1973).

A second new wave of Marxist criminology emerged in the late 1970s, when a group of critical sociologists focused on the role of law in defining the parameters of acceptable behavior in society; laws were also a source of structural or "built-in" inequality and, by extension, crime (Colvin and Pauly 1983:513). They often linked economic inequality to violence, homicide, rape, and prostitution.[1] This group also believed that capitalists exclude children from the labor market but expect them to take on the values of that market, which produces unique strains that find individual and group expression in adolescent rebellion and delinquency (Colvin and Pauly 1983; Greenberg 1981; Schwendinger and Schwendinger 1985).

The members of the first of these two paradigms were **instrumental Marxists** because they saw the political state an *instrument* of oppression used by capitalists against the workers. The latter were **structural Marxists** because they adopted a *structuralist* method of analysis: the political state is not always and in all ways subject to the will of the ruling elite, since in some ways the state may be autonomous of capitalism. That is, political states create some laws that are at odds with the interests of the ruling elite, while others exclusively serve their interests. Each paradigm contributed significantly to criminology. We begin with the instrumental Marxists' views on crime and justice.

Instrumental Marxism and Crime

The Dutch criminologist Willem Adriaan Bonger (1876–1940), arguably the first Marxist criminologist, saw capitalism as promoting greed and self-interest, what he called **excessive egoism.** According to Bonger (1969[1916]), capitalism encourages citizen's to seek ends that benefit themselves with little regard for others, resulting in excessive egoism. Sounding much like the conflict theorists of Chapter 9, Bonger believed that those with power criminalized only the greed of the poor, allowing the wealthy (i.e., themselves) to pursue their desires with impunity. In a key departure from conflict theorists, however, Bonger contended that capitalism stood at the core of the problem: The poor commit crimes out of need or a sense of injustice, when they come to realize the inequities created by capitalism. Poverty alone did not cause crime, but merged with other negative social forces, including individualism, racism, materialism, and the false masculinity derived from violence, creating conditions conducive to the rise of criminality.[2]

Bonger viewed socialism as a solution to this problem. Socialism, he wrote, would promote the general welfare of all citizens and alleviate the legal bias enjoyed by the rich and destabilize the evil influences of capitalism (Bonger 1969 [1916]). A form of selfless altruism that Bonger associated with socialism would flourish and allow the beneficent growth of communities, as opposed to the destructive egoism of capitalism. As the following box suggests, Bonger's theory, which has rarely been tested, is enjoying resurgence nearly 70 years after this death.[3]

Contemporary Marxist criminologists, such as Richard Quinney, William Chambliss, and Barry Krisberg, expanded the instrumentalists' basic arguments about the ties between the state, laws, and crime. One of the most interesting of this group is Richard Quinney.

Crime and Demystification   According to Quinney (1973:vi), crime is best understood as a product of "how the capitalist ruling class establishes its control over those it must oppress." Quinney (1973) argued for the **demystification** of false consciousness about crime, a state creation, which enables oppression to continue. As William Chambliss and Robert Seidman (1982:315) observe about mystification:

> Everywhere, the legal order shrouds itself in weird rituals, outlandish costumes, incomprehensible language. It clothes itself in mystification. Many of these forms rose in other historical contexts for reasons that seemed valid. Why do they continue to this day? ... [M]any forms of mystification serve to persuade both dissident elements of the ruling class and the mass of the population that the law lies so far beyond their understanding that they can only accept it.

Quinney (1980) demystified crime by defining its many forms, tying each to Marxist class conflict. For Quinney, crime takes two main forms: (1) crimes of the working class and (2) crimes of the elite. Working-class crimes include crimes of accommodation and crimes of resistance. **Crimes of accommodation** do not challenge the social order but take place within it. For example, predatory crimes of accommodation mimic capitalism, in that offenders get property from their victims (e.g., robbery, theft, burglary, and auto theft). Violent crimes of accommodation—including homicide, rape, and assault—reflect capitalism's own use of institutionalized brutalization.

COMPARATIVE CRIMINOLOGY—WORLD VIEWS ON CRIME AND JUSTICE: A Comparative Test of Bonger's Theory of Criminality and Economic Condition

Critical criminologists, but especially instrumentalists, tend to avoid and even demean quantitative studies of crime and justice. The result has been that criminologists have never fully investigated the ideas of many early Marxists, including Bonger. Olena Antonaccio and Charles R. Tittle provide an exception to this generalization in their test of two hypotheses derived from Bonger's theory of criminality and economic conditions. Their hypotheses were straightforward:

- The degree of capitalism among societies should be related positively to crime rates in those societies, with the most capitalist societies having the highest crime rates and the least capitalistic having the lowest crime rates.

- Demoralization serves as a mediating link between capitalism and crime, with the degree of demoralization positively related to crime rates.

The researchers included information taken from 100 nations, the data coming from the World Bank, International Labor Organizations, the United Nations Statistics Division, and the United Nations Office on Drugs and Crime, sources generally viewed as providing both reliable and valid information. They selected homicide as the study's single dependent variable, since previous studies concluded that this statistic has the most validity and reliability of all crime figures for cross-national comparisons. They used four indicators of capitalism: (1) social security taxes as a percent of income, (2) private health expenditures as a percent of total health spending, (3) union density, and (4) an index of income inequality. As a mediator variable placed between capitalism and crime, they chose an index of corruption for each nation, as derived from national polls of experts and general surveys reported by the World Bank.

Antonaccio and Tittle found that capitalism is a significant predictor of homicide rates. However, corruption—their single indicator of egoism and demoralization—did not mediate the effects of capitalism, but rather had an independent and direct influence on homicide rates. At the same time, the extent of the predictions was relatively low, and other factors, including structural ones (e.g., sex ratio) and cultural ones (e.g., corruption and religion) also impact homicide rates "independently of the degree of capitalism or by serving as a contingency," or special situation in which homicide is more likely (p. 947). For example, in nations with a predominant Eastern Orthodox religion, the link between capitalism and homicide is the reverse of that found for nations with other dominant religions. Finally, the authors suggest that Bonger's theory could benefit from a merger with Messner and Rosenfeld's institutional anomie theory (Chapter 6) and social control theory (Chapter 7) that were unknown to criminologists in Bonger's day.

SOURCE: Antonaccio and Tittle (2007).

Crimes of resistance are working-class reactions to the ruling elite's exploitation. These crimes include both predatory and violent crimes, with both revolutionary and nonrevolutionary goals. For example, a revolutionary group—whose members are rarely from the working class—could engage in crimes of violence against the state, such as bombing court buildings or other governmental facilities. Revolutionaries also commit predatory crimes, such as bank robbery and kidnapping, to finance their cause and to hit capitalists where it hurts the most.

The class conflict aspects of some crimes of resistance are harder to comprehend, but the radicalization of prison inmates gives some insight. While incarcerated, some prison inmates during the turbulent1960s, especially people of color, begin to view their crimes as directed against capitalism and so defined themselves as **political prisoners** (Cleaver 1968; Seale 1968). For example, the inmate leaders of New York's Attica State Prison uprising in 1971 used Marxist rhetoric in making their public demands of prison officials (Abadinsky 2008; Winfree 1995).

The crimes of the elite take three forms. First, as elites, capitalists commit **crimes of domination** and **crimes of repression** to protect their interests, property, and profits. They engage in crimes intended to create economic domination, such as bid rigging and price-fixing. Elites commit violent acts directly against the public, such as selling faulty or dangerous products even after they are aware of the dangers (Michalowski 1985; Pepinsky and Jesilow 1984). Corporate America also commits crimes directly against its own workers and the public, by failing to conform to worker safety standards (Michalowski 1985).

The third form of elite crimes, **crimes of control,** involves police, courts, and corrections, the ruling class's instruments of social control. In particular, capitalists view the lumpenproletariat as "social dynamite" (Spitzer 1975).[4] Nineteenth- and early twentieth-century capitalists could call upon the apparatus of crime control, and sometimes the military, to protect its interests against those of workers and the unions that sought to improve working conditions—strikes were criminalized and unions crushed. At other times, social control agents serve capitalism in ways that are more implicit, by arrest and detainment practices, sentencing patterns, and prison conditions, which protect them from dangerous members of the working class.

Finally, the **crimes of government** are both complex and important. They include criminal acts in which governments violate constitutional guarantees and the civil rights of citizens (Balkan, Berger, and Schmidt 1980; Chambliss 1989a). Those who commit these crimes do so on behalf of the state. According to this view, governments commit crimes when engaging in military operations that violate the sovereignty of other nations (Chambliss 1988; Clinard and Quinney 1967; Roebuck and Weeber 1978). For example, shortly after the U.S. invasion of Panama and the arrest of its ruler, Manuel Noriega, scholars questioned the legality of those actions (Lewis 1990). Earlier, the U.S. government, primarily using the Central Intelligence Agency, aided heroin traffickers in order to further governmental interests against communist forces during the Vietnam War (McCoy 1991). In Central America and the Middle East, drugs and weapons smuggling figured prominently in the 1980s Iran–Contra scandal. Critical criminologists linked governmental motives to ideological positions, although profit motives definitely played a role as well (Chambliss 1989a). Barry Krisberg, another instrumental criminologist, favored a far broader perspective in his critique of privilege.

Crime and Privilege   Krisberg's *Crime and Privilege,* published in 1975, was a clear testament of a new way to view criminology, a movement known as **New Criminology,** which criticized traditional (i.e., "old") criminology as serving the power elite's interests. Krisberg was harsh in his comments about liberal sociologists, whom he called "hip sociologists." They understood the nature of political struggles but, he claimed, succumbed to institutionalized cynicism and simply stopped "tilting at windmills." They bemoaned the unfairness of a modern capitalist state but did nothing to change it.

Krisberg felt that crime studies should be framed by broader concern for **social justice,** which is best viewed as a condition of equality, self-determination, and liberation that results in the elimination of all conditions of human suffering. The origin of much such suffering is the misuse of privilege. **Privilege** is "the possession of that which is valued by a particular social group in a given historical period" (Krisberg 1975:20). The specific things that are valued—be it land or wealth—may change with time and place, but class, power, and status remain essential and interrelated aspects of privilege systems. Krisberg (1975:20) viewed the conflict arising from the misuse of privilege systems as an injustice. Thus, from initial police contacts to processing through the court and correctional structures, privilege systems associated with race, class, and economic statuses determine one's fate. The poor, the lower classes, and minorities do not commit more crime, but are simply more likely to suffer negative processing at the hands of the "(in) justice system" (Krisberg 1975).

This characterization numbers women among society's "disprivileged." Although women commit quantitatively less crime than men, they "are often subjected to harsher conditions than men," including disrespect and brutality at the hands of criminal justice officials (Krisberg 1975:25), a topic to which we return in Chapter 11. Generally, however, when the privileged engage in rules violation, observed Krisberg, they rarely find themselves accorded the status of criminal, a notion that fits well with Bonger's earlier characterization of capitalists in general. Even when they are on the receiving end of justice processing, the penalties are generally far lighter than those accorded the crimes of the disprivileged, when—*and if*—they receive them in a court of law. Figure 10.1 summarizes instrumental Marxist crime theory.

Structural Marxism and Crime

Structuralist Marxists also view the state as a vehicle for ensuring the long-term dominance of capitalism as a way of life (Chambliss and Seidman 1982:313). Consequently, the state must balance the interests of many groups, at times even allowing the less powerful the appearance of victory. A jury may find the

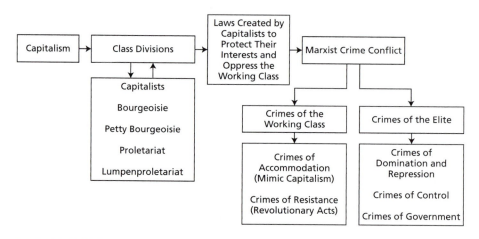

F I G U R E 10.1 Instrumental Marxist Theories of Criminality

---

COMMENTS AND CRITICISMS: Does the Government Always Get What It Wants?

The U.S. government's treatment of irregular or unlawful enemy combatants (i.e., individuals who engage in military or paramilitary actions against the U.S. government or its troops, but fail to wear uniforms or follow traditional military discipline) provides recent and controversial examples of possible crimes of government. U.S. and allied troops captured such personnel from various spots around the globe after 9/11. For the most part, the U.S. government held these detainees in a prison camp located on the U.S. naval base at Guantanamo Bay, Cuba. It was the position of President George W. Bush's administration that since this camp was not technically on America soil, inmates detained there were not eligible for the niceties of U.S. legal protections.

In 2004, in *Hamdi v. Rumsfeld,* the U.S. Supreme Court ruled 8–1 that while the government has a right to detain such unlawful combatants, those who are U.S. citizens have the ability to seek redress before an impartial tribunal.[5] However, no single opinion commanded a majority of the Court's votes, as all eight justices had a different take on the government's actions. Two years later, in *Hamdan v. Rumsfeld,* the U.S. Supreme Court disagreed in a 5–3 decision, which again contained multiple concurring and dissenting opinions, with President George Bush's assertion that military courts that had been set up to try these enemy combatants could proceed. The High Court asserted that such courts violated the Geneva Convention, to which the U.S. was a signatory, and the Uniform Code of Military Justice, which incorporated much of the Geneva Convention.

Sometimes even the powerful meet roadblocks in their quest for their own unique brand of justice. However, the complex and convoluted opinions of the U.S. Supreme Court revealed that even among the nation's legal elites, opinions on these matters were varied and often at odds with one another.

SOURCES: *Hamdi v. Rumsfeld* (2004); *Hamdan v. Rumsfeld* (2006).

---

odd white-collar criminal guilty and even send him (or less often her) to prison, but such events remain rare, from a structuralist point of view. The ultimate goal remains the same: the preservation of capitalism's dominance and the benefits that accrue for its successful adherents. As the following Comments and Criticisms suggests, even the most powerful in the land, the chief executive of the United States, does not always get what he wants.

Crime and the Law   We can find a key contribution to structural Marxism in the analysis of late medieval English property and vagrancy laws by William Chambliss. As feudalism declined—and was replaced by capitalism—formal laws concomitantly emerged, especially laws designed to protect the interests of emergent capitalists (Balkan, Berger, and Schmidt 1980:48–49). For example, Chambliss (1964, 1976) observed that English vagrancy laws reflected the interests of the economic elites. A compelling force in the creation of vagrancy laws was the bubonic plague, which decimated the labor force. The elites used the first English vagrancy law, passed in 1349, to force work from beggars, set low wages for their labor, and limit their movement through the countryside (Chambliss 1976:71).

The growth of commerce and trade intensified the need for the cheap labor previously supplied by feudalism's serfs. And these are not merely historical facts. Until recent court decisions eliminated broad and ill-defined vagrancy laws, law enforcement officials often enforced them during harvest time in agribusiness states. Selective enforcement increased the transitoriness of migrant workers, as police moved them to other job sites, guaranteeing cheap labor (Spradley 1970).

Theft laws protect property, capitalism's cornerstone. Jerome Hall (1952) notes that no systematic laws protecting private property existed in England before 1473. As feudalism gave way to commerce and trade, landowners lost control of the lawmaking process to the emerging economic elites. However, the new elites could not rely on existing laws because they were too unsophisticated and narrowly defined. In fact, they commonly prohibited only theft by servants (Chambliss 1976:85); the act of stealing by a so-called carrier transporting goods from one city to another was not a crime. In the carriers case of 1473, an English court found a carrier guilty, and thereby created a law "which was central to the well-being of the emergent class of capitalist traders and industrialists" (Chambliss 1976:86).[6]

A parallel situation emerged in the United States, where, during the nineteenth and early twentieth centuries, the Supreme Court thwarted federal legislative efforts to aid children. For example, in 1918 and again in 1922, the Court ruled unconstitutional federal laws intended to restrict the use of child labor. In the first case, a father fought for the right of his minor children—one under age 14 and the other between 14 and 16—to find employment in North Carolina's cotton mills (*Hammer v. Dagenhart et al.* 1918). In the second case, a North Carolina furniture manufacturer successfully fought the imposition of federal taxes intended to restrict the use of child labor (*Bailey et al. v. Drexel Furniture Company* 1922a). In both cases, the Court ruled that the federal government had no business restricting the rights of parents or the exercise of free trade (*Bailey et al. v. George et al.* 1922b).

Power, Authority, and Crime   John Hagan (1989a) saw power relations as central to crime. Hagan viewed power as relational; that is, power is meaningful only in terms of how it connects social actors to one another and ultimately to crime. He described two such relationships:

1. **Instrumental power relationships** occur when those with power manipulate it to achieve certain goals. Corporate criminals use their resources—such as disposable capital or local, state, national, and international political influence—to commit "white-collar" crime; similarly, street-level criminals have power resources at their disposal, such as semiautomatic weapons or brute strength.

2. **Symbolic power relationships** are ones in which society comes to view certain individuals or groups as less vulnerable to control agents because they have comparatively more power. The corporate criminal may only appear to be more reputable and credible than the street-level criminal.

More importantly, these two forms of power relationships often occur simultaneously and complement each other. Consider the following hypothetical examples of both types of power relationships:

■   Many in society view domestic marijuana growers as drug purveyors, living off human weaknesses. Local, state, and federal law enforcement agencies hunt these individuals, who face major sanctions as manufacturers, growers, and distributors of an illegal substance. They may have instrumental power, including vast financial resources and increasingly high-tech farming methods. However, their symbolic power relationships are typically low, owing to the way most in society views their work.

- Tobacco growers and tobacco producers have immense instrumental power relationships, ranging from *Fortune* 500 status to federal farm subsidies. Historically, based on their symbolic power relationships, they were reputable and credible—simply agribusiness persons trying to earn a living. Yet little room for debate exists, outside the tobacco lobby, about the human costs of tobacco versus marijuana. Interestingly, as the tobacco giants started losing personal damage suits, they began to diversify, buying companies with public-friendly images, such as baby food producers, perhaps to rehabilitate their symbolic power relationships.

The distinction between social class as a status position and as a power relationship is important to understanding some crimes (Curran and Renzetti 1994: 270–71). Hagan defined class in relation to ownership and authority. Some social actors, the owners of businesses and those in positions of occupational authority, have greater resources, including the resources to commit crimes that have great impact on society, such as polluting the environment or engaging in price-fixing. Those with little authority and no ownership commit relatively unimportant crimes—important to only a few, such as the immediate victims or their friends and families (Hagan 1989a:4).

Perhaps no single criminologist better reflects the many twists and turns found in critical criminology than Richard Quinney, a point addressed in the following Comments and Criticisms.

Assessing Marxist Crime Theories

Instrumental Marxists view traditional criminological research, employing scientific determinism, as supporting state interests (Gibbons 1984; Nettler 1984). Many instrumentalists adopt analytical techniques more common to muckraking and yellow journalism than social science (Friday 1977). Moreover, proponents generally ignore or overlook contradictory evidence. Critics argue that instrumental Marxism has become more of a *crime ideology* than a *crime theory* (Akers 1979, 1994; Inciardi 1980). After all, instrumental Marxists recognize no source of conflict beyond social class and economic power, a position at odds with most conflict theories (Vold 1979). Moreover, should we expect the criminal justice system to secure the goals of social justice?

Structural Marxists' theories include responses to the instrumentalists' criticisms. Chambliss, for one, emphasized the complexity of laws in action, by acknowledging that people who occupy various social class positions—and not merely the powerful or rich—can respond to those who create and enforce laws. For example, even those people occupying positions of limited social or economic power have the ability to command the attention of the press, politicians, and others possessing far more power and greater resources with which to

---

COMMENTS AND CRITICISMS: Quinney and the Social Reality of Crime

In order to understand Quinney the Marxist criminologist, one must also appreciate Quinney the conflict theorist.[7] In 1970, three short years before he wrote *Critique of the Legal Order: Crime Control in a Capitalist Society,* Quinney authored *The Social Reality of Crime,* in which he developed six propositions about the social reality of crime in contemporary society. As you read these propositions, reflect back on generic conflict theory (Chapter 9) and the philosophical movement between that position and both Quinney's social reality of crime (below) and his critique of capitalist crime control.

- Proposition 1—Definition of Crime: Crime is a definition of human conduct created by authorized agents in a politically organized society.

- Proposition 2—Formulation of criminal definitions: Criminal definitions describe behaviors that conflict with the interests of the segments of society that have the power to shape public policy.

- Proposition 3—Application of criminal definitions: Those segments of society that have the power to shape the enforcement and administration of criminal law apply criminal definitions.

- Proposition 4—Development of behavioral patterns in relation to criminal definitions: Behavior patterns are structural in segmentally organized society in relation to criminal definitions, and within this context persons engage in actions that have relative probabilities of being defined as criminal.

- Proposition 5—Construction of criminal conceptions: Conceptions of crime are constructed and spread throughout society by various means of communications.

- Proposition 6—The social reality of crime: The social reality of crime is constructed by the definition of crime, the formulation and application of criminal definitions, and the development of criminal behavior patterns, and the construction of criminal conceptions, that is, the sum total of the previous propositions.

What elements did Quinney add to his critique of the legal order? How do these propositions differ from what Quinney and Krisberg propose in this chapter? Think "demystification." An understanding of the answers to these questions helps us gain a "criminology of knowledge," or a study of how thinking about crime, criminals, and society's response to both evolves over time, a topic that we have addressed throughout this book and to which we return in Chapter 12. We suggest that after reading the next chapter, you may wish to perform a similar analysis of instrumental-Marxist John Hagan's many contributions to criminology.

SOURCES: Quinney (1970, 1973).

---

respond to the police, courts, and correctional systems. Hagan went beyond narrow definitions of class and economic struggles to include power relationships such as those reflected in gender, race, and ethnicity. Hagan's (1989a, 1994) research supports his thesis. Studies of the structural elements in punishment reveal relationships similar to those contained in Hagan's structural criminology.[8]

By the early twenty-first century, even diehard instrumental-Marxist criminologists began to succumb to the logic of structural Marxism. Akers and Sellers (2009) contend that these distinctions could not long be maintained: "Both agree that the long term historical tendency of the legal system is to reflect and protect the interest of the capitalist class and oppress the masses" (p. 240). Indeed, structural Marxists sometimes share a shortcoming with their instrumental brethren: They ignore contradictory evidence. Jeffrey Adler (1989) contended that Chambliss's emphasis on economics as a motivating force behind the English vagrancy laws was misplaced. Adler claimed that more than economics was at work to create these laws, social; rather significant religious, political, and historical forces shaped England of the fourteenth and fifteenth centuries.[9] This criticism aside, Chambliss (1964) reminds us that we must consider the social and historical context in which laws emerge.

Several observations hold for both instrumental and structural Marxist criminology:

- *Law does not cause behavior.* As with labeling and generic conflict theorists, critical criminologists may put too much emphasis on the role of law in creating crime.

- *Avoids quantitative analyses.* Instrumental Marxists tend to view quantitative data analyses as an extension of positivistic criminology and, as a result, generally avoid such studies in their own work and criticize it as positivist criminology.

- *Tends to ignore contradictory evidence.* While structural Marxists show an inclination to use quantitative analyses, they, like instrumental Marxists, are prone to ignore contradictory evidence or alternative interpretations.

- *Impossible to test fully.* Given the strong ideological bent of much Marxist criminology, full tests of its implications for crime and justice may not be possible. Specifically, providing conceptual and operational definitions that pass both scientific and ideological muster may be impossible.

- *Lacks definitional comparability.* Even among critical criminologists, there is great disagreement as to the nature of their paradigm (cf., Arrigo 2000; Henry and Milovanovic 1991; Milovanovic 2002). This makes conducting any kind of research on critical criminology or constructing adequate tests of its assertions difficult tasks.

- *The explanatory language is stilted.* In Chapter 1, Travis Pratt (2008) suggests that criminologists should simplify their terminology, but especially the verbiage they use to explain the causes of crime. Marxists use special terms, such as *false consciousness*, *perfectibility*, and *purpose-driven*, ones not likely to find much cache outside of Marxist criminology. Such terms are also unlikely to endear these theories to anyone except "true believers."

Structural Marxists respond to critics by substituting issues of inequality, gender, race, urban density, and opportunity structures with Marxist rhetoric. However, the subsequent "new formulation" closely resembles Marxist theory. Ronald Akers (1994:169) was far more blunt: "Except for the nuances of emphasis and terminology, [structural Marxism] becomes indistinguishable from other theories of crime."

Marxism, Public Policy, and Criminal Justice Practices

The chief Marxist policy implication is utopian—the replacement of a capitalist or imperfect communist economic system with a truly classless society. Because capitalists will not peacefully relinquish economic, political, and social control, Marxists must resort to violent revolution. Until then, radical criminologists must work with the leaders of oppressed groups in the quest for social justice.

As Ian Taylor, Paul Walton, and Jock Young (1973:282) noted, "The task is to create a society in which the facts of human diversity, whether personal, organic, or social, are not subject to the power to criminalize."

Structural Marxists, while no less critical of capitalism, are far less idealistic and utopian than instrumentalists. The policies they propose seek to alter the causes of crime. For example, Stanley Cohen (1984, 1985) believed that the state must play a positive role in closing the income inequality gap, specifically targeting the lowest-income groups. Elliott Currie (1985) also argued that the government must provide for its neediest citizens, including children, single mothers, the disabled, the elderly, and the physically and mentally ill. The proponents of a "realistic critical policy" also targeted work conditions, the goal being to create a "more humane, just and workable alternative" to repressive capitalist control (Cohen 1986:23). All workers should "earn a substantial living wage with full benefits, including day care and household help for working mothers, health and welfare subsidies, [and] enriched education" (Davis and Stasz 1990:78).

Law Enforcement Practices   Marxists view the police as primary offenders when it comes to crimes of control. As Raymond Michalowski (1985:196) observed about police work, "'The policeman's lot is not a happy one'—so the saying goes. And indeed, the policeman's lot in America is not enviable. This is primarily because police work is 'dirty work.'" The police find their work to be both socially stigmatizing and fraught with contradictions. They must enforce the laws against capitalism's "social junk," and, like the trash collector, stand between much of society and its less desirable elements. As a result, we often view police with disdain; much of society, which sees them and their work as distasteful, tends to shun them.

The contradictions, noted Michalowski (1985:196), derive from the fact that the police often feel that they must violate the law to preserve the social order. For example, they may resort to illegal searches and seizures, excessive use of force, or illegally obtained confessions. Society condemns only *excessively* brutal or discriminatory abuses. In any case, "state legitimacy rests on the ideology of fair and equal treatment under a legal system dispassionately enforced by professional police. When police behavior appears to contradict this image, the state must respond to protect its legitimacy" (Michalowski 1985:197). These contradictions are not lost on the police, who often feel abandoned when legal authorities question their behavior (Skolnick 1966).

Judicial Practices   Marxists view courts with suspicion. Instrumentalists see them as reifying capitalistic values, and structuralists view judges as using power to respond to society's pluralistic demands. Mainly rich, old, white, and male, judges ultimately serve and preserve capitalism. At times, the powerless appear to win, but this simply promotes acquiescence to a rule of law that serves as protection for capitalists (Chambliss and Seidman 1982).

Structural Marxists observe that being different makes a difference. Even when caught, criminals from the upper social classes often avoid prosecution and imprisonment more frequently than do their lower-class counterparts. For example, Clayton Mosher and Hagan (1994) studied sentencing patterns for narcotics offenders in Canada from 1908 to 1953. Early in the twentieth century, judges handed down harsh sentences for working-class offenders. By the middle of the century, when arrests of middle- and upper-class drug offenders was on the rise, such individuals received disproportionately more lenient sentences than did working-class offenders.

Correctional Practices   From a Marxist perspective, prisons and jails serve to control the dangerous class, the lumpenproletariat. Instrumental Marxists also believe that prisons warehouse surplus labor in times of economic downturns, which makes these inmates political prisoners. Central themes for instrumental Marxists are what they call the "struggles inside," in which prison inmates speak of the pain of imprisonment. These themes were popular in the 1960s and early 1970s. Today's prison inmates are more likely to be part of a prison gang, and not any group espousing radical or any other political views (Mays and Winfree 2009).

Structural Marxists point to the race, class, and power dimensions of punishment. The crimes of the less powerful—street crime—result in prison terms. Crime in the "suites" often results in only fines or forfeitures and, infrequently, in brief stays at minimum-security prisons. Race, too, plays a significant role in who goes to prison. As Michalowski (1985:238) pointed out, "The black proportion of prison inmates is just slightly less than double the black proportion of those arrested, indicating that once arrested blacks face a significantly greater likelihood of being incarcerated than their white counterparts." The structure of penal law may account for some racial disparities. We detail the apparent connections (and resulting inequities) between race and judicial decision making in Chapter 11.

LEFT REALISM AND PEACEMAKING CRIMINOLOGY

In the final two decades of the twentieth century, criminologists offered several new but somehow familiar theories. One, originating in Great Britain, had its roots in the New Criminology of the 1970s. The New Criminology fit well with Britain's postwar **social democracy.** That is, after World War II, the British state assumed ever-increasing responsibility for providing everything from power and public transportation to health care, housing, and education, essentially creating a welfare state. The New Criminology influenced this social democracy's justice policies through the admonition that official labeling contributes to the crime problem. For example, consider Young's work on the police role in deviance amplification for drug users (see Chapter 8). The tendency of the police to make a bad situation worse is central to the New Criminology's view of institutional power.

Left Realism and Crime Control

Britain's social and economic climate changed with the 1979 national elections, and widespread policy changes occurred throughout the 1980s. In particular, the elevation of Margaret Thatcher to prime minister signaled the New Right's emergence in Britain. Thatcher, who shared much ideological ground with U.S. President Ronald Reagan, served as prime minister from 1979 to 1990. She set about dismantling Britain's social democracy, known for its socialized welfare system. Violent offenders, especially as related to street crime and drugs, became targets of what British criminologists called **right realism** (Matthews and Young 1992). Right realists view crime's origins as being not within society but within the individual; people *choose* crime. Rehabilitation and the search for crime causes are, in their view, wasted efforts. Right realists argue strongly for conservative approaches to crime control, including more prisons, harsher penalties, longer prison terms, and the death penalty.

In response to right realism, a group of British criminologists, largely led by British sociologist and criminologist Jock Young, made a break with basic Marxist tenets. They dismissed instrumental Marxists as **left idealists** who (1) romanticize working-class criminals who, after all, prey mainly on their own class; (2) emphasize crime in corporate suites to the literal exclusion of predatory crime and its devastating impact on society; (3) ignore the impact of society's structure on crime, including such things as unemployment and poverty, and instead highlight crime control ideologies; and (4) provide no insights into what can be done within the existing capitalist system to facilitate law and order (Lea and Young 1984; see also DeKeseredy and Schwartz 1996:245–58).[10]

Young and his colleagues proposed **left realism** as an alternative (Lea and Young 1984). The perspective is leftist because it calls for increased governmental involvement in the lives of citizens. It is realistic because proponents view working-class crime as a real problem for the working class and recognize the need to work within the existing socioeconomic system.

Left realism also is rooted in what Young (1992) calls the **square of crime.** Traditional criminology considered only the triangle of crime: the offender, the state, and, rarely, the victim. Four elements—the four corners of the square—define crime; they include the victim, the offender, the state, and the society or community. As Young (1992:27) noted about the square of the crime, "It is the relationship between the police and the public which determines the efficacy of policing, the relationship between the victim and the offender which determines the impact of crime, the relationship between the state and the offender which is a major factor in recidivism." Anticrime measures, to be effective, must address all four corners—all the stakeholders in crime—simultaneously.[11]

Finally, left realists emphasized relative deprivation's role in leading to crime. **Relative deprivation** is a sociological principle whereby, no matter how much material wealth someone possesses, someone else always has more. However, in order for relative deprivation to mean anything, people must first learn about how little they have and how much others possess. In this sense, people's own reference groups—the constructed social entities in which they come to believe that they share membership with others based on education, occupation, or place of residence—assume great importance. It is through the perceived advantages of the reference group, or what the members believe they have in common with everyone else in the group, that individuals learn about their disadvantages.

The causal explanation proposed by left realists is simple and straightforward: "Relative deprivation equals discontent; discontent plus lack of political solution equals crime" (Lea and Young 1984:88).

Peacemaking Criminology

By the late 1980s and early 1990s, a new way of viewing the relationship between crime, criminals, and victims began to take shape in American criminology. **Peacemaking criminology** emerged from the collaborative efforts of Quinney and Harold Pepinsky. Their coedited book, *Criminology as Peacemaking* (1991), clearly shows peacemaking's Marxist roots. Peacemaking criminologists view crime as another form of violence perpetrated on humanity, much like war, racism, sexism, poverty, and human rights violations. Society should stop using the "war" metaphor to resolve social problems. There must be peace, claim proponents, between the criminal and the victim. Quinney (1991:11) wrote that crime is suffering and can be ended only through the establishment of peace. A state of peace and justice will occur—and crime will be eliminated—only when we transform our social, economic, and political structure (Quinney 1991:12).

Besides its critical and Marxist roots, peacemaking criminology has close ties to anarchism, humanism, Christian socialism, Eastern meditative thought, and feminism. Indeed, peacemaking typically takes one of two forms: sacred or secular. The sacred form emphasizes the spiritual and transcendental elements of nonviolence as a path to truth and righteousness. The secular form places great emphasis on such legalistic practices as mediation, reconciliation, conflict resolution, and reintegration of the offending parties.

As with left realism, peacemaking criminology is not so much a causal theory as a prescription for social change. Peacemakers reject the repressive and punitive policies of right realists; at times, they, like earlier Marxists, sound **utopian,** or morally, socially, and politically ideal, perhaps beyond the reach of reality. However, proponents endorse several unique and interesting practices intended to achieve peace between the victim, the offender, the criminal justice community, and the community at large.

Assessing Left Realism and Peacemaking Criminology

The lack of empirical studies hampers the assessment of left-realist and peacemaking criminology. Most assessments look at its assumptions. For example, Ira Schwartz (1991:119–20) noted that left realism's best contribution may be that it places a realistic assessment of crime squarely in the limelight. Victimization is not limited to criminals; the state also victimizes. However, left realism fails to address the concerns of feminists and other critical criminologists, but especially the excesses of state-sponsored right realism (DeKeseredy and Schwartz 1991). Left realists employ an oversimplified view of "the community" and fail to adequately define who is included and excluded in the definition of community. For example, it is conceivable that the community could be extremely heterogeneous, made up of groups that disagree on every major sociopolitical issue (DeKeseredy and Schwartz 1996:257). Finally, left realists seem not to understand that they could become another tool of state oppression (Schwartz 1991).

Peacemaking criminology sets lofty, if not unattainable, goals, at least in the worldwide context. Peacemaking, with its ties to social justice, may add little to what we already know about crimes injustices (see also Akers 2000). The same criticism is true of left realism (Gibbons, 1994, 2000). Perhaps most critically, peacemaking criminology, like left realism, generates no testable hypotheses about crime. As Akers (2000:214) wrote about peacemaking criminology, "Explanations of crime and the criminal justice system might or might not be consistent with the religious and other precepts espoused by peacemaking criminologists, but these precepts do not themselves constitute a testable theory." Don Gibbons (2000: xxix) observed that replacing the pain and injustice of crime with a new sense of community through peacemaking is laudable; however, he also doubts the long-term viability of this approach in criminology.

Left Realism, Peacemaking Criminology, Public Policy, and Criminal Justice Practices

Left-realist and peacemaking criminologists call for a new awareness of the "costs of crime," especially to the powerless and disenfranchised in society. Left realists support the use of both qualitative and quantitative information to support decision-making by policy makers. Thus, they have conducted local surveys on a wide range of topics, including crime victimization and the fear of crime, abuse of women, and perceptions of law enforcement (DeKeseredy and Schwartz 1996).[12] Left-realists used the results to argue for a local policy responses, suggesting that the community best knows its problems and likely solutions (DeKeseredy and Schwartz 1996:249; see also Lea and Young 1984).

Peacemaking criminology places crime in the larger context of world peace. Crime is but one form of violence; war, poverty, sexism, and racism are others. Reducing crime means working for peace. Societies should abandon the philosophy of declaring "war" on social problems, as in the "War on Crime," the "War on Drugs," or, even, the "War on Poverty." War dehumanizes the "enemy," an important idea if the enemy is one of us. In peacemaking, crime control has a community-based component, much as in left realism. Alternative sentencing options include "an apology, restitution (paying back the victim), volunteer work (paying back the community through free labor), a charitable donation, and victim–offender mediation" (DeKeseredy and Schwartz 1996:271).

Judicial Practices   The Indian peoples of North America also well understand the concept of peacemaking (Dumont 1996; Hoyle 1995; Tso 1996). American Indian **peacemaker courts** offer a unique example of peacemaking in action (Yazzie and Zion 1995). Navajos view crime and violence as tears in the social fabric; crime and other social ills upset the community's balance (Yazzie and Zion 1995). Only through the timely intervention of a peacemaker—an elder skilled in listening and gentle persuasion—can the community restore the lost

TABLE 10.1 Marxist Theories, Left Realism, Peacemaking Criminology, and Crime

Theory	Major Figures	Central Assumptions	Causal Arguments (Key Terms)	Strengths	Weaknesses
Marxist criminology Instrumental Marxist theory Structural Marxist theory	Marx, Engels Quinney, Spitzer, Chambliss, Krisberg Chambliss, Seidman, Hagan	*All:* A historical "class struggle" exists between capitalists and workers; a revolution will eventually occur that signals the end of capitalism and the beginning of communism.	*Marxism:* Workers (*proletariat*) crimes against the wealthy (*capitalists*) are revolutionary; the crimes of society's least desirable elements (*lumpenproletariat*) are reactionary; the crimes of capitalists are the true crimes. *Instrumental Marxism:* Emphasizes the instrumental role of law and government in achieving subjugation of the working class; the crimes of the elite and government are key constructs. *Structural Marxism:* Laws protect the ruling class's interests; power relationships are central to understanding crime.	*Marxism and instrumental Marxism:* Provides a rather naive view of crime and justice issues. *Structural Marxism:* Applies a more sophisticated view of the relationship between elites and power; provides unique and disturbing insights into the operation of the nation's government and corporate elites.	*Marxism and instrumental Marxism:* Is a theology for true believers; is anti-empirical. *Structural Marxism:* May ignore contradictory evidence; empirical results have been mixed. Both perspectives suggest few policy implications of their own outside the revolutionary model; however, they do provide insights into criminal justice practices.
Left realism and peacemaking criminology	Young, Matthews, Lea, Quinney, Pepinsky	*Left realism:* Violent crime has real consequences for the disenfranchised and the poor. *Peacemaking:* Working for peace will eliminate crime.	*Left realism:* Working locally with the square of crime will reduce conditions causing crime. *Peacemaking:* Working for peace will eliminate crime	*Left realism:* Brings local resources to bear on crimes that directly affect them. *Peacemaking:* Views peace as a solution to crime.	*Left realism:* Is a prescription, not a testable theory. *Peacemaking:* Rests on utopian principles; yields research results, using traditional quantitative methods that are mixed and inconclusive; however, legal analyses and qualitative methods yield far more support.

balance (see Chapter 8's treatment of shaming and restorative justice). For example, the Navajos use peacemaker courts in cases of domestic violence and other family-based problems (Bluenose and Zion 1996). The peacemaker also uses the sacred **harmony ceremony** to reestablish balance both at the micro-level between the offended and offending parties, and at the macro-level within the Navajo Nation itself.

Correctional Practices   Peacemaking and other restorative practices have been adopted to the prison setting, either to assist with adjustment to prison life or prepare the soon-to-be released convict for life outside prison. Rather than repeat an explanation of those programs and practices here, we refer you back to Chapter 8.

SUMMARY

The theories in this chapter share several features with those in the previous chapter. Power is the most obvious one. Marxists, left realists, and peacemakers explore the role of power in defining crime and criminals. Although the definitions differ slightly from theory to theory, power's role as a causal factor is relatively invariant: Some groups or individuals have power, use it to further their own interests, and are not above exploiting it to control (i.e., make deviant, criminalize, or otherwise discredit) the conduct of those perceived to be threats. The theorists in this chapter argue that all members of the community must share power, even if it takes revolutionary acts to achieve this goal.

Second, the theories are essentially deterministic in nature. Like conflict and labeling theories (Chapters 8 and 9), they blame forces outside the control of individuals for causing the criminal condition. Critical or Marxist criminologists typically adopt one of two strategies in exploring the relationship between power and crime. They may hold capitalism at fault and look at the criminal justice system as the instrument of repression. Alternatively, they may critique society's structure as creating, endorsing, and maintaining basic social, racial, and economic inequities that benefit the interests of capitalists at the expense of workers.

Third, power's insertion into any discussion of crime results in confusion about what to call the resulting theories. Marxist theory, besides its instrumental and structural forms, is known as radical conflict and critical theory. However, some criminologists see any theory that questions power's use as a critical theory (Bohm 1982; Davis and Stasz 1990; Friedrichs 1982).

Critical or Marxist theorists in the 1960s advanced the idea that economic exploitation of workers by a repressive and oppressive capitalist system leads directly to crime. There was a resurgence of interest in these perspectives in the late twentieth and early twenty-first centuries. The key difference between the two epochs is that when they first emerged, these power-based theories were acclaimed for their intuitive and logical insights into crime but condemned for their reliance on rhetoric and disregard of empirical proof, whereas the new critical conflict theories place a far greater premium on the links between theory, methods, and practice.

A point not addressed in the previous chapter relates to the criminal justice system. The theories reviewed in this chapter are as much about that system's operation and impact on society as they are about crime causation. They are theories of criminal justice and criminological outcomes (see, e.g., Akers 2000:165–235). We could say the same, of course, about labeling, reintegrative shaming, or generic conflict theory. This final observation relates directly to the first point made in this summary: Those with power can criminalize literally whatever conduct they wish, particularly if that conduct or those who engage in it threaten their interests.

Finally, what distinguishes the theories in this chapter from other power-based theories (see Chapters 8 and 9) is that they give faces to those abusing power for their own self-interests: They are capitalists, they are men, and they are Caucasians. Unless Marxist-oriented criminologists gain the attention of policy makers, as happened in Britain in the 1960s and 1970s, the chances of meaningful changes based on their theories seem slim. American Marxists tried frontal attacks throughout much of the 1970s, but they met with little success. This fact may account for the popularity among radical-liberal academics of left realism and peacemaking criminology. It is an open question whether this intellectual popularity will translate into policy and practices.

KEY TERMS

alienation

anarchism

bourgeoisie

capitalists

class war

crimes of accommodation

crimes of control

crimes of domination

crimes of government

crimes of repression

crimes of resistance

critical criminology

demoralization

demystification

excessive egoism

false consciousness

harmony ceremony

instrumental Marxists

instrumental power relationships

left idealists

left realism

lumpenproletariat

Marxism

New Criminology

peacemaker courts

peacemaking criminology

perfectibile

petite bourgeoisie

privilege

political prisoners

proletariat

relative deprivation

right realism

social democracy

social justice

square of crime

structural Marxists

symbolic power relationships

utopian

CRITICAL REVIEW QUESTIONS

1. Compare and contrast instrumental Marxist and structural Marxist explanations of crime. Which approach makes the most sense? (Note: "Neither" is an unacceptable answer!)

2. Why are critical criminologists unapologetic in their disdain for positive crime theories?

3. What point made by Quinney do you believe is important even beyond its use by Marxist criminologists? Explain your selection.

4. Explain what instrumental Marxists meant by "social justice." Do people other than criminologists use this term? If so, in what context?

5. Are there other instances, besides vagrancy and property laws, in which Chambliss's analysis of law in action makes sense?

6. In the opening section of this chapter, we mentioned both the tobacco and handgun manufacturing industries as fitting Hagan's structural criminology, although at that time you did not know the name of the theory. We did not later refer to the handgun industry in the text. Explain how its power relationships fit within Hagan's model.

7. In which area of criminal justice policy or practice do Marxist-derived theories provide the best insights? Where is their application the weakest? (Note: See Question 1.)

8. Richard Quinney is arguably one of the most influential criminologists of the twentieth century. He has also contributed broadly to American culture beyond the study of crime and justice. How does his eclecticism make his criminological contributions more credible? In what ways do you think that his diversity of interests troubles criminologists?

9. Left realism has strongly influenced the crime and justice policies of another common law nation, Great Britain. Do you think it is unlikely to shape crime policies in the United States? Under what circumstances might left realists have such an influence?

10. Peacemaking criminology has grown in importance just as the United States has expanded its use of war as a mechanism of social change worldwide. How could the ideas of peacemaking criminology reshape the nation's internal policies on the War on Drugs or the War on Terror?

NOTES

1. The following works are instructive in learning more about these topics: Blau and Blau (1977, 1982); Braithwaite (1984); Messerschmidt (1986); Miller (1986); Schwendinger and Schwendinger 1983; Wallace and Humphries (1981).

2. Later generations of critical criminologists addressed the use of such tactics as racism, sexism, and economic exploitation against targeted groups, including working-class immigrants, women, and both racial and ethnic minorities.

In situations where these statuses overlap, as in the case of a working-class minority female-immigrant, the oppression is often even greater than it would be for only one or two such statuses (Hopkins and Burke 2001).

3. As German troops invaded his native Holland in 1940, Bonger committed suicide, knowing that his name was prominent among the Dutch intelligentsia targeted by the Nazis.

4. One could argue that capitalists are more likely to use the lumpenproletariat—for example, organized–crime–capitalism connection—than fear it since the rich are rarely victims of true lumpen-criminals. False consciousness involves a media-political focus on crimes most likely to be committed by the underclass, while resources for investigating corporate crime is limited accordingly

5. Associate Justice Clarence Thomas was the sole judge who wrote in favor of the government's position, also supported by the Fourth Circuit's ruling. Justice Thomas supported the view that the important security interests at stake and the president's broad war-making powers negated the rights of the enemy combatants.

6. Law derived from court decisions is part of common law, or what we call case law.

7. Richard Quinney possesses arguably one of the most eclectic minds in criminology. During the early and mid-1960s, working with Marshall B. Clinard, a traditional positivist-criminologist and contributor to anomie theory, Quinney prepared a systematic assessment of criminological typologies. By the late 1960s, Quinney began to write about the social reality of conflict, attributing to conflict a far more causal role in criminology, as we acknowledged in Chapter 8. The late 1970s saw him shift to far more Marxist verbiage in works such as *Critique of the Legal Order: Crime Control in a Capitalist Society* (1974) and *Class, State and Crime* (1977), where he endorsed a kind of "religious socialism" within the dialectic of class struggle. Then by the 1980s, Quinney began to contribute to the peacemaking literature. Somewhere along the line, he found time to write about religion (*Providence*, 1980), natural history, photography, and general philosophy. For more on Quinney, especially his contribution to peacemaking criminology, see Wozniak (2002).

8. The following works provide instructive insights into Hagan's structural criminology: (Bridges and Crutchfield 1988; Daly 1987b; Hagan and Parker 1985).

9. Chambliss (1989b:231) saw Adler as the latest in a series of critics in whom "prejudice and ignorance combine to distort Marxist criminology." He recognized only two forms of criminology: Marxist and anti-Marxist (Chambliss 1989:237).

10. As DeKeseredy and Schwartz (1996:246) observed, left realists do not identify left idealists by name but attack their ideas in broad general terms.

11. In Chapter 8, several of the RJ practices based on reintegrative shaming emphasize a circle approach to mending communities. The circle includes the victim, if possible, and the victim's friends and relatives, the offender and the offender's friends and relatives, representatives of the community, and at least one representative of state interests. In this regard, the square of the crime conceptually resembles the aboriginal sentencing circle as a philosophical practice or, in more specific terms, family group conferencing that originated in Australia and New Zealand.

12. For more on left realists' research into crimes of inequality, see the following: Crawford, Jones, Woodhouse, and Young (1990); Jones, MacLean, and Young (1986); Kinsey, Lea, and Young (1986); Mooney (1993).

11

Gender, Race, and Crime Theories

CHAPTER OVERVIEW

Gender and Race: Definitional Issues

Defining Gender and Race

Measuring Gender, Race, and Crime

Gender and Criminological Theories

Mainstream Criminological Theorizing about Gender

Critical Criminology and Gender

Assessing Gender-Inclusive Theorizing

Gender, Public Policy, and Criminal Justice Practices

Race and Criminological Theories

Mainstream Criminological Theorizing about Race

Critical Criminology and Race

Assessing Race-Inclusive Theorizing

Race, Ethnicity, Public Policy, and Criminal Justice Practices

LEARNING OBJECTIVES

In this chapter, you will learn the following:

- The central definitional, measurement, and theoretical issues that drive the search for explanations that are sensitive to offenders' gender, race, or ethnicity.

- The extent to which mainstream crime theories have ignored or downplayed the impact of both gender and race as causal or even mediating factors.[1]

- The types of theories that have explicitly included either gender or race or, in some cases, have included both as key features in their causal explanations.

- The breadth of feminist- and race-inclusive theorizing about criminality, and the insights such theorizing provides about the criminal activities of men compared to women, and ethnic minorities compared to non-Hispanic whites.

INTRODUCTION

Race is important to criminology. To many people, race is *the* defining feature in viewing someone as a "likely suspect" or, minimally, someone to avoid in certain public places. Age strengthens the stereotyping: The person many people, including minorities, would likely avoid on an otherwise empty street late at night is an adolescent minority male.

Correctional researchers paint a bleak future for minorities, but especially African American males: While 7 percent of all persons born in 2001 may eventually go to prison, nearly five times that number of black males may end up in prison (Bonzcar 2003). In 2007, 40 percent of male prison inmates were black, about 25 percent being Hispanic or Latino; 33 percent were non-Hispanic whites, and the rest (2 percent) were other races (West and Sabol 2008). The **disproportionate minority contact (DMC)** phenomenon, whereby minority group members account for a far larger percentage of the criminal justice system's clientele than their respective proportion in the national population, is a major policy issue in American criminal justice (Mays and Ruddell 2008; Walker 2006). Race is such a strong force in American society, that we treat it as a separate concern in our trip across the landscape of criminological theorizing.

Gender is also an important criminological concept, but for different reasons. Mainstream criminologists have largely ignored women, primarily because women come to the attention of the criminal justice system less often than do men.[2] Women account for a small percentage of convicted felons. In 2007, about 7 percent of all federal and state prisoners were women; black women accounted for 28 percent of female prison inmates—a figure far below that of black males—Latinas added 17 percent, and the rest were non-Hispanic Caucasian women (48 percent) or women of other races (7 percent) (West and Sabol 2008). As pundits have noted about female criminality, the squeaky wheel gets the oil; in this case, the squeaky wheel is the male offender.

In this chapter, we explore two questions related to gender and race. First, what can the criminological theories reviewed to this point tell us about the criminality of females compared to males, and racial or ethnic minorities compared to non-Hispanic whites? Mainstream criminology has accorded both topics short shrift; even critical theories, which give race and gender special attention, offer incomplete insights. Hence, our second question: What specialized theories have evolved to fill the gaps in our knowledge about the roles played by race and gender in the study of crime and criminals? Before turning to these questions, however, we address several central issues concerning gender and race (as well as the related term *ethnicity*). While you may think that each term is easily defined, even here we find disagreement.

GENDER AND RACE: DEFINITIONAL ISSUES

- Male and female. Woman and men. Do the terms *sex* and *gender* mean the same thing? What are their special meanings? Why are the distinctions important?

- When we talk about a person's race, to what are we referring? Similarly, ethnicity is a term with equally widespread application in contemporary society. To what does it refer? Why are these distinctions important?

Our first task is to define the central terms used in this chapter. What will become clear is that even for terms like *sex,* there are options that can redirect our search for answers. The same is true of race, especially as used by laypersons compared to social scientists—let alone biologists and other physical scientists. Second, we review the breadth and depth of crimes in the U.S. that are committed by men, contrasted with women and racial or ethnic minorities, contrasted with all others. Finally, we look at how definitions and crime statistics shape criminological thinking about women and minority group members.

Defining Gender and Race

Science is based on shared definitions. Nowhere is this research norm more important than in any attempt to look at the roles gender and race play in the study of crime and criminals. Nearly all crime-related definitions have at least three critical forms: social, legal, and political. Gender and race are no exceptions to this generalization.

From Sex to Gender to Feminism   For biologists, the term *sex* provides the means to group humans based on physical sexual characteristics and reproduction functions, hence the term generally known as **biological sex.** Given this scientific definition, we can divide biological sex into two primary categories: males and females.

Gender refers to culturally defined and socially agreed upon conduct norms governing behaviors deemed as appropriate for men and women. There need be no biological basis for a person's **gender identity,** or the self-conception as either male or female that is independent of a person's biological sex. Gender identity answers the following question: With which gender, male or female, do you most closely identify? Sometimes people use the term **sexual orientation** rather than gender identity. If you look up *gender* in a dictionary, you are likely to see that it is also used as a colloquial term for biological sex. Gender, then, is often used interchangeably with biological sex, although some physical and social scientists might argue against such a practice as being scientifically inaccurate.

Besides its scientific and social significance, gender has legal implications, as well. One's sex is included on most government documents. Criminal, civil, or administrative laws tend to respond differently to men and women. For example, there are bathrooms and prisons reserved for each sex; marriage is generally restricted to opposite-sex couples, although this legal restriction is under increasing public scrutiny and modification.

Gender also has political cache, especially at the intersection of gender and feminism. **Feminism** refers to the belief that men and women should have equal political, social, sexual, and economic rights. Feminists engage in discourse about gender and sexual differences between males and females, advocate for women's equality, and campaign for women's rights. One target is any form of **sexism,** a belief or attitude that one gender or sex is inferior to or less valuable than the other, as well as discriminatory practices based on one's sex or gender; the latter defined as **sexual discrimination.**[3]

During the nineteenth and early twentieth centuries, **first-wave feminists** worked for the extension of basic human rights to woman—rights denied them under male-dominated legal systems—especially the right to vote.[4] During this epoch, black feminists, like Isabella Van Wagener, also known as Sojourner Truth (1797–1883), argued that their experiences were unique and distinct from those of white women. In the 1960s and 1970s, the women's liberation movement, largely made up of **second-wave feminists,** argued for greater economic and social rights for women; they worked to end discrimination and all forms of inequality based on sex or gender. For example, the "Equal Rights Amendment" to the U.S. Constitution sought to extend equal-rights across the board, eliminating any legal distinctions based on sex; however, it failed to achieve necessary state-level ratification.[5] Second-wave feminist and activist Betty Friedan (1921–2006) wrote about a condition that had no name, but from which many of her female contemporaries suffered: the feminine mystique. **Third-wave feminists,** starting in the 1990s, moved beyond what they viewed as the limiting experiences of their predecessors, which they criticized as class-bound (i.e., upper-class only) and race-bound (i.e., white only). Hence, third-wave feminists focus on interconnections between class, gender, and race, while allowing adherents to define feminism as they see fit and addressing such disparate topics as reproductive rights, objectification of females, maternity-leave policies, eating disorders, body imaging, and other topics of *social justice* (Walker 1995; Wurtzel 1999).

Feminism has given rise to a wide range of theories and ideologies. All three waves engendered social and political activism in adherents. For example, before enactment of the Nineteenth Amendment to the U.S. Constitution in 1920, suffragettes regularly marched, lobbied, and otherwise campaigned for women's right to vote. Supporters of the women's liberation movement held public demonstrations, where they chronicled the social and economic inequalities that remained legally in force. In the twenty-first century, performances such as *The Vagina Monologues,* organizations such as Take Back the Night, and magazines such as *Bitch* present the social and political agenda of third wave feminists. Current feminist theoretical orientations include, for example, Marxist feminism, radical feminism, liberal feminism, black feminism, and multiracial feminism, all of which have influenced criminological thinking over the past 30-plus years. In the following box, feminists of the three waves speak for themselves.

IN THEIR OWN WORDS: Feminists on the Condition of Women in Society

---

We can learn a great deal about feminism and sexism from the words of feminists in the different epochs.

First-wave feminist Sojourner Truth on "Aren't I a woman?": "That man . . . says that women need to be helped into carriages, and lifted over ditches, and to have the best places everywhere. Nobody ever helps me into carriages, or over mud puddles, or gives me any best place, and aren't I a woman? . . . I have plowed, and planted, and gathered into barns, and no man could head me—and aren't I a woman? I could work as much and eat as much as a man (when I could get it), and bear the lash as well—aren't I a woman? I have borne thirteen children and seen them most all sold off into slavery, and when I cried out with a mother's grief, none but Jesus heard—and I aren't I a woman?"

Second-wave feminist Betty Naomi Friedan on rejecting the feminist mystique: "A girl should not expect special privileges because of her sex, but neither should she 'adjust' to prejudice and discrimination. She

must learn to compete . . . not as a woman, but as a human being. . . . Who knows what women can be when they are finally free to become themselves? Who knows what women's intelligence will contribute when it can be nourished without denying love? . . . The time is at hand when the voices of the feminine mystique can no longer drown out the inner voice that is driving women to become complete."

Third-wave feminists Jennifer Baumgardner and Amy Richard on consciousness raising among young women: "Consciousness among women is what caused this [change], and consciousness, one's ability to open their mind to the fact that male domination does affect the women of our generation, is what we need. . . . The presence of feminism in our lives is taken for granted. For our generation, feminism is like fluoride. We scarcely notice we have it—it's simply in the water."

SOURCES: Baumgardner and Richard (2000); Friedan (1963); Truth (1851).

Race and Ethnicity   In common usage, people sometimes talk about a person's *race* when they are referring to his or her *ethnicity*. **Race** divides human beings into distinct groups based on hereditary characteristics. In order to belong to a given race, the characteristics of that race must be biologically determined and independent of any social factors. Anthropologists were first to apply this term as they sought to categorize the species *Homo sapiens*. Early racial identifications turned on physical characteristics, such as skin color, hair texture, facial features, and stature. Differing combinations of these characteristics provided the basis for the four major racial groups that dominated discussions of race in the early twentieth century: Caucasoid, Mongoloid, Negroid, and Australoid.[6]

Racial distinctiveness depends on physical, geographical, national, and cultural isolation. In the twentieth century, such groupings had less biological and anthropological significance. Nowhere is that more clearly demonstrated than in America, where racial distinctions have blurred even further in the children of mixed-race parents. The Human Genome Mapping Project (Chapter 3) has shed light on this issue. Genetically, individuals in two different races may be more similar to each other than to others in their respective racial categories (Keita, Kittles et al. 2004). The fact that genetic differentiation allows scientists to identify individuals as to their ancestor's geographic origins does not equate to race. Human variation is simply too great to support the idea of race as we now use it (Keita, Kittles et al. 2004:519). Researchers also note that the absence of a scientific concept of race does not mean the elimination of the sociological phenomenon of *racism*.

Ethnicity, by contrast, is an **ethnoym,** or name given to a specific ethnic group, that refers to the group's common social or cultural traits. Ethnic groups may have their own language, religion, and customs.[7] Perhaps the most important element of ethnicity is the in-group identification shared by members, the sense that as a group they are traditionally distinct from the larger society. **Ethnic identity,** like *gender identity,* refers to how we see ourselves, and may or may not have anything to do with how others see us.

Based on these two definitions, African Americans are a racial group, whereas Hispanics are an ethnic group. However, several racial groups claim the cultural modifier of Hispanic or Latin, making classification complicated. There are Hispanics of European descent (from Spain, for example); there are Hispanics of Afro–Caribbean descent (from the Dominican Republic or Puerto Rico, for example), who are also descended from people whose origins are African and Spanish; and there are Hispanics descended from both Spanish colonialists and various indigenous peoples throughout the Americas.

In the early 1990s, the American Anthropological Association (AAA) entered the debate. The AAA criticized the race and ethnic distinctions offered by the Office of Management and Budget (OMB) for use by the U.S. federal government and nearly all state and local governments. The OMB recognized five races: American Indian or Alaskan Native, Asian, Native Hawaiian or Pacific Islander, black or African American, and white; it recognized two ethnic designations: Hispanic and non-Hispanic. However, the OMB admitted that it had no scientific basis for this classification system. What the AAA suggested was that race is more useful in social and cultural contexts than in a biological one, as genetic science has established. The AAA acknowledged that some Hispanics consider being Hispanic a racial designation (see also Gerber and de la Puente 1996; Rodriguez and Cordero-Guzman 1992). In the final analysis, the AAA (1998) concluded that race as a means of distinguishing among different groups of peoples may have outlived its usefulness. To date, the OMB allows people to identify with more than one race, but the ethnicity choice is still either Hispanic or non-Hispanic.

In sum, sociologists and anthropologists over the past 20 years have repeatedly issued a warning: The term *race,* as used since the days of Swedish taxonomist Carolus Linnaeus (1707–1778) in the eighteenth century, currently provides virtually meaningless and unscientific classifications. Race, whether it has any scientific cache, is a divisive and politically charged term. Groups across the political spectrum have adopted race as their watchword, challenging others to dispute their interpretations, often, as the following Comments and Criticisms suggests, with horrific consequences.

Measuring Gender, Race, and Crime

In Chapter 1, we provided a trend analysis of overall crime by type. Here, the focus is on the same forms of criminal conduct, but we provide analyses by gender and race.

COMMENTS AND CRITICISMS: Scientific Racism

Racism refers to an ideology that one's own race is superior to all others.[8] No one racial group "owns" racism; all so-called races have, at some time and at some place, expressed racist attitudes and practiced exclusionary or restrictive behavior based on race, the latter being **racial discrimination.** In the U.S., the Founding Fathers' racist attitudes and practices led them to devalue the lives of Africans, justifying the latter's legal status as slaves. Indeed, racism has a grim history in the history of humankind, extending back to Greek and Roman civilizations, and perhaps even earlier. We can find racism in ancient laws and codicils, works of great literature, and the policies and practices of the colonial powers, such as Spain, Portugal, France, Great Britain, Belgium, and the United States.

Scientific racism—a pejorative term that refers to the use of science or pseudoscience to prove that one race is superior in certain (or all) aspects to others (or all)—provides an example of what can happen when ideology seeks scientific validation. In the nineteenth century, French aristocrat Joseph Arthur, Comte de Gobineau (1816–1882), argued that **Aryans,** a mythical "race" whose language derived from the Indo-European language group and evolved into the Nordic racial ideal type, were the **master race,** a racially pure group that should rule over all others. Gobineau influenced others in the late nineteenth and early twentieth century, including French anthropologist Georges Vacher de Lapouge (1854–1936), who used skull measurements to contrast European Aryan heads to those of European Jews, and English

Germanophile, political philosopher, and naturalist Houston Stewart Chamberlain (1855–1927), who wrote about the natural racial superiority of the "Germanic peoples." Their collective work gave rise to race theories at the core of the political beliefs, social attitudes, and genocidal behavior associated with Germany's National Socialist party, or the Nazis, from the 1920s to 1945.

In 1935, the Nazis created the *Ahnenerbe,* a racist "think tank" whose sole purpose was to provide "scientific evidence" of the anthropological and cultural history—and superiority—of the Aryan race. They sponsored German racial anthropologist Bruno Beger, who participated in a 1938 expedition to Tibet looking for the roots of Aryanism. Other worldwide expeditions looked for examples of racial inferiority and superiority. In its bleakest form, scientific racism served as the basis for racial and eugenic experiments conducted at concentration camps during the Nazi era. Beyond pseudoscientific experiments to alter eye color and test a person's life expectancy in freezing water or after exposure to malaria, *Ahnenerbe* anthropologists were charged with hand-selecting Jewish men, women, and children from the Auschwitz concentration camp complex for the Nazi's infamous Jewish skeleton collection.[9] Such perversions of science explain contemporary resistance to biological and genetic arguments about crime and criminals.

SOURCES: Levey and Greenhall (1983); Mosse (1968); Pringle (2006); Stackelberg and Winkle (2003); Theodorson and Theodorson (1969).

Gender Comparisons of Crime Prevalence   Table 11.1 contains useful information about male–female crime comparisons and offense–specific trends between 1998 and 2007. Two pieces of information—or statistics—about crime are contained in this table. The first statistic is the absolute number of arrests, which is not adjusted for population changes. Since we are looking at the same information for both groups, we can compare the percentage increases (or decreases) for men with the same increases (or decreases) for women, revealing trends in arrests. For example, we learn that arrests for males declined by 6.1 percent over the 10 years in question, while arrests for women increased by 6.6 percent. For men, the declines in arrests for some crimes were dramatic, including the index crimes of forcible rape, larceny-theft, and motor vehicle theft, with an increase only in robbery arrests. For women, the index-crime figures were inconsistent: robbery and burglary increased, while the rest decreased. Women's arrests were up overall due to increases in categories with large base numbers (i.e., large total number of arrestees), such as driving under the influence, drug law violations, and all other offenses, categories where men actually declined or experienced far smaller increases. In short, female arrests increased in categories not historically associated with female criminality (English 1993; Simon and Landis 1991; Steffensmeier and Streifel 1992); there were decreases in the latter (i.e., prostitution, forgery and counterfeiting, and fraud).

The second set of statistics is the proportion of arrests accounted for by men or women. For example, in the total arrest category, the percentage of men arrested is 78 percent in 1998, compared to 76 percent in 2007. We can use this information in two ways. First, it tells us that the overall male proportion of arrests declined slightly over the 10 years in question (and arrests for women increased by that amount). Second, cases where the proportion of male or female arrests deviates from this percentage can be taken as a reflection of whether males or females dominate a specific crime. Since men account for such a high proportion of all arrests in 1998 and 2007 (78 and 76 percent, respectively), we arbitrarily selected 87 percent as a proportion that is indicative of a male-dominated crime; as women accounted for a smaller proportion of all arrests in each year (22 and 24 percent, respectively), we arbitrarily selected 33 percent as indicative of a crime in which women were substantially overrepresented.[10] In both 1998 and 2007, males dominated such crimes as murder and nonnegligent manslaughter, forcible rape, robbery, burglary (1998 only), motor vehicle theft—all index crimes. In these same years, men also dominated such nonindex crimes as gambling (1998 only), drunkenness (1998 only), weapons offenses, and sex offenses (except forcible rape and prostitution). Women, on the other hand, were overrepresented among arrestees for larceny-theft, forgery and counterfeiting, embezzlement, prostitution and commercialized vice, and runaways.

There is little doubt that the arrest patterns for women in 2007 have changed since 1998. In every category where the number of arrests for men increased, the increases for women were higher; and women increased in some categories where the number of arrests for men declined. However, most of the increases for women—and nearly all of the large increases—were for nonindex crimes, many having to do with substance use and abuse. Clearly, women are arrested for proportionately fewer crimes than men. Moreover, women's arrest patterns are different from those of men, although the magnitude of these differences is closing. Can theory help us understand why these patterns exist?

Race and Ethnic Comparisons of Crime Prevalence   Table 11.2 provides a one-year picture of arrests by race. Unlike Table 11.1, we do not have trend analyses of arrest by race, as the U.S. Bureau of Justice Statistics (BJS) rarely provides such analyses. Later in this chapter we examine variations over time by race for a single crime, that of homicide.

Blacks have accounted for between 11 to 12 percent of the nation's population since the late 1990s; the percent of Hispanics surpassed blacks early in 2001 and stands at over 14 percent (Bureau of the Census 2009). Nearly 70 percent of all 2007 arrests summarized in Table 11.2 involved white suspects, about 28 percent were black, and the rest were other races. Using these figures as the "expected" proportion for a given race, any figure with a difference of more

T A B L E   11.1   Ten-Year Arrest Trends, by Sex, 1998–2007[1]

Offense charged	Total arrests		Male arrests					Female arrests				
	1998	2007	1998		2007		98-07	1998		2007		98-07
	N	N	N	%	N	%	Percent change	N	%	N	%	Percent change
TOTAL[2]	8,397,065	8,118,197	6,550,864	78.0	6,150,145	75.8	-6.1	1,846,201	21.8	1,968,052	24.2	+6.6
Murder and nonnegligent manslaughter	8,232	7,301	7,342	89.2	6,519	89.3	-11.2	890	11.2	782	10.2	-12.1
Forcible rape	17,148	13,212	16,942	98.8	13,079	99.0	-22.8	206	1.2	133	1.1	-35.4
Robbery	68,353	72,355	61,410	89.8	64,004	88.5	+4.2	6,943	10.0	8,351	11.6	+20.3
Aggravated assault	290,851	257,464	234,040	80.5	202,588	78.7	-13.4	56,811	9.6	54,876	21.3	-3.4
Burglary	195,696	182,552	170,504	87.1	154,607	84.7	-9.3	25,192	12.5	27,945	14.5	+10.9
Larceny-theft	791,085	689,037	514,574	65.0	413,125	60.0	-19.7	276,511	34.7	275,912	40.0	-0.2
Motor vehicle theft	80,925	62,766	68,494	84.6	51,382	81.9	-25.0	12,431	15.7	11,384	17.7	-8.4
Arson	10,055	9,094	8,606	85.6	7,685	84.5	-10.7	1,449	14.7	1,409	15.8	-2.8
Violent crime[3]	384,584	350,332	319,734	83.1	286,190	81.7	-10.5	64,850	16.8	64,142	18.2	-1.1
Property crime[4]	1,077,761	943,449	762,178	70.7	626,799	66.4	-17.8	315,583	28.9	316,650	33.4	+0.3
Other assaults	768,038	754,280	593,042	77.2	560,655	74.3	-5.5	174,996	22.4	193,625	25.2	+10.6
Forgery and counterfeiting	67,870	58,832	41,508	61.2	36,217	61.6	-12.7	26,362	38.9	22,615	38.2	-14.2
Fraud	213,800	147,985	114,751	53.7	82,340	55.6	-28.2	99,049	45.8	65,645	44.1	-33.7
Embezzlement	11,115	14,065	5,584	50.2	6,849	48.7	+22.7	5,531	48.8	7,216	51.5	+30.5
Stolen property; buying, receiving, possessing	78,371	72,904	66,132	84.4	57,865	79.4	-12.5	12,239	15.5	15,039	20.4	+22.9
Vandalism	173,617	168,815	147,331	84.9	139,748	82.8	-5.1	26,286	15.2	29,067	17.0	+10.6
Weapons; carrying, possessing, etc.	109,533	106,080	100,973	92.2	97,822	92.2	-3.1	8,560	7.9	8,258	7.8	-3.5

Prostitution and commercialized vice	50,082	39,081	20,745	41.4	11,485	29.4	−44.6	29,337	57.8	27,596	68.1	−5.9
Sex offenses (except forcible rape and prostitution)	52,527	45,871	48,658	92.6	42,369	92.4	−12.9	3,869	8.2	3,502	8.8	−9.5
Drug abuse violations	878,355	1,033,203	723,435	82.4	833,941	80.7	+15.3	154,920	17.5	199,262	18.8	+28.6
Gambling	5,067	3,289	4,568	90.2	2,769	84.2	−39.4	499	10.4	520	9.0	+4.2
Offenses against the family and children	85,823	71,305	67,843	79.0	53,754	75.4	−20.8	17,980	21.7	17,551	25.3	−2.4
Driving under the influence	803,030	788,864	676,911	84.3	626,371	79.4	−7.5	126,119	15.6	162,493	20.8	+28.8
Liquor laws	375,009	332,231	294,553	78.5	242,820	73.1	−17.6	80,456	21.4	89,411	27.8	+11.1
Drunkenness	468,796	410,583	409,100	87.3	345,502	84.1	−15.5	59,696	12.8	65,081	16.0	+9.0
Disorderly conduct	387,534	358,428	293,691	75.8	261,327	72.9	−11.0	93,843	23.3	97,101	26.3	+3.5
Vagrancy	17,994	16,388	14,281	79.4	12,761	77.9	−10.6	3,713	20.6	3,627	22.2	−2.3
All other offenses (except traffic)	2,185,863	2,267,145	1,732,271	79.2	1,744,417	76.9	+0.7	453,592	20.5	522,728	23.0	+15.2
Suspicion	3,463	1,299	2,766	79.9	1,031	79.4	−62.7	697	20.4	268	20.8	−61.5
Curfew and loitering law violations	104,976	73,217	73,163	69.7	51,116	69.8	−30.1	31,813	30.5	22,101	30.8	−30.5
Runaways	97,320	61,850	40,412	41.5	27,028	43.7	−33.1	56,908	58.2	34,822	56.1	−38.8

1. 7,946 agencies; 2007 estimated population 171,876,948; 1998 estimated population 154,013,711.
2. Does not include suspicion.
3. Violent crimes are offenses of murder and nonnegligent manslaughter, forcible rape, robbery, and aggravated assault.
4. Property crimes are offenses of burglary, larceny-theft, motor vehicle theft, and arson.
SOURCE: FBI (2008); modified by authors.

T A B L E   11.2   Arrests by Race, 2007[1]

Offense charged	Total arrests				Percent distribution[2]			
	Total	White	Black	Other[3]	Total	White	Black	Other
TOTAL	10,656,710	7,426,278	3,003,060	227,372	100.0	69.7	28.2	2.1
Murder and nonnegligent manslaughter	10,067	4,789	5,078	200	100.0	47.6	50.4	2.0
Forcible rape	17,058	10,984	5,708	366	100.0	64.4	33.5	2.1
Robbery	96,584	40,573	54,774	1,237	100.0	42.0	56.7	1.3
Aggravated assault	326,277	208,762	109,985	7,530	100.0	64.0	33.7	2.3
Burglary	228,346	156,442	68,052	3,852	100.0	68.5	29.8	1.7
Larceny-theft	894,215	610,607	261,730	21,878	100.0	68.3	29.3	2.4
Motor vehicle theft	88,843	55,229	31,765	1,849	100.0	62.2	35.8	2.1
Arson	11,400	8,510	2,666	224	100.0	74.6	23.4	1.9
Violent crime[4]	449,986	265,108	175,545	9,333	100.0	58.9	39.0	2.1
Property crime[5]	1,222,804	830,788	364,213	27,803	100.0	67.9	29.8	2.2
Other assaults	980,512	641,991	316,217	22,304	100.0	65.5	32.3	2.2
Forgery and counterfeiting	77,757	54,136	22,460	1,161	100.0	69.6	28.9	1.5
Fraud	184,446	127,377	54,575	2,494	100.0	69.1	29.6	1.3
Embezzlement	16,954	10,813	5,818	323	100.0	63.8	34.3	1.9
Stolen property; buying, receiving, possessing	91,937	57,870	32,570	1,497	100.0	62.9	35.4	1.6
Vandalism	220,055	166,201	48,642	5,212	100.0	75.5	22.1	2.4
Weapons; carrying, possessing, etc.	142,369	82,311	57,745	2,313	100.0	57.8	40.6	1.6

Offense							
Prostitution and commercialized vice	59,307	34,190	23,251	1,866	100.0	57.6	39.2	3.1
Sex offenses (except forcible rape and prostitution)	62,586	45,961	15,372	1,253	100.0	73.4	24.6	2.0
Drug abuse violations	1,382,783	880,742	485,054	16,987	100.0	63.7	35.1	1.2
Gambling	9,141	2,199	6,805	137	100.0	24.1	74.4	1.5
Offenses against the family and children	88,437	60,124	26,090	2,223	100.0	68.0	29.5	2.5
Driving under the influence	1,050,803	929,453	97,472	23,878	100.0	88.5	9.3	2.3
Liquor laws	474,726	406,221	49,434	19,071	100.0	85.6	10.4	4.0
Drunkenness	449,117	375,440	62,278	11,399	100.0	83.6	13.9	2.6
Disorderly conduct	537,809	342,169	183,810	11,830	100.0	63.6	34.2	2.2
Vagrancy	25,584	15,493	9,474	617	100.0	60.6	37.0	2.5
All other offenses (except traffic)	2,936,233	1,969,862	905,656	60,715	100.0	67.1	30.8	2.1
Suspicion	1,571	904	649	18	100.0	57.5	41.3	1.2
Curfew and loitering law violations	109,575	69,950	37,532	2,093	100.0	63.8	34.3	1.9
Runaways	82,218	56,975	22,398	2,845	100.0	69.3	27.2	3.5

1. 11,929 agencies; 2007 estimated population 225,477,173.

2. Because of rounding, the percentages may not add to 100.0.

3. Others include American Indian or Alaska Native and Asian or Pacific Islander.

4. Violent crimes are offenses of murder and nonnegligent manslaughter, forcible rape, robbery, and aggravated assault.

5. Property crimes are offenses of burglary, larceny-theft, motor vehicle theft, and arson.

SOURCE: FBI (2008a); modified by authors.

than 10 percent—plus or minus—merits special attention, essentially looking at cases where white or black arrests are higher than expected. For example, we find that white arrests for all index crimes are within this arbitrary 10 percent rule. Whites are overrepresented in three nonindex crimes, including driving under the influence, liquor laws, and drunkenness. Blacks have higher than expected arrests for two violent index crimes—murder and nonnegligent manslaughter and robbery—and four nonindex crimes—weapons, prostitution and commercialized vice, gambling, and suspicion.

In most of the racial comparisons, offense-specific differences are relatively small; that is, the proportion of most crimes committed by whites, blacks, and others is very similar to that reported for overall arrests. Having said this, differences by race exist for 10 offense comparisons. Moreover, we are unable to make trend comparisons from these crime statistics. Such cross-time analyses are available for homicide, a crime where blacks not only experience higher than expected arrest rates, but also account for more than half of them. In addition, we are able to include gender and age as variables.

The Special Case of Homicide: The Intersection of Gender, Race, and Age   Homicide is a unique crime, one of the few where the number of reported crimes is close to the actual number of offenses.[11] The BJS provides a 30-year window into homicide by race and gender (Fox and Zawitz 2007). In Figure 11.1, the offending rate per 100,000 for whites shows little fluctuation over time, and the general trend, since peaking in 1981, has been downward, reduced by 40 percent in 2005 from its peak. The rate for blacks shows greater fluctuation over time, peaking twice, once in 1980 and again in 1991; the 2005 reported rate is nearly 50 percent below these peaks, having been relatively stable since the late 1990s. What should not be lost in this discussion, however, is that the per capita rate for blacks is 10 times that for whites.

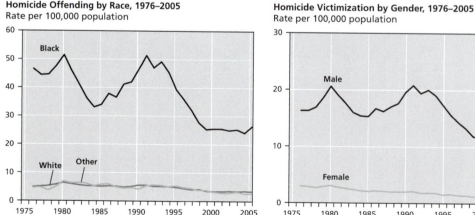

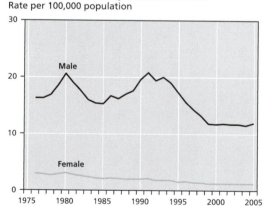

F I G U R E   11.1   Homicide Offending (per Capita) by Race and Victimization by Gender, 1976–2005

If we look only at gender, we again see a downwardly spiraling trend for males and females, although males—like blacks—had three peaks: 1980, 1991 and 1993. The rate for 2005 is about 80 percent below the peaks. For females, the trend is also generally downward; their 2005 rate was reduced over the 1976 and 1980 rates by more than half.

Examining homicide rates by gender and race, plus breaking it down by age, clarifies the significance of the intersection of all three variables in homicide studies (see Figure 11.2). First, in all four cases, the highest per capita rates, irrespective of gender and race, were for 18- to 24-year-old individuals, the age group that also experiences the highest victimization rates for this crime (and most violent crimes). Second, the homicide rate trend for women, irrespective of race or age, has been downward over the years, with a few upward spikes. Third, while black women, especially those in the 18- to 24-year-old age group, had higher homicide rates in 1976 than did white males, by the early 1980s these differences largely disappeared. The homicide rates for black females were still higher than those for white females, the rates for the latter having barely changed except to

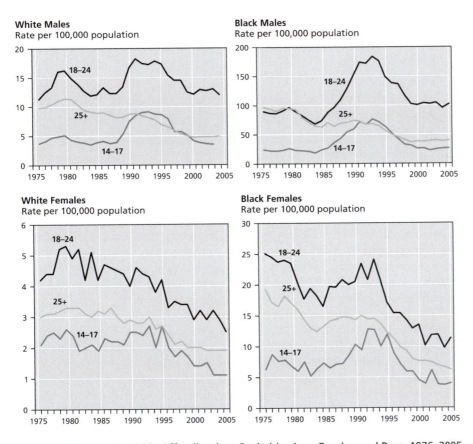

FIGURE 11.2 Homicide Offending (per Capita) by Age, Gender, and Race, 1976–2005

go down. Finally, the graph of the rates of black males looked like that of white males over time with one significant difference: No matter what age was considered, the rates for black males were 10 times that reported for white males. Hence, black males are killed at a rate 10 times that of white males, no matter what the year or age category we examine.

In sum, the intersection of gender, race, and age provides otherwise hidden information about homicide. These variables have clear implications for the study of homicide, and, we would argue, all crimes where there is a race or gender imbalance in who gets arrested and who goes on to further justice system processing.

GENDER AND CRIMINOLOGICAL THEORIES

- If you are female and have a brother, did your parents treat you the same when you were growing up, especially during your teenage years? Did you both have the same rules, curfews, and behavioral expectations? [Males can also answer these questions.] While odds are that your brother or sister is not an offender, is it possible that gender-specific socialization can account for some of the differences in the crimes reported for males compared to females?

- How would you respond to the charge that the criminal justice system responds differently to women who are either economically disadvantaged or minority-group members? Is this political rhetoric or social reality?

At the end of the nineteenth century, the classical school of criminology relegated women to the same legal category as children. These criminologists viewed both groups as incapable of making rational decisions and so excused them from criminal responsibility, assigning it instead to the *paterfamilias,* the senior male in the family. The ascent of positivistic criminology did little to draw criminologists to female criminality. For one thing, crime committed by women was a rare phenomenon. And when Lombroso (see Chapter 3) and Freud (see Chapter 4) offered explanations of female criminality, they did so in uniformly sexist ways. They described criminal women as too masculine or acquisitive, or as lacking in maternal instincts. The crimes of women were limited largely to prostitution, shoplifting, and aiding and abetting their male counterparts.

The model of overmasculinized and conniving criminal women went largely unchallenged until the 1970s. The prevailing model, however, did come under fire after World War II. The intervening contributions of Otto Pollak (1950) are worth noting. Pollak (1908–1998) addressed the nearly 10-to-1 difference in the arrest rates of men and women. He claimed that three aspects of women's crime selection accounts for their underrepresentation in arrest statistics. First, their crimes (e.g., shoplifting, domestic theft, and theft by prostitutes) have a low likelihood of detection. Second, when detected, it is unlikely that the victims will report the crimes to the police. Third, when the crimes are detected and reported, owing to a double standard for men and women, police are less likely to arrest and prosecutors are less likely to seek convictions against female offenders, especially those with dependent children. Even the male criminal, reported Pollak, adopts a "chivalrous" attitude toward his female counterpart, showing reluctance to implicate her.

The tendency to discount female offenders continued well into the twentieth century. Two trends emerged in the study of female criminality by the mid-1980s. The first was the use of mainstream theories to examine the influence of gender's obvious influence on crime; the second was to provide alternative theorizing about the gender–crime nexus. We begin with the role of mainstream crime theories.

Mainstream Criminological Theorizing about Gender

Gender may play either a mediating or conditional role on criminality. That is, since gender has social as well as biological aspects, children, during a time when their gender identities are emerging, are simultaneously exposed to crime-causing forces in their social, psychological, or physical environments. Gender could mediate—or come between—these forces and the presence or absence of criminal conduct. Or, it is also possible that gender plays a conditional role: the causal factors work in different ways for men compared to women. Hence, both of these perspectives suggest that we must provide separate gender-sensitive analyses of extant theories to determine what exactly is happening to women and girls compared to men and boys.[12]

Gender as a Mediating or Conditional Factor in Criminality   Social bonding theory addresses gender differences in misbehavior. A breakdown in the social bond better predicts drug use by females than it does for males (Dull 1983), a prediction that holds for true for overall female delinquency compared to male patterns (Hindelang 1973; Jensen and Eve 1976). Control theory yields insights into why female criminals differ from their male counterparts (Box 1981). According to Jill Rosenbaum (1987:129), males and females share the same motivations to commit misbehavior; however, males enjoy more freedom to engage in "occasional delinquency without jeopardizing their relationships with others or their chances of success." For a female to violate rules, her bonds must be weaker than a male's for the same level of offending to occur.

Bonds may also function differently for males and females. Angela Huebner and Sherry Betts (2002), examining a sample of school-age children, found that while the level of involvement with family predicts delinquency for both boys *and* girls, attachment functions to protect females to a far greater extent than males. This latter finding suggests that attachment, an emotive condition, works better with females, whose gender socialization tends to emphasize intimacy and supportive social networks more than is the case for males (Boss 1988; Miller 1991; Seiffge-Krenke 1995). Leanne Alarid and associates (2000), in a study of incarcerated male and female felons, reported that parental attachments are a better predictor of violent offending among women than men (i.e., the higher the attachment, the lower the participation in violent offending); at the same time, they reported that differential association has more consistent effects, especially for men. It would appear, then, that in the case of these two theories—bonding and differential association—there are gender-specific differences in how they function.

Self-control theory recognizes gender differences in control levels. As discussed earlier, self-control theory emphasizes parental monitoring and surveillance of children. Generally, girls are regarded as more at risk in a dangerous world and in need of higher levels of monitoring than are boys. Caregivers tend to pay more attention to the socialization of girls, given contemporary society's norm of female dependency (Heimer and DeCoster 1999). If then, parents and other caregivers subject girls to higher levels of monitoring and surveillance, and practice greater accountability for the misbehavior of females, the result should be higher levels of self-control.

Researchers have explored whether self-control levels can account for gender differences in offending. The results have been mixed. Burton and associates (1998), using an adult random sample from a U.S. city, report that holding the level of self-control constant eliminates the effects of gender on self-reported offending. LaGrange and Silverman (1999), using a sample of Canadian children, found that measures of self-control appear to reduce the association between gender and self-reported offending. However, Gibbs and associates (1998) indicate that gender has both a direct impact on the self-reported noncriminal deviance of college students and an indirect effect through self-control levels. Finally, Tittle and associates (2003), also using an adult sample of urban dwellers and Grasmick's attitudinal scale for measuring self-control, provide confirmation of some self-control claims. That is, generally, self-control works well to predict crime and deviance for both males and females. Importantly, however, self-control exhibits gender differences: the cognitive (i.e., mental processing measures) levels of self-control found in male and female subjects are the same; the behavioral (i.e., the scale measures of behavior and the variety of self-reported individual behavior) are not, with males exhibiting less self-control.[13] Moreover, as was the case with Gibbs and associates, controlling for self-control levels does not eliminate the gender's direct influences on self-reported offending.

Changing Status of Women as a Causal Factor in Female Criminality   The works of Freda Adler (1975) and Rita Simon (1975a) generated considerable public interest in gender-specific crime theories. Adler stresses a nearly epidemic-like involvement of women in almost every major crime category and forecasted a blurring of the traditional male–female gender-role distinctions. The women's liberation movement inadvertently opened up new crime opportunities as well, an idea advanced by Adler. As Steffensmeier and associates (1989) reveal in the following box, it is possible to test these ideas in a comparative criminological context with interesting results.

After reviewing the women's liberation movement and alleged increases in female criminality, Adler described the events using the rhetoric of second-wave feminists. Simon (1975a) presents a different interpretation of these statistics,

COMPARATIVE CRIMINOLOGY—WORLD VIEWS ON CRIME AND JUSTICE: National Development and Female Crime Rates

Economic development is often associated with an increase in female crime, especially as measured by female arrests. Four arguments support this link: (1) gender equality that comes with economic development; (2) female economic marginality that can accompany economic development favoring the status of men over women; (3) enhanced opportunities for female offending related to economic development; and (4) economic development leading to increased formalization of criminal justice processing, which makes female crime far more visible as record keeping improves, enforcement efforts expand, and criminal responsibility transfers to women from other family members. Darrell Steffensmeier and associates (1989) provide a unique look into these arguments, using INTERPOL statistics for 69 nations between 1970 and 1976. The crimes of interest were homicide, major property crime (i.e., robbery and burglary), and minor property crime (i.e., a combination of larceny-theft and fraud). The female percentage of arrests (FP/A) is a percentage of all arrests for each offense category that are females, after controlling for the distribution of males and females in the population at large.[14]

The analyses performed by Steffensmeier and associates found support for two arguments, while the other two were poor predictors. Specifically, increased opportunities for female-based consumer crimes—the number of radios per capita—and the formalization of social control—the number of years a given nation had participated in the INTERPOL data collection between 1952 and 1976—were each good predictors of FP/A. Conversely, the equality of women—the percentage of university students in a nation that are female—and economic marginality of females—the proportion of working women who would have to change jobs in order to gain equality for women across all occupations—performed poorly in predicting FP/A.

The researchers acknowledge that their measures may be suspect and that other forces may be at work, mediating the influence of economic development on female arrests relative to males. Nonetheless, the significance of female-based consumer crimes and enhanced justice system processing for female arrests cannot be ignored.

SOURCES: Steffensmeier, Allan, and Streifel (1989).

making several important points: (1) Female involvement in violent crime is decreasing; (2) female involvement in other serious crime is increasing; and (3) we cannot directly link increases in female crime to the women's movement; instead, they are a result of increased opportunities in the labor market (Simon 1975a:19, 38–39, 46). Simon's analysis does not turn on the presence of liberated women. But the inference remains, as the increased labor–market opportunity is one victory claimed by the women's liberation movement.

Roy Austin (1982) explored what became known as the **liberation hypothesis** by looking at gender-role theory for conceptual support. First, he plotted the divorce rates and labor force participation rates for females. Increases in both rates, he observed, coincided with the founding of the National Organization for Women. Moreover, female contributions to crime rates followed the same patterns of growth along the same timeline. Austin (1982:421) believed that the rise in female arrest rates fit the causal criteria of association and temporal order with the women's liberation movement, supporting the hypothesis.

Challenges to the concept of the "new female offender" soon appeared. Joseph Weis (1976) suggested, "The new female criminal is more a social invention than an empirical reality." His analysis of self-reported data led him to favor a

COMMENTS AND CRITICISMS: Is the Gender Gap Closing?

The official picture of crime—as represented in the UCR—gives us pause to reconsider the claims of the 1970s second-wave feminists. But other forces may be at work. Comparing longitudinal data from the UCR, the NCVS (where the victim identifies the offender's sex), and two major self-report studies of the nation's youth, Steffensmeier and associates fail to find support for the official picture of female crime as escalating. What they suggest, instead, is an increase in girls' arrest-proneness due to net-widening efforts such as the following: (1) expanded definitions of violence to include incidents that in the past would not have been noted by authorities; (2) increased policing of

family-based violence, including violence in previously sacrosanct environments such as the school and home; and (3) decreased tolerance toward female juvenile offenders exhibited by a wide range of stakeholders, including parents and the community. They conclude: "It is not so much that girls have become more violent; it is that the avenues to prevent or punish violence have grown so enormously" (p. 397). The claims that female violence have increased, then, are more social construction than empirical reality.

SOURCES: Steffensmeier, Schwartz, et al. (2005).

sex-specific opportunity theory (see the comparative criminology box above). That is, increased participation by women in the work world has given them more opportunities to commit crime. He noted the historical exclusion of women from certain means of success, both conventional and unconventional. Before women became CPAs or physicians in significant numbers, for example, they represented no real threat to embezzle funds or write phony prescriptions.

Even in the 1970s, many criminologists expressed skepticism about the "new female offender" (Giordano and Cernkovich 1977; Jacobs 1975; Kramer and Kempinen 1978). In particular, Darrell Steffensmeier challenged the statistics cited by Simon and Adler (Steffensmeier 1978, 1980, 1983a,b; Steffensmeier and Cobb 1981; Steffensmeier and Steffensmeier 1980). He saw the increases in female arrest rates as (1) more artifacts than actual differences due to "flawed arrest rates"; (2) limited to certain nonviolent offense categories such as shoplifting, fraud, and larceny; and (3) the result of changes in reporting and policing behaviors. Steffensmeier saw no conclusive evidence for a crime-rate convergence of the sexes, as he makes clear in the above box.

Two recent trends suggest that the inclusion of gender in mainstream criminological theories is likely to increase: gendered pathways and gendered contexts (Akers and Sellers 2009:281–86). The **gendered pathways** approach examines the life experiences and developmental trajectories of females as contrasted to males, and is similar to the life course perspective (Chapter 12). Mainstream theories that acknowledge close ties between being a victim and being an offender, such as general strain theory's inclusion of the anger and depression that surrounds being a victim as a force moving the victim closer to becoming an offender, stand as examples of gendered pathways. Such insights, however, seem more descriptive than explanatory (Akers and Sellers 2009:284).

The **gendered context** approach addresses differences in male and female socialization experiences, as well as the differentials in opportunity afforded each to engage in miscreant behavior. This approach tacitly acknowledges observations made by critics of such theories as differential association/social learning, social, and anomie theory: They account for only minor forms of misbehavior. If we want to understand serious offending, we need to include a gendered context (Steffensmeier and Allan 1996). As noted earlier in this section, contemporary society continues to differentiate men from women in important ways. Why should we not expect such differences to impact criminality? As Steffensmeier and Allan (1996) cogently observe, husbands rarely kill their wives because they fear them, but the same cannot be said of wives who kill their husbands.

In sum, mainstream criminology contributes much to our understanding of gender–crime disparities. Before recent efforts to make mainstream criminology more gender-inclusive, critical criminologists developed gendered ways of viewing crime and criminals.

Critical Criminology and Gender

Critical criminologists look at crime–gender links differently than do mainstream criminologists. Traditionalists explore male and female criminality with an eye to the biological, psychological, and sociological forces that help determine who in each gender category is more likely to turn to crime or delinquency. Critical criminology is a branch of criminology that critiques parts of the existing social order (e.g., capitalism, economic disparities, racism, sexism) as creating both crime and criminals.

Radical Feminism: Patriarchal Society, Oppressed Females, and Survival   In spite of questions about Adler's and Simon's interpretations, patriarchal and chivalry arguments continue to inform criminologists. **Radical feminists** look at masculine power and privilege as the chief cause of all inequities in social relations (see Jaggar and Rothenberg 1984). For example, Meda Chesney-Lind (1973), an early proponent of the chivalry argument, observes that many youthful female crimes are "status offenses," or law violations related to the offender's age (e.g., incorrigibility, truancy, and running away). Criminologists, she argues, often dismiss these offense types as inconsequential and unimportant. Therefore, positivistic theories do not address the types of offending most important to an understanding of female crime. Mainstream male-dominated and male-oriented criminal justice research also fails to tell us much about how the criminal justice system responds to female offenders, young or old (Chesney-Lind 1989:18–19).

Chesney-Lind also dismisses the liberation hypothesis as flawed. She argues instead for a feminist theory of delinquency. She defines young girls' misbehavior—particularly running away and incorrigibility—as "survival strategies," or methods of dealing with dangerous or abusive environments.[15] They may make what is for them rational and logical, if extralegal, choices, such as engaging in minor criminality, to survive. In her theory, young women are the victims of a **patriarchal authority** system that physically, sexually, and mentally abuses them. Laws intended to "protect" youths instead criminalize their survival strategies, especially those of young girls. And youth and family courts extend the patriarchal power of the fathers beyond the family. As Chesney-Lind (1989:24) observes, "Young women in conflict with their parents (often for very legitimate reasons) may actually be forced by present laws into petty criminal activity, prostitution, and drug use." From a radical feminist perspective, the patriarchal legal and judicial systems thus leave girls few options.

Girls' responses to this conflict, along with the results of criminal justice system processing, endure long after adolescence. Serious adult delinquency also may be tied to the implementation of earlier survival strategies. In particular, sexual victimization at home is often linked to prostitution and drug use as street survival techniques. These behaviors continue in adulthood because these women "possess truncated educational backgrounds and virtually no marketable occupation skills" (Chesney-Lind 1989:23).

Chesney-Lind saw a feminist perspective on female delinquency as appropriate for two reasons. First, although both boys and girls are victims of violence and sexual abuse, girls' victimization, unlike that of boys', shapes their status as young women. Second, the victimizers of young women, who are, more often than not, adult males, can use formal control agencies to keep the young women at home. Girls' survival strategies provide not only their only hope but also the high potential for further criminalization and progressive movement into even more serious types of offending.

Socialist Feminism: Power–Control Theory   Socialist feminists recognize the importance of both class and gender, but neither factor assumes preeminence over the other, as class and gender are seen as interacting with one another. As James Messerschmidt (1986:42) observes, class and gender interact to create gender-based positions within class structures, resulting in different crimes for upper-level men and women, compared to men and women in society's lower levels, as well as differing opportunities to engage in these crimes. Class is structured by gender and gender by class; hence it is impossible to appreciate one without including the other.

Beginning in the late 1970s, John Hagan (1990) and his colleagues expressed the idea that we can best understand the relationship between gender and delinquency by focusing on intrafamilial power relations.[16] Hagan (1989a) saw family structure as incorporating patterns of power between spouses. The relative positions of the husband and wife in the workplace and in the home determine spousal power. For example, in patriarchal families, wives have little power compared with husbands, and daughters have little freedom compared with sons. These differences decrease in families with egalitarian structures, in which the spouses share power or in which the father is missing.

Hagan described a family dynamic. Patriarchal families generally produce daughters whose futures lie in domestic labor and consumption, and expect that sons will take part in economic production. In egalitarian families, the two power–control models overlap. Two sets of forces act to produce these different family types (Hagan, Simpson, and Gillis 1979; see also Hagan 1989a). In patriarchal families, the expectation is that fathers, as social control agents, will control daughters more than sons. The control of children, then, socially reproduces the parents' power relationships. In contrast, parents in egalitarian families share control efforts, so that controls imposed on daughters are similar to those imposed on sons.

Besides differential control patterns, relationships between parents and daughters in patriarchal families promote a reduced preference for risk taking by daughters. Hagan (1989a) defined risk-taking behavior as the antithesis of the passivity inherent in the daughter's role in patriarchal families. Conversely, sons in patriarchal families are encouraged to develop risk-taking tendencies. Patriarchal families see risk taking as a prerequisite for the development of entrepreneurial skills and other activities within the production and power spheres. In egalitarian families, both daughters and sons are encouraged to develop risk-taking attitudes.

Delinquency is a risk-taking activity. Consequently, power–control theory predicts larger gender-based differences in delinquency for patriarchal families than egalitarian families. The core assumption is that the presence of power and the absence of controls combine to create conditions conducive to common forms of delinquency (Hagan, Simpson, and Gillis 1985). Males continue to exhibit a higher proclivity for crime and delinquency, but in egalitarian families, the gender-ratio differences are less pronounced. Figure 11.3 contains summaries of Chesney-Lind's and Hagan's feminist theories of crime.

Marxist Feminism: The Critique of Sexual Politics   Marxist feminists follow the writings of Engels, who saw both class and gender divisions of labor as accounting for the relative social class positions of men and women (Beirne and Messerschmidt 2000:205). The evolution of capitalism, say **Marxist feminists,** assures men's dominant role. Male dominance clearly reflects the ideology of a society that is willing to subjugate women, first to capital and second to men. Capitalism often trivializes the labor of women as homemakers. However, such labor is essential in that it profits the capitalist class. Marxist feminists also point out that women's crimes, including shoplifting and prostitution, represent a twisted view of enforced domesticity. When they commit violent crimes, they show a preference for kitchen knives rather than guns (Balkan, Berger, and Schmidt 1980:211).

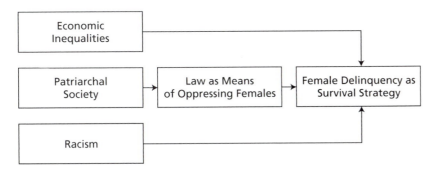

MARXIST AND FEMINIST THEORIES

(a) Chesney-Lind's Patriarchal Society Thesis

FIGURE 11.3a Feminist Theories of Crime

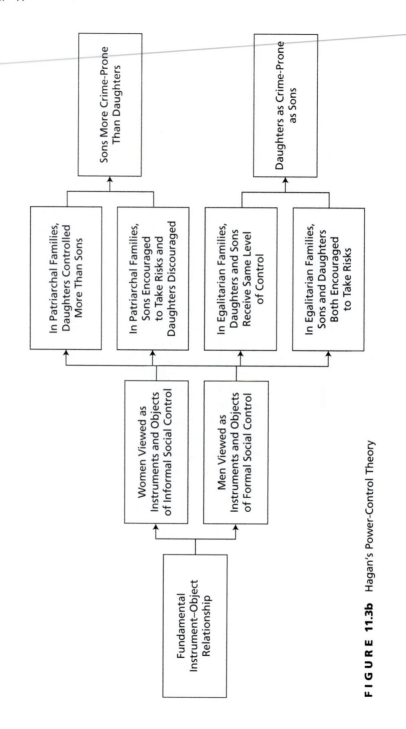

FIGURE 11.3b Hagan's Power-Control Theory

Julia and Herman Schwendinger's analysis of rape (1983) provides a powerful illustration of a Marxist-feminist critique. Societies without "commodity production" exhibit high levels of egalitarianism, and violence against women is almost nonexistent. When these societies begin to produce items for exchange, however, men gain control of the emerging "industry," resulting in a division of labor with men at the top. The position of women in society declines, and rapes and other violence against women increase.

Assessing Gender-Inclusive Theorizing

We have already assessed mainstream criminology's efforts to be gender-inclusive. At this point, we answer the following three questions about feminist theorizing: (1) What is the current state of research findings? (2) How have feminist theorists responded to critics? (3) How have feminist theories influenced criminology?

What Is the Current State of Research Findings?   Feminists tend to discount early liberation hypothesis studies (Gora 1982; Steffensmeier 1980). Marxist feminists and radical feminists offer explanations that are, like earlier instrumental Marxist explanations, more ideologies than theories, making any tests difficult. Moreover, unless male domination and other aspects of patriarchal society are shown to vary, nearly any tests will be impossible (Akers 1994:177).

For its part, tests of power–control explanations have yielded generally positive results for delinquency (Hagan and Kay 1990; Singer and Levine 1988). As a rule, however, these studies find nearly identical gender difference between patriarchal and egalitarian families (Morash and Chesney-Lind 1991; Blackwell 2000). Some critics question whether social class should be included in power–control theory at all (Jensen and Thompson 1990), although a restructured power–control theory (see below) gives it high prominence (McCarthy, Hagan, and Woodward 1999).

Including gender *and* power–control provides a gendered context for self-control theory. Brenda Blackwell and Alex Piquero (2005), using a random sample of adult urban dwellers, found that while low self-control was related to self-reported misconduct, the influence of power–control elements was undeniable. Parental monitoring was an important predictor for males and females, except for women raised in less patriarchal households. Blackwell and Piquero explain that to understand gender-based differences in the influences of self-control on crime, we should consider the element of power: Who has it in the family, and is it shared? The authors conclude that Gottfredson and Hirschi failed to give gender its proper deference in their theory. The nexus between parental socialization, family power-dynamics and gender, contend Blackwell and Piquero, are central to unraveling the influence of self-control on crime and analogous behavior.

How Have Feminist Theorists Responded to Critics?   Hagan's original idea was to look at the reproduction of gender relations across generations of parents and children. The focus was on patriarchal family structures, which Hagan and his associates believed would perpetuate the higher delinquency rates of males. Extensions of this theory through the 1980s and 1990s addressed what might happen as women entered the job market: They predicted that the rates of delinquency among their daughters would increase (Hagan et al. 1990; Grasmick, Tittle, et al. 1993). Feminists attacked these extensions of power–control theory (Chesney-Lind and Shelden 1992; Messerschmidt 1993; Naffine 1987). Why, they ask, would daughters become more like their brothers as their mothers entered the workforce? Wasn't it possible, they speculate, that instead of daughters becoming like sons, sons might become *less* delinquent?

John McCarthy and associates (1999) offers a feminist view of mothers' influence on sons in less patriarchal families. They note that boys and girls are exposed to many "gender activity" schemas about what is and is not appropriate behavior, and that these schemas vary across family structures. McCarthy and associates (1999:784) found that, consistent with traditional power–control theory, in the more patriarchal families, "males are more likely than females to support patriarchal schemas and offend." And consistent with the extended theory, "mothers in less patriarchal families appear to have made some inroads in challenging male resistance by altering their sons' support for conventional views" (McCarthy et al. 1999:785). The original power–control theory clearly overlooked the mothers' complex role in shaping the values and outlooks of their sons.

Brenda Blackwell (2000) extends this thesis by considering the fathers' role.[17] Her findings are consistent with previous power–control research. However, Blackwell includes informal social controls, such as embarrassment and shame, in her power–control model. Males raised in less patriarchal families perceive greater threats of embarrassment than do similarly situated females. Blackwell attributes this finding to the fact that in less patriarchal families, fathers assume more child-rearing responsibilities. In such families, sons, anxious to please their fathers, are more responsive to informal social controls. The net result may be that fathers in such families have a significant impact on their children's propensity for crime, but especially their male children.

How Have Feminist Theories Influenced Criminology?   Feminist critiques of male-dominated "mainstream" criminology caused mainstream criminologists to reevaluate the impact of gender on crime. Over the past 30 years, they have used it to study, among other things, youth gangs, street robberies, homicide victimization rates, intimate killings, and urban crime rates.[18] Moreover, gender's inclusion in tests of mainstream criminological theories, once a rarity, is on the rise. Increasingly, criminologists seek to understand the single best predictor of criminality: a person's biological sex.

Gender, Public Policy, and Criminal Justice Practices

Feminists, like conflict and Marxist theorists, argue for power sharing. Due to the broad range of perspectives under the feminist umbrella, some calls to action resemble the policies endorsed by conflict theorists, and others express themselves in the militant tones of radical Marxists. For example, Daly and Chesney-Lind (1988) argue that men's violence toward women must be given a higher priority by the justice system, particularly sexual and physical abuse. Daly and Chesney-Lind (1988:521–24) question the role of the state in supporting, perpetuating, and encouraging this violence. As evidence, they cite efforts to control pornography and prostitution, whereby local police engage in these activities only reactively, in response to public pressures, and discontinue them when the spotlight moves on to something new. Daly and Chesney-Lind also address the tacit acceptance of spousal violence and rape. They point to such policies as "presumptive arrest" of spouse abusers as a positive, if measured, attempt by the state to gain control; however, they doubt whether it will greatly reduce violence against women.

Many feminists further contend that equality with men is not their ultimate goal, as they have no interest in viewing the lives of men as a worthy behavioral norm. Under the doctrine of equality, "nearly all women's legal claims are construed as 'special treatment'" (Daly and Chesney-Lind 1988:524). Thus, the liberal feminist position of equal treatment is coming under increasing scrutiny and criticism. Invoking the imagery of racial discrimination, feminist legal scholars suggest that society may need to adopt new definitions of gender discrimination, ones that recognize "special needs." Some feminists are concerned that equal treatment of women in court, particularly at sentencing, "will prove unjust and may work ultimately against women," as in divorce and child custody laws (Daly and Chesney-Lind 1988:525). Women may also suffer from correctional policies that call for equal treatment, ignoring women's unique health problems and problems with incarceration (Daly and Chesney-Lind 1988:526).

No unified feminist-derived crime control policies exist. Most feminists do agree that the evaluation of any public policies should include the "gender question." According to Daly and Chesney-Lind (1988:525),

> A focus on gender and gender differences is not simply a focus on women or on what some scholars term "women's issues" in a narrow sense. It is and should be a far more encompassing enterprise, raising questions about how gender organizes the discipline of criminology, the institutions that fall within its scope, and the behavior of men and women.

The implications for criminology and criminal justice, then, extend beyond simply inserting gender into a given analysis; as proponents of critical race theory (see below) suggest, criminology should embrace a critical perspective on the development of criminological knowledge, including how we know what we know and why that knowledge is important.

Given these observations, a complete discussion of the implications of these theories for criminal justice procedures is beyond the scope of this text. Instead, to stimulate discussion and debate, we present representative examples.

Law Enforcement Practices   Feminists look for discriminatory practices based on gender. Race appears to confound our understanding of female contacts with police, as reflected in the feminist/women-of-color perspective. Christy Visher

(1983) observed that police chivalry exists only for white female offenders; black offenders were far more likely to be arrested. Similarly, white female victims receive preferential treatment from the police, especially when compared to their black counterparts (Smith, Visher, and Davidson 1984). As Sally Simpson (1989:614) noted, "Although chivalry may be alive and well for white women, it appears to be dead (if it ever existed) for blacks." We return to this topic in the next section of this chapter.

Judicial Practices   Early in feminist criminology, judicial decision making emerged as the point in the administration of justice at which the operation of sexist, paternalistic, or antifeminist attitudes could be observed (cf. Adler 1975:252; Simon 1975a:107). Court sentencing has been a traditional focus of feminist critiques of the criminal justice system. Evidence of the extent and nature of **gendered justice** (Simpson 1989:614) may depend upon the theoretical perspective that frames the research. For example, researchers using a liberal feminist argument reported that women receive lenient treatment early in the process, such as less restrictive and less expensive methods of release from jail before trial (Nagel 1983). At sentencing, however, the results were extremely variable. They ranged from more lenient sentences to no differences, once the researchers eliminated differences due to offense type and prior records (cf. Bernstein, Kick, Leung, and Schulz 1977; Farrington and Morris 1983; Wilbanks 1987). However, women who commit nontraditional female crimes or violate female sexual norms may face harsher sentences (Bernstein et al. 1977; Chesney-Lind 1973).

Daly (1987a:154) observed other evidence of gendered justice decisions. Gendering occurs when the court formally recognizes that women are responsible for the care of others and that men must provide for their families' financial support. **Familied decisions** occur when the court perceives that removing either the man or the woman would cause hardship. Courts often view men or women without family responsibilities in nearly identical fashion: They receive harsher treatment than do persons with family responsibilities. Women with families receive the most lenient treatment of all due to "the differing social costs arising from separating [women] from their families" (Daly 1987b:287). Thus, outright gender-based discrimination may not cause differential court treatment. Rather, the courts' behavior may best be understood as an attempt to protect nuclear families and the value systems associated with them (Daly 1989; Eaton 1986).

For critical feminists, male control of social power explains gendered justice. From this perspective, pretrial release and sentencing are best understood, after eliminating the confounding effects of criminal record and offense seriousness, in terms of the interaction between family and gender. Candace Kruttschnitt (1982) reported that women are more likely to receive probation if they are dependent upon fathers or husbands.

Correctional Practices   Liberal feminists call women in prison "the forgotten offenders" (Pollock-Byrne 1990:59; Simon 1975b). This label may stem from the relative paucity of female prison inmates, accounting as they do for less than 10 percent of the adult prison population; moreover, women's prisons are generally smaller than those for men, and there are far fewer such prisons (West and Sabol 2008). Finally, female inmates receive little attention from reformers because they, unlike their male counterparts, call little attention to themselves through such institutional behaviors as prison riots and uprisings (Bartollas and Conrad 1992:467).

The conditions of confinement for female inmates range from lenient to harsh (Simpson 1989:615). As Clemens Bartollas and John Conrad (1992:474) reported, the place of confinement is typically uniform in appearance:

> Women's prisons, unlike men's, often resemble college campuses rather than fortress penitentiaries. There are no gun towers, armed guards, or stonewalls. With few exceptions, there are no fences strung on top with concertina wire…. These institutions are frequently rural, pastoral settings that suggest tranquility and "easy time" for the inmate. Women's prisons may be more attractive than men's prisons, but this peaceful appearance is deceptive.

The "campus model," which emerged in the 1930s, was supposed to instill "traditional" feminine value systems and work habits (Clear and Cole 1997:300–301; Mays and Winfree 1998:158–59). Rehabilitation programs included cosmetology, parenting skills, and domestic training. These programs stressed moral and social improvement, goals borrowed from the early twentieth-century "reformatory era" (Champion 1990:448–50).

Feminist views of prisons vary widely (Simpson 1989:615–17). Radical feminists see prisons for women as institutionalized attempts to control female sexuality (Chesney-Lind 1973). For example, if diseased prostitutes were incarcerated, their cure was a condition of release (Rasche 1974). Socialists often describe female prisoners in terms of gender, race, and class. Prisons were for evil and immoral women, where primarily black female felons were treated like men; reformatories were intended for white working-class misdemeanants, who were "fallen women" and salvageable (Rafter 1985; Rasche 1974). For Marxist feminists, women's prisons are places for the retooling of "deviant women for gender-appropriate roles in capitalist patriarchal societies…. Societal control of female deviance serves the needs of capitalism. When those needs change, so too will the mechanisms and directions of social control" (Simpson 1989:616–17). In the women's prison of the early twentieth century, Marxism met feminism, as correctional institutions wrestled with the fates of criminal women.

RACE AND CRIMINOLOGICAL THEORIES

- What did you conclude from the crime statistics for each racial and ethnic group? If, as physical and social scientists contend, race is a sociological construct and not a biological one, who (or what) gets the blame for the observed disparities?

- Recently there has been much talk about race and ethnicity no longer being important in a blended and enlightened America, especially one that elected its first African American president. Given what you have read about race and crime links, are these people being premature or overly optimistic?

Race and ethnicity are a "third-rail" in criminology. No one who touches it can expect to escape unscathed.[19] Race is a topic, like gender, about which nearly everyone has an opinion, particularly when it comes to crime and justice. Eric Holder, the nation's first black attorney general, observed this about race in America: "Though this nation has proudly thought of itself as an ethnic melting pot, in things racial we have always been and I believe continue to be, in too many ways, essentially a nation of cowards" ("America is a 'nation of cowards' on racial matters, Holder says" 2009:4A). Initial reactions to his challenge that Americans fail to talk about race relations—its history and its present context— in meaningful ways were mixed, but clearly Holder touched the third-rail of race in America.

Our goal here is to separate fact from fiction, lay opinion from informed opinion, and theory from ideology. Attempts to explain the disproportionate minority contacts represented in the official crime statistics have taken criminologists down many different paths since the early nineteenth century. One possible explanation is that economically deprived persons are more likely to commit the types of crime that come to the attention of the police. Such overrepresentation may also reflect overt discrimination in the policies and practices of individual actors and agencies within the criminal justice system These practices and policies, combined with the depressed socioeconomic levels of many in minority communities, place minority-group members at distinct disadvantages when they come in contact with members of the criminal justice community, be it police on the streets, judges and juries in court, or correctional officers in prison or jail. Studies of differential arrest rates for adults and juveniles do not find a link between police conduct and the disproportionate number of minority youth coming in contact with the police (Pope and Snyder 2003; Sorenson, Hope, and Stemen 2003). However, race and ethnicity do appear to influence processing decision for adults and juveniles in about two-thirds of all court cases (Pope and Freyerherm 1990a, 1990b, 1991).

Institutionalized racism, a form of prejudicial treatment whereby criminal justice decisions place persons of color at a significant disadvantage, may be a core feature of the American criminal justice system, but that determination is beyond the scope of this book. Critical criminologists are sensitive to arguments that explore endemic racism as a source of conflict. Mainstream criminologists too have sought to contextualize their causal arguments by including race and ethnicity. In both instances, irrespective of whether the theories have conservative, liberal, or even radical ideology behind them, the messenger is often pilloried with the message. This should come as no great surprise, since criminology—beginning with Beccaria's statements on the unfairness inherent in contemporary justice processing and official reactions to his claims—has had a sociopolitical subtext. Much current theorizing about race, crime, and justice has the same proclivity for controversy or, at the very least, dissent.

Mainstream Criminological Theorizing about Race

The inclusion of race in criminological theories has a checkered history. As with gender, mainstream criminologists have considered race as a causal factor and as a mediating or conditional factor. In spite of the fact that the biological and genetic evidence tells us that race is not viable as a scientific measure, as a sociological measure it still has a great deal of cache. That is, people may be responding to a person's race as a social threat, rather than the race itself causing anyone's behavior, an idea to which we return later in this section. First, we must review various mainstream claims associated with race, including the claim that it causes intelligence, which itself is the cause of crime.

Race as a Causal Factor   Psychologist Arthur Jensen (1969) suggested a race–IQ–crime link in an essay on genetic heritage. Like his mentor Hans Eysenck, Jensen was a differential psychologist, interested in how and why people behaved differently from one another. He divided intelligence into Level I—**associative learning,** the simple retention of input, or rote memorization of simple facts and skills—and Level II—**conceptual learning,** the ability to manipulate and transform information. Jensen believed that IQ tests measured Level II intelligence. Interested in how culture, development, and genetics influence IQ, Jensen began extensive testing of minority group children in the 1960s, leading him to two conclusions. First, he believed that 80 percent of intelligence was based on heredity (nature) and the remaining 20 percent on the environment (nurture). Second, he contended that, although all races were equal in terms of Level I intelligence, Level II occurred with significantly higher frequency among whites than blacks, and among Asian Americans somewhat more than whites. Given his first premise, he was led to the conclusion that whites are inherently better able to engage in conceptual learning than are blacks, a conclusion viewed by many as racist (Lederberg 1969).

Jensen found a champion in Robert Gordon, who carried the argument to its next level. In an early statement supporting the connection between race, IQ, and delinquency, Gordon (1976) cited Jensen's belief about the dominant role of genetics in IQ. He saw striking parallels between IQ scores and delinquency rates in court records and juvenile commitment data. Gordon, largely without supporting evidence, connected race and IQ to delinquency. Gordon (1987) later completed this argument in an attack on the sociological claim that what is being measured is socioeconomic status (SES), and not IQ. He subsequently endorsed a race–IQ–delinquency thesis. After conducting a series of analyses of lifetime delinquency prevalence rates, he reported that IQ is a better predictor of delinquency than SES (Gordon 1987:91). As for the race–IQ–crime connection, Gordon (1987:92) stated that "it is time to consider the black–white IQ difference seriously when confronting the problem of crime in American society."

An IQ-based model, he claimed, best explained black–white differences in delinquency rates.

In *The Bell Curve,* Herrnstein and Murray, like Jensen and Gordon, argue that race is a precursor of IQ. Hence, certain races, but particularly blacks, genetically fated to lower-than-normal intelligence, also exhibit a similarly higher tendency to commit crimes. Herrnstein and Murray did allow that not all low-cognitive-ability persons commit crime. Moreover, crime rate changes cannot be attributed solely to changes in cognition, as other factors place low-cognition persons at greater risk than in the past. At the same time, they ignored the suggestion that standardized tests have a dark side, as such tests can disguise racist motives (Chabris 1998; Fraser 1995). Indeed, persons raised in more privileged economic circumstances—homes with higher socioeconomic status—have a higher IQ regardless of race. So what does IQ really measure?

Race as a Mediating or Conditional Factor   Mainstream criminological theories recognize the significance of race as a mediating or conditional factor. Many tests of social process theorists, especially those theories claiming to be general theories of crime, address the role of race or ethnicity. For example, the measures of self-control perform in very similar ways to predict the self-reported crime and analogous behavior of African American and Native American adolescents compared to non-Hispanic whites (Morris, Wood, and Dunaway 2006; Vazsonyi and Crosswhite 2004). Earlier, we related that social bonding, self-control, and social learning theories also work well in a cross-cultural context (see Chapter 7); that is, these theories, and their concepts and associated variables, transcend national and even cultural barriers. These collective findings suggest that the social processes experienced by all youths are very similar, although some differences exist by gender but not by race (Rosenbaum 1987; Vazsonyi and Crosswhite 2006). In sum, race is a relatively unimportant factor in understanding the influence of social process factors on who is likely to commit crimes.

Social organizational theories also show sensitivity to the construct of race. However, it is not race alone that concerns them, but rather the nexus of race and socioeconomic conditions. For example, Karen Parker and Scott Maggard (2005), when measuring urban disadvantage (e.g., poverty rates, labor market conditions, and income inequality) and social disorganization (e.g., family disruption by divorce and level of residential mobility) in 168 major U.S. cities, provide race-specific analyses of drug arrests. A national shift away from manufacturing jobs between 1980 and 1990 significantly affected black arrests for drug possession. Moreover, social disorganization proved equally important for African Americans and whites.

Institutional anomie may also be a salient race-sensitive force; however, the results of race-specific analyses are inconclusive. In one study, this time using a sample of urban residents and institutionalized offenders, Stephen Cernkovich and associates (2000) reveal that African Americans maintain a stronger belief in the American Dream than do whites. They considered success goal orientation—for example, commitment to material things or willingness to sacrifice for a career—as indicators of the American Dream. However, a stronger commitment of success goal orientation does not translate into support for bonding theory's suggestions about ties to social institutions and offense involvement for either whites or blacks. When Cernkovich and associates looked at the extent to which strains to success modeled behavior, they found that such strains only explained the illegal conduct of whites, not blacks. They suggest that perhaps whites more than blacks feel the impact of being blocked from success. As Cernkovich and associates (2000:163) summarize it: "In short, even though African Americans experience greater levels of objective deprivation, whites may experience greater levels of subjective or relative deprivation." Blacks have had to deal with such barriers from birth; whites are unaccustomed to them. Hence, confronted with these specific strains, whites more than blacks may resort to crime as a legitimate response.

Structural theories that focus on subcultural responses provide unique insights into the role of race as a conditional factor in criminological studies. In his study of homicides in Philadelphia, Marvin Wolfgang (1958) found that most criminal homicides—those not premeditated or caused by some serious mental disease or defect—occur predominantly among the members of certain social groups living in certain neighborhoods. These homicides followed relatively trivial events. Wolfgang speculated that the events took on greater significance due to the meanings attached to them by participants, mostly minority-group males. What was this special meaning? Many criminal homicides, Wolfgang (1958:188–89) believed, followed a predictable pattern:

> The significance of a jostle, a slight derogatory remark, or the appearance of a weapon in the hands of an adversary are stimuli differentially perceived and interpreted by Negroes and whites, males and females. Social expectations of response in particular types of social interactions result in differential "definitions of the situation." A male is usually expected to defend the name or honor of his mother, the virtue of womanhood.... When such a cultural norm response is elicited from an individual engaged in social interplay with others who harbor the same response mechanism, physical assaults, altercations, and violent domestic quarrels that result in homicide are likely to be common.

Working with Franco Ferracuti, Wolfgang developed a theory of homicide, suggesting that many murderers are young, nonwhite, lower-class males who share the conduct norms of a **subculture of violence** (Wolfgang and Ferracuti 1967:153). Echoing Sellin, they viewed such individuals as in conflict with the dominant culture's values: The latter value life; the former value pride, self-respect, dignity, and status in the community more highly than life. When someone in the subculture verbally or physically challenges another, the conduct norms may require action. Only by this means can he or she counter the loss created by the challenger's actions. If both are members of the subculture of violence, the event may quickly escalate into a deadly confrontation. Wolfgang and Ferracuti (1967:156) likened it to a wartime situation in which "it is either him or me."

In sum, Wolfgang and Ferracuti observe that middle-class families and communities avoid routine corporal punishment, do not take exceptional umbrage at derogatory remarks or incidental slights, and view violence as unacceptable in dispute resolution. In lower-class families and communities, attempts to end disputes by words rather than actions often meet with ridicule and derision. Wolfgang and Ferracuti (1967:163) acknowledge that these differences are endemic and that lower-class residents culturally transmit them to successive generations, especially males.

Critical Criminology and Race

In this section, we review two orientations to the race–crime connection. First, we reexamine conflict theories that emphasize the role of race as a mediator or conditional variable. As we discussed previously, the use and abuse of power is central to the causal statements present in critical theories, whether they derive from group, legal, cultural, or economic arguments. Second, we review *critical race theory,* an emergent perspective on the race–crime link that not only shares an emphasis on power, but also adds additional arguments that challenge traditional liberal views on crime.

Conflict and Race   As the twentieth century progressed, conflict theorists turned their attention increasingly to the role of race as a central factor in conflicts, both intranationally and internationally. A key idea contained in these studies is the evolution of the idea of the *symbolic threat.* To say that something is a symbolic threat does not mean that it is not a real threat to those perceiving it. Rather, in this context, a **symbolic threat** is some characteristic, in this case a person's race, that comes to stand for—is a symbol of—something larger, that being the replacement of the dominant group or race in the social hierarchy by this "competing" race. In fact, the dominate group may see even expansions in the size of minority groups as a threat (Blumer 1958; Blalock 1967).

The idea of race serving as a symbolic threat—often described as the **racial-threat hypothesis**—merged with conflict theory in the late twentieth century as a means of explaining, among other things, police and judicial conduct.[20] For example, *racial profiling* by police is one topic that has captured the imagination of criminologists and laypersons alike. Phrases like "driving while black" and "driving while brown" have entered the criminological lexicon since the merger of lawsuits and research efforts in the late 1990s (ACLU 1999). The research results, in a word, are inconsistent (Petrocelli et al. 2003; Lange, Johnson, and Voas 2005). Black drivers appear slightly more likely to be stopped than others, but do not suffer other legal consequences as a result. A study of police actions in Richmond, Virginia, found that while blacks are stopped more often than are whites, they are not more likely to be searched and are actually less likely to be arrested than are whites (Smith and Petrocelli 2001). Matthew Petrocelli and associates (2003), looking at police decisions to stop, search, and arrest in the same city, found that the sole factor in the decision to stop is the crime rate in the surrounding neighborhood (i.e., the higher the crime rate, the greater the likelihood of being stopped); however, when those stops occur in a black neighborhood, the likelihood of a search is greater than if the neighborhood is predominantly white;

finally, a higher crime rate and higher percent black population result in lower arrest rates. They suggest that given the tendency to search black suspects, a "correction" of sorts occurs (i.e., a tendency to warn and release rather than arrest blacks compared to whites), as the bar for a legal stop and search had not been met in most such cases.

Malcolm Holmes and associates (2008), in a unique study of police resource allocation across the southwestern U.S. border region, also used conflict theory as a key explanatory variable. Their results were also mixed. While major cities across the region allocate police resources based on the percent of black residents, a finding consistent with conflict theory, the same was not true of Hispanics. Proximity to the border and social class may hold some insights into these inconsistent findings. Specifically, cities at a greater distance from the border with Mexico spent less money on police, a finding that supports the idea that it is undocumented immigrants that pose the greatest symbolic race threat (see also Calavita 1996; Hasian and Delgado 1998). The researchers further suggest that while many blacks in the region are economically impoverished, Hispanics as a group are less impoverished and more socially integrated into the southwestern border region. Importantly, the researchers acknowledge that research such as theirs typically oversimplifies what are often complex conflict arguments.[21]

Conflict criminologists, then, have made race an essential part of their studies of U.S. police and court practices, particularly in situations where discretion can and often does play a central role in decision making. As the following comparative box reveals, the racial-threat phenomenon is not solely an American problem.

Critical Race Theory Early in the twentieth century, sociologist, historian, and social critic W.E.B. Du Bois (1903) warned that racism would serve as a major social problem for the foreseeable future. In the opinion of proponents of critical race theory, who see in Dubois (1868–1963) a prescient visionary, he was right then and he is right now. Critical race theory has long been associated with a branch of critical legal studies that addresses questions of racial subordination, discrimination, and racism. We can define **critical race theory (CRT)** as follows: "A framework or set of basic perspectives, methods, and pedagogy that seeks to identify, analyze, and transform those structural and cultural aspects of society that maintain the subordination and marginalization of People of Color" (Solórzano 1997:6).[22] To this end, CRT adherents, or **race–Crits** as they refer to themselves, see their mission as challenging the traditional race and racism discourses; they focus on how the legal system facilitates and perpetuates the discrimination and subordination of certain ethnic groups (Bell 1995).

Since its beginnings in legal critical circles, the CRT perspective has also found its way into education, history, sociology, and criminology. No matter what the subject matter, CRT follows four general themes (Solórzano 1997). First, race-Crits—like Du Bois before them—see race and racism as timeless, endemic, and permanently entwined in the social fabric of American society. Second, they challenge the liberal ideals of objectivity and racial sensitivity as a form of constructed ideology, arguing that such ideals are blinds intended to hide

COMPARATIVE CRIMINOLOGY—WORLD VIEWS ON CRIME AND JUSTICE: The Racial-Threat Hypothesis and Criminal Sanctions

The racial-threat hypothesis yields interesting ways in which to view comparative justice practices. The idea that racial minorities suffer imprisonment at higher rates than nonminorities is central to a race-inclusive conflict argument. Internationally, who is a racial (or ethnic) minority varies from nation to nation. As we noted earlier in this chapter, no single race owns the concept of racism. If the minority-threat hypothesis is correct, it is the presence of a race-based minority that is important, not the race of that minority.

One way to operationalize minority threat is to examine population heterogeneity. This is what Rick Ruddell and Martin Urbina did in their cross-national study of the abolition of the death penalty and imprisonment rates in 140 nations. In order to examine the impact of population heterogeneity, they statistically eliminated the effects of modernization, political repression, violent crime, and economic stress factors. What they found was that nations with diverse populations incarcerate more people, while nations with less diversity ban the death penalty. Ruddell and Martin suggested that the concept of minority threat be extended to include indicators of language and religion, as well as race and ethnicity, extensions that Sellin would have appreciated.

One could argue that, given different political practices, such a wide array of nations could cloud the influence of minority threat on imprisonment. Jacobs and Kleban (2003) used a panel (1970 to 1995) of 13 progressive democracies and looked at ties between incarceration rates (i.e., annual number of prisoners per 100,000 population) and the following factors: offense rates (i.e., homicide and all crime rates), social disorganization levels (i.e., infant mortality rate and out-of-wedlock birthrate), and political arrangements (i.e., centrally managed democracies or the corporatist model versus decentrally managed democracies or the federalist model). Racial threat was, once again, reflected by the percentage of minorities in a given nation's population. Their analyses revealed that high levels of social disorganization predicts high incarceration levels. Corporatism yields lower incarceration rates, while the reverse is true of federalism. That is, imprisonment rates are most substantial when the public has the greatest political influence. Centralism contributes to a penal system that is restitutive and less exclusionary than in decentralized governments. Finally, large minority populations produce higher incarceration rates, again supporting the cross-national utility of the minority-threat hypothesis.

SOURCES: Jacobs and Kleban (2003); Ruddell and Urbina (2004).

the hegemonic or ruling practices of the dominant groups in America, principally Caucasian males. Third, race-Crits exhibit a strong commitment to *social justice,* particularly as related to the eradication of racial subjugation (Arrigo 2001). Finally, CRT encourages the expansion and inclusion of the experiential knowledge of women *and* people of color. Such knowledge, primarily available through their lived experiences and oral or written histories, is both legitimate and central to any understanding of subjugated or "forgotten peoples" (Solórzano 1997).

Race-Crits use the language and words of the oppressed as central features of their work. Storytelling and **counterstorytelling,** the latter referring to reexamining previously related stories told about people of color by those who do not fully appreciate CRT, are their central methods. The experiences of the people of color, told directly by them alone, have the power to reveal endemic, systemic, and institutionalized racism and its consequences, as well as to suggest ways to reduce its negative impact on the oppressed. In *Critical Race Theory: The Cutting Edge,* editors Richard Delgado and Jean Stefancic (2001a) provide dozens of research exemplars. For example, Ian Haney Lopez's (2001) finding that over a period of nearly 200 years, various Supreme Court decisions, from

Dred Scott v. Sanford [23] to *Plessy v. Fergusson*[24] and a host of others, helped create the primacy of whites in social, political, and economic arenas. For another, George Martinez's (2001) claim that judicial decisions concerning the "whiteness" of Mexican Americans largely depended on whether it would hurt the interests of Mexican Americans, in which case they were white, but if the decision made no difference in the status of Mexican Americans, they were nonwhite. In this same vein, James Gordon's (2001) genealogical studies that speculate on the claim that Associate Justice John Harlan, author of the dissent in *Plessey v.Fergusson,* where he argued for racial equality, had a black brother. Collectively, the works in this volume present a view of race and American society at times sharply conflicts with the one portrayed by the non-race-Crit researchers of crime and justice issues.

According to race-Crits, such narratives expose three mainstream myths: (1) that color-blind policies will yield a society free of racism, arguing instead that endemic racism is difficult if not impossible to purge from society; (2) the idea that racism is only perpetuated by extremists, seeing it, instead, as the resulting from the actions and inactions of mainstream society; and (3) the notion that racism exists in isolation, adopting instead the perspective that it is inexplicably related to other forms of oppression, including sexism, homophobia, and classism (Valdes, Culp, and Harris 2002).[25] Hence, it is the operation of the racist criminal justice system, as a reflection of endemic racism of American society, that creates the social and legal conditions conducive to the overrepresentation of blacks in crime statistics and the nation's prisons (see also In Their Own Words, for how race and racism were viewed by two of critical racial theory's intellectual forefathers living almost a century apart).

Assessing Race-Inclusive Theorizing

The IQ–crime connection was thoroughly assessed in Chapter 5. Here it seems sufficient to reiterate that as race has lost its biological/genetic utility as a categorical variable, what we are left with is race as a sociological factor. That is, if the IQs of African Americans and other minorities were indeed lower than those of non-Hispanic whites, then those lower scores are due to social forces, not biological ones. Other factors, such as racism or racial stereotyping, intervene between the identification of a child as a minority group member and a score on an IQ test, irrespective of the ties between IQ and crime (see Chapter 5).

Critics of the subculture-of-violence thesis question its racial motivations; hence, the theory is sometimes called the **black subculture-of-violence thesis**.[26] Liqun Cao and associates (1997), among others, questioned whether blacks are more likely than whites to express violent tendencies. Using a national survey of males under the age of 65, they found that white males are significantly more likely to express violent tendencies in defensive situations, and that there are no racial differences in offensive situations. Although this study does not resolve the issue, blacks as a group are no more likely than whites to embrace a subculture of violence (Cao, Adams, and Jensen 1997:376).

IN THEIR OWN WORDS: Critical Race Theorists on Being Black in American Society

Critical race theory has its origins in the scholarship of W.E.B. Du Bois. However, modern versions are strongly tied to the work of critical law scholar Derrick Bell. Below are sampling of their writings.

W.E.B. Du Bois on the souls of "black folk": It is a peculiar sensation, this double-consciousness, this sense of always looking at one's self though the eyes of others, to measuring one's soul by the tape of a world that looks on in amused contempt and pity. One ever feels his two-ness,—an American, a Negro; two souls, two thoughts, two unreconciled strivings; two warring ideals in one dark body, whose dogged strengths alone keeps it from being torn asunder" (p. 887).

Derrick Bell on being black: "Black people are the magical faces at the bottom of society's well. Even the poorest whites, those who must live their lives only a few levels above, gain their self-esteem by gazing down on us. Surely, they must know that their deliverance depends on letting down their ropes. Only

by working together is escape possible. Over time, many reach out, but most simply watch, mesmerized into maintaining their unspoken commitment to keeping us where we are, at whatever cost to them or to us" (p. v).

Derrick Bell on racial equality and critical thinking: "The goal of racial equality is, while comforting to many whites, more illusory than real for blacks. For too long, we have worked for substantive reform, then settled for weakly worded and poorly enforced legislation, indeterminate judicial decisions, token government positions, even holidays. I repeat. If we are to seek new goals for our struggles, we must first reassess the work of the racial assumptions on which, without careful thought, we have presumed too much and relied on too long" (p. 14).

SOURCES: Bell (1992); Du Bois (1903) quoted in Wideman (2001).

Adding race to power-based theories, especially the racial-threat hypothesis, essentializes this important construct in criminology. Studies of conflict and symbolic threats have tended to focus on two topics: police–citizen interactions and criminal sanctioning generally, but especially the use of imprisonment. While the racial profiling practices of police yield inconsistent results, research that looks at drug-related arrest and sentencing practices (Mosher 2001), civil rights complaints (Holmes 2000; Lersch 1998), or juvenile court decision-making (MacDonald 2003) tend to find race differentials, although there are exceptions to this generalization (Franklin and Fearn 2008; Rodriguez 2007). David Eitle and associates (2002) took a different approach: They obtained indicators of black-on-white crime from South Carolina's National Incident-Based Reporting System, which they took as reflecting black-crime threat, part of the racial-threat hypothesis. These types of crime increased black arrest levels: As the percent of offenses involving a black perpetrator and white victim crime goes up, the likelihood of a black individual being arrested increases; the same is not true of black-on-black crime. As a general observation, then, conflict theories, but especially those using a racial-threat component, yield important and interesting insights into the administration of criminal justice.

Besides these specific assessments of race-inclusive theories about crime and delinquency, we offer the following criticisms of CRT:

- *CRT's status as a theory or a social movement.* Some race-Crits suggest strongly that CRT is a movement, not a theory (Crenshaw et al. 1995). In its current form, CRT is an ideology about the creation of inequities in

American society that has clear connections to, *inter alia,* DMC. As importantly, to the extent that it is a theory, CRT lacks the structure needed to tests its basic assertions.

- *Use of highly subjective data may limit attempts to test CRT.* The use of narratives and storytelling (and counterstorytelling) is highly subjective, leading to multiple interpretations of the same set of facts (Delgado and Stefancic 2001a,b). Race-Crits also place limits on who can use CRT, which may cause some observers to question the perspective's objectivity and generalizability. Specifically, in order to use this orientation as a research tool, the researcher must be a member of a group under the conceptual umbrella of "victims" (Bergerson 2003).[27]

- *Attack on social liberals by race-Crits is a resurrected form of the same criticisms offered by Marxists in the 1970s against the liberal establishment.* The race-Crits are highly critical of social liberals, whom they accuse of caving to the demands of powerful white interests in society. This is the same criticism leveled by Marxists and some feminists against liberals, who, critics claimed, knew that capitalism was the root cause of crime, but rather than work against that system, they worked within it and became corrupted by capitalism. Given CRT's origins in Marxist critique, this is not a surprising criticism (Schneider 2001:90).

- *CRT employs a flawed method for the postmodernist era.* In a nutshell, postmodernists reject the usefulness of narratives and storytelling as a way to achieve superior knowledge, viewing them as modernist artifacts with limited utility (Henry and Milovanovic 1996). This critique has created a schism between postmodernist theorizing and CRT (Schneider 2001).

Race, Ethnicity, Public Policy, and Criminal Justice Practices

One policy option suggested by race-inclusive theories is to create local, state, and federal programs that provide alternative cultural messages. However, this approach resembles the existing public education system, one heavily criticized by Race-crits in particular. Wolfgang, Ferracuti, Curtis, and others also warned that several other policies have a dark side. For example, one possibility is the forced removal of an entire generation from these subcultures, allowing the undesired and offensive norms and values to die out. The U.S. government tried this method to eradicate American Indian culture, using the Bureau of Indian Affairs' Indian Schools. Another possibility is to isolate the entire subculture. These alternatives resemble the practices of totalitarian regimes, both in fact (Nazi Germany) and in fiction (*Brave New World, 1984*).

Curtis (1975a,b), in particular, suggests that a full understanding of race-based violence requires an appreciation for the general social conditions that underlie its creation. Curtis blamed repressive police violence directed at black ghettos and a general absence of legitimate opportunities for success. As Curtis argued, attempts to reduce the subculture of violence must do more than dilute its influence and give hope for assimilation. Policy makers must also address the root causes of the subculture in the first place.

Elijah Anderson (1994) elaborated on Curtis's theme, viewing the reduction of alienation among minority-group inner-city youths as a precursor to providing alternatives to a unique street code that promotes violence. He warned against the "get tough" approach:

> Many feel not only that they have little to lose by going to prison but they have something to gain. The toughening-up experienced in prison can actually enhance one's reputation on the streets. Hence the system loses influence over the hard core who are without jobs with little perceptible stake in the system. (Anderson 1994:94)

Instead, Anderson (1999) theorized that adopting the street code insulated street youths in highly disorganized, high-crime communities, gaining them respect among peers and potential assailants alike. However, Eric Stewart and associates (2006) tested this **code of the streets hypothesis.** Based on a longitudinal study of African American adolescents in such neighborhoods, they concluded that adopting the code of the streets only makes a bad situation worse: Youths who adopt the code run the risk of higher victimization levels than would normally occur in dangerous and disorganized communities.

This return to the streets as a way to understand criminogenic situations, looking at foreground causes of crime and delinquency as contrasted with background causes (e.g., sociobiological factors), is consistent with the admonitions of Bill McCarthy and John Hagan (1992:625): "The finding that variables measuring situational adversity are salient in the causation of street delinquency is important not only because it redirects and broadens our theoretical perspective on crime and delinquency, but also because it extends our understanding of street life more generally." It is the conditions on the street, they claim, that may yield the best insights into crimes and their prevention.

Law Enforcement Practices   The race-inspired practices of police, in the face of mounting empirical evidence, are undeniable. Whether they are the intentional acts of a few "bad apples" as some contend (which is a difficult position to justify given their widespread nature); the result of recruitment practices that select into police work persons who are prone to authoritarian attitudes, including racism (which calls into question the entire selection process); a protective response learned through repeated interactions with criminals and others at the margin of society (which suggests that police administrators should revisit systems of punishers and rewards) or an endemic condition in American society that is simply mirrored in police work (which is a position endorsed by many conflict and critical race theorists) is the subject of much speculation and research (see also Chapters 6, 7, and 8 for more on these subjects).

Perception is often more important than reality. For example, minority group members are far more likely than non-Hispanic whites to see a divide in the administration of justice based on race: Non-Hispanic whites perceive fewer instances of injustice than both African Americans and Hispanics, and African

Americans perceive more injustice than Hispanics, placing Hispanics in the middle ground on the question of perceived injustices between non-Hispanic whites and blacks (Buckler and Unnever 2008; see also Hagan, Shedd, and Payne 2005). Hence, the extent to which police feed this image of reacting differently to non-Hispanic whites compared to all others only serves to reinforce the misperception. Police sensitivity to image-management and interpersonal skills during interactions with high potential for conflict may ameliorate an already difficult situation, the contentious police–citizen interaction.

Judicial Practices   Race-inclusive criminological theories offer several suggestions for judicial relief, especially the conclusions of race-Crits. Besides their own narratives and counternarratives, race-Crits endorse attacks on the use of racially charged words, especially when used against the interests of racial minorities. First, they question whether race-hatred speech and associated acts are protected; second, they ask whether the U.S. Constitution should protect them. For example, in 1990, a group of male youths in St. Paul, Minnesota, burned a cross in the front yard of a local black family. They were charged with the violation of St. Paul's Bias-Motivated Crime Ordinance. The state claimed the act constituted a *hate crime* while the defendants exerted their rights to free speech, which, they claimed, included the act of cross burning. Two years later, the U.S. Supreme Court agreed, striking down the ordinance and vacating the conviction of one of the defendants. In *R.A.V. v. City of St. Paul* (505 U.S. 377), Associate Justice Antonin Scalia, writing for the Supreme Court's 9–0 majority, condemned the act itself as reprehensible, but went onto reaffirm the primacy of the First Amendment. As Scalia wrote:

> The State may choose to prohibit only that obscenity which is the most patently offensive in *its prurience*—i.e., that which involves the most lascivious displays of sexual activity. But it may not prohibit, for example, only that obscenity which includes offensive *political* messages. And the Federal Government can criminalize only those threats of violence that are directed against the President, since the reasons why threats of violence are outside the First Amendment (protecting individuals from the fear of violence, from the disruption that fear engenders, and from the possibility that the threatened violence will occur) have special force when applied to the person of the President.

Mari Matsuda and associates (1993) attacked the 9–0 decision and Justice Scalia's opinion as totally devoid of historical and social context. Race-Crits argue, contrary to Scalia's First Amendment protection argument, that when acts of speech, such as the cross burning, are used to intimidate and portray violence, they must be considered within the historical context and viewed as attempts to control and dominate the subject group. While the CRT argument did not prevail in *R.A.V.*, race-Crits often provide support for legal cases involving hate crimes, where they present *amicus curiae* briefs, a legal strategy whereby someone without legal standing can present an argument to the court in the form of a written statement, to aid the court in dealing with what are often complex social and legal issues such as those reflected in *R.A.V.*

Correctional Practices   Race is central to understanding the nation's burgeoning prison population. The various race-sensitive theories contained in this chapter tend to focus on race-specific contacts with the police or at sentencing. It makes sense that if far larger numbers of racial and ethnic minorities—like males generally—enter the "justice funnel," then there will be far more of them to endure the other elements of justice processing, including imprisonment. Once in prison, race dynamics likely impact a person's daily life as much if not more than on the outside. Within prisons, there is often conflict over power and control. Inmate cliques—and those with ties to extrainstitutional gangs and subcultures unique to prisons—can further erode already tenuous nature of inmate–inmate relations by increasing the tensions associated with the competition for scarce goods and commodities, including power and control. The dynamics of inmate–staff relations—between the keepers and the kept—also mirror to a great extent the same tensions between law enforcement and minority communities—the police and the policed. As such, we refer the reader back to the various chapters that explore the ties between various theories and correctional practices.

Intertwining race, crime, and for-profit imprisonment, Michael Hallett (2006) offers a highly critical look at the industry of private prisons in America. He notes that in the post-9/11 era of "Fortress America," privatization of prisons has emerged from a period of neglect. Hallett provides a detailed historical review of for-profit prisons, linking them to post–Civil War forced servitude and England's use of transportation to the colonies, first the Americas and then Australia, as a source of cheap labor. He is particularly critical of the **convict lease system,** whereby wardens sell the labor of inmates, as an extension of slavery into the twentieth century. As non-race-Crits also observe, shifts in political agendas, particularly the "war on drugs" has disproportionately cost the black community compared to whites. Indeed, Hallett claims that policy makers specifically targeted black America, and that corporate America benefits, through the growth of private, for-profit prisons. These new-wave private prisons target nonviolent, low-level offenders, ones whom Hallett claims are largely African American serving mandatory minimum sentences for one-time drug possession charges. It is his contention that the DMC issue, as reflected in microcosm by the private prison movement, is a reflection of colonial America's designation of black slaves as a dangerous class. Like many race-Crits before him, Hallett spends more time focusing on the problem than on suggesting ways to reduce it, other than to curtail the privatization of prisons.

SUMMARY

This chapter has been a study in contrasts and similarities (see Table 11.3). For decades, mainstream criminology focused nearly exclusively on males, the dominant players in the marketplace of crime. In the past 30-plus years, gender has

T A B L E 11.3   Feminist and Race-Inclusive Crime Theories

Theory	Major Figures	Central Assumptions	Causal Arguments (Key Terms)	Strengths	Weaknesses
Liberal feminism	Adler, Simon, Austin, Kruttschnitt	Society is patriarchal; women are second-class citizens and undeserving of the same legal protections as men; in times past, to reinforce this view, women were legally defined as the chattel of their husband.	*Liberal feminism:* With equal treatment, gender-specific differences in criminality will disappear.	Helps us understand the tremendous disparities in offending proclivities between men and women; points out basic gender-role socialization processes, especially those found in families; more radical forms offer arguments similar to various forms of Marxist criminology.	Yields research results, using traditional quantitative methods, that are mixed and inconclusive; however, legal analyses and qualitative methods yield far more support.
Radical feminism	Chesney-Lind, Daly		*Radical feminism:* Society criminalizes women for being "bad" (e.g., using drugs, prostitution), behaviors they use to escape society's oppression.		
Marxist feminism	Schwendingers		*Marxist feminism:* Females' place in the workplace is defined first by capitalism and second by men.		
Socialist feminism	Messerschmidt, Hagan (and associates)		*Socialist feminist:* Crime is best understood by blending class and gender.		
Critical race theory (CRT)	Delgado, Stefancic, Arrigo, Schneider	Racism is endemic and (perhaps) intractable; only suitably credentialed minority-group members can be race-Crits	*Storytelling* and *counterstorytelling* reveal the truth about the influence of race on crime and justice.	Provides first-person narratives and other personalized accounts of racism's impact on people of color, especially as it relates to crime and justice issues.	May be more movement than theory; cannot be subjected to testing in its current form.

become an essential variable in two criminological enterprises: theorizing and research. The result is often more questions than answers. At least the questions are being asked, whereas in the past they were largely ignored.

Second, race—a third rail of American criminology and perhaps American society on the whole—has emerged in this same time frame as another critical force in criminology. From reaching a consensus as to what the term means to how it is measured to what those measurements mean, there have been great strides made in theorizing about the race–crime link since the racism-inspired theorizing of the late nineteenth and early twentieth centuries. Race continues to confound criminologists, but they better understand its role in individual and organizational decision making—whether one is becoming a criminal or responding to a person suspected of a crime—now than they did just 30 years ago.

Third, criminologists today recognize that if they are to understand crime, they must sensitize their theories to the intersection of race *and* gender (Franklin and Fearn 2008). **Multiracial feminism,** which includes all waves of feminism and places them in a racial context that Sojourner Truth would have understood, is one way to achieve this goal (Burgess-Proctor 2006), as are critical race theory, or the gender- and race-inclusive versions of mainstream theories. What is important is the recognition that crime theories, if they are to enjoy any credibility within both society and the criminal justice community, must come to grips with the realities of crime in the twenty-first century, and those realities include understanding the roles of race and gender in crime causation.

KEY TERMS

Ahnenerbe	ethnicity	Marxist feminists
Aryans	ethnocentrism	master race
associative learning	ethnoym	misandry
autonyms	exonyms	misogyny
biological sex	familied decisions	multiracial feminism
black subculture-of-violence thesis	feminism	*paterfamilias*
code of the streets hypothesis	first-wave feminism	patriarchal authority
conceptual learning	gender	race
convict lease system	gender identity	race-Crits
counterstorytelling	gendered context	racial discrimination
critical race theory (CRT)	gendered justice	racial-threat hypothesis
ethnic identity	gendered pathways	racism
	institutionalized racism	radical feminists
	liberation hypothesis	second-wave feminism

sexism   scientific racism   symbolic threat

sexual orientation   socialist feminists   third-wave feminism

sexual discrimination   subculture of violence

CRITICAL REVIEW QUESTIONS

1. Define *feminism*. Which "feminist theory" makes the most sense to you, and why?

2. What single piece of information gleaned from the gender-based analyses of crime were you not expecting? [NOTE: "None of it was unexpected" is not a particularly good answer.]

3. Which mainstream theory helped you best understand the lower involvement of women in crime? Explain your answer.

4. Suppose you are discussing gender-inclusive theories with a group of friends. One of them says, "Criminologists must be stupid. Of course gender's an important variable in criminality." What do you say in defense of criminology?

5. In which area of criminal justice policy or practice do feminist theories provide the best insights? Where is their application the weakest? (Note: See Question 1.)

6. Define *racism*. What evidence can you marshal to support the idea that DMC is an indicator of endemic racism in the United States? What evidence can you marshal on the other side of the argument? Which evidence is more compelling?

7. What single piece of information gleaned from the race-based analyses of crime were you not expecting? [NOTE: "None" or "all" are not particularly good answers.]

8. Which mainstream theory helped you best understand the DMC of minorities? Explain your answer.

9. Which race-sensitive theory helped you best understand the DMC of minorities? Explain your answer.

10. Some criminologists argue that it is only at the intersection of race and gender that we can truly understand their influence on criminality. What do you think?

NOTES

1. We use "mainstream" as a way to identify crime theories that evolved out of the traditional perspectives on crime and criminals such as deterrence, biogenic, psychogenic, and most sociogenic theories. Labeling, shaming, conflict, and Marxist theories are tributaries of mainstream theories.

2. Recall from Chapter 1 that the kinds of high-profile crimes attributed to women have been primarily intrafamilial. Consider, too, what happened in the case of the

Wineville (California) chicken-ranch murders: In real life, the mother-accomplice suffered a far less punitive sanction than did her son. While some murdering mothers and other female criminals do suffer society's most severe sanctions—think Aileen Wuornos—as a rule, criminologists accord female criminals less attention, unless their acts stray outside culturally defined and societally accepted female roles.

3. Being a sexist, whether the object is a woman (**misogyny**) or a man (**misandry**), is not illegal, hence feminists seek to enlighten and change attitudes; if ideas turn to actions, then feminists seek to expose those engaging in it to legal action.

4. These distinctions derive in part from Krolokke and Sorensen (2005).

5. The Equal Rights Amendment, as passed by Congress and approved by President Richard Nixon, began its movement through the states in 1972, as ratification by 38 state legislatures was necessary for it to become part of the Constitution. It had seven years to achieve this goal, but failed to garner the support of more than 36 state legislatures by 1979. See Held, Herndon, and Stager (1997) for more on the ERA.

6. The AAA views racial groupings such as these as vestiges of *scientific racism*. See Coon (1962) for more on their use.

7. Ethnonyms have two forms: (1) **exonyms,** created by outsiders for the ethnic group; and (2) **autonyms,** created and used by the ethnic group itself. For example, the Navajo Nation, an American Indian tribe, employs the ethnonym Navajo, an exonym given to them by the Apaches and the U.S. government; they refer to each other by the autonym of Diné, meaning "the People."

8. Racism is a form of **ethnocentrism,** the latter defined as an attitude or orientation that requires the holder to judge other cultures solely in terms of how they compare to the holder's culture of origin, since different cultures are inferior ones.

9. Pringle (2006) notes that several of the *Ahnenerbe*'s anthropologists seamlessly rejoined German academic circles after the war, becoming well-respected scholars and suffering no real negative consequences for their work with the Nazis.

10. Inferential statistics cannot be used to find significant differences with a census of all arrests; moreover, given the law of large numbers, almost any difference would appear statistically significant. Instead, we created a range by averaging the percentages for each year and adding or subtracting 10 percent.

11. As discussed in Chapter 1, homicide is one of the few offenses, given its high degree of reliability and validity, which allows for cross-cultural comparisons.

12. The world's most dangerous criminal organizations generally do not allow female members (for example, the Mafia, Triads, outlaw motorcycle clubs, and Mexican and Colombian drug cartels). While street gangs may have a "female auxiliary," they are male-only groups (Abadinsky 2010).

13. Tittle and associates (2003) also included age categories in their analyses. Importantly for the theory, self-control does not perform equally well across these categories, which is a direct contradiction of its claim to be age-invariate.

14. In developed nations compared to developing nations, the sex ratio is skewed toward higher numbers of females; correcting for these disparities, Steffensmeier and associates (1989) are less likely to report differences that are statistical artifacts.

15. The use of the term *girls* is not meant to demean young women. We use it in the spirit of recent discussions by feminists about restoring the status of girlhood as a

transition between childhood and adulthood (Adler 1997). Moreover, much of the misbehavior of these girls is status offending (e.g., running away or incorrigibility), while other conduct is clearly criminal (e.g., prostitution or street-level drug sales).

16. See, for example, the following: Hagan, Simpson, and Gillis (1979, 1985, 1987); Hagan, Gillis, and Simpson (1988, 1990).

17. McCarthy and associates (1999) allow that fathers in less patriarchal families may have a positive impact; however, they give more attention to mothers' roles.

18. See, for examples, Esbensen and Deschenes (1998); Esbensen and Winfree (1998); Freng and Winfree (2004); Gauthier and Bankston (1997); Miller (1998); Marvell and Moody (1999); and Steffensmeier and Haynie (2000).

19. The "third rail" idea derives from electrified subways where trains run on two rails and the third one carries electricity. Anyone who touches the third rail courts disaster. As a metaphor, the third rail refers to an untouchable or highly charged topic. In politics, citizen identification cards are a third-rail issue. In criminology, biogenic explanations, including race-based ones, are third-rail issues.

20. For more on racial threat and police practices, see Alpert, Dunham, and Smith (2007); Brunson (2007); Curreton (2000); Harris (2007); Holmes (2000); Holmes, Smith et al. (2008); Lersch (1998); Mosher (2001); Petrocelli, Piquero, and Smith (2003); for more on racial threat and court practices, see Brennan (2006); Franklin and Fearn (2008); MacDonald (2003); Rodriguez (2007); Schlesinger (2005).

21. The economically deprived commit the type of crime likely to upset communities and draw the attention of police at a higher rate, and, in current American society, greater number of blacks are economically deprived than whites. Prisons are always filled with poor persons—at an earlier time these were mostly white persons (Mays and Winfree 2009).

22. For more on the evolution of critical race theory see Crenshaw, Gotanda, et al. (1995) and Delgado and Stefancic (2001a, 2001b).

23. *Dred Scott v. Sanford* (1857) established, *inter alia,* that persons descended from African slaves, whether free or slave, were not citizens of the United States as defined by the U.S. Constitution.

24. *Plessy v. Ferguson* (1896) upheld the constitutionality of racial segregation in public accommodations (e.g., railroads and bathrooms), under the doctrine of "separate but equal."

25. Race-Crits have founded Latino/a critical race studies, Asian American critical race studies, and American Indian critical race studies (Delgado and Stefancic 1998: Lintner 2007; Romero 2002; Yosso 2005). In critical white studies, both nonwhites and white learn what it means to be white in contemporary society (Delgado and Stefancic 1997).

26. See, for example, Adler, Mueller, and Laufer (1994); Barlow (1996); Coser, Nock, et al. (1990); Siegel (1992); Messner (1983); Parker (1989).

27. This requirement is *necessary* (i.e., a race-Crit must be a minority), but not *sufficient* (i.e., being a minority by itself is not enough). Race-Crits reserve strong criticism for minority intellectual elites who fail to get involved in "the struggle."

12

The Future of Crime Theory

CHAPTER OVERVIEW

Question 1: Are New Research Priorities or Different Methods Needed?

Research Exemplar 1: The City Project

Research Exemplar 2: Domestic Violence and Arrest Policies

Question 2: Are New Theories Needed?

Old Wine in New Barrels or New Wine in Old Barrels?

Integrated Theories

Theoretical Exemplar 1: Control Balance Theory

Theoretical Exemplar 2: Life-Course and Developmental Criminology

Question 3: Are New Questions or New Paradigms Needed?

Overcoming Disciplinary and Political Philosophical Barriers

The Case for the Paradigm Shifts in the Study of Crime and Criminals

Postmodernism: A New Paradigm for the Study of Crime and Criminals?

LEARNING OBJECTIVES

In this chapter, you will learn the following:

- The outcomes associated with shifting research priorities and the use of different methods on crime studies.

- About criminological efforts to create new theories and reexamine old ones.

- That the search for knowledge about crime and criminals is *both* academic and political.

- The crime-related challenges and opportunities that await criminologists—and the nation—in the twenty-first century.

INTRODUCTION

What is a crime? Who is the criminal? Answers to these two questions provided us with an initial set of definitions and guidelines. Later we added two more questions: Why is there crime? Why do people engage in law-violating behavior? The search for answers to these and other questions has taken us through the domains of many academic disciplines, including biology, chemistry, psychology, psychiatry, sociology, economics, political science, and philosophy. This journey covered hundreds of years, although much of the "real work" occurred in the twentieth century.

Several generalizations emerged in response to our guiding questions. First, much is known about why people commit crimes and why the level of crime is so high. Second, there is considerable variability in research support for crime theories, ranging from virtually none to consistently high levels. Third, supported or not, many theories exhibit interesting linkages to criminal justice policies and practices.

Given the obvious—and often not-so-obvious—ties between crime theories and criminal justice policies and practices, separating the wheat from the chaff takes on even greater significance in the search for logically consistent and empirically verified theories. Poor empirical support for a given theory might reveal more about contemporary research designs and analytic capabilities than it does about the theory. Moreover, new ways of thinking about old theories also hold much promise, as in new views on deterrence and shaming, new conceptualizations of labeling, and new definitions of strain.

We are near the conclusion of our journey across the landscape of crime theory. Yet, in many important ways, this journey has just begun. Answers to three general questions may assist criminologists to more fully inform criminal justice policies and practices. Before you explore these questions, we issue a caveat: This material is meant to stimulate *your* thinking about crime. Nothing in the following pages should be construed as a mandate. Rather, the questions and answers represent divergent points of view that should spur you to speculate further about existing theories, research, policies, and practices, and those that will evolve over the course of the twenty-first century.

QUESTION 1: ARE NEW RESEARCH PRIORITIES OR DIFFERENT METHODS NEEDED?

Much of what is known about crime and criminals comes from official statistics, victimization surveys, and self-report studies. Official statistics, such as the Uniform Crime Report, provide data on crime and punishment trends and little else. However, painting a complete picture of crime is beyond their scope; they merely reveal who and what comes to the attention of the law enforcement community. Victimization studies, like the National Crime Victimization Surveys, explore the nature and extent of offenses by studying households across the nation at regular intervals; however, the picture they provide is also incomplete. Numerous self-report studies tend to focus on known offender populations and on youths. As Gresham Sykes and Francis Cullen (1992:88) observed, "No national study has been made of adult criminality, and knowledge of self-reported adult crime remains rudimentary." In other words, adult crime-related outlooks, orientations, and activities, an important piece of the puzzle, are largely unknown.

Over the past 20 years, two forms of research have assumed greater visibility and importance in criminological studies: the **longitudinal panel study,** where the same people are followed over an extended period of time and researchers look for changes in attitudes, orientations, and behavior; and the **classic experimental design,** where subjects are divided randomly into at least two groups, with one receiving an experimental treatment and the other becoming a control group. Politicians and other policy makers, as stakeholders in the crime control marketplace, generally understand the significance of both types of studies. After all, these research designs play major roles in health-related studies, such as determining the efficacy of a new disease treatment. Primary stakeholders could not make laws or engage in other public policy–related activities without knowing the crime trends or patterns over time. This observation is true for crime control policies as well. In fact, Congress created the Bureau of Justice Statistics to provide it with just this kind of information about crime and justice issues.

The application of experimental designs to crime studies is a difficult task. Many researchers consider the classical experimental design, with its control groups and treatment or experimental groups, to be the best way to establish cause-and-effect relationships (Babbie 1983). In classical experiments, researchers must maintain high levels of control over test and control subjects, something that is difficult in any human research employing human subjects, let alone criminological studies. The classical design is best used in a laboratory setting, which critics condemn as too artificial for crime studies (Chow and Hemple 1977). The randomized experiment, where assignment to the experimental and control groups is beyond the researcher's control, remains the "gold standard" of evidence in evaluation research, given its ability to demonstrate that changes in treatment variables caused changes in the outcomes being measured (Cook and Campbell 1979; Shadish, Cook, and Campbell 2002).

An alternative is the **natural experiment,** one that occurs in a real-world setting and is subject to some researcher manipulation and control. The findings generated by this design are limited by the extent to which nature or some other force exerts its influence over that of the scientist. Far more likely is the **quasi-experimental design,** one that employs parts of the classical design, but may lack randomization, a control group, or researcher manipulation and control. However, the following Comments and Criticisms box chronicles what can happen when researchers try random assignment.

We review two research projects below. This review is by no means exhaustive or necessarily representative. The projects were selected because they (1) included either a longitudinal or an experimental design (or both), (2) have had far-ranging and long-lasting impacts on criminal justice policymaking, and (3) have implications for crime theories. In each case, we summarize the research projects and their

COMMENTS AND CRITICISMS: Unexpected Consequences of Random Assignment in Criminal Justice Evaluations

In spite of its obvious strengths, randomized experiments are rarely conducted in criminological and criminal justice studies. Perhaps even more than methodological issues, there are perceived ethical concerns. In any experiment, only some of the subjects receive a treatment; the rest receive perhaps a **placebo**, a false stimulus or treatment. In medical research, this could mean that someone is cured while someone else dies. In crime-related experiments, this could mean that someone is victimized while someone else is not, or that someone is "cured" of criminal proclivities while the control subjects continues their criminal practices or are denied access to a potentially life-altering treatment. Thus, crime-based experiments have a high potential for being viewed as morally and ethically questionable. We offer two examples, where justice-system stakeholders sought to interfere in a proposed or ongoing evaluation using such a design.

In 1997, Lynette Feder sought to evaluate a program for men convicted of misdemeanor domestic violence. She wanted to randomly assign men to either an experimental group that received probation and completed a mandatory 26-week batterer counseling program or a control group that received only probation. Besides evaluating the program, Feder proposed to test competing domestic violence theories. The local prosecutor's office threatened to stop the study on legal grounds (i.e., the random assignment was a misuse of judicial discretion) and ethical grounds (i.e., the denial of treatment was based on chance). Feder requested a friend-of-the-court (*amicus curiae*) brief

from the American Society of Criminology's Executive Board, which provided its own response: "The principle is that random assignment to treatment options is the best scientific method for determining the effectiveness of options such as those proposed in this case" (p. 296).

Prosecutors were not the only ones to object. In 1996, Thomas Winfree and associates obtained permission from a municipal court to randomly assign persons convicted of DWI to either normal court processing or a treatment program, a DWI-Drug Court administered by the court's senior judge. All went well for six months, with researchers making assignments randomly; no one objected on the theory that there were only a fixed number of slots available in the experimental treatment program and that everyone in the applicant pool was eligible. Allowing "fate" (or in this case a random-number generator) to determine who got what did not bother defendants or their attorneys. When the senior judge unexpectedly resigned, a new judge refused to allow further random assignments, for the same reasons cited by the prosecutor in the Feder case. In fact, the judicial interference reached a peak when magistrate judges from the surrounding county, who operated a similar DWI-drug court, threatened the researchers with contempt if they did not make it clear in the final report that the study did not include *their courts*. The new municipal court judge participated in the proceedings, in the spirit of judicial collegiality.

SOURCE: Breckenridge, Winfree, et al. (2000); Short, Zahn, and Farrington (2000); Winfree and Giever (2000).

ties to the present topic, along with the current state of knowledge about each topic, and its ties to theory, policies, and practices.

Research Exemplar 1: The City Project

In the 1980s, social scientists began a major longitudinal study of crime-related issues in Chicago, a city known for its class, racial, and ethnic diversity, and in which no single group represented a majority of the population. The **Project on Human Development in Chicago Neighborhoods** (hereafter the **City Project**) divided Chicago's communities into neighborhood clusters, based on similar income, family structure, and racial and ethnic composition.[1] From these clusters, the researchers identified 80 neighborhoods that showed enough variability to allow the detection of neighborhood-level effects.

Origins and Implementation   The City Project had two parts. The first included (1) a community survey of nearly 9,000 residents, (2) an observational study (called **systematic social observations**) that videotaped all interactions and physical evidence of disorder (e.g., garbage on the streets, litter, graffiti, abandoned cars, and needles and syringes) occurring on 23,000 blocks in 196 neighborhoods, 12 hours per day, seven days per week, and (3) a survey of nearly 3000 randomly selected community leaders in education, religion, business, politics, law enforcement, and community organization.

The second part consisted of six age cohorts (birth, 3, 6, 9, 12, 15, and 18), each with roughly 500 males and 500 females, all randomly selected from the 80 Chicago neighborhoods. The first wave of contacts with over 6,000 subjects— and their primary caregivers—ran from 1994 to 1997; data collection continued for two more waves (1997–1999 and 2000–2002). In the final wave, researchers obtained responses from nearly 5,000 subjects ranging in age from 8 to 26 years. Thus, the researchers used an **accelerated panel design,** meaning that they staggered their subjects through the age cohorts and followed them for a fixed period, yielding information about the subjects from birth to 26 years of age. At each wave, City Project researchers gathered information about school, peers, family, and individual differences, with all questions rooted in biological, sociological, and psychological theories.

The Current State of the City Project   Data collection and codification for the City Project ended several years go, providing numerous observations and conclusions:

- *Community survey results* (Sampson and Bartusch 1999). Chicago's black and Latino/a residents were significantly less tolerant of crime than whites, particularly when it came to perceptions of teenage fighting. Levels of **legal cynicism**—the idea that laws and societal rules are not binding on one's actions—was higher for blacks and Latinos/as than for whites; moreover, those with low socioeconomic status (SES) were twice as likely as those with high SES to report high levels of legal cynicism. The researchers reported that the neighborhood of residence affects attitudes. Minority-group members in neighborhoods characterized by poverty and instability were more cynical than whites; once the economic disadvantage found in a neighborhood was taken into account, the legal cynicism of whites and blacks converged. Blacks appeared to be more cynical only because they were more likely to live where disadvantage is concentrated.

- *Cohort study* (Earls 1998; Obeidallah and Earls 1999). Among 12- and 15-year-old white, African American, and Latina girls, nearly 50 percent more of those who were mildly to moderately depressed compared to nondepressed girls engaged in property crime, and 100 percent more engaged in crimes against persons. The results for antisocial aggressive behavior were even more startling: Mildly and moderately depressed girls exhibited rates that were more than four times higher than those for the nondepressed. In the first-wave cohort of 9-, 12-, and 15-year-old youths, exposure to violence—hearing gunfire or witnessing a knife attack or a shooting—was strongly correlated with self-reported violent behavior. Such findings suggest a neighborhood influence, as some neighborhoods clearly were safer than others.

- *Surveys and observational study* (Sampson and Raudenbush 2001). Wilson and Kelling's (1982) "broken window" hypothesis puts a community's crime squarely on its level of disorder (e.g., soliciting prostitutes, loitering, and committing other incivilities). Using systematic social observations (i.e., videotaping of neighborhood interactions and activities) as objective and independent measures of disorder, City Project researchers linked it to several measures of crime, including residents' perceptions of crime and police records. They also created a subjective measure called **collective efficacy,** or the mutual trust level between neighbors and a willingness to intervene on behalf of the common good. The researchers reported that, contrary to the broken windows hypothesis, disorder did not cause crime directly, as collective efficacy and neighborhood features proved far stronger influences. Once these factors were taken into account, but especially poverty and concentration of immigrants, the disorder–crime connection vanished in most instances. A major exception was robbery; the authors suggested that visual cues associated with social and physical disorder entice robbers to act, which supports the "broken windows" hypothesis.

The City Project and Public Policy   The City Project is rich in policy implications and theoretical value. First, given the neighborhoods' influence, "policymakers and agents of the criminal justice system would do well to consider the role of community social norms" (Sampson and Bartusch 1999:2). Second, the findings support one of the oldest crime theories—social disorganization—and cast doubt on the broken windows hypothesis at the heart of aggressive policing intended to eradicate disorder in the nation's inner cities. According to Sampson and Bartusch (1999:5; emphasis in original), "The findings strongly suggest that policies intended to reduce crime by eradicating disorder solely through tough law enforcement tactics are misdirected.... Eradicating disorder *may* reduce crime indirectly by stabilizing neighborhoods." While it is too early to document the total impact of this project, the scientific significance of the reports and academic articles generated by the researchers and others who have gained access to the data is substantial (Liberman 2007).

In sum, the City Project was perhaps the most ambitious and expensive single study of crime ever conducted. As law professor Michael Tonry noted, "By a factor of 10 or maybe a factor of 20, it's the largest social science research project undertaken in this country concerning crime and delinquency" (Coughlin 1994:A8). The information collected by City Project researchers has been archived by the Interuniversity Consortium for Political and Social Research, a data repository at the University of Michigan.

Research Exemplar 2: Domestic Violence and Arrest Policies

A confluence of forces in the mid–1980s led to a new awareness about domestic violence, a crime traditionally accorded low status in police work. Police saw it as more of an order maintenance or social work activity than real law enforcement (Chaney and Saltzstein 1998; Zorza 1992). The implementation of mandatory arrest policies, in which the aggressor—typically a male—is arrested at the crime scene by responding officers, owes much to lobbying by battered-women's advocates in the 1970s and 1980s (Frisch 1992; Zorza 1992). Litigation also played a role, as negligence and tort claims against police agencies mounted (Zorza 1992). These pressures aside, what appears to have solidified support for mandatory arrest is the belief, based on empirical data, that such a policy actually deters future conduct (Jaffe, Wolf, Telford, and Austin 1986). The empirical data in question were provided by the **Minneapolis Domestic Violence Experiment.**

In 1981, the Police Foundation, an independent policy research institute, conducted a yearlong study in Minneapolis, where police officers were instructed to use one of three strategies when responding to simple (misdemeanor) domestic assaults: (1) Arrest the suspect, (2) send him from the scene of the assault for eight hours, or (3) give advice and mediate. A random lottery system predetermined officers' responses to domestic violence assault calls. At the experiment's conclusion, Larry Sherman and Richard Berk (1984a,b) had data on three randomly assigned responses to domestic violence cases, which they followed up on to see if there was further violence. Sherman and Berk (1984a) reported that arrest was the most effective of the three responses. Giving advice and sending assailants away from the home were far less effective in deterring future violence.

In response to the research, Minneapolis changed its policy toward "wife beaters" from avoiding an arrest to arresting the assailant. Other state legislatures quickly enacted either a **mandatory arrest policy** or a **presumptive arrest policy.** In the former, officers must either arrest the aggressor or, if that person's identity cannot be determined, all parties involved; in the latter situation an arrest must be made "unless there are good, clear reasons why an arrest would be counterproductive" (Sherman and Berk 1984b:272). The Minneapolis experiment became a policy maker's dream: It provided clear and unequivocal evidence that arresting the abuser deterred future offending. Or did it?

Challenges to the Minneapolis Experiment Findings   Five follow-up studies—called the **Spouse Assault Replication Program (SARP)**—failed to duplicate the original findings. In Omaha, Nebraska, arrest was no more effective than either mediation or separation measured at six-month and one-year intervals (Dunford 1992). Researchers in Milwaukee, Wisconsin, reported variable effects: a short-term deterrent effect and lower violence for whites, married arrestees, and those who were employed, but higher violence levels for blacks, the unemployed, the unmarried, and high school dropouts (Sherman et al. 1992). Employment status had a similar positive impact on arrest's deterrent effects in Colorado Springs, Colorado; however, an arrest could make a bad situation even worse (Berk,

Campbell, Klap, and Western 1992). A fourth study conducted in Charlotte, North Carolina, found that the batterer's previous criminal record might be the strongest indicator of whether arrest is the best policy (Hirschel and Hutchinson 1992). A fifth experiment conducted in Metro-Dade County, Florida, found marginal support for mandatory arrest, as recidivism dropped only slightly (Pate and Hamilton 1992).

Arnold Binder and James Meeker (1988) criticized the Minneapolis experiment for methodological weaknesses and implementation problems, questioning the wisdom of touting its findings as definitive when they were in fact weak and inconclusive. And when the SARP failed generally to replicate its findings, Binder and Meeker (1993:887) again assailed the experiment: "The consequence was a dramatic change in public policy with potentially substantial negative effects on many people and an unwarranted large expenditure of public monies." Jannell Schmidt and Sherman (1993) added fuel to the debate when they questioned the efficacy of mandatory arrest policies; they further feared that mandatory arrest might do more harm than good (Schmidt and Sherman 1996).

The Minneapolis Domestic Violence Experiment, Public Policy, and Criminal Justice Practices   More than 20 years after the Minneapolis experiment, nearly 9 in 10 U.S. law enforcement agencies follow written policies on discretionary arrest and domestic disputes, affecting about 97 percent of all sworn officers (Hickman and Reaves 2001:19). Mandatory arrest remains a fixed part of the law enforcement policy lexicon.

Research into police responses to domestic violence continues and reveals that, although arrest policies appear to dominate police practices, bureaucratic discretion remains high (Chaney and Saltzstein 1998). Moreover, restraining-order violations in domestic violence incidents appear to have the highest impact on arrest probability when the victim's risk of injury is low, and fall off as that risk increases (Kane 2000; Mignon and Holmes 1995). In a reanalysis of the SARP, Christopher Maxwell and associates (2001) reported findings consistent with Sherman's original claims. The predicted relationship between the suspect's arrest and later aggression was observed, even controlling for differences across research sites. They described it as "a consistent and direct, though modest deterrent effect of aggression by males against their female intimate partners" (Maxwell, Garner, and Fagan 2001:9). They concluded that the reanalysis provided sufficient evidence supporting the argument that arresting male batterers may reduce subsequent intimate partner violence (Maxwell, Garner, and Fagan 2001).

Finally, the Minneapolis experiment extended theorizing about domestic violence. Couching their arguments in terms of deterrence theory, labeling theory, and the "stake in conformity" hypothesis, Sherman and associates (1992) found that, contrary to deterrence theory, arrest did not reduce either official or victim-reported recidivism. Rather, consistent with labeling theory, offenders with a low stake in conformity actually increased their recidivism after arrest. This theory-based analysis led to Sherman's recanting of his earlier position on mandatory arrest (Schmidt and Sherman 1993, 1996).

In sum, experiments and longitudinal studies contribute to criminology, but not without costs. These methods tend to devalue more qualitative approaches (see the next In Their Own Words). When it comes to crime research, it may not be a good idea to put all your eggs in one basket. Longitudinal studies are often expensive and may not be appropriate for some causal questions, a topic revisited later in this chapter. Experiments often generate controversy, even though policies, procedures, and laws allow for their use (Boruch, Victor, and Cecil 2000; Krisberg and Schuman 2000). Another motivation centers on funding for social science research: The National Institute of Justice, a major source of funding for criminal justice–related research, prefers randomized experiments (Garner and Visher 1988; Liberman 2009). Given sufficient safeguards, randomized experiments may answer seminal questions about program efficacy and causal sequencing.

Whatever other reasons underlie their application, social scientists should recall the experiences of medical researchers: "Progress toward more sustained use of experimental research in social settings is also likely to be driven by the lesson that social interventions, just like medical ones, may do more harm than good" (Oakley 2000:326). The qualified answer to the first question, then, is yes—that is, employ both longitudinal and experimental designs where appropriate, but not to the exclusion of other methods.

IN THEIR OWN WORDS: Research Subjects Speak for Themselves

Jody Miller interviewed 94 girls, about half of whom were in gangs and all of whom lived in areas with gang activity, and captured their attitudes about women in gangs:

> In describing themselves as "one of the guys," young women highlighted what they perceived to be the importance of being tough and physically aggressive and of not being preoccupied with "feminine" concerns. As Veronica noted earlier, girls who "get scared" or "don't wanna break their nails and stuff like that" don't belong in gangs. Tonya complained about girls who "don't fight, ones that think they too cute to fight, ones that be scared to sell drugs, just scared. . . . You can't be scared and be a gang member."

Kenneth Tunnell interviewed 60 male, chronic property offenders who collectively had committed nearly 50,000 crimes. From one he learned the following lesson about legal sources of money:

> I went to the bank four different times. I went to four or five different loan companies, you know the ones that say, "Come on in and borrow money on your word" and all this. That a crock of shit. They ain't anybody going to lend you nothing. I mean it's there for the taking, but it ain't there for the lending.

Neal Shover studied 50 convicted ordinary property offenders, 40 and older. Many intended to quit the life, but not all, including one who observed about returning to crime:

> Well, at this stage in my life I think that's the only thing left open to me, that I can really profit from. I'm not going to be successful working. . . . I don't want that day-to-day grind and I don't want that regimentation that goes along with working a job.

SOURCE: Miller (2001:182); Shover (1985:45); Tunnell (1992:64–65).

QUESTION 2: ARE NEW THEORIES NEEDED?

Many criminologists, concerned about the future of crime theory, have asked another question: Are new theories needed? According to John Braithwaite (1990), much criminological decay is due to the fact that more energy is spent criticizing scholarly work than building upon that work. As Braithwaite (1990:163–64) further stated:

> Criminology as a science has failed to put us in a position to say sensible, empirically informed things about protecting the community from crime. . . . When a science fails us so utterly in this way, we must look to its fundamentals—its theory. The policy failure is a failure of explanation; we cannot solve it by retreating from the need to explain. The fruits of the atheoretical policy-oriented criminology of recent decades are not on the trees waiting to be plucked. The quick policy fixes are just not out there waiting to be discovered. . . . The mission of criminology as a science should be to build theories of as general a scope as we can manage. Then, one would hope that policy-makers would work through these theories as alternative frameworks for thinking about particular policy interventions.

Contemporary criminological theories must contribute policy-relevant explanations, while aspiring to even higher goals.[2] For example, Don Gottfredson (1989:1) wrote that most criminological theories are "unclear and lacking in justifiable generality." Nor do they, as Braithwaite and others have observed, offer practical guidance that "does not require heroic leaps of conjecture." Gottfredson (1989:15) further suggested that theorists should provide as much detail as possible— including any assumptions about crime, criminals, and society; the measurement of key concepts and other abstract information; and any limits on the generalizability of the theory—to allow those who come after them the means to determine the adequacy of the theory. Moreover, criminologists should, suggested Gottfredson, use the evidence to reexamine and, if necessary, revise the theory.

Old Wine in New Barrels or New Wine in Old Barrels?

As suggested by Gottfredson, then, new theories provide but one means to alter the current state of criminological theorizing. In point of fact, this text contains few truly original theories proposed after 1970, outside of perhaps Cornish and Clarke's rational choice theory (Chapter 2), Cohen and Felson's routine activities theory (Chapter 2), Gottfredson and Hirschi's self-control theory (Chapter 7), Hagan's power–control theory (Chapter 9), and Tittle's control-balance theory (this chapter). Some critics might argue that, with few exceptions, even these theories are examples of "old wine in new barrels"—that is, old ideas represented as something new. There is nothing inherently wrong with this approach, so long as the ideas are recognized for what they are: Both the new and old varieties make the same or very similar assumptions and assertions about crime, criminals, and society. Researchers are guided to essentially the same places for answers, and they employ nearly identical concepts and variables in both the original and the "new barrel" variety. Thus, rational choice theory exhibits close ties to cost–benefit analysis and classical deterrence theory; self-control theory is a restatement of classical deterrence and rational choice principles bound up in a bonding theory framework.

If there is old wine in new barrels, what about new wine in old barrels? That is, are old theories about crimes and criminals being modified, refined, or repackaged and put into the theory marketplace as reincarnations of themselves? To answer these questions we need only refer to the resurgence of interest in biocriminology (Chapter 3), social disorganization and strain theories (Chapter 6), labeling theory (Chapter 8), and critical race theory (Chapter 11), all of which could be considered old wine in new barrels, especially given their clear and well-stated ties to the original theories.

Two exemplars include psychopathy (Chapter 4) and shaming theory (Chapter 8), both of which criminal justice practitioners widely endorse. First, psychopathy, an idea largely discounted by sociological criminologists by the early 1970s, remerged early in this century with new measurement techniques (e.g., Hare Psychopathy Checklist-Revised) and a body of correctional research touting its validity and reliability. Second, shaming, one of the oldest known mechanisms of social control, morphed into Braithwaite's reintegrative shaming in the 1990s and found widespread acceptance as the theoretical basis for restorative justice practices throughout the world's criminal justice systems.

In sum, this analogy (old wine/new barrels, new wine/old barrels) is only a device to look at the following: If the ideas (wine) are old and simply repackaged (barrels) as something new, it is old wine in new barrels; if the ideas are acknowledged as old, but have been "re-barreled" with new ways of thinking about or measuring them, it is new wine in old barrels. To reiterate, neither approach is wrong or deceptive, as the goal is to provide better insights into crime and criminals. Another tactic is to take ideas found in two or more theories, combining them into an integrated theory, our next topic.

Integrated Theories

Criminologists have long used either theory falsification or theoretical competition as a means of reducing the number of theories. **Theory falsification** involves discarding those theories whose predictions are inconsistent with empirical observations (Bernard and Snipes 1996). In a case of **theoretical competition,** two or more theories that make contradictory predictions are tested together, and those whose predictions are inconsistent with the data are discarded (Liska et al. 1989). Another approach is theoretical integration. *Integration* is a common term in theoretical discussions, as all theory "'integrates,' or unifies, empirical findings" (Liska et al. 1989:2). The phrase **theoretical integration** is usually reserved for "an activity that involves the formulation of linkages between different theoretical arguments. Theoretical integration is best viewed as one means of theorizing—i.e., as one strategy for developing more cogent explanations and for explaining theoretical growth" (Liska et al. 1989:2). Another definition provides a more prescriptive set of instructions: "Theoretical integration can be defined as *the act of combining two or more sets of logically interrelated propositions into one larger set of interrelated propositions, in order to provide a more comprehensive explanation of a particular phenomenon*" (Thornberry 1989:52; emphasis in original).

Many previously considered crime theories are integrated theories. Terms like *integrate, integration, combined,* and *synthesized* figured prominently in discussions of the similarities between differential association and social learning theories, social control and self-control theories, and classical deterrence and constitutional-learning theories. These theories and others reviewed in this book result from one of the following integrative strategies suggested by Allen Liska and associates (1989:15–17):

- **Theoretical elaboration.** This strategy, which involves the full development of existing theories, is based on the following idea: "Extant theories of deviance and crime are so underdeveloped that we might better spend our time and energies on developing them rather than on integrating them" (Liska et al. 1989:16). The preceding section ("Old Wine in New Barrels or New Wine in Old Barrels?") described this approach, and represents intentional (new wine in old barrels) and unintentional (old wine in new barrels) forms of theoretical elaboration.

- **Conceptual integration.** Many theories may have similar or nearly identical core concepts. If we can reduce the conceptual information to common elements and consistent definitions, then the next step, propositional integration, is simplified (see Thornberry's definition of *integration*). For example, Ronald Akers (1990, 1994) has argued that the concepts contained in numerous theories (e.g., classical deterrence, rational choice, social control, strain) can be "subsumed" under existing social learning concepts. Belief, a central part of social control theory, is similar to social learning theory's definitions; strain theory's blocked opportunities is similar to social learning theory's differential reinforcements; the peer influences and moral judgments found in rational choice theory are, in Akers'(1990:655) words, "derived" from social learning theory.

- **Propositional integration.** Existing theories are part of even more general theories, and the goal is to first take concepts and propositions from different theories and determine how they fit together, followed by an empirical assessment of their goodness of fit (Liska et al.1989). For example, the differential opportunity structures found in Cloward and Ohlin (i.e., the ability to learn illegitimate means) are part of Sutherland's differential association theory and are not at all incompatible with Merton's strain theory. This approach is arguably the highest form of theoretical integration.

Irrespective of the approach employed, the end product should meet two goals (Liska et al. 1989). First, the "new theory" should be logically coherent; that is, the synthesis of concepts or propositions should make sense, and not simply increase predictability. Second, the products of such activities should provide criminologists with intellectual puzzles. Ultimately, the ideas that emerge from

---

COMPARATIVE CRIMINOLOGY—WORLD VIEWS ON CRIME AND JUSTICE: Testing Integrative Theory in a Global Context

Travis Pratt and Timothy Godsey draw upon three macro-level crime theories to develop a single analytical model of homicide. They suggest that such a model should include social support elements drawn from Braithwaite's reintegrative shaming—measured by the percent of a nation's gross domestic product spent on health care—and Messner and Rosenfeld's institutional anomie and economic inequality—measured by the ratio of median incomes of a nation's richest to poorest 20 percent of citizens. Both variables should have direct effects on crime; in this case, homicide rates.

Pratt and Godsey take these ideas a step further and contend that Agnew's general strain theory also predicts that these variables should have both direct and interactive effects on crime. People have difficulty coping with general strains in situations of low social support; inequality can lead to increased relative deprivation, and as people perceive inequality, they come to understand that they cannot get what they want legitimately. At that point, the effects of high income inequality should be greatest on homicide rates when coupled with low social support. In sum, Pratt and Godsey suggest that general strain theory helps us understand how social support levels and inequality independently and interactively influence homicide rates.

The researchers use reasonably reliable and valid information from the World Health Organization and the United Nations Statistics Division concerning 68 fairly well-developed, industrialized nations. They found significant relationships among social support, inequality and the per-capita homicide rate, and, as predicted, social support and income inequality interacted to provide even more predictive power: the criminogenic effects of income inequality increase when found with low levels of social support. They conclude that while these relationships were resilient for homicide, the same might not be true for other crimes, especially given variable definitions across nations.

SOURCE: Pratt and Godsey (2003).

---

theoretical integration should open up new research opportunities and provide greater insights into the crime problem. The research exemplar in the above box clearly exceeds these goals.

The following sections examine two rather different examples of recent attempts to extend crime theorizing. The first, control balance theory, is a general theory on crime and arguably the last new theory of the twentieth century. It was selected because it (1) is a logically coherent, unique, and broad-ranging theory; (2) represents propositional integration, the most complex form of theory integration; (3) provides in its orienting concept—balance—a challenge to traditional criminological thinking; (4) has been subjected to empirical testing; and (5) yields policy implications. The second, life-course/developmental criminology, is a general explanatory perspective on crime that includes sociological, psychological, and biological factors. This orientation to crime studies looks at different life stages, and provides the conceptual grounding for Chicago's City Project (Sampson, Raudenbush, et al. 1997), Dunedin (New Zealand) Multidisciplinary Mental Health and Development Study (Moffitt 1993a,b), and the Pittsburgh Youth Study (Loeber, Farrington, et al. 1998). We begin with control balance theory.

Theoretical Exemplar 1: Control Balance Theory

In 1995, Charles Tittle offered a revision of control theory in his book *Control Balance: A General Theory of Deviance*. Tittle's **control balance theory** did not represent a break with traditional control theory, as he accepted that control is essential to conformity. However, Tittle extended this idea, noting that it is not the absolute presence or absence of social control efforts that is important, itself a break with the linear thinking that dominates crime theories (i.e., crime is related in straight-line fashion to more or less of something). He addressed the balance between the control one can exert and that to which one is subjected. Tittle expressed this relationship as a ratio, placing the former in the denominator and the latter in the numerator. Unless both forms are the same, an imbalance exists, and the *probability* of deviance increases.

Control Deficits and Surpluses   Tittle described two types of control imbalance. The first is **control deficit,** which occurs when the amount of control to which one is subjected exceeds the control one has over others. For example, a child may have control over some aspects of the behavior of his or her younger siblings but may experience a deficit when it comes to parental control.

Persons with control deficits engage in **repressive deviance,** which takes one of three forms. The goal of each form is to escape the control deficit and reestablish control balance. First, **predation** is physical violence committed with the intent to harm others (e.g., sexual assault and robbery). These offenders "prey" on other humans due to *marginal* control deficit imbalance. Second, **defiance,** a result of *medium* control-deficit imbalance, consists of acts that challenge the dominant rules, especially those that are creating the deficit but that do not harm another person. Therefore, these individuals are rarely criminal or delinquent, with the exception of vandals and truants. Other forms of defiant behavior may, depending on the age of the "offender," violate laws or ordinances (e.g., drug usage and sexual activity). Third, **submission** is a total loss of control, where people resort instead with "passive, unthinking and slavish obedience" to what they think others want (Tittle 1995:139). Submission, resulting from *extreme* control-deficit imbalance, includes turning on those seen as less powerful to gain acceptance from those perceived to be more powerful (e.g., an act of aggression against a suspected gay person to gain the attention and respect of like-minded but higher-status homophobes). Submissives also allow themselves to be humiliated and degraded by others.

In those cases in which people's control over others exceeds that imposed on them, Tittle saw **control surplus,** a condition associated with **autonomous deviance,** which also takes three forms. First, **exploitation** resembles predation with a key difference, one related to minimal control surplus. Autonomous deviants have the ability to control others, so they hire, co-opt, coerce, or otherwise secure the assistance of individuals who commit the actual miscreant acts. A powerful person who wishes to unseat a rival could, for example, hire a professional killer to do the deed. Second, **plunder,** a concept related to the idea of the "spoils of war," results from medium control-surplus imbalance. For example, a conqueror may feel so powerful that he or she takes what is desired from the vanquished, (e.g., rape, property, or genocide). Plunderers do it because they can, and no one is powerful enough to stop them. Third, **decadence,** involves irrational, spontaneous acts committed without much forethought. This form of autonomous deviance is due to maximum control-surplus imbalance.[3]

Control imbalances increase the probability for deviance, but they do not guarantee deviance. To explain individual responses, Tittle borrowed heavily from such theories as Sutherland's differential association, Merton's anomic trap, Marxist conflict, labeling, deterrence, and routine activities, and, of course, Hirschi's control theory. For example, following the logic of routine activities theory (see Chapter 2), Tittle contended that what determines whether an imbalance in control—too much or too little—produces deviance is largely determined by an individual's predispositional motivations, situational motivations, constraints, and, opportunities. **Predispositional motivations** are themselves a product of innate physical and psychological needs and desires; for example, in Tittle's view we all need food or desire autonomy. **Situational motivations** (or provocations) are more immediate and relate to an individual's perception of a power imbalance—for example, the person who is rejected by a supposed friend or, conversely, who perceives that another is easily intimidated or threatened by a word or look.

Motivations alone will not produce deviance; rather, they must interact with **constraints,** which are "the actual probability that potentially controlling reactions will be forthcoming" (Tittle 1995:167). Thus, a person who becomes aware of an imbalance is naturally drawn to act upon that condition—by either escaping a deficit or extending a surplus—and in the absence of sufficient constraints (deterrent effects) has a heightened probability of engaging in those deviant acts that will offset the imbalance. The final element, *opportunity,* is nearly always present. It is the convergence of high motivations, low constraints, and high opportunity, in the presence of a perceived control imbalance, that increases the probability of deviance.

Assessing Control Balance Theory   Braithwaite (1997) suggested four refinements to control balance theory. First, he proposed simplifying the major assumption: People always want more control, no matter how much they currently possess. Second, given conceptual imprecision between categories of autonomous deviance, they should be collapsed into one form. Third, he saw Tittle's work as a theory of predation, because the various forms of defiance are merely different techniques for engaging in self-benefit by taking advantage of someone or something. Finally, Braithwaite would have Tittle treat submissiveness as a separate, nondeviant response.

Tittle (1997) responded that the distinction between maintaining a deficit and extending a surplus was essential. As for the qualitative distinctions, Tittle acknowledged that they were imprecise and agreed that they should be abandoned; however, he further noted that Braithwaite's proposed simplification jeopardized a central component of the theory. In similar fashion, he rejected Braithwaite's suggestion that control balance was a predation-only theory: "To reduce it to a strict theory of predation would not really achieve anything and it would sacrifice a lot" (Tittle 1997:104). Although acknowledging problems with submission, Tittle remained unconvinced that it should be excluded, preferring instead to allow researchers to confirm or deny the correctness of its inclusion. Tittle (2004:397) later observed that central causal process in the theory is "a cognitive 'balancing' of the gain in *control* to be achieved form engaging in deviant behavior against the potential counter control that a particular act of deviance is likely to stimulate" (emphasis in original). He also suggested including an individual's level of self-control as a conditioning factor: Low self-control would make people vulnerable to provocation, as they would react instantly and would be unlikely to consider the costs and gains of their actions; high control persons, conversely, under less provocation to act immediately, would consider what their actions would do to their control balances.

Alex Piquero, Matthew Hickman, and various associates have provided several key operationalizations of control balance's basic concepts.[4] For example, Piquero and Hickman (1999) wrote that self-reported rates of predation and defiance acts among college students were, as predicted, high among those with control deficits; however, the rates were also high for those with control surpluses. In an examination of gender differences, Hickman and Piquero (2001) again obtained mixed results. Contrary to Tittle's theory, both forms of imbalance predicted both repressive and autonomous deviance with gender variations. That is, control imbalance works well to explain repressive deviance for female college students but not males, and it explains autonomous deviance for males but not females. Adding rational choice elements, Piquero and Hickman (2001) observed that the ability of imbalances to predict the intent to commit predatory offenses was greatest under conditions of high pleasure and low risk. Piquero and associates (2001, 2003) also extended the theory to victims and found that persons with both forms of control imbalance were more likely to be theft victims than were balanced persons. Finally, Hickman and associates (2001) applied the theory to police deviance. Using a survey of randomly selected patrol officers, they found support for Tittle's theory, albeit for a minor form of police deviance: Officers with control deficits were more likely to violate the police code of silence by reporting fellow officers' involvement in illicit behavior; however, the same was not true for control surpluses.

Tests of control balance theory tend to involve either relatively minor offending or college-student populations. In an exception to this generalization, Stephen Baron and David Forde (2007) sampled homeless street youths in British Columbia, Canada, presenting their subjects with scenarios involving three forms of deviance, including property and assault crimes and asking a series of questions about their subjects' reactions to the scenarios. Using measures of control—those circumstances over which they have control versus circumstances that exert control over them—similar to those used by Piquero and associates, Baron and Forde found that both control surpluses and deficits relate to engagement in violent and serious theft; only when peers were introduced as a variable did these control elements explain minor theft offending. However, Baron and Forde's work did not support Tittle's (2004) contention that self-control levels conditionally impact control surpluses and deficits (see also Piquero and Hickman 2001).

Generally, then, critics note several problems with the theory, including the following:

- *Logical inconsistencies, definitional difficulties, and other lapses.* Joachim Savelsberg (1996, 1999) and Gary Jensen (1999) assailed Tittle's assumptions about the human condition; the vagueness of his definitions of deviance, power, and control; and the theory's general conceptual ambiguities. In striving to present a general theory, claimed the critics, Tittle provided too little concreteness.

- *Expressions of control imbalance.* The idea of an imbalance resembles Sutherland's differential association principle, and the same question is relevant here: How much of an imbalance, asked Braithwaite (1997) is required? Tittle described small, medium, and large imbalances but did not reveal the differences.

- *Inconsistent results involving minor forms of misconduct.* Control imbalances—both surpluses and deficits—may be related to deviance in certain contexts, including defiant law-breaking acts by college students, such as marijuana smoking and frequent drunkenness (Curry and Piquero 2003) and exploitation of their peers, such as using another to obtain class notes (Higgins and Lauterbach 2004). Moreover, in a study of corporate misbehavior, Nicole L. Piquero and Alex Piquero (2006) found support for the notion that white-collar exploitative conduct, such as taking advantage of a peer in the workplace, relates best to situations of control surpluses rather than control deficits.

Control Balance and Public Policy   While Tittle (1997, 2001) specifically avoided policy concerns, Braithwaite (1997) nonetheless saw a number of policy implications in control balance theory, as predation, exploitation, and plunder threaten **republican freedom,** or "freedom as non-domination, liberty that is assured by legal, social, and economic guarantees that those with greater power will have their ability to dominate us checked" (p. 89). From the standpoint of republication freedom, then, control balance theory has several implications, including these:

1. *Greater equality of control.* This idea entails redistributing control from those with surpluses to those with deficits. One way to achieve this is by redistributing wealth from the rich to the poor.

2. *Republication virtue in the exercise of control.* Control is essential, and so is commitment to a rule of law, in which no one feels above the law even in the exercise of control. However, the favored republication way to exercise control is through dialogue, whereby the objects of control give their consent.

3. *Greater acceptance of control.* A key goal in any community must be to help those who resist being controlled to understand the necessity of it. According to Braithwaite (1997:92), "We should support those controls that in their ultimate effects increase freedom as non-domination, [and] resist controls that reduce republication freedoms."

4. *Stronger social bonds, social support, and communities.* Extreme inequalities wilt in the face of strong social bonds, social support, and communities. "When

social bonds are strong in a society, shaming of domination, pride in non-domination and respectfulness are more likely to prevail. So is shaming of the predation that arises from the control imbalances that remain" (Braithwaite 1997:93).

These policy implications are broad and abstract, as is the theory. Similar observations were made about other crime theories when they first emerged. As control balance is tested and refined, the policy statements should become more focused and concrete.

In sum, control balance theory is one of the few truly new theories of the late twentieth century. Moreover, Tittle has responded to his critics by extending and refining the theory in the best spirit of theoretical elaboration. While tests of the theory to date are limited in their scope and samples, the theory nonetheless merits further attention to clarify its position as a criminological theory (Baron and Forde 2007).

Theoretical Exemplar 2: Life-Course and Developmental Criminology

Criminals rarely emerge suddenly without any prior warnings, no matter what causal factors are at work. Over the past 20 years, this observation has pushed criminologists in different directions. In the early 1980s, criminologists debated the issue of criminal propensity versus criminal careers. The impetus was a longitudinal study conducted in Philadelphia by Marvin Wolfgang and his associates (1972), who explored delinquency in a single birth cohort (i.e., all persons sharing the same birth year). They found that 6 percent of the juveniles accounted for 52 percent of all juvenile–police contacts and an astounding 70 percent of all juvenile contacts for felony offenses.

Criminologists disagreed over the theoretical and practical implications of Wolfgang's cohort study. One group's position was summed up in *Criminal Careers and "Career Criminals,"* a two-volume report authored by Albert Blumstein and his associates (1986). They saw **career criminals** as chronic offenders who engage in a high volume of crime over a long time. A **criminal career** is simply a description of the type, volume, nature, and length of a person's involvement in crime. Some careers are short, and others are long. Career criminal advocates focused on high-frequency offenders and examined the **onset** (beginning) and **desistance** (ending) of their careers, as well as the seriousness and duration of their criminal activity. They challenged the long-held belief that rates of offending rise rapidly in the mid-teens, peak in the late teens or early 20s, and drop steadily throughout the 20s. The contrasting idea embodied in the career criminal concept was that frequency of offending does not change, but rather the pool of offenders dips, owing to death or incarceration. Hence, anyone committing crimes after age 20 was a career criminal and a threat to public safety, which lent support to the idea of selectively incapacitating persons designated as career criminals (see Chapter 1).[5]

Michael Gottfredson and Travis Hirschi (1989) opposed the career criminal thesis, proposing instead the **criminal-propensity thesis**—that some people are simply more prone to commit crime than others. Variations in the amount of offending follow the same age–crime curve for all types of crime-prone individuals. The greatest involvement occurs in the late teens, followed by declining involvement. Thus, the curve's appearance is the same for low-crime-prone persons and high-crime-prone ones. The magnitude—the peak offending level—is what differs. Whatever other forces are at work, claimed Gottfredson and Hirschi, as they mature people outgrow criminality. Attempts to identify career criminals are a wasted effort, and more importantly, selective incapacitation simply will not work as a crime reduction technique.

This debate was healthy for criminology.[6] Gottfredson and Hirschi developed event-propensity theory, what others call self control theory (Chapter 7). Adherents to the career criminal position explored theoretical reasons for Blumstein's empirical claims. Out of this latter work came developmental crime theories, a movement which paralleled the development of life-course criminology.

Life-Course Criminology Life-Course Criminology has roots in a 1930s study by Sheldon and Eleanor Glueck (Chapter 3), who collected a wealth of information on two samples of youths, one delinquent and the other nondelinquent, matched in terms of general intelligence, ethnicity, and residence in underprivileged areas. Robert Sampson and John Laub (1993) reanalyzed the Gluecks' qualitative and quantitative data, employing an integrated theory that drew heavily upon social control and labeling theories, with a strong appreciation for large-scale structural forces such as poverty.

Sampson and Laub (1993) use social control as an organizing principle as a means to explore life-course social bonding and included institutions of formal *and* informal social control. They use two concepts: (1) **trajectories,** or long-term developmental pathways over the life course, and (2) **transitory events,** or short-term, specific life events that are part of trajectories and may mark movement from one status to another. These forces operate on individuals according to their age-graded status: (1) becoming juvenile delinquents, (2) making the behavioral transitions that accompany the transition from juvenile status to adulthood, and (3) becoming an adult offender.

According to Sampson and Laub, the family context associated with delinquency includes a lack of supervision, erratic or harsh discipline, and parental rejection. Structural background factors, including family SES, residential mobility, and household crowding, combined with individual differences, including early conduct disorders and difficult temperament, to influence the social bonding associated with family and school. They also acknowledged the relative stability of deviance over the life course, given that the best predictor of future delinquency is past involvement in delinquency. However, change is also an important feature of life-course development. The key issue for Sampson and Laub was how many doors the past misconduct had closed for the individual (see labeling theory), something they called **cumulative continuity,** leading to a type of forced stability. *Transitory events,* then, *may* lead to **turning points,** or changes in life-course trajectories (Laub, Sampson, and Allen 2001:100). For example, social capital emerged as a crucial force for change; those adults with strong ties to friends, family, and job have an investment in conformity even if they were seriously involved in delinquency as late adolescents and young adults. In the absence of transitory events—a new prosocial relationship or an epiphany or awakening after a particularly traumatic event in the person's life, such as the murder of a close friend—cumulative continuity pushes the offender forward throughout his or her criminal career.

Persistent and Limited Offending Psychologist Terrie Moffitt (1993a,b), while studying a panel of New Zealand residents over time, observed two crime trajectories or pathways. **Life-course persistent (LCP) offenders** embark on paths that begin at a very early age. At age 4 and younger, LCP offenders engage in "acting out" behavior such as biting and hitting; by age 10 they are shoplifters and truants. Crime seriousness increases with age, so that by their 20s they are engaging in robbery and rape, and by their 30s are committing fraud and child abuse. Moffitt found that many LCP offenders have neurological problems throughout childhood, perhaps even attention deficit disorder (Chapter 3) and certainly learning difficulties during their school years. As youths they miss out on the acquisition of interpersonal and prosocial skills for two reasons: (1) They are rejected and even avoided by their peers, and (2) their own parents become frustrated with them and often psychologically abandon them (Moffitt 1993a). Living in disorganized homes and violent neighborhoods only exacerbates the LCP offenders' growing tendencies toward antisocial behavior.

LCP offenders are in the minority, as most are **adolescent-limited (AL) offenders,** who begin offending with the start of adolescence and cease causing trouble (desist) around age 18. These offenders differ in several other ways from LCP offenders. First, they lack the LCP offenders' histories early and persistent antisocial behavior. Second, AL offenders learn to get along with others, something LCP offenders rarely master. Third, AL offenders do not exhibit the same depth and duration of neurological problems. Fourth, although the frequency of offending for AL offenders may mimic that of LCP offenders, and neither group can be distinguished in terms of most antisocial and problem behavior indicators in earlier childhood, this changes during the teenage years. Fifth, AL offenders more so than LCP offenders become involved in expressions of autonomy from adult control, including vandalism, alcohol and drug offenses, truancy, and running away. Lastly, unlike the LCP offenders, AL offenders in their late teens can abandon their miscreant ways should they interfere with adult-like goals, such as getting a full-time job or going to college.

In sum, Moffitt's theory blends neuropsychology and developmental psychology. Her work on different trajectories to delinquency and crime helps explain the unique social control threats posed by a small group of early-onset, long-term offenders. It also explains why most delinquents, as AL offenders, have the developmental histories and skills to explore alternative life pathways.

Developmental Criminology   Rolf Loeber and Marc LeBlanc (1990) coined the term **developmental criminology** to provide three sets of insights into criminals:

1. Explore within-individual changes, allowing for comparisons between the subject's offending at different times.

2. Identify those causal factors that predate delinquency and, consequently, impact its course, making it possible to clarify not only the possible causes of onset, escalation, deescalation, and desistance in offending, but also individual differences in these factors among offenders.

3. Study life cycle transitions and other factors as they affect offending.

Developmental criminology owes a debt to the propensity/criminal career debate. Loeber and LeBlanc (1990) contend that only by studying and describing within-individual differences in criminal careers can criminologists hope to understand why some youths become more deeply involved than others. Developmental criminologists assume that the influence of causal factors throughout the cycle is a constant.

Loeber and D. F. Hay (1994) described three developmental pathways to offending. The first is an **authority-conflict pathway,** which children begin before age 12, starting with stubborn conduct, moving to defiance, and settling into authority avoidance. While often a nuisance, adherent to this pathway pose minimal threats to society. A **covert pathway** consists of minor hidden behavior as the first step; however, the misconduct escalates quickly to property damage (e.g., vandalism and arson) and moderate forms of delinquency (e.g., burglary, car theft, and fraud). An **overt pathway** tends to manifest itself as aggression and violence; bullying and annoying behavior are the first step, followed by fighting and, finally, major aggressive acts, including assault and rape.

Identifying a child as an **experimenter** type or a **persister** type is important to developmental criminologists (Loeber, Keenan, and Zhang 1997). Both may start on their respective paths at an early age, but one stops (desists), while the other continues. Given an emphasis on within-individual changes, classification requires more than one assessment over time—hence developmental criminologists' use of longitudinal research.

Overt and covert aggressive acts pose differential threats to the community (Loeber and Stouthamer-Loeber 1998). *Behaviorally* overt aggressors commit their acts in the open and in direct contact with victims; covert aggressors do not like confrontations, preferring to be sneaky, dishonest, or concealed. In developmental criminology terms, then, violent crimes are examples of overt aggression, whereas property crimes are acts of covert aggression. *Emotionally* anger is more important to overt aggression; covert aggression entails far less emotionality. *Cognitively* people who use overt aggression are hostile and exhibit cognitive deficiencies associated with violence-proneness, qualities missing in people who use covert aggression. *Developmentally* overt aggression generally begins early in life (see Moffitt's life-course persistent offenders), but not all overt aggressors come to their acts early. **Late-onset offenders,** criminals who begin their careers well

COMPARATIVE CRIMINOLOGY—WORLD VIEWS ON CRIME AND JUSTICE: An International Perspective on Life-Span Offending

The developmental perspective is one of the most globalized in criminology. For example, Lisa Broidy and colleagues report on developmental trajectories found in six different studies conducted in the U.S., Canada, and New Zealand. They looked at the aggression's developmental course, focusing on its roots in children and its manifestation in adolescence. They found that chronic, repetitive occurrences of physical aggression in the elementary school years increased the risk for later physical violence and even nonphysical forms of delinquency, especially during adolescence. However, they observed these patterns across all studies and nations only for boys. That is, there does not appear to be a clear link between early physical aggression and adolescent offending for the girls in their samples. Even girls who exhibited chronic physical aggression in elementary school did not necessarily develop into problem delinquents later in life, although the same cannot be said of similarly disposed boys.

This comparative study is important for several reasons. First, it provides clear support for the notions advanced in Chapter 11 that when theorizing about female criminality, especially that found among young girls, criminologists have much room for improvement. Second, it also suggests that when researchers explore their causal arguments across time and space, the results can be rewarding. Finally, it reinforces the conclusion that while developmental models are useful in predicting some forms of early onset offending, crime across the life-course remains an elusive target.

SOURCE: Broidy, Tremblay, et al. (2003).

after adolescence, constitute a minority within the offender population and are rarely studied (Loeber and Stouthamer-Loeber 1998).

In sum developmental criminology, with its emphasis on longitudinal research designs and within-individual analyses, seeks to identify "keystone" behaviors for subsequent criminality. "In other words, we should know at what ages or developmental stages certain potential targets for intervention become more stable and less malleable" (Loeber and Loeber-Stouthamer 1996:22). Once these keystones are identified, treatments for them can be designed and subsequent criminality reduced. The above box provides strong evidence that such ideas have cache outside the American experience.

Assessing Life-Course and Developmental Criminology   Sampson and Laub found that the Gluecks' 1930s data comported well with a life-course analysis. Bonds to school, family, and peers were among the strongest features, with the operation of the latter two forces leading one criminologist to wonder about the theory's ties to differential association and social learning theories (Akers 2000:251). Some tests have centered on central themes. For example, marriage is a key turning point. Using the Glueck data, John Laub and his associates (1998) found that marriage leads to a reduction in crime and delinquency, although this process of desistance appears to be gradual and cumulative. Mark Warr (1998) also found that marriage has an ameliorative impact on offending. However, marriage may not be the turning point, but a transition to other forces. That is, marriage reduces the time spent with delinquent friends and provides alternative peer associations, adding credibility to the notion that social learning forces may be at work as well. Critics note that to date researchers have emphasized change and desistance from criminal conduct, largely ignoring other key parts of the theory (Mazerolle 2000).

Do developmental models/taxonomies/theories/hypotheses fit the data? The research results are mixed. Studies by developmental criminologists, including a merger of Pittsburgh and Dunedin (New Zealand) youths, support divergent crime pathways (Caspi, Moffitt, et al. 1994; Moffitt, Lynam, and Silva 1994). Stephen Tibbetts and Alex Piquero (1999) tested one of Moffitt's hypotheses— the interaction between increased risk for neuropsychological disorders and disadvantaged childhood environments. They found—consistent with Moffitt—that these factors interact to predict early-onset but not late-onset offending. Tibbetts and Piquero also specified gender-specific models: Males had the interactions, but females did not. Although Moffitt's theory distinguished between early and later initiators of violence, Todd Herrenkohl and associates (2001) found that youths who initiated violence early *and* late follow similar pathways during adolescence. Rather than more pathways, there may be fewer, or the pathways may be more complex than previously thought, differing for males and females, a point that configures well with the gender-inclusive theorizing described in Chapter 11.

Developmental criminology assumed a prominent research position in the last decade of the twentieth century. Not only are the questions posed and the answers provided theoretically important, but also, as with the Philadelphia cohort study and the crime propensity/criminal career debate, the results generated more questions, including these:

- *Are developmental theories really theories, or are they hypotheses or taxonomies?* Loeber and associates described their efforts as moving in the direction of a theory. They provided assumptions for developmental theory and many pathways, models, and testable hypotheses; however, clearly stated conceptual linkages are missing. Moffitt described her efforts as taxonomical, meaning the focus was on classifying offenders into discrete categories, describing their collective characteristics, and trying to determine the forces responsible for their membership in a given category.

- *Is developmental criminology anything more than a merger and restatement of personality theories, the IQ–crime hypothesis, and various behavioral theories?* Moffitt and others who have looked at neuropsychological risk tended to use test scores and psychological assessments not unlike those explored in Chapter 5 (Simons, Johnson, et al. 1998; Tibbetts and Piquero 1999). It is even possible that youths on high-risk pathways, including the chronic offenders identified by Wolfgang, were psychopaths (Vaughan and DiLisi 2008). It is unclear how these conceptual arguments about pathways escape the limitations associated with personality theories, impulsivity hypotheses, and IQ testing.

- *How many developmental paths are there?* Moffitt identified two paths, inferring the possibility of more. Loeber and Loeber-Stouthamer described three pathways. After studying the paths taken by British boys, Daniel Nagin and Kenneth Land (1993) outlined four: (1) Moffitt's adolescence-limited offenders; (2) high-level chronic offenders, basically lifetime-persistent offenders; (3) low-level chronic offenders, individuals who reached a relatively low

---

COMMENTS AND CRITICISMS: How Do Criminologists View Crime Theories?

Anthony Walsh and associates periodically survey criminologists as to how they assess current crime theories. In 1988, they surveyed presenters at the annual meeting of the **American Society of Criminology**,[7] who put social control and social learning at the top of their list of theories capable of explaining both serious/persistent offending and delinquency/minor offending. When it came to specific forces motivating serious/persistent offenders, the presenters most often cited "an economic system that prevents participation of some individuals." They blamed delinquent and minor offending on "poor supervision in the home or unstable and uncaring family."

Presenters at the 1997 ASC meetings saw social control as the one theory best able to explain serious/persistent offending. They linked delinquency/less serious offending to low self-control. Social learning fell out of the top five, while differential association moved up for both types of offending. They again saw a frustrating economic system as the most important single cause of serious/persistent offending, but in this survey they considered peer influences as among the most important factors associated with delinquent/minor offending.

After a 10-year hiatus, Walsh and associates again surveyed criminologists in 2007. Rather than rely on participants at the ASC annual meetings, they asked all members of the ASC to participate in an online survey,

and about one-third of the membership complied. With respect to which theories best explain serious/persistent offending, the members capped their top 10 list with social learning, followed in descending order by life-course/developmental, social control, social disorganization, self-control, social disorganization, biosocial, rational choice, conflict, critical, and differential association theories. Delinquent and minor adult offending presented a slightly different list, topped again by social learning theory, following by social control, differential association, social disorganization, routine activities, self-control, life-course/developmental, labeling, biosocial, and rational choice theories. Lack of empathy and concern for others edged out a frustrating economic system to top the list of broad causal factors for serious and persistent offending; delinquency and minor adult offending, on the other hand, caused by peer influences also edged out lack of supervision and monitoring by the family as a broad causal factor.

These surveys beg an interesting question: What influences criminologists when they look for a theory? Can you answer that question for yourself? That is, what have you come to look for in a criminological theory?

SOURCE: Ellis and Hoffman (1990); Ellis and Walsh (1999); Ellis, Cooper, and Walsh (2008).

---

plateau of offending early on and stayed there after turning 18 (or subdivisions of Moffitt's life-course persistent offenders); and (4) never-convicted offenders. Given the developmental criminologists' methodology, the task of uncovering pathways may be unending or divisible into increasingly smaller pathway groups.

Overall, developmental theories serve as a rich source of speculation about the mix of neuropsychological conditions, prenatal and perinatal events, and environments that produce offenders. They are an equally rich source of policies and practices. And, as the following Comments and Criticisms suggests, criminologists increasingly see them as a viable alternative to other theorizing about crime.

Life-Course/Developmental Theories, Public Policy, and Criminal Justice Practices   Life-course and developmental theories have important public policy implications. For example, Moffitt's theory of life-course persistent offenders suggests that impulsivity, early neuropsychological problems, and cyclical interactions with parents intensify the childhood misbehavior problems common to most adolescents. These troubles manifest themselves as school-based difficulties, especially as related to impulsivity, and eventually as delinquency and adult crime. Understanding impulsivity alone may assist in changing the lives of many high-risk children. Interrupting a troubling trajectory can potentially lower the probability of criminality.

These theories suggest that prenatal and early interventions by trained medical staff may offset criminality trajectories. For example, David Olds and his associates (1998) reported on a 15-year follow-up of prenatal and early-childhood home visitations conducted in upstate New York. The researchers randomly assigned volunteer test subjects to one of four treatment conditions, including some combination of the following: prenatal care, free transportation, sensory and developmental screening services, clinical evaluations and treatment, and nurse visitations in the home (the number of visits before and after birth varied widely). The children were reexamined 15 years later, through self-reports, probation or family court data, and school or teacher report data. The findings supported the idea that program effects were greatest with regard to early-onset antisocial behavior (in contrast to more common and less serious puberty-related antisocial behavior). Compared to the other groups, adolescents born to women who received nurse visits during pregnancy and postnatally—and who had high risk factors for antisocial behavior (e.g., unmarried mothers and mothers in low-SES households)—reported less incidence of running away; fewer arrests, convictions, and probation violations; fewer lifetime sex partners; and fewer days of having consumed alcohol in the past six months (Olds et al. 1998). Their parents reported that their children had fewer behavioral problems related to the use of alcohol and other drugs.

In the absence of prenatal and early childhood interventions, other interventions hold promise. That is, the timely treatment of early neuropsychological problems or the introduction of special classes in parenting skills with high-risk children may lower the risk for school failure (Greenwood, Model, et al. 1996). An experiment in Montreal, Quebec, explored this question by randomly assigning boys (and their volunteer families) identified as disruptive in kindergarten to either an experimental group, where their parents received special training, or a control group (Tremblay et al. 1992). Parents in the experimental group received training based on the Oregon Social Learning Center's program of consistent, nonphysical discipline (Patterson 1982; Patterson, Reid, et al. 1975).[8] After two years of training, which included social skills training for the boys, and a total elapsed time of five years, the experimental subjects were less physically aggressive in school, were in age-appropriate regular classrooms, and reported fewer delinquent behaviors. However, there may be limits to the ability of preschool programs to impact positively the lives (and crime pathways) of children with serious medical conditions observed after birth (Pagani, Tremblay, et al. 1998).

The Office of Juvenile Justice and Delinquency Prevention (OJJDP), part of the National Institute of Justice, launched its Strengthening America's Families Initiative in the mid-1980s and serves as a clearinghouse for family-oriented programs (Coolbaugh and Hansel 2000). Family-strengthening programs make direct or implicit references to Bandura and other behaviorists (Chapter 5) as providing the theoretical grounding for their programs. In nearly all, the family is central both to the problem and to the solution, with key causal forces described in terms familiar to learning theorists, while others use a developmental approach to delinquency and drug use prevention and intervention.

Among the programs' goals are helping parents learn effective parenting and avoid abusive parenting and child-rearing practices (Bavolek 2000). In 1992, Prevent Child Abuse America created Healthy Families America, and by 2001 this organization was serving 420 communities in 39 states, the District of Columbia, and Canada, providing services prenatally or at birth along with risk factor assessment and treatments (Erickson 2001:1).

The specific role of agents of social control under the umbrella of developmental criminology is unclear. The theory describes pathways beginning as young as age 3 or 4 and recommends early interventions. Hence, there is little that law enforcement or corrections can do to aid in this process. Police removal of youths from abusive families or diversion of the family into one of the family-strengthening programs is one possibility, as the police are often the first respondents in cases of parent–child conflicts. The courts, especially family and juvenile courts, may also play a role in altering a given pathway by ordering participation in one of the programs, although voluntary participation is generally best. Removal of an at-risk child from an abusive family situation is another alternative.

In sum, the quest for new theories is laudable and equally fraught with difficulties. The resulting work, as Braithwaite pointed out and as exemplified by Tittle's control balance theory, often comes under unusually critical scrutiny, especially when they offer general theories. Theoretical elaborations continue, as evidenced by the body of work reviewed in this text. Perhaps we have not exhausted the ability of existing theories to yield meaningful insights into crimes and criminals. In answer to the second question, then, criminologists most likely will continue on multiple paths. Some will pursue theoretical elaboration; others will integrate existing concepts, propositions, and theories; and a few will offer genuinely new and unique insights into crime and criminals.

QUESTION 3: ARE NEW QUESTIONS OR NEW PARADIGMS NEEDED?

Developing new questions may prove to be the broadest and most difficult strategy to implement. As a strategy, it suggests that the questions currently informing criminologists either are inadequate to the task or have yielded all possible insights into crime and criminals. Ironically, before we can even begin to frame new questions, a number of historical and entrenched barriers to thinking about new questions must be broached.

Overcoming Disciplinary and Political Philosophical Barriers

Our quest for knowledge is often delimited by those who have preceded us in that search or, more often, those who educated us. Existing knowledge, complete with ideological, philosophical, academic disciplinary, and political components, defines the issues and questions, which is good because it provides structure. However, structure is also confining, meaning that where we can look for possible answers is often defined for us by these same ideologies, philosophies, academic disciplines, and politics.

One person's theory is another person's ideology, and what is ideology for some may be theology for others. In a given crime theory, then, it is possible that what we are seeing is something that has taken on a life of its own or, to use a Latin term, *sui generis*. Challenging a particular theory or its underlying assumptions may assume the status of heresy. Similar problems exist for criminologists who suggest that the nature–nurture dichotomy inhibits thinking about crime. Life, they observe, is rarely a matter of *either* nature *or* nurture. Attempts to discern which is the more important force may be the modern equivalent of the Gordian knot, an insoluble problem with a simple solution: Appreciate the differences but treat both forces as essential and interrelated.

Disciplinary Barriers   Existing disciplinary barriers inhibit the creation of new questions. For example, such theorists as biocriminologist Ellis (Chapter 3) and psychological-behaviorist Eysenck (Chapter 5) have suggested that we must look beyond parochial academic disciplines, such as biology, chemistry, psychology, sociology, or economics, as the source of answers to all questions of crime and criminality. Crime is, after all, a complex problem requiring complex and multidisciplinary answers. Indeed, Ray Jeffery (1978:149–50) described how in the late 1940s three "giants" in the behavioral sciences—the legal philosopher Jerome Hall, the sociologist Edwin Sutherland, and the behavioral psychologist B. F. Skinner—worked within a hundred yards of each other on the Indiana University campus but had no significant mutual interaction. Such is the strength of disciplinary boundaries, ones criminologists such as Jeffery suggest have outlived their usefulness in the study of crime. Indeed, as his Indiana University example illustrates, they constitute barriers to the free exchange of ideas.

A number of sociologists contend that criminology should be a social science in its own right. In Marvin Wolfgang's (1963) opinion, criminology has amassed its own information and theories. Individuals who devote all or most of their scholarly time and resources to the study of crime and its control should be designated as criminologists. Daniel Glaser (1965:773) writes that criminology should be regarded as a "synthesizing discipline." Don Gibbons (1979:4) observes that much criticism has focused on the fact that mainstream criminology is ignorant of criminal law and criminal procedure, two important elements in criminal justice. Moreover, "other commentators on the criminological enterprise have taken note of its a historical character, its silence on the question of psychological forces in criminality, and other signs of *academic provincialism*" (Gibbons 1979:4; emphasis added).

Some sociologists are less than sanguine about the prospect of nonsociological criminology. For example, Ronald Akers (1992) maintained that sociology remains "very much the intellectual 'center of gravity' in criminology, and criminology remains an important part of sociology." He defined criminology not as a separate discipline, but rather as an area of study in sociology. Akers drew upon the basic definition of criminology offered by Sutherland (1947): Criminology is the study of the making of law, the breaking of law, and the social reaction to laws. There is nothing in this definition that designates a particular approach or perspective; rather, all that is mentioned is the object of study. To be a discipline, argued Akers, there must be some sort of perspective—such as a sociological, economic, biological, or psychological perspective—that defines how crime is studied.

This theme was driven home in Chapter 3, but especially in the research and observations of Rafter (2008) and Wright and associates (2008a,b) concerning sociological biases against biocriminology in its historical and current forms. The twentieth century was criminology's sociological century. It is doubtful that a single discipline will dominate the work of criminologists in the twenty-first century.

Political Barriers   Science must be autonomous, that is, free from external restrictions and constraints (Kaplan 1963). This statement does not mean that science need be free from criticisms or comments. Peer review—a process by which other researchers or scientists review findings to determine if they are devoid of bias or mistakes—is intended to keep scientists honest. Moreover, as we learned in the section on experimental designs, replications keep scientists honest. It is particularly distressing for scientists, therefore, when their work is subject to political pressures.

Value-neutrality, first advanced for sociology by Max Weber, means that "sociology, like other sciences, needed to be unencumbered by personal values if it is to make a special contribution to society" (Babbie 1983:465). However, questions about crime theory, crime research, and crime policy have become increasingly political—and tied to various value-laden positions—over the past 30 years, certainly since researchers began to question what works and at what cost (Martinson 1974). Political barrier appear to merge with academic barriers. Bridging both may prove to be the most difficult single task confronting twenty-first century criminologists.

As Akiva Liberman (2009:1) notes, if criminologists want to influence criminal justice policies and practices in a positive fashion, they need to demonstrate the value of **evidence-generating policies,** which he defines as "advocating that policy-makers treat policy changes as experimental and expected outcomes as hypotheses, and implement those policies in such a way as to generate reasonable evidence about their effect." This is the distinction between "trying a policy" and committing to it before the policy has been tried to its alleged effects. In light of the latter approach, unforeseen and sometimes unintended consequences can result: this happened with three-strikes legislation and various drug-control sentencing practices on the nation's prison population generally and on blacks in particular (Mays and Ruddell 2008; Walker 2006). The question remains, which criminologists are willing to politicize their theoretical and research efforts?

The Case for the Paradigm Shifts in the Study of Crime and Criminals

Thomas Kuhn (1970), physicist and philosopher, coined the term **scientific revolutions** to explain how quantum leaps in knowledge, or paradigm shifts, occur in the sciences. *paradigm* is, according to Kuhn (1970), a fundamental model or scheme that organizes our view of something; it is "a set of recurrent and quasi-standard illustrations of various theories in their conceptual, observational, and instrumental applications." A paradigm may not give us the answers to our questions, but it tells us where to look by governing "not a subject matter but rather a group of practitioners" (Kuhn 1970:180).

After a period of growth in which scientific knowledge evolves, many sciences are characterized by periods of paradigm validation, followed by normal, incremental growth and, perhaps, intellectual stagnation. The old truths (and old paradigms) become the only truths. Any challenges to those truths are heresy and universally condemned by "true scientists." According to Kuhn, the big breakthroughs in science—paradigm shifts resulting in scientific revolutions—occur when new thinkers enter the arena and challenge the status quo. The clarity of their arguments and the level of their proof carry the day, the science moves forward, often undergoing a radical transformation, and thus creates a scientific revolution. As evidence of this process, Kuhn cited examples from chemistry and physics, such as the replacement of Newtonian physics by Einstein's relativity. Kuhn believed that scientific revolutions were not limited to the physical sciences, a suggestion taken to heart by more than a few social scientists.

Two paradigms dominate the criminology: classicalism and positivism. Within positivism, the nature–nurture controversy created a second-layer paradigm. These paradigms have been challenged by conflict (Chapter 9), Marxist (Chapter 10), critical race (Chapter 11), and feminist paradigms (Chapter 11), each suggesting different questions and different solutions. In the twenty-first century, it is possible that new insights into crime will come from an emerging perspective: postmodernism.

Postmodernism: A New Paradigm for the Study of Crime and Criminals?

The 1960s were a decade of change in American society and culture. To some social critics, the 1960s were ripe with secular humanism, a philosophy directed toward the attainment of a wide range of human interests but generally at the expense of traditional religious doctrines and practices. These critics called the 1960s "the Fall" (Woodiwiss 1993)—for some of them, the beginning of the end of the **modern era.** The beginning of the modern era is variously attributed to the 1930s New Deal era and the post–World War II era of American preeminence; it ended, according to most critics, in the late 1980s (Woodiwiss 1993:13). The modern era was notable for its emphasis on unchecked economic growth both as an end in itself and as a precursor to other positive changes (Cobb 1993). Dissatisfaction with the modern era, grounded as it was in laissez-faire capitalism, led to both antimodern sentiments and a belief that society must go beyond the modern to some new level. The worldview that evolved from seventeenth-century science—and the collective works of Galileo, Descartes, Bacon, and Newton—was rejected, a view that defined the **postmodern era.**

Postmodernism "refers to a diffuse sentiment rather than to any common set of doctrines—the sentiment that humanity can and must go beyond the modern" (Griffin and Falk 1993:xii). The fact of the postmodern era is taken as a given; what to do about it is open to debate. Postmodernists contend that there are two ways of achieving this goal (Griffin and Falk 1993; Rosenau 1992). **Deconstructive postmodernists** wish to completely abandon the past, the modern era. They adopt an antiworldview that calls for the elimination of all the ingredients necessary to create a worldview, including "God, self, purpose, meaning, a real world, and truth as correspondence" (Griffin and Falk 1993: xii), a position some might label nihilistic (i.e., a total rejection of laws and institutions, morality, and judgments). **Constructive postmodernists** call not for the total dissolution of the modern era, but rather for a revision of those premises and traditional concepts that are a part of modernism. In short, constructive postmodernists separate and save the wheat of the modernist era while disposing of its chaff.

Postmodern Society and Culture   Postmodernism has several implications for society. According to one view, a generation of youths is being socialized into a mass-media-generated culture (Mead 1970), with an accompanying loss of historical consciousness in the youth-oriented media's "cut and paste" temporal orientation (MTV's "Rock the Vote" campaign in 1992) and an embracement of "just do it" youthful pragmatism. This postmodern culture reflects a loss of stable social-identity references and a sense of community. For example, Robert Bellah and associates (1985) noted the loss of community ties in the United States and an increasing emphasis on **instrumentalism** (i.e., making money) and **expressive individualism** (i.e., exploring oneself). The theme of instrumental individualism, especially as related to the cultural trend of "by any means necessary," is central to Steven Messner and Richard Rosenfeld's (1994) institutional anomie (Chapter 6). In a postmodern world, competing images and symbols not only appear in contemporary life, but also are viewed as commodities and marketed worldwide by media and informational technologies in what has become an important structural feature of current capitalist society. One has only to consider the public interest in and merchandising of O. J. Simpson's trial for double homicide or the popularity of movies like *The Silence of the Lambs* to understand the blurring of the distinction between fiction and reality in the postmodern era.

Media dominance in shaping culture is a popular theme in postmodernist literature (Baudrillard 1988). Norman Denzin (1991), for example, noted that the sociological metaphor of the "dramaturgical" society has become interactional reality (see also Goffman's contributions to the dramaturgical approach in Chapter 8). Postmodernism emphasizes the idea that culture has become more fluid and relative, appropriated by the individual actor to meet situational needs. Because culture is itself a fusion of competing images, each individual has the more complex task of interpreting both behavior and the rapidly shifting cultural environment. The "self" becomes crafted by conflicting media symbols and images—images that are less cohesive and more "schizophrenic" (Deleuze and

Guattani 1983; Jameson 1984). As a result, people have trouble making sense of their environment or their place in space and time (Harvey 1989).

Losers and Winners in the Postmodern Era   Shifts in power, loss of individual and community identity, culture in flux—postmodernism would seem, on the surface, to provide new grist for the social science mill through the incorporation of cultural themes as variables in existing empirical and theoretical work. However, as Pauline Marie Rosenau (1992) noted, the extremes of postmodernist thought, particularly "skeptical" or "deconstructionist" postmodernists, have created a serious challenge for social scientists. Skeptical postmodernists question the existence of a body of knowledge that can be regarded as "social scientific," that is, positivistic. They argue that no criteria of evidence can be used to empower one claim of truth over another, and they doubt whether any social science can adequately describe or "represent" the experiences of another person or group (Baudrillard 1988). The skeptics tend to follow the lead of the German philosopher Friedrich Nietzsche, "taking... 'perspectivist' and 'relativist' positions that theories, at best, provide partial perspectives on their objects, and that all cognitive representations of the world are historically and linguistically mediated" (Best and Kellner 1991:4).

Besides challenging positivism, many postmodernists also call into question Marxist images. In particular they criticize Marxists' analyses of capitalism for relying on historical and linguistic interpretations that are, for postmodernists, highly suspect (Woodiwiss 1993). However, neo-Marxist postmodernists (see, e.g., Harvey 1989; Jameson 1991) also theorize that postmodernism is a historical phase of capitalism. They argue that "the present consumer or post-industrial phase of capitalist development, far from contradicting Marx's earlier analysis, in fact represents a purer, more developed, and more realized form of capitalism" (Best and Kellner 1991:185). Depending on whom you read, Marxism is either refuted or supported by postmodern theory (Best and Kellner 1991; Giddens 1990; Habermas 1981; Woodiwiss 1993). A paradigm shift to postmodernism could mean new life for criminological theories based on the relative concept of power—especially, it would appear, power over the media.

Clear winners in the postmodern era include qualitative methodologies, such as symbolic interactionism, social phenomenology, and ethnomethodology. The relativism of postmodern theory seems comparable to the symbolic interactionist position that social reality is fluid, constantly recreated and reproduced in new situations. Denzin (1991), for one, was concerned with control over popular culture, definitions of the American Dream, happiness, gender, class, and the like, which are developed by the new power elite of journalists, politicians, and advertisers. As Denzin (1991:24) further noted, the postmodern tradition follows the methodological tradition "that society in the here-and-now, society-at-hand, is best understood as an interactional accomplishment... mediated by localized, interactional practices." Critical analysis also receives support from revisionist post-modernists: Although emphasizing critical theoretical positions that are largely antipositivistic, they provide new images of reform and revitalization for the social sciences (Arrigo and Bernard 1997; Rosenau 1992).

Postmodernism and the Study of Crime   Postmodernism has several implications for the study of crime. Linguistic postmodernist criminologists would
have us reject most, if not all, of criminology as another oppressive offshoot
of the failed Enlightenment (Henry and Milovanovic 1991). However, the media's role in creating a pliable image of American culture is far more difficult to
dismiss; some argue that criminologists should counter with a **newsmaking
criminology** that provides an alternative reality (Barak 1988). It is becoming
increasingly difficult to tell reality from fiction, truth from lie. The questions
asked are similar to those discussed in Chapters 8 and 9: Who is in control of
creating these images? Whose interests do they serve? Stuart Henry and Dragan
Milovanovic (1991:110) offered answers to these questions in **constitutive
criminology:**

> Constitutive criminology is concerned with identifying the way in
> which the interrelationships between human agents and their social
> world constitute crime, victims, and control as realities. It is oriented to
> how we may deconstruct these realities and to how we may reconstruct
> less harmful alternatives. Simultaneously, it is concerned with how
> emergent socially constructed realities themselves constitute human
> agents with the implication that, if crime is to be replaced, this neces-
> sarily must involve a deconstruction and reconstruction of the human
> subject.

Postmodernism emphasizes critical assessment, particularly radical neo-Marxist
postmodernists and race-Crits (Chapter 11; see also Arrigo and Barrett 2008).
A postmodernist criminology would likely be concerned with deconstructing
the texts of "law producers," in line with the work of Chambliss and Seidman
(Chapter 9). Given postmodernists' overriding cultural concerns, a critical question for postmodern criminology would be the following: Is criminal behavior
simply another human response to the overwhelming aspects of contemporary
postmodern society?

In sum, the movement toward new questions and new paradigms is difficult
to predict. In the final decade of the twentieth century, postmodernist criminologists added their voices to those questioning the dominant paradigms (Arrigo
and Barrett 2008). Little contemporary mainstream criminology would survive
in a postmodernist criminology. It seems unlikely that all knowledge about crime
as we know it will be abandoned. However, as Kuhn noted (1970), a mature
science is one with a single paradigm. By this measure criminology is far from a
mature science.

Theorists and researchers alike have questioned the wisdom of viewing
the various paradigms as mutually exclusive. New theoretical perspectives have
been merged with old ones, creating exciting and highly promising ways of
viewing the "crime problem." The old reasons for rejecting various unappealing
explanations for current crime problems no longer seem to hold currency.
Existing historical, ideological-philosophical, disciplinary, and political barriers
seem anachronistic in the first decade of the twenty-first century. Instead of

answering this section's question, we are left with a new one: Are we approaching a scientific revolution involving studies of crime and criminals?

SUMMARY

The three questions addressed in this chapter reflect the merger of theory, research, policy, and practices explored in Chapter 1 and throughout the text. Our somewhat qualified answers to each (see Table 12.1) were meant to stimulate discussion about them rather than end debate. As Shakespeare wrote in *The Winter's Tale,* "What's past is prologue." We offer this work as a prologue to crime theory in the twenty-first century. Criminology has come a long way since the days of Lombroso. Feeble, ill-defined, and poorly articulated theories have given way to stronger ones; new methods of theory testing have replaced armchair conjecture and anecdotal evidence. Much work remains to be done, and part of that work must include the development of a spirit of cooperation that transcends the limitations we noted in this chapter.

Criminologists must, in the words of Bernard (1990), seek the falsification of theories (negative learning) simultaneously with the verification of knowledge (positive learning); that is, they must separate the good theories from the bad. Only then can science—in this case the study of crime, criminals, and society's reactions to both—assume a set of "findings and move beyond them to add to

T A B L E 12.1   Summary of Key Questions (and Answers)

Questions	Basic Idea(s)	Strengths	Weaknesses	Overall Assessment
Focus on specific methods?	Two research methods—experimental and longitudinal designs—have the potential to answer the difficult causal questions buried within most crime theories.	Provides structured, highly scientific procedures to follow; yields high-quality information about any phenomenon for which time is a variable.	Is expensive and time-consuming; may lead to an overreliance on quantitative methods at the expense of far richer and contextualized qualitative ones.	Proceed cautiously. Experiments and longitudinal studies are expensive and often time-consuming; they may not yield definitive answers.
Create new theories?	Criminology has reached a creative dead end; new theories are needed to jump-start the search for crime explanations.	Allows new ideas to enter criminology and old ones to be revisited, possibly merging the two.	May divert attention from highly fruitful existing theories, ones that only need better data, better analysis, or better conceptualizing.	May yield new theoretical and empirical leads; researchers should proceed with caution and avoid conflicting assumptions.
Ask new questions/ employ new paradigms?	We have exhausted the creative energy of "modern" ideas and theories, and are entering a new era with new theories, opportunities, and directions.	Provides something new that is attractive for what it represents: the potential to reveal truths hidden within something that is as of yet untried.	*See strengths;* offers new questions/paradigms that may require new methods and analytic procedures, along with new ways to test and build theories.	Some criminologists will explore new directions, but most energy will be expended in pursuit of existing paradigms.

the depth and breadth of knowledge in the context of that theory," or what Kuhn called "normal science" (Bernard 1990:326). Problematically, Thomas Bernard (1990:329) saw "nothing in criminology that researchers can simply assume and move beyond when they organize new research," the first step in defining scientific progress.

Little will happen to change Bernard's characterization of crime theory until and unless all extant theories are critically examined, tested, and either accepted or rejected, for both their empirical soundness and their practical utility. As the psychologist Kurt Lewin (1951:169) is quoted as saying, "Nothing is as practical as a good theory." A generation before, Lewis Madison Terman (1906:72), the psychologist responsible for instituting the IQ test in America, wrote, "Theory that does not some way affect life has no value." These emphases guided this textbook's orientation to the study of theory.

In conclusion, we offer two final caveats. First, we have throughout this text sought to provide explanations of theory for the "theoretically challenged." Therefore, at times we have lowered the level of conceptual abstraction and, perhaps for theoretical purists, thereby slightly altered the original theory. We hope that this has not occurred with any regularity. Second, in this final chapter we made some marginally outrageous statements and suggestions about crime theories and the future. There is nothing in these strategies that should be viewed as a blueprint for success. We sought only to challenge you to think critically about crime theory. We hope we have succeeded.

KEY TERMS

accelerated panel design

adolescent-limited (AL) offenders

American Society of Criminology

authority-conflict pathway

autonomous deviance

career criminals

City Project

classic experimental design

collective efficacy

conceptual integration

constitutive criminology

constraints

constructive postmodernists

control balance theory

control deficit

control surplus

covert pathway

criminal career

criminal-propensity thesis

cumulative continuity

decadence

deconstructive postmodernists

defiance

desistance

developmental criminology

evidence-generating policies

exploitation

experimenter

expressive individualism

instrumentalism

late-onset offenders

legal cynicism

life-course criminology

life-course persistent (LCP) offenders

longitudinal panel study

mandatory arrest policy

Minneapolis Domestic Violence Experiment

modern era

natural experiment

newsmaking criminology

onset

overt pathway

persister

placebo

plunder

postmodern era

postmodernism

predation

predispositional motivation

presumptive arrest policy

Project on Human Development in Chicago Neighborhoods

propositional integration

quasi-experimental design

repressive deviance

republican freedoms

scientific revolutions

situational motivations

Spouse Assault Replication Project (SARP)

submission

systematic social observations

theoretical competition

theoretical elaboration

theory falsification

theoretical integration

transitory events

trajectories

turning points

value-neutrality

CRITICAL REVIEW QUESTIONS

1. How would you go about convincing a state or federal legislator to sponsor a longitudinal or experimental study? What logical arguments would you use in support of your position?

2. Using the researchers' names or the City Project's formal name, search the Web or your library for more recent findings from this study. What did you find?

3. What is the official policy of your local law enforcement agency on whom to arrest at a domestic violence call? If they have this policy, why? If not, why not?

4. Can you think of any theories reviewed in this book that might provide a conceptual base for mandatory or presumptive arrests in misdemeanor domestic violence cases?

5. What do you consider to be the most important lesson about criminological research employing experimental or longitudinal designs?

6. What type of theory integration do you think has the most potential to advance criminological thinking? What is the basis of your answer?

7. Each chapter contains at least one comparative criminological example. How have they helped you understand the various theories? What specific goals would help advance the comparative examination of crime theories?

8. Which barrier do you think is most counterproductive—a disciplinary barrier or a political barrier? What is the basis of your answer?

9. Compare and contrast postmodernism and the theories contained in this text. Are there any that might exist in a postmodernist-dominated criminology?

10. Is it true that the public's perspective on criminals is already in the postmodernist era, and that criminology simply has not caught up to that fact? [HINT: Think reality TV.]

NOTES

1. Much of the following is from Sampson and Raudenbush (2001) and Marz and Stamatel (2005).

2. McCord (1989) and Petersilia (1991) address this concern in considerable detail.

3. A seeming contradiction is that those with the least control deficits engage in the most serious forms of crime—predation. Tittle explained it in this way: When deficits are small, people will usually be deterred, but when they commit violations, the acts are far more serious in nature; when deficits are large, people are "less able to imagine that such behavior will escape controlling responses from others" and so engage in less serious forms of crime (Tittle 1995:187). Surpluses function differently. Those with control surpluses commit acts that are proportionately as serious as the control surplus level they perceive.

4. Piquero, prominent in the testing of self-control theory (see Chapter 7), was also instrumental in operationalizing and measuring balance control.

5. The aging process affects criminals whose crime requires physical attributes such as strength and dexterity. Many years ago, as a parole officer in New York, one of the authors (Abadinsky) was assigned a rather proficient burglar whose arrest and conviction resulted from a fluke accident. The man swore that he would never return to his previous line of work. When his parole officer expressed skepticism, he explained: "Oh, I'm not reformed, just flatfooted." A check of prison records indicated that during his incarceration, he had become severely flatfooted. He was an exemplary parolee.

6. The career criminal/crime propensity controversy eventually evolved into a related debate about the type of data necessary to test theories. Gottfredson and Hirschi (1987) argued that, because the age–crime relationship is invariant (unchanging over time), researchers need only employ cross-sectional studies. Blumstein, Jacqueline Cohen, and David Farrington (1988) argued for longitudinal studies. Still others argued that it is not a question of *either* crime propensity *or* criminal careers, of *either* cross-sectional *or* longitudinal studies. Rather, criminology has room for both (Nagin and Land 1993).

7. The American Society of Criminology (ASC) is an organization dedicated to the exchange of ideas and information about crime, criminals, and criminal justice. Members, according to its charter, "pursue scholarly, scientific, and professional knowledge concerning the measurement, etiology, consequences, prevention, control, and treatment of crime and delinquency" (ASC 2009).

8. Gerald Patterson (1982) saw the families of delinquency-prone youths as inadvertently reinforcing antisocial behavior and failing to reinforce prosocial behavior.

References

Abadinsky, H. (1998). *Law and Justice: An Introduction to the American Legal System*, 4th ed. Belmont, CA: Wadsworth.

———. (2000). *Organized Crime*, 6th ed. Belmont, CA: Wadsworth.

———. (2001). *Drug Abuse: An Introduction*, 4th ed. Belmont, CA: Wadsworth.

———. (2002). *Probation and Parole: Theory and Practice*, 7th ed. Upper Saddle River, NJ: Prentice-Hall.

———. (2008). *Drug Use and Abuse: A Comprehensive Introduction*, 6th ed. Thousand Oaks, CA: Wadsworth.

———. (2009). *Probation and Parole: Theory and Practice*, 10th ed. Upper Saddle Creek, NJ: Prentice-Hall.

———. (2010). *Organized Crime*, 9th ed. Belmont, CA: Wadsworth.

Abadinsky, H., and L. T. Winfree, Jr. (1992). *Crime and Justice: An Introduction*. Chicago: Nelson-Hall.

Abraham, H. J. (1975). *The Judicial Process: An Introductory Analysis of the Courts of the United States, England, and France*. New York: Oxford University Press.

Adams, R. (1973). "Differential association and learning principles revisited." *Social Problems* 20: 458–70.

———. (1974). "The adequacy of differential association theory." *Journal of Research in Crime and Delinquency* 11: 1–18.

Addiction Research Unit/SUNY at Buffalo. (1998).

Adler, A. (1963). *The Individual Psychology of Alfred Adler*. New York: Basic Books.

———. (1968)[c.1928]. *Understanding Human Nature*. Trans. W. B. Wolfe. London: G. Allen and Unwin.

Adler, F. (1975). *Sisters in Crime: The Rise of the New Female Criminal*. New York: McGraw-Hill.

———. (1986). "Jails as a repository of former mental patients." *International Journal of Offender Therapy and Comparative Criminology* 30: 225–36.

Adler, F., G. O. W. Mueller, and W. S. Laufer. (1994). *Criminal Justice*. New York: McGraw-Hill.

Adler, J. S. (1989). "A historical analysis of the law of vagrancy." *Criminology* 27: 209–29.

Adorno, T., E. Frenkel-Brunswick, D. L. Levinson, and R. N. Sanford. (1985). *The Authoritarian Personality*. New York: Harper and Row.

Agnew, R. (1985). "A revised strain theory of delinquency." *Social Forces* 64: 151–67.

———. (1991). "A longitudinal test of social control and delinquency." *Journal of Research in Crime and Delinquency* 28: 126–56.

———. (1992). "Foundation for a general strain theory of crime and delinquency." *Criminology* 30: 47–87.

———. (1995). "Strain and subcultural theories of criminality." In *Criminology: A Contemporary Handbook*, ed. Joseph F. Sheley. Belmont, CA: Wadsworth.

Agnew, R., and D. Peterson. (1989). "Leisure and delinquency." *Social Problems* 36: 332–48.

Agnew, R., F. T. Cullen, V. S. Burton, Jr., T. D. Evans, and R. G. Dunaway. (1996). "A new test of classic strain theory." *Justice Quarterly* 13: 681–704.

Aichhorn, A. (1973) [1935]. *Wayward Youth*. New York: Viking Press.

Akers, R. (1968). "Problems in the sociology of deviance: Social definitions and behavior." *Social Forces* 46: 455–65.

———. (1973). *Deviant Behavior: A Social Learning Approach*. Belmont, CA: Wadsworth.

———. (1979). "Theory and ideology in Marxist criminology." *Criminology* 16: 527–44.

———. (1985). *Deviant Behavior: A Social Learning Approach*, 3d ed. Belmont, CA: Wadsworth.

———. (1990). "Rational choice, deterrence, and social learning theory in criminology: The path not taken." *Journal of Criminal Law and Criminology* 81: 653–76.

———. (1991). "Self control as a general theory of crime." *Journal of Quantitative Criminology* 7: 201–11.

———. (1992). "Linking sociology and its specialties: The case of criminology." *Social Forces* 71: 1–16.

———. (1994). *Criminological Theories: Introduction and Evaluation*. Los Angeles: Roxbury.

———. (1996). "Is differential association/ social learning theory cultural deviance theory?" *Criminology* 34: 229–47.

———. (1998). *Social Learning and Social Structure: A General Theory of Crime and Deviance*. Boston: Northeastern University Press.

———. (2000). *Criminological Theories: Introduction and Evaluation*, 3d ed. Los Angeles: Roxbury.

Akers, R. L., and R. Matsueda. (1989). "Donald Cressey: An intellectual portrait of a criminologist." *Sociological Inquiry* 29: 423–38.

Akers, R. A., and C. S. Sellers. (2009). *Criminological Theories: Introduction, Evaluation, and Application*. New York: Oxford.

Akers, R. L., and A. Silverman. (2004). "Toward a social learning model of violence and terrorism." In *Violence: From Theory to Research*, ed. M. A. Zahn, H. H. Brownstein, and S. L. Jackson. Cincinnati, OH: LexisNexis-Anderson Publishing.

Akers, R. L., N. S. Hayner, and W. Grunninger. (1974). "Homosexual and drug behavior in prison: A test of the functional and importation models of the inmate system." *Social Problems* 21: 410–20.

Akers, R. L., M. D. Krohn, L. Lanza-Kaduce, and M. Radosevich. (1979). "Social learning and deviant behavior: A specific test of a general theory." *American Sociological Review* 44: 448–62.

Alarid, L. F., V. S. Burton, Jr., and F. T. Cullen. (2000). "Gender and crime among felony offenders: Assessing the generality of social control and differential association theory." *Journal of Research in Crime and Delinquency* 37: 171–99.

Alex, N. (1976). *New York Cops Talk Back*. New York: Wiley.

Alexander, F., and W. Healy. (1935). *Roots of Crime*. New York: Knopf.

Alexander, F., and H. Staub. (1956). *The Criminal, the Judge and the Public*. Glencoe, IL: Free Press.

Allan, E. A., and D. J. Steffensmeier. (1989). "Youth, under-employment, and property crime: Differential effects of job availability and job quality on juvenile and young adult arrest rates." *American Sociological Review* 54: 107–23.

Allen, G. E. (2001). "The biological basis of crime: An historical and methodological study." *Scientific Studies in the Physical and Biological Sciences* 31: 183–222.

Allman, W. F. (1994). "Why IQ isn't destiny: A new book's focus on IQ misses many of the mind's wondrous talents." *U.S. News & World Report*, 24 October: 73–80.

Alper, J. S. (1995). "Biological influences on criminal behaviour: How good is the evidence?" *British Medical Journal* 310: 272–273.

Alpert, G. P. (1993). "The role of psychological testing in law enforcement." In *Critical Issues in Policing*, ed. R. G. Dunham and G. P. Alpert. Prospect Heights, IL: Waveland.

Alpert, G. P., R. G. Dunham, and M. R. Smith. (2007). "Investigating racial profiling by the Miami–Dade police department: A multimethod approach." *Criminology and Public Policy* 6: 25–56.

Alpert, L. (1981). "Learning about trial judging: Socialization of state trial judges." In *Courts and Judges*, ed. J. A. Cramer. Beverly Hills, CA: Sage.

Alvarado, R., and K. Kumpfer. (2000). "Strengthening America's families." *Juvenile Justice* 7(3): 8–18.

American Civil Liberties Union. (1999a). "Should 'driving while black' be a crime?" http://www.aclu.org/features/nytimesad100698.html

———. (1999b). "Driving while black: Racial profiling on our nation's highways." New York: ACLU.

American Society of Criminology. (2009). "About ASC." Retrieved 5 March 2009 at http://www.asc41.com/about.htm.

Anderson, E. (1994). "The code of the streets." *Atlantic Monthly,* May: 80–94.

———. (1999). *Code of the Streets: Decency, Violence and the Moral Life of the Inner City.* New York: Norton.

Anderson, T. L., and R. R. Bennett. (1996). "Development, gender, and crime: The scope of the routine activities approach." *Justice Quarterly* 13: 31–56.

Andreski, S., ed. (1971). *Herbert Spencer: Structure, Function, and Evolution.* New York: Scribner.

Andrews, D. A. (1980). "Some experimental investigations of the principles of differential association through deliberate manipulation of the structure of service systems." *American Sociological Review* 44: 448–62.

Andrews, D. A. and J. Bonta. (1994). *The Psychology of Criminal Conduct.* Cincinnati: Anderson.

———. (1998). *Psychology of Criminal Conduct,* 2d ed. Cincinnati, OH: Anderson.

Andrews, D. A., I. Zinger, R. D. Hoge, J. Bonta, P. Gendreau, and F. T. Cullen. (1990). "Does correctional treatment work? A clinically relevant and psychologically informed meta-analysis." *Criminology* 28: 369–404.

Ang, I., and J. Stratton. (1996a). "Asianing Australia: Notes toward a critical transnationalism in cultural studies." *Cultural Studies* 10(1): 16–36.

———. (1996b). "A cultural studies without guarantees: Response to Kuan-Hsing Chen." *Cultural Studies* 10(1): 71–77.

Angier, N. (2000). "Do races differ? Not really, genes show." *New York Times,* 22 August: F1.

Anonymous. (2000). "About the International Center." http://www.ojp.usdoj.gov/nij/international/about_text.htm

Anson, R. J., D. Mann, and D. Sherman. (1986). "Niederhoffer's cynicism scale: Reliability and beyond." *Journal of Criminal Justice* 14: 295–305.

Antonaccio, O., and C. R. Tittle. (2007). "A cross-national test of Bonger's theory of criminology and economic conditions." *Criminology* 45: 925–58.

Antonaccio, O., and C. R. Tittle. (2008). "Morality, self control, and crime." *Criminology* 46: 479–510.

Appelbaum, R. (1979). "Born-again functionalism? A reconsideration of Althusser's stucturalism." *Insurgent Sociologist* 9: 18–33.

Armstrong, E. G. (2000). "Constructions of cultural conflict and crime." *Sociological Imagination* 37: 114–26.

Arneklev, B. J., J. K. Cochran, and R. R. Gainey. (1998). "Testing Gottfredson and Hirschi's 'low self-control' stability hypothesis." *American Journal of Criminal Justice* 23: 107–27.

Arneklev, B. J., H. G. Grasmick, and R. J. Bursik, Jr. (1999). "Evaluating the dimensionality and invariance of 'low self-control.'" *Journal of Quantitative Criminology* 15: 307–31.

Arrigo, B. (2000). "Social justice and critical criminology: On integrating knowledge." *Contemporary Justice Review* 3: 7–37.

———. (2001). "Critical criminology, existential humanism, and social justice: Exploring the contours of conceptual integration." *Critical Criminology* 10: 83–95.

Arrigo, B. A., and T. J. Bernard. (1997). "Postmodern criminology in relation to radical and conflict criminology." *Critical Criminology* 8: 39–60.

Arrigo, B. A., and L. Barrett. (2008). "Philosophical criminology and complex systems science: Towards a critical theory of justice." *Critical Criminology* 16: 165–84.

Arrigo, B. A., and S. Shipley. (2001a). "The confusion over psychopathy (I): Historical considerations." *International Journal of Offender Therapy and Comparative Criminology* 45: 325–44.

———. (2001b). "The confusion over psychopathy (II): Implications for forensic (correctional) practice." *International Journal of Offender Therapy and Comparative Criminology* 45: 407–20.

Arsovska, P., and P. Verduyn. (2008). "Globalisation, conduct norms and 'culture conflict': perceptions of violence and crime in an ethnic Albanian context." *British Journal of Criminology,* 48(2): 226–46.

Associated Press. (2009). "America is 'nation of cowards' on racial matters, Holder says." *USA Today,* 19 February: 4A.

Atkins v. Virginia (00-8452), 260 Va. 375, 534 S.E. 2d 312 (2002).

Aubert, V. (1983). *In Search of Law: Sociological Approach to Law*. Totowa, NJ: Barnes and Noble.

Auerhahn, K. (2001). *Incapacitation, Dangerous Offenders, and Sentencing Reform*. Albany, NY: State University of New York Press.

———. (2002). "Selective incapacitation, three strikes, and the problem of aging prison populations: Using simulation modeling to see the future." *Criminology & Public Policy* 3: 353–88.

Austin, R. L. (1982). "Women's liberation and increases in minor, major and occupational offenses." *Criminology* 20: 407–30.

Austin, J., and J. Irwin. (2001). *It's about Time: America's Imprisonment Binge*, 3d ed. Belmont, CA: Wadsworth.

Austin, J., and B. Krisberg. (1981). "Wider, strong, and different nets: The dialectics of criminal justice reform." *Journal of Research in Crime and Delinquency* 18: 165–96.

Austin, J., J. Clark, P. Hardyman, and D. A. Henry. (1998). "Three strikes and you're out": The implementation and impact of strike laws." Washington, DC: National Institute of Justice.

Ayers, R. M. (1977). "Case studies of police strikes in two cities—Albuquerque and Oklahoma City." *Journal of Police Science and Administration* 5: 19–31.

Aylward, J. (1985). "Psychological testing and police selection." *Journal of Police Science and Administration* 13: 201–10.

Babbie, E. (1975). *The Practice of Social Research*. Belmont, CA: Wadsworth.

———. (1983). *The Practice of Social Research*, 3d ed. Belmont, CA: Wadsworth.

Babbie, E. R. (2007). *The Practice of Social Research*, 11th ed. Belmont, CA: Wadsworth.

Bachman, R., R. Paternoster, and S. Ward. (1992). "The rationality of sexual offending: Testing a deterrence/rational choice conception of sexual assault." *Law and Society Review* 26: 343–72.

Bailey et al. v. Drexel Furniture Company, 259 U.S. 20, 42 S.Ct. 449, L.Ed. 817 (1922a). *Bailey et al. v. George et al.*, 259 U.S. 16, 42 S.Ct. 419, 66 L.Ed. 816 (1922b).

Bailey, W. C. (1976). "Use of the death penalty v. outrage at murder." *Crime and Delinquency* 20: 37.

———. (1998). "Deterrence, brutalization, and the death penalty: Another examination of Oklahoma's return to capital punishment." *Criminology* 36: 711–33.

Bailey, W. C., and R. D. Peterson. (1989). "Murder and capital punishment in the evolving context of the post-Furman era." *Social Forces* 66: 774–807.

Balbus, I. (1973). *The Dialectics of Legal Repression*. New York: Russell Sage Foundation.

Balch, R. W., C. T. Griffiths, E. L. Hall, and L. T. Winfree, Jr. (1976). "The socialization of jurors: The voir dire as a rite of passage." *Journal of Criminal Justice* 4: 271–83.

Baldus, D. C., C. Pulaski, and G. Woodworth. (1983). "Comparative review of death sentences: An empirical review of the Georgia experience." *Journal of Criminal Law and Criminology* 74: 661–753.

Baldwin, J. D. and J. I. Baldwin. (1998). *Behavior Principles in Everyday Life*, 3d ed. Upper Saddle River, NJ: Prentice Hall.

Balkan, S., R. J. Berger, and J. Schmidt. (1980). *Crime and Deviance in America: A Critical Approach*. Belmont, CA: Wadsworth.

Ball, R. A., C. R. Huff, and J. R. Lilly. (1988). *House Arrest and Correctional Policy: Doing Time at Home*. Beverly Hills, CA: Sage.

Bandura, A. (1974). "Behavioral theory and the models of man." *American Psychologist* 28: 859–69.

———. (1977). *Social Learning Theory*. Englewood Cliffs, NJ: Prentice-Hall.

———. (1989). "Human agency in social cognitive theory." *American Psychologist* 44: 1175–84.

Bandura, A., and A. Huston. (1961). "Identification as a process of incidental learning." *Journal of Abnormal and Social Psychology* 63: 311–18.

Bandura, A., D. Ross, and S. Ross. (1963). "Vicarious reinforcement and imitative learning." *Journal of Abnormal and Social Psychology* 67: 601–07.

Banks, T., and J. M. Dabbs. (1996). "Salivary testosterone and cortisol in a delinquent and violent urban subculture." *Journal of Social Psychology* 36: 49–57.

Barak, G. (1988). "Newsmaking criminology: Reflections on the media, intellectuals, and crime." *Justice Quarterly* 5: 565–87.

Barberet, R. (2001). "Global competence and American criminology—An expatriate's view." *Criminologist* 26: 1, 3–5.

Barlow, H. D. (1996). *Criminology*. New York: HarperCollins.

———. (1997). *Criminology*. Reading, MA: Addison-Wesley.

Barnes, C. Wolff, and R. S. Franz. (1989). "Questionably adult: Determinants and effects of the juvenile waiver decision." *Justice Quarterly* 6: 117–35.

Barr, R., and K. Pease. (1990). "Crime placement, displacement and deflection." In *Crime and Justice: A Review of Research*, vol. 12, ed. M. Tonry and N. Morris. Chicago: University of Chicago Press.

Baron, S. W., and D. R. Forde. (2007). "Street youth crime: A test of control balance theory." *Justice Quarterly* 24: 334–55.

Bartol, C. R., and H. A. Holanchock. (1979). "A test of Eysenck's theory of criminality on an American prisoner population." *Criminal Justice and Behavior* v6: 245–49.

Bartol, C. R. (1991). *Criminal Behavior: A Psychological Approach*, 3d ed. Englewood Cliffs, NJ: Prentice-Hall.

———. (1999). *Criminal Behavior: A Psychosocial Approach*, 5th ed. Upper Saddle River, NJ: Prentice-Hall.

Bartollas, C., and J. Conrad. (1992). *Introduction to Corrections*, 2d ed. New York: HarperCollins.

Bartollas, C., and S. Dinitz. (1989). *Introduction to Criminology: Order and Disorder*. New York: Harper and Row.

Baudrillard, J. (1988). *America*. London: Verso.

Baumer, E. P., R. Wright, K. Kristindottir, and H. Gunnlaugsson. (2002). "Crime, shame, and recidivism." *British Journal of Criminology* 41: 40–59.

Baumgardner, J., and A. Richards. (2000). *Manifest A: Young Women, Feminism, and the Future*. New York: Farrar, Straus, and Giroux.

Bavolek, S. J. (2000). "The nurturing parenting program." *OJJDP Juvenile Justice Bulletin*, November.

Bazemore, G., and M. Schiff. (2001). *Restorative Community Justice: Repairing Harm and Transforming Communities*. Cincinnati, OH: Anderson.

Bazemore, G., and M. Umbreit. (2001). "A comparison of four restorative conferencing models." *Juvenile Justice Bulletin*, February. Washington, DC: Office of Juvenile Justice and Delinquency Prevention.

Beaver, K. M., J. P. Wright, M. Delisi. (2007). "Self-control as an executive function: Reformulating Gottfredson and Hirschi's parental socialization thesis." *Criminal Justice and Behavior* 34: 1345–61.

Beccaria, C. (1963)[1764]. *On Crimes and Punishments*. Trans. H. Paolucci. Indianapolis, IN: Bobbs-Merrill.

Beck, A. J., and J. C. Karberg. (2001). "Prison and jail inmates at midyear 2000." Washington, DC: U.S. Bureau of Justice Statistics.

Beck, A. J., and L. M. Maruschak. (2001). "Mental health treatment in state prisons, 2000." Washington, DC: U.S. Bureau of Justice Statistics.

Becker, G. S. (1968). "Crime and punishment: An economic approach." *Journal of Political Economy* 76: 169–217.

Becker, H. S. (1963). *Outsiders: Studies in the Sociology of Deviance*. New York: Free Press.

———. (1973). *Outsiders: Studies in the Sociology of Deviance*, rev. ed. New York: Free Press.

Beirne, P., and J. Messerschmidt. (2000). *Criminology*, 3d ed. Boulder, CO: Westview Press.

Bell, D. (1992). *Faces at the Bottom of the Well: The Permanence of Racism*. New York: Basic Books.

———. (1995). "Who's afraid of critical race theory?" *University of Illinois Law Review* 893–910.

Bellah, R. N., and associates. (1985). *Habits of the Heart*. New York: Perennial.

Bellair, P. E. (1997). "Social interaction and community crime: Examining the importance of neighbor networks." *Criminology* 35: 677–703.

Benekos, P., and A. Merlo. (1995). "Three strikes and you're out! The political sentencing game." *Federal Probation* 59: 3–9.

Benner, A. W. (1986). "Psychological screening of police applicants." In *Psychological Services in Law Enforcement*, ed. J. T. Reese and H. A. Goldstein. Washington, DC: U.S. Government Printing Office.

Bennett, R. R. (1991). "Routine activities: A cross-national assessment of a criminological perspective." *Social Forces* 70: 147–63.

Bennett, R. R., and Theodore Greenstein. (1975). "The police personality: A test of the predisposition model." *Journal of Police Science and Administration* 3: 439–45.

Bentham, J. (1948)[1789]. *An Introduction to the Principles of Morals and Legislation*. New York: Kegan Paul.

Berg, B., E. True, and M. Gertz. (1984). "Police, riots, and alienation." *Journal of Police Science and Administration* 12: 186–90.

Bergerson, A. A. (2003). "Critical race theory and white racism: Is there room for white scholar in fighting racism in education?" *International Journal of Qualitative Studies in Education* 16: 51–63.

Bergesen, A., and M. Herman. (1998). "Immigration, race, and riot: The 1992 Los Angeles uprising." *American Sociological Review* 63: 39–54.

Berk, R. A. (1993). "Policy corrections in the ASR." *American Sociological Review* 58: 889–90.

Berk, R. A., Alec Campbell, Ruth Klap, and Bruce Western. (1992). "A Bayesian analysis of the Colorado Springs spouse abuse experiment." *Journal of Criminal Law and Criminology* 83: 170–200.

———. (1992). "The deterrent effect of arrest in incidents of domestic violence: A Bayesian analysis of four field experiments." *American Sociological Review* 57: 698–708.

Berman, H. J., and W. R. Greiner. (1980). *The Nature and Functions of Law*, 4th ed. Mineola, NY: Foundation Press.

Berman, L. (1938). *The Glands Regulating Personality*. New York: Macmillan.

Bernard, T. J. (1984). "Control criticisms of strain theories: An assessment of theoretical and empirical adequacy." *Journal of Research in Crime and Delinquency* 21: 353–72.

———. (1990). "Twenty years of testing theories: What have we learned and why?" *Journal of Research in Crime and Delinquency* 27: 325–47.

Bernard, T. J., and Jeffery B. Snipes. (1996). "Theoretical integration in criminology." Pp. 301–348 in *Crime and Justice: A Review of Research*, ed. Michael Tonry. Chicago: University of Chicago Press.

Bernberg, J. G., and M. D. Krohn. (2003). "Labeling, life chances, and adult crime: The direct and indirect effects of official interventions in adolescence on crime in early childhood." *Criminology* 41: 1287–317.

Bernberg, J. G., M. D. Krohn, and C. J. Rivera. (2006). "Official labeling, criminal embeddedness, and subsequent delinquency: A longitudinal test of labeling theory." *Journal of Research in Crime and Delinquency* 43: 67–88.

Bernstein, I. Nagel, E. Kick, J. Leung, and B. Schulz. (1977). "Charge reduction: An intermediary stage in the process of labeling criminal defendants." *Social Forces* 56: 362–84.

Berry, B., and J. D. Kasarda. (1977). *Contemporary Urban Ecology*. New York: Macmillan.

Bersani, C. A. (1989). "Reality therapy: Issues and a review of research." In *Correctional Counseling and Treatment*, 2d ed., ed. P. C. Kratcoski. Prospect Heights, IL: Waveland Press.

Best, S., and D. Kellner. (1991). *Postmodern Theory: Critical Interrogation*. New York: Guilford Press.

Bevis, C., and J. B. Nuttler. (1977). "Changing street layouts to reduce residential burglary." Paper presented to the American Society of Criminology, Atlanta, GA.

Bhati, A. S., J. K. Roman, and A. Chalfin. (2008). "To treat or not to treat: Evidence on the prospects of expanding treatment to drug-involved offenders." Washington, DC: The Urban Institute.

Biderman, A. J., et al. (1967). Report on a pilot study in the District of Columbia on victimization and attitudes toward law enforcement, Field Surveys 1. *President's Commission on Law Enforcement and Administration of Justice*. Washington, DC: U.S. Government Printing Office.

Binder, A., and J. W. Meeker. (1988). "Experiments as reforms." *Journal of Criminal Justice* 16: 347–58.

———. (1993). "Implications of the failure to replicate the Minneapolis experimental findings." *American Sociological Review* 58: 886–88.

Black, D. (1976). *The Behavior of Law*. Orlando, FL: Academic Press.

Blackstone, W. (1962)[1760]. *Commentaries on the Laws of England*. Boston: Beacon Press.

Blackwell, B. S., and A. R. Piquero. (2005). "On the relationship between gender, power control, self-control, and crime." *Journal of Criminal Justice* 33: 1–17.

Blair, R. J., and U. Frith. (2000). "Neurocognitive explanations of the antisocial personality disorder." *Criminal Behavior and Mental Health* 10(4): S66–S81.

Blalock, H. M. (1967). *Towards a Theory of Minority Group Relations*. New York: John Wiley.

Blau, J. R., and P. M. Blau. (1977). *Inequality and Heterogeneity: A Primitive Theory of Social Structure*. New York: Free Press.

————. (1982). "The cost of inequality: Metropolitan structure and violent crime." *American Sociological Review* 47: 114–29.

Blomberg, T. G. (1980). "Widening the net: An anomaly in the evaluation of diversion programs." In *Handbook of Criminal Justice Evaluation*, ed. M. Klein and K. Teilmann. Beverly Hills, CA: Sage.

Bluenose, P., and J. Zion. (1996). "Hozhooji Naat' Aanii: The Navajo justice and harmony ceremony." In *Native Americans, Crime and Justice*, ed. M. A. Nielsen and R. A. Silverman. Boulder, CO: Westview Press.

Blumer, H. (1958). "Race prejudice as a sense of group position." *Pacific Sociological Review* 1: 3–7.

Blumstein, A., and J. Cohen. (1987). "Characterizing criminal careers." *Science* 237: 985–91.

Blumstein, A., J. Cohen, and D. Farrington. (1988). "Criminal career research: Its value for criminology." *Criminology* 26: 1035.

Blumstein, A., J. Cohen, and D. Nagin, eds. (1978). *Deterrence and Incapacitation: Estimating the Effects of Criminal Sanctions on Crime Rates*. Washington, DC: National Academy of Sciences.

Blumstein, A., J. Cohen, J. Roth, and C. Visher, eds. (1986). *Criminal Careers and "Career Criminals."* 2 vols. Washington, DC: National Academy Press.

Boeringer, S., C. L. Shehan, and R. L. Akers. (1991). "Social contexts and social learning in sexual coercion and aggression: Assessing the contribution of fraternity membership." *Family Relations* 40: 558–64.

Boesel, D., R. Berk, W. E. Groves, B. Edison, and P. H. Rossi. (1969). "White institutions and black rage." *Trans-Action* 6: 24–31.

Bohm, R. (1982). "Radical criminology: An explication." *Criminology* 19: 565–89.

Bonczar, T. P. (2003). "Prevalence of imprisonment in the U.S. population, 1974–2001." *Bureau of Justice Statistics Bulletin*. Washington, DC: U.S. Department of Justice.

Bonger, W. (1969)[1916]. *Criminality and Economic Conditions*. Bloomington: Indiana University Press.

Bonnie, R. J. (1990). "The competence of criminal defendants with mental retardation to participate in their own defense." *Journal of Criminal Law and Criminology* 81: 419–46.

Booth, A., and D. Wayne Osgood. (1993). "The influence of testosterone on deviance in adulthood: Assessing and explaining the relationship." *Criminology* 31: 93–117.

Bootzin, R. R. (1975). *Behavior Modification and Therapy: An Introduction*. Cambridge, MA: Winthrop.

Bopp, W. J., P. Chignell, and C. Maddox. (1977). "The San Francisco police strike of 1975: A case study." *Journal of Police Science and Administration* 5: 32–42.

Boruch, R. F., T. Victor, and J. S. Cecil. (2000). "Resolving ethical and legal problems in randomized experiments." *Crime and Delinquency* 46: 330–53.

Borum, R., and H. V. Stock. (1993). "Detection of deception in law enforcement practices." *Law and Human Behavior* 17: 157–60.

Boss, P. (1988). *Family Stress Management*. Newbury Park, CA: Sage.

Botchkovar, E. V., and C. R. Tittle. (2005). "Crime, shame, and reintegration in Russia." *Theoretical Criminology* 9: 401–42.

Botstein, D., and N. Risch. (2003). "Discovering genotypes underlying human phenotypes: Past successes for mendelian disease, future approaches for complex diseases." *Nature Genetics* 33: 228–37.

Bottcher, J., and M. E. Ezell. (2005). "Examining the effectiveness of boot camps: A randomized experiment with a long-term follow up." *Journal of Research in Crime and Delinquency* 42: 309–332.

Boudon, R. (2003). "Beyond rational choice theory." *Annual Review of Sociology* 29: 1–21.

Bowers, W. J., and J. H. Hirsch. (1987). "The impact of foot patrol staffing on crime and disorder in Boston: An unmet promise." *American Journal of Police* 6: 17–44.

Box, S. (1981). *Deviance, Reality and Society*. London: Holt, Rinehart and Winston.

Boyle, J. (1992). "Natural law and the ethics of traditions." Pp. 3–30 in *Natural Law Theory*, edited by R. P. George. Oxford, England: Oxford University Press.

Bozarth, M. A. (1994). "Pleasure systems in the brain." Pp. 5–16 in *Pleasure: The Politics and the Reality*, ed. D. M. Warburton. New York: John Wiley & Sons.

Braithwaite, J. (1984). *Corporate Crime in the Pharmaceutical Industry*. London: Routledge and Kegan Paul.

———. (1989). "The state of criminology: Theoretical decay or renaissance?" *Australian and New Zealand Journal of Criminology* 22: 129–35.

———. (1990). "The state of criminology: Theoretical decay or renaissance?" In *Advances in Criminological Theory*, vol. 2, ed. W. S. Laufer and F. Adler. New Brunswick, NJ: Transaction.

———. (1997). "Charles Tittle's control balance and criminological theory." *Theoretical Criminology* 1: 77–97.

———. (1999). "Restorative justice: Assessing optimistic and pessimistic accounts." In *Crime and Justice: A Review of Research*, ed. M. Tonry. Chicago: University of Chicago Press.

———. (2000). "Shame and criminal justice." *Canadian Journal of Criminology* 42: 281–99.

Braithwaite, J., and P. Pettit. (1990). *Not Just Deserts: A Republican Theory of Criminal Justice*. Oxford, UK: Oxford University Press.

Brantingham, P., and P. Brantingham. (1991). "How public transportation feeds private crime: Note on Vancouver 'Skytrain' experience." *Security Journal* 2: 91–95.

———. (1993). "Environment, routine situation, and situation: Toward a pattern theory of crime." In *Advances in Criminal Theory*, ed. R. V. Clarke and M. Felson. New Brunswick, NJ: Transaction.

Braga, A. A., D. Weisburd, E. Waring. L. Green-Mazzerolle, W. Spelman, F. Gajewski. (1999). "Problem-oriented policing in violent crime places: A randomized controlled experiment." *Criminology* 37: 541–80.

Breckenridge, J., L. T. Winfree, Jr., J. W. Maupin, and D. L. Clason. (2000). "Drunk drivers, DWI 'drug court' treatment, and recidivism: Who fails?" *Justice Research and Policy* 2(1): 87–105.

Breed v. Jones, 421 U.S. 519 (1975).

Brennan, P. K. (2006). "Sentencing female misdemeanants: An examination of the direct and indirect effects of race/ethnicity." *Justice Quarterly* 23: 60–95.

Brennan, P. A., S. Mednick, and J. Volavka. (1995). "Biomedical factors in crime." In *Crime*, ed. J. Q. Wilson and J. Petersilia. San Francisco: Institute for Contemporary Studies.

Bridges, G., and R. Crutchfield. (1988). "Law, social standing, and racial disparities in imprisonment." *Social Forces* 99: 699–724.

Brion, F., and F. Tulkens. (1998). "Conflit de culture et delinquance. Interroger L'evidence" ("The conflict between culture and crime: Questioning the evidence"). *Déviance et société* 22: 235–63.

Britt, C. L. (2000). "Comment on Paternoster and Brame." *Criminology* 38: 965–70.

Broberg, G., and N. Roll-Hansen, eds. (1996). *Eugenics and the Welfare State: Sterilization Policy in Denmark, Sweden, Norway, and Finland*. Lansing: Michigan State University Press.

Broidy, L. M., R. E. Tremblay, B. Brame, D. Fergusson, J. L. Horwood, R. Laird, T. E. Moffitt, D. S. Nagin, J. E. Bates, K. E. Dodge, R. Loeber, D. R. Lynam, G. S. Pettit, and F. Vitaro. (2003). "Developmental trajectories of childhood disruptive behaviors and adolescent delinquency: A six-site, cross-national study." *Developmental Psychology* 39: 222–45.

Brounstein, P. J., P. Hatry, D. Altschuler, and L. H. Blair. (1990). *Substance Use and Delinquency among Inner City Adolescent Males*. Washington, DC: Urban Institute.

Brown, J. (2001). "The Taliban's bravest opponents." Salon.com Life. http://www.salon.com/mwt/feature/2001/10/02/fatima/

Brown, W. K., T. Miller, R. L. Jenkins, and W. A. Rhodes. (1991). "The human costs of 'giving the kid another chance.'" *International Journal of Offender Therapy and Comparative Criminology* 35: 296–302.

Brownstein, H. H., and P. J. Goldstein. (1990). "A typology of drug-related homicides." In *Drugs, Crime and the Criminal Justice System*, ed. R. Weisheit. Cincinnati, OH: Anderson.

Brown, L. P., and M. A. Wycoff. (1986). "Policing Houston: Reducing fear and improving service." *Crime and Delinquency* 33: 71–89.

Bruen, M. (2007). "City man accused in three break-ins in Tolland, Coventry." *The Courant*, 1 August.

Bruinius, H. (2006). *Better for All the World: The Secret History of Forced Sterilization and America's Quest for Racial Purity*. New York: Knopf.

Bruinsma, G. (1992). "Differential association theory reconsidered: An extension and its empirical test." *Journal of Quantitative Criminology* 8: 29–42.

Brunner, H. G., M. Nelson, X. D. Breakefield, H. H. Ropes, and A. van Oost. (1994). "Abnormal behavior associated with a point mutation in the structural gene for monamine oxidase A." *Science* 262: 578–80.

Brunson, R. K. (2007). " 'Police don't like black people': African-American young men's accumulated police experiences." *Criminology and Public Policy* 6: 71–102.

Bryant, K. M., and J. M. Miller. (1997). "Routine activity and labor market segmentation: An empirical test of a revised approach." *American Journal of Criminal Justice* 22: 71–100.

Buck v. Bell, 274 U.S.C. 200 (1927).

Buckler, K., and J. D. Unnever. (2008). "Racial and ethnic perceptions of injustice: Testing the core hypotheses of comparative conflict theory." *Journal of Criminal Justice* 36: 270–78.

Buikhuisen, W. (1987). "Cerebral dysfunction and persistent juvenile delinquency." In *The Causes of Crime: New Biological Approaches*, ed. S. A. Mednick, T. E. Moffitt, and S. A. Stack. New York: Cambridge University Press.

Bureau of Justice Statistics (2008). "National Incident-Based Reporting System (NIBRS) implementation program." Washington, DC: Office of Justice Programs. Retrieved 9 November 2008 at http://www.ojp.usdoj.gov/bjs/nibrs.htm

Bureau of the Census. (2009). USA QuickFacts from the Bureau of the Census. Washington, DC: Department of Commerce. Retrieved 14 February 2009 at http://quickfacts.census.gov/qfd/states/00000.html

Burgess, R., and R. L. Akers. (1966). "A differential-association-reinforcement theory of criminal behavior." *Social Problems* 14: 128–47.

Burgess-Proctor, A. (2006). "Intersections of race, class, gender, and crime: Future directions for feminist criminology." *Feminist Criminology* 1: 27–47.

Bursik, R. J. (1986). "Ecological stability and the dynamics of delinquency." In *Communities and Crime*, ed. A. J. Reiss, Jr., and M. Tonry. Chicago: University of Chicago Press.

———. (1988). "Social disorganization and theories of crime and delinquency: Problems and prospects." *Criminology* 26: 519–51.

Burton, Jr., V. S., F. T. Cullen, T. D. Evans, L. F. Alarid, and R. G. Dunaway. (1998). "Gender, self-control, and crime." *Journal of Research in Crime and Delinquency* 35: 123–47.

Cadoret, R. J., E. Troughton, and T. W. O'Gorman. (1987). "Adoption studies: Historical and environmental factors in adoptee antisocial personality." *European Archives of Psychiatry and Neurological Science* 239: 231–40.

Calavita, K. (1996). "The new politics of immigration: 'Balanced budget conservativism' and the symbolism of proposition 187." *Social Problems* 43: 284–305.

Cao, L., A. Adams, and V. J. Jensen. (1997). "A test of the black sub-culture of violence thesis: A research note." *Criminology* 35: 367–79.

Cardozo, B. (1924). *The Growth of the Law.* New Haven, CT: Yale University Press.

Carey, G. (1992). "Twin imitation for antisocial behavior: Implications for genetic and family environment research." *Journal of Abnormal Psychology* 101: 18–25.

Carnegie Taskforce. (1994). "Starting points: Meeting the needs of our youngest children." Waldorf, MD: Carnegie Corporation of New York.

Carter, D. (1990). "Drug-related corruption of police officers: A contemporary typology." *Journal of Criminal Justice* 18: 85–98.

Carver, C. S., and M. F. Scheier. (2000). *Perspectives on Personality*, 4th ed. Boston: Allyn & Bacon.

Cason, H. (1943). "The psychopath and the psychopathic." *Journal of Criminal Psychopathology* 4: 522–27.

———. (1946). "The symptoms of the psychopath." *Public Health Reports* 61: 1833–68.

Cason, H., and M. J. Pescor. (1946). "A statistical study of 500 psychopathic prisoners." *Public Health Reports* 61: 557–74.

Caspi, A., T. E. Moffitt, P. A. Silva, M. Stouthamer-Loeber, R. F. Krueger, and P. A. Schmutte. (1994). "Are some people crime-prone? Replications of personality-crime relationship across countries, genders, races, and methods." *Criminology* 32: 163–96.

Castle, T., and C. Hensley. (2002). "Serial killers with military experience: Applying learning theory to serial murder." *International Journal of Offender Therapy and Comparative Criminology* 46: 453–65.

Catalano, R. F., and J. D. Hawkins. (1986). "The social development model: A theory of antisocial behavior." Pp. 149–192 in *Delinquency and Crime: Current Theories*, ed. J. D. Hawkins. New York: Cambridge University Press.

Cavalli-Sforza, L. L. (2000). *Genes, People, and Languages.* New York: Farrar, Straus and Giroux North Point.

Cernkovich, S. A., and P. C. Giordano. (1979). "Delinquency, opportunity, and gender." *Journal of Criminal Law and Criminology* 70: 145–51.

———. (1992). "School bonding, race, and delinquency." *Criminology* 30: 261–90.

Cernkovich, S. A., P. C. Giordano, and J. L. Rudolph. (2000). "Race, crime and the American Dream." *Journal of Research in Crime and Delinquency* 37: 131–70.

Chabris, C. E. (1998). "IQ since *The Bell Curve.*" *Commentary* 106: 33–40.

Chambliss, W. J. (1964). "A sociological analysis of the law and vagrancy." *Social Problem* 12: 67–77.

———. (1976). "The state and criminal law." In *Whose Law, What Order? A Conflict Approach to Criminology,* ed. W. J. Chambliss and M. Mankoff. New York: Wiley.

———. (1988). *Exploring Criminology.* New York: Macmillan.

———. (1989a). "State-organized crime." *Criminology* 27: 188–90.

———. (1989b). "On trashing Marxist criminology." *Criminology* 27: 231–38.

Chambliss, W. J., and R. Seidman. (1982). *Law, Order and Power.* Reading, MA: Addison-Wesley.

Chamlin, M., and J. K. Cochran. (1995). "Assessing Messner and Rosenfeld's institutional anomie theory: A partial test." *Criminology* 33: 411–29.

———. (1997). "Social altruism and crime." *Criminology* 35: 203–27.

Champion, D. J. (1990). *Corrections in the United States: A Contemporary Perspective.* Englewood Cliffs, NJ: Prentice-Hall.

Chaney, C. K., and G. H. Saltzstein. (1998). "Democratic control and bureaucratic responsiveness: The police and domestic violence." *American Journal of Political Science* 42: 745–68.

Chen, K. -H. (1996). "Not yet the postcolonial era: The (super) nation-state and transnationalism of cultural studies: Response to Ang and Stratton." *Cultural Studies* 10(1): 37–70.

Chermak, S. T., and S. P. Taylor. (1995). "Alcohol and human physical aggression: Pharmacological versus expectancy effects." *Journal of Studies on Alcohol* 56: 449–56.

Chesney-Lind, M. (1973). "Judicial enforcement of the female sex role." *Issues in Criminology* 8: 51–69.

———. (1989). "Girls' crime and woman's place: Toward a feminist model of female delinquency." *Crime and Delinquency* 35: 5–29.

Chesney-Lind, M., and R. C. Shelden. (1992). *Girls' Delinquency and Juvenile Justice.* Pacific Grove, CA: Brooks/Cole.

Chesno, F. A., and P. R. Kilmann. (1975). "Effects of stimulation intensity on sociopathic avoidance learning." *Journal of Abnormal Psychology* 84: 144–50.

Chira, S. (1994). "Study confirms worst fear on U.S. children." *New York Times,* 12 April: 1, 11.

Chiricos, T., K. Barrick, W. Bales, and S. Bontrager. (2007). "The labeling of convicted felons and its consequences for recidivism." *Criminology* 45: 547–81.

Chow, E. N., and W. E. Hemple. (1977). "Laboratory organizational experiments for corrections: An alternative method." *Criminology* 14: 513–26.

Christiansen, K. O. (1977). "A review of studies of criminality among twins." In *Biosocial Bases of Criminal Behavior,* ed. S. Mednick and K. O. Christiansen. New York: Gardner.

Cicourel, A. (1976). *The Social Organization of Juvenile Justice.* New York: Wiley.

Clarke, R. V. (1992). "Introduction." In *Situational Crime Prevention: Successful Case Studies,* ed. R. V. Clarke. Albany, NY: Harrow and Heston.

———. (1999). "Situation crime prevention: Theory and practice." *British Journal of Criminology* 20: 136–47.

Clarke, R. V., and D. Weisburg. (1994). "Diffusion of crime control benefits: Observation on the reverse of displacement." In *Crime Prevention Studies,* vol. 3, ed. R. V. Clarke. Monsey, NJ: Criminal Justice Press.

Clark, G. R., M. A. Telfer, D. Baker, and M. Rosen. (1970). "Sex chromosomes, crime and psychosis." *American Journal of Psychiatry* 126: 1569.

Clear, T., and G. F. Cole. (1986). *American Corrections.* Pacific Grove, CA: Brooks/Cole.

———. (1990). *American Corrections,* 2d ed. Pacific Grove, CA: Brooks/Cole.

———. (1997). *American Corrections,* 4th ed. Belmont, CA: Wadsworth.

Clear, T. R., G. F. Cole, and M. D. Reisig. (2009). *American Corrections*, 8th ed. Belmont, CA: Wadsworth.

Cleaver, E. (1968). *Soul on Ice*. New York: McGraw-Hill.

Cleckley, H. (1976). *The Mask of Sanity*. St. Louis, MO: Mosby.

Clemmer, D. (1940). *The Prison Community*. Boston: Christopher.

Clinard, M. B. (1964). *Anomie and Deviant Behavior: A Discussion and Critique*. New York: Free Press.

Clinard, M. B., and R. F. Meier. (1985). *Sociology of Deviant Behavior*, 6th ed. New York: Holt, Rinehart and Winston.

Clinard, M. B., and R. Quinney. (1967). *Criminal Behavior Systems: A Typology*. New York: Holt, Rinehart and Winston.

Clinard, M. B., P. C. Yeager, J. Brissette, D. Petrashek, and E. Harries. (1979). *Illegal Corporate Behavior*. Washington, DC: U.S. Government Printing Office.

Cloninger, S. (1993). *Theories of Personality: Understanding Persons*. Englewood Cliffs, NJ: Prentice-Hall.

Cloward, R., and L. Ohlin. (1960). *Delinquency and Opportunity: A Theory of Delinquent Gangs*. Glencoe, IL: Free Press.

Clynch, E., and D. W. Neubauer. (1981). "Trial courts as organizations: A critique and synthesis." *Law and Policy Quarterly* 3: 69–94.

Coates, R., and J. Gehm. (1989). "An empirical assessment." In *Mediation and Criminal Justice*, ed. M. Wright and B. Galaway. London: Sage.

Cobb, J. B. (1993). "A presidential address on the economy." In *Postmodern for a Planet in Crisis*, ed. D. R. Griffin and R. Falk. Albany: SUNY Press.

Cochran, J., M. B. Chamlin, and M. Seth. (1994). "Deterrence or brutalization? An impact assessment of Oklahoma's return to capital punishment." *Criminology* 32: 107–34.

Cochran, J. K., P. B. Wood, C. S. Sellers, W. Wilkerson, and M. Chamlin. (1998). "Academic dishonesty and low self-control: An empirical test of a general theory of crime." *Deviant Behavior* 19: 227–55.

Cohen, A. K. (1955). *Delinquent Boys: The Culture of the Gang*. New York: Free Press.

———. (1965). "The sociology of the deviant act: Anomie theory and beyond." *American Sociological Review* 30: 5–14.

Cohen, A. K., and J. F. Short, Jr. (1958). "Research in delinquent subcultures." *Journal of Social Issues* 14: 20–37.

Cohen, L. E., and M. Felson. (1979). "Social change and crime rate trends: A routine activity approach." *American Sociological Review* 44: 588–608.

Cohen, L. E., J. R. Kluehel, and K. C. Land. (1981). "Social inequality and predatory criminal victimizations: An exposition and test of a formal theory." *American Sociological Review* 46: 505–24.

Cohen, L. E., and B. J. Vila. (1995). "Self-control and social control: An exposition of the Gottfredson–Hirschi/Sampson–Laub debate." *Studies on Crime and Prevention*. 5: 125–50.

Cohen, S. (1984). "The deeper structure of the law or 'beware the rulers bearing justice.'" *Contemporary Crises* 8: 83–93.

———. (1985). *Vision of Social Control*. Cambridge, England: Polity.

———. (1986). "Taking decentralization seriously: Values, visions, and policies." In *The Decentralization of Social Control*, ed. J. Lowman, R. J. Menzies, and T. Palys. London: Gower.

Colvin, N. (1982). "The 1980 New Mexico prison riot." *Social Problems* 29: 449–63.

Colvin, M., and J. Pauly. (1983). "A critique of criminology: Toward an integrated structural-Marxist theory of delinquency production." *American Journal of Sociobiology* 89: 513–51.

Comings, D. E. (1995). "The role of genetic factors in conduct disorder based on studies of Tourette syndrome and attention-deficit hyperactivity disorder probands and their relatives." *Developmental and Behavioral Pediatrics* 16: 142–57.

Conger, R. (1976). "Social control and social learning models of delinquency: A synthesis." *Criminology* 14: 17–40.

Connors, E., T. Lundregan, N. Miller, and T. McEwen. (1996). "Convicted by juries, exonerated by science: Case studies in the use of DNA evidence to establish innocence after trial." Washington, DC: U.S. Department of Justice.

Cook, T. D., and D. T. Campbell. (1979). *Quasi-Experimentation: Design and Analysis Issues of Field Settings*. Chicago: Rand-McNally.

Cook, L. F., and B. A. Weinman. (1988). "Treatment alternatives to street crime." In *Compulsory Treatment of Drug Abuse Research and Clinical Practice*, ed. C. G. Leukefeld and F. M. Tims. Rockville, MD: National Institute of Drug Abuse.

Cooke, D. J., S. D. Hart, and C. Michie. (2004). "Cross-national differences in the assessment of psychopathy: Do they reflect variations in rates' perceptions or symptoms?" *Psychological Assessment* 16: 335–39.

Coolbaugh, K., and C. J. Hansel. (2000). "The comprehensive strategy: Lessons learned from the pilot sites." *OJJDP Juvenile Justice Bulletin*, March.

Cooley, C. H. (1922). *Human Nature and the Social Order.* New York: Scribner.

Coon, C. (1962). *The Origins of Races.* New York: Alfred A. Knopf.

Cornish, D. B., and R. V. Clarke. (1986). *The Reasoning Criminal: Rational Choice Perspectives on Offending.* New York: Springer-Verlag.

Corporate Fraud Task Force. (2008). *Report to the President.* Washington, DC: U.S. Government Printing Office.

Cose, E. (1994). "Color-coordinated truths: When blacks internalize the white stereotype of inferiority." *Newsweek*, 24 October: 62.

Coser, L. A. (1971). *Masters of Sociological Thought.* New York: Harcourt Brace Jovanovich.

Coser, L. A., S. L. Nock, P. A. Steffan, and D. Spain. (1990). *Introduction to Sociology.* San Diego, CA: Harcourt Brace Jovanovich.

Costello, B. (1997). "On the logical adequacy of cultural deviance theory." *Theoretical Criminology* 1: 403–28.

Costello, B. J., and P. R. Vowell. (1999). "Testing control theory and differential association: A reanalysis of the Richmond Youth Project data." *Criminology* 37: 815–42.

Coughlin, E. K. (1994). "Pathways to crime: $32-million study will try to determine what leads some people into delinquency." *Chronicle of Higher Education*, 27 April: A8–9.

———. (1995). "Recollections of childhood abuse: Contending research traditions face off in the debate of 'recovered memory.'" *Chronicle of Higher Education*, 27 January: A8, A9, A16.

Crawford, A., T. Jones, T. Woodhouse, and J. Young. (1990). *Second Islington Crime Survey.* London: Middlesex Polytechnic Centre for Criminology.

Crawford, C. (2000). "Criminal penalties for creating a toxic environment: *Mens rea*, environmental criminal liability standards, and the neurotoxicity hypothesis." *Boston College Environmental Affairs Law Review* 27: 341–90.

Crenshaw, K., N. Gotanda, G. Peller, and K. Thomas, eds. (1995). *Critical Race Theory: The Key Writings that Formed the Movement.* New York: New Press.

Cressey, D. R. (1965). "Changing criminals: The application of the theory of differential association." *American Journal of Sociology* 61: 116–20.

"Criticized Freud show is revised and on." (1998). *New York Times*, 8 July: E1.

Crowe, T. D. (2000). *Crime Prevention through Environmental Design*, 2d ed. Woburn, MA: Butterworth-Heineman.

Cullen, F. T. (1988). "Were Cloward and Ohlin strain theorists? Delinquency and opportunity revisited." *Journal of Research in Crime and Delinquency* 25: 214–41.

———. (1995). "Assessing the penal harm movement." *Journal of Research in Crime and Delinquency* 32: 338–58.

Cullen, F. T., P. Gendreau, G. Roger Jarjoura, and J. P. Wright. (1997). "Crime and the bell curve: Lessons from intelligent criminology." *Crime and Delinquency* 43: 387–411.

Cullen, F. T., and K. E. Gilbert. (1982). *Reaffirming Rehabilitation.* Cincinnati: Anderson.

Cullen, F. T., P. J. L. Sundt, and J. F. Wozniak. (2001). "The virtuous prison: Toward a restorative rehabilitation." Pp. 265–286 in *Contemporary Issues in Crime and Criminal Justice: Essay in Honor of Gilbert Geis*, ed. H. N. Pontell and D. Shichor. Upper Saddle Creek, NJ: Prentice-Hall.

Curran, D., and C. M. Renzetti. (1989). *Social Problems.* Boston: Allyn & Bacon.

———. (1994). *Theories of Crime.* Boston: Allyn & Bacon.

Currie, E. P. (1968). "Crime without criminals: Witchcraft and its control in Renaissance Europe." *Law and Society Review* 3: 7–32.

———. (1985). *Confronting Crime: An American Challenge.* New York: Pantheon.

———. (1993). *Reckoning: Drugs, the Cities, and the American Future.* New York: Hill and Wang.

Curreton, S. R. (2000). "Justifiable arrests or discretionary justice: Predictors of racial arrest differentials." *Journal of Black Studies* 30: 703–19.

Curry, G. D. (1998). "Book review: *Control Balance: Toward a General Theory of Deviance. Social Forces* 76: 1147–49.

Curry, D., and A. R. Piquero. (2003). "Control ratios and defiant acts of deviance: Assessing additive and conditional effects with constraints and impulsivity." *Sociological Perspectives* 46: 397–415.

Curtis, L. (1975a). *Criminal Violence: National Patterns and Behavior.* Lexington, MA: Heath.

———. (1975b). *Violence, Race, and Culture.* Lexington, MA: Heath.

Dabbs, J. M., T. S. Carr, R. L. Frady, and J. K. Riad. (1995). "Testosterone, crime, and misbehavior among 692 male prison inmates." *Personality and Individual Differences* 18: 627–33.

Dabbs, J., R. Frady, T. Carr, and N. Beach. (1986). "Saliva, testosterone and criminal violence in young adult prison inmates." *Psychosomatic Medicine* 48: 73–81.

D'Alessio, S., and L. Stolzenberg. (1998). "Crime, arrests, and pretrial jail incarceration: An examination of the deterrence thesis." *Criminology* 36: 313–31.

Dahrendorf, R. (1958). *Class and Class Conflict in Industrial Society.* Stanford, CA: Stanford University Press.

Dalton, K. (1961). "Menstruation and crime." *British Medical Journal* 2: 1752–53.

———. (1964). *The Premenstrual Syndrome.* Springfield, IL: Thomas.

Daly, K. (1987a). "Discrimination in the criminal courts: Family, gender, and the problem of equal treatment." *Social Forces* 66: 152–75.

———. (1987b). "Structure and practice of familial-based justice in a criminal court." *Law and Society Review* 21: 267–90.

———. (1989). "Gender and varieties of white-collar crime." *Criminology* 27: 769–93.

Daly, K., and M. Chesney-Lind. (1988). "Feminism and criminology." *Justice Quarterly* 5: 497–538.

Darwin, C. (1872). *The Expression of Emotion in Men and Animals.* London: Murray.

———. (1981)[1871]. *Descent of Man, and Selection in Relation to Sex.* Princeton, NJ: Princeton University Press.

Davenport, C. B. (1915). *The Feebly Inhibited.* Publication No. 236. Washington, DC: Carnegie Institute of Washington.

David, D., J. Schnur, and J. Birk. (2004). "Functional and dysfunctional feelings in Ellis' cognitive theory of emotion: An empirical analysis." *Cognition and Emotion* 18: 869–80.

Davidson, R. N. (1981). *Crime and Environment.* New York: St. Martin's.

Davies, W., and P. Feldman. (1981). "The diagnosis of psychopathy by forensic specialists." *The British Journal of Psychiatry* 138: 329–31.

Davis, L. A. (2000). "People with mental retardation in the criminal justice system." Silver Springs, MD: The Arc. http://www.open.org/~people1/articles/article_criminal_justice.htm

Davis, N. J., and C. Stasz. (1990). *Social Control of Deviance: A Critical Perspective.* New York: McGraw-Hill.

Decker, C. (1995). "Los Angeles Times Poll." *Los Angeles Times*, 8 October.

"Decoding the human body." (2000). *Newsweek*, 10 April: 52.

De Fleur, M., and R. Quinney. (1966). "A reformulation of Sutherland's differential association theory and a strategy of empirical verification." *Journal of Research in Crime and Delinquency* 3: 1–22.

De Zulueta, F. (1993). *From Pain to Violence: The Traumatic Roots of Destructiveness.* London: Whurr.

———. (2001). "Understanding the evolution of psychopathology and violence." Editorial. *Criminal Behavior and Mental Health* 11: S17–S22.

DeFrances, C. J., and G. W. Steadman. (1998). "Prosecutors in state courts, 1996." Washington, DC: U.S. Bureau of Justice Statistics.

Degler, C. N. (1991). *In Search of Human Nature: The Decline and Revival of Darwinism in American Thought.* New York: Oxford University Press.

DeKeseredy, W. S., and M. D. Schwartz. (1991). "British and U.S. left realism: A critical comparison." *International Journal of Offender Therapy and Comparative Criminology* 35: 248–62.

———. (1996). *Contemporary Criminology.* Belmont, CA: Wadsworth.

Del Caren, Rolando, and J. T. Walker. (2006). *Briefs of Leading Cases in Law Enforcement.* New York: Nexis/Lexis, Matthew Bender.

Del Carmen, R. V., and J. T. Walker. (1991). *Briefs in 100 Leading Cases in Law Enforcement.* Cincinnati, OH: Anderson.

Deleuze, G., and F. Guattari. (1983). *Anti-Oedipus.* Minneapolis: University of Minnesota Press.

Delgado, R., and J. Stefancic. (1997). *Critical White Studies: Looking Behind the Mirror.* Philadelphia, PA: Temple University Press.

———. (2001a). *Critical Race Theory: The Cutting Edge.* Philadelphia, PA: Temple University Press.

———. (2001b). *Critical Race Theory: An Introduction.* New York: New York University Press.

Denno, D. (1985). "Sociological and human development explanations of crime: Conflict or consensus?" *Criminology* 23: 711–41.

———. (1993). "Considering lead poisoning as a criminal defense." *Fordham Urban Law Journal* 20: 377–85.

Denzin, N. K. (1991). *Images of Post-modern Society.* London: Sage.

Devlin, B., M. Daniels, and K. Roeder. (1997). "The heritability of IQ." *Nature* 388: 468–71.

Dodson, A. J. (2000). "DNA 'line-ups' based on reasonable suspicion standard." *University of Colorado Law Review* 71: 221–54.

Donovan, D. M. (1988) "Assessment of addictive behaviors: Implications for an emerging biopsychosocial model." Pp. 3–48 in *Assessment of Addictive Behaviors,* ed. D. M. Donovan and G. A. Marlatt. New York: Guilford.

Dorschner, J. (1989). "The dark side of force." In *Critical Issues in Policing: Contemporary Readings,* ed. R. G. Dunham and G. P. Alpert. Prospect Heights, IL: Waveland Press.

Doyle, A. C. (2005/1892). *The adventure of the copper beeches.* Whitefish, MT: Kessinger Publishing.

Dred Scott v. Sanford, 60 U.S. 393 (1857).

Driver, E. D. (1972). "Charles Buckman Goring." In *Pioneers in Criminology,* ed. H. Mannheim. Montclair, NJ: Patterson Smith.

Du Bois, W. E. B. (1903). *The Souls of Black Folk.* Chicago: McClurg.

Dugan, L., G. LaFree, and A. R. Piquero. (2005). "Testing a rationale choice model of airline hijacking." *Criminology* 43: 1031–65.

Dull, T. (1983). "Friend's drug use and adult drug and drinking behavior: A further test of differential association theory." *Journal of Criminal Law and Criminology* 4: 608–19.

Dumont, J. (1996). "Justice and native peoples." In *Native Americans, Crime and Justice,* ed. M. A. Nielsen and R. A. Silverman. Boulder, CO: Westview Press.

Dunford, F. (1992). "The measurement of recidivism in cases of spousal assault." *Journal of Criminal Law and Criminology* 83: 122–30.

———. (2000). "Determining program success: The importance of employing experimental research designs." *Crime and Delinquency* 46: 425–34.

Dunford, F., D. Huizinga, and D. S. Elliott. (1986). "The role of arrest in domestic assaults: The Omaha police experiment." *Criminology* 28: 183–207.

Dunford, F., D. W. Osgood, and H. F. Weichselbaum. (1981). *National Evaluation of Juvenile Diversion Projects.* Washington, DC: National Institute of Juvenile Justice and Delinquency Prevention.

Durham v. United States, 214 F. 2d 862, D.C. Cir. (1954).

Durkheim, E. (1951)[1897]. *Suicide.* Trans. J. A. Spaulding and G. Simpson. New York: Free Press.

———. (1961)[1925]. *Moral Education.* Glencoe, IL: Free Press.

———. (1966)[1895]. *Rules of the Sociological Method.* Trans. W. D. Halls. Chicago: University of Chicago Press.

Duyme, M. (1990). "Antisocial behaviour and postnatal environment: A French adoption study." *Journal of Child Psychology and Psychiatry* 31: 699–710.

Earls, F. (1998). "Linking community factors and individual development." *Research Preview.* Washington, DC: National Institute of Justice, September.

Eaton, M. (1986). *Justice for Women? Family, Court, and Social Control.* Philadelphia: Open University Press.

Echeburua, E., and J. Fernandez-Montalvo. (2007). "Male batterers with and without psychopathy: An exploratory study in Spanish prisons." *International Journal of Offender Therapy and Comparative Criminology* 51: 254–63.

Eck, J. (1993). "The threat of crime displacement." *Criminal Justice Abstracts* 25: 527–46.

Eck, J. E., and W. Spelman. (1987). "Who ya gonna call? The police as problem-busters." *Crime and Delinquency* 33: 31–52.

Edney, R. (2004). "To keep me safe from harm? Transgender prisons and the experience of imprisonment." *Deakin Law Review* 17: 327–38.

Edwards v. United States, U.S. S.Ct. 96-1492, 61 CrL3015 (1997).

Egger, S. A. (1990). *Serial Murder: An Elusive Phenomenon*. New York: Praeger.

Ehrlich, I. (1975). "The deterrent effect of capital punishment: A question of life and death." *American Economic Review* 65: 397–417.

Einstadter, W., and S. Henry. (1995). *Criminological Theory: An Analysis of Its Underlying Assumptions*. Fort Worth, TX: Harcourt Brace.

Eisenstein, J., and H. Jacobs. (1977). *Felony Justice: An Organizational Analysis of Criminal Courts*. Boston: Little, Brown.

Eitle, D., S. J. A'Alessio, and L. Stolzenberg. (2002). "Racial threat and social control: A test of the police, economic, and threat of black crime hypotheses." *Social Forces* 81: 557–76.

Elliott, D. S., and S. S. Ageton. (1980). "Reconciling race and class differences in self-reported and official estimates of delinquency." *American Sociological Review* 45: 95–110.

Elliott, D. S., and D. Huizinga. (1984). "The relationship between delinquent behavior and ADM problems." Paper presented at the AD-AMHA/OJJDP State-of-the-Art Research Conference on Juvenile Offenders with Serious Drug, Alcohol, and Mental Health Problems, Rockville, MD.

Elliott, D. S., D. Huizinga, and S. S. Ageton. (1985). *Explaining Delinquency and Drug Use*. Beverly Hills, CA: Sage.

Elliott, M. A. (1967). "Social disorganization." In *Dictionary of Sociology and Related Sciences*, ed. H. Pratt. Totowa, NJ: Littlefield, Adams.

Ellis, L. (1990). "Conceptualizing criminal and related behavior from a biosocial perspective." In *Crime in Biological, Social, and Moral Contexts*, ed. L. Ellis and H. Hoffman. Westport, CT: Praeger.

———. (1991). "Monoamine oxidase and criminality: Identifying an apparent biological marker for antisocial behavior." *Journal of Research in Crime and Delinquency* 28: 227–51.

Ellis, L., and H. Hoffman. (1990). "Views of contemporary criminologists on causes and theories of crime." In *Crime in Biological, Social, and Moral Contexts*, ed. L. Ellis and H. Hoffman. Westport, CT: Praeger.

Ellis, L., and A. Walsh. (1999). "Criminologists' opinions about the causes and theories of crime and delinquency." *The Criminologist* 24: 6, 1, 14, 26–27.

Ellis, L., and A. Walsh. (2000). *Criminology: A Global Perspective*. Boston: Allyn & Bacon.

Ellis, L., J. A. Cooper, and A. Walsh. (2008). "Criminologists' opinions about causes and theories of crime and delinquency: A follow-up." *The Criminologist* 33: 23–6.

Emerson, R. M. (1969). *Judging Children*. Chicago: Aldine.

Empey, L. (1967). "Delinquency theory and recent." *Journal of Research in Crime and Delinquency* 4: 28–42.

———. (1982). *American Delinquency*. Homewood, IL: Dorsey.

Empey, L., and Maynard L. Erickson. (1972). *The Provo Experiment: Evaluating Community Control of Delinquency*. Lexington, MA: Heath.

Engels, F. (1958[1845]). *The Condition of the Working Class in England*. Oxford, UK: Blackwell.

Englebert, P. (2000). "Pre-colonial institutions: Post-colonial states, and economic development in tropical Africa." *Political Research Quarterly* 53: 7–36.

English, K. (1993). "Self-reported crime rates of women prisoners." *Journal of Quantitative Criminology* 9: 357–82.

"Environment beats heredity in determining IQ, study finds." (1997). (Las Cruces) *Sun News*, 31 July: A7.

Erickson, M. H. (1928). "A study of the relationship between intelligence and crime." *Journal of Criminal Law and Criminology* 19: 592–635.

Erickson, K. T. (1966). *Wayward Puritans*. New York: Wiley.

Erickson, N. (2001). "Healthy Families America." *OJJDP Fact Sheet*. Washington, DC: National Institute of Justice, June.

Erickson, R., and K. Carriere. (1994). "The fragmentation of criminology." In *The Futures of Criminology*, ed. D. Nelken. London: Sage.

Erlanger, H. S. (1974). "The empirical status of the subculture of violence thesis." *Social Problems* 22: 280–92.

Ermann, M. D., and R. Lundman. (1992). *Corporate and Governmental Deviance: Problems of Organizational*

Behavior in Contemporary Society. New York: Oxford University Press.

Esbensen, F.-A. (1987). "Foot patrol: Of what value?" *American Journal of Police* 6: 45–65.

Esbensen, F.-A., and E. P. Deschenes. (1998). "A multisite examination of youth gang membership: Does gender matter?" *Criminology* 36: 799–827.

Esbensen, F.-A., and D. Huizinga. (1990). "Community structure and drug use from a social disorganization perspective: A research note." *Justice Quarterly* 7: 691–709.

Esbensen, F.-A., and D. W. Osgood. (1997). "National Evaluation of G.R.E.A.T." *Research in Brief.* Washington, DC: National Institute of Justice, November.

Esbensen, F.-A., D. W. Osgood, T. J. Taylor, D. Peterson, and A. Freng. (2001). "How great is G.R.E.A.T.? Results from a longitudinal quasi-experimental design." *Criminology and Public Policy* 1: 87–118.

Esbensen, F.-A., and L. T. Winfree, Jr. (1998). "Race and gender differences between gang and non-gang youths: Results of a multi-site survey." *Justice Quarterly* 15(3): 505–26.

Evans, T. D., F. T. Cullen, V. S. Burton, Jr., R. G. Dunaway, and M. L. Benson. (1997). "The social consequences of self-control: Testing the general theory of crime." *Criminology* 35: 475–504.

Eysenck, H. J. (1973). *The Inequality of Man.* San Diego, CA: Edits.

———. (1977). *Crime and Personality*, 2d ed. London: Routledge and Kegan Paul.

Eysenck, H. J., and I. H. Gudjonsson. (1989). *The Causes and Cures of Criminality.* New York: Plenum.

Eysenck, H. J., and L. Kamin. (1981). *The Intelligence Controversy.* New York: Wiley.

Faderman, L. (1998). *I Begin My Life All Over: The Hmong and the American Immigrant Experience.* Boston: Beacon Press.

Fadiman, A. (1997). *The Spirit Catches You and You Fall Down: A Hmong Child, Her American Doctors, and the Collision of Two Cultures.* New York: Farrar, Straus and Giroux.

Fagan, J. (1989). "The social organization of drug use dealing among urban gangs." *Criminology* 27: 633–67.

Fagan, J., and K.-L. Chin. (1991). "Social processes of initiation into crack." *Journal of Drug Issues* 21: 313–43.

Fagan, J., E. Piper, and M. Moore. (1986). "Violent delinquents and urban youth," *Criminology* 24: 439–71.

Fagan, J., and S. Wexler. (1987). "Family origins of violent delinquents." *Criminology* 25: 643–69.

Falk, G. (1966). "The psychoanalytic theories of crime causation." *Criminology* 4: 1–11.

Farabee, D. (2002). "Examining Martinson's critique: A cautionary note for evaluators." *Crime and Delinquency* 48: 189–202.

Farnworth, M., and M. Lieber. (1989). "Strain theory revisited: Economic goals, educational means, and delinquency." *American Sociological Review* 54: 263–74.

Farrington, D. P. (2003). "British randomized experiments on crime and justice." *Annals* 589: 150–67.

———. (2005). "Childhood origins of antisocial behavior." *Clinical Psychology and Psychotherapy* 12: 177–90.

Farrington, D. P., L. Biron, and M. LeBlanc. (1982). "Personality and delinquency in London and Montreal." In *Abnormal Offenders, Delinquency, and the Criminal Justice System*, ed. J. Gunn and D. P. Farrington. Chichester, England: Wiley.

Farrington, D. P., and A. Morris. (1983). "Sex, sentencing, and reconviction." *British Journal of Criminology* 23: 229–48.

Farrington, D. P., and R. Tarling. (1985). *Prediction in Criminology.* Albany: SUNY Press.

Feder, L., and R. F. Boruch. (2000). "The need for experiments in criminal justice settings." *Crime and Delinquency* 46: 291–94.

Federal Bureau of Investigation (2008a). "Uniform Crime Reporting: National Incident-Based Reporting System." Retrieved 9 November 2008 at http://www.fbi.gov/hq/cjisd/ucr.htm

———. (2008b) "Table 1. Crime in the United States." Retrieved 9 November 2008 at http://www.fbi.gov/ucr/cius2007/data/table_01.html

Felkenes, G. T. (1975). "The prosecutor: A look at reality." *Southwestern University Law Review* 7: 98–103.

———. (1991). "Affirmative action in the Los Angeles Police Department." *Criminal Justice Research Bulletin* 6: 1–9.

Felson, M. (1987). "Routine activities and crime prevention in the developing metropolis." *Criminology* 25: 911–31.

———. (1993). "Review of Choosing Crime by K. Tunnell." *American Journal of Sociology* 98: 1497–99.

———. (1994) *Crime and Everyday Life*. Thousand Oaks, CA: Pine Forge.

———. (1998). *Crime and Everyday Life*, 2d ed. Thousand Oaks, CA: Pine Forge.

———. (2000). "The routine activities approach as a general crime theory." Pp. 205–16 in *Of Crime and Criminality*, ed. S. S. Simpson. Thousand Oaks, CA: Pine Forge.

———. (2001). "The routine activities approach: A very versatile theory of crime." Pp. 43–46 in *Explaining Criminals and Crime*, ed. R. Paternoster and R. Bachman. Los Angeles: Roxbury.

———. (2002). *Crime and Everyday Life*, 3rd ed. Thousand Oaks, CA: Sage.

Felson, M., and L. E. Cohen. (1980). "Human ecology and crime: A routine activity approach." *Human Ecology* 8: 389–406.

Ferraro, K. (1989). "The legal response to battery in the United States." In *Women, Policing, and Male Violence*, ed. J. Hanmer, J. Radford, and E. Stanka. London: Tavistock.

Feshbach, S., and R. D. Singer. (1971). *Television and Aggression*. San Francisco: Jossey-Bass.

Finckenauer, J. O. (1982). *Scared Straight and the Panacea Phenomenon*. Englewood Cliffs, NJ: Prentice-Hall.

Fishbein, D. H. (1990). "Biological perspectives in criminology." *Criminology* 28: 27–72.

———. (1992). "The psychobiology of female aggression." *Criminal Justice and Behavior* 12: 99–126.

Fishbein, D. H., and S. E. Pease. (1988). "The effects of diet on behavior: The implications for criminology and corrections." *Research in Corrections* 1: 1–44.

Flynn, L. E. (1986). "House arrest: Florida's alternative eases crowding and tight budgets." *Corrections Today* 48: 64–68.

Flynn, J. T., and M. Peterson. (1972). "The use of regression analysis in police patrolman selection." *Journal of Criminal Law, Criminology, and Police Science.* 63: 564–69.

Fogel, D. (1975). "... We are the living proof ..." In *The Justice Model for Corrections*. Cincinnati: Anderson.

Forst, B. E. (1983). "Capital punishment and deterrence: Conflicting evidence?" *Journal of Criminal Law and Criminology* 74: 927–42.

Foshee, V., and K. E. Bauman. (1992). "Parental and peer characteristics as modifiers of the bond–behavior relationship: An elaboration of control theory." *Journal of Health and Social Behavior* 33: 66–76.

Fox, J. A., and M. W. Zawitz. (2007). *Homicide trends in the United States*. Washington, DC: Bureau of Justice Statistics. Retrieved 15 February 2008 at http://www.ojp.gov/bjs/homicide/homtrnd.htm.

Frank, S. (1999). *Crime, Cultural Conflict, and Justice in Rural Russia, 1856–1914*. Berkley, CA: University of California Press.

Franklin, C. A., and N. E. Fearn. (2008). "Gender, race, and formal court-decision making: Chivalry/paternalism, conflict theory, or gender conflict?" *Journal of Criminal Justice* 3: 279–0.

Fraser, S. (1995). *The Bell Curve Wars: Race, Intelligence, and the Future of America*. New York: Basic Books.

Freedman, J. L. (1984). "Effects of television violence on aggressiveness." *Psychological Bulletin* 96: 227–46.

———. (1986). "Television violence and aggression: A rejoinder." *Psychological Bulletin* 100: 372–78.

Freidrich-Cofer, L., and A. C. Huston. (1986). "Television violence and aggression: A rejoinder." *Psychological Bulletin* 100: 364–71.

Freng, A., and L. T. Winfree, Jr. (2004). "Exploring race and ethnic differences in a sample of middle school gang members." Chapter 6 in *American Youth Gangs at the Millennium*, ed. F. -A. Esbensen, L. K. Gaines, and S. G. Tibbetts. Long Grove, IL: Waveland Press.

Freud, S. (1933). *New Introductory Lectures on Psychoanalysis*. New York: Norton.

Friday, P. C. (1977). "Changing theory and research in criminology." *International Journal of Criminology and Penology* 5: 159–70.

Friedan, B. N. (1963). *The Feminine Mystique*. New York: W.W. Norton and Company.

Friedrichs, D. O. (1982). "Crime, deviance, and criminal justice: In search of a radical humanistic perspective." *Humanity and Society* 6: 200–226.

Friend, T. (2000). "Genetic map is hailed as 'new power.' Fruits of historic achievement could be seen in 5 years." *USA Today*, 27 June: 1a.

Frisch, L. A. (1992). "Research that succeeds, policy that fails." *Journal of Criminal Law and Criminology* 83: 209–16.

Fuchs, J. (1965). *Natural Law: A Theoretical Investigation.* New York: Sheed and Ward.

Gabor, T. (1990). "Preventing crime: Current issues and debates." *Canadian Journal of Criminology* 32: 1–212.

Gallagher, P. (1998). "The man who told the secret: It took a non-Swede to get the full story of a government sterilization program." *Columbia Journalism Review,* January–February. http://www.cjr.org/year/98/1/Sweden/asp

Gardner, H. (1983). *Frames of Mind: The Theory of Multiple Intelligence.* New York: Basic Books.

Gardner, L., and D. J. Shoemaker. (1989). "Social bonding and delinquency: A comparative analysis." *Sociological Quarterly* 30: 481–500.

Garfinkel, H. (1956). "Conditions of successful degradation ceremonies." *American Journal of Sociology* 61: 420–24.

Garner, J., and C. A. Visher. (1988). *Policy Experiments Coming of Age.* NIJ Reports. Washington, DC: National Institute of Justice.

Gartner, A., C. Greer, and F. Reissman. (1974). *The New Assault on Equality: IQ and Social Stratification,* New York: Harper and Row.

Gates, H. L. (1995). "Thirteen ways of looking at a black man." *New Yorker,* October: 59.

Gauthier, D., and W. B. Bankston. (1997). "Gender equality and sex ratio of intimate killing." *Criminology* 45: 577–700.

Gay, W. G., T. H. Schell, and S. Schack. (1977). *Routine Patrol: Improving Police Productivity.* Washington, DC: U.S. Government Printing Office.

Gee, E. G., and D. Jackson. (1977). "Hand in hand or fist in glove?" In *Learning and the Law* 34.

Geerken, M. R., and W. R. Gove. (1975). "Deterrence: Some theoretical considerations." *Law and Society Review* 9: 497–513.

Gendreau, P., M. Irvine, and S. Knight. (1973). "Evaluating response styles on the MMPI with prisoners: Faking good adjustment and maladjustment." *Canadian Journal of Behavioral Sciences* 5: 183–94.

Gerber, E., and M. de la Puente. (1996). "The development and cognitive testing of race and ethnic origin questions for the year 2000 decennial census." Washington, DC: U.S. Bureau of Census. Retrieved 3 March 2009 at http://www.census.gov/prod/2/gen/96arc/iiiagerb.pdf

Gerbner, G., and L. Gross. (1976). "Living with television: the violence profile." *Journal of Communication* 26(2): 173–99.

———. (1980). "The violent face of television and its lessons." Pp. 149–62 in *Children and the Faces of Television: Teaching, Violence, Selling,* ed. E. L. Palmer and A. Dorr. New York: Academic.

Gibbons, D. C. (1977). *Society, Crime, and Criminal Careers,* 3d ed. Englewood Cliffs, NJ: Prentice-Hall.

———. (1979). *The Criminological Enterprise: Theories and Perspectives.* Englewood Cliffs, NJ: Prentice-Hall.

———. (1984). "Forcible rape and sexual violence." *Journal of Research in Crime and Delinquency* 21: 251–69.

———. (1992). *Society, Crime, and Criminal Behavior,* 6th ed. Englewood Cliffs, NJ: Prentice-Hall.

———. (1994). *Talking about Crime and Criminals.* Englewood Cliffs, NJ: Prentice-Hall.

———. (2000). "Introductory chapter: Criminology, criminologists, and criminological theory." In *Crime and Criminality,* ed. S. S. Simpson. Thousand Oaks, CA: Pine Forge.

Gibbs, J. (1968). "Crime, punishment and deterrence." *Southwest Social Science Quarterly.* 48: 515–30.

———. (1972). *Sociological Theory Construction.* Hinsdale, IL: Dryden.

———. (1975). *Crime, Punishment, and Deterrence.* New York: Elsevier.

———. (1985). "The methodology of theory construction in criminology." In *Theoretical Methods in Criminology,* ed. R. F. Meier. Beverly Hills, CA: Sage.

———. (1987). "The state of criminological theory." *Criminology* 25: 821–40.

Gibbs, J. J., and D. Giever. (1995). "Self control and its manifestations among university students: An empirical test of Gottfredson and Hirschi's general theory." *Justice Quarterly* 12: 231–55.

Gibbs, J. J., D. Giever, and J. S. Martin. (1998). "Parental management and self-control: An empirical test of Gottfredson and Hirschi's general theory." *Journal of Research in Crime and Delinquency* 35: 40–75.

Giddens, A. (1990). *Consequences of Modernity*. Stanford, CA: Stanford University Press.

Gill, A. (1978). "The misuse of genetics in the race-IQ controversy." *San Jose Studies* 4: 23–43.

Giordano, P., and S. A. Cernkovich. (1977). "Male theories and female crimes: Understanding the impact of social change." Paper presented at the annual meeting of the Midwest Sociological Society, Minneapolis, MN.

Glaser, D. (1956). "Criminality theories and behavioral images." *American Journal of Sociology* 61: 433–44.

———. (1960). "Differential association and criminological prediction." *Social Problems* 8: 6–14.

———. (1965). "Criminology." *Encyclopedia Britannica*, vol. 6. Chicago: Gilmore.

———. (1978). *Crime in Our Changing Society*. New York: Holt, Rinehart and Winston.

Glaser, D. and M. S. Ziegler. (1974). "Use of the death penalty v. outrage at murder." *Crime and Delinquency* 20: 337.

Glasser, W. (1975). *Reality Therapy*. New York: Harper and Row.

———. (1980). "Reality therapy: An explanation of the steps in reality therapy." In *Therapy*, ed. W. Glasser. New York: Harper and Row.

Glueck, S. (1956). "Theory and fact in criminology." *British Journal of Delinquency* 7: 92–109.

Glueck, S., and E. Glueck. (1950). *Unraveling Juvenile Delinquency*. New York: The Commonwealth Fund.

———. (1956). *Physique and Delinquency*. Cambridge, MA: Harvard University Press.

Goddard, H. H. (1914). *Feeblemindedness: Its Causes and Consequences*. New York: Macmillan.

———. (1921). "Feeblemindedness and delinquency." *Journal of Psycho-Asthenics* 25: 168–76.

Goenner, T. (2000). "Conflict, crime, communication, cooperation—Restorative justice as a new way of dealing with the consequences of criminal acts." Unpublished paper. Tuebingen, Germany: University of Tuebingen.

Goffman, E. (1963). *Stigma*. Englewood Cliffs, NJ: Prentice-Hall.

Gold, E. R. (1999). "Hope, fear and genetics: Judicial responses to biotechnology." *Judicature* 83: 132–38.

Gold, M. S., A. M. Washton, and C. A. Dackis. (1985). "Cocaine abuse: Neurochemistry, phenomenology, and treatment." In *Cocaine Use in America: Epidemiology and Clinical Perspective*, ed. N. J. Kozel and E. H. Adams. Rockville, MD: National Institute on Drug Abuse.

Gold, S. (1980). "The CAP control theory of drug abuse." In *Theories of Drug Abuse: Selected Contemporary Perspectives*, ed. D. J. Lettieri, M. Sayers, and H. W. Pearson. Rockville, MD: National Institute on Drug Abuse.

Goldberg, S. B., E. D. Green, and F. E. A. Sanders. (1985). *Dispute Resolution*. Boston: Little, Brown.

Goleman, D. (1987). "Embattled giant of psychology speaks his mind." *New York Times* 25 August: 17, 18.

———. (1990). "Scientists pinpoint brain irregularities in drug addicts." *New York Times*, 26 June: B5.

Goode, E. (1984). *Drugs in American Society*, 2d ed. New York: Knopf.

Gora, J. G. (1982). *The New Female Criminal: Empirical Reality or Social Myth?* New York: Praeger.

Gordon, J. W. (2001). "Did the first Justice Harlan have a black brother?" Chapter 12 in *Critical Race Theory: The Cutting Edge*, 2d ed., ed. R. Delgado and J. Stefancic. Philadelphia, PA: Temple University Press.

Gordon R. (1976). "Prevalence: The rare datum in delinquency measurement and its implications for the theory of delinquency." In *The Juvenile Justice System*, ed. M. W. Klein. Beverly Hills, CA: Sage.

———. (1987). "SES versus IQ in the race– IQ–delinquency model." *International Journal of Sociology and Social Policy* 7: 42–62.

Gottfredson, D. M. (1989). "Criminological theories: The truth as told by Mark Twain." In *Advances in Criminological Theory*, vol. 1, ed. W. S. Laufer and F. Adler. New Brunswick, NJ: Transaction.

Gottfredson, D. C., A. Cross, and D. A. Soulé. (2007). "Distinguishing characteristics of effective and ineffective after-school programs to prevent delinquency and victimization." *Criminology & Public Policy* 6: 289–318.

Gottfredson, M. R., and D. M. Gottfredson. (1988). *Decision Making in Criminal Justice: Toward the*

Rational Exercise of Discretion, 2d ed. New York: Plenum.

Gottfredson, M. R., and T. Hirschi. (1986). "The true value of lambda would appear to be zero: An essay on career criminals, criminal careers, selective incapacitation, cohort studies, and related topics." *Criminology* 24: 213–34.

———. (1987). "The methodological adequacy of longitudinal research on crime." *Criminology* 25: 581–614.

———. (1989). "A propensity-event theory of crime." Pp. 57–67 in *Advances in Criminological Theory*, vol. 1, ed. W. S. Laufer and F. Adler. New Brunswick, NJ: Transaction.

———. (1990). *A General Theory of Crime*. Stanford, CA: Stanford University Press.

Gough, H. G. (1965). "The F minus K Dissimulation index for the MMPI." *Journal of Consulting Psychology* 14: 408–13.

Gould, L. (1999). "The impact of working in two worlds and its effect on Navajo police officers." *Journal of Legal Pluralism* 44: 53–71.

Gould, S. J. (1981). *The Mismeasure of Man*. New York: Norton.

———. (1995). "Curveball." In *The Bell Curve Wars: Race, Intelligence and the Future of America*, ed. S. Fraser. New York: Basic Books.

Gove, W. R. (1980). *The Labeling of Deviance: Evaluation of a Perspective*. Beverly Hills, CA: Sage.

Gove, W. R., and C. Wilmoth. (1990). "Risk, crime, and neurophysiologic highs: A consideration of brain processes that may reinforce delinquent and criminal behavior." In *Crime in Biological, Social, and Moral Contexts*, ed. L. Ellis and H. Hoffman. Westport, CT: Praeger.

Grasmick, H. G., and R. J. Bursik. (1990). "Conscience, significant others, and rational choice: Extending the deterrence model." *Law and Society Review* 24: 837–61.

Grasmick, H. G., C. R. Tittle, R. J. Bursik, and B. J. Arneklev. (1993). "Testing the core empirical implications of Gottfredson and Hirschi's general theory of crime." *Journal of Research in Crime and Delinquency* 30: 5–29.

Greenberg, D. F. (1981). *Crime and Capitalism: Readings in a Marxist Criminology*. Palo Alto, CA: Mayfield.

———. (1999). "The weak strength of social control theory." *Crime and Delinquency* 45: 61–81.

Greenberg, S., and W. M. Rohe. (1984). "Neighborhood design and crime: A test of two perspectives." *Journal of the American Planning Association* 50: 48–61.

Greenberg, S., W. M. Rohe, and J. R. Williams. (1982). *Safe and Secure Neighborhoods: Physical Characteristics and Informal Territorial Control in High and Low Crime Neighborhoods*. Washington, DC: National Institute of Justice.

Greenfield, L. A. (1998). *Alcohol and Crime*. Washington, DC: U.S. Department of Justice, Bureau of Justice Statistics.

Greenleaf, R. G., and L. Lanza-Kaduce. (1995). "Sophistication, organization, and authority-subject conflict: Rediscovering and unraveling Turk's theory of norm resistance." *Criminology* 33: 565–86.

Greenwood, P. W., and A. Hawken. (2002). *An Assessment of the Effects of California's Three Strikes Law*. Malibu Lake, CA: Greenwood and Associates.

Greenwood, P. W., K. E. Model, C. P. Rydell, and J. Chiesa. (1996). *Diverting Children from a Life of Crime*. Santa Monica, CA: Rand.

Griffin, B. S., and C. T. Griffin. (1978). "Drug use and differential association." *Drug Forum* 7: 1–8.

Griffin, D. R., and R. A. Falk. (1993). *Postmodern Politics for a Planet in Crisis: Policy, Process and Presidential Vision*. Albany: SUNY Press.

Gross, J. (1992). "Collapse of innercity families creates America's new orphans: Death, drugs, and jail leave voids in childhood." *New York Times*, 28 March: A1.

Grossman, L., T. W. Haywood, E. Ostrov, O. Wasyliw, and J. L. Cavanaugh. (1990). "Sensitivity: MMPI validity scales." *Journal of Personality Assessment* 54: 220–35.

Guy, E., J. J. Platt, I. S. Zwelling, and S. Bullock. (1985). "Mental health status of prisoners in an urban jail." *Criminal Justice and Behavior* 12: 29–33.

Guze, S. B. (1976). *Criminality and Psychiatric Disorders*. New York: Oxford University Press.

Habermas, J. (1981). "Modernity versus postmodernity." *The German Critique* 22: 3–14.

Hacker, A. (1992). *Two Nations: Black and White, Separate, Hostile, Unequal*. New York: Scribner.

Hagan, F. (1989). *Research Methods in Criminal Justice and Criminology*, 5th ed. Boston: Allyn & Bacon.

Hagan, J. (1974). "Extralegal attributes and criminal sentencing: An assessment of a sociological viewpoint." *Law and Society Review* 8: 357–83.

———. (1989a). *Structural Criminology*. New Brunswick, NJ: Rutgers University Press.

———. (1989b). "Why is there so little criminal justice theory? Neglected macro- and micro-level links between organization and power." *Journal of Crime and Delinquency* 26: 116–35.

———. (1990). "The structuration of gender and deviance: A power control theory of vulnerability to crime and the search for deviant role exits." *Canadian Review of Sociology and Anthropology* 27: 137–56.

———. (1991). "Destiny and drift: Subcultural preferences, status attainment, and the risk and rewards of youth." *American Sociological Review* 56: 567–82.

———. (1994). *Crime and Disrepute*. Thousand Oaks, CA: Pine Forge.

———. (1995). "Rethinking crime theory and policy: The new sociology of crime and disrepute." Pp. 29–42 in *Crime and Public Policy: Putting Theory to Work*, ed. H. Barlow. Boulder, CO: Westview Press.

———. (1997). "Defiance and despair: Subcultural and structural linkages between delinquency and despair in the life course." *Social Forces* 76: 119–34.

———. (2005). *Research Methods in Criminal Justice and Criminology*. Boston: Allyn & Bacon.

Hagan, J., A. R. Gillis, and J. H. Simpson. (1988). "Feminist scholarship, relational and instrumental control and a power-control theory of gender and delinquency." *British Journal of Sociology* 39: 301–36.

———. (1990). "Clarifying and extending power control theory." *American Journal of Sociology* 95: 1024–37.

Hagan, J., G. Hefler, G. Classen, K. Boehnke, and H. Merkens. (1998). "Subterranean sources of subcultural delinquency beyond the American dream." *Criminology* 36: 309–41.

Hagan, J., and F. Kay. (1990). "Gender and delinquency in white-collar families: A power-control perspective." *Crime and Delinquency* 36: 391–407.

Hagan, J., and P. Parker. (1985). "White collar crime and punishment: The class structure and legal sanctioning of securities violations." *American Sociological Review* 50: 802–20.

Hagan, J., W. Rymond-Richmond, and P. Parker. (2005). "The criminology of genocide: The death and rape of Darfur." *Criminology* 43: 525–61.

Hagan, J., C. Shedd, and M. R. Payne. (2005). "Race, ethnicity, and youth perceptions of injustice." *American Sociological Review* 70: 381–407.

Hagan, J., J. H. Simpson, and A. R. Gillis. (1979). "The sexual stratification of social control: A gender-based perspective on crime and delinquency." *British Journal of Sociology* 30: 28–38.

———. (1985). "The class structure of gender and delinquency: Toward a power-control theory of common delinquent behavior." *American Journal of Sociology* 90: 1151–78.

———. (1987). "Class in the household: A power-control theory of gender and delinquency." *American Journal of Sociology* 92: 788–816.

Hagedorn, J. M. (1998). *People and Folks: Gangs, Crime and the Underclass in a Rustbelt City*. Chicago: Lake View Press.

Hall, J. (1952). *Theft, Law, and Society*, rev. ed. Indianapolis, IN: Bobbs-Merrill.

Hall, R. W. (1989). "A study of mass murder: Evidence underlying cadmium and lead poisoning and brain involving immunoreactivity." *International Journal of Biosocial and Medical Research* 11(2): 144–52.

Hallett, M. A. (2006). *Private Prisons in America: A Critical Race Perspective*. Urbana and Chicago: University of Illinois Press.

Hamdan v. Rumsfeld, 548 U.S. 557 (2006).

Hamdi v. Rumsfeld, 542 U.S. 507 (2004).

Hammer v. Dagenhart et al., 247 U.S. 251, 38 S.Ct. 529, L.Ed. 1101 (1918).

Hammond, H. A., and C. T. Caskey. (1997). "Automated DNA typing: Method of the future." *NIJ Research Preview*, February. Washington, DC: U.S. Department of Justice.

Hamparian, D. M., L. K. Estep, S. M. Muntean, R. R. Prestino, R. G. Swisher, P. L. Wallace, and J. L. White. (1982). *Youth in Adult Courts: Between Two Worlds*. Columbus, OH: Academy of Contemporary Problems.

Hancock, L. (1994). "In defiance of Darwin: How a public school in the Bronx turns dropouts into scholars." *Newsweek*, 24 October: 61.

Hare, R. D. (1996a). "Psychopathology: A clinical construct whose time has come." *Criminal Justice and Behavior* 23: 25–54.

———. (1996b). "Psychopathy and antisocial personality disorder: A case of diagnostic confusion." *Psychiatric Times* 13: 39–40.

———. (1998). "The PCL-R: Some issues concerning its misuse." *Legal and Criminological Psychology* 3: 99–119.

———. (2003). *Manual for Hare Psychopathy Checklist-Revised*. 2d ed. Toronto, Ontario, Canada: Multi-Health Systems.

Hare, R. D., D. Clark, M. Grann, and D. Thornton. (2000). "Psychopathy and the predictive validity of the PCL-R: An international perspective." *Behavioral Sciences and the Law* 18: 623–45.

Harris, D. A. (1999). *Driving While Black: Racial Profiling on Our Nation's Highways*. New York: American Civil Liberties Union.

———. (2007). "The importance of race and policing: Making race salient to individuals and institutions within criminal justice." *Criminology and Public Policy* 7: 5–24.

Harris, G. T., T. A. Skilling, and M. E. Rice. (2001). "The construct of psychopathy." *Crime and Justice* 28: 197–264.

Harris, N., J. Braithwaite, and L. Walgrave. (2003). "Emotional dynamics in restorative conferences." *Theoretical Criminology* 8: 191–210.

Harris, N., and S. Maruna. (2006). "Shame, sharing, and restorative justice: A critical appraisal." Pp. 452–60 in *Handbook of Restorative Justice: A Global Perspective*, ed. D. Sullivan and L. Tifft. New York: Routledge.

Harry, J., and W. W. Minor. (1985). "Intelligence and delinquency reconsidered: A comment on Menard and Morse." *American Journal of Sociology* 91: 956–62.

Hartjen, C. A., and S. Kethineni. (1999). "Exploring the etiology of delinquency across country and gender." *Journal of Crime and Justice* 22(2): 55–90.

Hartjen, C. A., and S. Priyadarsini. (2003). "Gender, peers, and delinquency: A study of boys and girls in rural France." *Youth & Society* 34: 387–414.

Harvey, D. (1989). *The Condition of Postmodernity*. Cambridge, England: Blackwell.

Hasian, Jr., M., and F. Delgado. (1998). "The trials and tribulations of racialized critical rhetorical theory: Understanding the rhetorical ambiguities of Proposition 187." *Communication Theory* 8: 245–70.

Hathaway, R. S., and E. D. Monachesi. (1953). *Analyzing and Predicting Juvenile Delinquency with the MMPI*. Minneapolis: University of Minneapolis Press.

Hawkins, G. (1976). *The Prison*. Chicago: University of Chicago Press.

Hawkins, G., and G. P. Alpert. (1989). *American Prison System: Punishment and Justice*. Englewood Cliffs, NJ: Prentice-Hall.

Hawkins, J. D., and J. Weis. (1985). "The social development model: An integrated approach to delinquency prevention." *Journal of Primary Prevention* 6: 73–97.

Hay, C. (1998). "Parental sanctions and delinquent behavior: Toward clarification of Braithwaite's theory of reintegrative shaming." *Theoretical Criminology* 2: 419–43.

———. (2001a). "Parenting, self-control, and delinquency: A test of self-control theory." *Criminology* 39: 707–36.

———. (2001b). "An exploratory test of Braithwaite's reintegrative shaming theory." *Journal of Research in Crime and Delinquency* 38: 132–53.

Hay, C., and W. Forrest. (2006). "The development of self-control: Examining self-control theory's stability thesis." *Criminology* 44: 739–772.

Hayeslip, D. W. (1989). *Local-Level Drug Enforcement: New Strategies*. National Institute of Justice Research in Action. Washington, DC: U.S. Government Printing Office.

Haynie, D. L., and D. W. Osgood. (2005). "Reconsidering peers and delinquency: How do peers matter?" *Social Forces* 84: 1109–30.

Healy, W., and A. F. Bronner. (1936). *New Light on Delinquency and Its Treatment*. New Haven, CT: Yale University Press.

Healy, W., A. F. Bronner, and A. M. Bowers. (1930). *The Structure and Meaning of Psychoanalysis*. New York: Knopf.

Heimer, K., and S. De Coster. (1999). "The gendering of violent delinquency." *Criminology* 37: 277–318.

Held, A., S. L. Herndon, and D. M. Stager. (1997). "The Equal Rights Amendment: Why the ERA remains legally viable and properly before the states."

William & Mary Journal of Women and the Law. 3: 113–36.

Heineke, J. H. (1988). "Crime, deterrence, and choice: Testing the rational behavior hypothesis." *American Sociological Review* 54: 303–05.

Henriques, D. B., with D. Baquet. (1993). "Investigators say bid-rigging is common in milk industry." *New York Times* 23 May: 1, 12.

Henry, S., and D. Milovanovic. (1991). "Constitutive criminology: The maturation of critical theory." *Criminology* 29: 293–315.

———. (1996). *Constitutive Criminology.* Thousand Oaks, CA: Sage.

Hepburn, J. R. (1976). "Testing alternative models of delinquency causation." *Journal of Criminal Law and Criminology* 67: 450–60.

Herrnstein, R. J. (1971). "I.Q." *Atlantic Monthly* 228: 43–64.

Herrnstein, R. J., and C. Murray. (1994). *The Bell Curve: Intelligence and Class Structure in American Life.* New York: Free Press.

Herronkohl, T. I., B. Huang, R. Kosterman, J. D. Hawkins, R. F. Catalano, and B. H. Smith. (2001). "A comparison of social development processes leading to violent behavior in late adolescence for childhood initiators and adolescent initiators of violence." *Journal of Research in Crime and Delinquency* 38: 45–63.

Hesseling, R. (1994). "Displacement: A review of the empirical literature." In *Crime Prevention Studies*, vol. 3, ed. R. V. Clarke. Monsey, NY: Criminal Justice Press.

Hickman, M. J., and A. R. Piquero. (2001). "Exploring relationships between gender, control balance, and deviance." *Deviant Behavior* 22: 323–51.

Hickman, M. J., A. R. Piquero, B. P. Lawton, and J. R. Greene. (2001). "Applying Tittle's control balance theory and police deviance." *Policing* 24: 497–519.

Hickman, M. J., and B. A. Reaves. (2001). *Local Police Departments 1999.* Washington, DC: U.S. Department of Justice.

Higgins, G. E., and C. Lauterbach. (2004). "Control balance theory and exploitation: An examination of contingencies." *Criminal Justice Studies* 17: 291–391.

Hindelang, M. J. (1972). "The relationship of self-reported delinquency to scales of CPI and MMPI."

Journal of Criminal Law, Criminology, and Police Science 63: 75–81.

———. (1973). "Causes of delinquency: A partial replication and extension." *Social Problems* 20: 471–87.

———. (1981). "Variations in sex-race-age-specific incidence rates of offending. *American Sociological Review* 46: 461–74.

Hippchen, L. (1978). *Ecologic-Biochemical Approaches to the Treatment of Delinquents and Criminals.* New York: Van Nostrand Reinhold.

———. (1982). *Holistic Approaches to Offender Rehabilitation.* Springfield, IL: Thomas.

Hirschel, J. D., and I. W. Hutchinson. (1992). "Female spouse abuse and the police response: The Charlotte, North Carolina, experiment." *Journal of Criminal Law and Criminology* 83: 73–119.

Hirschi, T. (1969). *Causes of Delinquency.* Berkeley: University of California Press.

———. (1972). *Causes of Delinquency.* Berkeley: University of California Press.

———. (1996). "Theory without ideas: Reply to Akers." *Criminology* 34: 249–56.

———. (2004). "Self-control and crime." In *Handbook of Self-regulation: Research, Theory, and Application*, ed. R. F. Baumeister and K. D. Vohs. New York: Guilford Press.

Hirschi, T., and M. Gottfredson. (1986). "The distinction between crime and criminality." Pp. 55–69 in *Critique and Explanation*, ed. T. Hartnagel and R. Silverman. New Brunswick, NJ: Transaction.

Hirschi, T., and M. J. Hindelang. (1977). "Intelligence and delinquency: A revisionist review." *American Sociological Review* 42: 571–86.

Hobbes, T. (1957)[1651]. *Leviathan.* Oxford, England: Basil Blackwell.

Hoebel, E. A. (1974). *The Law of Primitive Man.* New York: Atheneum.

Hoffer, P. C. (1997). *The Salem Witchcraft Trials: A Legal History.* Lawrence: University Press of Kansas.

Hoffman, B. F. (1977). "Two new cases of XYY chromosome complement." *Canadian Psychiatric Association Journal* 22: 447–55.

Hoffman, J. P. (2002). "A contextual analysis of differential association, social control, and strain theories of delinquency." *Social Forces* 81: 753–85.

Hollin, C. R. (1989). *Psychology and Crime: An Introduction to Criminological Psychology*. London: Routledge.

———. (1990). *Cognitive-Behavioral Interventions with Young Offenders*. New York: Pergamon Press.

Holmes, R. M. (1990). *Profiling Violent Crimes*. Newbury Park, CA: Sage.

Holmes, M. D. (2000). "Minority threat and police brutality: Determinants of civil rights criminal complaints in U.S. municipalities." *Criminology* 38: 343–67.

Holmes, M. D., D. W. Smith, A. B. Freng, E. A. Muñoz. (2008). "Minority threat, crime control, and police resource allocation in the southwestern United States." *Crime and Delinquency* 54: 128–52.

Holten, N. G., and L. L. Lamar. (1991). *The Criminal Courts: Structures, Personnel, and Processes*. New York: McGraw-Hill.

Holzman, H. (1979). "Learning disabilities and juvenile delinquency: Biological and sociological theories." In *Biology and Crime*, ed. C. R. Jeffery. Beverly Hills, CA: Sage.

Hooton, E. (1939). *The American Criminal: An Anthropological Study*. Cambridge, MA: Harvard University Press.

Hopkins Burke, R. (2001). *An Introduction to Criminological Theory*. Cullompton: Willan.

Horgan, J. (1993). "Eugenics revisited." *Scientific American* 254: 122–31.

Horney, J. (1978). "Menstrual cycles and criminal responsibility." *Law and Human Behavior* 2(190): 25–36.

Horney, J., and I. H. Marshall. (1992). "Risk perceptions among serious offenders: The role of crime and punishment." *Criminology* 30: 575–92.

Horowitz, I. L. (1967). *The Rise and Fall of Project Camelot: Studies in the Relationship between Social Science and Practical Politics*. Cambridge, MA: MIT Press.

Houston, J. (1995). *Correctional Management: Functions, Skills and Systems*. Chicago: Nelson-Hall.

Hoyle, M. L. (1995). "'A fitting remedy': Aboriginal justice as a community healing strategy." In *Popular Justice and Community Regeneration*, ed. K. M. Haslehurst. Westport, CT: Praeger.

Hubka, V. E. (1975). *The Fate of Idealism in Lawyers*. Ph.D. dissertation, University of California, Berkeley. University Microfilms International BMJ76-15069.

Huebner, A. L., and S. C. Betts. (2002). "Exploring the utility of social control theory for youth development: Issues of attachment, involvement, and gender." *Youth and Society* 34: 123–45.

Hughes, E. C. (1945). "Dilemmas and contradictions of status." *American Journal of Sociology* 50: 353–59.

Huizinga, D., R. Loeber, and T. P. Thornberry. (1995). *Urban Delinquency and Substance Abuse: Recent Findings from the Program of Research on the Causes and Correlates of Delinquency*. Washington, DC: U.S. Department of Justice, Office of Justice Programs, Office of Juvenile Justice and Delinquency Prevention.

Hunt, D. M. (1999). *O.J. Simpson Facts and Fiction: New Rituals in the Construction of Reality*. New York: Cambridge University Press.

Hunt, J. (1985). "Police accounts of normal force." *Urban Life* 13: 315–41.

Hunter, H. (1966). "YY chromosomes and Klinefelter's syndrome." *Lancet* 1: 984.

———. (1977). "XYY males." *British Journal of Psychiatry* 121: 468–77.

Hurwitz, S., and K. O. Christiansen. (1983). *Criminology*. London: Allen and Unwin.

Hutchings, B., and S. A. Mednick. (1977). "Criminality in adoptees and their biological parents: A pilot study." In *Biosocial Bases of Criminal Behavior*, ed. S. A. and K. O. Christiansen. New York: Gardner.

Inciardi, J. A., ed. (1980). *Radical Criminology: The Coming Crises*. Beverly Hills, CA: Sage.

———. (1992). *The War on Drugs II: The Continuing Epic of Heroin, Cocaine, Crack, Crime, AIDS, and Public Policy*. Mountain View, CA: Mayfield.

———. (2007). *War on Drugs IV: The Continuing Saga of the Mysteries and Miseries of Intoxication, Addiction, Crime, and Public Policy*, 4th ed. Boston: Allyn & Bacon.

In re Gault, 387 U.S. 1; 18 L.Ed. 2d 527, 87 S.Ct. 1428 (1967).

In re Winship, 397 U.S. 358 (1970); 397 U.S. 358 (1971).

International Crisis Group. (2009). *Crisis in Darfur*. Retrieved 9 January 2009 at http://www.crisisgroup.org/home/index.cfm?id=3060.

Irwin, J. (1980). *Prisons in Turmoil*. Boston: Little, Brown.

Jackson, P. (1984). "Opportunity and crime: A function of city size." *Sociology and Social Research* 68: 172–93.

Jacobs, C. (1975). "The criminality of women." Unpublished paper presented to the Western Social Science Association, Denver, CO.

Jacobs, J. (1961). *The Death and Life of Great American Cities*. New York: Vintage Books.

Jacobs, D., and R. Kleban. (2003). "Political institutions, minorities, and punishment: A pooled cross-national analysis of imprisonment rates." *Social Forces* 80: 725–55.

Jacobs, P. A., M. Bruton, M. Melville, R. P. Brittain, and W. F. McClemont. (1965). "Aggressive behavior, mental sub-normality and the XYY male." *Nature* 208: 1351–52.

Jaffe, P., D. A. Wolf, A. Telford, and G. Austin. (1986). "The impact of police charges in incidents of wife abuse." *Journal of Family Violence* 1: 37–49.

Jaggar, A. M., and P. Rothenberg. (1984). *Feminist Frameworks*. New York: McGraw-Hill.

Jameson, F. (1984). "The politics of theory: Ideological positions in the postmodernism debate." *New German Critique* 33: 53–65.

———. (1991). *Postmodernism, or the Cultural Logic of Late Capitalism*. Durham, NC: Duke University Press.

Jeffery, C. R. (1965). "Criminal behavior and learning theory." *Journal of Criminal Law, Criminology, and Police Science* 56: 294–300.

———. (1971). *Crime Prevention through Environmental Design*. Beverly Hills, CA: Sage.

———. (1978). "Criminology as an inter-disciplinary science." *Criminology* 16: 149–67.

———. (1985). *Criminology: An Interdisciplinary Approach*. Englewood Cliffs, NJ: Prentice-Hall.

———. (1993). "Genetics, crime, and the canceled conference." *Criminologist* 18: 1, 6–8.

Jeffery, C. R., L. B. Myers, and L. A. Wollan. (1991). "Crime justice, and their systems: Resolving the tension." *Criminologist* 16: 1, 3–6.

Jensen, A. R. (1969). "How much can we boost I.Q. and scholastic achievement?" *Harvard Educational Review* 39: 1–123.

Jensen, G. F. (1972). "Parents, peers, and delinquent action: A test of the differential association perspective." *American Journal of Sociology* 78: 63–72.

———. (1999). "A critique of control balance theory." *Theoretical Criminology* 3: 339–43.

Jensen, G. F., and D. Brownfield. (1983). "Parents and drugs." *Criminology* 21: 543–54.

Jensen, G. F., and R. Eve. (1976). "Sex differences in delinquency." *Criminology* 13: 427–48.

Jensen, G. F., and D. G. Rojek. (1998). *Delinquency and Youth Crime*, 3d ed. Prospect Heights, IL: Waveland Press.

Jensen, G. F., and K. Thompson. (1990). "What's class got to do with it? A further examination of power-control theory." *American Journal of Sociology* 95: 1009–23.

Johnson, R. E. (1979). "Are adolescent theft, vandalism, and assault due to the same causal processes?" *International Journal of Comparative and Applied Criminal Justice* 3: 59–69.

Johnson, V. (1988). "Adolescent alcohol and marijuana use: A longitudinal assessment of a social learning perspective." *American Journal of Drug and Alcohol Abuse* 14: 319–39.

Jones, O. W. (2006). "Behavioral genetics and crime, in context." *Law and Contemporary Problems* 69: 81–100.

Jones, T., B. MacLean, and T. Young. (1986). *The Islington Crime Survey*. Aldershot, England: Gower.

Jung, C. G. (1921). *Psychological Types*. Zurich: Verlag.

———. (1961)[1933]. *Modern Man in Search of a Soul*. New York: Harcourt, Brace and World.

Kanarek, R. B. (1994). "Nutrition and violent behavior." In *Understanding and Preventing Violence*, vol. 2, ed. A. Reiss, K. Miczek, and J. Roth. Washington, DC: National Academy Press.

Kane, R. J. (2000). "Police responses to restraining orders in domestic violence incidents: Identifying the custody-threshold thesis." *Criminal Justice and Behavior* 27: 561–80.

Kaplan, A. (1963). *The Conduct of Inquiry*. Scranton, PA: Chandler.

Kappeler, V. E., and R. V. Del Carmen. (1990). "Civil liability for failure to arrest intoxicate drivers." *Journal of Criminal Justice* 18: 117–31.

Katz, J., and W. J. Chambliss. (1991). "Biological paradigms." In *Exploring Criminology*, ed. W. Chambliss. New York: Macmillan.

Keane, C., P. S. Maxim, and J. J. Teevan. (1993). "Drinking and driving, self-control, and gender: Testing a general theory of crime." *Journal of Research in Crime and Delinquency* 30: 30–46.

Keita, S. O. Y., R. A. Kittles, C. D. M. Royal, G. E. Bonney, P. Furbert-Harris, G. M. Dunston, and C. N. Rotimi. (2004). "Conceptualizing human variation." *Nature Genetics Supplement* 36: S17–S20.

Kelley, B.Tatem, T. P. Thornberry, and C. A. Smith. (1997). "In the wake of child maltreatment." *Juvenile Justice Bulletin*, August. Washington, DC: Office of Juvenile Justice and Delinquency Prevention.

Kelling, G., T. Pate, D. Dieckman, and C. Brown. (1974). *The Kansas City Preventive Patrol Experiment: A Summary Report*. Washington, DC: Police Foundation.

Kennedy, L. W., and S. W. Baron. (1993). "Routine activities and a subculture of violence: A study of violence on the streets." *Journal of Research in Crime and Delinquency* 30: 88–112.

Kenney, D. J., and S. Watson. (1990). "Intelligence and the selection of police recruits." *American Journal of Police* 9: 39–64.

Kent v. United States, 383 U.S.C. 541 (1966).

Kephart, W. M. (1957). *Racial Factors and Urban Law Enforcement*. Philadelphia: University of Pennsylvania.

Keppel, R. (2005). *The Riverman: Ted Bundy and I Hunt for the Green River Killer*. New York: Pocket Books.

Kessler, S., and R. H. Moos. (1970). "The XYY karyotype and criminality: A review." *Journal of Psychiatric Research* 7: 164.

Khantzian, E. J. (1985). "The self-medication hypothesis of addictive disorders: Focus on heroin and cocaine dependence." *American Journal of Psychiatry* 142: 1259–64.

Kimbrough v. United States, 128 S. Ct. 558 (2007).

King, R., D. Curtis, and G. Knoblich. (1996) "Biological factors in sociopathy: Relationships to drug abuse behaviors." Chapter 5 in *Vulnerability to Drug Abuse*, ed. M. D. Glantz and R. Pickens. Washington, DC: American Psychological Association.

Kinsey, R., J. Lea, and J. Young. (1986). *Losing the Fight against Crime*. Oxford, UK: Basil Blackwell.

Kleck, G. (1996). "Crime, culture conflict and the sources of support for gun control." *American Behavioral Scientist* 39: 387–404.

Kleck, G., B. Sever, S. Li, and M. Gertz. (2005). "The missing link in general deterrence research." *Criminology* 43: 623–59.

Klein, L. R., B. Forst, and V. Filatov. (1978). "The deterrent effect of capital punishment: An assessment of the estimates." In *Deterrence and Incapacitation: Estimating the Effects of Criminal Sanctions on Crime Rates*, ed. A. Blumstein, J. Cohen, and D. Nagin. Washington, DC: National Academy of Sciences.

Klochko, M. A. (2006). "Time preference and learning versus selection." *Rationality and Society* 18: 305–331.

———. (2008). "Individual time preferences in prison population: the effects of rehabilitation programs on women vs. men in Ukraine." Pp. 185–206 in *Beyond Little Vera: Women's Bodies, Women's Welfare in Russia and Central/Eastern Europe, Ohio Slavic Papers*, vol. 7, ed. A. Brintlinger and N. Kolchevska. Columbus, OH: The Ohio State University.

Knoblich, G., and R. King. (1992). "Biological correlates of criminal behavior." Pp. 1–21 in *From Facts, Frameworks, and Forecasts: Advances in Criminological Theory*, Volume 3, J. McCord, ed. Piscataway, NJ: Transaction Publishers.

Knoppers, B. M., and R. Chadwick. (2005). "Human genetics research: Emerging trends in ethics." *Nature Reviews: Genetics* 6: 75–79.

Kornhauser, R. (1978). *Social Sources of Delinquency*. Chicago: University of Chicago Press.

Kovandzic, T., J. J. Sloan III, and L. M. Vieraitis. (2002). "Unintended consequences of politically popular sentencing policy: The homicide promoting effects of 'three strikes' in U.S. cities (1980–1999)." *Criminology & Public Policy* 1: 399–424.

Kramer, J. H., and C. Kempinen. (1978). "Erosion of chivalry? Changes in the handling of male and female defendants from 1970 to 1975." Paper presented at the annual meeting of the Society for the Study of Social Problems, San Francisco.

Kreuz, L., and R. Rose. (1972). "Assessment of aggressive behavior and plasma testosterone in a young criminal population." *Psychosomatic Medicine* 34: 321–32.

Krisberg, B. (1975). *Crime and Privilege: Toward a New Criminology*. Englewood Cliffs, NJ: Prentice-Hall.

Krisberg, B., and J. F. Austin. (1993). *Reinventing Juvenile Justice*. Newbury Park, CA: Sage.

Krisberg, B., and K. F. Schumann. (2000). "Introduction." *Crime and Delinquency* 46: 147–55.

Krohn, M. D., and J. Massey. (1980). "Social control and delinquent behavior: An examination of the elements of social bond." *Sociological Quarterly* 21: 529–44.

Krohn, M. D., W. F. Skinner, J. L. Massey, and R. L. Akers. (1985). "Social learning theory and adolescent cigarette smoking: A longitudinal study." *Social Problems* 2: 4455–71.

Krolokke, C., and A. S. Sorensen. (2005). "Three waves of feminism: From suffragettes to grrls." Chapter 1 in *Gender Communication Theories and Analyses: From Silence to Performance*. Thousand Oaks, CA: Sage.

Kropotkin, P. (1970)[1927]. *Kropotkin's Revolutionary Pamphlets: A Collection of Writings by Peter Kropotkin*, ed. R. N. Baldwin. New York: Dover.

Kruttschnitt, C. (1982). "Women, crime, and dependency." *Criminology* 19: 495–513.

Kuhn, T. S. (1970). *The Structure of Scientific Revolutions*, 2d ed. Chicago: University of Chicago Press.

Kumpfer, K., and C. M. Tait. (2000). "Family skills training for parents and children." *OJJDP Juvenile Justice Bulletin*, April. NCJ180140.

Kurki, L. (1999). "Incorporating restorative and community justice into American sentencing and corrections." *Sentencing & Corrections: Issues for the 21st Century*, no. 3. Washington, DC: U.S. Office of Justice Programs.

Kvale, S. (1992). *Psychology and Postmodernism*. London: Sage.

LaGrange, T. C., and R. A. Silverman. (1999). "Low self-control and opportunity: Testing the general theory of crime as an explanation for gender differences in delinquency." *Criminology* 37: 41–69.

Lanier, M. M., and S. Henry. (1998). *Essential Criminology*. Boulder, CO: Westview Press.

Lange, J. E., M. B. Johnson, and R. B. Voas. (2005). "Testing the racial profiling hypothesis for seemingly disparate traffic stops on the New Jersey turnpike." *Justice Quarterly* 22: 193–223.

Lange, M., J. Mahoney, and M. vom Hau. (2006). "Colonialism and development: A comparative analysis of Spanish and British colonies." *The American Journal of Sociology* 111(5): 1412–62.

Langworthy, R. H. (1987a). "Comment—Have we measured the concept(s) of police cynicism using Niederhoffer's cynicism index?" *Justice Quarterly* 4: 277–80.

———. (1987b). "Police cynicism: What we know from the Niederhoffer scale." *Journal of Criminal Justice* 15: 17–35.

Lanza-Kaduce, L., and R. G. Greenleaf. (1994). "Police-citizen encounters: Turk on norm resistance." *Justice Quarterly* 11: 605–23.

———. (2000). "Age and race deference reversals: Extending Turk on police-citizen conflict." *Journal of Research in Crime and Delinquency* 37: 221–36.

Lanza-Kaduce, L., and M. Klug. (1986). "Learning to cheat: The interaction of moral-development and social learning theories." *Deviant Behavior* 7: 243–59.

Larsen, R. W. (1980). *Bundy: The Deliberate Stranger*. Englewood Cliffs, NJ: Prentice-Hall.

Latimer, J., C. Dowden, and D. Muise. (2005). "The effectiveness of restorative justice practices: A meta—analysis." *The Prison Journal* 85: 127–44.

Laub, J. H. (1983). "Urbanism, race, and crime." *Journal of Research in Crime and Delinquency* 20: 183–98.

Laub, J. H., D. S. Nagin, and R. J. Sampson. (1998). "Trajectories of change in criminal offending." *American Sociological Review* 63: 225–38.

Laub, J. H., and R. Sampson. (1991). "The Sutherland–Glueck debate: On the sociology of criminological knowledge." *American Journal of Sociology* 96: 1402–40.

Laub, J. H., R. J. Sampson, and L. C. Allen. (2001). "Explaining crime over the life course: Toward a theory of age-graded informal social control." Pp. 97–112 in *Explaining Criminals and Crime*, ed. Raymond Paternoster and Ronet Bachman. Los Angeles: Roxbury.

Lea, J., and J. Young. (1984). *What Is to Be Done about Law and Order?* New York: Penguin Books.

Leacock, E. B. (1971). *Culture of Poverty: A Critique*. New York: Simon and Schuster.

Leavitt, G. (1999). "Criminological theory as an art form: Implications for criminal justice policy." *Crime and Delinquency* 45: 389–99.

Lederberg, J. (1969). "The meaning of Dr. Jensen's study of IQ disparities." *Washington Post*, 29 March.

Lemert, E. (1951). *Social Pathology*. New York: McGraw-Hill.

Lersch, K. M. (1998). "Police misconduct and malpractice: A critical analysis of citizens' complaints." *Policing* 21: 80–96.

Leudtke, G., and E. Lystad. (1970). *Crime in the Physical City. Final Report*. LEAA Grant 169-078. Washington, DC: U.S. Government Printing Office.

Leverant, S., F. T. Cullen, B. Fulton, and J. F. Wozniak. (1999). "Reconsidering restorative justice: The corruption of benevolence revisited?" *Crime and Delinquency* 45: 3–27.

Levey, J. S., and A. Greenhall, eds. (1983). *The Concise Columbia Encyclopedia*. New York: Columbia University Press.

Levinthal, C. F. (1988). *Messengers of Paradise: Opiates and the Brain*. Garden City, NY: Doubleday.

Lewin, K. (1951). *Field Theory in Social Science: Selected Theoretical Papers*, ed. Dorwin Cartwright. New York: Harper and Row.

Lewis, N. A. (1990). "Scholars say arrest of Noriega has little justification in law." *New York Times*, 10 January: A12.

Liberman, A. (2007). "Adolescents, neighborhoods, and violence: Recent findings from the Project on Human Development in Chicago Neighborhoods." *NIJ Research in Brief*. Washington, DC: U.S. Department of Justice.

———. (2009). "Advocating evidence-generating policies: A role for the ASC." *The Criminologist* 34: 1, 3–5.

Lindner, R. (1944). *Rebel without a Cause*. New York: Grove.

Lintner, T. (2007). "Critical race theory and the teaching of American history: Power, perspective, and practice." *Social Studies Research and Practice* 2: 103–16.

Lipset, S. M. (1969). "Why cops hate liberals—and vice versa." *Atlantic Monthly* 223: 76–83.

Lipsey, M. W., G. L. Chapman, and N. A. Landenberger. (2001). "Cognitive-behavioral programs for offenders." *Annals* 578 (November): 144–57.

Lipton, D. (1994). "The correctional opportunity: Pathways to drug treatment for offenders." *Journal of Drug Issues* 24: 331–48.

Lipton, D., R. Martinson, and J. Wilks. (1975). *The Effectiveness of Correctional Treatment: A Survey of Treatment Evaluation Studies*. New York: Praeger.

Liska, A. E. (1971). "Aspirations, expectations, and delinquency: Stress and additive models." *Sociological Quarterly* 12: 99–107.

Liska, A. E., and M. B. Chamlin. (1984). "Social structure and crime control among macrosocial units." *American Journal of Sociology* 90: 383–95.

Liska, A. E., M. B. Chamlin, and M. D. Reed. (1985). "Testing the economic production and conflict models of crime control." *Social Forces* 64: 119–38.

Liska, A. E., and Jiang Yu. (1992). "Specifying and testing the threat hypothesis: Police use of deadly force." Pp. 53–69 in *Social Threat and Social Control*, ed. A. E. Liska. Albany, NY: The State University of New York Press.

Liska, A. E., M. D. Krohn, and S. F. Messner. (1989). "Strategies and requisites for theoretical integration in the study of crime and deviance." In *Theoretical Integration in the Study of Deviance and Crime: Problems and Prospects*, ed. S. F. Messner, M. D. Krohn, and A. E. Liska. Albany: SUNY Press.

Liska, A. E., and S. F. Messner. (1999). *Perspectives on Crime and Deviance*, 3d ed. Upper Saddle River, NJ: Prentice-Hall.

Little, C. M. (2003). "Female genital circumcision: Medical and cultural considerations." *Journal of Cultural Diversity* 10: 30–4.

Locurto, C. (1991). *Sense and Nonsense about IQ: The Case of Uniqueness*. New York: Praeger.

Loeber, R., and D. F. Hay. (1994). "Developmental approaches to aggression and conduct problems." In *Development through Life: A Handbook for Clinicians*, ed. M. L. Rutter and D. F. Hay. Oxford, UK: Blackwell.

Loeber, R., and M. LeBlanc. (1990). "Toward a developmental criminology." Pp. 375–473 in *Crime and Justice*, ed. N. Morris and M. Tonry. Chicago: University of Chicago Press.

Loeber, R., and M. Stouthamer-Loeber. (1996). "The development of offending." *Criminal Justice and Behavior* 23: 12–24.

———. (1998). "Development of juvenile aggression and violence: Some common misconceptions and controversies." *American Psychologist* 53: 242–59.

Loeber, R., D. Farrington, D. P., M. Stouthamer-Loeber, T. E. Moffitt, and A. Caspi (1998). "The development of male offending: Key findings from the first decade of the Pittsburgh Youth Study." *Studies on Crime and Crime Prevention* 7: 141–71.

Loeber, R., K. Kennan, and Q. Zhang (1997). "Boys' experimentation and persistence in developmental pathways toward serious delinquency." *Journal of Child and Family Studies* 6: 321–57.

Lofland, J. (1969). *Deviance and Identity*. Englewood Cliffs, NJ: Prentice-Hall.

Loftus, E. F., and K. Ketcham. (1994). *The Myth of Repressed Memory*. New York: St. Martin's.

Loh, W. D. (1984). *Social Research in the Judicial Process: Cases, Readings and Text*. New York: Russell Sage Foundation.

Lombroso, C. (1876). *L'uomo Delinquente* [The Criminal Man]. Milan: Hoepli.

———. (1968)[1911]. *Crime: Its Causes and Remedies*. Montclair, NJ: Patterson-Smith.

———. (1876[2006]). *Criminal Man*. Translated and with a new introduction by M. Gibson and N. H. Rafter. Durham, NC: Duke University Press.

Lombroso-Ferrero, G. (1979)[1911]. *Criminal Man, According to the Classification of Cesare Lombroso*. New York: Putnam.

London, P. (1964). *The Modes and Morals of Psychotherapy*. New York: Holt Rinehart and Winston.

Longshore, D., J. A. Stein, and S. Turner. (1998). "Reliability and validity of a self-control measure: A rejoinder." *Criminology* 36: 175–82.

Longshore, D., S. Turner, and J. A. Stein. (1996). "Self-control in a criminal sample: An examination of construct validity." *Criminology* 34: 209–28.

Lopez, I. F. H. (2001). "The social construction of race." Chapter 15 in *Critical Race Theory: The Cutting Edge*. 2d ed., ed. R. Delgado and J. Stefancic. Philadelphia, PA: Temple University Press.

Louscher, K., R. E. Hossford, and C. S. Moss. (1983). "Predicting dangerous behavior in a penitentiary using Megargee typology." *Criminal Justice and Behavior* 10: 269–84.

Lu, Hong. (1998). *Community Policing—Rhetoric or Reality? The Contemporary Chinese Community-Based Policing System in Shanghai*. Ph.D. dissertation, Arizona State University.

Lynskey, D. P., L. T. Winfree, Jr., F.-A. Esbensen, and D. L. Clason. (2000). "Linking gender, minority group status and family matters to self-control theory: A multivariate analysis of key self-control concepts in a youth-gang context." *Juvenile and Family Court Journal* 51: 1–19.

Macallair, D., and M. Males. (1999). *Striking Out: The Failure of California's "Three Strikes and You're Out Law."* San Francisco, CA: Justice Policy Institute.

MacDonald, H. M. (1961). "Government under law." Pp. 3–21 in *The Rule of Law*, edited by A. L. Harding, Dallas, TX: Southern Methodist University Press.

MacDonald, J. M. (2003). "The effect of ethnicity on juvenile court decision making in Hawaii." *Youth and Society* 35: 243–63.

MacDougall, W. (1908). *An Introduction to Social Psychology*. London: Methuen.

MacKenzie, D. L. (1993). "Shock incarceration as an alternative for drug offenders." In *Drugs and the Criminal Justice System: Evaluating Public Policy Initiatives*, ed. D. L. MacKenzie and C. Unchida. Newbury Park, CA: Sage.

MacKenzie, D. L., A. R. Gover, G. S. Armstrong, and O. Mitchell. (2001). "A national study comparing the environments of boot camps with traditional facilities for juvenile offenders." *Research in Brief*. Washington, DC: National Institute of Justice, August.

MacKenzie, D. L., J. W. Shaw, and V. B. Gowdy. (1993). *An Evaluation of Shock Incarceration in Louisiana*. Washington, DC: National Institute of Justice.

Magnusson, D., B. Klinteberg, and H. Stattin. (1994). "Juvenile and persistent offenders: Behavioral and physiological characteristics." Pp. 81–92 in *Adolescent Problem Behaviors and Issues*, R. D. Ketterlinus and M. E. Lamb, ed. Hillsdale, NJ: Robert Erlbaum Associates.

Maguire, K., and A. L. Pastore. (2000). *Sourcebook 1999*. Washington, DC: U.S. Department of Justice.

Makkai, T., and J. Braithwaite. (1994). "Reintegrative shaming and compliance with regulatory standards." *Criminology* 32: 361–83.

Mankoff, M. (1976). "Societal reaction and career deviance: A critical analysis." In *Whose Law, What Order? A Conflict Approach to Criminology*, ed. W. J. Chambliss and M. Mankoff. New York: Wiley.

Marcos, A. C., and S. J. Bahr. (1988). "Control theory and adolescent drug use." *Youth and Society* 19: 395–425.

Marcos, A. C., S. J. Bahr, and R. E. Johnson. (1986). "Test of bonding/association theory of adolescent drug use." *Social Forces* 65: 135–61.

Martens, W. H. J. (2000). "Antisocial and psychopathic personality disorders: Causes, course, and remission—A review article." *International Journal of Offender Therapy and Comparative Criminology* 44: 406–30.

Martin, R., R. J. Mutchnick, and W. T. Austin. (1990). *Criminological Thought: Pioneers Past and Present.* New York: Macmillan.

Martin, S. O. (1980). *Breaking and Entering: Policewomen on Patrol.* Berkeley: University of California Press.

Martinez, G. A. (2001). "Mexican American and whiteness." Chapter 35 in *Critical Race Theory: The Cutting Edge*, 2d ed., ed. R. Delgado and J. Stefancic. Philadelphia, PA: Temple University Press.

Martinson, R. (1974). "What works?—Questions and answers about prison reform." *Public Interest* 35: 22–54.

———. (1979). "New findings, new views: A note of caution regarding sentencing reform." *Hofstra Law Review* 7: 243–58.

Marvell, T. B., and C. E. Moody. (1999). "Female and male homicide victimization rates: Comparing trends and regressors." *Criminology* 37: 879–902.

———. (2001). "The lethal effects of three strikes laws." *The Journal of Legal Studies* 30: 89–106.

Marx, K. (1956). *Selected Writings in Sociology and Social Philosophy*. Trans. T. B. Bottomore. New York: McGraw-Hill.

———. (1993[1853]). "On capital punishment." In *Crime and Capitalism: Readings in Marxist Criminology*, ed. D. Greenberg. Philadelphia, PA: Temple University Press.

———. (1963[1862]a). "Class conflict and law." In *Karl Marx: Selected Writings for Sociology and Social Philosophy*, ed. T. B. Bottomore and M. Rubel. Middlesex, UK: Penguin.

———. (1963[1862]b). "Theories of surplus value." In *Karl Marx: Selected Writings for Sociology and Social Philosophy*, ed. T. B. Bottomore and M. Rubel. Middlesex, UK: Penguin.

Marz, K., and J. Stamatel. (2005). "Project on human development in Chicago neighborhoods (PHDCN) data now available." *ICPSR Bulletin*. XXVII(1): 13–17.

Masters, R. D. (1997). "Brain chemistry and social status: The neurotoxicity hypothesis. In *Intelligence, Political Inequality, and Public Policy*, ed. E. White. Westport, CT: Praeger.

Masters, R. D., B. Hone, and A. Doshi. (1998). "Environmental pollution, neurotoxicity, and criminal violence," In *Environmental Toxicology: Current Developments*, ed. J. Rose. New York: Taylor and Francis.

Matsuda, M. J., C. R. Lawrence III, R. Delgado, and K. W. Crenshaw. (1993). *Words That Wound: Critical Race Theory, Assaultive Speech, and the First Amendment*. Boulder, CO: Westview Press.

Matsueda, R. L. (1982). "Testing control theory and differential association: A causal modeling approach." *American Sociological Review* 47: 489–504.

———. (1988). "The current state of differential association theory." *Crime and Delinquency* 34: 277–306.

———. (1992). "Reflected appraisals, parental labeling, and delinquency: Specifying a symbolic interactionist theory." *American Journal of Sociology* 97: 1577–1611.

———. (1997). "'Cultural deviance theory': The remarkable persistence of a flawed term." *Theoretical Criminology* 1: 429–52.

Matsueda, R. L., and K. Heimer. (1987). "Race, family structure and delinquency: A test of differential association and social control theories." *American Sociological Review* 52: 826–40.

Matthews, R., and J. Young. (1992). *Issues in Realist Criminology*. London: Sage.

Matza, D. (1964). *Delinquency and Drift*. New York: Wiley.

Matza, D., and G. Sykes. (1961). "Juvenile delinquency and subterranean values." *American Sociological Review* 26: 712–19.

Maxwell, C. D., J. H. Garner, and J. A. Fagan. (2001). "The effects of arrest on intimate partner violence: New evidence from the spouse assault replication program." *Research in Brief*. Washington, DC: National Institute of Justice, July.

May, D. C. (2003). "Nonsocial reinforcement and violence: Can juvenile justice policies be effective against intrinsic gratification received from violent activity among youth?" *Journal of Juvenile Justice and Detention Services* 18: 9–31.

Mays, G. L., and R. Ruddell (2007). *Making Sense of Criminal Justice: Policies and Practices*. New York: Oxford University Press.

Mays, G. L., and L. T. Winfree, Jr. (2006). *Juvenile Justice*. Long Grove, IL: Waveland Press.

Mays, G. L., C. Fields, and J. A. Thompson. (1994). "Preincarceration patterns of drug and alcohol abuse." *Criminal Justice Policy Review* 5: 40–52.

———. (2000). *Juvenile Justice*. New York: McGraw-Hill.

Mays, G. L., and L. T. Winfree, Jr. (1998). *Contemporary Corrections*. Belmont, CA: Wadsworth.

———. (2002). *Contemporary Corrections*, 2d ed. Belmont, CA: Wadsworth.

———. (2009). *Essentials of Corrections*. Belmont, CA: Wadsworth.

Mazerolle, P. (1998). "Gender, general strain, and delinquency: An empirical examination." *Justice Quarterly* 15: 65–91.

———. (2000). "Understanding illicit drug use: Lessons from developmental theory." Pp. 179–204 in *Of Crime and Criminality: The Use of Theory in Everyday Life*, ed. S. S. Simpson, Boston: Pine Forge.

McBride, D. C., and J. A. Swartz. (1990). "Drugs and violence in the age of crack cocaine." In *Drugs, Crime and the Criminal Justice System*, ed. R. Weisheit. Cincinnati, OH: Anderson.

McCarthy, B., and B. J. McCarthy, Jr. (1991). *Community-Based Corrections*, 2d ed. Pacific Grove, CA: Brooks/Cole.

McCarthy, B., and J. Hagan. (1992). "Mean streets: The theoretical significance of situational delinquency among homeless youths." *American Journal of Sociology* 98: 597–627.

McCarthy, B. R., and B. L. Smith. (1986). "The conceptualization of discrimination in the juvenile justice process: The impact of administrative factors and screening decisions on juvenile court dispositions." *Criminology* 24: 41–64.

McCarthy, J. D., J. Hagan, and T. S. Woodward. (1999). "In the company of women: Structure and agency in a revised power-control theory of gender and delinquency." *Criminology* 37: 761–88.

McCold, P., and B. Wachtel. (1998). *Restorative Policing Experiment: The Bethlehem, Pennsylvania, Police Family Group Conferencing Project*. Pipersville, PA: Community Service Foundation.

McCord, J. (1978). "A thirty-year follow-up of treatment effects." *American Psychologist* 33: 384–89.

———. (1989). "Theory, pseudohistory, and metatheory." In *Advances in Criminological Theory*, vol. 1, ed. W. S. Laufer and F. Adler. New Brunswick, NJ: Transaction.

McCord, W., and J. Sanchez. (1983). "The treatment of deviant children: A twenty-five-year follow-up study." *Crime and Delinquency* 29: 238–53.

McCoy, A. W. (1991). *The Politics of Heroin: CIA Complicity in the Global Drug Trade*. Brooklyn, NY: Lawrence Hill Books.

McDermott, T. (2005). *Perfect Soldiers. The Hijackers: Who They Were, Why They Did It*. New York: Harper-Collins.

McDougall, William. (1908). *An Introduction to Social Psychology*. London: Methuen.

McGloin, J. M., and T. C. Pratt. (2003). "Cognitive ability and delinquent behavior among inner-city youth: A life-course analysis of main, mediating, and interaction effects." *International Journal of Offender Therapy and Comparative Criminology* 47: 253–71.

McGloin, J. M., T. C. Pratt, and J. Maahs. (2004). "Rethinking the IQ-delinquency relationship: A longitudinal analysis of multiple theoretical models." *Justice Quarterly* 21: 602–35.

McInerney, J. D. (1999). "Genes and behavior: A complex relationship." *Judicature* 83: 112–15.

McKay, H. D. (1960). "Differential association and crime prevention: Problems of utilization." *Social Problems* 8: 25–37.

McKiever v. Pennsylvania, 403 U.S. 528, 91 S.Ct. 1976, 29 L.Ed. 2d 6 (1971).

McShane, M. D., and W. Krause. (1993). *Community Corrections*. New York: Macmillan.

Mead, G. H. (1918). "The psychology of punitive justice." *American Journal of Sociology* 23: 586–92.

———. (1934). *Mind, Self and Society*. Chicago, IL: University of Chicago Press.

Mead, M. (1970). *Culture and Commitment: A Study of the Generation Gap*. Garden City, NY: Natural Press/Doubleday.

Mednick, S., P. Brennan, and E. Kandel. (1988). "Predispositions to violence." Special edition of *Current Theoretical Perspectives on Aggressive and Antisocial Behavior* 14: 25–33.

Mednick, S. A., W. Gabrielli, and B. Hutchings. (1984). "Genetic influences in criminal convictions: Evidence from an adoption cohort." *Science* 224: 891–94.

Mednick, S. A., T. E. Moffitt, and S. A. Stacks, eds. (1987). *The Causes of Crime: New Biological Approaches*. Cambridge, England: Cambridge University Press.

Megargee, E. I. (1972). *The California Psychological Inventory Handbook*. San Francisco: Jossey-Bass.

———. (1977). "The need for a new classification system." *Criminal Justice and Behavior* 20: 355–60.

Megargee, E. I., and J. L. Carbonell. (1985). "Predicting prison adjustment with MMPI correctional scale." *Journal of Consulting and Clinical Psychology* 53: 874–83.

Meier, R. F. (1977). "Introduction." In *Theory in Criminology: Contemporary Views*, ed. R. F. Meier. Beverly Hills, CA: Sage.

———. (1989). *Crime and Society*. Boston: Allyn & Bacon.

Meier, R. F., and W. T. Johnson. (1977). "Deterrence as social control: The legal and extralegal production of conformity." *American Sociological Review* 42: 292–304.

Menard, S., and D. Elliott. (1990). "Longitudinal and cross-sectional data collection and analysis in the study of crime and delinquency." *Justice Quarterly* 7: 11–55.

Menard, S., and B. J. Morse. (1984). "A structuralist critique of the IQ–delinquency hypothesis: Theory and evidence." *American Journal of Sociology* 89: 1347–78.

———. (1985). "IQ and delinquency: A response to Harry and Minor." *American Journal of Sociology* 91: 962–68.

Mercer, J. (1994). "A fascination with genetics: Pioneer Fund is at center of debate over research on race and intelligence." *Chronicle of Higher Education*, 7 December: A28–A29.

Merton, R. K. (1938). "Social structure and anomie." *American Sociological Review* 3: 672–82.

———. (1957). *Social Theory and Social Structure*. New York: Free Press.

———. (1968). *Social Theory and Social Structure*, 2d ed. New York: Free Press.

———. (1997). "On the evolving synthesis of differential association and anomie theory: A perspective from the sociology of science." *Criminology* 35: 517–25.

Messerschmidt, J. (1986). *Capitalism, Patriarchy, and Crime: Toward a Socialist Feminist Criminology*. New York: Rowman and Allenheld.

———. (1993). *Masculinities and Crime*. Lanham, MD: Rowman and Allenheld.

Messner, S. F. (1983). "Regional and racial effects on the urban homicide rate: The subculture of violence revisited." *American Journal of Sociology* 88: 997–1007.

Messner, S. F., and J. R. Blau. (1987). "Routine leisure activities and rates of crime: A macro-level analysis." *Social Forces* 64: 1035–52.

Messner, S. F., Z. Lu, L. Zhang, and J. Liu. (2007). "Risks of criminal victimization in contemporary urban China: An application of lifestyle/routine activities theory." *Justice Quarterly* 24: 496–522.

Messner, S. F., and R. Rosenfeld. (1994). *Crime and the American Dream*. Belmont, CA: Wadsworth.

———. (2001). *Crime and the American Dream*, 3rd ed. Belmont, CA: Wadsworth.

Michalowski, R. L. (1977). "Perspective and paradigm: Structuring criminological thought." In *Theory in Criminology: Contemporary Views*, ed. R. F. Meier. Beverly Hills, CA: Sage.

———. (1985). *Order, Law and Crime: An Introduction to Criminology*. New York: Random House.

Miethe, T. D., H. Lu, and E. Reese. (2000). "Reintegrative shaming and recidivism risks in drug court: Explanations for some unexpected findings." *Crime and Delinquency* 46: 522–41.

Miethe, T. D., and R. C. McCorkle. (1997). "Gang membership and criminal processing: A test of the 'master status' concept." *Justice Quarterly* 14: 407–27.

Miethe, T. D., and R. F. Meier. (1990). "Opportunity, choice and criminal victimization: A test of a theoretical model." *Journal of Research in Crime and Delinquency* 27: 243–66.

Miethe, T. D., M. C. Stafford, and J. S. Long. (1987). "Social differentiation in criminal victimization: A test of routine activities/lifestyle theories." *American Sociological Review* 27: 243–66.

Mignon, S. I., and W. M. Holmes. (1995). "Police responses to mandatory arrest laws." *Crime & Delinquency* 41: 430–44.

Miller, E. (1986). *Street Women*. Philadelphia: Temple University Press.

Miller, J. (1991). "The development of women's sense of self." Pp. 11–26 in *Women's Growth in Connection: Writings from the Stone Center*, ed. J. Jordan, A. Kaplan, J. Miller, I. Stiver, and J. Surrey. New York: Guilford.

———. (1998). "Up it up: Gender and the accomplishment of street robbery." *Criminology* 36: 37–66.

———. (2001). *One of the Guys: Girls, Gangs and Gender*. New York: Oxford University Press.

Miller, J., and D. Lyman. (2001). "Structural models of personality and their relations to antisocial behavior: A meta-analytic review." *Criminology* 39: 765–98.

Miller, W. B. (1958). "Lower class culture as a generating milieu of gang delinquency." *Journal of Social Issues* 14: 5–19.

Millman, N. (1996). "$100 Million fine in ADM guilty plea." *Chicago Tribune*, 16 October: 1, 27.

Millon, T., M. E. Simonsen, M. Birket-Smith, and R. D. Davis, eds. (1998). *Psychopathy: Antisocial Criminal, Violent Behavior*. NY: Guilford Press.

Mills, J. A. (1998). *Control: A History of Behavioral Psychology*. New York: NYU Press.

Milovanovic, D. (2002). *Critical Criminology at the Edge*. Westport, CT: Praeger.

Minor, W. W. (1977). "A deterrence-control theory of crime." In *Theory in Criminology: Contemporary Views*, ed. R. F. Meier. Beverly Hills, CA: Sage.

Mischel, W. (1976). *Introduction to Personality*, 2d ed. New York: Holt, Rinehart and Winston.

Moffitt, T. (1993a). "Adolescence-limited and life-course-persistent anti-social behavior: A developmental taxonomy." *Psychological Review* 100: 674–701.

———. (1993b). "The neuropsychology of conduct disorder." *Development and Psychopathology* 5: 135–51.

Moffitt, T., D. Lyman, and P. Silva. (1994). "Neuropsychological tests predicting persistent male delinquency." *Criminology* 32: 277–300.

Moffitt, T. E., W. F. Gabrielli, S. A. Mednick, and F. Schulsinger. (1981). "Socioeconomic status, IQ, and delinquency." *Journal of Abnormal Psychology* 90: 152–56.

Moffitt, T. E., and P. Silva. (1988). "IQ and delinquency: A direct test of the differential detection hypothesis." *Journal of Abnormal Behavior* 97: 330–33.

Mogul, J. (undated). "Lesbians and the death penalty." Women and Prison: A Site for Resistance. Retrieved 8 November 2008 at http://www.womenandprison.org/sexuality/joey-mogul.html

Moltich, M. (1937). "Endocrine disturbance in behavior problems." *American Journal of Psychiatry*, March: 1179.

Monachesi, E. (1973). Cesare Beccaria. In *Pioneers in Criminology*, 2d ed., ed. Herman Mannheim. Montclair, NJ: Patterson Smith.

Monaghan, P. (1992). "Professor of psychology stokes a controversy on the reliability and repression of memory." *Chronicle of Higher Education*, 23 September: A9–A10.

Mooney, J. (1993). *The Hidden Figure: Domestic Violence in North London*. Enfield, UK: Middlesex University, Centre for Criminology.

Moore, E., and T. Hogue. (2000). "Assessment of personality disorder for individuals with offending histories." *Criminal Behavior and Mental Health* 10: s34–s90.

Moore, M. H., and R. Trojanowicz. (1988). *Policing and the Fear of Crime*. Washington, DC: U.S. Government Printing Office.

Morash, M. (1983). "Gangs, groups, and delinquency." *British Journal of Criminology* 23: 309–31.

Morash, M., and M. Chesney-Lind. (1991). "A reformulation and partial test of the power control theory of delinquency." *Justice Quarterly* 8: 347–78.

Morganthau, T. (1994). "IQ: Is it destiny? An angry book ignites a new debate over race, intelligence and class." *Newsweek*, 24 October: 53–60.

Moriarty, L. J., and J. E. Williams. (1996). "Examining the relationship between routine activities theory and social disorganization: An analysis of property crime victimization." *American Journal of Criminal Justice* 21: 43–59.

Morris, G. D., P. B. Wood, and R. G. Dunaway. (2006). "Self-control, native traditionalism, and Native American substance use: Testing the cultural invariance of a general theory of crime." *Crime and Delinquency* 52: 572–98.

Morse, M. (1997). "Facing a bumpy history." *Smithsonian* 28(24).

Mos, L. P. (1999). "Behaviorism: An ideology of science without vision." *Canadian Journal of History* 34: 417–21.

Mosher, C. (2001). "Predicting drug arrest rates: Conflict and social disorganization perspectives." *Crime and Delinquency* 47: 84–104.

Mosher, C., and J. Hagan. (1994). "Constituting class and crime in upper Canada: The sentencing of narcotics offenders, circa 1908–1953." *Social Forces* 72: 613–41.

Mosse, G. L. (1968). "Introduction to the 1968 edition." Page ix in H. S. Chamberlain, *Foundations of the Nineteenth Century*. Vol. I. Translated by J. Lees. New York: Howard Fertig.

Moyer, I. (1986). "An exploratory study of role distance as a police response to stress." *Journal of Criminal Justice* 14: 363–73.

Moynihan, D. P. (1969). *Maximum Feasible Misunderstanding: Community Action in the War on Poverty*. New York: Free Press.

Mueller, C. W. (1983). "Environmental stressors and aggressive behavior." In *Aggression*, vol. 2, ed. R. G. Green and E. I. Donnerstein. New York: Academic Press.

Mueller, I. (1991). *Hitler's Justice: The Courts of the Third Reich*. Cambridge, MA: Harvard University Press.

Mujanovic, E., J. Nash, and L. T. Winfree. (2008). "Maloljetnicko prestupnistvo i upotreba psihoaktivnih supstanci medju adolescentima u Bosni I Hercegovini-prevalencije i korelacije (studija Eurogang)" *Kriminalisticke Teme-Casopis za Kriminalistiku, Kriminologiju i Sigurnosne Studije* 8: 133–148.

Murray, C. A. (1976). *The Link between Learning Disabilities and Juvenile Delinquency*. Washington, DC: U.S. Government Printing Office.

Mustaine, E. E (1997). "Victimization risks and routine activities: A theoretical examination using a gender-specific and domain-specific model." *American Journal of Criminal Justice* 22: 41–70.

Mustaine, E. E., and R. Tweksbury. (1998). "Predicting risks of larceny theft victimization: A routine activities analysis using refined lifestyle measures." *Criminology* 36: 829–57.

Myers, D. J. (1997). "Racial rioting in the 1960s: An event history analysis of local conditions." *American Sociological Review* 62: 94–112.

Naffine, N. (1987). *Female Crime: The Construction of Women in Criminology*. Sydney, Australia: Allen and Unwin.

Nagel, I. (1983). "The legal/extra-legal controversy: Judicial decision in pretrial release." *Law and Society Review* 17: 481–515.

Nagin, D. S. (1978). "General deterrence: A review of the empirical evidence." Pp. 95–139 in *Deterrence and Incapacitation: Estimating the Effects of Criminal Sanctions on Crime Rates*, ed. A. Blumstein, J. Cohen, and D. S. Nagin. Washington, DC: National Academy Press.

Nagin, D. S., and K. Land. (1993). "Age, criminal careers, and population heterogeneity: Specification and estimation of a nonparametric mixed Poisson model." *Criminology* 31: 163–89.

Nagin, D. S., and G. Pogarsky. (2004). "Time and punishments: Delayed consequences and criminal behavior." *Journal of Quantitative Criminology* 30: 295–317.

Nagourney, E. (2008). "Link seen between crime and fitness." *New York Times* 17 June: F6.

National Advisory Commission on Criminal Justice Standards and Goals. (1973). *Corrections*. Washington, DC: U.S. Government Printing Office.

National Institute of Corrections. (1983). *New Generation Jails*. Boulder, CO: Library Information Specialists.

National Institute of Drug Abuse. (1998). "Genetics of drug addiction vulnerability." Washington, DC: National Institute of Drug Abuse.

National Institute of Justice. (2008). "Increasing efficiency in crime laboratories." *In Short: Towards Criminal Justice Solutions*. Washington, DC: U.S. Department of Justice.

National Research Council. (1996). *The Evaluation of Forensic DNA Evidence*. Washington, DC: National Institute of Justice.

Neff, J. L., and D. E. Waite. (2007). "Male versus female abuse patterns among incarcerated juvenile offenders: comparing strain and social learning variables." *Justice Quarterly* 24: 106–32.

Nelson, W. R. (1988). "Cost saving in new generation jails: The direct supervision approach." *National Institute of Justice Construction Bulletin.* Washington, DC: U.S. Government Printing Office.

Nettler, G. (1984). *Explaining Crime*, 3d ed. New York: McGraw-Hill.

Newkirk, T. C., and M. A. Robertson. (1998). "Insider trading: A U.S. perspective." Speech to SEC staff. Retrieved 8 November 2008 at http://www.sec.gov/news/speech/speecharchive/1998/spch221.htm

Newman, G. (1978). *The Punishment Response.* New York: Pantheon.

Newman, O. (1972). *Defensible Space.* New York: Macmillan.

New York Special Commission on Attica. (1972). *Attica.* New York: Praeger.

Niederhoffer, A. (1969). *Behind the Shield: The Police in Urban Society.* Garden City, NY: Anchor.

Nietzel, M. T., D. A. Bernstein, G. P. Kramer, and R. Milich. (2003). *Introduction to Clinical Psychology*, 6th ed. Upper Saddle River, NJ: Prentice Hall.

Nye, F. I. (1958). *Family Relationships and Delinquent Behavior.* New York: Wiley.

Oakley, A. (2000). "A historical perspective on the use of randomized trials in social science settings." *Crime and Delinquency* 46: 315–29.

Obeidallah, D. A., and F. Earls. (1999). "Adolescent girls: The role of depression in the development of delinquency." *Research Preview.* Washington, DC: National Institute of Justice, July.

O'Brien, R. M. (1983). "Metropolitan structure and violent crime: Which measure of crime?" *American Sociological Review* 48: 434–47.

O'Connor, A. (2008). "The claim: Identical twins have identical DNA." *New York Times*, 11 March: F5.

Office of National Drug Control Policy. (2001). "Drug treatment in the criminal justice system." ONDCP Drug Policy Information Clearinghouse: Fact sheet. Washington, DC: ONDCP (March).

"O. J. Simpson found guilty on all counts." (2008). *Las Vegas Sun*, 3 October.

Olds, D., C. R. Henderson, Jr., R. Cole, J. Eckenrode, H. Kitzman, D. Luckey, L. Pettit, K. Sidora,

P. Morris, and J. Powers. (1998). "Long-term effects of nursing home visitation on children's criminal and antisocial behavior: 15-year follow-up of a randomized controlled trial." *Journal of the American Medical Association* 280: 1238–44.

Olweus, D., A. Mattson, D. Schalling, and H. Low. (1980). "Testosterone, aggression, physical and personality dimensions in normal adolescent males." *Psychosomatic Medicine* 42: 253–69.

Omer, H., and P. London. (1988). "Metamorphosis in psychotherapy: End of the systems era." *Psychotherapy* 25: 171–80.

Orcutt, J. (1983). *Analyzing Deviance.* Homewood, IL: Dorsey.

Osgood, D. W., and A. L. Anderson. (2004). "Unstructured socializing and rates of delinquency." *Criminology* 45: 519–50.

Osgood, D. W., J. K. Wilson, P. M. O'Malley, J. G. Bachman, and L. D. Johnston. (1996). "Routine activities and individual deviant behavior." *American Sociological Review* 61: 635–55.

Özbay, Ö., and Y. Z. Özcan. (2006). "A test of Hirschi's social bonding theory: Juvenile delinquency in the high schools of Ankara, Turkey." *International Journal of Offender Therapy and Comparative Criminology* 50: 711–26.

Pagani, L., R. E. Tremblay, F. Vitaro, and S. Parent. (1998). "Does preschool help prevent delinquency in boys with a history of perinatal complications?" *Criminology* 36: 245–68.

Palarma, F., F. T. Cullen, and J. C. Gertsen. (1986). "The effects of police and mental health intervention on juvenile deviance: Specifying contingencies in the impact of formal reaction." *Journal of Health and Social Behavior* 27: 90–105.

Pallone, N. J., and J. J. Hennessy. (1992). *Criminal Behavior: A Process Psychology Analysis.* New Brunswick, NJ: Transaction.

Palmer, T. B., M. Bohnstedt, and R. Lewis. (1978). *The Evaluation of Juvenile Diversion Projects: Final Projects.* Sacramento: Division of Research, California Youth Authority.

Parker, R. N. (1989). "Poverty, subculture of violence and type of homicide." *Social Forces* 67: 983–1007.

Parker, K. F., and S. R. Maggard. (2005). "Structural theories and race-specific drug arrests: What structural factors account for the rise in race-specific drug arrests over time?" *Crime and Delinquency* 51: 521–47.

Passas, N. (1990). "Anomie and corporate deviance." *Contemporary Crises* 14: 157–78.

Passingham, R. E. (1972). "Crime and personality: A review of Eysenck's theory." In *Biological Bases of Individual Behavior*, ed. V. D. Nebylitsyn and J. A. Gray. New York: Academic.

Pate, A. M., and E. E. Hamilton. (1992). "Formal and informal deterrents to domestic violence: The Dade County spouse assault experiment." *American Sociological Review* 57: 691–97.

Paternoster, R. (1987). "The deterrent effect of perceived severity of punishment: A review of the evidence and issues." *Justice Quarterly* 4: 173–217.

———. (1989a). "Absolute and restrictive deterrence in a panel of youth: Explaining the onset, persistence/desistance, and frequent offending." *Social Problems* 36: 289–309.

———. (1989b). "Decision to participate in and desist from four types of common delinquency: Deterrence and the rational choice perspective." *Law and Society Review* 23: 7–40.

Paternoster, R., and R. Bachman. (2001). *Explaining Criminals and Crime: Essays in Contemporary Criminological Theory*. Los Angeles: Roxbury.

Paternoster, R., and R. Brame. (1998). "The structural similarity of processes for generating criminal and analogous behaviors." *Criminology* 36: 633–69.

———. (2000). "On the associations between self-control, crime, and analogous behavior." *Criminology* 38: 971–82.

Paternoster, R., and L. Iovanni. (1989). "The labeling perspective and delinquency: An elaboration of the theory and an assessment of the evidence." *Justice Quarterly* 6: 359–94.

Paternoster, R., and P. Mazzerole. (1994). "General strain theory and delinquency: A replication and extension." *Journal of Research in Crime and Delinquency* 6: 379–94.

Patterson, G. R. (1975). *Families: Applications of Social Learning to Family Life*. Champaign, IL: Research Press.

Patterson, G. (1982). *Coercive Family Process: A Social Learning Approach*, vol. 3. Eugene, OR: Castalia.

Patterson, G. R., B. D. Debarshe, and E. Ramsey. (1989). "A developmental perspective on antisocial behavior." *American Psychologist* 44: 329–335.

Patterson, G., J. B. Reid, R. R. Jones, and R. E. Conger. (1975). *A Social Learning Approach to Family Intervention*, vol. 1: *Families with Aggressive Children*. Eugene, OR: Castalia.

Payne, A. A., and S. Salotti. (2007). "A comparative analysis of social learning and social control theories in the predict of college crime." *Deviant Behavior* 28: 553–75.

Pearl, D., L. Bouthilet, and J. B. Lazar, eds. (1982). *Television and Behavior: Ten Years of Scientific Progress and Implications for the Eighties*, vols. 1 and 2. Washington, DC: U.S. Government Printing Office.

Pearson, F. S., D. S. Lipton, C. M. Cleland, and D. S. Yee. (2002). "The effects of behavioral/cognitive-behavioral programs on recidivism." *Crime and Delinquency* 48 (July): 476–96.

Penry v. Lynaugh, 109 S.Ct. 2934 (1989).

Penry v. Lynaugh, 492 U.S. 302 (1989).

Peers, W. R. (1979). *My Lai Inquiry*. New York: Norton.

Pepinsky, H., and P. Jesilow. (1984). *Myths That Cause Crime*. Cabin John, MD: Seven Locks.

Perrone, D., L. J. Sullivan, T. C. Pratt, and S. Magaryan. (2004). "Parental efficacy, self-control, and delinquency: A test of a general theory of crime on a nationally representative sample of youth." *International Journal of Offender Therapy and Comparative Criminology* 48: 298–312.

Peters, M., D. Thomas, and C. Zamberlan. (1997). *Boot Camps for Juvenile Offenders: Program Summary*. Washington, DC: OJJDP.

Petersilia, J. (1991). "Policy relevance and the future of criminology – The American Society of Criminology. 1990 presidential address." *Criminology* 29: 1–15.

Peterson, J. L., and M. J. Hickman. (2005). "Census of publicly funded forensic crime laboratories, 2002." Bureau of Justice Statistics Bulletin. Washington, DC: National Institute of Justice.

Peterson, R. D., L. J. Krivo, and M. A. Harris. (2000). "Disadvantage and neighborhood violent crime: Do local institutions matter?" *Journal of Research in Crime and Delinquency* 37: 31–63.

Petrocelli, M., A. R. Piquero, and M. R. Smith. (2003). "Conflict theory and racial profiling: An empirical analysis of police traffic stop data." *Journal of Criminal Justice* 31: 1–11.

Pickens, R. W., and D. S. Svikis. (1988). "Genetic vulnerability to drug use." In *Biological Vulnerability to Drug Use*, ed. R. W. Pickens and D. S. Svikis. Rockville, MD: National Institute of Drug Abuse.

Pileggi, N. (1990). *Wise Guy: Life in a Mafia Family*. New York: Pocket Books.

Piliavin, I., R. Gartner, C. Thornton, and R. L. Matsueda. (1986). "Crime, deterrence, and rational choice." *American Sociological Review* 51: 101–19.

Piquero, A. R., and J. A. Bouffard. (2007). "Something old, something new: A preliminary investigation of Hirschi's redefined self-control." *Justice Quarterly* 24: 1–27.

Piquero, A. R., and M. Hickman. (1999). "An empirical test of Tittle's control balance theory." *Criminology* 37: 319–41.

———. (2001). "The rational choice implications of control balance theory." Pp. 85–107 in *Rational Choice and Criminal Behavior*, ed. A. R. Piquero and S. G. Tibbetts. New York: Routledge.

———. (2003). "Extending Tittle's control balance theory to account for victimization." *Criminal Justice and Behavior* 30: 283–301.

Piquero, A. R., R. MacIntosh, and M. Hickman. (2000). "Does self-control affect survey response? Applying exploratory, confirmatory, and item response theory analysis to Grasmick et al.'s self-control scale." *Criminology* 38: 897–928.

———. (2001). "Applying Rasch modeling to the validity of a control balance scale." *Journal of Criminal Justice* 29: 493–505.

Piquero, A. R., and A. B. Rosay. (1998). "The reliability and validity of Grasmick, et al.'s self-control scale: A comment on Longshore, et al." *Criminology* 36: 157–73.

Piquero, N. L., and A. R. Piquero. (2006). "Control balance and exploitative corporate crime." *Criminology* 44: 397–429.

Pistone, J. D. (2004). *The Way of the Wiseguy*. Philadelphia, PA: Running Press.

Piven, F. F., and R. A. Cloward. (1971). *Regulating the Poor: The Functions of Public Welfare*. New York: Vintage.

Plessy v. Ferguson, 163 U.S. (1896).

Plomin, R. (1989). "Environment and genes: Determinants of behavior." *American Psychologist* 44: 105–11.

Pogrebin, M., and E. D. Poole. (1988). "Humor in the briefing room: A study of the strategic uses of humor among police." *Journal of Contemporary Ethnography* 17: 183–210.

Polk, K. (1991). "Book review—*A General Theory of Crime*." *Crime and Delinquency* 37: 575–79.

Pollak, O. (1950). *The Criminality of Women*. Philadelphia: University of Pennsylvania Press.

Pollock, J. M. (1994). *Ethics in Crime and Justice: Dilemmas and Decisions*, 2d ed. Belmont, CA: Wadsworth.

———. (2003). *Ethics in Criminal Justice: Dilemmas and Decisions*, 4th ed. Belmont, CA: Wadsworth.

Pollock-Byrne, J. M. (1990). *Women, Prison and Crime*. Pacific Grove, CA: Brooks/Cole.

Pope, C., and W. Freyerherm. (1990a). "Minority status and juvenile justice processing. Part I." *Criminal Justice Abstracts* 22: 327–36.

———. (1990b). "Minority status and juvenile justice processing. Part II." *Criminal Justice Abstracts* 22: 527–42.

———. (1991). *Minorities and Juvenile Justice System: Final Report*. Washington, DC: U.S. Department of Justice.

Pope, C., and H. N. Snyder. (2003). *Disproportionate Minority Confinement: A Review of the Literature from 1989 through 1991*. Washington, DC: U.S. Department of Justice.

Powell, M. (2009). "Police polish image, but concerns persist." *New York Times*, 5 January: 21, 26.

Powers, E., and H. Witmer. (1951). *An Experiment in the Prevention of Juvenile Delinquency: The Cambridge–Somerville Youth Study*. New York: Columbia University Press.

Poyner, B. (1983). *Design against Crime: Beyond Defensible Space*. London: Butterworth.

Pranis, K. (1997). "Peacemaking circles." *Corrections Today*, December: 72, 74, 76, 122.

Pratt, T. C. (2008). "Rational choice theory, crime control policy, and criminological relevance." *Criminology & Public Policy* 7: 43–52.

Pratt, T. C., and F. T. Cullen. (2000). "The empirical status of Gottfredson and Hirschi's general theory of crime: A meta-analysis." *Criminology* 38: 931–64.

———. (2005). "Assessing macro-level predictors and theories of crime: A meta-analysis." *Crime and Justice* 32: 373–449.

Pratt, T. C., F. T. Cullen, K. R. Blevins, L. E. Daigle, and T. D. Madensen. (2006). "The empirical status of deterrence theory: A meta-analysis." Chapter 13 in *Taking Stock: The Status of Criminological Theory*, ed. F. T. Cullen, J. P. Wright, and K. R. Blevins. Edison, NJ: Transactions Books.

Pratt, T. C., F. T. Cullen, C. S. Sellers, L. T. Winfree, Jr., T. D. Madensen, L. E. Daigle, N. E. Fairn, and J. C. Gau. (2008). "The empirical status of social learning theory: A meta-analysis." Unpublished manuscript. Phoenix, AZ: Arizona State University.

Pratt, T. S., and T. W. Godsey. (2003). "Social support, inequality, and homicide: A cross-national test of an integrated theoretical model." *Criminology* 41: 611–43.

Presidential Commission on Law Enforcement and Administration of Justice. (1967). *The Challenge of Crime in a Free Society*. Washington, DC: U.S. Government Printing Office.

Price, W. H., J. A. Strong, P. B. Whatmore, and W. R. McClemont. (1966). "Criminal patients with XYY sex-chromosome complement." *Lancet* 1: 565–66.

Prichard, J. C. [(1835)/1973]. *Researches into the Physical History of Man*. Reprinted. Chicago: University of Chicago Press.

Pringle, H. (2006). *The Master Plan: Himmler's Scholars and the Holocaust*. New York: Hyperion.

Project on Human Development in Chicago Neighborhoods. (n.d.). Chicago: Project on Human Development.

Purcell, N., L. T. Winfree, Jr., and G. L. Mays. (1994). "DNA (deoxyribonucleic acid) evidence and criminal trials: An exploratory survey of factors associated with the use of 'genetic fingerprinting' in felony prosecutions." *Journal of Criminal Justice* 22: 145–57.

Quadragno, J. S., and R. J. Antonio. (1975). "Labeling theory as an over-socialized conception of man: The case of mental illness." *Sociology and Social Research* 60: 33–45.

Quinney, R. (1970). *The Social Reality of Crime*. Boston: Little, Brown.

———. (1973). *Critique of Legal Order: Crime Control in Capitalist Society*. Boston: Little, Brown.

———. (1980a). *Class, State and Crime*, 2d ed. New York: Longman.

———. (1980b). *Providence: The Reconstruction of Social and Moral Order*. New York: Longman.

———. (1991). "The way of peace: On crime, suffering, and service." In *Criminology as Peacemaking*, ed. H. Pepinsky and R. Quinney. Bloomington: Indiana University Press.

R.A.V. v. City of St. Paul, 505 U.S. 377 (1992).

Rafter, N. H. (1985). *Partial Justice: Women in State Prisons: 1800–1935*. Boston: Northeastern University Press.

———. (1992). "Criminal anthropology in the United States." *Criminology* 30: 525–45.

———. (1997). *Creating Born Criminals*. Urbana and Chicago, IL: University of Illinois Press.

———. (2004). "Earnest A. Hooton and the biological tradition in American criminology." *Criminology* 42: 735–72.

———. (2008). *The Criminal Brain: Biological Theories of Crime*. New York: New York University Press.

Raine, A. (1993). "The psychopathology of crime: Criminal behavior as a clinical disorder." San Diego, CA: Academic Press.

Raine, A., P. Brennan, and S. A. Mednick. (1997). "Interaction between birth complications and early maternal rejection in predisposing individuals to adult violence: Specificity to serious, early-onset violence." *American Journal of Psychiatry* 154: 1265–71

Raine, A., M. O'Brien, N. Smiley, A. S. Scerbo, and C. J. Chan (1990). "Reduced lateralization in verbal dichotic listening in adolescent psychopaths." *Journal of Abnormal Psychiatry* 99: 272–77.

Raine, A., P. H. Venables, and M. Williams. (1990). "Relationship between central and autonomic measures of arousal at age 15 years and criminality at age 25 years." *Archives of General Psychiatry* 47: 1003–07.

Raine, A., T. Lencz, S. Bihrle, L. LaCasse, and P. Colletti. (2000). "Reduced prefrontal gray matter volume and reduced autonomic activity in antisocial personality disorder." *Archives of General Psychiatry* 57: 119–27.

Rainwater, L. (1966). "Fear and the home-as-haven in the lower class." *Journal of the American Institute of Planners* 11: 35–47.

Ramirez, Jr., R., and M. T. Lee. (2000). "On immigration and crime." Washington, DC: Department of Justice.

Rankin, J. H., and L. E. Wells. (1990). "The effects of parental attachments and direct control on delinquency." *Journal of Research in Crime and Delinquency* 27: 140–65.

Rasche, C. (1974). "The female offender as an object of criminological research." *Criminal Justice and Behavior* 1: 301–20.

Read, D., and N. L. Read. (2004). "Time discounting over the lifespan." *Organizational Behavior and Human Decision Processes* 94: 22–32.

Rebellon, C. J. (2006). "Do adolescents engage in delinquency to attract the social attention of peers? An extension and longitudinal test of the social reinforcement hypothesis." *Journal of Research in Crime and Delinquency* 43: 387–411.

Reckless, W. C. (1961). "A new theory of delinquency and crime." *Federal Probation* 25: 4–46.

Reed, G. E., and P. C. Yeager. (1996). "Organizational offending and neoclassical criminology: Challenging the reach of a general theory of crime." *Criminology* 34: 357–82.

Regoli, R. M. (1976). "An empirical assessment of Niederhoffer's scale." *Journal of Criminal Justice* 4: 231–41.

Reichel, P. L. (2008). *Comparative Criminal Justice Systems: A Topical Approach*, 5th ed. Upper Saddle River, NJ: Prentice-Hall.

Reid, J. B., G. R. Patterson, and J. Snyder, eds. (2002). *Antisocial Behavior in Children and Adolescents: A Developmental Analysis and Model for Intervention*. Washington, DC: American Psychological Association.

Reiff, P., ed. (1963). *Freud, Therapy and Techniques*. New York: Crowell-Collier.

Reilly, P. R. (1991). *Surgical Solution: A History of Involuntary Sterilization in the United States*. Baltimore, MD: Johns Hopkins University Press.

Reiman, J. (2007). *The Rich Get Richer and the Poor Get Prison*, 8th ed. Boston: Allyn & Bacon.

Reiss, A. J. (1951). "Delinquency and the failure of personal and social controls." *American Sociological Review* 16: 196–207.

Reiss, A. J., and A. L. Rhodes. (1964). "An empirical test of differential association theory." *Journal of Research in Crime and Delinquency* 1: 5–18.

Reiss, A. J., and J. Roth. (1993). *Understanding and Preventing Violence*. Washington, DC: National Academy Press.

Rennison, C. M. (2002). "Hispanic victims of violent crime, 1993–2000." *Bureau of Justice Statistics Special Report*. Washington, DC: Bureau of Justice Statistics.

Reno, J. (1999). "Message from the Attorney General." In *Postconviction DNA Testing: Recommendations for Handling Requests*. Washington, DC: National Institute of Justice.

Reppetto, T. A. (1976). "Crime prevention and the displacement phenomenon." *Crime and Delinquency* 22: 166–77.

Ressler, R. K., A. W. Burgess, and J. E. Douglas. (1988). *Sexual Homicide: Patterns and Motives*. Lexington, MA: Lexington-Heath.

Reuter, P. (1987). *Racketeering in Legitimate Industries: A Study in the Economics of Intimidation*. Santa Monica, CA: RAND Corporation.

Reyes, Jessica Wolpaw. (2007). "Environmental Policy as Social Policy? The Impact of Childhood Lead Exposure on Crime," *The B.E. Journal of Economic Analysis & Policy*: Vol. 7: Iss. 1 (Contributions), Article 51.

Reyna, V. F., and F. Farley. (2007). "Is the teen brain too rational?" *Scientific American Mind* (December/January): 59–65.

Reynolds, M. (2004). *Dead Ends: The Pursuit, Conviction and Execution of Female Serial Killer Aileen Wuornos, the Damsel of Death*. New York: St. Martins.

Riechers, L., and R. R. Roberg. (1990). "Community policing: A critical review of underlying assumptions." *Journal of Police Science and Administration* 17: 105–14.

Rilling, M. (2000). "How the challenge of explaining learning influenced the origins and development of John B. Watson's behaviorism." *American Journal of Psychology* 113: 275–301.

Robbins, M. S., and J. Szapocnik. (2000). "Brief strategic family therapy." *OJJDP Juvenile Justice Bulletin*, April. NCJ 179285.

"Robber not ready for crime time." (2008). *New York Daily News*, 1 April: 17.

Roberg, R. R., and J. Kuykendall. (1993). *Police and Society*. Belmont, CA: Wadsworth.

Robins, L. N. (1966). *Deviant Children Grow Up: A Sociological and Psychiatric Study of Sociopathic Personality*. Baltimore: Williams and Wilkins.

Robison, S. M. (1936). *Can Delinquency Be Measured?* New York: Columbia University Press.

Rodriguez, C. E., and H. Cordero-Guzman. (1992). "Placing race in context." *Ethnic and Racial Studies* 15: 523–42.

Rodriguez, N. (2007). "Juvenile court context and detention decisions: Reconsidering the role of race, ethnicity, and community characteristics in juvenile court process." *Justice Quarterly* 24: 629–56.

Rodriguez, O., and D. Weisburd. (1991). "The integrated social control model and ethnicity: The case of Puerto Rican-American delinquency." *Criminal Justice and Behavior* 18: 464–79.

Roebuck, J., and S. C. Weeber. (1978). *Political Crime in the United States: Analyzing Crime by and against Government.* New York: Praeger.

Rokeach, M. (1956). "Political and religious dogmatism: An alternate of the authoritarian personality." *Psychological Monographs* 70: 1–43.

Rokeach, M., M. G. Miller, and J. A. Snyder. (1977). "A value gap between the police and the policed." *Journal of Social Issues* 27: 155–71.

Romero, V. C. (2002). "Critical race theory in three acts: Racial profiling, affirmative action, and diversity visa lottery." *Albany Law Review* 66: 325–41.

Rommen, H. A. (1998). *The Natural Law: A Study in Legal and Social History and Philosophy.* Translated by T. R. Hanley. Indianapolis: Liberty Fund.

Roncek, D. W. (1981). "Dangerous places: Crime and residential environment." *Social Forces* 60: 74–96.

Roncek, D., and R. Bell. (1981). "Bars, blocks, and crimes." *Journal of Environmental Systems* 11: 35–47.

Roncek, D., and P. Maier. (1991). "Bars, blocks, and crimes revisited: Linking the theory of routine activities to the empiricism of 'hot spots.'" *Criminology* 29: 725–50.

Roncek, D., and M. A. Pravatiner. (1989). "Additional evidence that taverns enhance nearby crime." *Sociology and Social Research* 73: 185–88.

Rose, S. (1972). *The Betrayal of the Poor: The Transformation of Community Action.* Cambridge, MA: Schenkman.

Rosenau, P. M. (1992). *Postmodernism and the Social Sciences.* Princeton, NJ: Princeton University Press.

Rosenbaum, J. L. (1987). "Social control, gender, and delinquency: An analysis of drug, property, and violent offenders." *Justice Quarterly* 4: 117–32.

Rosenbaum, J. L., and J. R. Lasley. (1990). "School, community context, and delinquency: Rethinking the gender gap." *Justice Quarterly* 7: 493–513.

Rosencrance, J. (1987). "A typology of presentence probation officers." *International Journal of Offender Therapy and Contemporary Criminology* 31: 163–77.

Roshier, B. (1989). *Controlling Crime: The Classical Perspective in Criminology.* Chicago: Lyceum.

Ross, H. L. (1982). *Deterring the Drinking Driver: Legal Policy and Social Control.* Lexington, MA: Lexington Books.

Ross, I. (1992) *Shady Business: Confronting Corporate Corruption.* New York: Twentieth Century Fund Press.

Rossi, G., and H. Sloore. (2008). "Cross-cultural reliability and generality of the Megargee offender classification system." *Criminal Justice and Behavior* 35: 725–40.

Roth, J. A., X. O. Breakefield, and C. M. Castiglione. (1976). "Monoamine oxidase and catechol-o-methyltransferase activities in cultured human skin fiboblast." *Life Sciences* 19: 1705–10.

Rotter, J. (1954). *Social Learning and Clinical Psychology.* New York: Prentice-Hall.

Rousseau, J. -J. (1954)[1762]. *The Social Contract.* Chicago: Regenery.

Rowe, D. C. (1983). "Biomedical genetic models of self-reported delinquent behavior: A twin study." *Behavior Genetics* 13: 473–89.

———. (1990). "Inherited dispositions toward learning delinquent and criminal behavior: New evidence." In *Crime in Biological, Social, and Moral Contexts,* ed. L. Ellis and H. Hoffman. Westport, CT: Praeger.

———. (2002). *Biology and Crime.* Los Angeles: Roxbury.

Rowe, D. C., and B. L. Gulley. (1992). "Sibling effects on substance use and delinquency." *Criminology* 30: 217–23.

Rowe, D. C., and D. W. Osgood. (1984). "Heredity and sociological theories of delinquency: A reconsideration." *American Sociological Review* 49: 526–40.

Rubin, R. T. (1987). "The neuroendro-crinology and neurochemistry of antisocial behavior. In *The Causes of Crime: New Biological Approaches,* ed. S. A. Mednick, T. E. Moffitt, and S. A. Slack. New York: Cambridge University Press.

Ruddell, R., and M. G. Urbina. (2004). "Minority threat and punishment: A cross-national analysis." *Justice Quarterly* 21: 903–31.

Rule, A. (2000). *The Stranger Beside Me*. Revised edition. New York: Signet.

Rushton, J. P. (1996). "Self-report delinquency and violence in adult twins." *Psychiatric Genetics* 6: 87–89.

Sagatun, I., L. McCollum, and L. P. Edwards. (1985). "The effect of transfers from juvenile to criminal court: A loglinear analysis." *Journal of Crime and Justice* 8: 65–92.

Sampson, R. J. (1993). "Linking time and place: Dynamic contextualism in the future of criminological inquiry." *Journal of Research in Crime and Delinquency* 30: 426–44.

———. (2001). "Foreword." In *Life-Course Criminology: Contemporary and Classic Readings*, ed. A. Piquero and P. Mazerolle. Belmont, CA: Wadsworth.

Sampson, R. J., and D. J. Bartusch. (1999). "Attitudes toward crime, police, and the law: Individual and neighborhood differences." *National Institute of Justice Research Preview*. Washington, DC: U.S. Department of Justice.

Sampson, R. J., and W. B. Groves. (1989). "Community structure and crime: Testing social disorganization theory." *American Journal of Sociology* 94: 774–802.

Sampson, R. J., and J. Laub. (1993). *Crime in the Making: Pathways and Turning Points through Life*. Cambridge, MA: Harvard University Press.

Sampson, R. J., and S. W. Raudenbush. (2001). "Disorder in urban neighborhoods—Does it lead to crime?" *Research in Brief*. Washington, DC: National Institute of Justice, February.

Sampson, R. J., S. W. Raudenbush, and F. Earls. (1997). "Neighborhood and violent crime: A multilevel study of collective efficacy." *Science* 277: 918–24.

Sarbin, T. R., and J. E. Miller. (1970). "Demonism revisited: The XYY chromosome anomaly." *Issues of Criminology* 5: 195–207.

Sarri, R. C. (1986). "Gender and race differences in criminal justice processing." *Women's Studies International Forum* 9: 89–99.

Savelsberg, J. J. (1996). "Review: *Control Balance: Toward a General Theory of Deviance*." *American Journal of Sociology* 26: 620–22.

———. (1999). "Human nature and social control in complex society: A critique of Charles Tittle's *Control Balance*." *Theoretical Criminology* 3: 331–38.

Sayad, A. (1999). "Immigration et « pensée d'État »" ("Immigration and state mentality"). *Actes de la recherche en sciences sociale* 129: 5–14.

Schafer, S. (1969). *Theories in Criminology: Past and Present Philosophies of the Crime Problem*. New York: Random House.

Schall v. Martin, 467 U.S. 253 (1984).

Scheff, T. J. (1988). "Shame and conformity: The deference–emotion system." *American Sociological Review* 53: 395–406.

———. (2001). "Shame and community: Social components in depression." *Psychiatry* 64: 212–24.

Schiraldi, V., J. Colburn, and E. Lotke. (2004). "Three strikes and you're out: An examination of the impact of 3-strikes laws 10 years after their enactment." Washington, DC: Justice Policy Institute. Retrieved 8 December 2008 at http://justicepolicy.org/images/upload/04-09_REP_ThreeStrikes Natl_AC.pdf

Schlesinger, T. (2005). "Racial and ethnic disparity in pretrial criminal processing." *Justice Quarterly* 22: 170–92.

Schmidt, J., and L. Sherman. (1993). "Does arrest deter domestic violence?" *American Behavioral Scientist* 36: 601–10.

———. (1996). "Does arrest deter domestic violence?" In *Do Arrests and Restraining Orders Work?* ed. E. Buzawa and C. Buzawa. Thousand Oaks, CA: Sage.

Schneider, C. J. (2001). "Integrating critical race theory and postmodernism implications of race, class, and gender." *Critical Criminology* 12: 87–103.

Schreiber, F. (1973). *Sybil*. Chicago: Regnery.

———. (1983). *The Shoemaker*. New York: Simon & Schuster.

Schur, E. (1968). *Law and Society: A Sociological View*. New York: Random House.

———. (1971). *Labeling Deviant Behavior: Its Sociological Implications*. New York: Harper and Row.

———. (1973). *Radical Non-Intervention: Rethinking the Delinquency Problem*. Englewood Cliffs, NJ: Prentice-Hall.

Schwartz, R. D., and J. Skolnick. (1962). "Two studies of legal stigma." *Social Problems* 10: 133–42.

Schwartz, I. (1991). "Removing juveniles from adult jails: The unfinished agenda." Pp. 216–26 in *American Jails: Public Policy Issues*, ed. J. A. Thompson and G. L. Mays. Chicago: Nelson-Hall.

Schwartz, M. D. (1991). "The future of critical criminology." In *New Directions in Critical*

Criminology, ed. B. MacLean and D. Milovanovic. Vancouver, BC: Collective Press.

Schwendinger, J. R., and H. Schwendinger. (1983). *Rape and Inequality*. New York: Praeger.

———. (1985). *Adolescent Subcultures and Delinquency*. New York: Praeger.

Scott, J. P. (1987). "Review essay: On genetics and criminal behavior." *Social Biology* 34: 256–65.

Seabrook, J. (2008). "Suffering souls: The search for the roots of psychopathy." *The New Yorker*, 10 November. Retrieved 6 February 2009 at http://www.newyorker.com/reporting/2008/11/10/081110fa_fact_seabrook

Seale, B. (1968). *Seize the Time*. New York: Random House/Vintage.

Seiffge-Krenke, I. (1995). *Stress, Coping and Relationships in Adolescence*. Mahway, NJ: Lawrence Erlbaum.

Sellers, C. S. (1999). "Self-control and intimate violence: An examination of the scope and specification of the general theory of crime." *Criminology* 37: 375–404.

Sellers, C. S., J. Cochran, and L. T. Winfree, Jr. (2002). "A social learning theory of courtship violence: An empirical test." Chapter 5 in *Advances in Criminological Theory: Social Learning Theory*, ed. R. L. Akers and G. Jensen. Chicago: University of Chicago Press.

Sellers, C. S., T. C. Pratt, L. T. Winfree, Jr., and F. T. Cullen. (2000). "The empirical status of social learning theory: A metaanalysis." Paper presented at the annual meeting of the American Society of Criminology, San Francisco.

Sellers, C. S., and L. T. Winfree, Jr. (1990). "Differential associations and definitions: A panel study of youthful drinking behavior." *International Journal of the Addictions* 25: 755–71.

Sellers, C. S., L. T. Winfree, Jr., and C. T. Griffiths. (1993). "Legal attitudes, permissive norm qualities, and substance use: A comparison of American Indians and non-Indian youth." *Journal of Drug Issues* 23: 493–513.

Sellin, T. (1938). *Culture Conflict and Crime*. New York: Social Science Research Council.

Sentencing Project, The. (2004). "Crack cocaine sentencing police: Unjustified and unreasonable." Washington, DC: The Sentencing Project.

Shadish, W. R., T. D. Cook, and D. T. Campbell. (2002). *Experimental and Quasi-Experimental Designs for Generalized Causal Inference*. Boston: Houghton-Mifflin.

Shah, S. A., and L. H. Roth. (1974). "Biological and psychophysiological factors in criminality." In *Handbook of Criminology*, ed. D. Glaser. Chicago: Rand McNally.

Sharpe, J. (1997). *Instruments of Darkness, Witchcraft in England 1550–1750*. Oxford, UK: Oxford University Press.

Shaw, C. R. (1930). *The Jack-Roller: A Delinquent Boy's Own Story*. Philadelphia: Saifer.

———. (1938). *Brothers in Crime*. Philadelphia: Saifer.

Shaw, C. R., and H. D. McKay. (1942). *Juvenile Delinquency and Urban Areas: A Study of Rates of Delinquency in Relation to Different Characteristics of Local Communities in American Cities*. Chicago: University of Chicago Press.

———. (1972). *Juvenile Delinquency and Urban Areas: A Study of Rates of Delinquency in Relation to Different Characteristics of Local Communities in American Cities*, rev. ed. Chicago: University of Chicago Press.

Sheldon, R. G., J. A. Horvath, and S. Tracey. (1989). "Do status offenders get worse? Some clarification on the question of escalation." *Crime and Delinquency* 32: 202–16.

Sheldon, W. (1949). *Varieties of Delinquent Youth*. New York: Harper and Row.

Shelley, L. (1981). *Crime and Modernization: The Impact of Industrialization and Urbanization on Crime*. Carbondale: Southern Illinois University Press.

Sherman, L. W. (1992). *Policing Domestic Violence: Experiments and Dilemma*. New York: Free Press.

———. (1993). "Defiance, deterrence, and irrelevance: A theory of the criminal sanction." *Journal of Research in Crime and Delinquency* 30: 445–73.

Sherman, L. W., and R. Berk. (1984a). The Minneapolis Domestic Violence Experiment." *Police Foundation Reports* 1: 10–18.

———. (1984b). "The specific deterrent effects of arrest for domestic assault." *American Sociological Review* 49: 261–72.

Sherman, L. W., D. P. Farrington, B. C. Welsh, and D. L. MacKenzie (2002). *Evidence-Based Crime Prevention*. London and New York, NY: Routledge.

Sherman, L. W., P. R. Gartin, and M. E. Bueger. (1989). "Hot spots of predatory crime." *Criminology* 27: 27–55.

Sherman, L., D. Gottfredson, D. MacKenzie, J. Eck, P. Reuter, and S. Bushway. (1997). "Preventing crime: What works, what doesn't and what's promising." Research report. Washington, DC: U.S. Office of Justice Programs.

Sherman, L., and D. P. Rogan. (1995). "Effects of gun seizures on gun violence: 'Hot spots' patrol in Kansas City." *Justice Quarterly* 12: 673–94.

Sherman, L. W., J. D. Schmidt, D. Smith, P. Gartin, E. G. Cohen, D. J. Collins, and A. R. Bacich. (1992). "The variable effects of arrest on criminal careers: The Milwaukee domestic violence experiment." *Journal of Criminal Law and Criminology* 83: 137–69.

Sherman, L. W., and D. Smith, with J. D. Schmidt and D. P. Rogan. (1992). "Crime, punishment, and stake in conformity: Legal and informal control of domestic violence." *American Sociological Review* 57: 680–90.

Sherman, L., and H. Strang (2008). *Restorative Justice: The Evidence*. London, UK: The Smith Institute.

Sherman, L., H. Strang, J. Barnes, J. Braithwaite, N. Ipken, and M. Teh (1998). "Experiments in restorative justice: A progress report to the National Police Research Unit in the Canberra Reintegrative Shaming Experiments (RISE)." Canberra: Australian Federal Police and Australian National University.

Sherman, L., and D. Weisburd. (1995). "General deterrent effects of police patrol in crime 'hot spots': A randomized controlled trial." *Justice Quarterly* 12: 625–48.

Sherman, Lawrence W., Heather Strang, G. C. Barnes, et al. (1998). "Experiments in restorative policing: A progress report to the National Police Research Unit." Canberra: Australian National University.

Shockley, W. (1967). "A 'try the simplest cases' approach to the heredity–poverty–crime problem." *Proceedings of the National Academy of Sciences* 57: 1767–74.

Shoham, S. G., and M. Seis. (1993). *A Primer in the Psychology of Crime*. New York: Harrison and Heston.

Short, J. F., Jr. (1957). "Differential association and delinquency." *Social Problems* 4: 233–39.

———. (1958). "Differential association with delinquent friends and delinquent behavior." *Pacific Sociological Review* 1: 20–25.

———. (1960). "Differential association as a hypothesis: Problems of empirical testing." *Social Problems* 8: 14–25.

———. (1968). *Gang Delinquency and Delinquent Subcultures*. New York: Harper and Row.

Short, J. F., Jr., and F. L. Strodtbeck. (1965). *Group Processes and Gang Delinquency*. Chicago: University of Chicago Press.

Short, J. F., Jr., M. Z. Zahn, and D. P. Farrington. (2000). "Experimental research in criminal justice settings: Is there a role for scholarly scientists?" *Crime and Delinquency* 46: 295–98.

Shover, N. (1985). *Aging Criminal*. Beverly Hills, CA: Sage.

Siegel, L. (1992) *Criminology*, 4th ed. St. Paul, MN: West.

Sigurdson, H. R. (1985). *The Manhattan House of Detention: A Study of Podular Direct Supervision*. Washington, DC: National Institute of Corrections.

———. (1987). *Larimer County Detention Center: A Study of Podular Direct Supervision*. Washington, DC: National Institute of Corrections.

Silberman, M. (1976). "Toward a theory of criminal deterrence." *American Sociological Review* 41: 442–61.

Simmel, Georg. (1955). *Conflict*. Trans. K. H. Wolff. Glencoe, IL: Free Press.

Simon, J. L. (1969). *Basic Research Methods in Social Science: The Art of Empirical Investigation*. New York: Random House.

Simon, R. J. (1967). *The Jury and the Defense of Insanity*. Boston: Little, Brown.

———. (1975a). *Women and Crime*. Lexington, MA: Heath.

———. (1975b). *The Contemporary Woman and Crime*. Washington, DC: National Institute of Mental Health.

Simon, R. J. and J. Landis. (1991). *The Crimes Women Commit, the Punishments They Receive*. Lexington, MA: Lexington Books.

Simons, R. L., and P. A. Gray. (1989). "Perceived blocked opportunity as an explanation of delinquency among lower-class black males: A research note." *Journal of Research in Crime and Delinquency* 26: 90–101.

Simons, R. L., C. Johnson, R. D. Conger, and G. Elder, Jr. (1998). "A test of latent trait versus life-course perspectives on the stability of adolescent antisocial behavior." *Criminology* 36: 217–44.

Simons, R. L., M. G. Miller, and S. M. Aigner. (1980). "Contemporary theories of deviance and female delinquency: An empirical test." *Journal of Research in Crime and Delinquency* 17: 42–57.

Simpson, S. (1989). "Feminist theory, crime and justice." *Criminology* 27: 605–27.

Singer, S. I., and M. Levine. (1988). "Power-control theory, gender, and delinquency: A partial replication with additional evidence on the effects of peers." *Criminology* 26: 627–48.

Skinner, B. F. (1974). *About Behaviorism.* New York: Knopf.

Skinner, W. F., and A. M. Fream. (1997). "A social learning theory analysis of computer crime among college students." *Journal of Research in Crime and Delinquency.* 34: 495–518.

Skogan, W. (1990). *Disorder and Decline: Crime and the Spiral of Decay in American Neighborhoods.* New York: Free Press.

Skogan, W., and M. A. Wycoff. (1986). "Storefront police offices: The Houston field test." In *Community Crime Prevention: Does It Work?* ed. D. Rosenbaum. Beverly Hills, CA: Sage.

Skolnick, J. (1966). *Justice without Trial: Law Enforcement in a Democratic Society.* New York: Wiley.

Smart, F. (1970). *Neurosis and Crime.* New York: Barnes and Noble.

Smith, D., and R. Paternoster. (1990). "Formal processing and future delinquency: Deviance amplification as selection artifact." *Law and Society Review* 24: 1109–31.

Smith, M. R., and M. Petrocelli. (2001). "Racial profiling? A multivariate analysis of police traffic stop data." *Police Quarterly* 4: 4–27.

Smith, D., C. A. Visher, and L. Davidson. (1984). "Equity and discretionary justice: The influences of race on police arrest decisions." *Journal of Criminal Law and Criminology* 75: 234–49.

Smith, J. L. (2001). "The legacy of behaviorism: Historical appraisal versus contemporary critique." *American Journal of Psychology,* Winter: 654–58.

Smith, M. E. (2001). "What future for 'public safety' and 'restorative justice' in community corrections?" *Sentencing & Corrections: Issues for the 21st Century,* no. 11. Washington, DC: U.S. Office of Justice Programs.

Smith, R. A. (1961a). "The incredible electrical conspiracy." *Fortune,* April: 132–37, 170, 175–76, 179–80.

———. (1961b). "The incredible electrical conspiracy." *Fortune,* May: 161–64, 210, 212, 217–18, 221–24.

Snarr, R. W., and B. I. Wolford. (1985). *Introduction to Corrections.* Dubuque, IA: Brown.

Snyder, J. J., and G. R. Patterson. (1995). "Individual differences in social aggression: A test of a reinforcement model of socialization in the natural environment." *Behavior Therapy* 26: 371–91.

Sofair, A. N., and L. C. Kaldjian. (2000). "Eugenic sterilization and a qualified Nazi analogy: The United States and Germany, 1930–1945." *Annals of Internal Medicine* 132: 312–19.

Solórzano, D. (1997). "Images and words that wound: Critical race theory, racial stereotyping, and teacher education." *Teacher Education Quarterly* 24: 5–19.

Solzhenitsyn, A. (1974). *The Gulag Archipelago, 1918–1956.* New York: Harper and Row.

Sorenson, J., R. Hope, and D. Stemen. (2003). "Racial disproportionality in state prison admissions: Can regional variation be explained by differential arrest rates?" *Journal of Criminal Justice* 31: 73–84.

Sorensen, J., R. Wrinkle, V. Brewer, and J. Marquart. (1999). "Capital punishment and deterrence: Examining the effect of execution on murder in Texas." *Crime and Delinquency* 45: 481–93.

Spano, R., J. D. Freilich, and J. Bolland. (2008). "Gang membership, gun carrying, and employment: Applying routine activities theory to explain violent victimization among inner city, minority youth living in extreme poverty." *Justice Quarterly* 25: 381–410.

Spelman, W., and J. E. Eck. (1987). *Problem-Oriented Policing.* Washington, DC: U.S. Department of Justice.

Spencer, H. (1961)[1864]. *The Study of Sociology.* Ann Arbor: University of Michigan Press.

Spitz, J. (2005). *Doctors from Hell: The Horrific Account of Nazi Experiments on Humans.* Boulder, CO: Sentient.

Spitzer, S. (1975). "Toward a Marxian theory of deviance." *Social Problems* 22: 638–51.

Spradley, J. P. (1970). *You Owe Yourself a Drink*. Boston: Little, Brown.

Srole, L. (1956). "Social integration and certain corollaries: An exploratory study." *American Sociological Review* 52: 709–16.

Stack, S. (1987). "The effect of temporary residences on burglary: A test of criminal opportunity theory." *American Journal of Criminal Justice* 19: 197–214.

Stackelberg, R. and S. A. Winkle. (2003). *The Nazi Germany Sourcebook: An Anthology of Texts*. New York: Routledge.

Stafford, M. C., and M. Warr. (1993). "A reconceptualization of general and specific deterrence." *Journal of Crime and Delinquency* 30: 123–35.

Stanfield, R. E. (1966). "The interaction of family variables and gang variables in the aetiology of delinquency." *Social Problems* 13: 311–417.

Stanford v. Kentucky, 429. U.S. 361 (1989).

Stark, R. (1987). "Deviant places: A theory of the ecology of crime." *Criminology* 25: 841–62.

Stattin, H., and I. Klackenberg-Larsson. (1993). "Early language and intelligence development and their relationship to future criminal behavior." *Journal of Abnormal Psychology* 102: 369–78.

State v. Soto-Fong, 187 Ariz. 186, 928 P.2d 610 (1996).

Steadman, H. J. (1972). "The psychiatrist as a conservative agent of social control." *Social Problems* 20: 263–71.

———. (2000). "Survey of DNA crime laboratories, 1998." U.S. Bureau of Justice Statistics Special Report. NCJ 179104.

———. (2002). "Survey of DNA crime laboratories, 2000." U.S. Bureau of Justice Statistics Special Report. NCJ 191191.

Steadman, G. W. (2001). "The survey of DNA crime laboratories." Washington, DC: Bureau of Justice Statistics.

Steen, R. Grant. (2001). *DNA and Destiny: Nature and Nurture in Human Behavior*. Cambridge, MA: De Capo Press.

Steffensmeier, D. (1978). "Crime and contemporary women: An analysis of changing levels of female property crime, 1960–1975." *Social Forces* 57: 566–84.

———. (1980). "Sex differences in patterns of adult crime, 1965–1977." *Social Forces* 58: 1080–90.

———. (1983a). "Organizational properties and sex integration in the underworld: Building a sociological theory of sex differences in crime." *Social Forces* 61: 1010–32.

———. (1983b). "Flawed arrest 'rates' and overlooked reliability problems in UCR arrest statistics: A thought on Wilson's 'The masculinity of violent crime—Some second thoughts.'" *Journal of Criminal Justice* 11: 167–71.

———. (1986). *The Fence: In the Shadow of Two Worlds*. Totowa, NJ: Rowman and Littlefield.

———. (1989). "On the causes of white collar crime: An assessment of Hirschi and Gottfredson's claims." *Criminology* 27: 345–50.

Steffensmeier, R., and E. Allan. (1996). "Gender and crime: Toward a gendered theory of female offending." *Annual Review of Sociology* 22: 459–87.

Steffensmeier, R., E. Allan, and C. Streifel (1989). "Development and female crime: A cross-national test of alternative explanations." *Social Forces* 68: 262–83.

Steffensmeier, D., and M. J. Cobb. (1981). "Sex differences in urban arrest patterns, 1934–1979." *Social Problems* 29: 37–50.

Steffensmeier, D., and D. Haynie. (2000). "Gender, structural disadvantage, and urban crime: A test and elaboration of power-control theory." *Criminology* 38: 403–38.

Steffensmeier, D., and R. N. Steffensmeier. (1980). "Trends in female delinquency: An examination of arrest, juvenile court, self-report, and field data." *Criminology* 18: 62–85.

Steffensmeier, R., and C. Streifel. (1992). "Time-series analysis of female percentage of arrests for property crimes, 1960–1985." *Justice Quarterly* 5: 53–80.

Steffensmeier, D., J. Schwartz, H. Zhong, and J. Ackerman. (2005). "An assessment of recent trends in girls' violence using diverse longitudinal sources: Is the gender gaps closing?" *Criminology* 43: 355–405.

Stephan, J. J., and J. C. Karberg. (2003). *Census of state and federal correctional facilities, 2000*. Washington, DC: U.S. Department of Justice.

Sternberg, R. J. (1985). *Beyond IQ: A Triarchic Theory*. New York: Cambridge University Press.

Stevenson, J., and P. Graham. (1988). "Behavioral deviance in 13-year-old twins: An item analysis." *Journal of American Academy of Child and Adolescent Psychiatry* 27: 791–97.

Stewart, E. A., C. J. Schreck, and R. L. Simons. (2006). "'I ain't gonna let no one disrespect me': Does the code of the street reduce or increase violent victimization among African American adolescents?" *Journal of Research in Crime and Delinquency* 43: 427–58.

Stoddard, E. R. (1968). "The informal 'code' of police deviancy: A group approach to 'blue-coat crime.'" *Journal of Criminal Law, Criminology, and Police Science* 59: 201–13.

Stolzenberg, L., and S. J. D'Alessio. (1997). "Three strikes and you're out: The impact of California's new mandatory sentencing law on serious crime rates." *Crime and Delinquency* 43: 457–69.

Strang, H. (2002). *Repair or Revenge: Victims and Restorative Justice.* Oxford, UK: Oxford University Press.

Strawbridge, P., and D. Strawbridge. (1990). *A Networking Guide to Recruitment, Selection and Probationary Training of Police Officers in Major Police Departments of the United States of America.* London: New Scotland Yard.

Streib, V. L. (1995). "Death penalty for lesbians." *National Journal for Sexual Orientation Law.* http://www.cs.cmu.edu/afs/cs/user/scotts/bulgarians/njsol/death_penalty_lesbian.txt

Stretsky, P. B., and M. J. Lynch. (2001). "The relationship between lead exposure and homicide." *Archives of Pediatric and Adolescent Medicine.* 155: 579–582.

Strong v. Repide, 213 U.S. 419 (1909).

Strueber, D., M. Lueck, and G. Roth. (2007). "The violent brain." *Scientific American Mind* (December/January): 20–27.

Sullivan, P. S. (1989). "Minority officers: Current issues." In *Critical Issues in Policing: Contemporary Issues*, ed. R. G. Dunham and G. P. Alpert. Prospect Heights, IL: Waveland Press.

Sullivan, R. F. (1973). "The political economics of crime: An introduction to the literature." *Crime and Delinquency* 19: 138–49.

Sumner, W. G. (1906). *Folkways: A Study of the Sociological Importance of Usages, Manners, Customs, Mores, and Morals.* Boston: Ginn.

Sutherland, E. H. (1929). "Crime and conflict process." *Journal of Juvenile Research* 13: 38–48.

———. (1931). "Mental deficiency and crime." Pp. 357–75 in *Social Attitudes*, ed. K. Young. NY: Henry Holt.

———. (1947). *Principles of Criminology.* Philadelphia: Lippincott.

———. (1949). *White Collar Crime.* New York: Holt, Rinehart and Winston.

———. (1951). "Mental deficiency and crime." Pp. 357–375 in *Social Attitudes*, ed. K. Young. New York: Holt.

———. (1973). *On Analyzing Crime*, ed. K. Schuessler. Chicago: University of Chicago Press.

Sutherland, E. H., and D. R. Cressey. (1974). *Criminology*, 9th ed. Philadelphia: Lippincott.

Suttles, G. (1968). *The Social Order of the Slum: Ethnicity and Territory.* Chicago: University of Chicago Press.

Swanson, C., L. Territo, and R. W. Taylor. (1998). *Police Administration: Structure, Processes, and Behavior.* Upper Saddle River, NJ: Prentice-Hall.

Swigert, V. L., and R. A. Farrell. (1976). *Murder, Inequality, and the Law.* Lexington, MA: Lexington Books/Heath.

Sykes, G., and F. T. Cullen. (1992). *Criminology*, 2d ed. New York: Harcourt Brace Jovanovich.

Sykes, G., and D. Matza. (1957). "Techniques of neutralization: A theory of delinquency." *American Journal of Sociology* 22: 664–70.

Sykes, G., and S. L. Messinger. (1960). "The inmate social system." In *Theoretical Studies in the Social Organization of the Prison*, ed. G. N. Grosser, R. McCleary, L. E. Ohlin, and S. L. Messinger. New York: Social Science Research Council.

Tannenbaum, F. (1938). *Crime and the Community.* New York: Ginn.

Tappan, P. (1960). *Crime, Justice and Correction.* New York: McGraw-Hill.

Taxman, F. S., and A. Piquero. (1998). "On preventing drunk driving recidivism: An examination of rehabilitation and punishment approaches." *Journal of Criminal Justice* 26: 129–43.

Taylor, I., P. Walton, and J. Young. (1973). *The New Criminology: For a Social Theory of Deviance.* New York: Harper and Row.

Taylor, R. B., and J. Covington. (1988). "Neighborhood changes in ecology and violence." *Criminology* 26: 553–89.

Taylor, R. B., and S. D. Gottfredson. (1986). "Environmental design, crime, and prevention: An examination of community dynamics." In *Communities and Crime*, ed. A. J. Reiss and M. Tonry. Chicago: University of Chicago Press.

Taylor, R. B., S. D. Gottfredson, and S. Brower. (1984). "Block crime and fear: Defensive space, local ties, and territorial functioning." *Journal of Research in Crime and Delinquency* 21: 303–31.

Teichman, D. (2005). "The market for criminal justice: Federalism, crime control and jurisdictional competition." *Michigan Law Review* 103: 1831–876.

Tennenbaum, D. J. (1977). "Personality and criminality: A summary and implications of the literature." *Journal of Criminal Justice* 5: 225–35.

Terman, L. M. (1906). "Genius and stupidity: A study of some of the intellectual process of seven 'bright' and seven 'stupid' boys." *Pedagogical Seminary* 13: 307–72.

Theodorson, G. A., and A. G. Theodorson. (1969). *Modern Dictionary of Sociology*. NY: Thomas Y. Crowell.

Thomas, C. W. (1970). "Toward a more inclusive model of the inmate contraculture." *Criminology* 8: 251–62.

Thomas, C. W., and J. M. Hyman. (1978). "Compliance theory, control theory, and juvenile delinquency." In *Crime, Law and Sanctions: Theoretical Perspectives*, ed. M. D. Krohn and R. L. Akers. Beverly Hills, CA: Sage.

Thomas, W. I., and F. Znaniecki. (1918). *The Polish Peasant in Europe and America*, vol. 1. Chicago: University of Chicago Press.

Thomas, W. I., and D. S. Thomas. (1928). *The Child in America*. New York: Knopf.

Thornberry, T. P. (1989). "Reflections on the advantages and disadvantages of theoretical integration: In *Theoretical Integration in the Study of Deviance and Crime: Problems and Prospects*, ed. S. F. Messner, M. D. Krohn, and A. E. Liska. Albany: SUNY Press.

Thornberry, T. P., M. D. Krohn, A. J. Lizotte, and D. Chard-Weischem. (1993). "The role of juvenile gangs in facilitating delinquent behavior." *Journal of Research in Crime and Delinquency* 30: 55–87.

Tibbetts, S. G., and A. R. Piquero. (1999). "The influence of gender, low birth weight, and disadvantaged environment in predicting early onset of offending: A test of Moffitt's interactional hypothesis." *Criminology* 37(4): 843–78.

Tilson, H. A. (1993). "Neurobehavioral methods used in neurotoxicology." Pp. 1–33 in *Assessing Neurotoxicity in Drugs of Abuse*, ed. L. Erinoff. Rockville, MD: National Institute on Drug Abuse.

Timmerman, I. G. H., and P. M. G. Emmelkamp. (2005). "An integrated cognitive-behavioural approach to the aetiology and treatment of violence." *Clinical Psychology and Psychotherapy* 12: 167–76.

Tittle, C. R. (1969). "Crime rates and legal sanctions." *Social Problems* 23: 3–18.

———. (1975). "Labeling or deterrence?" *Social Forces* 53: 399–410.

———. (1983). "Social class and criminal behavior: A critique of the theoretical foundation." *Social Forces* 65: 405–32.

———. (1985). "The assumption that general theories are not possible." In *Theoretical Methods in Criminology*, ed. R. F. Meier. Beverly Hills, CA: Sage.

———. (1995). *Control Balance: Toward a General Theory of Deviance*. Boulder, CO: Westview Press.

———. (1997). "Thoughts stimulated by Braithwaite's analysis of control balance theory." *Theoretical Criminology* 1: 99–110.

———. (2000). "Theoretical developments in criminology." Pp. 51–101 in *The Nature of Crime: Continuity and Change*, ed. Gary LaTree. Washington, DC: U.S. Government Printing Office.

———. (2001). "Control balance." Pp. 316–34 in *Explaining Criminals and Crime*, ed. R. Paternoster and R. Bachman. Los Angeles: Roxbury.

———. (2004). "Refining control balance theory." *Theoretical Criminology* 8: 395–428.

Tittle, C. R., and E. V. Botchkovar. (2005). "Self-control, criminal motivation and deterrence: An investigation using Russian respondents." *Criminology* 43: 307–53.

Tittle, C. R., M. J. Burke, and E. F. Jackson. (1986). "Modeling Sutherland's theory of differential association: Toward an empirical clarification." *Social Forces* 65: 405–32.

Tittle, C. R., and A. R. Rowe. (1974). "Certainty of arrest and crime rates: A further test of the deterrence hypothesis." *Social Forces* 52: 455–62.

Tittle, C. R., and W. J. Villemez. (1977). "Social class and criminality." *Social Forces* 56: 474–502.

Tittle, C. R., D. A. Ward, and H. G. Grasmick. (2003). "Gender, age, and crime/deviance: A challenge to self-control theory." *Journal of Research in Crime and Delinquency* 40: 426–53.

Toby, J. (1957). "The differential impact of family disorganization." *American Sociological Review* 22: 505–12.

———. (1959). "Review of *Family Relationships and Delinquent Behavior* by F. Ivan Nye." *American Sociological Review* 24: 282–83.

———. (2000). "Are the police the enemy?" *Society* 37: 38–42.

Tonry, M. (1999). "Parochialism in U.S. sentencing policy." *Crime and Delinquency* 45: 48–65.

The Training School at Vineland. (2009). "History." Retrieved 11 January 2009 at http://www.vineland.org/history/trainingschool/history/history.html.

Transgender Law and Policy Institute. (2009). "Non-discrimination laws that include gender identity and express." Retrieved 9 February 2009 at http://www.transgenderlaw.org/ndlaws/.

Tremblay, R. E., B. Boulerie, L. Arsenault, and M. Junger. (1995). "Does low self-control during childhood explain the association between delinquency and accidents in early adolescence?" *Criminal Behaviour and Mental Health* 5: 439–51.

Tremblay, R. E., F. Vitaro, L. Bertrand, M. LeBlanc, H. Beauchesne, H. Boileau, and L. David. (1992). "Parent and child training to prevent early onset of delinquency: The Montréal longitudinal-experimental study." Pp. 117–138 in *Preventing Antisocial Behavior: Interventions from Birth through Adolescence*, ed. J. McCord and R. Tremblay. New York: Guilford.

Tricarico, D. (1984). *The Italians of Greenwich Village*. Staten Island, NY: Center for Migration Studies of New York.

Trojanowicz, R. (1987). "Community policing: Attacking crime at its roots." *Police Chief*, August: 16.

Trojanowicz, R., R. Baldwin, D. Banas, D. Dugger, D. Hale, H. Harden, P. Marcus, S. McGuire, J. McNamara, F. Medrano, C. Smith, P. Smyth, and J. Thompson. (1982). *An Evaluation of the Neighborhood Foot Patrol Program in Flint, Michigan*. Lansing: Michigan State University.

Truth, S. (1851). Speech at Woman's Rights Convention, Akron, Ohio. Pp. 482–83 in *Bartlett's Familiar Quotations*, ed. J. Bartlett. Boston, MA: Little-Brown.

Tsai, J. L. (2001). "Cultural orientation of Hmong young adults." *Journal of Human Behavior in the Social Environment* 3: 99–104.

Tso, Chief Justice T. (1996). "The process of decision making in tribal courts." In *Native Americans, Crime and Justice*, ed. M. A. Nielsen and R. A. Silverman. Boulder, CO: Westview Press.

Tsoukala, A. (2002). "Le traitement médiatique de la criminalité étrangère en Europe" ("Media coverage of foreign crime in Europe"). *Déviance et société* 26: 61–82.

Tunnell, K. D. (1992). *Choosing Crime: The Criminal Calculus of Property Offenders*. Chicago: Nelson-Hall.

Turk, A. (1969). *Criminality and Legal Order*. Chicago: Rand-McNally.

———. (1976). "Law as a Weapon in Social Conflict." *Social Problems* 23: 276–291.

Turner, J. J. (1978). *The Structure of Sociological Theory*. Revised Edition. Homewood, IL: Dorsey Press.

Tyler, T. P., L. Sherman, and H. Strang. (2007). "Reintegrative shaming, procedural justice, and recidivism: The engagement of offender's psychological mechanisms in the Canberra RISE drinking and driving experiment." *Law and Society Review* 41: 553–84.

Udry, R. M. (1990). "Biosocial models of adolescent problem behaviors." *Social Biology* 37: 1–10.

Umbreit, M. S. (1994). *Victim Meets Offender: The Impact of Restorative Justice and Mediation*. Monsey, NY: Willow Tree Press.

Unnever, J. D., F. T. Cullen, and R. Agnew. (2006). "Why is 'bad' parenting criminogenic? Implications from rival theories." *Youth Violence and Juvenile Justice* 4: 1–31.

U.S. Bureau of Labor Statistics. (2003). *Census of fatal occupation industries*. Washington, DC: U.S. Department of Labor.

U.S. Bureau of Justice Statistics. (2000). *Correctional Populations in the United States, 1997*. Washington, DC: U.S. Department of Justice.

———. (2002a). "Key facts at a glance: Correctional populations." http://www.ojp.usdoj.gov/bjs/glance/tables/corr2tab.htm

———. (2002b). "Key facts at a glance: Incarceration rate, 1980–2001." http://www.ojp.usdoj.gov/bjs/glance/tables/inrttab.htm

Useem, B., C. G. Camp, G. M. Camp, and R. Dugan. (1995). *Resolution of prison riots.* Washington, DC: U.S. Department of Justice.

U.S. Department of Justice. (1992). *Census of State and Federal Correctional Facilities, 1990.* Washington, DC: U.S. Government Printing Office.

———. (1994). *Census of State and Federal Correctional Facilities, 1992.* Washington, DC: U.S. Government Printing Office.

———. (1999). *Census of State and Federal Correctional Facilities, 1997.* Washington, DC: U.S. Government Printing Office.

———. (2000). *Census of State and Federal Correctional Facilities, 1998.* Washington, DC: U.S. Government Printing Office.

———. (2002). *Census of State and Federal Correctional Facilities, 2000.* Washington, DC: U.S. Government Printing Office.

———. (2008a). "Former top SAS cargo group executive agrees to plead guilty to participating in price-fixing conspiracy." Press release: 28 July.

———. (2008b). "LG, Sharp, Chunghwa agree to plead guilty, pay total of $585 million in fines for participating in LCD price-fixing conspiracies." Press release: 12 November.

U.S. Government Accounting Office. (1980). *Jail Inmates' Mental Health Care Neglected: State and Federal Attention Needed.* Washington, DC: U.S. Government Printing Office.

U.S. Office of Justice Programs. (2001). Grants to Encourage Arrest Policies and Enforcement of Protection Orders Program. Fiscal Year 2001 Application and Program Guidelines. Washington, DC: U.S. Government Printing Office.

U.S. Sentencing Commission. (1995). *Cocaine and Federal Sentencing Policy.* Washington, DC: U.S. Government Printing Office.

Vago, S. (1990). *Law and Society,* 3d ed. Englewood Cliffs, NJ: Prentice-Hall.

———. (2009). Law and Society, 9th ed. Upper Saddle Creek, NJ: Prentice-Hall.

Valdes, F., J. Culp, and A. Harris, eds. (2002). *Crossroads, Directions, and a New Critical Race Theory.* Philadelphia, PA: Temple University Press.

Van den Haag, E. (1975). *Punishing Criminals: Concerning a Very Old and Painful Question.* New York: Basic Books.

Van Dusen, K. T., S. A. Mednick, W. F. Gabrielli, and B. Hutchings. (1983). "Social class and crime in an adoption cohort." *Journal of Criminal Law and Criminology* 74: 249–54.

Van Maanen, J. (1973). "Observations on the making of policemen." *Human Organization* 32: 407–18.

Van Ness, D. (n.d.) "Restorative justice in prisons." Washington, DC: Prison Fellowship International.

Van Ness, D., and K. H. Strong. (2006). *Restoring Justice: An Introduction to Restorative Justice.* Cincinnati, OH: Anderson.

Van Ommen, G. -J. B., E. Bakker, and J. T. den Dunnen (1999). "The human genome project and the future of diagnostics, treatment and prevention." *The Lancet* 354: S5–S10.

Vaughan, M. G., and M. DeLisi. (2008). "Were Wolfgang's chronic offenders psychopaths? On the convergent validity between psychopathy and career criminality." *Journal of Criminal Justice* 36: 33–42.

Vazsonyi, A. T., and L. M. Belliston. (2007). "The family low self-control deviance: A cross-cultural and cross-national test of self-control theory." *Criminal Justice and Behavior* 34: 505–30.

Vazsonyi, A. T., and J. M. Crosswhite. (2004). "A test of Gottfredson and Hirschi's general theory of crime in African American adolescents," *Journal of Research in Crime and Delinquency* 41: 407–32.

Vazsonyi, A. T., L. E. Pickering, M. Junger, and D. Hessing. (2001). "An empirical test of a general theory of crime: A four-nation comparative test of self-control and the prediction of deviance." *Journal of Research in Crime and Delinquency* 38: 91–131.

Vermeiren, R., D. Deboutte, V. Ruchkin, and M. Schwab-Stone. (2002). "Antisocial behavior and mental health: Findings from three communities." *European Child & Adolescent Psychiatry* 11: 168–75.

Vermeiren, R., S. M. Jones, V. Ruchkin, D. Deboutte, and M. Schwab-Stone. (2004). "Juvenile arrest: A cross-cultural comparison." *Journal of Child Psychology and Psychiatry* 45: 567–76.

Veysey, B., and S. F. Messner. (1999). "Further testing of social disorganization theory: An elaboration of Sampson and Grove's 'community structure and crime.'" *Journal of Research in Crime and Delinquency* 36: 156–74.

Vien, A., and A. R. Beech. (2006). "Psychopathy: Theory, measurement, and treatment." *Trauma, Violent, & Abuse* 7: 155–74.

Visher, C. (1983). "Gender, police arrest decisions, and notions of chivalry." *Criminology* 21: 5–28.

———. (1994). "Op/Ed." American Sociological Association, *Crime, Law and Deviance Newsletter*, Fall/Winter: 1, 5–7.

Vito, G. F., and T. J. Keil. (1988). "Capital sentencing in Kentucky: An analysis of the factors influencing decision making in the post-Gregg period." *Journal of Criminal Law and Criminology* 79: 483–503.

Vold, G. B. (1958). *Theoretical Criminology*. New York: Oxford University Press.

———. (1979). *Theoretical Criminology*, 2nd ed. New York: Oxford University Press.

Vold, G. B., and T. J. Bernard. (1986). *Theoretical Criminology*, 3d ed. New York: Oxford University Press.

Vold, G. B., T. J. Bernard, and J. B. Snipes. (2001). *Theoretical Criminology*, 5th ed. New York: Oxford University Press.

Volkow, N. D., G. -J. Wang, J. S. Fowler, J. Logan, S. J. Gatley, A. Gifford, R. Hitzemann, Y. -S. Ding, and N. Pappas. (1999). "Prediction of reinforcing responses to psychostimulants in humans by brain dopamine D2 receptor levels." *American Journal of Psychiatry* 156: 1440–43.

von Hirsch, A. (1976). *Doing Justice*. New York: Hill and Wang.

Voracek, M. (2004). "National intelligence and suicide rates: An ecological study of 85 countries." *Personality and Individual Differences* 37: 543–53.

———. (2007). "National intelligence and suicide rates across Europe: An alternative test using educational attainment data." *Psychological Reports* 101: 512–18.

Voss, H. L. (1964). "Differential association and reported delinquency behavior: A replication." *Social Problems* 12: 78–85.

Votey, H. L. (1984). "The deterioration of deterrence effects of driving legislation: Have we been giving the wrong signals to policy makers?" *Journal of Criminal Justice* 12: 115–30.

Wagatsuma, H., and A. Rosett. (1986). "The implications of apology: Law and culture in Japan and the United States." *Law and Society Review* 20: 461–98.

Waldo, G., and T. Chiricos. (1972). "Perceived penal sanctions and self-reported criminality: A neglected approach to deterrence research." *Social Problems* 19: 522–40.

Waldo, G., and S. Dinitz. (1967). "Personality attributes of the criminal: An analysis of research studies." *Journal of Research in Crime and Delinquency* 4: 185–202.

Waldron, J. A., and H. R. Angelino. (1977). "Shock probation: A natural experiment on the effect of a short period of incarceration." *The Prison Journal* 57: 45–52.

Walker, S. (1983). *The Police in America: An Introduction*. New York: McGraw-Hill.

———. (1992). *The Police in America: An Introduction*. New York: McGraw-Hill.

———. (1994). *Sense and Nonsense about Crime and Drugs: A Policy Guide*, 3d ed. Belmont, CA: Wadsworth.

———. (1998). *Popular Justice: A History of American Criminal Justice*, 2d ed. New York: Oxford University Press.

———. (2006). *Sense and Nonsense About Crime and Drugs: A Policy Guide*, 6th ed. Belmont, CA: Wadsworth.

Walker, R. (1995). *To Be Real: Telling the Truth and Changing the Face of Feminism*. New York: Anchor.

Wallace, D., and D. Humphries. (1981). "Urban crime and capital accumulation: 1950–1971." In *Crime and Capitalism*, ed. D. Greenberg. Palo Alto, CA: Mayfield.

Wallace, W. L. (1971). *The Logic of Science in Sociology*. Chicago: Aldine.

Walsh, A., and L. Ellis. (1999). "Political ideology and American criminologists' explanations for criminal behavior." *Criminologist* 24: 1, 14.

———. (2007). *Criminology: An Interdisciplinary Approach*. Thousand Oak, CA: Sage Publications.

Walsh, A., and H.-H. Wu. (2008). "Differentiating antisocial personality disorder, psychopathy, and sociopathy: Evolutionary, genetic, neurological, and sociological considerations." *Criminal Justice Studies* 21 (June): 135–152.

Walters, G. D. (1992). "A meta-analysis of the gene-crime relationship." *Criminology* 30: 595–614.

———. (1999). "Crime and chaos: Applying nonlinear dynamic principles to problems in criminology." *International Journal of Offender Therapy and Comparative Criminology* 43: 134–53.

———. (2004). "The trouble with psychopathy as a general theory of crime." *International Journal of Offender Therapy and Comparative Criminology* 48(2): 133–48.

Wang, Shu-Neu, and G. F. Jensen (2003). "Explaining delinquency in Taiwan: A test of social learning theory." Pp. 65–84 in *Advances in Criminological Theory*, ed. R. L. Akers and G. F. Jensen. Chicago: University of Chicago Press.

Warr, M. (1998). "Life-course transitions and desistance from crime." *Criminology* 36: 183–216.

———. (2002). *Companions in Crime: The Social Aspects of Criminal Conduct*. Cambridge, England: Cambridge University Press.

Wasyliw, O. E., L. S. Grossman, T. W. Haywood, and J. Cavanaugh. (1988). "The detection of malingering in criminal forensic groups: MMPI validity scales." *Journal of Personality Assessment* 52: 321–33.

Watson, J. D. (1990). "The human genome project: Past, present and future." *Science*. April: 44–49.

Watson, J. B. (1913). "Psychology as the behaviorist views it." *Psychological Review* 20: 158–77.

———. (1914). *Behavior: An Introduction to Comparative Psychology*. New York: Holt.

———. (1930). *Behaviorism*, rev. ed. New York: Norton.

Weber, M. (1947)[1918]. *The Theory of Social and Economic Organizations*. Trans. A. M. Henderson and Talcott Parsons. New York: Free Press.

———. (1967)[1925]. "On Law." In *Economy and Society*, ed. M. Rheinstein and E. Shils. New York: Simon and Schuster.

Weeks, H. A. (1958). *Youthful Offenders at Highfields*. Ann Arbor, MI: University of Michigan Press.

Weidner, R. R., and W. Terrill. (2005). "A test of Turk's theory of norm resistance using observational data on police-suspect encounters." *Journal of Research in Crime and Delinquency* 42: 84–109.

Weiner, C. (2001). "Drawing the line in genetic engineering: Self-regulation and public participation." *Perspectives in Biology and Medicine* 44: 208–220.

Weis, J. (1976). "Liberation and crime: The invention of the new female criminal." *Social Justice* 1: 17–27.

Weisburd, D., and J. E. Eck. (2004). "What can police do to reduce crime, disorder and fear?" *Annals of the American Academy of Political and Social Sciences* 593: 42–65.

Weisburd, D., and L. Green. (1995). "Measuring immediate spatial displacement: Methodological issues and problems. In *Crime and Place: Crime Prevention Studies*, vol. 4, ed. J. Ecks and D. Weisburd. Monsey, NY: Willow Tree Press.

Weisburd, D., C. M. Lum, and A. Petrosino. (2001). "Does research design affect study outcomes in criminal justice?" *The ANNALS of the American Academy of Political and Social Science* 578: 50–70.

Weisburd, D., L. A. Wyckoff, J. Ready, J. E. Eck, J. C. Hinkle, and J. Gajewski. (2006). "Does crime just move around the corner? A controlled study of spatial displacement and diffusion of crime control benefits." *Criminology* 44: 549–92.

Wellford, C. (1975). "Labeling theory and criminology: An assessment." *Social Problems* 22: 332–45.

Welsh, W. N., P. H. Jenkins, and P. W. Harris. (1999). "Reducing minority overrepresentation in juvenile justice: Results of community-based delinquency prevention in Harrisburg." *Journal of Research in Crime and Delinquency*. 36: 87–110.

Welsh, W. N., R. Stokes, and J. R. Green. (2000). "A macro-level model of school disorder." *Journal of Research in Crime and Delinquency* 37: 243–83.

West, H. A., and W. J. Sabol. (2008). "Prisoners in 2007." *Bureau of Justice Statistics Bulletin*. Washington, DC: U.S. Department of Justice.

Westley, W. (1970). *Violence and the Police: A Sociological Study of Law, Custom and Morality*. Cambridge, MA: MIT Press.

Wexler, D. B. (1975). "Behavior modification and other behavior change procedures: The emerging law and proposed Florida guidelines." *Criminal Law Bulletin* 11: 600–16.

Wheeler, D. L. (1992a). "U. of Md. Conference that critics charge might foster racism loses NIH support." *Chronicle of Higher Education*, 2 September: A6–7.

———. (1992b). "Meeting on possible links between genes and crime cancelled after bitter exchange." *Chronicle of Higher Education*, 16 September: A7–8.

———. (1995). "A growing number of scientists reject the concept of race." *Chronicle of Higher Education*, 17 February: A8, A9, A15.

Whyte, W. F. (1955). *Street Corner Society*. Chicago: University of Chicago Press.

Wiatrowski, M. D., D. B. Griswold, and M. R. Roberts. (1981). "Social control and delinquency." *American Sociological Review* 46: 525–41.

Wideman, J. E. (2001). *My Soul Has Grown Deep: Classics of Early African-American Literature*. Philadelphia: Running Press.

Widom, K. S., (1989). "Child abuse, neglect, and violent criminal behavior." *Criminology* 27: 251–71.

Widom, C. S. (1989). "Child abuse, neglect, and violent criminal behavior." *Criminology* 27: 251–71.

Wilbanks, W. (1987). *The Myth of a Racist Criminal Justice System*. Monterey, CA: Brooks/Cole.

Wilcox, P., T. D. Madensen, and M. S. Tillyer. (2007). "Guardianship in context: Implications for burglary victimization risk and prevention." *Criminology* 45: 771–804.

Wilkins v. Maryland State Police, No. CCB-93–468 (1996).

Wilkins, L. (1965). *Social Deviance: Social Policy, Action and Research*. Englewood Cliffs, NJ: Prentice-Hall.

Willging, T. E. and T. G. Dunn. (1982). "The moral development of law students: Theory and data on legal education." *Journal of Legal Education* 31: 306–58.

Williams, III, F. P. (1984). "The demise of the criminological imagination: A critique of recent criminology." *Justice Quarterly* 1: 91–106.

Williams, III, F. P., and M. McShane. (1988). *Criminological Theory*. Englewood Cliffs, NJ: Prentice-Hall.

Williams, F. P., and M. D. McShane. (2004). *Criminological Theory*, 4th ed. Upper Saddle Creek, NJ: Prentice-Hall.

Williams, K., and R. Hawkins. (1986). "Perceptual research on general deterrence: A critical overview." *Law and Society Review* 20: 545–72.

Williams, L. E., L. Clinton, L. T. Winfree, and R. E. Clark. (1992). "Family ties, parental discipline, and delinquency: A study of youthful misbehavior by parochial high school students." *Sociological Spectrum* 12: 381–401.

Wilson, D. B., L. A. Bouffard, and D. L. MacKenzie. (2005). "A quantitative review of structured, group-oriented, cognitive-behavioral programs for offenders." *Criminal Justice and Behavior* 32 (April): 172–204.

Wilson, J. Q., and R. J. Herrnstein. (1985). *Crime and Human Nature*. New York: Simon and Schuster.

Wilson, J. Q., and G. Kelling. (1982). "Broken windows: The police and neighborhood safety." *Atlantic Monthly*, March: 29–38.

Wilson, W. J. (1987). *The Truly Disadvantaged: The Inner City, the Under-class, and Public Policy*. Chicago: University of Chicago Press.

Wilt, G. M., and J. D. Brannon. (1976). "Cynicism or realism: A criticism of Niederhoffer's research into police attitudes." *Journal of Police Science and Administration* 4: 38–45.

Winfree, Jr., L. T. (1985). "Peers, parents and adolescent drug use in a rural school district: A two-wave panel study." *Journal of Youth and Adolescence* 14: 499–512.

———. (1995). "Attica." In *Encyclopedia of American Prisons*, ed. M. D. McShane and F. P. Williams III. New York: Garland.

Winfree, Jr., L. T. (2003). "Peacemaking and community harmony: Lessons (and admonitions) from the Navajo peacemaking courts." Pp. 285–306 in *Restorative Justice: Theoretical Foundations*, ed. E. G. M. Weitekamp and H. J. Kerner. Devon, UK and Portland, OR: Willan Publishing.

———. (2004). "New Zealand Police and restorative justice philosophy." *Crime & Delinquency* 40: 189–213.

———. (2009). "Restorative policing and law enforcement in the USA: Problems and prospects." In *Victimology, Victim Assistance and Criminal Justice*, ed. O. Hagemann, P. Schaefer, and S. Schmidt. Mönchengladbach, Germany: Mönchengladbach University Press.

Winfree, Jr., L. T. and J. K. Akins. (2008). "Extending the boundaries of social structure/social learning theory: The case of suicide bombers in Gaza."

International Journal of Crime, Criminal Justice, and Law 3: 146–58.

Winfree, Jr., L. T., and F. Bernat. (1998). "Social learning, self-control, and substance abuse by eighth grade students: A tale of two cities." *Journal of Drug Issues* 28: 539–58.

Winfree, Jr., L. T., F. Bernat, and F.-A. Esbensen. (2001). "Hispanic and anglo gang membership in two southwestern cities." *Social Science Journal* 38: 105–17.

Winfree, Jr., L. T., F. -A. Esbensen, and D. W. Osgood (1996). "Evaluating a school-based gang-prevention program." *Evaluation Review* 20: 181–203.

Winfree, Jr., L. T., and D. M. Giever. (2000). "On classifying driving-while-intoxicated offenders: The experiences of a city-wide D.W.I. drug court." *Journal of Criminal Justice* 28: 1–9.

Winfree, Jr., L. T., and C. T. Griffiths. (1983). "Youth at risk: marijuana use among native American and Caucasian youth." *International Journal of the Addictions* 18: 53–70.

Winfree, Jr., L. T., C. T. Griffiths, and C. S. Sellers. (1989). "Social learning theory, drug use, and American Indian youth: A cross-cultural test." *Justice Quarterly* 6: 501–23.

Winfree, Jr., L. T., and L. Kielich. (1979). "Criminal prosecution and the labeling process: An analysis of the application of official sanctions." In *Legality, Morality and Ethics in Criminal Justice*, ed. Nicholas Kittrie and Jackwell Susman. New York: Praeger.

Winfree, Jr., L. T., L. Kielich, and R. Clark. (1984). "On becoming a prosecutor: Observations on the organizational socialization of law interns." *Work and Occupations: An International Sociological Journal* 11: 207–26.

Winfree, Jr., L. T., G. L. Mays, and T. Vigil-Backstrom. (1994). "Youth gangs and incarcerated delinquents: Exploring the ties between gang membership, delinquency, and social learning theory." *Justice Quarterly* 11: 229–55.

Winfree, Jr., L. T., C. S. Sellers, and D. Clason. (1993). "Social learning and adolescent deviance abstention: Toward understanding reasons for initiating, quitting and avoiding drugs." *Journal of Quantitative Criminology* 9: 101–25.

Winfree, Jr., L. T., T. J. Taylor, Ni He, and F. -A. Esbensen. (2006). "Self-control and variability over time: Multivariate results from a 5-year, multisite panel of youths." *Crime & Delinquency* 52: 253–86.

Winfree, Jr., L. T., T. Vigil-Backstrom, and G. L. Mays. (1994). "Social learning theory, self-reported delinquency, and youth gangs: A new twist on a general theory of crime and delinquency." *Youth and Society* 26: 147–77.

Wirth, L. (1931). "Culture conflict and misconduct." *Social Forces* 9: 484–92.

Witkin, H. A., Sarnoff, A. Mednick, F. Schulsinger, E. Bakkestrom, K. O. Christiansen, D. R. Goodenough, K. Hirschhorn, C. Lundstean, D. R. Owen, J. Philip, D. R. Rubin, and M. Stocking. (1977). "Criminality, aggression, and intelligence among XYY and XXY men." In *Biosocial Bases of Criminal Behavior*, ed. S. A. Mednoff and K. O. Christiansen. New York: Gardner Press.

Witte, A. D. (1993). "Some thoughts on the future of research in crime and delinquency." *Journal of Research in Crime and Delinquency* 30: 513–25.

Wolf, D. R. (1991). *The Rebels: A Brotherhood of Outlaw Bikers*. Toronto: University of Toronto Press.

Wolfgang, M. E. (1958). *Patterns of Criminal Homicide*. Philadelphia: University of Pennsylvania.

———. (1963). "Criminology and criminologists." *Journal of Criminal Law, Criminology and Police Science* 54: 155–62.

Wolfgang, M. E., and F. Ferracuti. (1967). *The Subculture of Violence*. London: Tavistock.

Wolfgang, M. E., R. M. Figlio, and T. Sellin. (1972). *Delinquency in a Birth Cohort*. Chicago: University of Chicago Press.

Wolny, P. (2005). *Colonialism: A Primary Source Analysis*. New York: Rosen Publishing Group.

Wong, D. (1996). *Paths to Delinquency: Implications for Juvenile Justice in Hong Kong and China*. Ph.D. dissertation: University of Bristol.

Wood, E. (1961). *Housing Designs: A Social Theory*. New York: Citizens' Housing and Planning Counsel of New York.

Wood, P. B., J. K. Cochran, B. Pfefferbaum, and B. J. Arneklev. (1995). "Sensation-seeking and delinquent substance use: An extension of learning theory." *Journal of Drug Issues* 25: 173–93.

Wood, P. B., W. R. Gove, and J. K. Cochran. (1994). "Motivation for violent crime among incarcerated adults: A consideration of reinforcement processes." *Journal of Oklahoma Criminal Justice Consortium* 1: 63–80.

Wood, P. B., W. R. Gove, J. A. Wilson, and J. K. Cochran. (1997). "Nonsocial reinforcement and habitual criminal conduct: An extension of learning theory." *Criminology* 35: 335–66.

Wood, P. B., B. Pfefferbaum, and B. J. Arneklev. (1993). "Risk taking and self-control: Social psychological correlates of delinquency." *Journal of Criminal Justice* 16: 111–30.

Woodiwiss, A. (1993). *Postmodernity USA: The Crisis of Social Modernism in Postwar America*. London: Sage.

Worthman, C. M., and E. Loftus. (1992). *Psychology*. New York: McGraw-Hill.

Wozniak, J. F. (2002). "Toward a theoretical model of peacemaking criminology: An essay in honor of Richard Quinney." *Crime and Delinquency* 48: 205–31.

Wright, J., and K. Beaver. (2005). "Do parents matter in creating self-control in their children? A genetically informed test of Gottfredson and Hirschi's theory of low self-control." *Criminology* 43: 1169–202.

Wright, J., K. Beaver, M. Delisi, and M. Vaughn. (2008). "Evidence of negligible parenting influences on self-control, delinquent peers, and delinquency in a sample of twins." *Justice Quarterly* 25: 544–69.

Wright, J., K. Beaver, M. Delisi, M. Vaughn, D. Boisvert, and J. Vaske. (2008). "Lombroso's legacy: The miseducation of criminologists." *Journal of Criminal Justice Education* 19: 325–338.

Wright, B. R. E., A. Caspi, T. E. Moffit, and P. A. Silva. (1999). "Low self-control, social bonds, and crime: Social causation, social selection or both." *Criminology* 37: 479–513.

Wright, B. R. E., A. Caspi, T. E. Moffitt, and R. Paternoster. (2004). "Does the perceived risk of punishment deter criminally prone individuals? Rational choice, self-control, and crime." *Journal of Research in Crime and Delinquency* 41: 180–203.

Wright, R. (1996). "Afterward." In *Life without Parole: Living in Prison Today*, by Victor Hassine. Los Angeles: Roxbury.

Wright, R. A., and J. M. Miller. (1998). "Taboo until today? The coverage of biological arguments in criminology textbooks, 1961 to 1970 and 1987 to 1996." *Journal of Criminal Justice* 26: 1–19.

Wrightsman, L. S., M. T. Nietzel, and W. H. Fortune. (1994). *Psychology and the Legal System*, 3d ed. Pacific Grove, CA: Brooks/Cole.

Wurtzel, E. (1999). *Bitch: In Praise of Difficult Women*. New York: Anchor Books.

Yablonsky. L. (1989). *The Therapeutic Community*. New York: Gardner Press.

Yazzie, R., and J. W. Zion. (1995). "'Slay the monsters': Peacemaker court and violence control plans for the Navajo nation." In *Popular Justice and Community Regeneration: Pathways of Indigenous Reform*. Westport, CT: Praeger.

Yeudall, L. T. (1977). "Neuropsychological assessment of forensic disorders." *Canadian Mental Health* 25: 7–15.

Yinger, M. J. (1960). "Contraculture and subculture." *American Sociological Review* 25: 625–35.

Yochelson, S., and S. E. Samenow. (1976). *The Criminal Personality*, vol. 1. New York: Aronson.

Yosso, T. J. (2005). "Who culture has capital? A critical race theory discussion of community cultural wealth." *Race, Ethnicity and Education* 8: 69–91.

Young, J. (1971). "The role of the police as amplifiers of deviancy, negotiators of reality, and translators of fantasy: Some consequences of our present system of drug control as seen in Notting Hill." In *Images of Deviance*, ed. S. Cohen. Middlesex, England: Penguin.

———. (1992). "Ten points of realism." In *Rethinking Criminology: The Realist Debate*, ed. Jock Young and R. Matthews. London: Sage.

Young, T. R. (1991). "Crime and chaos." *Critical Criminologist* 3(2): 17–21.

Zatz, M. (1985). "Los Cholos: Legal processing of Chicano gang members." *Social Problems* 33: 13–30.

Zickler, P. (1999). "NIDA studies clarify developmental effects of prenatal cocaine exposure." http://165.112.78.61/NIDA_Notes/NNVol143/Prenatal.html

Zimring, F. E., and G. J. Hawkins. (1973). *Deterrence: The Legal Threat in Crime Control*. Chicago: University of Chicago Press.

Zingraff, M. T., J. Leiter, K. A. Myers, and M. C. Johnsen. (1993). "Child maltreatment and youthful problem behavior. *Criminology* 31: 173–202.

Zingraff, M. T., W. R. Smith, and D. Tomaskovic-Devey. (2000). "North Carolina Highway Traffic and Patrol Study: 'Driving While Black.'" *Criminologist* 25: 1, 3–4.

Zorza, J. (1992). "The criminal law of misdemeanor domestic violence, 1970–1990." *Journal of Criminal Law and Criminology* 83: 46–72.

Zuckerman, M. (2006). "Rich man, poor man." *U.S. News and World Report*, 12 June: 71–72.

Zupan, L. (1991). *Jails: Reform and the New Generation Philosophy*. Cincinnati, OH: Anderson.

Zupan, L., and B. Menke. (1988). "Implementing organizational change: From traditional to new generation jail operations." *Policy Studies Review* 7: 615–25.

Zupan, L., and M. K. Stohr-Gillmore. (1987). "Doing time in the new generation jail: Inmate perceptions of gains and losses." *Policy Studies Review* 7: 626–40.

Author Index

Subject Index